ARKANA

THE NEW WHOLE FOODS ENCYCLOPEDIA

REBECCA WOOD, who learned gardening and foraging techniques from her grandparents and studied with leading experts in macrobiotics and traditional Oriental medicine, has taught and written about organic food, whole grains, and seasonal produce since 1970. Her food columns have appeared in *Whole Foods Magazine, Health Foods Retailer,* and other publications, and she was food editor for *East-West Journal* and *Whole Foods Digest.* Her most recent book, *The Splendid Grain,* won both a James Beard Award and a Julia Child/IACP Award. Wood & Associates, created in 1981, was educational consultant to numerous organizations in the natural foods industry. Rebecca Wood also co-founded and directed the East-West Center in Boulder, Colorado, and has established cooking schools in London and Colorado. Today, between speaking engagements and whole foods cooking classes, Wood is working to distill different cultures' knowledge of the energetic and medicinal properties of food.

PEGGY MARKEL, who provided the illustrations for *The New Whole Foods Encyclopedia,* has directed *La Cucina al Focolare,* a traditional Tuscan culinary program outside of Florence, Italy, since 1992. More recently she inaugurated the Ligurian School of Poetic Cooking in Tellaro. When not in Italy, Markel resides with her family on a small farm outside of Boulder, Colorado.

PENGUIN

ARKANA

An A to Z of Selection, Preparation, and Storage for More Than 1,000

Common and Uncommon Fruits, Vegetables, Grains, and Herbs—

Including How to Heal with Ayurveda, Western Nutrition, and

Traditional Chinese Medicine

Rebecca Wood

Foreword by Paul Pitchford
Illustrations by Peggy Markel

The New
Whole Foods Encyclopedia

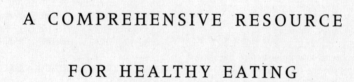

A COMPREHENSIVE RESOURCE

FOR HEALTHY EATING

PENGUIN/ARKANA

PENGUIN BOOKS
Published by the Penguin Group
Penguin Putnam Inc., 375 Hudson Street,
New York, New York 10014, U.S.A.
Penguin Books Ltd, 27 Wrights Lane,
London W8 5TZ, England
Penguin Books Australia Ltd, Ringwood,
Victoria, Australia
Penguin Books Canada Ltd, 10 Alcorn Avenue,
Toronto, Ontario, Canada M4V 3B2
Penguin Books (N.Z.) Ltd, 182–190 Wairau Road,
Auckland 10, New Zealand

Penguin Books Ltd, Registered Offices:
Harmondsworth, Middlesex, England

The Whole Foods Encyclopedia first published in the United
States of America by Prentice Hall Press 1988
This revised and updated edition published in Penguin
Books 1999

10 9 8 7 6 5 4 3 2

Copyright © Rebecca Wood, 1988, 1999
Illustrations copyright © Peggy Markel, 1999
All rights reserved

A NOTE TO THE READER
The New Whole Foods Encyclopedia is a reference volume.
Because individuals differ widely in their reactions to
food, this book is not intended to treat, diagnose, or
prescribe. Neither the author nor the publisher shall be
liable or responsible for any harm, damage, or illness
arising from the use of the information contained
herein. If you have a medical concern, consult a qualified health-care practitioner. Ideally, your practitioner is
knowledgeable about using whole foods as one facet of
maintaining (or regaining) well-being. Consult with
her/him about some of the specific ideas presented
herein.

Grateful acknowledgment is made for permission to reprint the following copyrighted works:

"Green Plum . . ." by Buson from *The Essential Haiku*,
edited by Robert Hass. Selection and translation copyright © 1994 by Robert Hass. Reprinted by permission
of The Ecco Press.

Excerpt from "Kudzu" from *The Whole Motion: Collected
Poems, 1945–1992* by James Dickey, Wesleyan University Press. © 1992 by James Dickey. Reprinted by permission of University Press of New England.

Excerpt from "The Hollow Men" from *Collected Poems
1909–1962* by T. S. Eliot. Copyright 1936 by Harcourt
Brace & Company. Copyright © 1964, 1963 by T. S.
Eliot. Reprinted by permission of Harcourt Brace &
Company and Faber & Faber Ltd.

"Song of the Taste" from *Regarding Wave* by Gary Snyder. Copyright © 1970 by Gary Snyder. Reprinted by
permission of New Directions Publishing Corp.

LIBRARY OF CONGRESS CATALOGING IN PUBLICA-
TION DATA
Wood, Rebecca.
  The new whole foods encyclopedia : a comprehensive
resource for healthy eating / Rebecca Wood : foreword
by Paul Pitchford : illustrations by Peggy Markel.
    p. cm.
  Includes bibliographical references.
  ISBN 0 14 02.5032 8
  1. Natural foods—Encyclopedias. I. Title.
TX369.W67   1999
641.5'63'03—dc21   98-47431

Printed in the United States of America
Set in Meridien Roman
Designed by Betty Lew

$\mathcal{F}$oreword

$\mathcal{I}$ first met Rebecca Wood when we were both teaching at a pristine mountain retreat center in the Canadian Rockies. I can still recall her delightful cooking class dishes composed of wild herbs, whole grains, recently harvested vegetables from the garden, and freshly plucked berries.

Meeting Rebecca, I found her attuned to the present and exuding a sense of ease. In speaking with her, I could only begin to plumb the depths of her life experience, which included her natural cure from cancer, and studies with expert cooks, shamans, and master healers. Through the medium of whole foods, she has invested incredible time and effort in bringing a healing message to the world.

A few years later, with her revision of the *Whole Foods Encyclopedia* in hand, I was enthralled by the lore, insights, recipes, properties of foods, and her intuitive awareness that so clearly touches every part of her writing. One senses mastery and integration.

After reviewing the notes on the health properties of foods and taking a pleasurable read through the rest of the text, I was reminded of a feature essential to our nutritional well-being—*quality*. How to know which foods are the best quality? What does a quality cabbage look like? Which potatoes taste best? When is the best time to buy apricots? *The New Whole Foods Encyclopedia* gives information that enables us to obtain optimum nutrition.

In addition, this massive reference informs us who benefits most from a specific food and, importantly, when a food is not appropriate or is contraindicated. I have never known a food or health product that is good for everyone, even though sales people may lead us to believe otherwise. Knowing the properties of foods is a valuable tool. For example, if you easily become chilled, you can warm up by emphasizing more warming foods and spices in your diet. Simply changing your thermal nature can help heal afflictions marked with thermal imbalance—as any affliction may be—from arthritis to premenstrual syndrome. Rebecca includes health benefits attributed to foods in Oriental and Western traditions to help us choose the best foods for thermal and other dimensions of balance in our lives.

The New Whole Foods Encyclopedia is a vital work for several reasons, among the first being its focus on unrefined, whole foods. Today, whole foods are greatly lacking in our diet. Most people cannot identify a grain of wheat; most do not know that unrefined oils exist or that unrefined cane sugar actually prevents tooth decay and nerve deterioration instead of causing them as refined sugars do. White rice, white bread, and the other white foods can promote blood sugar imbalances, which in turn can lead to emotional instability and addictions. The denaturing of foods into separated ingredients over the last hundred years or so parallels the movement of our culture into hyperspecialization and societal fragmentation.

Perceiving food solely according to scientific data is a dull experience. Whole foods in particular are immeasurably more than mere nutrients. They are imbued with subtle life energies, colors, aromas, thermal natures, and various healing properties. Food also sustains awareness—our thoughts are influenced by it, as is life itself. To help us understand this gestalt, let's briefly contrast whole foods with refined foods.

Whole foods means foods that are in their unrefined edible state, for example, whole wheat and whole grain pasta, whole fruits, and unrefined oils, salt, and sweeteners. After some four million years of evolution, humanity has just recently (ca. 1850) started consuming highly refined foods. Refined foods, such as white flour used in bread, pastry, and pasta, are not just missing a few ingredients that can be replaced by enrichment with three or four vitamins. They lack up to 50 different minerals and trace minerals, a number of vitamins, virtually all the fiber and precious oils, and untold numbers of phytochemicals that support full immune function.

These nutrients are required for complete metabolism to occur. As a result of consuming refined foods, the missing nutrients are extracted from the bones, tissues, and nerves. This is why in a land of great excess and obesity, there is so much underlying deficiency. It is precisely this etiology of deficiency that leads to cravings, addictions, emotional turmoil, and nearly every degenerative disease, including diabetes, cancer, heart disease, and arthritis, to mention the most common. Whole vegetal foods, with fiber and all nutrients intact, can reverse most cases of heart and artery disease in as little time as four weeks.

The nutrients in whole foods clean, build, and maintain the body. Refined foods rob us of our birthright—a vital body and mind during our entire life span. Hence, the great need for this encyclopedic text. It has the potential to awaken the entire food industry, as well as to educate many individuals and families about quality, healthful foods and healthy food practices. In my experience, people want good nutrition; however, they've been misinformed by incomplete or misapplied food sciences that claim refined foods are acceptable.

This pattern contains a message. If we continue with lifeless, denatured, refined food (and the refined medicines that accompany them), we lose our connection with nature. We are led unerringly to degeneration. A lifestyle of wholeness fosters strength and unity. This book helps us to respect food for the gift it is and affirms that we are at the forefront of a quiet, whole-foods revolution.

A quintessential factor in our nutritional well-being, once we accept the idea of wholeness, is freshness. Recently prepared whole foods impart this. Nearly everyone can taste the liveliness in a meal of fresh foods. We hear this reminder throughout this text and receive many pointers for gathering, preparing, and locating the best-quality fresh foods.

In summary, what distinguishes *The New Whole Foods Encyclopedia* is the blend of wisdom and wit, the personal stories, the anecdotes as well as the hard science you would expect from such a seasoned researcher as Rebecca Wood. She has studied, grown, written about, sought out, and taught whole foods and their cookery over the last thirty years. I can think of no one else in America with her expertise. No other reference is as complete. This book is a superb resource. May you be inspired to dive in and delight in foods that are elegantly simple.

Paul Pitchford
Author of *Healing with Whole Foods:*
Oriental Traditions and Modern Nutrition and
Director of Oriental Healing Arts & Nutritional Training
Heartwood Institute
Garberville, California
January 1999

Acknowledgments

Sincere thanks to my excellent editor, Dawn Drazl; her assistant editors, Jariya Wanapun and Nelly Bly; Leda Scheintaub and the talented Penguin team; to copy editor Susan Derecskey for her superb craftsmanship; Rose Grant for her precise index; and for her assistance with typing, Mary Gilley.

Deepest gratitude to Paul Pitchford and Amadea Morningstar whose classes, books, and friendship have helped form my understanding of food and who have kindly read the text for accuracy. Thanks to my first food energetic teachers, Michio and Aveline Kushi, the late Naboru Muramoto, and Jack Worsley. Thanks to Brigitte Mars, Deni Bown, Gernot Katzer, Sally White, and Charlene Weidner.

To all my cooking students for their questions, support, and enthusiasm about healing with whole foods. What a thrill for me to watch your and your families' transformations as you fine-tune your diets.

My community gardening friends who help sustain me with camaraderie, flowers, and awesome produce: Kevin Betts, Bryn Brocklesby, Caroline Conway, Elizabeth Ducette, Hourt Feng, Dea Jacobson, Eldon Krugman, Barbara Leach, Janet Mativi, Deb Pointowsky, Bonnie Steele, Lynn Stoody, Donna Vogel, and Sarah and Sharon Weidner.

To dear friends Evelyn Anglim, Judith Marie Diederich, Carl and Julia Farrer, Lisa and John Fenton-Free, Pat Lewiter, Abbie Kay Marschner, Jeff and Peggy Markel, Yuji Matsumura, Betty and Gordon McBride, Nancy Morgan, Christine Palafox, Jane Randolph, Jo-Ann and Bernard Rosenberg, Carol Summer, and Chris and Penny Webster.

Thank you Shirley Hill. How the beauty of your people and the far north have captured my heart. To everyone at Crestone Mountain Zen Center and Rocky Mountain Shambhala Center, the spacious retreat centers where I completed this manuscript.

To Mark Retzloff and Hass Hassan who first encouraged me to write this book. Thanks also to the readers of the first and second editions whose sustained interest encouraged me to revise it yet again.

Deepest gratitude to my parents. And to my children, Elizabeth, Asa, Roanna, and my son-in-law, Marc—I wouldn't change a single hair of your heads.

$\mathcal{C}$ontents

 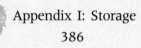

Introduction

In the pages that follow, you will find an alphabetical listing of available grains, vegetables, fruits, nuts, seeds, seaweeds, fungi, sweeteners, fats, oils, and culinary herbs and spices.

You'll find entries for turnips, turnip greens, and beets, but not beet greens. Turnip tops stand on their own; beet tops don't. A couple of baby beet greens might find their way into a bowl of mesclun—and I always add them to borscht—but they're not served solo and so do not appear solo.

I've included traditional food products that once were homemade. Most of these I prepare—or have prepared—from scratch, including bulgur, barley malt, rice syrup, vinegar, masa, umeboshi, koji, soy sauce, miso, natto, tempeh, ghee, tofu, amasake, seitan, and even maraschino cherries. Well, that was in my mother's kitchen. These food products are all part of a healthful, plant-based diet and, cherries excepted, most are available in their traditional versus their hi-tech form.

While culinary herbs are covered in some detail, I've not included strictly medicinal herbs. Even though in the heart of my garden I grow echinacea and St. John's wort for tinctures—and I recommend them to you—they're not included here. Parsley and sage have entries because they're culinary ingredients. Chamomile, too, since it is our most common tisane.

Cornsilk squeaked in because, although my primary use of it is medicinal (it is a diuretic and treats kidney stones) rather than culinary, it makes an oh-so-sweet stock. Besides, the next time you're shucking corn, its silk will be right there in your hand—free for the taking—ready to be dried.

You won't find entries for alcoholic beverages, supplements, meat, fish, eggs, dairy products (except butter), or other animal foods—the scope is the vegetable realm. I include butter for its inimitable medicinal and culinary properties. I've included honey (sometimes classified as an animal food) because it is a useful whole foods ingredient. I've included several foods sold as supplements: microalgae and barley and wheat grass juice. Unlike other supplements that are isolated food components, these are remarkable whole foods, ones that I heartily recommend to you.

I will alert you to a few noxious food products (noted with the Ø symbol) masquerading as healthful, such as canola oil and fruit juice sweeteners. Because there's more misinformation perpetrated—and profit made—with vegetable oils and sweeteners than any other products, I will provide you with guidelines for determining their quality.

I include some information about foraging for freely given foods, but more as a tease. This is not a foraging guide. If, however, you find yourself out in the open spaces with gathering basket in hand, so much the better. Food foraging is, after all, humanity's oldest profession. Wild foods offer superior nutrients and medicinal properties and make you feel, in a word, wild. There are three guidelines for foraging. One, identify plants carefully since some varieties—especially mushrooms—are toxic. There are numerous regional plant guides available to help with identification. Two, gather only in areas that you are confident are free from chemical contamination. Do not gather along heavily traveled roadsides. Lastly, do not overforage. Always leave enough healthy plant specimens to assure their propagation.

Wild foods with commercial availability include hand-harvested wild rice, mesquite, ramps, fiddlehead ferns, glasswort, purslane, lamb's-quarters, some mushrooms, most seaweeds, some wildflower blossoms, wild blue-green algae, and pine nuts.

Watch for roadside fruit stands—sometimes just a cardboard table set out on a country lane—offering wild berries, fruits, and nuts. Back in town, let your greengrocer be your ally and inform you when there's a wild harvest coming in.

WHAT ENTRIES INCLUDE

Entries provide a description of the food, suggestions for its use, buying tips, and its health benefits. When a foodstuff has specific storage needs, they are specified within the text. (General storage information is described on pages 386–389.)

Entries are cross-referenced. In the case of mushrooms, citrus, beans, and others, refer to the specific food as well as the family. If an entry does not contain a section on Health Benefits or Buying, you can find its properties by looking up the cross-references.

This book is short on formulas, the reason being that formulas work best when they're formulated just for you. An apple cider remedy for arthritis, for example, may help your neighbor, but if you happen to suffer also from low energy and frailty, it will exacerbate your condition—especially with long-term use. Preventive medicine is not symptomatic. Rather, it seeks the underlying cause of imbalance and then modifies diet and lifestyle as a first step toward regaining health.

A PERSONAL NOTE

Where did my interest in food as medicine begin? The foundations were laid at my grandpa's farm in Tremonton, Utah. How I loved being at his side, about bursting with pride for both of us that "since that last rain, them sugar beets are leafing out real pretty." With him or with Grandma, there was the thrill of the find when foraging pine nuts and mushrooms, with or without cousins. And there was feasting upon the find. There was always enough to set some by and to share with friends and those in need. My mother and her four sisters all tried outdoing each other with marvelous made-from-scratch foods. My father and uncles, avid fishermen and hunters, provided wild game for the table. From an early age, how could I not compare the energy in a pheasant or sage hen to a chicken, in a pan-fried brook trout to fish sticks, or in wild asparagus to store-bought.

After college, I ended up in Boston in the home of macrobiotic teachers Michio and Aveline Kushi. In 1969, we were a community of 25 living in two large "study houses." Aveline cooked, Michio taught, and I experienced how daily foods affected physical, emotional, and mental health. As a community, we observed and discussed the same, and we explored the effects of diet on world cultures. It was a fascinating study.

I next studied Five Elements medicine at the Traditional College of Oriental Medicine in Kenilworth, England. Meanwhile, I was teaching and writing about whole foods cookery. Back in the Rocky Mountains, my own study of food energetics deepened as I raised my children and tried to keep ahead of my students' questions. This work continues to delight and nourish me as I see its practical benefits enhance other people's lives.

EARLY EDITIONS OF THE WHOLE FOODS ENCYCLOPEDIA

The original edition of this book, written in 1983, was entitled *Whole Foods: A Guide for Employees of Natural Food Stores*. It was part of my training program for Alfalfa's Market in Boulder, Colorado, and it became the primary industry reference text. I then traveled throughout the United States conducting workshops and seminars and giving lectures for natural foods businesses. This opportunity enabled me to meet many farmers, producers, distributors, and retailers and to learn even more about our foods, how they're produced and processed, and about their quality. Over the years, I've especially enjoyed meeting the people who grow our staple foods. I love walking fields and orchards and talking crops and soil with farmers. Five years later, the book was revised for Prentice Hall as *Whole Foods Encyclopedia: A Shopper's Guide*.

To a large degree, the quality of our food determines our health. Let us better understand our daily foods that we may more fully enjoy them and be nourished by them. Foods aren't the whole picture—add exercise, healthy lifestyle, right livelihood, and you have preventive medicine at its best.

Cooking need not be drudgery. Over the years, I've discovered the critical ingredient in food preparation is intention. I have found that how I cultivate, prepare, serve, and eat a food affects how the food will taste and how I will assimilate it. So make your hearth a bright and welcoming place. Enjoy touching carrots and cabbages as you wash and chop. And enjoy the incomparable aromas as you simmer and serve. Then, as we sit to break bread together, may we all be renewed by earth's bounty.

R.W.
Crestone, Colorado, March 1999

Health Benefits

Foods have multiple energetic properties, and discerning and using these properties to enhance well-being are an age-old activity. Hunter-gatherer peoples had extensive knowledge of local plant species and knew each one's edibility and medical value.

This knowledge helped form Western herbology and traditional Asian medical systems. In the West, however, the seventeenth-century Cartesian view that matter is subject to mechanical laws squelched this wisdom. It has remained vital, however, in India and China. Written records of a food's medicinal applications for humans extend unbroken for more than four thousand years. Ayurvedic and traditional Chinese medicine have the most sophisticated and time-proven pharmacopoeias in existence.

Reclaiming this wisdom and weaving it in with contemporary knowledge of nutrition enables us—from a biochemical vantage—to select foods that encourage healthful metabolic processes. Here is an overview of how to determine a food's specific medicinal value. (Refer to the bibliography for sources of more detailed information concerning traditional Chinese medicine and Ayurveda.) If any of these models is too unscientific for you, consider it a poetic device and digest it a bit at a time. Or bypass it entirely. A year from now you might consider reconsidering it.

Whole Foods

Favoring whole, intact foods supports optimum health. Fragmented foods, even whole wheat flour as compared to the whole wheat berry itself, impart less energy. Eating integral foods that are capable of regenerating themselves supports our own regeneration. Nutritionally, there's no difference between the whole wheat flour in a bagel and a handful of wheat grain; energetically, there's a world of difference.

Fresh Foods

Fresh produce, in a word, enlivens. It offers more than canned, frozen, or past-their-prime fruits and vegetables can. Beans, most grains, seaweed, some spices, sweeteners, and seeds remain fresh for a year or more when properly stored. Due to their higher fat content, nuts—once shelled—quickly become stale. Unrefined vegetable oils are so fragile that to remain healthful, they demand special processing, handling, and storage.

The same holds true for freshly cooked foods. They impart more energy the day they're prepared rather than the next day—or in the case of packaged foods, the next month or the next year.

Cooked Foods

Historically, people have mainly eaten cooked foods because they are easier to assimilate and therefore more nourishing and energizing. In addition, cooking offers a greater range of sensory pleasures. As delicious as a fresh peach or carrot is, think how limiting it would be if we could only eat it raw.

When your diet contains many stale, denatured foods, raw foods have greater appeal. As you reduce your consumption of packaged, highly refined, leftover, and stale foods, the craving for raw foods decreases.

People with strong digestion and abundant energy better assimilate salads and raw fruit. On the other hand, people suffering from low energy, congestion, allergies, or weak digestion better assimilate cooked foods.

True, prolonged cooking at high temperatures destroys enzymes and water-soluble vitamins. But that's all. Moderate cooking does not destroy carbohydrates, proteins, fatty acids, fat-soluble vitamins, minerals, or micronutrients. Most of our ills today are not from a deficiency of enzymes and water-soluble vitamins.

Freshly cooked foods give energy. If you doubt this, try for one week to eat only microwaved, leftover, stale, frozen, or canned foods. Physically, emotionally, and mentally, you'll probably feel lousy.

Thermal Properties of Foods

When consumed, foods have an overall cooling, neutral, or warming effect. This observation helped form Western herbalism and medicine from Greek times until the seventeenth century. It remains a critical tenet in traditional Chinese medicine as well as in Ayurvedic medicine.

While all systems agree that garlic is heating and watermelon cooling, exceptions occur, arising from each one's scope. For example, in traditional Chinese medicine the overall effect of radishes is considered cooling. But in Ayurvedic medicine, radishes increase *agni*, or digestive fire, and are therefore considered warming. Both are correct within context. For consistency, I follow the traditional Chinese medical way of evaluating thermal properties.

Here are seven rules of thumb that suggest a food's thermal properties:

1. Foods that take longer to grow, like cabbage and winter squash, are more warming than foods that grow quickly, like lettuce and summer squash.
2. A food is more cooling when eaten raw than when it is cooked.
3. Chilled food is more cooling than warm or room-temperature food.
4. Blue, green, or purple foods are more cooling than similar foods that are red, orange, or yellow; thus a lime cools more than a lemon.
5. Cooking a food with more time, more oil or fat, less water, greater pressure, or at higher temperatures makes that food more warming.
6. Foods cooked over gas or wood heat impart more warmth than foods cooked with electricity. A microwave-cooked food holds and conveys even less warmth than food cooked on an electric range.
7. Tropical and subtropical foods tend to be more cooling than foods grown in temperate zones.

Organic Foods

Favor organic foods whenever possible for their extra flavor and greater nutritional value and energy. Chemically grown foods take their toll on our kidneys and liver (the organs that filter chemicals) as well as the environment. We're barely three generations into ingesting artificial chemicals, and judging from the results, it's been a dangerous experiment.

If your budget for organic foods does not cover all of your food purchases, then spend it first on the fattiest foods. Because toxins concentrate in fatty acids, avoid commercial-quality meat, dairy, oils, nuts, seeds, and grains—in that order.

Seasonal and Regional Produce

Seasonality is not an issue for shelf-stable whole grains and beans. Produce is a different matter. I grow watermelon, grapes, and zucchini in my garden, but not in January. I could buy these cooling foods fresh in winter, shipped in from a different region, but their thermal properties won't help me stay warm in zero temperatures. Besides, a long-distance zucchini has no flavor. It makes sense to eat zucchini in season when it tastes like zucchini.

Prior to the advent of refrigerated trucking in the 1940s, people ate seasonal produce or what they had set by. Period. In cold weather, my grandmother's fresh vegetable options were a few cold-loving greens like broccoli and kale from the garden; parsley from the pot on her windowsill; and potatoes, onions, cabbages, turnips, parsnips, rutabagas, carrots, and squash from the root cellar. In addition to dried or preserved fruits, she had stored apples and pears.

Eating seasonally doesn't mean that we must limit ourselves. But at the supermarket, favor hardier produce in cold weather. The best way of attuning to seasonal vegetables is to garden.

Until very recently, people consumed only regional foods. Unlike us, most people knew the hands that grew and milled, tended and slaughtered, and cooked the food. Today, few of the foods we consume are regional unless they are homegrown or purchased at a farmers' market.

Purchasing regional foods strengthens your local economy—besides offering superior flavor. From an energetic point of view, it also makes sense. Foods of your region help you to be in balance with and attuned to your specific environment.

DOCTRINE OF SIGNATURE

In natural healing systems worldwide, people have discovered that a food's appearance often indicates its medicinal potential. Thus a beet's color correctly indicates that beets build blood. The milky sap of mature lettuce aptly infers that lettuce supports lactation. Beef and chicken liver support our liver function.

COROLLARY VEGETABLE PARTS

Similar to the doctrine of signature is that each plant part has a propensity to support the corollary body part. From the bottom up, here's a quick sketch.

- **Roots** Vegetable roots correlate to our roots—our intestines, kidneys, and regenerative organs. Roots are the most mineral-dense plant part and the most strengthening. Consider the types of roots to further determine their potential. Of a radish, turnip, and carrot, the carrot penetrates the earth more deeply and is, energetically, more strengthening to the kidneys than the others.
- **Tubers** Growing below ground as the thickened, fleshy parts of underground stems, tubers lack the mineral density of true roots. Potatoes, Jerusalem artichokes, and sweet potatoes are tubers. Traditional medical systems recommend tubers for people wishing to gain weight, as is suggested by a tuber's amorphous, undifferentiated mass. Other vegetables have a distinct top, bottom, and, often, core. A tuber's energy is more grounding than a stalk or flower.
- **Stalks and Stems** The stalk of a vegetable transports. Vegetable stalks are good for moving our energy and may perk up someone whose energy is stuck or who has a limited view. Vegetables with pronounced stalks include asparagus, bok choy, cardoon, celery, Chinese cabbage, and fennel.
- **Leaves** Chlorophyll is to a plant what blood is to an animal. Since leaves are richest in chlorophyll, eating leafy greens supports blood formation and liver function. In addition, leaves also breathe by converting carbon dioxide

into oxygen, and so eating leafy greens supports our lungs. Greens with greater surface area, like a sprig of parsley, offer more lung and liver support than narrow leaves, like a scallion blade.

- **Flowers**   Our eyes are drawn to faces and flowers. It's where the essence is more clearly seen. Eating broccoli flowers and cauliflower brings energy up to the head. Eating actual blossoms revivifies the spirit. It's amazing how intense the energy packed in even a tiny blossom is.
- **Seeds**   A seed, like an egg, is the self-contained embryonic plant, which holds the future. Seeds act upon our regenerative organs. Seeds contain more precious and protective fatty acids than other plant parts. Grains, the most biologically advanced plants, are both the seed and the fruit in one.
- **Fruit**   Most fruits are the ripened ovary or ovaries of a seed-bearing plant, which contain the seed. Lush and juicy fruits engender softness and a sense of ease, or relaxation. A diet with excessive fruit, however, can make one too soft, unfocused, or ungrounded.

WESTERN NUTRITION

Structural in view, Western nutrition takes things apart and looks at the pieces, literally. Years ago, we learned that carrots are good for the eyes because they're high in vitamin A. Next, we learned of the pre–vitamin A factors, carotenoids. Now carotenoids have been further subdivided into alpha, beta, gamma, and delta. We can anticipate that as scientists continually reduce nutrients to smaller parts, termed phytochemicals, the supplement industry will have an unending supply of newly discovered micronutrients to address specific health problems. It's a valuable contribution, but not the whole picture.

This mechanistic view, resulting from Cartesian philosophy, treats symptoms rather than causes. It is not preventive medicine.

YIN AND YANG

Many Eastern healing modalities are based on a yin-yang system that promotes health and harmony through balance. The original system, used for millennia, remains the most widely accepted and is used in this book. The newer hybrid yin-yang systems, including the macrobiotic model, deviate from the original.

Yin refers to the relatively more passive processes that are more like water in substance. Our body's fluids and tissues (hormones, blood, lymph, flesh, bones, and so on) are yin. Conversely, yang processes are relatively more active and tend to be more fiery and energetic. Our energy, mental and spiritual processes, and driving life spark are yang.

The yin-yang system is useful for describing foods' medical action. For instance, according to its thermal nature, a yin food tends to cool us down, a yang food to warm us. Imagine eating watermelon on a frizzling-hot summer afternoon. The melon's cooling fluid (yin) helps balance out the hot (yang) weather. If you're suffering from the common cold, cooking with fresh ginger helps resolve it. Ginger's hot, ascending, dispersing yang qualities help dry up the yin (watery mucus deposits) and drive out the invading pathogens.

A balance of yin and yang promotes health and harmony. Use this system to understand imbalances within your body and then choose appropriate foods or herbs to support your overall health.

TRADITIONAL CHINESE MEDICINE

Chinese medicine assumes that we maintain optimum health through a balanced diet and lifestyle. A diet of wholesome, easy-to-assimilate foods promotes digestion, and whatever promotes digestion supports the health of the entire organism. Health concerns (imbalances) are adjusted with diet and lifestyle modifications. If a problem persists, intervention is accelerated, starting with the least invasive such as herbal medicines and progressing, as necessary, up to more invasive treatments like acupuncture.

The use of foods and herbs as medicine is based upon a science of functional relationships, which, using the principles of yin and yang, considers the thermal properties of a food and the Five Elements. Yin foods, for example, are cooling; their flavor is salty, bitter, or sour; they build blood and fluids; and their energy descends in the body. Conversely, yang foods are warming; their flavors are sweet or pungent; they increase overall energy; and their energy ascends.

Five Elements takes its name from the elements. Each is associated with a season, color, flavor, direction, organ/meridian system, and numerous other attributes.

ELEMENT	wood	fire	earth	metal	water
SEASON	spring	summer	Indian summer	fall	winter
COLOR	green/blue	red	yellow	white	black/dark
FLAVOR	sour	bitter	sweet	pungent/spicy	salty
DIRECTION	rising	floating	centering	descending	sinking
ORGAN SYSTEM	liver/ gallbladder	heart/small intestine	stomach/ spleen-pancreas	lungs/colon	kidneys/ bladder
ENVIRONMENTAL INFLUENCE	wind	heat	damp/moist	dry/astringent	cold

Using this outline, a food that is green and sour tasting, like sorrel, acts upon the liver. Watercress, also green, acts upon the liver; its pungent flavor gives it lung/colon action; and as a water plant it influences the kidneys. Coffee's black color indicates kidney action; its rising energy implicates liver; and its bitter/sweet taste involves the heart/small intestine and stomach/spleen-pancreas. People who drink more coffee than is good for them often develop symptoms associated with dysfunction of these organs.

Environmental Influences

The environmental influence of each element offers yet another important way to determine a food's potential healing property. Each of the Five Elements has an environmental influence. Cold and heat are the respective environmental influences for the water and fire elements and are described in thermal properties (see page xxi). The remaining influences are damp, dry, and wind.

In nature, mix too much water with earth and you'll have a sticky environment. Excessive moisture challenges the spleen-pancreas (earth element) and so living in a humid environment may exacerbate digestive imbalance. Also, eating too many sweets (the earth element flavor) often creates a too-damp, sticky digestive system that is the perfect environment for an overgrowth of fungi, bacteria, and candida-type yeast infections. To support balance, minimize the use of foods that promote dampness such as dairy products, eggs, meat, pineapple, salt, soy products, and sweeteners. Also, use bitter tasting and/or aromatic foods that dry dampness, including amaranth, aduki beans, asparagus, bitter melon, celery, lettuce, garlic, turmeric, turnips, and vinegar.

Living in a dry climate, or when the body tends to be dry, challenges the lungs/colon (metal element). When our homes are overly dry, we can create equilibrium with a humidifier or an abundance of houseplants. With diet we can support balance by minimizing the use of drying foods and increasing the use of moistening foods (see above).

Wind is associated with the liver. While a spring breeze is conducive to energy movement, a strong wind often agitates a person with a stressed liver and heightens irritability. Such people do well to avoid being in a strong wind, to use sour-tasting foods, and to avoid foods that stress the liver. One way a liver imbalance may manifest itself is as too much wind—belching or intestinal gas.

AYURVEDA

As with Chinese medicine, Indian Ayurvedic medicine was developed by a culture using a plant-based diet of whole, fresh, seasonal, and regional foods. Its purpose was to promote health and to prevent disease. An interesting difference between Ayurvedic and Chinese medicine arises from the fact that India is predominately a subtropical region and China is predominately a temperate region. Because of this dramatic climactic difference, Ayurvedic cuisine uses more sweat-inducing spices and is overall a more cooling and cleansing diet.

The Five Elements in Ayurveda correspond closely to the old European system of the humors. They are earth, water, fire, air, and ether. People are a combination of these elements and can be described as one of three *doshas*, or types, which are *vata*, *pitta*, and *kapha*. Each person is a combination of these three *doshas*. A person's constitutional *dosha* as well as his or her current condition is considered in formulating a treatment. Foods described as *tridoshic* are balancing to all conditions. A more detailed discussion of Ayurveda and which foods support which body types can be found in the appendix on page 394.

Vata, a combination of air and ether elements, embodies the very essence of life energy and is considered dry, light, cold, clear, hard, subtle, and mobile. It relates most directly to the nervous system but also rules respiration, movement, will, and sense acuity. Foods that reduce an excessively *vata* condition are nurturing, soft, soothing, and warm and have a sweet flavor.

Pitta, the fire element, governs internal heat, digestion, hormones, circulation, thirst, courage, and intelligence. Foods that reduce excess fire are drying, soothing, and cooling. They have a bitter, astringent, or sweet flavor.

Kapha, the water and earth element, is cold, wet, heavy, and slow; it builds the body and fosters peacefulness and patience. Foods that reduce excess *kapha* are drying, warm, and cleansing, with spicy, bitter, and astringent flavors.

Looking at coffee again, but from an Ayurvedic vantage, it overstimulates the already overly mental *vata* type and is too exciting for the already excitable *pitta* person. For the lethargic *kapha* person, however, a cup of coffee can provide a useful start-up energy.

MACROBIOTICS

The core tenet of macrobiotics is a modified yin-yang theory. Macrobiotics, a term coined in Japan in the 1930s, was popularized in the United States by Michio and Aveline Kushi. At its best, it's a plant-based diet of whole, seasonal, regional, and organic foods. Through their literature and wholesale and retail businesses, the proponents of macrobiotics helped define and implement the budding natural foods industry in the 1960s and 1970s. In addition, the macrobiotic movement is primarily responsible for introducing or reintroducing to our cuisine such quality foods as whole grains, seaweed, and many unpasteurized, fermented foods.

My criticism of macrobiotics is that its dualistic yin-yang answer for every food and phenomenon renders it simplistic and, in its worst applications, counterproductive to a healthy balance. Traditional, time-tested healing systems draw from a vastly more comprehensive base.

END NOTE

I hope my description of these healing systems helps you decipher a food's medicinal properties. But don't fill your head with too many food facts and figures. Rather, fill your belly with good food. Then notice how it makes you feel.

As you attune yourself to a food's potential, watch your relationship to that food deepen. In any relationship, the more deeply we know the other—be it a neighbor, the cat, or an apple—the more that relationship offers. We don't expect depth from a stranger. Anonymous foods provide calories, but they lack succor. Let your everyday food choices help ameliorate specific health problems and support optimum health.

How to Implement a Nourishing Diet

We all wish to enjoy health, happiness, and well-being—and we sincerely extend that wish to others. Knowing that a good diet effectively supports overall health, we also know that food is not the whole answer. Vibrant well-being is supported by a healthy lifestyle, meaningful work that doesn't harm others, exercise, and—I believe—contemplative prayer, yoga, or meditation. In addition, the healthiest people I know actively give back to others and to their communities.

How does good food support health? From observing my own family and countless students, I believe gaining a deeper understanding of our foods—knowing their stories and energetic actions and discerning their quality—supports our well-being. Herein lies the raison d'être of this book. While knowledge about individual foods is a good starting place, it's not enough. Two relevant questions remain.

First, how do you efficiently implement a whole foods diet? With minimal time to spend in the kitchen, how can it be organized and equipped so that meal preparation is effortless?

Second, what diet works best for your specific needs? While this or that food may be good for thus and so, how are various foods combined to achieve a balanced diet that supports an individual's unique being?

SETTING THE STAGE

When I come home tired and hungry after a long day and there's nothing ready to eat, the kids are hungry, groceries need putting away, and the sink is full of dirty dishes, then convenience food is the option. In this situation, to cook from scratch—and to digest the results—is impossible. When cooking is drudgery, don't cook.

To enjoy cooking, I need an orderly space with each pot, hot pad, and spatula in its place. When washing rice, for example, I need a strainer, so I open the cupboard door under the sink and, without even looking or thinking, my hand removes the strainer from its hook. If I had to rummage through a drawer to find the same, I'd grumble "Now, *where* is that strainer?" The creative juice of food preparation slips away in proportion to the time wasted searching for a strainer.

When each tool of my craft is in its own place, and when I have the basic ingredients at hand, then cooking becomes a dance. As with any creative art—no matter how great our expertise or lack thereof—we can be renewed and enlivened by its practice. When I enjoy making the soup, that soup also tastes better and imparts better energy.

Therefore, to make a good soup, organizing your kitchen might be the first step. Part of organizing might include recycling poor-quality or stale ingredients as well as nonfunctional cookware and all those gadgets you never use. Scrubbing down surfaces, removing clutter, and giving the refrigerator a deep cleaning can transform your kitchen into an artist's studio.

Equipment

As a culinary artist, quality tools assist your art. If I offered you two cups of hot tea, one in a Styrofoam cup and the other in a glass cup, which would you choose? The one tasting *only* like tea and not like Styrofoam-spiked tea. The ions and molecules in both raw and cooked foods react with metallic and synthetic ions in cookware, storage containers, and service. Whenever possible, favor nonreactive cookware such as enamel, earthenware, or glass.

Even though heavy-gauge stainless or surgical steel is the least reactive metal, remove cooked food from metal as soon as it is cooked to minimize its metallic taste.

Stainless is a superior choice over aluminum or a synthetic (including the popular nonstick surfaces and the glass/polymer Vision Ware). While cast iron is good for dry foods or batters, it taints soups, watery dishes, or acid foods with harsh-tasting (and not bioavailable) iron.

As you are able to do so, upgrade your equipment. In the meantime, scour and organize what you have. Lacking a dream kitchen with top-quality equipment is a poor excuse for not starting today with what you have at hand.

Basic Cooking Elements

Most cooking applications require heat, water, salt, and oil. The quality of each of these primary elements affects the food as well as our overall energy and well-being. Foods cooked over wood or gas fuel have more flavor and impart more energy than the same foods cooked by electricity or microwave. If you doubt this statement, do a comparison and your taste buds will clearly inform you. Consider upgrading your kitchen range with your next remodel. In the meantime, you might recycle your microwave, or if it's built in, unplug it and use it as a bread box.

Overnight Soaking and the Crock-Pot

As your kitchen takes shape with quality basics, staples, and equipment claiming their commonsense space, the next thing to organize is meal plans. This brings us to my best strategy for eating well—being close to a satisfying meal when I'm hungry. If I'm hungry now, odds are I'll eat what is available. It's the healthy animal within us all. When hungry, we eat. If what I eat is vital and flavorful, then I am satisfied. On the other hand, if what I eat is stale, denatured, or lacking, then I feel stale, denatured, and lacking. And, probably, I'll overeat because a shoddy meal doesn't succor. Even though I may be physically full, I'll keep nibbling, trying to assuage a deeper hunger.

In an organized and well-equipped kitchen, planning a meal and dividing some of the preparation into stages make cooking effortless. For example, tonight I'll take three minutes to soak a pot of quinoa for breakfast. Tomorrow morning, all I need do is turn on the stove and, while I'm in the shower, breakfast—and the base for lunch or dinner—will be effortlessly cooking. I'll enjoy quinoa as a hot breakfast cereal, and I'll use the leftovers in a quinoa salad for lunch or I'll add it to a stir-fry for dinner. From experience, I know that having to stop and organize when I come home hungry or when I am rushing about in the morning is asking too much.

I believe the mind-set of "not having time to cook" has little to do with actual time. Having the first step of meal preparation accomplished gives you the psychological ease of knowing that nurture is near at hand. Your already-started breakfast simply awaits the second step—turning on the stove. Later, driving home from work, you can almost taste the remaining quinoa with arugula and tempeh or cubed chicken breast. It's a much different feeling than the edge of panic in, "What can I fix for dinner tonight?"

In addition to making meal preparation easier, soaking grains and beans overnight makes them easier to digest. Many people also rely on a slow cooker, or Crock-Pot, which enables them to wake up, or come home, to a hot meal.

These are some of my methods for organizing my kitchen and meal plans. Try them. In the process, you'll discover your own techniques for supporting your own good dietary habits.

YOUR OPTIMUM DIET

Here are three useful guidelines. The first is to examine historical precedent to determine your optimum diet; the second is to be informed about human digestion in general; and the third is to attune your cooking to your unique digestive processes.

Historical Precedence

Examine the dietary habits of traditional peoples living in temperate zones, hunter-gatherer peoples excepted. Until the past one hundred years or so, they consumed a grain-based diet of whole, seasonal, regional, fresh or preserved unrefined foods, with minimal animal foods. They ate no highly refined, chemical-laden foods. Where such peoples had the benefit of adequate calories, their overall health was superior to peoples eating a contemporary Western diet.

This traditional diet, with its four- to six-thousand-year success rate, provides us with useful guidelines to assess food trends, new diets, and fabricated foods. Regard media hype with skepticism. The same with research data. Often research is funded by private interest concerns. Even with more objective testing, scientific inquiry cannot access the sum total of a foods' energetic properties.

Human Digestive System

No matter how nutritious a carrot, it must be assimilated to provide you with nutrients. Because our culture doesn't support good digestive habits, it's useful to recall Grandmother's advice. Give thanks for our food, chew well, and sit down to eat. Do not eat in front of the television. Rather, enjoy the camaraderie of family and friends. If you habitually eat alone, remove extra chairs from the dining area so the room doesn't feel empty, put photos of your loved ones right on the table, light a candle, put on some beautiful music, and enjoy dining with your own good company.

To support digestion, avoid the following: late-night eating, intoxicants, frequent snacking, overeating, or eating denatured, refined, or poor-quality foods.

People requiring additional dietary support include the very young, the elderly, and convalescents. For them, prepare easy-to-digest, quality foods that are soft, low-fat, and mild tasting.

Food Combining

The way we combine foods also affects digestion. Different enzymes in the digestive system exist to digest specific foods, and some of them work solo. For example, when you eat fruit and grain at the same time, the fruit-digesting enzymes go to work first. Meanwhile, the grain waits in your warm and moist stomach. Put grain in a warm and moist environment and it starts to ferment. Such fermentation is useful when malting barley for beer but not for digestion. Symptoms of poor food combining include acid indigestion, sinusitis and other mucus-type problems, gastrointestinal complaints, bowel irregularity, and/or bloating.

Does this mean banishing peach pie? Fortunately, no. Fruit and grain combinations are less of a problem in the following cases. Cooked foods are easier to assimilate than raw. Imagine your reaction to peach pie versus fresh peach slices over oatmeal. We can intuitively sense which one is more digestible. Herbs and spices enhance digestion—such as cinnamon and ginger in peach pie. Lastly, because *agni,* or digestive function, decreases with age, people often note that food combining becomes more important as the years pass. For such individuals, digestive enhancers are available, including enzymes, probiotics, and various herbal formulas.

General food-combining guidelines for people with sensitive digestion include:

- Eat fruit by itself as a snack rather than combined with other foods; or when it's pie for dessert, give your digestive process some time between dinner and dessert.
- Milk is most easily digested when consumed alone.
- Proteins and starches are easiest to digest when eaten at separate meals and accompanied by nonstarchy vegetables, so enjoy bean soup or fish and a salad at one meal, bread or rice with stir-fried vegetables at another meal.

If the concept of food combining is new to you, don't let it overwhelm you. Experiment with it at a comfortable pace, and discover what works. Many students report that this single tool helps them feel better than ever before. Simply note—it's useful to write it down—how you feel when you follow food combining and how you feel when you don't. This exercise also encourages a new bodily awareness of cause and effect. Because we like to feel good, this body-centered knowing what makes us feel good is a powerful aid for implementing healthy dietary habits.

Your Specific Diet

Today, the number of people with compromised assimilation is immense. Challenged digestion is implicated in environmental and food allergies, candida-type yeast infections, chronic fatigue, diabetes, hypoglycemia, depression, challenged immune systems, arthritis, diabetes, and cancer. Enhancing digestive function is critical to regaining health. In addition, some people may need to follow a restricted diet temporarily. Others may need a parasite elemination program. Some may require the assistance of a qualified health care practitioner.

Factors contributing to the general decline in health include the use of broad-spectrum antibiotics, antiseptic mouthwashes, alcoholic beverages, and chlorinated water. These substances destroy our intestinal flora population. Healthy intestinal flora supports complete assimilation of food and also serves as a barrier against pathogens.

Your Diet and Other People

In an ideal world, your family, friends, and coworkers will not only support your dietary upgrades but may even be curious enough to try what you're doing and incorporate relevant changes themselves. If this is your situation, be thankful. Unfortunately, some people—possibly because they're battling or ignoring their own food issues—are less than helpful. Here are some suggestions.

Create a healthy-eating support system. If this isn't in your home, find it elsewhere. Bring a Crock-Pot of soup to share at work to help initiate a network; start a study group; join natural foods cooking classes; or find like-minded friends online. Support is out there as more people increasingly make positive dietary choices.

Don't try to change your family and friends. Tossing out their favorite junk food or lecturing them doesn't work. Claim ownership for what you're doing and grant others the dignity of making their own choices. With young children, however, having only healthful options available at home is ideal.

Being Good to Yourself

Be loving and compassionate with yourself. Effectively implementing dietary upgrades takes time. If you find yourself eating something—say a Big Mac and Coke—that you'd promised yourself never to eat again, relax. Don't worry. Acknowledge both your intention and what you're actually doing. Bless that burger and then really taste it. Savor its textures, be with its flavors, note how it feels in your stomach, pay special attention to how you feel right after eating it, and then tune in to how you feel one and two hours later. This kind of body awareness helps inform future food choices.

We tend to be a compulsive, all-or-nothing culture. Many of us have dieted for one week and binged for the next two. With this whole foods dietary upgrade, consider the more realistic Ayurvedic one-quarter approach. If you want to give up coffee, for example, reduce the amount you drink by one-fourth until you are comfortable at this new plateau. Then, reduce coffee consumption by another one-fourth and so on. This approach brings about lasting freedom from undesired habits. It also makes it possible for you, when you choose to treat yourself to an occasional cup of coffee, to savor it with abandon. Remorse, good-bye!

The New
Whole Foods Encyclopedia

ACHIOTE See **Annatto.**

ACORN
(Quercus)

If you've ever wondered why the wooden pulls attached to Venetian blind cords are shaped like acorns, it's because of Thor. This Norse god ruled both thunder and oak trees. Surely, therefore, oaks were protected from lightning, and hanging an acorn talisman at one's window might prevent it from striking indoors.

Oaks grow throughout the northern hemisphere and range from the 150-foot stately English oak to thickets of scrubby Gambles oak in the Rocky Mountains. Oak fruits, acorns, figured prominently in the diets of hunter-gatherer peoples and are still eaten today during times of famine. Chestnutlike in texture, the thin-shelled, starchy seed is nestled in a tiny basal cup. It is considered "one of the most palatable wild foods" by H. D. Harrington who ate his way through uncounted edibles while researching his classic reference work, *Edible Native Plants of the Rocky Mountains.*

Health Benefits The acorn is 8 percent protein and 5 percent fat and contains 68 percent carbohydrates. It helps to stabilize blood sugar and so is used both for hypogly-

---

ACORN TEA PARTY

My children used to forage acorns. As the woody caps make perfect doll-size tea cups, we had a seasonal supply of the nutmeats. We ground them in a blender and soaked them in several changes of water until they tasted sweet. Leaching, which takes from a few hours to a few days depending upon acorn variety, is as easy as soaking a pot of beans. Next we added the moist acorn meal to muffin or cookie batter for their excellent flavor—and for the fun of it.

cemia and for hyperglycemia. Acorns contain a bitter tannic acid that must be leached out before use. They are a nurturing food, helping build mass and supporting the stomach and spleen-pancreas meridians.

Use Traditionally, acorn meal is used alone or in combination with other grains in mush, soups, bread, and quick breads. When leached and roasted, they are also a tasty snack food.

Buying/Foraging The only commercial source of acorns of which I'm aware is as an ingredient in the rich coffee substitute Yannoh. This Belgian import is available in natural food stores.

See **Nuts.**

ACORN SQUASH
(Cucurbita pepo)

Shaped like a deeply ribbed acorn, this winter squash is a longtime American favorite. Newer varieties are super sweet; the heirloom varieties are mildly sweet. An acorn's hard skin is usually dark green but some squashes are orange or may become orange upon maturity. Compared to a buttercup or butternut squash, the acorn flesh is pale yellow rather than orange, dryer, less dense, and somewhat stringy. For beautiful flower shapes, slice this squash crosswise into thin rounds.

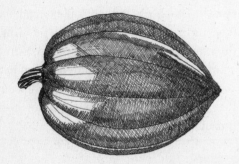

See **Winter Squash.**

ADUKI
Adzuki, Azuki
(Phaseolus angularis)

According to the Japanese, who feature the aduki in their finest dishes—from soup to dessert—it is the "king of beans." Cultivated for centuries in Asia, aduki beans are now grown commercially in the United States. In cooking, substitute the aduki freely for other common beans.

Health Benefits Aduki beans tonify the kidneys and have diuretic properties. This action is enhanced when aduki beans are cooked with sweet rice or when just the liquid from cooked aduki beans is drunk 20 minutes before a meal. The aduki is easier to assimilate than most other beans. Aduki reduces *vata* (in moderation), *pitta,* and especially *kapha.*

Buying Aduki beans imported from Japan are lightly polished to a bright sheen and are the most costly. Domestic and most Chinese beans are not polished and, as a result, have a barely noticeable gritty texture.

See **Beans and Legumes.**

AGAR
Agar-Agar, Kanten
(Pterocladia, Gracilaria et al.)

Contrary to popular belief, gelatin is not made from cattle hooves and horns. Commercial gelatin is extracted from the cartilage, ligaments, tendons, bones, and hides of cattle, horses, and pigs. This information gives agar—an unprocessed, nutritious gelling agent—extra appeal. Agar, which you may remember from high school days, is the growth medium found in petri dishes.

Vegetable Jell-O is another term for this type of red marine algae known as agarophytes (agar yielding), which contain a complex starch that makes an ideal gelling agent.

Health Benefits The healthful agar gel not only enhances the flavors of other foods but also acts as a mild laxative and lends bulk. Agar soothes the entire digestive tract, making it an excellent invalid and infant food. It bonds with toxic and radioactive pollutants and dispels them from the body. Agar is rich in iodine, calcium, iron, phosphorus, and vitamins A, B-complex, C, D, and K. Agar reduces *vata* and *pitta*.

When the accompanying recipe is made with only the fruit and juice of apples and/or pears, it soothes inflamed bronchia and lungs.

Use Throughout the world agar is used as a gelling agent in such products as jam, yogurt, and candy. Agar is easy to use and contains absolutely no calories. It does not gel when combined with acetic acid, found in wine and distilled vinegar, or with oxalic acid, found in chocolate, rhubarb, and spinach. To gel 1 cup of liquid, use ½ teaspoon fine agar powder (or 1 teaspoon granulated agar or 1½ tablespoons kanten flakes).

Buying Agar is available in a variety of forms including flaked, powdered, granular, and bars. The bars, called kanten, consist of numerous agar varieties. Flakes and powdered or granulated agar are usually made from one agar variety harvested off the Pacific coast of South America.

See Kanten; Seaweed.

AGAR-AGAR See Agar.

BETTER THAN JELL-O

Here's a dessert that takes three minutes to cook and just one hour to set. Because agar enhances other flavors, the dish will taste even more delicious than the fruit juice and fruits you use to flavor it with. Use a 100 percent natural juice and you'll be pleased with this unpretentious and satisfying dessert.

4 cups apple juice or fresh apple cider
2 teaspoons agar powder (or 4 teaspoons granular agar or 6 tablespoons kanten flakes)
2 cups fresh strawberries, sliced

Pour the juice into a saucepan and add the agar. Bring to a boil over medium heat. Watch closely to prevent boiling over, stir to blend, and simmer for 1 minute. Pour the liquid into a shallow dish. Strew with strawberries. Allow to sit, uncovered, in a cool place until set, about 1 hour. To expedite setting, refrigerate.

ALARIA
(Alaria marginata)

My friend Shep Erhart, who makes a living foraging different kinds of seaweed in Maine, reports that alaria "is the most beautiful to look at, the most delicate to the taste, and the most dangerous to harvest." Alaria loves rocky, windswept peninsulas where it curls and crashes with every breaking wave. At the lowest tides of the new and full moon during late spring, Shep hand-cuts these native greens, handful by handful.

IMMERSED IN SENSUALITY

Harvesting alaria I enter into another time/space consciousness, mesmerized by the motions of undulating alaria fronds, the ocean's rhythms, and sunlight. Immersed in the sensuality of it all with deep joy, I fill my sacks and then carry them ashore across the slippery, rocky, ocean-washed terrain. . . . As I do this work, I feel thankful and honored from my depths to be able to continue to be with the alaria, remembering that along with it goes the obligation to work for protection of the ocean and her inhabitants.
—John and Eleanor Lewallen, *Sea Vegetable Gourmet Cookbook and Wildcrafter's Guide*

Alaria is biologically very similar to Japanese wakame but is wilder tasting and requires longer cooking. Alaria is high in protein and calcium; it is also high in other minerals and nutrients.

See **Seaweed.**

ALBI See Taro.

ALFALFA SPROUTS
Lucerne
(Medicago sativa)

Alfalfa originated in Arabia and was called *al fasfasah* meaning "father of all foods." To learn how such a tiny seed earned such a big name, look to its roots. This legume's amazing root system penetrates 100 feet into the ground and pulls up minerals and trace minerals unavailable to radishes and most of our other vegetables, whose roots range from a few inches to a few feet.

Health Benefits Alfalfa is a cooling herb that detoxifies and tonifies damp conditions, controls bleeding, lowers cholesterol, acts as a diuretic and appetizer, and augments the urinary system and the intestines. It aids in the assimilation of protein, fats, and carbohydrates. In addition, alfalfa contains the phytoestrogens *daidzein* and *genistein*, which block some cancers and ease menopausal distress. Alfalfa sprouts reduce *kapha* and *pitta*.

If you have an autoimmune disease such as rheumatoid arthritis or lupus, eat only mature alfalfa sprouts or leaves which are, in fact, medicinal for such conditions. Alfalfa seeds and immature sprouts, however, contain the amino acid canavanine that can exacerbate those conditions. It's easy to distinguish immature from mature sprouts— the latter have set forth their first two leaves.

Alfalfa is up to 30 percent protein by dry weight and is an excellent source of chlorophyll, vitamins K and P (bioflavonoids), and carotene. Almost as good as seaweed as a food mineral source, alfalfa contains calcium, iron, magnesium, potassium, manganese, phosphorus, sodium, sulfur, silicon, chlorine, cobalt, and zinc.

Use While mature alfalfa is typically fermented into silage for cattle, for human consumption it is sprouted and its pea-flavored leaves are used in salads or as a medicinal tea and herbal supplement.

See **Sprouts.**

ALGAE See Microalgae; Seaweed.

ALMOND
(Prunus dulcis)

A cousin of peaches, plums, and apricots, the almond is our oldest cultivated nut; wild almonds have been found in excavated Greek archaeological sites dating from 8000 B.C. Two types of almonds are grown—sweet and bitter. Sweet almonds are used primarily as a nutmeat. Bitter almonds are used in French and Italian confections, made into almond extract, and also used in cosmetics. One hundred percent of the commercial almonds grown in the United States come from vast orchards in the San Joaquin and Sacramento valleys in California. Almonds are the seventh largest U.S. food export.

Health Benefits Almonds are generally regarded as superior to other nuts in terms of their medicinal action. They restore, tone, and nurture. They support the digestive tract and the nervous system. The almond is the only nut that helps to mildly alkalinize the system. Like the pits of plums and its other relatives, the almond contains cyanidelike substances that—besides giving a feeling of well-being—have strong medicinal action including inhibition of cancer. The more recent discovery of almond's phytonutrient phytosterol also attests to its anticancer activity and its ability to lower cholesterol.

As a kitchen remedy, almonds are used for the relief of a dry cough (but not a productive cough). They relieve constipation, kidney stones, and gallstones. They build mental and spiritual proclivity and strengthen the bones, nerves, and reproductive system, according to Ayurvedic medicine. Almonds are *tridoshic* and are especially calming to *vata*.

Almonds contain about 18 percent protein, several B vitamins, calcium, iron, potassium, and phosphorus. They are one of the richest sources of alpha-tocopherol vitamin E. Like most nuts, they are high in unsaturated fats.

Use Almonds are easiest to digest when soaked overnight (or all day) and then eaten raw or toasted. The brown skin is bitter and a mild stomach irritant; remove it by rubbing soaked or blanched almonds between your hands.

Buying On a shelled almond, the thin brown skin should be intact since it provides some protection from rancidity.

See **Nuts.**

ALMOND BUTTER See **Nut and Seed Butters.**

ALMOND MILK

Almonds make a delicate but satisfying dairyfree and soyfree milk. Use this sweet

---

DELICIOUS ALMOND MILK IN MINUTES

3 tablespoons organic almonds

1 cup water

1 teaspoon honey or maple syrup (optional)

Soak the almonds overnight in water to cover. Strain and discard the soaking water. Rub the almonds between your hands to remove the skins. Place in a blender, add the water and sweetener if desired. Blend at high speed until smooth. Pour through a strainer for a smooth consistency.

nut milk in smoothies, soups, casseroles, desserts, and by the glassful.

Check the ingredients in the almond milk in aseptic packaging to see if it meets your criteria for quality. If not, homemade almond milk is easy to make, tastes even better, and is certainly fresher and therefore more healthful.

ALOE VERA
Medicine Plant
(Aloe vera)

> Nicodemus . . . brought a mixture of myrrh and aloes, weighing about a hundred pounds. They took the body of Jesus and wrapped it with the spices in linen cloths, following the Jewish burial custom.
>
> —John 19:39–41

Since the time of the Egyptian pharaohs, the gel from the aloe plant was used medicinally for many purposes, including an embalming agent. Aloe vera grows in clustering rosettes of stiff, upright leaves. There are many aloe species, but aloe vera (which means "true aloe" in Latin) is considered to be the most therapeutic.

Health Benefits Aloe has antibiotic, antiviral, astringent, and antiparasitic properties. It inhibits pain, enhances immune system function, stimulates growth, and acts as a coagulating agent. Aloe vera juice is widely used as a bowel regulator; it is nonabrasive and soothing to the intestinal tract and relieves ulcers. Aloe is a balancing beverage for summer heat and is a yin tonic. It treats premenstrual pain and menopausal heat and is good for women who have had hysterecto-

mies. It is *tridoshic*. The whole leaf, available powdered, is intensely purgative—consult with your natural health care practitioner regarding dosage. Because aloe stimulates the uterus, it is not used during pregnancy.

For external use, aloe contains a wound hormone that accelerates the rate of healing for injured and burned surfaces. The enzymatic activity of aloe reportedly reduces or eliminates scars.

Use If you've a decorative aloe plant in your home, there's your optimum aloe supply. For external use, snip a piece of leaf, split it open, and dab the gel on burns, irritated skin, or wounds. For a beverage, scrape off two tablespoons of gel from a split leaf, stir into a glass of water or juice, and drink, or follow your health care practitioner's recommendation.

Buying Aloe vera is available in many forms: concentrate, drink, powdered extract (used only as a laxative), gel, and juice. Purchase only *unrefined* or unfiltered aloe vera products; they taste bitter but contain active ingredients.

AMARANTH
(Amaranthus)

Domesticated more than five thousand years ago in Mexico, amaranth once was the sacred food of the Aztecs, as important as corn until the conquering Spaniard, Hernando Cortés, forbade its cultivation. (It suffered the same fate as did the Incas' revered

THE BEST PLANTS TO SLEEP WITH— ORCHIDS AND ALOE

Most houseplants release oxygen and absorb carbon dioxide during the day; aloe, orchids, snake plants, and bromeliads, however, do the opposite. By upping the oxygen while you sleep, they make ideal bedroom companions. In addition, they remove toxins.

Dr. B. C. Wolverton, the noted scientist who created a breathable environment for the NASA lunar habitat, pioneered the study of the value of houseplants for our health and has written *How to Grow Fresh Air: 50 House Plants That Purify Your Home or Office*. In addition to increasing humidity and oxygen, houseplants remove human bioeffluents (substances emitted through normal biological processes), including carbon dioxide, carbon monoxide, hydrogen, methane, alcohol, and others. Houseplants are also superior filters of common environmental pollutants such as ammonia, formaldehyde, and benzene.

"Houseplants," writes Dr. Wolverton, "are no longer luxuries, but essential to health. They are nature's 'eco-friendly' living air purifiers, with years of documented scientific evidence to prove it."

grain, quinoa.) Farther north, Zuni legends relate that amaranth had been brought up from the underworld at the time of their emergence.

The United Nations Food and Agriculture Organization has encouraged amaranth's use since 1967 because wherever amaranth is consumed there is little or no malnutrition. The amaranth family includes more than 60 different species, mostly wild, on five of the seven continents. In fact, the genus is recognized as one of the world's most successful weeds. The four groups of amaranth can be grown for grain, leaf, dye, or as a garden ornamental. While I grow amaranth for its seeds and magenta-colored greens, it is undoubtedly my garden's most stately ornamental. Amaranth seeds are as small as poppy seeds and their color ranges from purple-black to buff yellow, although most are golden, cream colored, or pink hued. One plant yields a massive number of seeds—up to 50 thousand—enough seed to plant two acres. Amaranth is a relative of spinach and quinoa and is a member of the goosefoot family.

Health Benefits Amaranth plants are members of an elite group of photosynthetic superperformers that botanists call the C4 group. C4 plants utilize a photosynthetic process or pathway that has above-normal efficiency in converting soil, sunlight, and water into plant tissue. Thus amaranth has enhanced environmental adaptation and is extraordinarily nutritious.

Amaranth is higher than milk in protein and calcium (including the supporting calcium cofactors, magnesium and silicon), making it an especially helpful food for nursing or pregnant women, infants, children, people who do heavy physical labor, and people wanting to gain weight. The seed is appreciated for its remarkable vitality.

Amaranth is a cooling, astringent food, beneficial to congested lungs. It controls bleeding and helps check diarrhea and excessive menstruation. Amaranth reduces *vata* and *kapha* and, when used in moderation, *pitta*.

Use Several packaged health foods contain an insignificant percentage of amaranth flour but are promoted as amaranth products. That's a scam. Likewise, don't look to a cold breakfast cereal, amaranth or otherwise, as healthful; it is too denatured to really nourish. If you want to benefit from amaranth's vitality, cook it as a grain and expect a wild and woolly flavor. Or cook a few tablespoons of amaranth with a cup of rice, quinoa, or another grain. It thickens soups and stews and is tasty when popped. A confection sold by street vendors, called *alegria* in Mexico and *ladoos* in India, is made of popped amaranth bound with a sweetener.

See **Amaranth Flour; Amaranth Greens; Grains.**

AMARANTH FLOUR

Amaranth flour has a distinctive flavor and blends well with other flours in numerous dishes. It is non-glutinous, so it is appreciated by people with grain or gluten sensitivities. Generally a small portion is used in leavened products. Flatbreads may have a higher percentage of amaranth flour.

See **Flour.**

AMARANTH GREENS
En Choy, Pigweed, Yin Tsoi
(Amaranthus)

Like basil, amaranth leaves may be green or magenta red. They are an earthy-tasting vegetable similar to spinach but with more substance and character. Amaranth leaves are soft but rough textured and grow in clusters on slender stalks from one to six feet tall. Their immature fleshy seed heads are eaten like broccoli.

Health Benefits Amaranth greens effectively treat diarrhea and other gastrointestinal disorders. Externally, they're used as a poultice or pack for nosebleeds, vaginal discharge, and ulcerated sores in the mouth. Amaranth greens rank at the top as a superior and easily digested source of calcium and iron; they're also rich in protein, beta carotene, and vitamin C.

Buying/Foraging/Harvesting You can find amaranth greens at an Asian greengrocer in late spring and early summer; they look like extra-large basil leaves but without serration. They can be oval or as narrow as mint.

If foraging or harvesting, collect the greens from the plant before it flowers. Gather the immature seed heads as they bud. It is, however, imperative to not gather amaranth (or any other plant) in polluted areas since the plant "easily picks up and accumulates high levels of nitrates . . . [which may] cause severe gastrointestinal discomfort, cramps, and nausea," warns foraging expert Tom Brown.

Use Use very young amaranth greens in salads. Larger leaves and stems are an excellent potherb. One of my favorite ways to cook amaranth greens is with purple potatoes in a spectacularly colored pink soup. You may also stir-fry, sauté, or steam them. Cook the leaves only until tender, about 5 minutes, since their color fades with overcooking.

AMASAKE

At the Crestone Mountain Zen Center, amasake is the nightcap. At the end of a long, rigorous silent practice day and while still formally seated in the *zendo*, a cup of the creamy, warm, sweet liquid is served. It feels so good in the belly and assures a good night's sleep.

Amasake is like a thick rice pudding with a unique, satisfying, and never cloying sweetness. It's fermented from koji and sweet rice and may be as thick and lush as a malted milk or as thin as milk. This traditional Japanese food is produced in the first fermentation of sake making; the name literally means sweet sake.

Health Benefits If I were running a marathon, I'd stash amasake at my aid stations because it is nutrient dense and predigested so it doesn't take energy—it gives it. This fermented rice is broken down into soluble complex carbohydrates and maltose (a grain-malt sugar), and it increases blood sugar slowly rather than rapidly like more simple sugars.

Amasake's primary sugar is still more complex than sugar, honey, or maple syrup, so it is a more healthful sweetener because it has a softer impact on blood sugar irregularity. It calms *vata* and *pitta*. Amasake is an excellent food for the very young, the elderly, and convalescents.

Use A prepared amasake beverage from the store can be either thick or thin. Serve it hot or cold with your favorite seasoning or with ginger, cardamom, and a drop of vanilla.

Buying/Making Amasake beverages are available in the refrigerated section and on open shelves at your natural food store with other nondairy milk. Amasake comes in various flavors. As is usual with fermented prod-

ucts like cheese and wine, brands vary in flavor and texture; experiment with different brands to find your favorite.

G.E.M. Cultures (see page 402), Asian markets, and some natural food stores sell the amasake inoculant, koji, which is packaged with directions for making homemade amasake. Making it is as easy as making yogurt. Mix 1 cup koji with 3 cups of freshly cooked, unsalted rice and, while it is still hot, cover it and incubate at 130 degrees for about 12 hours. For a variation, I enjoy making amasake from other grains; currently posole is my favorite.

See **Fermented Foods**.

ANAHEIM CHILE See Chile Pepper.

ANASAZI BEAN
(Phaseolus vulgaris)

The mottled maroon-and-white anasazi bean is similar to a Jacob's cattle bean but smaller and plumper. When cooked, it is sweet and has a slightly gritty texture. It may be freely substituted for black, pinto, bolita, or pink beans in Mexican-style dishes.

Compared to other beans, anasazi beans are easier to assimilate. Compared to a pinto, for example, they contain 75 percent less of the flatulence-causing trisaccharides.

See **Beans and Legumes**.

ANCHO CHILE See Chile Pepper.

ANGELICA
(Angelica archangelica)

To name an herb archangel is some indication of its value in Europe. And that angelica is a tonifying herb second only to ginseng in Asia makes a strong case for its value. There's little culinary use of angelica today outside of crystallized stems for decorating confections. However, if you can find it fresh, blanch the young stems as a salad ingredient. The seeds, roots, stems, and leaves are used for digestive, urinary, and female problems.

See **Carrot Family; Herbs and Spices.**

ANISE
Anise Seed
(Pimpinella anisum)

Of my mother's vast cookie repertoire, my favorite is a minuscule anise cake. One teaspoon of batter per morsel rests on a cookie sheet overnight. When baked the next day, the moist interior batter puffs up under the dried surface to create an iced, double-decker appearance. The cookie's whimsical shape befits the sweet but racy anise seeds sprinkled throughout.

The tiny fruits or seeds of this parsley family plant of Mediterranean origin have remained popular since ancient Egyptian times. Because its licoricelike aroma is so similar to fennel, in Asian countries the two are used interchangeably; of the two, however, anise has a rounder, sweeter licorice flavor compared to fennel's bite. Today, Turkey is the primary anise producer, though Spain produces a superior crop.

Health Benefits Anise has a sweet flavor and a strong licorice aroma. It benefits the liver, stomach, kidneys, and spleen-pancreas. It is warming, builds *chi* and energy, supports lactation, aids digestion, clears asthma that has underlying cold symptoms, and relieves bronchitis. It helps control excessive menstruation, and it relieves spasms and other wind-related imbalances. James Duke, in his *Green Pharmacy*, notes that anise also has anticarcinogenic properties. Traditionally, anise was considered an aphrodisiac. It has mild abortive properties and so its medicinal use is not recommended during pregnancy.

Use Today, inexpensive and synthetic anise flavorings have displaced anise's prior culinary popularity. Anise still flavors some sausages and stews and is occasionally found in cakes or festive breads or confections made of dried fruit. Its primary use is, however, in anise-flavored liquors, including arak, raki, ouzo, and pernod.

In Peru, anise ranks with chamomile as a popular herbal tea and is listed on many restaurant menus. In Mediterranean regions, fresh anise greens are used as a salad ingredient and a cooked vegetable.

See **Herbs and Spices.**

ANJOU PEAR See **Pear.**

ANNATTO
Achiote, Lipstick Tree
(Bixa orellana)

The rust-colored seeds of the annatto evergreen are a potent, almost neon orange-red colorant. The intensity of color is comparable to turmeric only it is predominantly salmon red rather than mustard yellow. The plant's alternate name, lipstick tree, denotes its cosmetic use; but long before the term lipstick was coined, Amazonians used annatto as a body dye and insect repellent.

Annatto was used in the original Aztec

ANNATTO OIL FOR HALLOWEEN
PAINT AND FUSION CUISINE

To infuse annatto, sauté ½ teaspoon annatto seeds in 1 tablespoon unrefined oil
or butter over low heat for 4 to 5 minutes, or until the oil turns a vivid scarlet-
orange. Strain, discarding the seeds. Stir
seasoned oil into soup, grain dishes,
stuffing for tamales or humitas, or use it
in marinades.

I infuse annatto as I need it. If, however, you would like to keep a supply on
hand, infuse 3 tablespoons annatto seeds
in 1 cup of oil or butter.

chocolate beverage to deepen the brew's
color. It continued as a common chocolate
ingredient in Europe through the sixteenth
century. Since then, annatto's main culinary
use is as to tint butter, margarine, and cheese.
Today, this small, bushy plant is grown commercially in the Philippines and throughout
tropical Americas—its place of origin.

Health Benefits Annatto is mildly bitter
and astringent. It contains a high rate of carotenoids and carotenoid factors, which explains its effectiveness as a dye and as a
medicinal herb. Annatto's vast ethnobotani-
cal uses include treatment for headaches,
cancer, diabetes, inflammation, jaundice, ep-
ilepsy, and tumors. It is also used as an aphrodisiac and douche.

Use Today, annatto tints fusion cuisine
and Latino dishes. Annatto also colors some
Philippine and other Asian dishes including
an unauthentic version of Beijing duck. An-

natto's faint, floral perfume and modest taste
does little, if anything, to flavor food.

Buying Annatto is available in Latino,
Asian, and natural food markets, whole,
ground into a paste, or sometimes oil infused. You can infuse your own using quality
oil or butter.

See **Herbs and Spices**.

APPLE
(Malus pumila)

Why is the protrusion in your neck called
Adam's apple? Apparently Adam couldn't
swallow that bite of forbidden fruit. The
apple originated not far from the mythical
Eden, in Almaty, Kazakhstan, in Central Asia,
where wild apple trees still cover the
foothills.

The apple, a rose family member, is the
most popular temperate-zone fruit, and it
grows in almost every state in the United
States. Washington produces more than half
of the apple crop, and most of it comes from
eastern Washington where some twelve billion apples are thinned and picked by hand.

Health Benefits Apples contain malic
and tartaric acids, which inhibit fermentation
in the stomach, making apples easier to assimilate than most other fruits. They are
cooling and act upon the spleen-pancreas
and stomach meridians. Apples are moistening and so ease thirst, reduce fever, and ease
dry, hot lungs. In addition, apples—especially green apples—cleanse the liver and
gallbladder and help soften gallstones. Their
pectin promotes beneficial intestinal flora
and supports normal colon function.

To reduce fever in children, serve them

grated raw apples. To ease a dry cough, steam apples with honey. To eliminate mucus from the lungs, prepare apples with agar. Apples are an excellent low-calorie source of pectin, fiber, and nutrients. Their flavonoids may reduce the risk of heart disease and inhibit the development of certain cancers. Apples reduce *pitta* and *kapha*. When cooked, they can be eaten in moderation for *vata*.

Use More than 7,500 apple varieties are grown throughout the world today. Because every apple seed contains unique genetic material, you can plant ten seeds from a single apple and get ten different kinds of apple trees. However, most of our commercial varieties lack genetic diversity. More commonly available apples, listed below, are classified according to use:

- **Eating Apples** Apples with a crisp, juicy, firm texture include Cortland, Criterion, Elstar, Fuji, Golden Delicious, Gala, Granny Smith, Jonagold, Jonathan, McIntosh, Newton Pippin, Stayman, and Winesap.
- **Pie and Applesauce Apples** Tart and juicy apples include Cortland, Criterion, Elstar, Golden Delicious, Granny Smith, Jonagold, Jonathan, McIntosh, Newton Pippin, Northern Spy, and Rome Beauty.
- **Baking Apples** Apples that become tender with baking while holding their shape and flavor include Rome Beauty (considered the best), Cropland, Golden Delicious, Granny Smith, Ida Red, Jonagold, Newton Pippin, and Northern Spy.

RED, BRIMMING WITH SUGAR, BLEMISHFREE, AND CHASTE

Antique apples have a vast flavor range, often a mottled skin, a less than symmetrical shape, and they have sex. With the help of bees and breezes, they beget diverse offspring.

In contrast, most of today's sugary-sweet, cosmetically perfect apples are grafted—rather than grown from seed—from the same parents (Red Delicious, Golden Delicious, Jonathan, McIntosh, and Cox's Orange Pippin). This genetic uniformity, according to an article in *The New York Times* by Michael Pollan, "makes the apple a sitting duck for its enemies. In the wild, a plant and its pests are continually coevolving, in a dance of resistance and conquest that can have no ultimate victor. But coevolution freezes in an orchard of grafted trees, since they are genetically identical. The problem is that the apples no longer get to have sex, which is nature's way of testing out fresh genetic combinations."

A genetically identical orchard enables bacteria, fungi, and viruses to grow unchecked as the trees quickly lose whatever resistance they may have once possessed. This helps explain why apples require more pesticides than almost any other crop.

Buying The fact that apples store well and are versatile helps account for their popularity. Select firm, crisp apples with a vivid color. Peak season for apples is from September to March. Some varieties in controlled-atmosphere storage hold as long as twelve months.

Freshly harvested apples have their own waxy coating that protects them from shriveling and weight loss. Once harvested, apples are washed, and washing removes about half of the original apple wax. Commercial apples are waxed with carnauba (from a Brazilian palm tree) or shellac (made from the resinous secretion of various insects of the *Lacciferinae* family). According to the Washington Apple Commission, it is a thin coat and requires but a few drops to cover each fruit. Organic fruits are not waxed and therefore have a reduced shelf life.

See **Fruit.**

APPLE BUTTER

A thick, brown paste made by concentrating applesauce. A quality apple butter is the most healthful and natural preserve found in a natural food store—and it is sweet and delicious. Other conserves are sweetened with fruit juice concentrate, sugar, or honey.

APPLE CIDER

Real apple cider is an effervescent beverage that makes apple juice pale by comparison. A regional commodity, it is not pasteurized and is best consumed within a week (before it ferments into an alcoholic drink or vinegar). Hard (alcoholic) cider was especially popular in America from prerevolutionary days up until Prohibition.

APPLE CIDER VINEGAR

Traditionally made cider vinegar is nothing but freshly pressed apple juice allowed to

---

COMMONSENSE CLEANLINESS

Since September 1998, the FDA requires that cider display a warning label saying the product may contain illness-causing bacteria. This ominous warning has effectively ended commercial cider availability in my region and possibly elsewhere.

What instigated this regulation is that tragically—and stupidly—a load of cider apples was hauled to a manufacturer in an unsterilized truck that had previously hauled manure. The virulent bacteria E.coli contaminated the apples and one child who consumed the cider died. If you or a neighbor have access to a cider press—and if you use commonsense cleanliness in pressing—you may still relish a harvest toast of fresh cider.

---

ferment over a four- to six-week period at room temperature. It contains no added clarifiers, enzymes, or preservatives. Rich with sediment and strongly acidic, a quality cider vinegar tastes like the apples from which it was pressed.

Health Benefits Vinegar immediately increases circulation and therefore moves stasis—be it emotional or physical. Due largely to its mineral content (especially potassium) and its ability to normalize the body's acid/alkaline balance, apple cider vinegar has long been valued as a versatile folk remedy. Internally, it cleanses the digestive tract; externally, it disinfects any skin wounds or abrasions. Its acidity reportedly aids in the removal of calcium deposits from joints and blood vessels without affecting normal calcium levels in the bones and teeth.

In the best-selling book *Folk Medicine,* Dr. D. C. Jarvis prescribes an old Vermont kitchen tonic—two teaspoons of apple cider vinegar and a teaspoon of honey in a cup of water—to treat chronic fatigue, headache, arthritis, colitis, obesity, food poisoning, kidney inflammation, insomnia, high blood pressure, dizziness, sore throat, and a host of other ailments in both humans as well as farm animals. Several centuries later, the effectiveness of this remedy is still attested to by countless individuals. It is a treatment, however, that I recommend only as a short-term symptomatic cure, since prolonged use does not address the root of the problem. As Paul Pitchford, teacher and author of *Healing with Whole Foods,* warns, regular use of a vinegar remedy can lead to a kind of vinegar dependency. Furthermore, he advises, it is contraindicated in cases of "weak digestion marked by loose, watery stools; general *deficiency* (frailty); muscular injury or weakness, including rheumatism." Vinegar is *rajasic* and calms *vata*.

Use Apple cider vinegar is used in dressings, sauces, condiments, marinades, and pickles.

Buying Unless a cider vinegar is specified as *certified* organic, unfiltered, and unpasteurized, I don't buy it. Commercial and even "natural" or "organic" cider vinegar by law may be diluted with water and treated with meta-bisulfite. Ideally, apple cider vinegar is stored in a lightfree environment to protect it from free radical activity and the breakdown of vital nutrients.

See Vinegar.

APRICOT
(Prunus armeniaca)

For those who have dallied amid apricot trees bearing ripe fruit, it makes perfect sense that nectar was the drink of the gods. Though my *Oxford English Dictionary* does not associate the apricot with nectar, common usage does, and it's an association that I have never doubted.

Apricot's malic and citric acid content give a lemony bite to this otherwise sweet, buttery fruit, a plum relative that originated in Asia. Today, California produces 90 percent of the domestic apricot crop; Washington, Colorado, Idaho, and Utah supply the rest.

Health Benefits Apricots have a lubricating action on the lungs and colon and are used for a dry throat, dry coughs, bronchitis, asthma, emphysema, and dry constipation. Excess consumption, however, may weaken the body or depress the central nervous system or respiratory functions. Apricots should be eaten in moderation during pregnancy.

An apricot's vibrant gold color marks it as a superior source of vitamin A and carotene. Its alpha, beta, gamma, and delta carotenoids serve as an antioxidant and protect DNA from free-radical damage. Dried apricots are a good source of iron, cobalt, and copper, and are an effective remedy for anemia. Extracts of laetrile, used in cancer therapy, are derived from the amygdalin of apricots and their kernels (see Almond). Apricots are *tri-*

doshic. If, however, they are sour, they are not recommended for *pitta.*

Use If you do not have access to just-harvested, ripe apricots, then dried apricots are your best choice. Rehydrate and use in fruit compote, as a sauce, or for filling. Eaten out of hand, fresh apricots are unsurpassed. They also lend themselves to fruit salad, home canning, and preserves.

Buying For an apricot to have a good flavor, it must be fully ripe when picked; it then keeps no more than three to four days. This explains why only 8 percent of the total commercial crop is sold fresh. Look for apricots during June and July and purchase those that yield to a soft touch and are golden all over with a rosy blush. If they are not, consider purchasing a dried apricot or a different fresh fruit.

See **Fruit.**

ARAME
(Eisenia bicyclis)

The sea vegetable arame is a brown kelp closely related to wakame and kombu, but in the package or cooked, it looks more like strands of black hiziki. Japan is the only country that is a significant producer of arame, but it has a mild, sweet taste that most Westerners enjoy from the start. Arame blades, which grow in wide leaves up to a foot in length, are sliced into long, stringlike strands, cooked for seven hours, sun dried, and packaged.

Health Benefits In addition to the numerous medicinal properties of seaweed in general, arame is noted for treatment of high blood pressure and, because it supports hormone functions, treatment of female disorders, including infertility, scanty lactation, and menstrual pain. It is an excellent source of protein. This ocean weed contains starch, sugar, unsaturated fat, vitamins A and B-complex, and significant amounts of iodine, calcium, and iron. It is especially calming to *vata.*

Use Arame is delicious sautéed alone, combined with land vegetables and eaten as a side dish, or used to fill turnovers and strudels. It may also be rehydrated and added directly to a salad.

See **Seaweed.**

ARBORIO RICE
(Oryza sativa)

This short-grain rice from the Piedmont region of Italy absorbs more liquid than other varieties do. Thus it yields a thick, creamy, and deliciously chewy rice dish—when, that is, it's made into risotto. Arborio rice is available, refined, in most markets with a wide selection of grains.

See **Rice.**

AREPAS

Arepas, the Central American and Cuban variety of posole, is made from a very large, starchy corn variety that's slaked in lye. Arepas signifies both the meal used to make flatbread and the flatbread itself. It is available in Cuban markets in the United States.

See **Posole.**

AROMATIC RICE See **Basmati Rice; Jasmine Rice; Pecan Rice; Red Rice.**

ARROWROOT
(Maranta arundinacea)

This fine-grained, white starch comes from the root of the tropical arrowroot plant; it is an excellent thickener, far superior to highly refined cornstarch. Most of our arrowroot comes from St. Vincent Island in the West Indies. The root is ground, sun dried, and then powdered.

Health Benefits Arrowroot flour is easily digestible, nutritive, and high in calcium, although medicinally it ranks well under my favorite thickening agent, kudzu. It helps soothe an inflamed gastrointestinal tract. For infant care, arrowroot is excellent for diaper rash. It is absorbent, soothing, natural, and nontoxic. It benefits *pitta* and *kapha*.

Use Arrowroot has a distinct advantage over flour in that, once thickened, it is crystal clear. Overstirring, however, may cause an arrowroot-thickened sauce to become thin again. When substituting arrowroot for cornstarch or flour, use 1 tablespoon arrowroot for 2¼ teaspoons cornstarch or for 1½ tablespoons all-purpose flour. Dissolve in cold water and use the slurry to thicken sauces, soups, icing, and desserts.

Buying I purchase arrowroot from the bulk herb section of my natural food store at 15 cents per ounce. At the supermarket, a two-ounce jar can cost as much as $3.50!

ARTICHOKE
(Cynara scolymus)

Back in 1948, Marilyn Monroe's first claim to fame was being crowned California's first Artichoke Queen. Today, artichokes need little endorsement. People love their buttered-popcorn aroma. Then there is the tiny nibble at the base of each leaf, whetting the appetite for the artichoke heart—which is actually the bud of the plant. The smooth, sweet taste of the artichoke and the leisurely manner of consuming it make this a popular vegetable.

This green vegetable of Arabian-Mediterranean origin is a close relative of the cardoon and a member of the sunflower family. Castroville, a town south of San Francisco that bills itself as the "Artichoke Center of the World," produces three-fourths of all California artichokes, and California grows America's entire domestic crop. The plants are cloned from rootstock.

Health Benefits Energetically speaking, the artichoke's most stellar phytochemical is *cynarin*, which improves the liver and gallbladder and lowers blood cholesterol levels. Artichokes increase bile secretion and thus may aid digestive disorders marked by poor assimilation of fat. Artichokes are easy to digest, increase overall energy, and have a neutralizing effect on some toxic substances. In addition, artichokes benefit heart activity and the speed of blood clotting. The artichoke relative milk thistle has similar biochemical properties for people with compromised immune systems or liver dysfunction—especially from alcohol-related liver diseases. This iodine-rich thistle is low in calories and high in fiber, vitamin C, folate, magnesium, chromium, manganese, potassium, iron, and calcium. Artichokes are *tridoshic*.

Use Artichokes are one of the few vegetables that I consistently pressure cook: Simmering them in a pot requires 50 minutes, while pressure steaming takes only 15 minutes. Baby artichokes may be trimmed, then halved or quartered, and sautéed, baked, or pickled. In larger artichokes, the choke (the fibrous center found under the smallest leaves and covering the heart) must be removed.

Buying In the spring, when the liver and the gallbladder most need support, artichokes are at their peak availability. Their secondary peak season is October, though they are in the markets year-round. Look for compact heads with fresh, vibrant green leaves; and look at the cut end of the stalk, which withers as it ages. Fall and winter artichokes may be darker or bronze tipped, or they may have a whitish, blistered appearance due to exposure to light frost, which actually increases their sweetness. The tip of each globe artichoke leaf ends in a sharp spine or pricker; newer spineless varieties often have a higher sugar content and less flavor.

Home gardeners in colder climes than California may grow this thistle for harvest in late summer. I've even harvested artichokes at 7,000-foot elevation in Colorado's San Luis valley. If you plant artichokes, plant enough for eating and plant extra for their mature blossoms. Dried or fresh, artichoke flowers make a stunning floral display.

See **Sunflower Family**.

ARUGULA
Rocket, Roquette, Rucola
(*Eruca vesicaria*)

The green vegetable arugula grows as a rosette of deeply lobed leaves. It has a sharp, bitter, peppery taste—like a radish—but with an almost musky aroma. Mediterranean in origin, it has long been valued in Europe and has recently become popular in the United States as well.

Health Benefits The oil extracted from arugula seeds was long considered an aphrodisiac in Europe. Its bitter and pungent properties make it a digestive tonic. Like mustard, it moves stuck energy and thus reduces *kapha*.

Use I keep a pot of arugula on my kitchen counter and snip the young leaves as a wake-up ingredient in a salad of otherwise mild-tasting greens. When the arugula is larger and more peppery in taste, I cook it in soups and stir-fries. It's a great substitute for basil in pesto, or it can be minced and strewn as a garnish.

Buying Avoid overgrown, yellowing, or wilted leaves or leaves from a plant that has flowered. Once garden arugula has gone to flower, though, you can use the blossoms in salads. Arugula is available most of the year—but is at its best in the spring and fall.

See **Cabbage Family**.

ASAFETIDA
Devil's Dung, Hing
(*Ferula assafoetida*)

I don't know what I love most about asafetida—its knock-your-socks-off sulfurous aroma (which explains its scatological name) or, once cooked, its pungent but pleasant and satisfying flavor. I also love the way the word rolls off my tongue: As'e-FET'E-da. Its name is from middle Latin and means fetid-smelling sap. Asafetida is the resin from a fennel species of the parsley family.

Health Benefits A favorite Ayurvedic remedy—*hing,* as they call it—this resin is used to strengthen and cleanse the liver and gastrointestinal tract. It aids digestion and helps relieve flatulence, constipation, bronchitis, and intestinal worms. It's one of the best herbs to help ground a high-strung *vata*-type person.

Use As its stink dissipates with cooking, asafetida is used primarily in cooked dishes—be they vegetable, grain, or bean. Use only a minuscule amount, and be certain to store asafetida in a tightly closed glass container.

Buying If the powdered resin you purchase is merely potent (as opposed to devilishly potent), it has been blended with wheat or rice flour. Asafetida is sold in small quantities in tightly closed containers. At one time, pure asafetida and even hardened lumps of the resinous sap were available, but on a recent shopping tour of Asian and Indian markets in New York City I was unable to find unadulterated asafetida.

See **Herbs and Spices.**

ASH PUMPKIN See Chinese Winter Melon.

ASIAN NOODLES See Pasta.

ASIAN PEAR
Apple Pear, Chinese Pear, Nashi, Sand Pear
(Pyrus pyrifolia)

Asian pears are the size of an apple and almost perfectly round, and the skin color ranges from yellow-green to brown. Asian pears are juicier and crisper than their relatives in the pear family. They are grown commercially in the United States.

Use Asian pears are delicious both raw and cooked and may be substituted for common pears in any recipe or dish. Cooking intensifies their flavor but doesn't compromise their shape and texture.

Buying There are numerous Asian pear varieties, but they are all marketed under the same name. Their size, appearance, and—

A POWERFUL ROMAN RECIPE

As did the ancient Romans, I keep asafetida-imbued pine nuts on hand and then use these netherworldly smelling seeds to flavor soups, stews, and roasted dishes. The fats in the pine nuts marry with the asafetida to create a pleasant flavor.

2 tablespoons pine nuts
1 teaspoon asafetida powder

Combine the ingredients in a small jar, tightly cover, and store in the refrigerator for several months. The seasoned pine nuts may be used in a few days but are at their best after a week or more. For a dish serving 4 people, crush and add 1 teaspoon of flavored pine nuts.

most importantly—flavor varies greatly; however, I select them by aroma since those with the most fragrance tend to have the most flavor. When ripe, they are hard to the touch. If unbruised, they can be stored in the refrigerator for a month.

See **Fruit.**

ASPARAGUS
(Asparagus officinalis)

Harvesters claim that asparagus spears grow so fast that when you are astride a row and bending to cut you either work briskly or get speared from behind. One spear may grow as much as ten inches in a day.

Compared to modern plants like roses, grass, and cabbage, asparagus looks ancient and phallic; indeed, it dates back to the age of reptiles, when ferns were the dominant plants. Botanically, asparagus is unusual in that there are distinct male and female plants—the male spears are skinny and the females plump. Their flavor depends upon freshness, however, and not sex, and only the young green shoots or spears should be eaten. If allowed to mature, a beautiful but inedible fern develops; the asparagus fern is in fact a popular hanging plant.

Health Benefits As the Indian name *shatavari* (she who possesses a hundred husbands) indicates, this rhyzome of an asparagus variety is the primary Ayurvedic root for strengthening female hormones, promoting fertility, increasing lactation, and relieving menstrual pain. It is *tridoshic*. In addition, the tubers of a Chinese asparagus variety are highly valued in Chinese herbology.

Asparagus from U.S. markets and ditch banks, however, is slightly warming in nature, with a bitter and mildly pungent flavor. It reduces phlegm and mucus, eases constipation, and soothes internal membranes. Asparagus contains asparagine, a diuretic that gives the urine a characteristic odor in people who lack the gene to break it down. While asparagus treats many types of kidney problems, do not use it when there is inflammation.

According to the National Cancer Institute, asparagus is the food highest in glutathione, an important anticarcinogen. Asparagus also contains a substance called rutin that helps prevent small blood vessels from rupturing. This explains its traditional use for heart palpitations. Rutin is also an antidote against X rays and other forms of radiation. Asparagus is also used for gout, rheumatism, and edema from heart failure. It contains good amounts of vitamins A, B-complex, C, and E, as well as potassium and zinc.

Use To remove the fibrous stalk end, hold the stalk by each end and bend it until it snaps in two. Use the stalk ends for soup stock; or peel to remove the fibrous skin and use the tender centers in salad or as finger food; or cook as you would the upper stalk. Steam the spears until tender. If just picked, steaming requires but two minutes, while older—and also thicker—stalks naturally require more time. Chopped, asparagus is delicious in stir-fried dishes, soups, and salads.

Buying/Foraging Wild asparagus is free for the harvesting along ditch banks and in meadows in the early spring. In the store, look for bright green, fresh-looking spears with compact tips. Avoid angular or flat stalks that are woody. For uniform cooking, select spears of similar thickness. Use asparagus as soon as possible after purchase or harvest. A pricey white, or blanched, asparagus popular in Europe is made by mounding earth above the plants to keep it from the sun and to prevent it from developing chlorophyll.

Once bought, store asparagus loosely covered in the refrigerator. To maintain freshness, wrap a moist paper towel around the stem ends or stand them upright in two inches of cold water.

ASPARAGUS BEAN See Yard-Long Bean.

ASPARAGUS LETTUCE See Celtuce.

Ø ASPARTAME
Equal, NutraSweet

Not recommended. The artificial sweetener aspartame is a chemical compound (phenylalanine and aspartic acid) synthesized from petrochemicals. It is two hundred times sweeter than sugar and is a popular sugar substitute in soft drinks, breakfast cereals, powdered beverages, and other dry packaged foods. Curiously enough, aspartame does not satisfy hunger; rather, it increases hunger, especially for sweets.

High levels of phenylalanine can have irreversible and toxic effects on the fetal brain and is implicated in liver damage (it breaks down into aldehyde, which damages liver cells). Symptoms include: behavioral changes in children, headaches, blindness, dizziness, epilepticlike seizures, menstrual problems, and an increased risk of cancer.

ATEMOYA
(Annona cherimola x A. squamos)

Cross a cherimoya and a sugar apple or sweetsop and the creamy result is an atemoya. This tough-skinned, grayish hybrid fruit is reminiscent of an artichoke in size and appearance. An atemoya's creamy, lush, ivory-colored flesh tastes like mango-flavored custard, but if not well ripened, its flavor is starchy. Native to the West Indies, atemoyas are grown commercially in Florida, Hawaii, California, New Zealand, and Australia.

Health Benefits For a fruit, the atemoya is unusually high in calories. It is an excellent source of vitamins C and K and potassium.

Use Atemoyas are used in fruit salads or can be riced and served as a fruit sauce. They're also eaten out of the rind, one spoonful at a time.

Buying/Storing This delicacy is available in the fall. Select thin-skinned atemoyas that are somewhat tender and unblemished. Allow to ripen at room temperature until they are soft, then consume immediately or refrigerate for a few days. Do *not* refrigerate until the fruit is ripened. Upon ripening, it may split at the stem end.

See **Tropical Fruit.**

ATOLE See Pinole.

AUBERGINE See Eggplant.

AVELLAN See Hazelnut.

AVOCADO
(Persea americana)

Superbowl Sunday is the third biggest food day for supermarkets (after Christmas and Thanksgiving), and the day that avocado sales peak. It seems that slathering chips with the avocado dip, guacamole, is a way TV viewers participate in this national ritual. Although technically a fruit and chemically more like a nut, the avocado is commonly used as a vegetable—a creamy, sensory vegetable.

Health Benefits Eighty-eight percent of an avocado's calories come from fat—primarily monosaturated fat—which makes avocados an excellent food for people wishing to put on weight and for the nourishment and building of blood and yin. They are also an excellent fat source for people who have difficulty assimilating other fatty foods. The fat accounts for their buttery texture, but also suggests discretionary use for those wishing to reduce their fat consumption.

Avocados are a good source of protein, potassium, and vitamin E. Avocados also reduce *vata*.

Use A versatile food, avocados are used raw in a variety of dishes—dips, gaspacho and other cold soups, fruit salads, desserts, and even ice cream. Avocados are a healthful substitute for sour cream or cream cheese in dressings, dips, and spreads.

Buying Many varieties of this native American plant are grown, but there are basically two different skin types: a smooth, green-skinned variety that remains green when ripe; and a dark, rough-skinned variety that blackens as it ripens. Hass is a dark-skinned summer fruit and Fuerte is a medium green fall and winter fruit.

Select avocados that are fairly heavy for their size and free of irregularities. When the fruit yields to gentle finger pressure, it is ripe. Store at room temperature until ripened, then refrigerate.

AZUKI BEAN See Aduki.

BABY LIMA See Lima Bean.

BABY RED HUBBARD See Kabocha Squash.

BAKING POWDER

Used as a yeast substitute since 1850, baking powder is a mixture of various simple chemical substances. When a baking powder is mixed into a batter, carbon dioxide gas is released from sodium (baking soda in our

---

ALUMINUMFREE BAKING POWDER

¼ cup baking soda
½ cup cream of tartar
½ cup arrowroot

Mix together and store in an airtight container. Substitute equal parts for commercial baking powder in any recipe. For a low-sodium variation, simply substitute potassium bicarbonate—available from a pharmacist—for the baking soda.

---

recipe) by the action of an acid or an acid salt (here, cream of tartar, the natural residue that occurs in juiced grapes). A moisture absorber, such as arrowroot, inhibits a premature reaction.

Commercial baking powder is a leavener that contains unhealthful and acrid-tasting aluminum compounds. An excellent alternative is homemade baking powder, which takes seconds to make, performs equally well, and leaves no bitter aftertaste.

See **Arrowroot; Cream of Tartar.**

BALSAMIC VINEGAR

From Modena, Italy, balsamic vinegar is made only from trebbiano grapes and is both sweet and sour. It is used on salads, in desserts, and—provided it has been aged over 50 years—is a delicious beverage. As the vinegar ages, it is concentrated in a series of casks made from different types of wood; the first is oak, then chestnut, cherry, ash, and mulberry. The casks flavor the vinegar; no other flavoring agent is added.

Buying The Consortium of Balsamic Producers in Modena specifies two different grades. One, quickly fermented and then aged, is *Aceto Balsamico di Modena;* the other, made traditionally, is *Aceto Balsamico Tradizionale di Modena.* The bottle of traditional vinegar is sealed with a serially numbered strip.

Peggy Markel, the illustrator of this book, operates a cooking school, La Cucina al Focolare, outside Florence, Italy. She describes the difference between the types of balsamic thusly: *"Balsamico Tradizionale* tastes perfect and complete; a nontraditional balsamic leaves you wanting."

See **Vinegar.**

BALSAM PEAR See Bitter Melon.

BANANA
(*Musa* esp. M. acuminata)

The banana grows in almost every tropical country, on a giant herb, which is probably the largest plant without a woody stem. A bunch of bananas is technically called a "hand," and each fruit is a "finger." They have a remarkably high yield per acre, making it our least expensive fruit. The United States consumes about 60 percent of the world's banana crop, coming primarily from Central and South America.

Health Benefits Ripe bananas are sweet tasting, highly nutritive, easily digested, antiulcerous, and soothing to the mucus lining of the stomach. They are used to treat constipation, ease thirst, and reduce *vata.* Underripe or green bananas are astringent and difficult to digest, and are used to relieve diarrhea and colitis and to reduce *pitta* and *kapha.*

Bananas are used in the treatment of hypertension because of their high potassium content. They have a high sugar content (about 17 to 19 percent) and are richer in minerals than any soft fruit except strawberries. They have twice as much vitamin C as apples and a high caloric value, but are low in carbohydrates and protein.

Buying The blunt-ended Cavendish variety has been the primary banana available but markets now regularly feature smaller and more colorful varieties, including small Lady Fingers, chunky Burro bananas, and plump, small red bananas. Dried bananas and banana flour are available but harder to find.

Bananas are picked green and gassed with ethylene to speed their ripening. Allow them to ripen at home at room temperature, placing them in a closed paper bag to speed the process. When the skin is yellow and speckled with brown, the banana is ripe. The browner the skin, the higher a banana's sugar content.

See **Plantain; Tropical Fruit.**

BANANA SQUASH
(*Cucurbita maxima*)

After several decades of avoiding banana squash, I happened upon a beautiful one at my local organic squash dealer and gave it another chance. Unfortunately, no matter how I prepared it, it lacked flavor and ended up in my chicken yard, not on my table. No wonder some people have a poor opinion of squash.

The banana squash is like a banana in

shape, with muted orange skin and slightly stringy, attractive orange flesh. It grows up to two feet in length and is about six inches in diameter.

See **Winter Squash.**

BANCHA TEA See Twig Tea.

BARBADOS MOLASSES See Molasses.

BARLEY
(Hordeum vulgare)

Barley and wheat, the world's oldest cereal crops, originated in Southwest Asia around 8500 B.C. The Roman gladiators were called *hordearri,* or barley men, after their primary staple, barley. Curiously enough, barley remains the staple of the physically strong peoples of the Himalayan region. Whole barley is a tan-colored grain, larger and plumper than all other grains except corn. Today, most people think of it in connection with soup—it makes a tasty, hearty soup base—but the bulk of barley is drunk in a malted form, otherwise known as beer.

Health Benefits Strengthening to the spleen-pancreas, barley regulates the stomach, stimulates the appetite, and is excellent in reducing *pitta* and *kapha.* It strengthens the intestines and blood and benefits the gallbladder and nerves. Barley is used for hepatitis and painful urination, and it helps reduce tumors. The most acidic of the grains, barley is made more alkaline and flavorful by roasting it a shade darker prior to cooking; this also eliminates whole barley's laxative property but it may exacerbate constipation, as does pearl barley. In England, barley water is used as a traditional convalescent food. It is not used for nursing mothers because it suppresses lactation.

Use Barley cooks into a chewy, sustaining dish. Try it plain, combined with brown rice, cooked with beans, or mixed with extra water to make a breakfast porridge. Barley is especially luscious cooked risotto style.

Buying Barley comes in several forms:

- **Whole Barley** Also called Scotch or pot barley, whole barley has its inedible hull removed but its bran is intact. Like brown rice, whole barley is darker, chewier, and more nutritious than its refined counterpart. In this form, its vitamin and mineral contents are intact, and it is significantly higher in protein, potassium, calcium, and iron than pearl barley. It also takes more time to cook. Whole barley includes hull-less or naked barley heirloom varieties, which easily thresh free from the hull and are an ideal grain for backyard gardeners and subsistence farmers.
- **Pearled or Pearl Barley** has had its bran polished off, has lost all of its fiber, and half of its protein, fat, and minerals. Pearled barley is the most commonly available barley. Often the pearled barley found in natural food stores has undergone less pearling than that found in a supermarket, as is indicated by its larger size.
- **Barley Flakes,** like rolled oats, make a tasty substitute in hot breakfast cereal and in granola and muesli.

The Himalayan diet is primarily *tsampa*—roasted ground barley mixed with black tea, salt, and yak butter. Peter Hackett, a high-elevation medical expert who lived in a small Everest-region village for a number of years, recently attended my cooking school. He recalled living on this amazing grain diet where his biggest food treat was an occasional turnip pickle. "They were a strong, healthy, hard-working people," Peter told me, "who subsisted almost entirely on *tsampa* or sometimes *sen*, a thick gruel made of ground roasted millet and water. It was not unusual for one person to eat two pounds at a sitting! The diet included potatoes but no other vegetables or fruits except when holiday foods were carried up from the lowlands. There was seldom meat."

- **Barley Grits** Tiny chunks of barley are quick to cook because of their size. Use grits as a hot breakfast cereal and even for barley "polenta." The grit size—and therefore cooking time—varies from manufacturer to manufacturer.

See **Black Barley; Grains.**

BARLEY FLOUR

Although, owing to its grayish crumb, barley bread may not look immedi-ately appetizing, those who acquire a taste for it are likely to become addicts. I am one. An addiction which is not always easily satisfied.

—Elizabeth David,
English Bread and Yeast Cookery

Barley flour is starchy and soft and has a sweet earthy taste. It yields a cakelike crumb and, curiously, imparts a grayish color when baked. Curious because both grain and flour are white. Whole barley flour yields a darker crumb than pearl barley flour and has a moister quality. In flavor, aroma, texture, and ease of handling, the difference between pearl and whole barley flours compares to the difference between white and whole wheat flour.

Barley is low in gluten. Generally no more than 15 percent barley flour is added to a yeast bread, and it imparts a more soft and dense texture. In cookies and cakes, it gives a light crumb. Toasting the flour prior to use heightens its flavor.

See **Flour.**

BARLEY GRASS JUICE

The juice of the chlorophyll-rich grass of young barley plants is nutritionally comparable to wheat grass juice as one of the most remarkable high-chlorophyll foods. Of the two, barley is more alkaline and therefore balanced, while wheat grass juice is stronger and faster acting. As excellent a protein source as meat, barley grass juice—and wheat grass juice—are nearly as high in chlorophyll and vitamin A as microalgae. In addition, barley grass offers important digestive enzymes, can resolve toxic substances, and contains nutrients that slow deterioration and mutation.

Barley grass juice is available at most natural food stores and juice bars, freshly juiced in one-ounce servings—a little is all it takes. It is also sold in tablet or powder form.

See **Wheat Grass Juice.**

BARLEY MALT SUGAR

Barley malt sugar is a buff-colored, crystalline powder made by evaporating the water out of barley malt syrup. Malt sugar is primarily used for brewing, although it is also available in high-quality stores as a superior sugar replacement. Unfortunately, it absorbs moisture very easily and then becomes rock hard. To prevent hardening, store sugar in a closed glass jar. Malt sugar is easy to substitute for sugar, and unlike natural liquid sweeteners, it gives the same tender crumb that sugar does. Substitute measure for measure. The result is a lighter sweetness with a pleasing malt flavor.

BARLEY MALT SYRUP

Hop flavored, and therefore intensely bitter, barley malt was sold "strictly as a sweetener" during Prohibition. This "sweetener," however, would have ruined anything but home brew. Sprout whole barley, roast it, and then extract it to a liquid form, and you've got barley malt syrup. Combine the syrup with hops and ferment with yeast, and the result is beer.

Barley malt is the least expensive of quality natural sweeteners. Compared to honey,

barley malt syrup is less sweet and more intensely flavored.

Health Benefits Barley malt is mostly carbohydrate, and though it contains small quantities of vitamins and minerals, the amount is negligible. Its primary sugars are maltose, and so like rice syrup, it more moderately impacts blood sugar levels than sugar, maple syrup, and honey. It is therefore more healthful. It reduces *vata* and *pitta*.

Buying Liquid barley malt is available in two forms: barley extracts and barley/corn malt. The extracts are 100 percent barley malt. Domestic extracts are strong tasting like blackstrap molasses. Imported malts are developed for table use and have a rich—but less intense—flavor with wider culinary application, but they are more costly than domestic malts. The pleasantly flavored and versatile blend of barley malt and corn is more readily available than the 100 percent extracts. The higher the percentage of corn, the less expensive the product and the milder the flavor. Corn cannot be malted by itself, but when corn grits are combined with malt, the barley enzymes reduce the corn starch to maltose. Some manufacturers mix commercial corn syrup with malt syrup to form an inferior product.

Store barley malt syrup in a glass or plastic container in a cool, dark cupboard. If stored for a long time (more than 12 months) or in a warm place, the malt may ferment. A sign of fermentation is bubbles percolating up through the malt. Should this occur, refrigerate and use quickly, or discard if it has an unpleasant aroma.

See **Sweeteners.**

BARTLETT PEAR See Pear.

BASIL
(Ocimum basilicum)

The French call basil *"l'herbe royale."* The Italians use this herb so copiously you'd think it's a vegetable. Basil's taste is reminiscent of its cousin mint—but with licorice, cinnamon, clove, lemon, and thyme tones. Apparently mosquitoes don't like all these flavors, and basil is an effective mosquito repellent: try planting it around windows and doors. A native of India, basil comes in more than 50 varieties, which are usually green but may be purple.

Health Benefits A pungent, warming herb, basil is restorative. It helps restore your balance, especially of lung- or stomach-related complaints. Basil is used to treat mild depression, headache, or menstrual pain. It calms the nerves, aids digestion, and treats fevers, whooping cough, constipation, nausea, insomnia, fatigue, colds, and the flu. It is effective against bacterial infections and intestinal parasites. Basil reduces *vata* and *kapha* and may be used, in moderation, for *pitta*. Basil seeds have an opposite thermal effect than the leaves and are added to cooling beverages in Ayurvedic cuisine.

Use A favorite in ethnic dishes from Indonesia to Italy, basil is especially savored as a pesto ingredient and has a great affinity for tomato, fish, bean, and egg dishes.

See **Herbs and Spices.**

BASMATI RICE
(Oryza sativa)

Basmati rice is a long-grain Himalayan rice. It has a buttery aroma, nutty flavor, and fluffy texture. Unlike other rice varieties, each grain almost doubles in length when cooked and yet changes little in thickness. Basmati rice is one of the few specialty varieties available both brown (whole) and white (refined).

There is a curious misconception about white basmati rice. In the 1970s, an Indian guru with a large American following proclaimed that white basmati was superior to whole grain brown rice. Today, many Americans still voice the same belief. Depending upon your vantage point, it may be superior or inferior. People often favor the particular varieties or preparations of their childhood foods. Basmati is an excellent—but not the only—aromatic rice. As with all refined grains, white basmati's nutritional and flavor profile is diminished and it lacks the *chi*, or vitality, of a whole grain.

Texmati and calmati are basmati hybrids now grown in Texas (and neighboring Arkansas) and in California.

See **Rice.**

BAY LAUREL See Bay Leaf.

BAY LEAF
Bay Laurel, Laurel, Sweet Laurel
(Laurus nobilis)

A laureate as lightning insurance? Just as the Old Norse peoples regarded oak trees (see Acorn), the Greeks believed that bay trees were protected from lightning. The plant was woven into wreaths to crown Olympic athletes. Today, we know that bay leaf does keep bugs at bay. To help prevent miller moths and weevils from hatching in stored grains, tuck several bay leaves into the grain.

One of our most common herbs, the bay leaf, usually dried, comes from an evergreen shrub native to the Mediterranean called the bay laurel. Turkey is one of the main bay exporters.

Health Benefits Aromatic, pungent, and slightly bitter, bay relieves hysteria, regulates delayed menstruation, relieves gas, colic, and indigestion. A bay decoction relieves rheumatism, sprains, and bruises. Bay reduces *vata* and *kapha*.

Use Bay leaves are typically used whole rather than ground. In my home, whoever finds a bay leaf in his or her soup gets to kiss the cook.

Bay leaves round the flavor of a wide variety of savory dishes, including soups, stews, sauces, pickles, sausages, and fish dishes. Bay is often included in the French *bouquet garni* and in Indian *masala*.

Buying High-quality bay leaves are aromatic and have a bright green color. The more faded the green color, the more bitter the leaves will be.

See **Herbs and Spices.**

BEAN CURD See Tofu.

BEAN FLAKES

Some beans are partially cooked and rolled like oats to shorten cooking time. They can generally be found in natural food stores,

but I leave them there. For full flavor and maximum energetic properties, favor intact beans.

BEAN FLOUR See **Chickpea Flour; Soy Flour.**

BEAN PASTE See **Miso.**

BEANS AND LEGUMES
(Leguminosus)

"Beans, beans, the musical fruit." Indeed, beans are technically a fruit, as the childhood rhyme accurately states. A bowl of beans is a more universal image of nurture than a loaf of bread. Unpretentious, filling, and warming, a pot of beans, peas, or lentils simmering on the back of the stove evokes home cooking at its humble best. One of the earliest—and most important—cultivated crops, beans and legumes are grown everywhere that people farm.

They grow on vines and are contained in pods; peanuts, with underground pods, also belong to the legume family. For millennia, farmers have dried beans and legumes in the field, then shelled, cleaned, and stored them. The same today. Beans are unrefined: They're not washed, parched, polished, gassed, preserved, or colored. Providing they're organic, their earthy sweetness is utterly unadulterated. No wonder they're so satisfying.

Health Benefits Beans and legumes strengthen the kidneys and adrenal glands and therefore promote physical growth and development. As does the protein in meat, bean protein builds body mass; but unlike meat, beans don't add cholesterol, saturated fat, or toxic nitrogen byproducts. A stick-to-the-ribs filling food, beans are more "grounding" than a salad.

A bean's color indicates the organ it most benefits, and so while beans *as a category* strengthen the kidneys, green-colored beans, like mung beans and split peas, also benefit the liver. Red beans, including aduki and kidney beans, influence the heart. Yellow beans, like chickpeas and soybeans, support the spleen-pancreas. Navy beans, limas, and other white beans energize the lungs and colon. Black beans are doubly supportive to the kidneys.

The phytochemical diosgenin, which appears to inhibit cancer cells from multiplying, is found in beans. Beans reduce the levels of serum cholesterol and so offer some protection against heart disease. They are a superior carbohydrate for people with diabetes or blood sugar imbalances, since they are slowly digested and cause only a gradual rise in blood sugar levels.

Most legumes range from 17 to 25 percent protein, roughly double cereals' protein and also higher than that of eggs and most meats. Soybeans rate exceptionally high, with 38 percent protein. Most beans are low in fat and are good sources of calcium, potassium, iron, zinc, and several B vitamins, including folate. The isoflavones in beans help prevent cancer and heart disease. In general, beans reduce *pitta* and *kapha*. Lentils, however, increase *pitta*, and soybeans—in excess—increase *kapha*.

Use From dumplings and *dosas* (an East Indian fermented pancake) to pasta and pies, for the past 30 years I've cooked with beans or their products daily. Sometimes it seems there aren't enough meals to match the number of delicious legume dishes that entice me.

A seasoned pot of beans with a garnish makes an excellent side dish. Add beans sparingly to a soup for their interesting shape and melting texture, or add generously to create a hearty soup, chili, or stew. In Central and South America, beans fill tamales, empanadas, and humitas. In China and Japan, they're sweetened and fill steamed buns. Or they're fermented into tempeh, miso, soy sauce, or natto. For bean cooking inspiration, peruse any ethnic cookbook. For cooking instructions, see sidebar, page 32.

Buying Purchase beans from a bulk bin or in a see-through wrapper. Favor those with a vibrant look, for they'll be the current crop beans. Dull, faded beans are older and tougher and take longer to cook. Select well-formed legumes with few broken, chipped, or split seeds. Uniformity of shape and color is not desirable—it indicates a hybrid, which is less vital than an heirloom variety.

I store my beans in airtight glass jars in a dark cupboard. A shelf with glass jars, each holding beans of a different color, may make a beautiful display, but all seeds—beans included—will best retain vitality away from heat and light. At least two nutrients found in beans, pyridoxine and pyridoxal (the natural forms of vitamin B_6), quickly deteriorate when exposed to light. Unlike grains, whole dried beans can be stored for several years or more. They do, however, toughen with age and require longer cooking.

See **Aduki; Anasazi Bean; Black-Eyed**

Pea; Black Soybean; Black Turtle Bean; Bolita Bean; Cannellini Bean; Chickpea; Cranberry Bean; Dal; Fava Bean; Flageolet; Great Northern Bean; Green Bean; Green Soybean; Jacob's Cattle Bean; Kidney Bean; Lentil; Lima Bean; Lupine; Mung Bean; Navy Bean; Nuña; Pea; Pigeon Pea;

SOAK THOSE BEANS

The problem with hard, poorly cooked beans is that they stress your digestive system, and this creates social distress. Regarding flatulence, be preemptive. Soak those beans. Soaking softens beans by leaching out their indigestible sugars (trisaccharides) and by activating enzymes that break down complex carbohydrates into simpler, easier to digest starches. (In addition, soaking eliminates the beans' phytic acid and that makes their minerals more bioavailable.)

Ideally, soak beans until they're uniformly soft. This may take, depending primarily upon the bean variety, from 2 to 24 hours. For long soaking, refrigerate to prevent the beans from souring. If unrefrigerated, or if in a hot and humid kitchen, change the soaking water after 8 hours or when it develops bubbles. For many people who have difficulty digesting beans, long soaking remedies this. People with delicate digestion may require a second step of partially sprouting beans (see Sprouts). This enables the beans' activated enzymes to more thoroughly "pre-digest" the complex carbohydrates. Sprout until the nascent sprouts just emerge and then cook as normal. I do not recommend the shortcut soaking method of boiling beans *before* soaking them because this prematurely kills their enzymes. Once soaked, strain, and rinse well. Next, add fresh water to cover the beans by two inches and boil furiously, without a lid, for ten minutes. In Ayurvedic terms, boiling without a lid allows the beans' gaseous (*vata*) properties to go up and out. Skim the hard-to-digest foam that rises to the top, then season, cover, and simmer until tender. If necessary, add additional water to keep the beans submerged.

After the boiling, add a 2-inch strip of kombu (if you wish, remove the kombu before serving) and ¼ teaspoon sea salt for each cup of dried beans, which work as softening agents and flavor enhancers. At this time, you can also add your favorite spices.

Other factors toughen beans, including lengthy storage time, the calcium in hard water, and acid ingredients. Therefore, if cooking old beans or if cooking in hard water, allow extra soaking and cooking time. Or if seasoning with added acidic ingredients (like tomatoes, citrus, or wine), add them *only* to softened beans.

Our grandmothers softened beans with baking soda. I don't recommend soda, though, as it destroys B vitamins and doesn't enhance flavor. But, when I have a pot of impervious beans and dinner guests are arriving, a pinch of soda seems a friendly alternative to gas.

MOM AT THE KITCHEN TABLE

As a child, my favorite thing about ham was anticipating the sure-to-follow navy bean soup with the ham bone. I so clearly recall Mother sitting at our Formica table before a small mound of white beans and culling the rejects. It's a timeless image. I always enjoy fingering my way through a pile of beans. It takes but a minute, and I feel at one with Mother and with all cooks, past and future.

Pink Bean; Pinto Bean; Rattlesnake Bean; Red Bean; Snow Pea; Soldier Bean; Soybean; Urad; Winged Bean; Yard Long Bean; Yellow-Eye Bean.

Bean Sprouts See Sprouts.

Bean Thread See Pasta.

Beavertail Cactus See Nopal.

Beefsteak Leaf See Perilla.

BEET
(Beta vulgaris)

The beet is the most intense of vegetables. The radish, admittedly, is more feverish, but the fire of the radish is a cold fire, the fire of discontent, not of passion. Tomatoes are lusty enough, yet there runs through tomatoes an undercurrent of frivolity. Beets are deadly serious.
—Tom Robbins, *Jitterbug Perfume*

Why is it that one day eating a beet turns your urine pink, whereas another day and another beet produce magenta stool? According to nutritionist Jeffrey Bland, Ph.D., pink urine may indicate an iron deficiency while magenta stool indicates adequate iron. Wild beets still grow along the Mediterranean coasts where they seem happiest just above high tide mark—a land-bound, but sea-loving, vegetable. Beets are a member of the ubiquitous goosefoot family.

Health Benefits As their color suggests, beets are a blood tonic and so are good for anemia, the heart, and circulation. They purify the blood, alleviate constipation, aid the liver, and promote menstruation. Beets reduce *vata* and *kapha*. Beet greens reduce *kapha*.

A starchy vegetable, beet roots are high in natural sugar. The greens have notable amounts of calcium, iron, magnesium, and phosphorus; they also contain vitamins A, B-complex, and C.

Use Like chard, beet greens are high in oxalic acid (and so are not to be eaten excessively), but when young and tender, they make for an excellent salad green. The greens may also be sautéed, steamed, or prepared like turnip greens. Beets are often pickled, boiled for use in salads, baked, or added to soups. A popular Russian soup, borscht, uses beets as a principal ingredient. Ground coriander, a delicious seasoning agent for beets, enables *pitta* types to better assimilate beets.

Buying Although some beets are gold (and some new varieties are white), most are identified by their bright red to dark purplish skin and flesh, which turn the cooking water red. Select firm, fresh-looking, plump beets. If their greens are intact, these should look vibrant.

See **Goosefoot Family.**

BELGIAN ENDIVE
Witloof
(Cichorium intybus)

The pale yellow Belgian endive, in the shape of a fat cigar, is a chicory grown in Belgium in trenches that are mounded over with fine soil to prevent the sun from turning it green. Belgian endive is a crisp, bitter salad green. It is delicious braised.

See **Chicory.**

BELL PEPPER See **Sweet Pepper.**

BERGAMOT See **Bitter Orange.**

BERMUDA ONION See **Onion.**

BESAN See **Chickpea Flour.**

BERRY See **Blackberry; Blueberry; Dewberry; Loganberry; Raspberry; Strawberry.**

BHUTANESE RED RICE
(Oryza sativa)

From the small Himalayan kingdom of Bhutan comes a small-grained red rice that is technically a long-grain rice variety. It is available scarified or rough milled; thus,

through its red bran layer, its lighter-colored endosperm is visible (see page 289).

See **Rice.**

BIBB LETTUCE See **Butterhead Lettuce.**

BILBERRY See **Blueberry.**

BITTER GOURD See **Bitter Melon.**

BITTER MELON
Balsam Pear, Bitter Gourd, Chinese Bitter Melon, Karela
(Momordica charantia)

The bitter melon is not a melon, but rather a summer squash similar to a cucumber in size and shape. Its lumpy, ridged skin and flesh are the color of pale jade.

Health Benefits The bitter melon, gaining acclaim for its use with AIDS patients, has long been popular as a diabetic remedy in China, India, Sri Lanka, and the West Indies. In clinical tests, it significantly improves glucose tolerance without increasing blood insulin levels. The *Research Reviews* of *HerbalGram* No. 39 reports that . . . "*In vitro* studies have shown that karela inhibits glucose absorption, increases insulin flow, and has insulinlike effects."

The bitter taste of bitter melon is due to its quinine content, which makes this a valued food and medicine. Bitter melon soothes irritated tissues, lowers fever, and cleanses toxins from the body. It also has diuretic and laxative properties. Nutritionally, it is comparable to summer squash. Eat bitter melon moderately, if at all, during pregnancy. Bitter melon reduces *pitta* and *kapha.*

Use In Indian and Asian cookery, the bit-

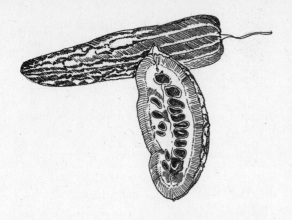

ter melon is a popular foil to strongly flavored foods. It is stir-fried, stewed, stuffed, braised, curried, and steamed. It is also pickled and used in chutneys. Cooking mellows its bitter flavor. To further reduce its bitterness, slice the melon in half lengthwise, remove and discard the brown seeds and pithy core, salt it generously, and allow to stand 15 minutes. Then rinse and squeeze dry before cooking.

Buying Favor bitter melons that are pale green—if dark green, they are immature and extremely bitter. If orange, they're over-mature, soft, and sweet. Select fruits with shiny, even-colored pale green skin, and store in the refrigerator. They are available from the summer into winter.

See **Gourd Family; Summer Squash.**

BITTER ORANGE
Bergamot, Seville Orange, Sour Orange, Yuzu
(Citrus aurantium)

The grandmother of all oranges, the bitter orange originated in northern India and is too intense to eat out of hand. Its astringency explains its alternative name—sour orange—but its bitterness predominates. This intense fruit came to Europe via the Moors and Seville, Spain—thus its alternate name. Bitter oranges are the most hardy citrus and, today, are grown as ornamentals as far north as Maryland. They're flatter than a sweet orange, with a thick, rough peel that fits loosely over its flesh. The bergamot, a close relative, has an even more aromatic rind.

Health Benefits Considered one of the strongest *chi* (energy) moving substances, bitter orange helps break up hardened masses, including lumps, tumors, and cysts. The peel is used for indigestion, abdominal distention, flatulence, constipation, stubborn coughs, and for colic in babies.

The essential oil of bergamot is used externally in douches for vaginal infections and in aromatherapy for stress and skin complaints. It reduces *pitta* and *kapha*.

Use The bitter orange is an indispensable ingredient in orange marmalade. Its juice adds piquancy to sauces, such as the Latin American *mojos*. Bitter orange complements duck and game. The peel may be candied, used to make orange-blossom water, or added to flavor teas, such as Earl Grey, and liqueurs, such as Grand Marnier.

Buying Winter is the best time to find bitter oranges at a specialty greengrocer or in an Asian market.

See **Citrus Family; Orange; Yuzu.**

BLACK BARLEY
(Hordeum vulgare)

The black of other black grains fades when cooked. Wild rice turns an earthy gray; Thai black sticky rice goes purple; and black quinoa becomes mottled buff with black specks.

But black barley, offered by Indian Harvest (see page 401), is the midnight beauty of grains. To deepen the hue of black barley, cook it with black sesame seeds.

Black barley, a variety of the more prosaic common barley, has an earthy sweetness. It is considered medicinal to the kidneys. Traditionally in Tibet, black barley was favored for beer making and light barley for their daily staple, *tsampa.*

Substitute black barley for whole barley in soup, risotto, or other grain dishes (if substituting it for pearl barley, increase the cooking time). As its color bleeds, do not cook it with cauliflower or white rice. Once cooked, however, combine it with different colored foods for a dramatic effect.

Western Trails (see page 401) also carries a tasty black barley. Theirs, however, is pale black, large, fruity flavored, and doesn't retain its color.

BLACK BEAN See Black Turtle Bean.

BLACKBERRY
Brambleberry
(Rubus ulmfolius)

The blackberry, plump and sweet, is closely related to the raspberry but is larger and juicier, with a grainier texture and a more assertive flavor. The core does not separate from the fruit. Although blackberries grow wild in temperate regions of the northern hemisphere, they're Asian in origin.

Health Benefits Blackberries are a mild diuretic and astringent and are therefore useful for diarrhea, dysentery, and hemorrhoids. The Romans used them as a gout treatment.

Blackberries are *tridoshic,* although they are best if eaten in moderation by *vata.* Blackberries are rich in vitamin C and pectin.

See **Fruit; Raspberry.**

BLACK CHANTERELLE See Trumpet Mushroom.

BLACK CUMIN See Cumin.

BLACK CURRANT
(Ribes nigrum)

That currant domestication is recent, a mere five hundred years, explains why this small, seedy berry is not very sweet. Although red, white, yellow, and black currants grow wild throughout the northern temperate regions of the world, the black currant has the greatest commercial availability. It grows on shrubs and emits a peculiar, heavy aroma.

No matter their color, they are hard to find in domestic markets. (They are more appreciated in Europe.) This is not a condemnation of them—currants have a matchless flavor, not exceptionally sweet, juicy, or tart but decidedly enjoyable. This smooth, small berry, from one-quarter- to one-half-inch wide, is thin skinned.

The white currant is the sweetest; the black is the most tart and is favored for preserves. Wild currants are comparable to the domesticated in all respects but size. The currant is related to the gooseberry but not to dried currants, which are raisins made from seedless corinth grapes. Look for shiny skins and plump berries from August. Refrigerate and use within three days.

See **Black Currant Seed Oil; Fruit.**

BLACK CURRANT SEED OIL

Oil from black currant seeds complements Omega-3 fatty acids and is a quality source of gamma-linoleic acid (GLA), a substance that contributes to prostaglandin synthesis and has a profound positive effect on health, especially in ameliorating premenstrual symptoms. Mother's milk, spirulina, evening primrose oil, and borage oil are other sources of GLA.

See **Essential Fatty Acids; Gamma-Linoleic Acid.**

BLACK-EYED PEA
China Bean, Cowpea
(Vigna unguiculata)

The classic New Year's Day menu in many southern homes includes black-eyed peas and collards—an excellent start for the New Year. This earthy-tasting legume originated in Africa around 3000 B.C., where it is still found growing wild. In the seventeenth century, it was introduced to the Americas by the Spanish and Portuguese. It is cream colored with a distinctive black spot. A "soft" or quick-cooking bean, the black-eyed pea is also enjoyed green, in the pod, or shelled. Even their leaves are consumed. The yard-long bean is a subspecies of the black-eyed pea.

Health Benefits Black-eyed peas are sweet tasting and tone the spleen-pancreas and stomach meridian. They help induce urination and relieve damp conditions like leukorrhea.

See **Beans and Legumes.**

BLACK FOREST MUSHROOM See **Shiitake.**

BLACK PEPPER See Pepper.

BLACK RADISH
(Raphanus sativus)

I love our most primitive radish, which evokes, for me, an image of an ancient kitchen and a bubbling cauldron. A designer vegetable it is not. This ancient Egyptian radish has a coarse black skin, but otherwise is turniplike in shape, taste, texture, and inner color. Black radishes are a liver tonic. Beloved and renowned Boulder, Colorado, herbalist Hannah Kroger used to use black radish and parsley in a formula for strep throat. Black radishes are available in the fall and winter and hold better through the winter than do other radishes.

Scrub the radish with a vegetable brush to remove any dirt and trim damaged or dehydrated spots. Peel only if the skin is tough and fibrous. Grate, dice, slice, or cut into little or big chunks and substitute black radish for daikon or turnip in soup, casseroles, or stir-fries or in steamed, blanched, or baked vegetable medleys. I love black radish grated, mixed with masa, and made into a tortilla. Food writer Susan Derecskey likes them grated or thinly sliced and salted.

See **Radish.**

BLACK RICE
(Oryza sativa)

There are several varieties of black rice marketed today under different names. One is contained in a blend. Lundberg Family Farms' Black Japonica is a combination of two varieties, black japonica and a brown mahogany rice, which grow together in the same field. Black rice varieties have a black or dark brown bran layer that covers a white endosperm. Black sticky rice is an exception.

See **Rice.**

BLACK SALSIFY See **Scorzonera.**

BLACK SESAME SEED
(Sesamum indicum)

The most common sesame seed is buff colored, but the black variety is more richly flavored. Available in natural food and Asian food stores, black sesame seeds are usually pretoasted. Unfortunately, the "black" sesame seeds sometimes found in Asian markets are dyed a shiny, monochromatic black. Unadulterated ones have a dull, matte finish and range in color from coal black to gray black with an occasional rust-colored seed.

Health Benefits The stronger flavor of black sesame seeds indicates that they are higher in minerals and trace nutrients than lighter-colored sesame seeds. Black sesame is a general building tonic: It nourishes blood and strengthens the kidneys and liver. It treats constipation, dry cough, blurry vision, ringing in the ears, low backache, weak knees, stiff joints, nervous spasms, headache, insufficient mother's milk, and dizziness. Black sesame seeds reduce *vata* beautifully.

See **Seeds; Sesame.**

BLACK SOYBEAN
(Glycine max)

Prior to an arduous journey, the Chinese fed black soybeans to their horses to boost their endurance. While most soybeans are a cream or yellow color, one type has a glossy black skin. It is easy to distinguish from the common black turtle bean. The black soy is round, plump, and glossy; the turtle is shaped like its relative, the pinto, but is smaller with a dull matte black skin. Like other soybeans, the black requires long soaking and long cooking, but fortunately, it is easier to digest than the yellow varieties. It has a rich, deep flavor.

Health Benefits Black soybeans are especially medicinal for the spleen-pancreas and kidneys, eliminating damp conditions and detoxifying the system. Black soybeans' nutrient profile is similar to yellow soybeans.

Use Soak black soybeans for 10 to 12 hours, bring to a boil, then simmer for 3 to 4 hours or until tender. They are also delicious toasted and cooked with brown rice. Toast ¼ cup unsoaked black soybeans in a skillet until their skins pop, about 5 to 7 minutes. Place the roasted beans in a pressure cooker with 2 cups of rice, 2½ cups water, and 1 teaspoon tamari. Pressure cook for 1 hour.

See **Black Turtle Bean; Beans and Legumes.**

BLACK STICKY RICE
(Oryza sativa)

Both Thai and Chinese black sticky rice are sweet rice varieties that have both a black bran and endosperm. Like other sweet rice varieties, they become sticky and glutinous when cooked and are considered medicinal to the kidneys. Both become a deep indigo. Thai black sticky rice is a long-grain variety and the Chinese is short-grain. Black sticky rice is used primarily in sweets and snacks.

See **Rice.**

BLACKSTRAP MOLASSES See **Molasses.**

BLACK TURTLE BEAN
Black Bean
(Phaseolus vulgaris)

This Mexican native is a member of the kidney bean family and may be interchanged with the pinto bean in any recipe; it will, however, color any other ingredients black. The black turtle is sweet, spicy, and robust, and is delicious in soups or refried (*refritos negros*).

At first glance a black turtle and black soybean may look like the same bean. The soy is shiny and rounded; the turtle has a dull appearance and is slightly square shaped.

See **Beans and Legumes; Black Soybean.**

BLACK WALNUT
(Juglans nigra)

The native American walnut, the black walnut, is related to the more common English walnut. The black, limited in availability and therefore in commercial use, is prized for its sweet and woodsy flavor. It is extremely difficult to crack, requiring a cement floor, a heavy hammer, and a hefty swing. Once split, each morsel of nut meat needs coaxing from its still unyielding shell. In the process, the black walnut oil leaves a deep brown stain on fingers, fabric—and even the cement. The amount of meat per nut is small, but its flavor is great. Just a bit of black walnut marvelously flavors a grain pilaf, a cake, or candy.

Health Benefits The black walnut is lower in fat and higher in protein and iron than the English walnut. It contains more vitamin A than any other nut. Black walnuts reduce *vata*.

See **Nuts; Walnut.**

SHORT STOP FOR BLACK WALNUTS

One October, I was driving near Fruita, Colorado, when I happened to see a handmade sign next to a large old Buick: "Black Walnuts." A couple sat in the front seat. A farmer in his seventies got out of the car to meet me, carrying a one-pound plastic bag of black walnuts. "Did you crack these yourself?" I asked, and he held out his brown-stained hands as evidence. We exchanged money, product, and names, and the Mrs. and I exchanged recipes. Michael Springmeyer said that his 36 black walnut trees don't produce uniformly but that there's always a crop to sell. At $12 a pound, the nuts were a steal.

BLADDER WRACK
Rockweed
(Fucus species)

Bladder wrack is highly regarded as an effective medicine for obesity, hypothyroid function, and edema. It is not, however, a diuretic as its name suggests. *Wraec* is an old English word for seaweed, and bladder refers to its swollen, bladderlike frond tips. Bladder wrack has a pleasing, sweet flavor but its slippery gel is a texture most people don't like. It is used primarily in stock or as an ingredient in food supplements. Bladder wrack is available by mail order (see pages 403–04).

See **Seaweed.**

BLOOD ORANGE See **Orange.**

BLUEBERRY
Bilberry
(Vaccinium corymbosum)

I once read an account of an explorer who, retracing Mackenzie's route to the Arctic ocean, found and feasted upon blueberries ten miles from the arctic circle. Imagine that.

Not too juicy and not too sweet, it is no wonder that the delectable blueberry is the second most popular berry after the strawberry. Because of its superior shipping properties, the blueberry is a sizable business in the northeastern states, especially Maine. The United States produces 95 percent of the world's blueberry crop. This native American plant is related to the huckleberry (*V. myrtillus*) and cranberry.

Health Benefits Medicinal for the blood and liver, bittersweet blueberries are a cooling food, support eye function, and have bacteria-fighting capabilities particularly useful in countering urinary-tract infections. For some allergic individuals, blueberries trigger hives and swelling of the face, lips, and eyes. Blueberries are an excellent source of vitamin C and manganese and a good source of vitamin A. Blueberry leaves effectively lower high blood sugar in adult-onset diabetes. Blueberries are *tridoshic* when eaten in moderation.

Use Fresh or frozen, blueberries are a colorful and tasty addition to cakes, shortcakes, pies, cobblers, preserves, and syrup. They dry well and are used in numerous prepared foods. Blueberries darken if stored in a metal container, and if combined with excessive alkalin (like baking soda), the berries turn a greenish blue.

Buying/Foraging Since blueberries are

BLUEBERRIES

Blueberries as big as the end of your
  thumb,
Real sky-blue, and heavy, and ready to
  drum
In the cavernous pail of the first one to
  come!
And all ripe together, not some of them
  green
And some of them ripe! You ought to
  have seen!

—Robert Frost

---

boxed with cellophane covering, it's hard to see their quality. Stains on the carton exterior indicate mashed and moldy berries. To know for sure, slip off the wrapper and look. Avoid withered and green fruits, and favor fresh, plump berries with a powdery bloom. This bloom is a natural, protective, waxy coat. Blueberries hold far better than other berries, but should be used within a week of picking. This lush berry is at its peak in midsummer.

The wild blueberry is still found in many parts of the country and is smaller and tarter than the commercial blueberry.

See Fruit.

BLUE CORN
Hopi Corn
(Zea mays)

Blue corn is literally blue, and it's sweeter and more delicately flavored than the yellow variety. This open-pollinated flint corn has remained a favorite of the Pueblo Indians for centuries.

BLESSED WITH BLUE CORNMEAL

One June I was invited to the Zuni pueblo in remote western New Mexico for their summer rain dance. It was incredible to join these people in their ages-old ceremonies and to experience directly how central corn is to their lives. At sunset we walked to the outskirts of the pueblo to watch the men and boys of the Deer Lodge clan and the Mudheads return from their day-long pilgrimage. Since dawn they'd walked, most of them barefoot, to a sacred salt mine to obtain salt for the ceremony. Upon returning to the village, they would dance through the night and until noon the next day. At noon a food giveaway would end the festivities.

The men of the Deer Lodge clan were bedecked with eagle feathers, fox pelts, evergreen ruffs, tortoiseshell rattles, and elaborate turquoise rings, bracelets, belts, and necklaces. The unadorned Mudheads were in plain brown garb with their heads enclosed in extraterrestrial-looking brown masks. Chanting prayers and walking gingerly on blistered and sore feet, the men and boys entered the village single file, dust covered, sweat streaked, and bone weary. The villagers, lined up along both sides of the road, silently blessed them for their sacrifice by placing a pinch of blue cornmeal on the shoulders of each passing pilgrim.

—Rebecca Wood, *The Splendid Grain*

Health Benefits Blue corn contains more complete protein and manganese than yellow corn. Many people prefer heirloom blue (and other open-pollinated varieties) because its energetic properties are superior to hybridized corn. While all corn is medicinal to the heart and kidneys, blue corn also supports the liver. Corn reduces *kapha,* and, in moderation, blue corn is easier on *pitta* than yellow corn.

Use Blue corn products such as blue cornmeal, atole, tortillas, chips, and pancake mix are available in natural food stores and some supermarkets. Substitute blue corn for yellow in any recipe for muffins, sauces, cookies, cake, bread, waffles, or beverage. The result will be a delicate gray blue.

Oddly enough, if you add an acid, such as lemon juice, the blue turns a stunning pink. I once made corn dumplings with a minced kumquat added to the batter and steamed them on a bed of collard greens. The citrus speckled the bluish dumplings with magenta and when they were served on the fresh steamed greens, they were striking, and so delicious.

See **Corn.**

BLUE-GREEN ALGAE See Wild Blue-Green Algae.

BOK CHOY
Celery Mustard, Pak Choy, Tai Sai
(*Brassica rapa* subsp. *chinensis*)

Bok choy is a small plant with a rosette of upright dark green leaves held on large, thick, flat white stalks. A popular vegetable in China since at least the fifth century, it is sweet, crisp, and mild tasting.

Health Benefits Bok choy is a cooling vegetable effective in cases of heat congestion in the lungs, which in the early stages would typically have symptoms such as fever, chills, dry cough, a sore throat, and thick mucus discharge. Bok choy reduces *pitta* and *kapha*.

It is an excellent source of vitamins A and C as well as the numerous phytonutrients common to the cruciferous (cabbage) family.

Use Bok choy stems are juicy and sweet and take a few minutes longer to cook than the mild-tasting greens. Delicious in stir-fries and soups, bok choy leaves are also used as a vegetable wrap for food morsels. If the plant is flowering, use the flowers as well.

Buying There are several varieties of bok choy, including baby types with up to 12-inch-long stemmed heads. The most common have white stalks, but one Shanghai variety has a green stalk. It is most typically available in the winter.

See Cabbage Family.

BOLETE
Cèpe, King Bolete, Porcino
(Boletus edulis)

Mushrooms don't get any more delicious than the bolete. Its texture is reminiscent of filet mignon—only more succulent. This large mushroom is spongy (with tubes rather than gills) under the cap and is famed throughout the northern hemisphere for its piny, earthy, memorable flavor.

Health Benefits In the folk medicine of Bohemia and Bavaria, bolete mushrooms are credited with cancer prevention. This folk wisdom is supported by studies at Sloan-Kettering Institute for Cancer. The bolete is also an ingredient in the Chinese medical formula "tendon-easing pills," which ease lumbago, leg pain, numbness in limbs, bone and tendon discomfort, and leukorrhea.

Bolete mushrooms are low in calories and a good vitamin D source. Medicinally, they are a cooling food, stimulate the appetite, and are best eaten in moderation. As an occasional food, they reduce *pitta* and *kapha*.

Use Some people discard the tubular spore-bearing part of the bolete, but not I. It develops a delicate, oysterlike texture when cooked, which I find particularly delicious. You may wish to allow longer cooking time for the more fibrous stem or cut it into smaller pieces so that it will cook at the same rate as the cap. Bolete mushrooms may be substituted in any recipe calling for cooked mushrooms. Lightly sautéed in olive oil with (or without) garlic and parsley is recipe enough. Do not serve raw. To rehydrate when dried, soak in water for twenty minutes or until softened.

Buying At this time, boletes are not grown commercially, but independent collectors do sell them in some markets. Occasionally fresh boletes are imported at an exorbitant price from France and Italy. Imported dried boletes, sold as porcini or cèpes, are more readily available in many markets.

Bolete mushrooms range in color from whitish to vivid orange to brick red. When fresh, this mushroom is highly perishable. Purchase boletes that are firm, bruisefree, and show no sign of insect infestation in the stem end. Since they deteriorate rapidly, plan to use them immediately.

See **Mushroom Family**.

BOLITA BEAN
(Phaseolus vulgaris)

A handful of bolita beans looks almost as diverse as pebbles in a creek. The color of bolitas is predominantly pink but ranges from buff to yellow. It's clear to see that they're pinto relatives despite their irregular size and shape. Such lack of cosmetic uniformity denotes an heirloom seed with great adaptability. Compared to the pinto, the bolita has a richer and sweeter flavor.

See **Beans and Legumes.**

BONIATO See **Sweet Potato.**

BORAGE
(Borago officinalis)

Borage is a large, beautiful European herb with velvety leaves and vivid, star-shape purple flowers. Its name probably comes from the Arabic *abu araq*, which means father of sweat.

Health Benefits As its Arab name suggests, borage stimulates sweat as well as lactation. A bland, cooling herb, borage stregthens the heart, reduces high fever and catarrh, is a mild laxative and a mild sedative and antidepressant. Borage seeds are an excellent source of the important gamma-linoleic acid (GLA), which regulates hormones and lowers blood pressure. It calms *pitta* and *kapha*.

Use Borage imparts a cucumberlike flavor. The leaves may be stuffed and rolled like grape leaves. When using raw, chop the leaves first to minimize their woolly texture. Use the leaves in salads, pasta sauces, beans with cooked vegetables, and as a garnish. When adding the blossoms to a salad, add as a garnish at the last moment to prevent the dressing from discoloring them. In Sicily and Italy, borage, hops, and endive are cooked and eaten as a spring tonic.

Buying Borage wilts so rapidly that unless it's plucked fresh from the garden, substitute dried borage.

See **Gamma-Linoleic Acid; Herbs and Spices.**

BOSC PEAR See **Pear.**

BOSTON LETTUCE See **Butterhead Lettuce.**

BOYSENBERRY
(Rubus ulmifolius x loganobaccus x idaeus)

In 1923, Rudolph Boysen crossed a black-

A GENTLE ANTIDEPRESSANT

Those of our time do use the floures in sallads to exhilerate and make the minde glad. There be also many things made of them, used for the comfort of the heart, to drive away sorrow, & increase the joy of the minde. The leaves and floures of Borrage put into wine make men and women glad and merry, driving away all sadnesse, dulnesse, and melancholy, as Discorides and Pliny affirme.

—John Gerard, *The Herball, or Generall Historie of Plantes*

berry, loganberry, and a raspberry and created a namesake. The boysenberry is red and more acidic than the blackberry. It is grown primarily for canning.

See Fruit; Blackberry; Loganberry; Raspberry.

BRAMBLEBERRY See Blackberry.

BRAN See Wheat Bran.

BRASSICA See Cabbage Family.

BRAZIL NUT
(Bertholletia excelsa)

A tropical evergreen that grows wild in the South American rain forest, the Brazil tree has thus far resisted attempts at cultivation in Florida. This makes the hard, toe-shape brown nut (technically a seed) one of the few foraged commercial nuts. Current crops come from Brazil, Peru, and Venezuela.

PLANTED WITH A BANG

Brazil nuts are collected from the ground, rather than being plucked from their 150-foot-tall trees. The trees' two- to four-pound woody fruits contain up to 24 nuts each, which fit together like orange segments. When these heavy fruits break off and come crashing down, they sometimes shatter open, driving (or, from another perspective, planting) the nuts into the ground. Harvesters wear protective headgear.

Health Benefits Brazil nuts are almost as fatty as macadamia and pine nuts. They are an excellent calcium source and reduce *vata*. The Brazil is also one of the few nuts that offers a significant amount of vitamin C.

Buying When purchasing shelled Brazil nuts, select those with their brown skin intact and that look plump and fresh; avoid those that are yellowed, dark, or bruised. Reddish brown shelled Brazils have been dyed for cosmetic purposes. Brazil nuts in the shell should feel heavy when shaken.

See Nuts.

BREWER'S YEAST See Nutritional Yeast.

BROAD BEAN See Fava Bean.

BROCCOFLOWER

A hybrid of broccoli and cauliflower, a broccoflower is almost chartreuse in color and is shaped like a cauliflower. It is milder and sweeter tasting than either of its parents.

See Broccoli; Cabbage Family; Cauliflower.

BROCCOLI
(Brassica oleracea var. italica)

Along with former President George Bush, I lack respect for broccoli. The higher a vegetable's commercial value, the more it has been tampered with to lengthen shelf life, and broccoli shows it. If you doubt me, do a taste comparison of broccoli with other equally nutritious cabbage family members. Broccoli tastes metallic and sulfurous; it's tough and grainy. An heirloom broccoli spear

NUTRIENTS ARE ONLY NUTRITIOUS WHEN DIGESTED

Raw broccoli in salad or as a crudité is a mistake. Its sulfury, metallic taste is one drawback, but how hard it is to digest is another. (Unless, that is, it is garden fresh and very young.) Broccoli steamed al dente, however, is quite another matter. The steaming brings up its color and flavor and reduces its otherwise harsh taste.

Cauliflower is more acceptable raw unless you're serving people with delicate digestive systems (the very young, the elderly, or convalescents).

fresh from the garden, on the other hand, is peppery sweet, rich, and heavenly.

Broccoli was introduced to the United States in the 1920s by Italian immigrants. The Salinis Valley in California provides 90 percent of the domestic broccoli crop.

Health Benefits Cooling in nature, broccoli treats the eyes and helps reduce eye inflammation. It is slightly diuretic in action. Broccoli reduces *pitta* and *kapha*. Broccoli contains twice the vitamin C of an orange, almost as much calcium as whole milk—and its calcium is better absorbed. Broccoli contains selenium, is a modest source of vitamin A and alpha-tocopherol vitamin E, and has value as an antioxidant.

Use The broccoli head is actually the plant's flower. Peel the fibrous skin of the stalks and use them, too. Use also the small leaves attached to the stem. In the cabbage family, the leafy greens (not the blossoms, as in cauliflower and broccoli) offer the most nutrients. Cook in plenty of boiling salted water until crisp-tender or steam until done.

Buying Select broccoli that has a fresh smell, bright and compact green florets, and firm stalks. Avoid any with a rank smell, yellow florets, or woody or hollowed stalks, all signs of an overmature vegetable.

See Cabbage Family; Sprouts.

BROCCOLI RABE
Broccoli Raab, Rapini
(*Brassica rapa* subsp. *parachinensis*)

Growing on slender stalks, with leafy dark greens and both green buds and yellow flowers, broccoli rabe is aggressively pungent and bitter. A nonheading broccoli closely related to the turnip, it adds zest to bland dishes and can hold its own with savory

INVITING THE RABE IN

When deciding which way to use broccoli rabe—or any other vegetable—consider how it will complement the main dish. If, for example, on a warm day I'm serving a substantial meaty or hard-to-digest dish, then I'll make the rabe light by steaming or blanching it and dressing it with nothing but a squeeze of lemon juice or umeboshi vinegar. If the weather wants the vegetables to be more warming and substantial, I'll sauté them with garlic and extra virgin olive or sesame oil; and if I want them warmer yet, I'll add ginger and fennel. On another day, the soup or stir-fry might invite the rabe into the pot.

ones. The Chinese variety, flowering Cabbage, is milder. Broccoli rabe reduces *kapha*.

Use Broccoli rabe is at its best when the leaves are fresh and free from discoloration and when the buds are still tight or just starting to open. Stalk, leaf, and flower are used.

See Broccoli; Cabbage Family.

BROCCOLI ROMANESCO
(Brassica oleracea)

The most fanciful and tender broccoli is the romanesco, a chartreuse vegetable mandala. Its sweet-tasting florets are spiraling conical turrets. Each floret is part of a spiral, and each tiny spiral is part of a larger spiral yet. It looks like computer-generated fractal art. Look for it at a farmers' market or grow it yourself. Romanesco withstands—and is in fact sweetened by—severe frost.

See Broccoli; Cabbage Family.

BROCCOLI SPROUTS See Sprouts.

BROWN ALGAE See Kelp.

BROWN RICE See Rice.

BROWN RICE PASTA See Rice Noodles.

BROWN RICE VINEGAR

Imported from Japan, brown rice vinegar that has been traditionally brewed and fermented has a smooth, mellow flavor and low acidity of 4.5 percent. If it does not say "traditionally brewed" on the label, I don't recommend it even if it's organic.

See Vinegar.

BROWN SUGAR

You can easily make your own brown sugar: Take some white sugar and stir in a bit of molasses or "caramel coloring" (burnt white sugar). Knowing how it's made dispels the "healthful" image that brown sugar once enjoyed. White sugar contains 99 percent sucrose, and brown sugar contains 98 percent sucrose.

When cooked, brown sugar adds a mild molasseslike flavor, a moister crumb, and a darker color. If you want these qualities plus a rich, round, smooth, and satisfying sweet flavor (rather than a cloying, angular sweetness), opt for the more healthful, unrefined rapadura that contains 82 percent sucrose.

See Rapadura; Sugar.

BRUSSELS SPROUT
(Brassica oleracea gemmifera)

Of all vegetables in the garden, Brussels sprouts look the strangest. From 20 to 40 auxiliary buds (or baby cabbages) grow close together along a tall, single stalk that's topped with small cabbagelike leaves. Brussels sprouts originated in Brussels, Belgium—ergo its name. The Germans more aptly called it *Rosenkohl,* or "rose cabbage."

Use In a traditional British Christmas dinner, Brussels sprouts are a given. Considering that these beauties are then at their peak and, when cooked properly, appropriate fare for the grandest of feasts, it's a custom I readily embrace.

To serve Brussels sprouts whole, trim, then cut an × into the base of each one to enable the heat to penetrate their center more quickly and cook through before the outer leaves are overdone. Blanch or steam until just tender but still a vibrant green. Brussels sprouts may also be halved, quartered, thinly sliced, or, for an elegant but time-consuming dish, separate each leaf. I also add Brussels sprouts to stir-fries and soups or to steamed, braised, or baked dishes.

Brussels sprouts at their prime need to be seasoned only with butter and salt or with extra virgin olive oil and vinegar. If they are not sweet, they invite more assertive flavorings. Deborah Madison in *Vegetarian Cooking for Everyone* recommends juniper and mustard or brown butter, capers, and lemon.

Buying Brussels sprouts become sweet and tender after a frost. Unfortunately, since our primary commercial supply of this vegetable comes from California's mild coastal area, Brussels sprouts generally lack sweetness. If your region has frost, seek out local Brussels sprouts.

See **Cabbage Family.**

BUCKWHEAT
(Fagopyrum esculentum)

The three-sided buckwheat groat is the shape and rusty color of a beechnut, and thus its Anglo-Saxon name was *boek* ("beech") *weite* ("wheat"). Although not a wheat, nor even a cereal grain, buckwheat is used like a grain. This rhubarb relative originated, and is still a staple, in Siberia and Manchuria. In medieval Russia, the word *kasha*, which today means roasted or cooked buckwheat, signified "meal" or "feast" because a meal was complete only with this staple present.

Health Benefits Of all the grains, buckwheat has the longest transit time in the gut and therefore is the most filling and stabilizing for blood sugar. Since it is a glutenfree,

noncereal grain, many people with food allergies rely upon buckwheat. It's a good blood-building food, as it neutralizes toxic acidic wastes. Buckwheat, however, is not recommended for someone with skin eruptions, which it may exacerbate. Likewise, it's not recommended for nervous, emotionally unstable people or people with extreme heat signs such as high fever, thirst, and high blood pressure.

Buckwheat contains the bioflavonoid rutin and therefore is medicinal to capillaries and blood vessels and increases circulation to the hands and feet. In addition, rutin is an antidote against X rays and other forms of radiation. In Japanese tradition, buckwheat is considered medicinal for the kidneys. In Ayurvedic medicine, it reduces *kapha.*

The most outstanding nutritional characteristic of buckwheat is the high proportion in it of all eight essential amino acids—especially lysine, which, at 6.1 percent, is greater in proportion in buckwheat than in any of the cereal grains. In addition, buckwheat has up to 100 percent more calcium than other grains, is rich in vitamin E, and contains almost the entire range of B-complex vitamins.

Use Buckwheat groats have a soft texture and, if roasted, a strong, robust flavor. Use

---

HOW A HORSE GETS SUNBURNED

A light-colored horse or cow grazing in a buckwheat field on a sunny day may become sunburned and suffer temporary hair loss. Buckwheat inhibits our tanning element, melanin, and judging from farmers' stories about sunburned livestock, apparently inhibits a horse's as well.

Perhaps this is why buckwheat is a staple of the dark-complexioned Siberian peoples but not of the fair-skinned Scandinavians. If you are dark skinned, a melanin inhibitor keeps your skin a shade lighter and thus enables you to absorb more of the sun's rays—and therefore more vitamin D, a hard-to-obtain vitamin during long, dark winters.

In our deep South, buckwheat was a old kitchen remedy for lightening the skin.

---

them as a hot breakfast cereal, a side dish, a grain entrée—either by itself or else cooked with other vegetables, nuts, or seeds as a grain pilaf. The cooked groats, when formed into croquettes and grilled or pan-fried, make an excellent patty or loaf.

Buying Buckwheat comes in several forms:

- **Buckwheat or Buckwheat Groats** White, unroasted buckwheat groats have a mild flavor. For maximum vitality, buy the unroasted groats and toast them just before cooking. To toast groats, place them in a wok or thin pan over high heat and stir constantly until the groats turn several shades darker, or to taste.
- **Kasha** Buckwheat that is factory toasted to a deep amber is called kasha. It has an almost scorched flavor that some people adore. To my taste, it is stale and as there is no telling how many months ago it was factory toasted, so I favor buckwheat.
- **Kasha Grits** These are available milled from coarse to fine in supermarkets, but I find no advantage to purchasing grits since whole kasha cook in a quick 10 minutes. Furthermore, a kasha grit, like any broken grain, lacks vitality.
- **Whole Buckwheat** With its black hull intact, whole buckwheat is suitable only for sprouting. The inedible hulls, incidentally, are used for stuffing cushions, *zabutons* (meditation cushions), and pillows.

See **Grains**.

BUCKWHEAT FLOUR

Buckwheat flour is made from unroasted groats. It is graded light, medium, or dark, depending on the amount of black hull contained in the flour. Since the hull is rich in lysine, an important amino acid, I favor the darker flour.

For a soft, aromatic cake or muffin with an earthy flavor, substitute 10 percent buckwheat flour for wheat flour. Add 30 percent or more buckwheat flour to bread and your loaf will have the density of a brick and the moistness of a pudding. Buckwheat flour is most familiar in pancakes, waffles, and crepes. Buckwheat flour, alone or combined with wheat, makes superlative pasta. As soba, it's Japan's most famous pasta. Buckwheat noodles, a specialty of Valtellina on the Italian-Swiss border, are combined with potatoes and cabbage in *pizzoccheri*. Throughout northern Italy, buckwheat flour is also made into a hearty black polenta, *polenta nera*.

See **Flour**.

BUDDHA'S HAND CITRON See **Citron**.

BULGHUR See **Bulgur**.

BULGUR
Bulghur

Steam, dry, and then crack whole wheat berries, and you've got bulgur. Why did Middle Eastern peoples devise this dish? Whole wheat is a long and hard chew, and cracked wheat is but a slight improvement. Bulgur, however, is light textured, has a tasty, nutty flavor, and needs considerably less cooking—in some cases, none at all.

Dark bulgur is made from hard red wheat. White bulgur, made from soft white wheat, has a more delicate flavor. As bulgur is a whole grain product, it does become rancid. Purchase bulgur that smells fresh and nutty. Store airtight in the refrigerator or freezer.

See **Grains; Wheat**.

BULLWHIP KELP See **Sea Whip**.

THE ULTIMATE BULGUR EXPERIENCE

Just as fresh pasta is incomparable to dry pasta, so is fresh bulgur a marvelously heightened taste experience over purchased bulgur. It's surprisingly easy to make. Soak 2 cups wheat berries in water to cover overnight. Drain, place berries and 4 cups water in a saucepan, cover, bring to a boil, and simmer for 1 hour or until the wheat is slightly tender. Drain and reserve cooking liquid for soup stock. Spread the wheat berries on a cookie sheet and sun dry. Or oven dry at 250 degrees for 45 to 60 minutes. Stir occasionally. When the wheat is completely dry, coarsely grind it in a grain mill, food processor, or blender. Store in a glass container until use.

BURDOCK
Gobo
(Arctium lappa)

If ever you've strolled through the autumn countryside and collected burrs on your sweater or socks, odds are that they were burdock fruits. One ingenious person examined the burr's minute hooks to see why it so effectively clings to things, went to the drawing board . . . and invented Velcro. When it comes to eating, though, it's the root—not the fruit—that is a prized vegetable.

Imagine the heady aroma of freshly dug earth—that's the aroma of burdock. Add sweet, and you've got its flavor, which is similar to artichoke hearts or salsify, only with a touch of bitter. Burdock skin is brown, while its somewhat fibrous flesh is white. Used in medieval Italy and long a favorite of the Japanese, who call it *gobo*, the burdock taproot grows up to two feet in length yet remains as slender as a carrot. It is a member of the sunflower family.

Health Benefits Burdock acts upon the lungs, stomach, kidney, and liver. It stimulates bile secretion and is an excellent source of the nutraceutical inulin, making it good for diabetic conditions. Burdock is one of the great alterative herbs, restoring the body to normal health by cleansing and purifying the blood, supporting digestion and the elimination of toxins, and helping to restore normal body function.

As an herbal ingredient, burdock appears in both European and Asian formulas as an anticarcinogen, as a treatment for arthritis, as a liver detoxifier, and for general kidney support. Burdock reduces *pitta* and *kapha*.

Burdock has more protein, calcium, and phosphorus than carrots and is an excellent source of potassium.

Use Ignore any recipe instructions that call to peel burdock's comely skin. Give it a light scrub with a vegetable brush and then cut and cook it like a carrot, allowing for longer cooking time. It's hard for me to imagine any cooked vegetable dish that is not enhanced by burdock's sweet, earthy flavor. I especially favor it in soups, stews, and stir-fries, or with sea vegetables. Burdock is not used raw.

Buying/Foraging Throughout many parts of the world, including the United States, burdock thrives as a common weed. You can identify it by its large, elephant ear–like leaves and its bothersome burrs. If foraging, harvest only the low-lying first-year plants before they develop tall stalks and set seed. Burdock is an easy plant to grow, but is really tough to harvest because it so tenaciously clings to the earth. It's always a real workout to dig it up. This spring I intend to plant it in a raised bed, alongside one of the boards that form the outside border. Come harvest, I'll remove the board and the burdock will fall into my waiting hands—or so I imagine.

Burdock is available in Asian markets and natural food stores throughout the year. Select plump, firm roots. (Limp roots are acceptable if they are not pithy or dehydrated.) Wrap in damp paper towels and refrigerate. Use within a week. If they dry, soak in water prior to use.

See **Sunflower Family.**

BUTTER

For baking, the most healthful and delicious fat is butter. Coconut butter equally withstands heat without becoming denatured.

Health Benefits In addition to baking, a second reason I use butter is to make ghee, which is the most easily digested culinary fat because it lubricates and enhances flow, and, where used moderately, is an anticarcinogen. Butter, especially salted butter, on the other hand, is heavy, congesting, and hard to digest.

If you have a cholesterol problem, then use butter or ghee in moderation. Otherwise, butter will actually protect against atherosclerosis as long as the overall diet is healthy.

Butter is a rich source of vitamin A and also contains vitamin D.

Buying Federal standards do not permit butter to contain preservatives or additives except for approved food colors (annatto and beta carotene). Nevertheless, do not purchase commercial butter. Cultured, unsalted, organic raw butter is decidedly the most delicious and healthful butter. In those states which prohibit the sale of raw butter, however, only butter made from pasteurized milk is available.

Sweet (unsalted) butter has a more delicate flavor and a shorter life than salted butter. Without salt to aid preservation, the manufacturer must use fresher cream—and the difference is a better-tasting butter. If you doubt this, a taste comparison of salted and unsalted butter will make you a believer.

Favor cultured butter, which means that the cream sat in a cool place for a day prior to being churned into butter. Our butter-churning grandmothers knew that cultured milk makes superior-tasting butter. Again, a taste test of cultured versus uncultured butter is telling. Ghee made from noncultured butter creates an inferior product.

Lastly, smell butter before purchasing it. Your nose will unerringly alert you—even through several layers of paper wrapping—to rancid butter. Good butter smells sweet and creamy.

See **Clarified Butter**; **Fat and Oil**; **Ghee**.

BUTTER BEAN See **Lima Bean**.

BUTTERCUP SQUASH
(Cucurbita maxima)

The buttercup squash has a dark green skin and is crowned with a blue-green "turban" at its blossom end. With bright orange flesh, it ranks just under kabocha as the sweetest squash. Creamy describes its texture. The buttercup is similar in shape to a turban squash but generally smaller and sweeter. Buttercups average around three pounds.

See **Kabocha Squash**; **Turban Squash**; **Winter Squash**.

BUTTERHEAD LETTUCE
Bibb Lettuce, Boston Lettuce
(Lactuca sativa)

The small butterhead lettuce has tender leaves bunched almost like rose petals. As its name suggests, butterhead is meltingly delicate.

See **Lettuce**.

BUTTERNUT SQUASH
(Cucurbita moschata)

The longest keeper in the squash family, butternut squash is reminiscent of a peanut in shape and color (thus its name), although it is actually more bell shaped. Its sweet, orange flesh is similar to the buttercup squash. Because a butternut's skin is thinner and lighter in color than other winter squash, I cook and purée it with the skin intact. This saves preparation time and increases nutritional value.

See **Winter Squash**.

CABBAGE

(Brassica oleracea capitata)

The word cabbage derives from the Latin word *caput*, meaning "head." And a head it is, indeed, with very little else save prerequisite roots.

The cabbage has more bad press than any vegetable because when overcooked it emits hydrogen sulfide (the rotten egg aroma), ammonia, and other foul smells. Take a cue and don't boil it to death or your intestinal gas will be similarly sulfurous. Cooked with care, though, cabbage is a delicious vegetable. Wild cabbages still grow in England and the Mediterranean area.

Health Benefits Valued for at least two millennia, cabbage is sweet and slightly cooling to the stomach. It therefore counters overheated conditions, such as inflammation and dry throat. It nourishes the spleen-pancreas, regulates the stomach, and relieves abdominal spasms, pain, and ulcers. It treats constipation, the common cold, mental depression, and irritability. Cabbage purifies the blood, acts as a vermifuge, and was used by the Romans as a hangover cure. Cabbage is an excellent source of numerous anticarcinogenic phytonutrients; it reduces *pitta* and *kapha*.

The outer, greener cabbage leaves contain more chlorophyll, vitamin E, and calcium than the inner, pale leaves. Cabbage is higher in vitamin C than oranges and is a superior source of vitamin U, an ulcer remedy. Cabbage is also a good source for many minerals. Phenolic compounds give red cabbage its characteristic color as well as additional antioxidant properties.

Use Cabbage can be eaten raw, as in slaws. When not overcooked, it is delicious and versatile in soups, or in simmered, sautéed, steamed, or baked dishes. The leaves make excellent wrappers for a savory filling. And pickled in sauerkraut it's delectable.

To further vivify the ruby of a red cabbage, cook it with a splash of acid like lemon juice, vinegar, or wine. When cooked in alkaline water or with mineral-rich foods, such as sea vegetables, it turns blue.

Buying Purchase cabbages with compact heads that are heavy for their size. Favor those that have their outer leaves in place; this indicates freshness. Cabbages may be either green or red, with round or pointy heads, and with smooth or crinkly leaves. The later, savoy cabbage, has a looser head, a sweeter, milder flavor, and a buttery smooth texture.

See **Cabbage Family.**

CABBAGE FAMILY
Brassica, Crucifer, Mustard

Historically and nutritionally, the cabbage, or brassica, family is one of the most important—if not *the* most important—vegetable family, and it is certainly one of the most diverse. It's hard to believe that kohlrabi and daikon are related unless you see them gone to seed. The four petals of each flower form a cross, from which the family gets its Latin name, *crucifer*.

Health Benefits The vegetables at the pinnacle of phytochemical research are the cabbage family. Their known phytonutrients aid the enzymes that ward off carcinogens and other outside invaders; they also inhibit cancer formation, detoxify carcinogens, and protect against colorectal, stomach, and respiratory cancers. Their leaves—especially their dark green leaves—often contain more phytochemicals than their other parts. Therefore, favor kale, collards, arugula, and Brussels sprouts over cauliflower or a pale cabbage, and even the leaves of broccoli over broccoli heads and stems.

MUSTARD OIL BURNS

The fiery mustard oil (isothiocyanate) present in brassica family members gives canola greens, horseradish, mustard, and wasabi their pungent wallop. Botanists surmise that the plants developed this oil as protection from grazing animals.

Mustard oil is volatile and cooking quickly dissipates it. So if you like it hot, eat it raw—but not when your digestive system is irritated, and certainly don't serve it to convalescents or the young. Laboratory-synthesized mustard oil is a chemical weapon used since World War I that burns the skin and mucus membranes.

Bok choy, Chinese cabbage, mizuna, and other mild-tasting cabbage family members have a much smaller amount of mustard oil.

Brassicas contain isothiocyanates, or mustard oil, which is partially responsible for their pungency and which has been used in higher concentrations as a toxic chemical weapon. Those with the highest mustard oil content are horseradish, watercress, wasabi, mustard, and canola (rape).

The cabbage family is goitrogenic, and therefore people with hypothyroidism would be wise to use it moderately.

When brassicas are cooked with warming spices and oil or are served warm, they are easier for *vata* to digest. Cabbage family members reduce and are therefore most useful for *kapha* and *pitta*.

Most dark leafy crucifers are exceptional

sources of calcium, magnesium, vitamins A and C, and beta carotene.

See Arugula; Bok Choy; Broccoflower; Broccoli; Broccoli Rabe; Broccoli Romanesco; Brussels Sprout; Cabbage; Canola Seed; Cauliflower; Chinese Broccoli; Chinese Cabbage; Collards; Cress; Daikon; Flowering Cabbage; Horseradish; Kale; Kohlrabi; Mizuna; Mustard Greens; Radish; Rutabaga; Tatsoi; Turnip; Watercress; Wrapped Heart Mustard Cabbage.

CACAO See Chocolate.

CACTUS PAD See Nopal.

CACTUS PADDLE See Nopal.

CACTUS PEAR See Prickly Pear.

CALABAZA
Cuban Squash, West Indian Pumpkin, Zapallo
(Cucurbita moschata)

A daily staple throughout the Caribbean, Central America, and South America, calabaza is a hard-shelled, round squash with a stellar orange flesh. Like its near relative butternut squash it is pleasingly moist and sweet. It has increasing availability in domestic markets, where it's often sold in large chunks. Calabaza, in Spanish, is a general term for squash.

See Butternut Squash.

CALMATI RICE See Basmati Rice.

CANE JUICE See Sugar.

CANNELLINI BEAN
(Phaseolus vulgaris)

This favorite Italian bean is white, with a creamy texture, and an earthy taste that is similar to a great northern bean; it is both longer and plumper than a navy bean. Cannellini are delicious in salads, puréed for spreads, or served warm with fresh rosemary, olive oil, and freshly ground black pepper.

See Beans and Legumes.

Ø CANOLA OIL

Prior to the canola oil hype, the rape plant, from which low erucic acid canola is hybridized, was used primarily as cattle feed. In the 1980s, a Canadian oil manufacturer saw a potential market and, because of his concern that "rape seed oil" would be a hard sell, created the name "canola." Contrary to what the media blitzkrieg has suggested, this product is not a superior culinary oil. In fact, it is toxic because it's highly refined. In addition, because of canola's 10 percent fragile Omega-3 fatty acids, it is even more toxic than other refined culinary oils that do not contain Omega-3.

About 1 percent of the canola oils available are unrefined; they must *never* be heated, however, and their shelf life is less stable than other quality monounsaturated oils like olive and sesame oil. Informed people favor hemp or flax oils as sources of essential fatty acids (EFAs).

Rape seed oil has a lengthy history of use in India and Europe. Note, however, that this oil was pressed fresh daily using simple presses that did not denature the fatty acids.

See Canola Seed; Essential Fatty Acids; Fat and Oil.

CANOLA SEED
Coleseed, Rape Seed
(Brassica napus)

Occasionally available toasted as a tasty condiment to sprinkle over salads or grains, rape seeds are black or reddish brown seeds about the size of millet. They have a mild bite, similar to radish seeds, and a peanut-like flavor. Rape greens are also used for salads or as a potherb.

See Cabbage Family; Seeds.

CANTALOUPE See Melon.

CAPE GOOSEBERRY See Ground Cherry.

CAPER
(Capparis spinosa)

The pickled or brined flower buds of a spiny Mediterranean shrub, capers are a pungent condiment. They are harvested from wild or cultivated caper bushes in southern Europe. Nasturtium or purslane buds are sometimes substituted for capers.

Health Benefits Astringent in action, capers are a stimulating digestive tonic useful for treating diarrhea, gout, and coughs. Nutritionist and Ayurvedic author Amadea Morningstar notes that the initial sour and salty flavor of capers seems to indicate that they are best for *vata;* however, their long-term astringency is aggravating to *vata.*

Use Capers have an intense resiny or tart flavor that vivifies sauces, dressings, and marinades. They're often combined with olives and anchovies and go especially well with fish.

Buying Nonpareils are the smallest, most flavorful, and therefore best quality. Capers are available pickled in jars or dried in salt.

CARAMBOLA See Star Fruit.

CARAWAY
(Carum carvi)

Shakespeare's Falstaff, invited to sup upon "a pippin and a dish of caraways," reminds us that caraway is more than a spice—it's also a vegetable. Pungent and aromatic, this member of the carrot family originated in the Middle East. The small, dark brown seeds have an explosive flavor.

Health Benefits Caraway is a stimulant that reduces spasms in the gastrointestinal tract and uterus. It is used to relieve menstrual cramps, poor circulation, and digestive problems, including hiatal hernia, indigestion, flatulence, stomach ulcer, and some intestinal parasites. It reduces *vata* and *kapha.*

In medieval Europe, a love potion called *Huile de Vénus* made from the oil of caraway was said to tone the muscles, soften the complexion, and aid digestion.

Use Caraway seeds may be chewed or infused as an herbal tea. The seeds are used to flavor breads, cakes, and pastries, and vegetable and meat dishes, especially in German, Austrian, and Scandinavian cuisine. The feathery, mild-flavored greens are used, before they flower, as an herb. Cook the taproot as you would a carrot.

See Carrot Family; Herbs and Spices.

CARDAMOM
(Elettaria cardamomum)

Cardamom, an Old World spice that tastes like lemon zest and eucalyptus, is a member of the ginger family. Its papery pods are about the shape, size, and color of a shelled pumpkin seed; they are hand harvested from a tall shrub that originated in tropical Southeast Asia. After saffron and vanilla, cardamom is the third most expensive spice. Today, cardamom is produced in India, Sri Lanka, and Mexico.

Health Benefits Cardamom is a sweet, pungent tonic that is warming in its thermal nature. It acts upon the spleen-pancreas, stomach, lung, and kidney meridians. It aids digestion, relaxes spasms, and cuts mucus, making it useful in lung tonics. Cardamom eases coughs, breathlessness, burning urination, incontinence, and hemorrhoids. It acts as an antidote to coffee's stress on the adrenal glands. Cardamom reduces *vata* and *kapha*.

Use Use whole cardamom in the pod or the seeds, just shelled and freshly ground. Once the protective pod is removed, cardamom develops an unpleasantly strong, camphorlike aroma and taste. For a subtle flavor, whole cardamom pods may be added to infused drinks or long-simmered dishes; extract the pod prior to serving. For more intensely flavored dishes, use ground seed.

Cardamom is widely used in sweet and savory dishes in Indian and Middle Eastern cuisines—especially in pilafs, curries, and desserts. In the Middle East and North Africa it is used to flavor coffee; elsewhere in Africa, to flavor tea. In German, Russian, and Scandinavian cuisines, cardamom is used in baked goods, pastries, fruit dishes, and beverages.

In the United States and France, cardamom is used to formulate perfumes.

Buying Cardamom is best purchased in small green pods that were air dried. If the pods are sandy white, they were sun dried and will be less flavorful. Larger, brown cardamom pods are not true cardamom; they have a harsh, inferior flavor.

Fresh cardamom seeds are plump and a uniform dark brown in color. As they age, they shrivel and develop a grayish blue.

I don't recommend purchasing powdered cardamom. If I mistakenly grind more cardamom than I'm using immediately, I don't attempt to save it because its flavor too quickly becomes camphorous.

See **Ginger Family; Herbs and Spices.**

CARDOON
(Cynara cardunculus)

A Mediterranean thistle, the cardoon is like a giant artichoke plant but with smaller, prickly flower heads that are not eaten. It is cultivated, rather, for the leafstalks and roots. This vegetable grows to a height of four feet and has gray-green leaves. The outer leaves are trimmed away before the plant reaches the market.

Properly trimmed, a cardoon yields even more waste than a globe artichoke: a six-pound bunch yields two pounds of edible stalk.

Health Benefits Similar to Artichoke.

Use Cardoons taste like artichokes—only more bitter. Very tender, young stalks

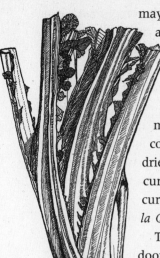

may be added raw to salads. Larger stalks are blanched and used as you would celery, in salads, soups, and stews. The root may also be used as a cooked vegetable. The dried flowers are used to curdle milk, as for the soft curd cheese *La Caillebotte à la Chardonette.*

To use, separate cardoons into stalks, rinse, and trim leaves. With a vegetable peeler, remove the indigestible stringy fibers, chop the stalk, and then parboil to reduce bitterness.

Buying Cardoons are available in specialty markets in the winter and early spring. Because they are blanched by enclosing the stalks in cardboard, they are an energy intensive crop, and therefore expensive. Look for fresh, crisp heads no larger than one foot long. Avoid heads with wilt or rust.

See **Artichoke; Sunflower Family.**

CARNAROLI RICE
(Oryza sativa)

This Italian import is a white, short-grain rice that absorbs more liquid than other grains but still stays firm during cooking. This makes it ideal for risotto and other creamy-but-chewy rice dishes. Because it is difficult to grow, it is the most expensive Italian rice. It is available in specialty shops.

See **Rice.**

CAROB
Saint John's Bread
(Ceratonia siliqua)

Saint John the Baptist lived in the wilderness on locusts and wild honey. In his case, locusts weren't crawling things but the leguminous pods of the locust tree, which we call carob. This explains the alternate name for carob.

Roasted and ground carob pods yield carob powder. The longer the pods are roasted, the more the taste approximates chocolate and the more perfumed it becomes. I use the term "approximates" loosely. Many people enjoy the carob flavor for what it is, namely, carob. To expect a real chocolate flavor from carob is asking too much of any legume. Carob pods are imported from the Mediterranean area and ground and roasted in the United States.

Health Benefits Sweet, light, and dry, carob is alkaline in nature. It nourishes the lungs. Carob contains tannin (as does cocoa), and because tannic acid reduces the absorption of protein through the intestinal wall, it may depress the growth rate of young animals. It is therefore recommended that carob be used in moderation, especially in children's diets.

Carob is an excellent source of calcium, containing more than three times as much calcium as milk. An extraordinarily rich source of potassium, it also has vitamin A and B, as well as other minerals. It has 8 percent protein and contains significantly less fat and calories than chocolate. Unlike chocolate, carob is free of caffeine and oxalic acids, and it is naturally sweet with 48 percent sugar, including sucrose.

Carob reduces *pitta* and *kapha* and, if moist, reduces *vata*.

Use Carob is available as a syrup or powdered as a baking ingredient. It is also a common ingredient in energy bars and other natural food confections.

CAROLINA RICE
(Oryza sativa)

Antebellum South Carolina was famous for a long-grain white rice with grains that were dry and separate when cooked. Although rice is not grown in the Carolinas today, the name is still used to evoke a high-quality rice.

See **Rice**.

Carrageen See Irish Moss.

CARROT
(Daucus carota subsp. sativus)

This Afghanistani native is our most valuable taproot crop. The carrot is derived from a wild carrot with a white root called Queen Anne's Lace. Old carrot varieties come in many colors, including yellow, dark red, white, and purple. New designer red carrots contain the pigment lycopene, which also colors tomatoes.

Health Benefits The ancient Greek word for carrot, *philon*, comes from the word "love"—as this root was considered an aphrodisiac. Carrots support the lungs, spleen-pancreas, and liver, and they tonify the kidneys. They are diuretic in action, supporting the elimination of waste, preventing constipation, lowering blood sugar, purifying the blood, and treating indigestion. Carrots relieve menstrual pain and premenstrual irritability. They improve night vision, skin health, and are anticarcinogenic. Carrots reduce *vata* and *kapha*.

Carrots are a rich source of vitamin A, carotenoids, and sugar. As a root crop, carrots are second only to beets in sweetness. They also contain B vitamins, phosphorus, iodine, calcium, and the phenol coumarin, which helps prevent blood clotting and has anticancer properties.

Use From soups to salads, from juice to cakes, carrots figure so prominently in our daily fare that it is hard to imagine life without them. Because the nutrients in carrots are concentrated in and near their skin, use them unpeeled. If the carrot is so old that the skin looks unappealing, then compost the carrot.

When fresh and young, the nutrient-rich carrot greens may be finely chopped and sautéed for a condiment or may be added to stir-fries or soups. Remove and discard the more fibrous stem first. Dried or fresh, carrot tops may be used like a strong-flavored parsley.

Buying There are several hundred varieties of carrots. Select carrots with the deepest orange color, indicative of the most vitamin A, and a good carrot aroma. The most popular in the United States is the Mediterranean type, which is fairly long, cylindrical, and orange.

See **Carrot Family; Carrot Juice.**

NOT ROBBING THE CRADLE

Peeled baby carrots—now ubiquitous in markets, restaurants, and salad bars—are not really babies. They are adult carrots whittled down to junior size, with the bits and pieces going into soups or TV dinners. These "babies" don't do much for me. As the late food writer M.F.K. Fisher observed in *The Art of Eating*, "All of them, whether tender or hard, thick skinned or thin, die when they are peeled . . . even as you and I."

Peeled carrots may develop a "white blush" (to use the industry term) if they're dehydrated. Soak them in water and they'll color back up again. Better yet, toss them and purchase fresh, whole carrots.

CARROT FAMILY
(Umbelliferae)

The umbellifer family is named for its clustered flowers, which resemble an upside-down umbrella. The most commonly used umbellifer is the carrot. The most important Chinese tonic after ginseng is angelica, another member of the carrot family.

See Angelica; Caraway; Carrot; Celeriac; Celery; Chervil; Cilantro; Cumin; Dill; Fennel; Lovage; Parsley; Parsley Root; Parsnip.

CARROT JUICE

A perennial favorite health drink, the fresh juice of carrots is excellent for liver rejuvenation and cleansing. The juice is more medicinal in action when taken on an empty stomach. Carrot juice applied directly to burns aids in their healing.

Use in moderation, as carrot juice is a refined food. This surprises people, especially those who like to juice their own carrots. But consider how many carrots go into one glass of juice and how much pulp remains. In a few gulps, the juice is gone. Imagine cramming that many whole carrots into your stomach in the same amount of time it takes to drink their juice. While whole carrots don't raise blood sugar because their fiber slows digestion, carrot juice is a liquid form of simple sugars, and it does raise blood sugar. Therefore, when serving it to children, dilute it first; and the next time you drink it, notice the rush of energy it gives.

CASABA See Melon.

CASHEW NUT
(Anacardium occidentale)

The cashew, native to Brazil, is one nut you'll never see in its shell. Its outer shell contains a toxic oil, cardol, which—if touched—burns the skin like its relative, poison ivy. Cardol is released from the uncracked nuts by roasting them at 350 degrees. Cashews are then cracked, roasted a second time to remove an inner shell, and sold "raw."

This sweet-tasting, kidney-shape nut grows in a curious manner. It hangs from a soft, swollen, pear-shape edible stalk called a cashew apple. This tasty apple spoils within twenty-four hours and so it is never exported. It is eaten fresh or made into beverages, preserves, or liquor. About 90 percent of our domestic supply of cashew nuts comes from India and East Africa. The remainder come from South America.

Health Benefits Cashew nuts are a nutritive and warming food. At 47 percent fat, they are lower in fat than most other nuts and most of their fat is unsaturated. They contain 20 percent protein, and high amounts of magnesium, phosphorus, and potassium. Cashews reduce *vata*.

Use Raw cashews are hard to digest, but roasting will enhance both their flavor and their digestibility. Like almonds, they may be made into a tasty nut milk. They are used as a dessert nut, cooked in stir-fried dishes and curries, or ground to thicken a sauce.

Buying Because they are not shelled domestically, cashews are frequently stale. Fresh cashews are crisp, solid, and white. Even though whole cashews are more expensive, they are definitely fresher and a better buy than cashew pieces.

See **Nuts**.

CASSAVA
Manioc, Yuca
(Manihot utilissima, M. esculenta)

A tuber staple throughout the tropics, cassava is primarily known in temperate regions as the source of tapioca. The cassava, an American native, looks like a sweet potato. It is cylindrical with a brown, bark-covered skin and flesh that is almost white, yellow, or red. Although a cassava can weigh over 50 pounds, market varieties are harvested at one to three pounds and are up to four inches in diameter. The cassava's near relative is the popular Christmas ornamental, the poinsettia.

While tapioca is processed from a bitter cassava (*M. esculenta*), the sweet varieties (*M. utilissima*) are eaten like a potato. Cassava is grown in Central and South America, Africa, and Asia.

Health Benefits Cassava is a soothing, calming food. Higher in calories than potatoes, it is an excellent source of potassium, vitamin C, and iron and a good source of thiamin and vitamin B_6.

Use Use the sweet cassava as a potato or sweet potato; but plan to use it immediately as it spoils rapidly. When peeled and cooked, its softly fibrous flesh becomes mildly sweet, buttery, chewy, and almost translucent. Remove its central, fibrous cord either before or after cooking. Some people love the tapiocalike texture of cassava; for others it's an acquired taste. Cassava absorbs the liquid in a soup, stew, or casserole. It may be deep-fried, baked, simmered, sautéed, puréed, or grated.

Buying As the cassava does not store well, take care to purchase a sound one. Select a cassava that is sweet smelling with no sign of mold, cracks, or sticky patches. The bark on the skin should be intact because if cut or damaged and not used immediately, it becomes toxic. Do not purchase a cassava that is sour or acrid smelling or has blue-gray mottled flesh. Ask your greengrocer to cut into one to assure that its flesh is clear without darkened areas near the skin. Or

On Sunday, December 16, 1492, an entry in Columbus's log describes a locally important cassava bread on the island he named Hispaniola (today known as the Dominican Republic). He also provides a terse recipe. "These fields are planted mostly with *ajes* [cassava]. The Indians sow little shoots, from which small roots grow that look like carrots. They serve this as bread, by grating and kneading it, then baking it in the fire." Today in this region, this same flatbread remains a dietary staple, according to contemporary food writer and historian Raymond Sokolov.

buy extra, and discard any discolored pieces. Do not refrigerate a cassava; rather, store it in a very cool, dry area for a day or two. Cassavas are available year-round in Latino markets and some specialty markets.

See **Tapioca.**

CASSAVA FLOUR

Throughout the tropics, cassava is ground into meal and used in porridge, sauces, stews, dumplings, and baked goods. Cassava flour thickens the onion, raisin, and cashew sauce of Brazil's national specialty, *feijaoda*, a dish of sausage and black beans. In the Caribbean, the flour is made into the unleavened, hard bread, *cassabe*. Look for cassava flour in Latino and Asian markets.

See **Flour.**

CASSIA See **Cinnamon.**

CAULIFLOWER
(Brassica oleracea botrytis)

Cauliflower is nothing but cabbage with a college education.
—Mark Twain, *Pudd'nhead Wilson*

The cauliflower is a compact, edible head of whitish undeveloped flower buds. The name means cabbage flower, and indeed the cauliflower is yet another member of the brassica, or cabbage family. Cauliflower originated in Crete or Cyprus. Our largest cauliflower supplier is California, followed by Arizona and Colorado.

Health Benefits Sweet in flavor and warming in action, cauliflower is similar to broccoli, although it contains lower amounts of vitamins, minerals, and chlorophyll. Cauliflower is considered a good brain food, according to the Doctrine of Signature. It reduces *pitta* and *kapha*.

Use Cauliflower greens contain the highest amount of calcium in the plant. Use the smaller greens, discarding, as necessary, the overly coarse parts. Although it is easier than broccoli to digest raw, cauliflower still benefits from light cooking. Like other cabbage family members, it develops a sulfurous aroma if overcooked.

Buying Cauliflower is in peak supply in the fall. Select one with a firm, compact head and a clean and creamy white color. (Newer varieties may range in color from purple and pink to lime-yellow.) Size is no indication of quality. If the head is wearing a collar of outer leaves, those should be fresh. Cauliflower with brown spots or spreading florets is past its prime. Refrigerate cauliflower, stem side up, loosely wrapped. This prevents moisture from collecting on the cauliflower top and thereby speeding deterioration.

See Broccoflower; Cabbage Family.

CAYENNE See Chile Pepper.

CECI See Chickpea.

CELERIAC
Celery Root, Knob Celery
(Apium graveolens rapaceum)

There's nothing tidy about celeriac. The swollen stem base, technically a corm, of a type of celery, celeriac tastes like a primitive heart of celery—only more so. Celeriac looks like an irregular brown turnip. Its upper part is covered with leaf scars from old leaves and the many gnarly roots and rootlets streaming from its base trap dirt and grit in its numerous whorls and crevices. Those roots and rootlets, if not trimmed away by the grocer, stretch out like octopus tentacles.

Health Benefits Celeriac is used for its diuretic properties and is useful for people with kidney stones and arthritic conditions. As a tonic, it stimulates the appetite, aids digestion, and supports the lymphatic, nervous, and urinary systems. It reduces *pitta* and *kapha*.

Use Peel away the mass of roots and rootlets. Julienne or grate and then marinate celeriac with a vinaigrette for a salad. Or dice or cut into chunks and cook the knob in soups and braised, sautéed, or baked dishes. If you're not going to cook the celeriac immediately, hold it in acidulated water. I also pickle celeriac. It blends beautifully with other foods, yet still retains its own celerylike flavor. If overcooked, it may become mushy.

Buying You rarely see celeriac with the stems intact. If you grow this vegetable, or find one with the greens, use them to flavor soups and stews—but use them judiciously since they are more bitter than celery.

Favor small celeriac; the large ones tend to be pithy. Press the stalk end with your thumb and select only those that are firm. Cut off any stems and refrigerate both. The root will keep up to week. Peel and discard the skin just prior to use. Celeriac is primarily available in the fall and winter.

See Carrot Family; Celery.

CELERY
(Apium graveolens dulce)

If you lived in Kalamazoo, Michigan, in 1874 and wanted to popularize a new celery variety, Pascal, how would you market it? The winning answer was: Pass it out free to train passengers traveling through Kalamazoo.

Pascal celery soon became—and today remains—our second most important salad crop. Our domestic crop is grown primarily in California, Florida, and Texas, with Michigan providing it in hot weather. Celery and its close relative parsley were once so similar that they were called by the same name in classical times.

Health Benefits The 1897 Sears Roebuck & Co. catalog advertised a celery tonic that was good for the nerves, reports Irena Chalmers in *The Great Food Almanac*. Since Greek times, celery has been valued as a hangover cure and blood cleanser. Clinical studies show that it significantly reduces the blood pressure by relaxing the muscle tissue in artery walls and thus enhancing blood flow.

As a kitchen medicine, celery is also used for constipation, as a diuretic, to break up gallstones, relieve liver congestion, and to heal wounds. Celery also treats arthritis, rheumatism, and gout. This vegetable has one of the highest sodium contents of all vegetables and treats diseases involving chemical imbalances. It is said to help bring energy up and is good if one is feeling stuck or heavy. Celery is a favorite reducing food, especially for *pitta* and *kapha*.

Use Celery sticks in a packed lunch, quickly braised, or simmered a long time in a soup. . . . Celery's versatility helps to make it one of our most used vegetables.

Buying Unfortunately, celery—along with mushrooms and iceberg lettuce—is one of the most chemically altered food crops. Virtually all supermarket celery is blanched with ethylene gas to reduce its bitter flavor. Stalks that are a vivid, deep green have not been blanched. For optimum nutrition, chlorophyll, and strengthening properties, favor organic, unblanched celery. It tastes much

---

A YOUNG WIFE'S DRUTHERS

According to a 1614 text by Giacomo Castelvetro, *A Brief Account of the Fruit, Herbs & Vegetables of Italy*, celery "is warm, and has great digestive and generative powers, and for this reason young wives often serve celery to their elderly or impotent husbands."

Back then, celery was intensely bitter. Its bitterness was bred out several centuries ago, making celery sweet enough now to munch on raw—but less effective as a remedy for young wives. If you had your druthers . . .

---

stronger but is delicious. Celery is available year-round.

Favor firm celery with no signs of damage; avoid celery with yellow leaves or wilted or cracked stalks.

See **Celeriac.**

CELERY ROOT See **Celeriac.**

CELLOPHANE NOODLES See **Mung Bean Pasta.**

CELTUCE
Asparagus Lettuce, Stem Lettuce
(*Lactuca sativa asparagina* x *Bailey*)

An Asian lettuce with a taste and texture like celery is called, logically enough, celtuce. Grown primarily for its foot-long, thick stem, it is topped with tender young leaves, which may be used like lettuce. The length of the stem, which is similar in taste to water chestnuts, is ridged with brown leaf scars from old leaves.

Celtuce is a relative newcomer to domestic markets; it is grown primarily in California. It is as easy to cultivate as lettuce. Celtuce is available throughout the year, except during the heat of the summer.

Use Peel the stem and use it raw or cooked, just as you would celery—it's tasty by itself or in combination with other vegetables. It is a favorite pickling vegetable of the Chinese and is delicious in stir-fries and soups. The leaves may be used in salad.

See Lettuce.

Cèpe See Bolete.

Cereal Grains See Grains.

Ceriman See Monstera.

CHAMOMILE
(Chamaemelum nobile, Matricaria recutita)

A member of the daisy family, chamomile is native to the Mediterranean region. Its Greek name, *melon khanai*, means apple on the ground, and indeed the chamomile section of my herb garden is a carpet of showy—if minuscule—white daisies with a plump yellow heart and an aroma similar to apples. The Spanish call it *manzanilla*, which means "little apple." Referring to its medicinal properties, the Germans call it *alles zutraut*, which means "capable of anything."

Health Benefits Chamomile is effective for nervousness, anxiety, stress, and insomnia. It improves the immune system and soothes the digestive tract, eases headaches and allergies, supports the gallbladder, and helps reduce gallstones. It expels gas, helps quiet spasms, and soothes a nervous stomach. It eases stomach ulcers, diverticulitis, and gastritis. Chamomile destroys some intestinal worms. It is *tridoshic*.

Herbalist Brigette Mars, writing of its value as a topical remedy for the skin in *Delicious!* magazine, notes that "chamomile was even more helpful in speeding skin healing time than cortisone. Not only does chamomile help promote skin growth over a wound, but it also can bring pain relief. Other external applications include: to relieve burns; as an eye wash, gargle, douche, or enema to calm irritated tissues; and as a sitz bath to relieve hemorrhoids." Speaking of baths, strain a pot of chamomile tea into your bath, sink in, and chamomile will not only soften your skin but ease away the day's fears and stresses. A chamomile bath also soothes cranky children, aids their sleep, and helps protect against nightmares.

While chamomile is safe, effective, and nonaddictive, it may be too relaxing to the uterus to consume often during pregnancy, for it might cause a miscarriage.

Buying Two types of chamomile are available—Roman (*C. Nobile*) (also known as English chamomile), and German or Hungarian (*M. recutita*). The latter is more commonly used, as it is less bitter, less expensive, and the superior source of pharmacological properties.

See Herbs and Spices; Sunflower Family.

CHANTERELLE
(Cantharellus cibarius)

The uncommonly beautiful and delicious chanterelle mushroom is egg yellow in color and like a curving trumpet in shape. It has a faint aroma reminiscent of apricots and is a tasty delicacy.

Use Use immediately. Subtly flavored dishes are enhanced by chanterelles. They are such a rare delicacy, however, that it's a shame to combine them with any other food. For maximum enjoyment lightly sauté this fungus in olive oil or ghee, and add a dash of salt or high-quality soy sauce.

Buying/Foraging Fresh wild chanterelles appear in some markets in the late summer and, where frost comes late, into the fall. In Ashland, Oregon, mushroom foragers routinely knock on restaurant doors peddling their wares. My daughter Roanna and her husband, Marc, purchase wild chanterelles and morels for a mere $7 per pound for their natural café, Pangea! Chanterelles are also available dried and canned. To hydrate dried chanterelles, soak in water for 20 minutes or until softened.

See Mushroom Family.

CHARD
Swiss Chard
(Beta vulgaris cicla)

Chard, a beet relative, takes its name from cardoon because of their similarly shaped leafstalks, which are long and broad. Chard may be either red or white, and its large leaf may be either crinkly—savoy style—or flat. Red chard is the showiest leafy green in the market.

Health Benefits Like other greens of the goosefoot family, chard contains oxalic acid and is therefore best used moderately by people with calcium deficiency. It is high in sodium and an excellent source of chlorophyll. Chard eases constipation in the elderly, is homeostatic and helps stop hemorrhage, and supports the liver and the lungs. Chard reduces *kapha;* in moderate amounts, it can be used by *vata* and *pitta.*

Use Chard is almost as quick cooking as spinach. It may be steamed, sautéed, or braised or it can be added to soups, stews, and casseroles. The Italians make an egg frittata with chard. I usually prepare the leaf and stem together, but they may be cooked and served separately as two different vegetables.

Buying Look for clear white or red ribs that show no discoloration and for crisp, curly leaves. Chard is available year-round.

See Beet; Goosefoot Family.

CHAYOTE
Christophine, Hop Yeung Qwa, Jeung Qwa, Mirliton, Vegetable Pear
(Sechium edule)

The squashlike chayote (cheye-YOH-teh) fruit is now commonly available in domestic markets. This gourd originated in Central America where the whole plant—roots, young leaves, fruits, seeds, and shoots—is an important food source.

The chayote is pear shape, with a thick

pale green skin divided by five grooves that run the length of it. The skin is usually smooth but may be covered with soft spines. A chayote is about five inches long and contains a single pit.

Use A fresh chayote has a delicate flavor and texture rather like the blend of a cucumber and pattypan squash. When old, it is flavorless. Substitute chayotes in any recipe calling for cooked summer squash. If tender, use its skin and—if you wish—its large seed. Roasting concentrates its flavor.

Buying Chayote is available year-round but with peak supplies in the winter. Look for a firm chayote with a solid appearance and an unblemished skin from pale green to ivory white in color. Store at 50 to 55 degrees for a week or more; when refrigerated, it holds for a month but loses much of its flavor.

See **Gourd Family.**

CHERIMOYA
Custard Apple
(Annona cherimola)

Inside a cherimoya's (cheh-ree-MOY-a) rough, armadillolike green shell is a lush treat. The silky smooth, sweet flesh has a slightly musky and decidedly tropical taste— part mango, part pineapple, part banana. It is related to the atemoya.

Cherimoya, a Quechua word which means "cold seeds," is native to the tropical Andes. Commercial crops are now growing in California, Australia, and South America, but the fruit is fragile and, despite increasing demand for its custardlike flesh, its availability may remain sketchy.

Use Cherimoya is usually eaten fresh, but is also used in salads, sauces, drinks, desserts, and ice cream. Spoon out the inedible black seeds as you would watermelon seeds.

Buying Cherimoyas are mostly available in the winter and early spring. They are harvested when hard. Purchase cherimoyas that are just beginning to soften but avoid brown or bruised ones. They may vary in size from half a pound to two pounds; size does not affect flavor. To increase sweetness, allow cherimoyas to ripen at room temperature just until they begin to brown but before they become overly soft. Once ripe, they may be refrigerated for up to five days. (Do not refrigerate a cherimoya before it softens.)

See **Tropical Fruit.**

CHERRY
(Prunus avium)

In New York, Broadway zags off course at the East 10th Street intersection because a cherry tree once grew there that was more valued than a tidy crossroads. Of temperate-zone stone fruits in the northern hemisphere, sweet cherries have, by far, the highest sugar content; but they're not only sweet—they're also lush, juicy, and, when tree ripened, delicious enough to zigzag roads for.

Like their plum relatives, cherries are a stone, or drupe, fruit. They are available in early summer. Sweet cherries are much more difficult to produce than sour cherries because, not uncommonly, a late spring frost will devastate the crop. Most cherries are produced in Washington, Colorado, Oregon, Idaho, and Utah.

Health Benefits Sweet cherries are a warming food that increases vital energy and tone the spleen-pancreas, liver, and kidneys. Also astringent, they treat involuntary seminal emission. Cherries remove excess body acids and blood stagnation and, when eaten regularly, are therefore therapeutic for gout, paralysis, numbness in the extremities, and rheumatic pain in the lower half of the body. Sweet cherries reduce *vata* and *kapha* and can be used in moderation by *pitta*.

Cherries are an excellent source of iron and contain some phosphorus, potassium, and calcium, as well as vitamin A.

Buying Cherries are one of the few remaining fruits that are truly seasonal. They are too fragile to import; only domestic cherries are available and then only from mid-June through July. (If you find them later than that, they've been held in storage too long to be worth much.)

Look for full-colored, soft cherries with a glossy, plump surface and fresh stems. Avoid overmature, dull-looking cherries with shriveled, dried, brown stems. Examine closely, since cherries decay easily and their decayed areas are often inconspicuous. Soft, leaking flesh, brown discoloration, and/or mold indicate decay.

There are fewer than ten commercial cherry varieties available fresh. Bing cherries—almost black-red—are the best known variety, with Lamberts close behind. The golden yellow Rainiers are the most fragile and costly.

Of all fresh fruits, commercial cherries, apples, and grapes generally contain the

---

MOTHER'S MARASCHINO CHERRIES

Every cherry season, my mother made one batch—seven quarts—of maraschino cherries. She first slaked Royal Anne cherries in alum to crisp them, then canned them in a heavy syrup flavored with cherry pits or almond extract and added red food color. The maraschinos had a delegated shelf spot among more than three hundred quarts of peaches, apricots, pears, raspberries, and regular cherries, plus pints of assorted jams and jellies—a respectably appointed fruit larder for our Mormon family of six in the 1940s and 1950s. Relative to commercial maraschinos, Mother's were softly colored and tender but crisp. They were an essential ingredient in my father's favorite cake, Poor Man's Cake.

The original maraschino was fermented in a liqueur made from the juice and crushed pits of *marasca*, a wild sour Italian cherry. Today's maraschino cherry that tops a banana split is tough, sugary (75 percent sugar), beggarly, and would wreck a Poor Man's Cake. The cake dates to a time when flour was a more prized ingredient than the maraschino cherries and nuts that filled it. The cake is tender (*not* like a holiday fruitcake) and a regal treat.

---

most toxic chemical residues. Favor organic cherries whenever possible.

Use A superior dessert fruit, most cherries are enjoyed raw, but they're also an excellent addition to salads and compotes. Enjoy them fresh, dried, juiced, or in preserves. They work in a pie, although sour cherries are preferred.

See **Fruit**; **Sour Cherry**.

CHERVIL
(Anthriscus cereifolium)

One of the first herbs to appear in the spring, chervil is a hardy annual that has been cultivated since Roman times; it still grows wild in damp places. Chervil is a member of the carrot family, related to parsley, celery, and fennel.

Health Benefits Chervil's mild, bitter flavor tonifies the liver and kidneys. As a tea, it makes an excellent wash for inflamed eyes and hemorrhoids. It calms *pitta* and *kapha*.

Use Chervil is a popular herb in central and western Europe and one of the four essential ingredients in the classic French blend *fines herbes* (the others being chives, parsley, and tarragon). According to Elisabeth Lambert Ortiz in *The Encyclopedia of Herbs*, chervil is "essential in French cooking, often supplanting parsley which it does resemble although the leaves are more feathery, and the flavor is reminiscent of anise."

Think of chervil like a delicate and refreshing parsley alternative. Use it in pesto, as a garnish, in salads, with asparagus and starchy vegetables like beets and potatoes, eggs, or seafood—especially oysters. It withstands neither prolonged heat nor drying. Use fresh and add at the last minute.

Buying Dried chervil lacks flavor and aroma. Because its delicate leaves are poor travelers it is not always available fresh. Fortunately, chervil flourishes indoors in a pot as easily as it does outside.

See **Carrot Family**; **Herbs and Spices**.

CHESTNUT
(Castanea sativa)

Unlike London, Paris, New York, or Boston where street vendors sell hot roasted chestnuts on nippy days, I'm yet to find the same here in the Rocky Mountains. My friend TuHan Holm remedies this oversight by roasting them at home, pouring them hot into everyone's pockets, and then heading out for a brisk winter walk. There's nothing like a pocketful of toasty chestnuts.

For hunter-gatherers and poor people in times of want, chestnuts were an important staple throughout the northern hemisphere. They remain a regular part of the diets of long-lived peoples in Central Asia. Chestnuts figure prominently in fine cuisine in both Europe and the Orient but less so in North America since a blight in the early 1900s destroyed all of our magnificent chestnut trees. Today, a few Japanese chestnuts are grown commercially on the West Coast but America's primary chestnut source is Europe.

Health Benefits The chestnut is a spleen-pancreas and kidney tonic; it tonifies the blood, removes coldness, strengthens the tendons, and nourishes the stomach, spleen-pancreas, and liver. It is sweet like a fruit, but unlike fruit builds and warms rather than cools and cleanses. It has an astringent nature, which controls diarrhea, coughing, whooping cough, and rheumatism and which helps check bleeding (anal bleeding, nosebleeds, vomiting of blood, or bloody sputum). The chestnut is especially calming to *pitta* and *vata*.

By nutritional profile, chestnuts are more

like a grain or bean rather than a nut because of their high carbohydrate content and their low oil content, making them the most easily digested nut.

Use Roasted, boiled, mashed like potatoes, sweetened, candied, or puréed, chestnuts are decidedly versatile. Delicious in both sweet and savory dishes, chestnuts can be added to grain, bean, vegetable, and fruit dishes. They're good in soup, stir-fries, casseroles, and even in hot breakfast cereal.

A favorite Roman way was to steam chestnuts with bitter greens. A Pakistani dish is roasted, puréed chestnuts topped with fresh walnut or hazelnut oil. The French garnish chestnut purée with crème fraîche for a dessert they call *mont blanc* after the largest peak in the Alps. Use purée as a delicious nondairy whip topping, frosting, or cream sauce.

Buying Although pricy, seasonal when fresh, and not in major markets when dry, seek them out. Having chestnuts in your larder is like having silk in your wardrobe.

- **Fresh Chestnuts** Available in the United States during the fall and winter in most supermarkets. Select fresh chestnuts in the shell with clear, silky smooth, brown shells rather than dry or brittle shells. To roast or bake them, first deeply score the shells with a paring knife; otherwise, they may explode. They also may be boiled and then shelled. Chestnuts are also available fresh-frozen, bottled or canned, either whole or puréed.
- **Dried Chestnuts** These are sweeter than fresh chestnuts since in the drying process carbohydrates convert to

sugar. Dried chestnuts are always more expensive than the fresh, but they are a great convenience and are available year-round. They may be rehydrated and cooked or ground into flour.

Dried chestnuts and chestnut flour are generally available in specialty food shops, Asian markets, and by mail order.

Storing Store fresh chestnuts in a paper bag in the refrigerator and use within a week. Store dried chestnuts in airtight containers and store in a cool, dark cupboard.

See **Chestnut Flour; Nuts.**

CHESTNUTS AND ROSE PETALS

Reading of traditional food uses often whets my appetite and sometimes inspires me with new ways to work with food. In the seventeenth century in Italy, a special covered perforated pan was used for roasting chestnuts. The filled pan was buried under hot ashes, and when roasted the nuts were shelled and served with salt and pepper. An old popcorn popper to hold over embers just might work for fire-roasted chestnuts.

The most inspiring treatment I've yet to find for dried chestnuts is to layer them with fresh rose petals to soften them. As the chestnuts draw moisture from the petals, they are imbued with rose essence. Next rose season, I'll give this a try.

CHESTNUT FLOUR

Fragrant, sweet, and fruity tasting, chestnut flour has a fine texture. It sweetens, lightens, and adds creaminess. It is not a thickening agent, but when combined with a grain flour, it makes a delicious pudding, sauce, or "cream" soup. Substitute ¼ cup chestnut flour per cup of flour.

Until this last century, chestnut flour was made into bread that was a staple for European people in mountainous regions where wheat did not grow and flour was a luxury. It is still used for a cake in Northern Italy.

Store chestnut flour in the refrigerator or freezer, tightly wrapped.

See **Chestnut; Flour.**

CHEWING GUM See Chicle.

CHIA SEED
(Salvia columbariae, S. hispanica)

From a member of the sage family, this tiny gray-black or golden tan seed looks like a flattened, washed-out poppy seed. The seeds are slippery to the touch. Chia grows in Mexico and the Southwest and is available in natural food stores.

Health Benefits Chia was long prized as an endurance food by Native Americans; today, we know that chia is, next to flax seed, the highest source of Omega-3 fatty acids. The gray-black (*S. columbariae*) variety is nutritionally superior to the golden chia variety. Chia becomes highly muciluginous when soaked; it lubricates dryness and relieves constipation, reduces nervousness, treats insomnia, and improves mental focus.

HAIRLESS HARRY GROWS GREEN HAIR

While alfalfa, mung, and other seeds easily sprout in a jar, chia does not. Because of its inordinate stickiness, chia requires a special earthenware container. Available in some gift catalogues, these Mexican-made containers are often shaped like a piglet or a human head; the later is dubbed "Hairless Harry." Sprinkle chia seeds on Harry's pate, water, and, within a few days, he'll sport green hair that has a tasty, watercresslike bite.

Chia reduces *vata* and *kapha* and can be used moderately by *pitta*.

Use Add soaked chia seeds to lemonade for a sustaining gelatinous beverage. Add the seeds, dried or ground, to baked goods, or to pinole flour for a sort of trail mix or endurance food. Chia seeds may be substituted for poppy or sesame seeds as a condiment and garnish.

See **Seeds.**

CHICKPEA
Ceci, Garbanzo
(Cicer arietinum)

A chickpea is unlike other legumes in two ways. First, while beans and lentils are smooth surfaced, a chickpea is not; it's wrinkled, roundish, but compressed and flattened at the sides with a projecting nascent radicle that looks like a chick's beak. Second, while most legumes share a pod with half a dozen or so other seeds, a chickpea has only one mature pea per pod.

Chickpeas were one of our first cultivated crops and today they are a popular legume throughout the temperate world. The most common chickpea in the United States is tannish in color, although there are red, white, brown, and black varieties available.

Health Benefits The chickpea is sweet in flavor and supports the spleen-pancreas, stomach, and heart. Indeed, it is shaped something like a heart, with two hemispheres, rounded at the top, and pointed at the bottom. Furthermore, its pod envelopes each pea much like a pericardium. Chickpeas reduce *pitta* and *kapha*. In Ayurvedic medicine, chickpeas are considered *rajasic* and valued for hard physical labor.

The chickpea provides more vitamin C, nearly double the usual amount of iron, and (soy excepted) three times more fat than most legumes.

Use If the only way you know chickpeas is from a salad bar, then you're eating canned chickpeas and missing a treat. Simmered until tender, with garlic and some toasted cumin seeds, chickpeas are one of the creamiest and tastiest of beans. Add them whole or mashed to soups, croquettes, vegetable dishes, or enjoy them plain as a side dish. They are the basis for the popular Mideastern dishes hummus and falafel. Cooked and then seasoned and roasted, they make a tasty nutlike snack food.

See **Beans and Legumes; Chickpea Flour.**

CHICKPEA FLOUR
Besan, Gram Flour

The high-protein flour made from hulled and roasted chickpeas is a common ingredient in the East Indian flatbread, *papadam,* and in Indian pasta and desserts. It is also used in southern Italy for *pauelle* (chickpea wafers), and in southern France for *socca* (chickpea wafers). It looks dry and powdery, almost chalky, and lends a sweet, rich chickpea flavor. In color, chickpea flour is like corn flour; in performance, it is more like millet flour. Since chickpea flour is gluten-free, it should be used in small quantities in leavened bread.

Chickpea flour is available in Indian, Italian, French, and natural food markets. It is more digestible than the other common legume flour, soy flour.

See **Flour.**

CHICLE
(Manilkara zapota, syn. Achras)

Picture yourself unwrapping a stick of spearmint gum, catching its cooling, minty aroma, and chewing away on the satisfying familiarity of one of life's simple pleasures. Yum! Let's hear it for petroleum-based synthetic polymers. I'm sorry to pop your bubble, but since the 1950s chewing gum has been plasticized. "Gum base" on the ingredient list is primarily styrene-butadiene rubber and polyvinyl acetate.

Prior to plastic, chewing gum was made of chicle, the gummy sap or latex of the giant sapodilla tree, which grows in the jungles of Mesoamerica. The ancient Maya chewed chicle as a way to clean their teeth and, presumably, for the fun of it.

The story of chicle chewing gum in North America starts in New York in the 1870s when one Thomas Adams experimented

---

AUNT ANNA'S CHEWING GUM

My Aunt Anna once collected several different kinds of saps, worked each one separately, flattened it with her thumb, shaped it into a stick of gum, and wrapped it in a gum wrapper for a multicolored and multiflavored package of decidedly unique home-chewed gum.

If you've never tried chewing wild gum, I recommend it. Select the semihard pitch of a pine or spruce and, in a word, chew. Rather, chew and spit, chew and spit. Spit out the mildly turpentine flavored saliva that forms but retain the gummy stuff. After a few chews-and-spits, the flavor mellows and what remains is a wad of pleasantly pine-flavored gum. Each kind of tree yields a different color, ranging from yellow to reddish brown. My favorite chews in the wild are ponderosa, which becomes a beautiful cinnamon color, and piñon, which turns a warm adobe pink. Each tastes like the aroma of the tree it came from.

Be sure to collect only almost hard sap that has oozed from a cut in the trunk or branches of a pine. Fresh pitch is sticky, gooey stuff, which wreaks havoc with dentures and sticks in your mouth for hours. Hardened sap crumbles rather than gums up.

---

with—but did not succeed in—vulcanizing chicle to make an inexpensive rubber substitute. A rubber tire chicle is not. I imagine Adams, in a moment of madness at his umpteenth failure, tearing at a piece of chicle with his teeth and . . . eureka! The rest is history. Adams stirred in some sugar and sassafras and patented Chiclets Chewing Gum. Soon this Central American product displaced North American gum, which was made from the sap of spruce or pine trees.

Buying Several brands of natural chewing gum made of chicle and natural flavors are available at natural food stores. Chicle, which has a pleasant mouth feel, comes in various tropical flavors, which all passed my children's taste test. Besides tasting good and chewing neatly, the important thing about chicle is that it provides a livelihood for indigenous peoples, *chicleros*, who harvest this renewable resource.

See **Sapodilla**.

CHICORY
(Cichorium endiva, C. intybus)

Chicory, a member of the sunflower family, is closely related to lettuce and dandelion; it grows wild throughout Europe, Asia, and North America. Its bitter leaves and root have been used from time immemorial for salads and as a medicinal plant. Cultivation has tamed its bitterness and produced numerous varieties. The family branch used mainly for its leaves is *C. endiva*.

C. intybus varieties, primarily Magdeburg and Brunswick, are grown for their large, bitter taproots. The roots are dried, roasted, and used to enhance—or, depending upon the amount used and one's point of view, to adulterate—coffee. Two *C. intybus* varieties used for their greens are radicchio and Belgian endive.

Health Benefits Chicory, both the root

and the greens, is an excellent bitter spring tonic that cleanses and helps regulate the liver and gallbladder. It purifies the blood, improves digestion, and nourishes the heart and circulatory system. Chicory contains inulin, which helps diabetics regulate their blood sugar levels. It reduces *pitta* and *kapha*. Chicory leaves are an excellent source of potassium and vitamin A and a good source of calcium.

Use Chicory greens are a popular salad vegetable and potherb. They may be blanched, braised, or roasted to reduce their bitter flavor. My favorite "spring tonic salad" dates to medieval Italy: wild chicory greens, some of the root, and some white shoots, seasoned with oil, vinegar, salt, and garlic. Couldn't be simpler, and couldn't be more delicious.

Buying/Foraging Chicory is one of the easiest plants to forage, it is nearly as common as dandelion, sports a perky telltale purple flour, and is readily recognized. Dig new roots in the spring or the fall. Roots more than a year old are extremely bitter. Harvest the new shoots and the leaves before the plant goes to flower.

Chicory root, dried and roasted, is available in the herb section of natural food stores or blended with coffee.

There are numerous green and red chicories, which may be shaped like a compact romaine lettuce or a loose-leaf lettuce. Their leaves range from very narrow and highly serrated (frisée) to almost semicircular (radicchio). Look for fresh, crisp greens and avoid those with wilt or browning.

In addition to the chicory varieties listed below, look for and experiment with some of the newer—to us—varieties, such as: Alouette, Coquette, Treviso, Verona, Scarola, Pain de Sucre (Sugarloaf), Chioggia, green heading chicory, Italian chicory, and green loose-leaf chicory.

See **Belgian Endive; Coffee Substitutes; Endive; Escarole; Frisée; Radicchio; Sunflower Family.**

CHICOS
Dried Sweet Corn, Shaker Dried Corn

At an open-air market in New Mexico, I asked the farmer how he dried his sweet corn kernels. If they were *horno chicos*, from a wood-fired, adobe oven, I was ready to put my money down.

"I roast 'em in an old car," he tersely said. Visualizing him torching a car, I asked for more detail.

"I load the car with corn, roll up the windows, the car gets hotter than hell and dries the corn just fine." I put my money down for car-roasted chicos.

The Shakers also sun-dried sweet corn for later reconstitution.

Use Sun-dried or *horno* chicos have a delicious caramel flavor and a chewy texture. This dried vegetable is rehydrated like beans and added to soups, stews, and bean dishes or cooked as a side dish in its own right.

Buying Chicos are available in Hispanic sections of supermarkets, many natural food stores, or by mail order from Coyoté Café General Store (see page 404). Freeze-dried sweet corn kernels, available in supermarkets, or the oven-dried Shaker corn are tasty but lack the caramel flavor of sun-dried chicos or *horno* chicos.

See **Sweet Corn.**

CHILE PEPPER
Chile, Chili, Hot Pepper, Red Pepper
(Capsicum)

Chile peppers, in a short four hundred years, have become the world's most highly consumed spice thanks to a single gene, the fiery, to-be-respected capsaicin. It's a lack of this gene that keeps sweet peppers cool. Capsaicin is the bitter, acrid, oily alkaloid found in chile peppers that may literally burn the skin, especially the eyes, nose, lips, and even the gastrointestinal tract. Nearly 90 percent of the capsaicin is concentrated in the white tissues to which the seeds are attached. Depending upon the chile heat you desire, exclude or include these membranes in your cooking.

Although chiles are most famous for their heat, behind that heat is their range of earthy sweet flavors. Chiles are popularly believed to be a mood enhancer because they increase the production of endorphins. This proposition lacks clinical data; if you eat a hot chile, however, you'll experience moments of heightened awareness.

Health Benefits Capsaicin is a fast-acting vasodilator that widens the blood vessels. This enhances blood circulation and therefore increases body temperature. The quick temperature rise causes perspiration, which cools the body back down.

The pungent flavor of chiles tonifies the spleen-pancreas, stomach, colon, lung, and heart meridians. They stimulate the digestive system. They have antioxidant properties that help preserve and detoxify food. Capsaicin often aids people with chronic bronchial problems. It protects against some chemical carcinogens and mutagens. Chiles warm and disperse cold, dry, and overly damp conditions and so treat colds, fevers, varicose veins, and asthma. Externally, capsaicin in an ointment relieves arthritis, shingles, neuralgia, and pleurisy (even though initially as the pain is drawn up and out, it may exacerbate the pain).

Chiles are not recommended for anyone with an inflamed colon. Ayurveda considers chiles *rajasic* and uses them primarily as a medicine. Chiles reduce *kapha*.

Green chiles are a superior source of vitamin C and red chiles a good source of vitamin A. Both also contain potassium and folic acid. They also contain fiber and iron. They are extremely low in calories.

Use Wear rubber gloves when you handle chiles, fresh or dried. Some people with less sensitive skin may handle chiles directly. If you are one, immediately wash your hands thoroughly with soap and water afterward, to prevent capsaicin burns to more sensitive areas. Should you develop a chile burn, washing with a mild bleach solution is a good antidote.

- **Dried Chiles** Crushed or powdered dried chiles are ready to use as an ingredient. To prepare whole dried chiles, rehydrate by soaking in hot water for an hour or so. Cut open and remove the seeds, stems, and veins.
- **Fresh Chiles** Fresh chiles are peeled prior to use. First, slit the skin near the stem. Place the chiles in a broiler pan about four inches from the heat source and broil until blistered and blackened (or grill or roast directly on a stovetop burner). Turn frequently. Immediately place the chiles in a brown paper bag, close the bag, and allow the chiles to steam for 15 minutes. The skins can then be easily slipped off from the peppers.

HOW HOT IS IT?

Here are some of the more commonly available chiles rated from cool to hot by Scoville unit according to Jean Anderson and Barbara Deskins in *The Nutritional Bible*. A rating of 1 is equivalent to 100–500 Scoville units; a rating of 10 is equivalent to 100,000 to 300,000 Scoville Units.

2 NuMex Big Jim
2–3 Anaheim (green or red), Hungarian cherry pepper, NuMex red chile, NuMex Eclipse, NuMex Sunrise, NuMex Sunset, NuMex miniature
3 Green or red poblano, espanola, ancho, mulato, Hungarian cherry pepper
3–4 Chawa, NuMex red chile
3–5 NuMex green chile, pasilla
5 Red or green jalapeño, peperocino
6 Red or green serrano, Dutch red chile, chiltepin, chipotle
7 DeArbol, Korean, serrano seco
8 Aji, cayenne, pequin, rocoto, tabasco, tepín, Thai
9 Scotch bonnet, Jamaican hot, malagueta
10 Habanero

Remove the skins and, if you wish, the seeds and veins.

Buying Hundreds of different chile varieties exist and many have more than one name. New varieties are frequently introduced and given a regional name. This prob-

PASS ON THE KETCHUP, PASS THE SALSA

When I was growing up, beef was a daily given, Velveeta and cheddar were the cheese options, strawberry ice cream a Sunday treat, and yogurt was an anomaly. That started changing in the early 1970s when the McGovern Select Senate Committee on Diet and Nutrition encouraged Americans to eat less red meat. Since then, our dairy consumption has increased at about the rate that cheese and ice cream choices have proliferated.

Tangentially, fiery foods have swept north from the Mexican border and east across the Pacific. And therein, I see a correlation. Here's why. Dairy foods in general are mucus forming and colon congesting. And cheese—especially hard and/or cooked cheese—is more efficient than any other food in colon obstruction. Period.

The spicy flavor, most remarkable in chiles, tonifies the large intestines. Recall how colon stimulating your early chile experiences were. As more cheese is consumed, Americans gravitate to more pungent foods in an effort to keep things moving.

lem is compounded when a fresh chile is called one thing but when dried goes by a different name.

This fruit of the nightshade family ranges in color, size, shape, and pungency. In general, the smaller and more pointed a chile, the hotter it is. A hot climate usually produces a hot chile. A fresh, green, immature chile is less fragile, stores longer, and therefore costs less than a mature chile, which may be red, purple, or yellow rather than green. Select fresh chiles that are firm and unblemished rather than limp or discolored. Dried chiles are available whole, crushed, or powdered.

Chiles are available pickled or canned, but I find their essence less compromised when dried or fresh.

Storing If you have a good supply of chiles, roast them together as instructed. Place them in a bag to steam, set aside until cool. Because a large clump of frozen chiles is unwieldy, pack them, as is, into small freezer bags, separated by butcher paper or another plastic bag, and freeze. Remove chiles from the freezer as needed. Hold under hot running water; the skin, seeds, and veins will quickly and easily separate from the flesh.

See **Nightshade Family; Paprika; Peppers; Sweet Pepper.**

CHILI See **Chile Pepper.**

CHINA BEAN See **Black-Eyed Pea.**

CHINA YELLOW BEAN
(Phaseolus vulgaris)

A traditional New England bean with a soft texture and pleasing mellow flavor. It is similar to a black-eyed pea.

See **Beans and Legumes.**

CHINESE ANISE See **Star Anise.**

CHINESE BITTER MELON See Bitter Melon.

CHINESE BROCCOLI
Chinese Kale, Gai Laan, Jie Lan
(Brassica oleracea var. alboglabra)

The two most delightful things about Chinese broccoli are its delicate edible flowers and its sweet flavor, which is like garden-fresh broccoli. Unlike market variety broccoli stems (stout) and leaves (puny), Chinese broccoli stems are tender, smooth, and slender (about ½ inch thick), and the plant is abundantly bestowed with broad, blue-green leaves.

Chinese broccoli was probably introduced to China by the Portuguese after 1517; it is a close relative of the Portuguese cabbage *couve tronchuda*.

Use Use as you would regular broccoli—sautéed, steamed, braised, boiled, and in soup. Chinese broccoli cooks in less time, however, since it's a less dense vegetable. The stems require longer cooking than the leaves, and the leaves longer cooking than the blossoms, so cut and cook the vegetable accordingly.

The blossoms, usually yellow but sometimes white, red, or pink, perk up any dish. Use them fresh as a garnish on the side of a plate or float them on a steaming bowl of soup. For stir-fried dishes, cook the blossoms for only the last minute so they retain their color.

Buying Look for Chinese broccoli with solid stems, unblemished leaves, and flower buds that are just starting to open. A year-round feature in Asian markets, this vegetable is becoming increasingly available in natural food markets and in farmers' markets.

See Cabbage Family.

CHINESE CABBAGE
Michihli Cabbage, Napa Cabbage
(Brassica rapa var. pekinensis)

Chinese cabbage has been described as a cabbage that even cabbage haters love. It is crisper, juicier, sweeter, and more tender than common cabbage. There are several varieties of Chinese cabbage. All form a head, but the head varies from round like cabbage to elongated like Romaine lettuce. In addition, the crinkly leaves may curl inward or outward.

Health Benefits Chinese cabbage is cooling and beneficial to the lungs, stomach, and liver channel. It is an anti-inflammatory, useful in cases of yellow mucus discharge and other heat symptoms, including fever. Chinese cabbage has but a fraction of cabbage's sulfur compounds. For people with chronic low energy, use Chinese cabbage moderately. It reduces *pitta* and *kapha*.

Chinese cabbage is very low in calories and in sodium. It is an excellent source of folic acid and vitamin A and a good potassium source.

Use Chinese cabbage's sweet flavor is enhanced with long simmering and the leaves become silky soft but still hold their form. Try it in soups, stews, baked or braised. It's also delicious when lightly cooked (stir-fries, steamed, blanched) or even raw in a salad. Its thin, crispy-crunchy leaves add great texture to a garden salad, and it makes an excellent salad base on its own. The blanched leaf makes a flexible and excellent wrapper that is, compared to common cabbage, easier to

SOME LIKE IT HOT

This easy-to-make Korean pickle, *kim chee*, is too hot for my taste. I adjust the recipe by decreasing, or even eliminating, the chile. As with other naturally fermented and unpasteurized pickles, *kim chee* is a rich source of enzymes and flora. A small serving will aid digestion.

1 head Chinese cabbage
1 tablespoon chile pepper
1 tablespoon sesame seeds, toasted
3 garlic cloves, minced
2 tablespoons minced ginger
1 tablespoon sea salt

Quarter the Chinese cabbage lengthwise, remove and discard the core, and cut into julienne. Toss with the remaining ingredients. Pack into a wide-mouth quart jar. (If the cabbage is extra large, pack the overflow into a smaller, preferably wide-mouth jar. It is not necessary to adjust the seasoning.)

Place the jar on a plate to collect the liquid that will form and seep out. Place a weight, such as a smaller water-filled jar, on top of the mixture so that it rests solidly upon the vegetable. This weight presses the vegetable down and keeps it submerged in the brine that will form.

Let stand for 3 to 5 days, or until the cabbage looks cooked and has lost its bright chlorophyll color. If the pickle is too hot, rinse under running water. If it is still too hot, allow it to soak in water for up to 15 minutes. Wash the sides of the jar, cover tightly, and refrigerate the *kim chee* for up to 6 weeks.

work with and, to my eye, more beautiful and delicate.

Pickled Chinese cabbage, *kim chee*, the signature dish of Korea, is as easy to make as sauerkraut, the pickled cabbage of equal prominence in German cuisine.

Buying In most markets, at least one form or another of Chinese cabbage is available year-round. Select fresh, light-colored greens with plump ribs. Chinese vegetable authority Rosa Lo San Ross advises squeezing the heads to find a firm, heavy one. Avoid those that have wilted leaves with any rot spots. Small dark specks, however, are naturally occurring. Chinese cabbage stores exceptionally well (but not so long as cabbage), and the flavor even improves when slightly wilted.

See Cabbage; Cabbage Family.

CHINESE CHIVE See Garlic Chive.

CHINESE FLOWERING CABBAGE See Flowering Cabbage.

CHINESE GOOSEBERRY See Kiwi.

CHINESE GREENS See Amaranth Greens; Bok Choy; Flowering Cabbage; Garland Chrysanthemum; Tatsoi; Wrapped Heart Mustard Cabbage.

CHINESE KALE See Chinese Broccoli.

CHINESE LANTERN See Ground Cherry.

CHINESE LONG BEAN See Yard-Long Bean.

CHINESE MUSHROOM See Shiitake.

CHINESE PARSLEY See Cilantro.

CHINESE PEAR See Asian Pear.

CHINESE SPINACH See Lamb's-Quarters.

CHINESE WINTER MELON
Ash Pumpkin, Wax Gourd, Winter Melon
(Benincasa hispida)

Crunch, rather than flavor, is what this bland-tasting, basketball-size squash is about. Chinese winter melon takes on the flavors of other foods it is cooked with yet retains its pleasing crispiness. The name "winter" refers to its lengthy storage capabilities and not its growing season, as it requires five months of warm temperatures. This member of the gourd family has a pale green skin with a thick and waxy bloom, which looks like frost or ashes, thus its other names, ash pumpkin or wax gourd. This wax (*petha*) is actually a wax source for candles in Asia.

Health Benefits Like a watermelon, a Chinese winter melon is 95 percent water; this explains why it is a cooling fruit with diuretic and anti-inflammatory properties. The melon contains anticancer terpenes. It is popularly used in China in reducing diets. In Ayurvedic medicine, it is used for lung ailments, coughs, and water retention.

Use When immature, winter melon is a favorite soup ingredient in Asian cuisine, especially in hot weather because of its cooling properties. It is also found in savory concoctions, candied, and pickled. The seeds may be roasted and eaten.

Buying/Storing Winter melons are available year-round, primarily in Asian markets. Select one that is firm and unblemished. A whole melon, when stored in a cool, dark, and dry place, will keep for many months. This large vegetable is often sold cut into slices, which should be used within several days of purchase. When buying by the slice, look for a firm-fleshed, evenly colored piece.

See **Gourd Family**.

CHIVE
(Allium schoenoprasum)

The German word for chive is *schnittlauch*, or cuttable leek, an apt name for the chive, which, like your front lawn, will thrive when the top half is clipped back. This feature is one reason why the chive is such a common—and rewarding—kitchen window box herb.

The chive grows wild from arctic Russia to the Mediterranean. A chive looks like a slender scallion without the swollen bulb. Its soft springtime flavor is more delicate than a scallion and also more arresting.

Health Benefits Chives, the least potent of the onion family, have lesser medicinal properties; furthermore, they are used in such small quantities that their energetic properties are negligible. They reduce *kapha*. Garlic chives, however, have potent medicinal properties.

Use The delicate chive flavor is lost when chives are dried at home; when industrially dried, more of the flavor is retained. Still, they're best fresh. Long cooking compromises most of their flavor. Chives are used most often as a garnish or in subtly flavored dishes. Feature their purple pompom blossoms in flower arrangements, or as a salad ingredient.

Buying This fragile onion family member is available year-round but must be very fresh to be worth the purchase. Avoid yellowed or wilted chives.

See **Garlic Chive; Herbs and Spices; Onion Family.**

CHLORELLA
(Chlorella)

Chlorella, the first plant form with a true nucleus, has been on earth since the pre-Cambrian period—over 2.5 billion years. The single-celled green algae grow in freshwater lakes and ponds. At 6 microns (6 millionths of a meter), chlorella is one of the smallest plants we eat, but possibly one of the most useful.

Health Benefits Chlorella is a superior source of assimilable chlorophyll, which helps cleanse and detoxify cells in the body. A clean, healthy cell can better utilize other nutrients. That is why chlorella relieves so many conditions. In addition, chlorella is one of the highest natural sources of DNA and RNA.

Chlorella is useful in a wide variety of maladies and conditions, including chronic gastritis, high blood pressure, some forms of cancer, diabetes, constipation, anemia, and high cholesterol. It helps clear toxic metals from the body. Chlorella has antitumor and anti-inflammatory properties and strengthens the immune system. The microalgae support normal growth and help maintain health in old age. They reduce *pitta* and *kapha* and, in moderation, are healing for *vata*.

A GROSS—BUT INFORMATIVE— STORY

To stave off starvation, pee into a pot, and grow chlorella. In her autobiography, *Wild Swans: Three Daughters of China,* Jung Chang describes an effective cure for edema caused by malnourishment: "Chlorella feeds on human urine and so people peed into spittoons and dropped the chlorella seeds in. They grew into something that looked like green fish roe in a couple of days and were scooped out, washed, and cooked with the rice. They were truly disgusting to eat but they did reduce the swelling."

In the great famine of 1959–1961, some 30 million Chinese starved to death. Chlorella, even grown in urine, had observable value. Today, chlorella from pristine, mineral-rich spring water and available in easy-to-pop tablets offers formidable nutrition.

Paul Pitchford, author of *Healing with Whole Foods,* observes that of the microalgae, chlorella is the "least cooling, the most tonifying, and most gently cleansing. . . . It is the safest to use for children, maintaining health in old age, healing injuries, and initiating growth where it has been stunted from disease or degeneration, including Alzheimer's disease, sciatica, palsy, seizures, multiple sclerosis, nervousness, and other nerve disorders. . . . This microalgae is generally not useful in the treatment of obesity."

Chlorella is similar to spirulina but with less protein and more nucleic acid and chlorophyll. It contains more than twenty differ-ent vitamins and minerals plus nineteen amino acids, including all of the essential amino and fatty acids. It is particularly rich in lysine and is one of the highest natural sources of chlorophyll. It is from 50 to 60 percent protein.

Use Chlorella, like other microalgae, is usually consumed as a dietary supplement. Due to its high processing costs, chlorella is one of the most expensive microalgae. It is available in pill and powder form.

See **Wild Blue-Green Algae.**

CHOCOLATE
Cacao, Cocoa
(Theobroma cacao)

Chocolate, native to tropical and Central America, was called *"xocoatl"* by the Maya and Aztecs, which means a bitter drink. It was a favorite beverage for the priests and royalty. The Swedish botanist Linnaeus tagged it *"theobroma,"* meaning, in Greek, food of the gods—few would disagree. Cacao beans were so valued that in Mexico they were used as standard currency as late as 1887.

The cacao tree is a tropical plant; its fruit pods look like small red or gold footballs. Each pod holds from 20 to 70 white beans about the size and shape of almonds. Today, Africa and Brazil supply more than 90 per-cent of the world demand for chocolate, but the finest quality comes from Venezuela and Costa Rica.

Cocoa beans are removed from the pod, fermented, dried, graded, and delivered to factories. They are then roasted (a process called torrefication), chopped up, and ground into an oily paste called chocolate mass or liquor. This liquor is nut particles suspended in cocoa butter, which is more than 50 per-cent fatty acids. The liquor gives the choco-late taste and color; the butter imparts a rich creamy mouth feel and glossy appearance.

To make cocoa powder used in beverages and baking, most of the cocoa butter is pressed from the liquor. The resulting paste may also be Dutch-processed, or further re-fined to improve its texture and flavor. There are many grades of cocoa powder to choose from—the darkest ones are the most bitter tasting and have the strongest cocoa flavor.

Chocolate for candy is made from the original, fat-rich liquor; fine chocolate is aug-mented with extra cocoa butter. In addition, superior chocolate undergoes an expensive mechanical conching, a process of grinding, mixing, and slightly heating the chocolate to enhance its texture and flavor. Lesser-quality chocolate is cut with inexpensive lecithin, vegetable oil, and/or synthetic substances. The taste of chocolate depends upon the va-riety of the cacao tree, the soil it was grown in, and what it is blended with as well as the processing.

Health Benefits Chocolate is bitter tast-ing and diuretic. It gives energy and was his-torically considered an aphrodisiac. It is rich in phenols that counter artery-clogging plaque, and it lowers blood pressure. It treats the severe chest pain of angina pectoris. Chocolate and cocoa are popularly believed to comfort the brokenhearted and to release the brain chemicals responsible for the feel-ing of being in love. This research remains unsubstantiated.

Historically, chocolate was used to treat

fevers, coughs, and complaints associated with pregnancy and childbirth. Today, however, we know that caffeine consumption during pregnancy contributes to birth defects, and chocolate's theobromine is a caffeine relative.

Theobromine, like caffeine, can trigger various nervous symptoms, including hyperactivity in children, anxiety, insomnia or disturbed sleep, heart disease, gastrointestinal complaints, and mood swings. Theobromine also relaxes the smooth muscle lining of the digestive tract and can soothe an upset stomach. On the other hand, because it also relaxes the lower esophageal sphincter, it may cause heartburn. In addition, chocolate and cocoa contain phenylethylamine and oxalic acid, both of which can inhibit calcium absorption. Overall calcium and mineral deficiencies are exacerbated by habitual chocolate consumption. Chocolate is one of the ten most common food allergens, and, in some individuals, it is implicated in migraine headaches.

Cocoa butter is used as an unguent for burns, skin irritation, and in cosmetics. In moderation, chocolate reduces *vata*.

Buying White chocolate excepted, all chocolate is a blend of cocoa liquor and cocoa butter. It may, or may not, contain other flavorings such as milk, vanilla, or sugar.

Quality chocolate is glossy and shiny. It should smell fresh and, when broken, should break cleanly rather than crumble.

- **Bitter (Unsweetened) Chocolate** Consists of 95 percent chocolate liquor with 5 percent added cocoa butter. It is used as an ingredient.
- **Bittersweet (Semisweet) Chocolate** Contains sugar and from 35 to 50 percent chocolate liquor, and 15 percent added cocoa butter.
- **Couverture** A rich chocolate, very high in cocoa butter and characterized by an exceptionally shiny finish.
- **Milk Chocolate** Contains sugar, added cocoa butter, milk solids, and chocolate liquor.
- **White Chocolate** Contains only cocoa butter and sugar, or, historically, chestnuts. It has a short shelf life and easily becomes rancid. In cheap, imitation white chocolate, vegetable oil is substituted for the cocoa butter.
- **Cocoa Powder** Contains only 18 percent total cocoa butter. The dry cake that remains after pressing cocoa butter is pulverized for use as an ingredient in baking, confectionery, and beverages.
- **Dutch-Process Cocoa Powder** Alkali-processed cocoa powder. The alkali, usually potassium carbonate, is used to neutralize the cocoa's acids and make it easier to dissolve. Also labeled European style.

CHOP SUEY GREENS See Garland Chrysanthemum.

CHOY SUM See Flowering Cabbage.

CHRISTOPHINE See Chayote.

CHRYSANTHEMUM See Garland Chrysanthemum.

CHUÑO
(Solanum tuberosum)

Don't be put off by chuño's appearance. A naturally freeze-dried potato or oca from the Andean altiplano, it looks more like a chunk of pumice than a food, but the earthy flavor and pleasing texture (something like deep-fried tofu) make chuños worth seeking out in a Latino market. The Quechuas and Aymaras preserve their just-harvested potatoes or ocas in this manner. They're left on the ground for several days, covered with a cloth to keep off the dew; each night they freeze. During the day, they are trampled by foot, to express their water. Once freeze-dried in this manner, they'll keep for years. Chuños are an excellent stew ingredient—taking on other flavors while imparting their own potato goodness.

Papa seca, or dried potato, another preserved Peruvian potato, is boiled but not trampled before being left out to freeze.

CILANTRO
Chinese Parsley, Coriander, Mexican Parsley
(Coriandrum sativum)

An ancient and popular herb since Egyptian times, cilantro is in the carrot family. The leaves have an aniselike taste (soapy when used in excess) and an earthy, fetid aroma. Because of this distinctive aroma, the Greeks named it *koris*, or bedbug. People either adore or are repulsed by cilantro; for the latter, even just a pinch of cilantro spoils a dish. If your first reaction was negative, I urge you to approach it again; odds are you'll become a convert. Cilantro is similar in appearance to parsley but lighter colored, with

larger and less curled leaves. Once dried, cilantro loses its overpowering aroma.

The seed, known as coriander, is tan and the size of a peppercorn. It is sweet and strongly aromatic, with a slight taste of orange peel.

Health Benefits Pungent and sweet in flavor, astringent and cooling (leaves), and neutral (seeds), cilantro supports the spleen-pancreas, stomach, bladder, and lung meridians. Cilantro and coriander help regulate energy, are diuretic, and specifically treat urinary tract infections. Both leaves and seeds are diaphoretic (support perspiration) and therefore treat fever. They aid digestion, relieve intestinal gas, pain, and distention, and support peristalsis. They treat nausea, soothe inflammation, rheumatic pain, headaches, coughs, and mental stress, and they quench thirst. The seeds and leaves are *tridoshic*.

Use Cilantro is basic in cuisine the world over; some say it is the most used herb, especially in warm regions, such as Mexico, the Middle East, Africa, Southeast Asia, and India. The leaves should not be overcooked.

Cilantro may be used like parsley, as a garnish and a flavoring herb. Use it sparingly with delicate ingredients, or its flavor overpowers. Or use it in large quantities in strongly flavored sauces and salsas. In Southeast Asian dishes, cilantro root is also used.

The slightly sweet, almost caramel-tasting seed acts as a catalyst to bring out the flavors of other ingredients, yet never masks or overpowers them. Coriander is an omnipresent ingredient in Indian curries and Ethiopian spice mixtures. Ground coriander quickly loses its pleasantly sweet taste and smell. It is preferable to use whole seeds or grind them just prior to use. To heighten the flavor of coriander, first toast the whole or ground seeds.

Buying Fresh cilantro is available in greengrocers year-round. In Asian markets, it is sold with the root attached, increasing its longevity. Select bunches that look fresh and bright. Cilantro quickly loses its flavor and develops a harsh, unpleasant taste; the leaves rapidly deteriorate, so use it soon after purchase.

Storing Cilantro is highly perishable and stores best when attached to its roots. Place the roots in a container of water, cover the greens with plastic, and refrigerate for up to a week. If purchased without roots, cover cilantro with a damp cloth, refrigerate in a perforated plastic bag, and use within four or five days.

Store whole coriander seeds and ground coriander in tightly closed containers in a dark, cool cupboard. The whole seeds keep a year or more. Once ground, coriander loses its savor less quickly than cardamom but faster

---

THE HEART OF A JAWBREAKER

For the Saturday matinee movie of my childhood, my siblings and I would walk three miles to the Country Club Theater. I don't recall much of the movies I saw. I do recall the manager periodically stopping the film to warn us to quiet down or he'd turn us out (he never did). And I can still almost taste my favorite penny candy, a jawbreaker.

One large ball filled a whole cheek plus and lasted the length of the movie. Layer upon layer, each a different color, of sugary candy would slowly dissolve. To give cheek muscles a rest, I'd occasionally pull out the jawbreaker to see if, indeed, there was any progress and to see what color level I was at.

At long last, the sugar all dissolved to reveal the central treasure—one tiny coriander seed. It provided a satisfying crunch and a burst of real flavor.

---

than cinnamon. Discard mild, flat-tasting ground coriander.

See **Carrot Family; Herbs and Spices.**

CINNAMON
Cassia
(Cinnamomum zeylanicum syn. C. verum, also C. cassia, C. burmannii)

The strongly aromatic, sweet-tasting, dried inner bark of a tree in the laurel family, cinnamon is one of humanity's oldest spices. Its recorded use in China and Egypt dates back to 2500 B.C.; it was one of the first spices traded in the Mediterranean area. Several cinnamon varieties exist in China, Indonesia, and Vietnam.

In many European languages, the name for cinnamon comes from the Latin *canella*, which means "small tube, pipe." This refers to how thin strips of the inner bark of the cinnamon tree are sun dried to form tightly curled quills.

Health Benefits Sweet and pungent, pleasant tasting and warming, cinnamon supports the spleen-pancreas, stomach, bladder, kidney, and liver meridians. It is one of the most commonly used warming Oriental herbs and has stimulant, analgesic, and astringent properties. Cinnamon can increase digestive fluid secretion and therefore ameliorate intestinal gas. It raises vitality and stimulates all the vital functions of the body, counteracting congestion and aiding the peripheral circulation of the blood. It is useful for treating diarrhea, nausea and vomiting, influenza, arthritis, menstrual cramps, rheumatism, and candidiasis. Its aroma relieves tension and helps steady the nerves.

Cinnamon is not recommended for pregnant women. It is *tridoshic* in action, although an excess could imbalance *pitta*.

Use In Western cuisine, cinnamon is commonly used in desserts. But considering that cinnamon aids absorption of nutrients, you might start using it more liberally. Elsewhere in the world, it is a common ingredient in savory dishes. My favorite way to use a cinnamon quill is to sauté it, along with any other spices, in warm oil until the quill unrolls, then add and cook the remaining ingredients. When using ground cinnamon, add it shortly before serving; it becomes bitter with prolonged cooking.

Buying Today, most ground cinnamon available in the United States is the mahogany red cassia. Cinnamon quills, *C. zeylanicum* or true cinnamon, have a more delicate aroma and tan color.

See **Herbs and Spices.**

CIPOLLINE See Onion.

CITRON
(Citrus medica)

Imagine a large, thick-skinned lemon with a lumpy rind as convoluted as a walnut—that's a citron. For a treat, soak the aromatic peel in salt brine and then candy it in sugar. Nubbins of candied citron abound in fruitcakes—and little else. The essential oil of citron peel is also used as a flavoring agent. The Corsican liqueur *cedratine* is made of citron.

The citron, which probably originated in India, was one of the first citrus fruits to be introduced to the Mediterranean region. Currently, it is grown there and in Puerto Rico. As a fresh fruit, it is available in specialty markets.

- **Buddha's Hand Citron** Composed of a cluster of green, fingerlike lobes. This citrus is considered a symbol of happiness in China.
- **Diamante Citron** Shaped like a green chile, up to 9 inches long. Grown predominately in southern Italy, the Diamante is almost all peel. What little flesh it has is not juicy and is packed with seeds.

A BOUNTIFUL FEAST OF THE TABERNACLES

The etrog, which represents abundance, is carried on myrtle boughs by celebrants at the Jewish Feast of the Tabernacles. The *Midrash* (Jewish Biblical commentaries) says, "Just as the Etrhog [*sic*] has taste and a pleasant fragrance, so there are in Israel men who are at once learned and strictly observant."

• **Etrog Citron** Grown in Israel. The Etrog has an almost orange rind and a pervasive fragrance than can linger for weeks at a time.

See **Citrus Family.**

CITRUS FAMILY
(Citrus)

From ruby grapefruit to Key limes, the number of citrus fruits is huge. Hundreds of varieties and subspecies grow throughout the tropics and subtropics. Add the endless number of hybrids for an unwieldy category, as well as the largest fruit industry.

Citrus plants are small evergreen trees or shrubs, which originated in China and Southeast Asia. The primitive citron was the original citrus fruit. Today, these fruits grow throughout the world, wherever there's ample moisture and little or no frost. Brazil and the United States are the world's largest citrus producers. Most of that fruit is processed rather than eaten out of hand.

Health Benefits Citrus fruits are remarkable in their wide range of healing properties. For example, mandarin oranges are specific for breast cancer whereas grapefruit pips are a potent treatment for candida. For specific medicinal properties, see each individual citrus fruit.

In general, citrus fruits are an effective cooling agent—be it for heat from a fever, from physical exercise, or from a menopausal hot flash. They are a general tonic for weak digestion and poor appetite. They contain 58 known anticancer agents.

Most citrus fruits are high in sugar, although lemons and limes are high in acids. All species are rich sources of vitamin C; they contain potassium and citric acid; and their peel contains valuable aromatic oils. Citrus pith contains bioflavonoids, needed by the body to absorb vitamin C. Citrus seed extract is a natural antibiotic and antifungal.

For people with food allergies, citrus ranks as one of the ten most common allergens.

Buying Citrus fruits are tree ripened and thus ready to eat from the market. Citrons, ugli fruits, and bitter oranges excepted, select heavy fruits with thin skins. As a rough skin indicates a thick skin, it also indicates a fruit with proportionately less flesh. A citrus that's light for its size is an old, dehydrated fruit. Avoid citrus with brown, bruised, or soft spots. Organic citrus lacks the uniform, cosmetic color of commercial citrus—as well as the chemical colorants and herbicides.

Refrigerate citrus fruit or store in a cool pantry. Do not keep in plastic bags; plastic draws moisture from the fruit and quickens spoilage.

See **Bitter Orange; Citron; Clementine; Grapefruit; Kaffir Lime; Kumquat; Lemon; Lime; Mandarin; Orange; Pummelo; Tangelo; Tangor; Ugli Fruit.**

THE CITRUS RELIGION

Almost religiously, many people consume citrus to ward off whatever ails—from a cold to cancer. I'm not one of those people. Favoring regional fruits best supports health. As right now I can see a snowstorm approaching from the north, a refreshing tangerine is not my choice. When I'm building sand castles in Palm Beach, that's another story. This common-sense wisdom of favoring regional foods is, however, a guideline, never a law.

There's a second reason I recommend citrus in moderation. Today, many people suffer from low energy, general weakness, cold extremities, and chronic illness. Reducing sugar, soft drinks, fruit juice, and tropical fruit consumption often ameliorates such problems.

On the other hand, citrus is frequently cited for its nutritional value and as an effective aid in preventing cancer. How do you figure out what's true for you? One way is to eat a lot of citrus, see how it makes you feel, and then proceed accordingly.

CITRUS PEEL
Citrus Zest

Don't toss organic orange peel. The outer part—not the pithy inner white part—is called zest and, as its name suggests, gives lots of flavor. Furthermore, it's remarkably medicinal.

Health Benefits It's curious that while citrus flesh and juice are cooling, its peel is warming. Warming because of its high oil concentration, which make it a useful medicine for cold and deficient symptoms. The peel contains numerous potent nutraceuti-

---

ZEST FOR LEMON

With an orange or lemon and a grater in hand, fresh zest is but a grate away. The easiest—and least messy—way to take zest is from an uncut fruit. Do not remove the white pith. Though lemon and orange are the most popular, you may use any citrus fruit.

- **Grated Zest** Grate citrus on the smallest opening of a handheld grater.
- **Sliced Zest** Peel the zest with a sharp knife, zesting tool, or vegetable peeler. Use the strips fresh in *bouquet garni*, in medicinal teas, or to flavor a jar of sugar.
- **Julienned Zest** Slice fresh zest strips lengthwise into thin julienne strips and use as garnish for sweet or savory dishes.
- **Dried Zest** Place zest strips on a saucer and allow to air or sun dry until brittle (about 2 to 4 days). Place the zest in a blender and pulverize. Store tightly covered.

cals. Liminoids, to name just one, are antioxidants that help combat carcinogens in the liver. Citrus peel enhances digestive energy and helps relieve intestinal gas, pain, swelling, and constipation. It helps decongest the lungs and reduce mucus conditions. As a liver tonic, lime, and secondly lemon, are more effective than grapefruit peel. *Tridoshic* in nature, citrus peel calms *vata, pitta*, and *kapha*.

Use Zest gives the concentrated flavor of the fruit without adding acid as would the flesh or juice. Use grated orange, lemon, or lime zest, fresh or dried, as a flavoring in savory and sweet dishes. Cut into julienne strips, zest is an attractive garnish. To make a tea, simmer fresh or dried peel, alone or with herbs, for fifteen minutes.

Buying Use only organic lemons, oranges, grapefruit, and limes for zest. Despite its pesticide residues and dyes, commercial citrus will up the flavor of a dish, but it will not up your health. Because the peel is not considered a food by the FDA, citrus is treated with toxic chemicals and dyes.

See **Herbs and Spices.**

CLARIFIED BUTTER

Clarified butter is a superb cooking fat that enhances flavor. It is the pure butterfat that remains when milk solids and water are removed from butter at a low to medium temperature. It contains 30 percent polyunsaturated fat and 65 percent saturated fat. Clarified butter can be stored for many months without becoming rancid because the whey and casein are removed.

See **Butter; Ghee.**

HOW TO CLARIFY BUTTER

To clarify butter, melt unsalted butter over medium heat. Remove from the heat and let stand for twenty minutes. With a slotted spoon, remove the foamy layer of milk solids from the top. Strain the pure liquid butterfat through a stainless steel mesh tea strainer. Take care to leave the residue (whey and salts) behind at the bottom of the pan.

CLEMENTINE
(Citrus reticulata)

A cross between a mandarin and a bitter orange, the clementine is Algerian in origin. It's named for one Brother Clement, a gardener at an orphanage who first cultivated this tree. When the clementine is grown in solid blocks (not near other citrus varieties), it is seedless, otherwise not. The clementine is a medium-size fruit with a slightly puffy peel and a deep orange, glossy color. It has a unique floral aroma and tastes something like apricot nectar. Available from October through March, it's a citrus fruit worth seeking out, seedless or not.

See **Bitter Orange; Citrus Family; Mandarin.**

CLOUD EAR See **Wood Ear.**

CLOVES
(Szygium aromaticum)

In ancient China, before an audience with the emperor, people had to chew cloves to freshen their breath. A clove is the dried, un-opened bud of an evergreen tree that originated in Moluccas, formerly the Spice Islands in what is now eastern Indonesia. For over 2,000 years, Molucca cloves have remained an important spice in Asia and Europe. They have an exceptionally strong aroma. Today, Zanzibar and Madagascar are the main clove producers, followed by Indonesia.

The name clove comes from the Latin word for nail, *clavus*, for indeed it looks like a small, dark nail with a rounded head.

Health Benefits Strongly aromatic, bitter, spicy, and warming, cloves tonify the kidney, spleen-pancreas, and stomach. When there are digestive problems due to "cold" in the stomach, cloves aid digestion, treat nausea, hiccups, and vomiting. They also treat impotence due to kidney deficiency. Cloves reduce *vata* and *kapha*. Oil of cloves is an effective toothache remedy.

Use Throughout Asia, North Africa, and many Arab countries, cloves are a favorite spice for meat, grain, and other savory dishes. In Europe and the United States, cloves are primarily used in sweets, especially cold-weather dishes like gingerbread or spice cookies. They are an ingredient in Worcestershire sauce and also a common ingredient in pickling spices. Whole cloves are used to decorate ham. A popular project for grade school children is to make a pomander holiday gift by embedding cloves into an orange or an apple. The cloves preserve the fruit and their perfume is long lasting.

To discourage Indonesians from chewing betel nuts, the Dutch introduced clove-spiked cigarettes. Unfortunately, these are even more toxic than tobacco. Even more unfortunately, the habit persists in Indonesia and India.

Buying Freshly dried whole cloves are mahogany red, oily, and with a pungent and sweet aroma. If they are black and shriveled, they're old. If ground cloves taste bitter and harsh, they're old and should be discarded.

See **Herbs and Spices**.

COBNUT See Hazelnut.

COCOA See Chocolate.

COCOANUT See Coconut.

COCONUT
Cocoanut
(Cocos nucifera)

The tall, tropical coconut palm tree is unusual in that it is so tolerant of salty, sandy soils that it grows right at the beach. This location, coupled with the fact that the fruit's buoyant, protective covering is impervious even to saltwater, has allowed edible coconuts, bobbing along on the Gulf Stream, to float as far as Norway. Unlike other transplanted foods dispersed by colonists and traders, self-sufficient coconuts set sail on their own and planted themselves throughout the tropics.

All parts of the coconut plant are used; the fronds for roofing material; the nut's hairy outer fiber for matting, ropes, and clothing; and, of course, the nutmeat as an important food and oil source. Although the coconut is popularly considered a nut—and is an exceptional source of lipids—it is technically a fruit.

Health Benefits Coconut is a warming food in the Oriental model: It has a sweet taste; it helps nurture the body in general; increase semen, and build energy, blood, and body mass. It is especially useful in terms of childhood malnutrition. It soothes internal membranes and has laxative properties.

Coconut tonifies the heart but is contraindicated for people with high cholesterol because it contains 60 percent fat and, unlike almost all other plant foods, that fat is primarily saturated fat. Coconut milk quenches thirst and is used in the treatment of diabetes, edema, and for clearing summer heat. Coconut and coconut milk are pacifying to *vata* and *pitta*.

HOW TO OPEN A COCONUT

To open a mature coconut, use a nut pick, awl, or nail and first pierce two of the eyes (the soft spots on the shell) at the rounded end of the coconut. Drain the coconut water and enjoy it as a refreshing beverage. Next, place the nut on a hard surface, like cement, and use several sharp blows from a hammer to crack it open. Hammer the halves again to break into smaller pieces. Use a table knife to pry out pieces. (The thin brown seed coat adhering to the white meat is edible and contains nutrients in addition to fiber.) Grate, slice, or shred the fresh coconut meat; eat it out of hand; or use it to prepare coconut milk.

Use White coconut meat is a popular ingredient. Toasting it caramelizes sugars on the surface, turning the coconut golden and enhancing its flavor and aroma. Use it with chocolate, fruit desserts, chutney, cakes, cookies, puddings, pies, and confections. Coconut is also excellent with curries and vegetable, fish, and grain dishes. While it's often coupled with highly flavorful (spicy or sweet) dishes, a little coconut added to a pot of millet or oatmeal elevates an otherwise basic staple. Shredded or flaked, coconut is a common ingredient in trail mixes. My favorite, however, is fresh coconut eaten out of hand as a snack.

Buying Coconuts are available year-round, with a peak supply from October through December.

- **Whole Coconut** Buy a coconut that is heavy for its size, that has no hairline cracks or soft or moldy spots on any of its eyes, and that sounds full of liquid when shaken.

  At my local supermarket, "quick-crack" coconuts are available. They come shrink-wrapped and scored about the middle to facilitate cracking. True, the scoring makes cracking easier. The shrink wrap, however, makes it impossible to detect any hairline cracks or know what the eyes looked like before they were sealed, and therefore increases the odds of purchasing an off fruit.

- **Shredded or Flaked Coconut** Available sweetened or not; frozen, canned, or in plastic. My choice is organic, nonsweetened coconut from a natural food store that has a quick turnover since coconut can become rancid. Commercial shredded coconut may contain propylene glycol and sugar. Better yet, shred your own in a processor or with a hand grater, using freshly shelled coconut for incomparable flavor and moist richness.

- **Water Coconut** An immature coconut. Today, cultivars are specifically bred to be sold at this stage. The thin flesh is jellylike and exceptionally delicious. Large water coconut pods are available in specialty markets cut down to form an eight-inch cube. Cut through the cube to get to the delicately flavored flesh within.

See **Coconut Milk and Cream; Dried Fruit; Fat and Oil; Nuts.**

COCONUT MILK AND CREAM

Coconut milk and cream are fragrant liquids extracted from fresh coconut meat. They give body and sweet flavor to sauces, desserts, and rice pilafs and are featured in Thai, Vietnamese, Indian, and Caribbean cuisine.

Coconut milk is widely available canned. The cream separates from and rises to the top of the milk. To blend the two, shake the can before you open it. Or after opening a can, lift off the cream and use it separately as a garnish or extra-rich ingredient. Cans labeled light coconut milk have had the cream removed. Bypass sugar-sweetened coconut milk intended for beverage use.

Canned coconut milk is available in most supermarkets and in Asian and Latino markets. Organic coconut milk is available in natural food stores.

Of course, coconut cream and milk are most appealing when made at home. For milk, add 1 cup boiling water to every packed cup of shredded, fresh coconut. Let the mixture rest for 20 minutes. Pour into a blender and purée. Strain through a double layer of cheesecloth, twisting and squeezing out as much milk as possible. Cover and store in the refrigerator for up to 5 days. To make cream, use 1 part water to 4 parts coconut. One coconut yields approximately 3 cups of milk.

See **Coconut.**

COCONUT OIL

For the past several decades, coconut oil (the fatty acids pressed from coconut meat) was falsely accused of raising blood cholesterol levels. Yes, it is a highly saturated fat—meaning that it is solid at room temperature—but it's an exceptionally healthy fat for vegetarians and people with low fat/cholesterol consumption. It and palm oil are the only unrefined vegetarian fats that are not denatured when heated above 240 degrees.

Health Benefits Unrefined coconut oil is lower in calories than most fats and oils. Moreover, it is over 50 percent medium-chain fatty acids, the kind that are not stored as fat. Rather, the body metabolizes medium-chain fatty acids into energy. This makes coconut oil a favorite food of dieters and athletes.

Possibly, however, coconut oil's most remarkable property is that it's one of the few significant plant sources of lauric acid. This

SUPER GRANOLA

My friend Elaine Gagné makes the best granola. She willingly shares its secret: Finger-rub coconut oil into the mixture so that the oil fully imbues the oats.

⅓ cup coconut oil, at room
    temperature
½ cup barley malt syrup
¼ cup maple syrup
1 teaspoon vanilla extract
3 cups rolled oats
1 cup chopped almonds
1 cup chopped pecans
1 cup currants, raisins, or other
    chopped dried fruit

Preheat oven to 325 degrees.

Combine the coconut butter, barley malt, maple syrup, and vanilla in a 3-quart mixing bowl and, using a wooden spoon, thoroughly blend. Add the oats, almonds, and pecans and mix well with the spoon. Then, using your fingertips, rub the mixture for several minutes or until the oats are thoroughly coated.

Spread evenly on a 17 × 11-inch jelly-roll pan and bake for 25 to 30 minutes. After 7 minutes, stir and spread the mixture out again in an even layer. Repeat after 7 minutes. Then stir every 5 minutes, or until the oats are crisp and brown but not burned. Remove from the oven and pour into a large wooden bowl to stop the cooking. Add the currants. Let cool thoroughly. Store in an airtight container in a cool spot. Makes 6 cups.

medium-chain fatty acid, which is also found in human milk, enhances brain function and the immune system.

Unrefined coconut oil is free of the toxic trans-fatty acids found in hydrogenated and refined oils. It does not clog the arteries or cause heart disease. It reduces *pitta* and *vata*.

Use For baking, pan-frying, and deep-frying, coconut oil is a superior oil. It has a toothsome texture with a pleasant mouth feel. Unlike other oils used for deep-frying, it is reusable because it remains stable and does not form toxic trans-fatty acids. When heated to high temperatures, however, coconut oil bubbles and froths. To prevent it from bubbling over, deep-fry in a large container and tend carefully. In some applications, using a fry-pan/pressure cooker, the type by Kuhn-Rikon, alleviates this problem.

It's easy to substitute coconut oil for shortening, lard, or butter in pastries. However, reduce the coconut oil measurement by 25 percent because it is almost pure fat. It's more concentrated than shortening, lard, and butter, which contain upwards of 20 percent moisture and/or milk solids.

Until now, unrefined coconut oil has been deodorized and therefore lacks flavor. Watch for the organic, full-flavored unrefined coconut oil now entering the marketplace.

Buying Organic, unrefined coconut oil is available by mail order from Omega Nutrition (see page 400) and in some natural food stores. Store coconut oil in a cool, dark place.

See **Coconut; Fat and Oil.**

COCOYAM See Yautia.

COFFEE
(Coffee arabica, C. canephora)

Coffee has been called liquid amphetamine, the devil's brew, or simply "power" by the Arabs, who obtained it from its native Ethiopia a thousand years ago. Everyone is in agreement that it's potent. How much—if any—of this power supports your well-being depends upon your constitution, current health, and individual tolerance. What is undisputed is coffee's popularity. Eighty percent of adults in America drink it at an annual rate of 28 gallons per capita.

Each small red fruit of the semitropical evergreen coffee shrub contains two white seeds (the beans). These seeds are removed from the berries in one of two methods. The traditional method, which involves fermentation, yields the most flavorful coffee. The second method is mechanical. Most American coffee is imported from Brazil.

Health Benefits Coffee is a warming, bitter-tasting stimulant with diuretic and purgative properties. Its caffeine, acid, and oils produce different effects. Caffeine stimulates the entire nervous system, stresses the adrenal glands, increases the pulse and blood pressure, raises the blood sugar level, suppresses the appetite, and gives a sense of high energy. Its acids corrode the small intestine's villi and therefore decrease nutrient absorption; heavy coffee drinkers often suffer from B vitamin shortages and have calcium and other mineral deficiencies. The oils in coffee can increase blood cholesterol.

Stressed adrenals translates in Oriental medicine as depleted kidney energy, reduced sexual vitality, and, in the case of pregnancy, increased rate of birth defects. As with any stimulant, coffee aggravates liver function (its acids break down stored fats in the liver) and therefore disturbs sleep and contributes toward irritability and anxiety. Coffee is a common allergen. Coffee, in moderation, reduces *kapha*.

Use Coffee is primarily used as a beverage but also to flavor foods and desserts. When combined with chocolate, it is called mocha, a name that also refers to a specific kind of coffee. Caffeine is used in some medications.

Buying Seventy percent of coffee comes from the superior flavored *C. arabica*, which is an upland species. An inferior-tasting, less expensive coffee—with double the caffeine—grows on a hardier, larger coffee tree, the robusta (*C. canephora*). Cultivated primarily in West Africa, Uganda, and Indonesia, it is mostly used in inexpensive blends and for instant coffee.

Ground coffee oxidizes quickly, becomes rancid, and loses flavor. The best option is to purchase whole beans and grind them just prior to use. Or to purchase small quantities of freshly ground coffee and keep it refrigerated.

- **Organic Coffee** Worth the extra price. The chemical residues in commercial coffee include traces of pesticides banned in the United States because they are known carcinogens.

- **De-acidified Coffee** Less detrimental to the gastrointestinal tract. When the acid is water extracted, it is a healthful process. Note that de-acidified coffee has reduced flavor.
- **Decaffeinated Coffee** A more healthful choice provided the caffeine is not removed with toxic solvents. Favor steam decaffeinated coffee.
- **Instant Coffee** Chemically processed, therefore not recommended.

HOW TO HAVE YOUR COFFEE AND DRINK IT, TOO

An Ayurvedic antidote to the depleting effect that coffee has on the adrenals and nervous system is to serve it with a pinch of cardamom and ginger.

A macrobiotic practice to counter coffee's acidity—and therefore ameliorate its damage to the gut—is to add a few grains of salt per cup.

To remove coffee's cholesterol-raising oils, drink filtered coffee.

So here's the formula, which happens to be delicious: Filtered coffee seasoned with cardamom, ginger, and salt.

What about a splash of cream? Hold it, advises Steve Gagné, author of *The Energetics of Food*. Drawing from over twenty years of nutritional counseling and teaching throughout the United States, Steve observes that a dietary habit common to people with colon polyps and most women with uterine or vaginal polyps, tumors, and cysts is drinking many cups of coffee with cream or milk. There's something about the synergy of coffee and cream or milk that contributes to the formation of fatty pockets and/or blocked energy in the lower organs.

COFFEE SUBSTITUTES

Postum, an old-time American hot beverage favorite, is still available as are another dozen healthful coffee substitutes. Each has a coffeelike aroma and flavor but lacks stimulants and acids. Domestic or imported from Europe, these coffee substitutes are available instant or needing to be brewed. With or without a splash of soymilk or milk, they are pleasing in their own right. Like coffee, they may be served hot or cold or used as a flavoring ingredient.

Most coffee substitutes, like Roma, Caffix, Pero, Inka, and Yannoh, are made of roasted barley or rye. They may contain chicory or other flavorants, beets for coloring, and often malted barley for sweetness. Two grainfree coffee substitutes are DaCopa, which is made from dahlia root, and Raja's Cup, which is a blend of Ayurvedic ingredients.

See **Acorn**; **Chicory**; **Dahlia**.

COLESEED See **Canola Seed**.

COLLARDS
(Brassica oleracea acephala)

A mild-tasting kale variety, collards are blue-green with large, smooth, nonheading paddlelike leaves. Collard greens, a favorite soul food of the American South, are available twelve months of the year. Collards contain nearly the same amount of calcium as does milk.

See **Cabbage Family; Kale.**

COMICE PEAR See Pear.

CONFERENCE PEAR See Pear.

CORIANDER See Cilantro.

CORN
Maize
(Zea mays)

What *Zea mays* is to a botanist, and maize to most of the world, is corn in North America. Corn, the most widely used native grain in the western hemisphere, originated nearly eight thousand years ago when the Indians of Mexico began selectively breeding a wild grass called teosinte. The early ears ranged in size from half an inch to two inches long. Columbus returned to Spain with seeds of Indian corn in 1493, and corn quickly spread around the world, following the trade routes of the early Portuguese navigators. With few exceptions, it seemed to adapt to whatever climate it was introduced to.

About 90 percent of domestic corn is fed to livestock. The rest is used for human consumption and in the production of paper, textiles, paints, explosives, and plastics. The United States, primarily in the corn belt, produces nearly 50 percent of the world's corn. Other important corn-producing regions include the European Danube basin and Po valley, northern China, northeastern Argentina, and southeastern Brazil.

There are five types of corn:

- **Dent Corn** A deep crease or dent forms on top of each kernel as its soft endosperm dries. Most corn grown today is a hybrid, yellow dent.
- **Flint Corn** This variety has the hardest, flintlike endosperm, making it difficult to grind. In the United States, colored flint corn is available on the cob primarily as a decoration. Flint corn was introduced to Europe in the 1500s and is still used in Italy, Romania, and Hungary to make polenta, mamaliga, and puliszka, respectively.
- **Flour Corn** The soft endosperm of this variety makes it easy to grind into flour.
- **Popcorn** The oldest strain of corn, with such an impervious hull that moisture trapped within it explodes when heated.
- **Sweet Corn** This new corn has a recessive gene that prevents its sugars from turning into starch, and so it is a vegetable, not a grain.

Health Benefits The thermal property of corn is neutral; its flavor is sweet; it strengthens overall energy (*chi*), blood, the stomach, and bladder. Corn is used in the treatment of heart disease, sexual weakness, and loss of appetite, as well as to stimulate bile flow, prevent the formation of urinary stones, lower blood sugar levels, and for cases of difficult urination or edema. Corn engenders joyfulness. It reduces kapha.

Corn is the only grain that contains vitamin A. Yellow corn is higher in vitamin A than white corn. Corn, relative to other cereal grains, is refreshing and an ideal hot weather grain. As with many other foods, you may assume that the darker and richer the color of a corn kernel, the more flavor it has. What is more, high flavor is an apt indicator of nutrient density.

Corn, especially dent corn products, is one of the ten most common food allergens. Very probably a contributing factor is corn syrup's pandemic use in most processed foods. Many people who are allergic to common commercial corn products find they can eat popcorn and the nutritionally superior blue corn, masa, or posole products.

Use Only popcorn, posole, and sweet corn are used in their whole form. Corn grits are used as a breakfast cereal.

Corn as an ingredient is found in over three thousand grocery food items. It appears in the following foods and ingredients: beer, bread, breakfast cereals, baked goods, candy, confections, corn flour, cornmeal, corn oil, corn solids (a filler), cornstarch, gin, snacks, soups, and whiskey. As a sweetener, it appears in the following forms: corn syrup, dextrose, fructose, high-fructose corn syrup, invert sugar, malitol, malt, and mannitol.

White corn has the blandest flavor; yellow

THE SACRED COLORS OF CORN

Stunning ears of flint corn are available in the fall for decoration. Their colors range—on any one ear—from black, blue, violet, red, pink to yellow and white. No two ears are alike in pattern or hue.

Traditional Pueblo Indians grow different colored corn for each of the sacred directions and for specific ceremonial uses. Not multicolored corn—rather, the kernels of each ear are one pure color. White corn represents the east and every morning a pinch of white cornmeal is offered to Sun Father. Blue corn is for the north, red for the south, yellow for the west, and black for above.

---

corn has a buttery flavor; and blue corn has the widest range of flavor components.

See Blue Corn; Chicos; Corn Flour, Grits, Cornmeal, and Pinole; Corn Oil; Corn Silk; Corn Syrup; Flour; Fructose; Grains; Huitlacoche; Masa; Masa Harina; Popcorn; Posole; Sweet Corn.

CORN FLOUR, GRITS, CORNMEAL, AND PINOLE

Ma made the cornmeal and water into two thin loaves, each shaped in a half circle. She laid the loaves with their straight sides together in the bake-oven, and she pressed her hand flat on top of each loaf. Pa always said he did not ask for any other sweetening when Ma put the prints of her hands on the loaves.

—Laura Ingalls Wilder,
Little House on the Prairie

Grind dried corn and the result is—from coarsest to finest—grits, meal, flour, and atole or pinole. Different in particle size, these products may be ground from whole or degerminated corn. While the degerminated corn has an indefinite shelf life, it is a vapid-tasting, limp, highly refined product that I don't recommend. Besides, degerminated corn flour is, by law, chemically enriched.

Commercial grades of corn flour and meal are usually made from dent corn, but pinole, a very fine corn flour, is ground from soft flour corn.

Use Ground corn absorbs more water than other flours and yields a drier, more crumbly product. Corn flour imparts a sweet, corn flavor and, when it's yellow corn flour, a beautiful golden color to cakes and cookies. Cornmeal, coarser than flour, is most often used in muffins, corn bread, or corn mush. In Africa and Asia, corn porridge is often fermented. Pinole, a corn-based dry meal, is made into a sustaining cereal or hot beverage.

Buying Favor stone-ground corn flour for its superior flavor and baking properties. Because whole corn has a high oil content, cornmeal and flour quickly become rancid. To avoid rancidity, purchase frequently in small quantities. Refrigerate corn flours in a tightly covered container.

Also available is the nutritionally improved "high-lysine cornmeal," with 70 percent more lysine than regular cornmeal. This corn boasts an improved balance of four critical amino acids (lysine, tryptophan, methionine, and cystine); it is superior in its protein profile to beans, milk, or beef. This new cornmeal has a sweet and nutty flavor. My preference, however, is for energetically superior, open-pollinated corn, rather than a hybridized variety.

See **Corn; Flour.**

Ø CORN OIL

A popular commercial oil, corn oil is a by-product of the corn industry. It requires high-tech processing to extract the small (5 percent) amount of oil from corn. I don't recommend corn oil.

See **Corn; Fat and Oil.**

CORN ON THE COB See **Sweet Corn.**

CORN SALAD See **Mâche.**

CORN SILK

The silk, or tassel (stylus of female flowers), from any corn variety makes a delicious herbal tea as well as a sweet-tasting stock. Use it as a diuretic to ease edema, reduce high blood pressure, and to help dissolve kidney and gall stones. Herbalist Michael Tierra observes that "Even though it is effective for kidney stones, it is one of the milder and safer diuretics."

Favor organic corn silk. Remove the corn husk, then the silk. Use it fresh in season or spread it on a dry surface to dry, which takes about three days. It will be brittle to the touch, look like celery green silk threads, and taste sweet and corny.

Corn silk is available in the bulk section of herb shops. The commercial silk is brown, matted, and less flavorful than homedried.

CORN SMUT See Huitlacoche.

Ø CORN SYRUP

Corn syrup is chemically purified cornstarch, water, and hydrochloric or sulfuric acid. It is available in conventional markets as light or dark Karo corn syrup. Dark corn syrup is artificially colored with caramel. This inexpensive sugar-in-solution is widely used as a glaze for meats and vegetables and as an ingredient in marinade, desserts, and candies. Other corn based sweeteners include invert sugar, dextrose, fructose, xylitol, and sorbitol. They are not recommended.

See **Sweeteners**.

COS LETTUCE See Romaine.

Ø COTTONSEED OIL

Cottonseed oil is not available on the retail level. It is, however, a common ingredient in shoddy salad dressing, margarine, and other processed foods. That it is used for human consumption is appalling. Here's why.

Because cotton has a long fruiting period, it is a veritable smorgasbord for the boll weevil and other insects, and so it is one of the most heavily sprayed cultivated crops. Furthermore, cotton is classified as a nonfood crop and so is treated with chemicals too toxic for food crops (see page 254). Since

---

FUNKY CANDY CANES

Compared to my Aunts Rosie and Barbara, who hand-dip chocolates, a candy maker I am not. At holiday time, however, my children and I open *Joy of Cooking* and we make candy. When a recipe calls for corn syrup—an ingredient I've never owned—we substitute maple syrup, honey, or rice syrup. When it calls for sugar, we use rapadura. Our English toffee looks like the real thing but, to be honest, our taffy that we color, twist, and shape into candy canes doesn't look store-bought. Besides the fun of making quality candies, the best part is their unrivaled flavor.

---

toxins concentrate in the fatty acids, cottonseed oil is the most tainted of oils. I anticipate the day when manufacturers stop using cottonseed oil. One way of voicing our opinion is not to purchase products containing it.

See **Fat and Oil**.

COUSCOUS

Featherlight couscous is a most delectable wheat product. Indigenous to North Africa, it is essentially a minuscule pasta. Traditionally, Berber women made it from a mixture of coarse and fine granules of moistened semolina that they rolled together between their palms and fingers. These granules were then sun dried. How I would love to see their hands at work—and then to taste their couscous. Today, the semolina granules are mechanically mixed (agglomerated) with water, shaped in a rotating drum roller, steamed, then oven dried. Our domestic couscous is manufactured in the United States. In North Africa, couscous may also be made of millet.

Use Traditionally, couscous is steamed in a *couscousière* and served with a stew that is also called couscous. For an authentic recipe, refer to any Moroccan cookbook.

For a quick-cooking dish, stir 1 cup of couscous into 1½ cups of seasoned boiling water and simmer for 1 minute, then let stand, covered, for 10 minutes. As a compliment to a heavy meal or a refreshing hot-weather grain, couscous is hit.

Buying In natural food stores, a tan, whole wheat couscous is available. Because it contains the germ, this product can become rancid. Select couscous, especially whole wheat couscous, that looks fresh and that has a fresh aroma and taste. Store whole wheat couscous in the refrigerator.

See **Israeli Couscous; Wheat.**

Cow Pea See **Black-Eyed Pea.**

CRACKED WHEAT

Cracked wheat is coarsely ground wheat and is used primarily as a hot breakfast cereal.

See **Wheat.**

CRANBERRY
(Vaccinium oxycoccus, V. macrocarpon)

A North American native, the cranberry (*V. oxycoccus*) grows in a mat-forming, ever-green shrub in moist woodlands and bogs. It is a blueberry relative and is small, dry, and intensely sour. The larger commercial variety (*V. macrocarpon*) is treated with growth hormones but generally not sprayed with insecticides. Most commercial cranberry production is in Massachusetts bogs, but cranberries are also produced in Washington, Oregon, New Jersey, Rhode Island, and Wisconsin.

Health Benefits The tannin, a chemical compound called proanthocyanidins, in cranberries increases urine acidity and inhibits bacteria (especially E. coli) from adhering to the bladder and urinary tract. This helps prevent and treats urinary infections; cranberry consumption also reduces some types of kidney stones. Because cranberries contain oxalic acid, they bind calcium and are best used in moderation, especially by individuals at risk of osteoporosis. Cranberries reduce *kapha*.

Use While cranberries are primarily associated with Thanksgiving relish, they are also delicious and colorful in cakes, muffins, jellies, and juice. Native Americans pounded them with jerked venison and nuts or fat to make pemmican.

Buying Commercial cranberry juice is usually sweetened; if using this beverage medicinally, consider favoring a cranberry supplement or making your own concentrate. To make your own, simmer the cranberries, covered, in water to cover for 40 minutes. Purée and sweeten to taste with a quality sweetener.

Look for cranberries that are bright red, plump, hard, and shiny. Avoid shriveled, soft, spongy, or browned fruits, which may produce an off flavor. Cranberries will keep

---

THE CRANE'S BERRY

To celebrate the spring solstice, I once joined friends to "boil a pot of bush tea" in the deep woods near Lake Athabasca in northeastern Alberta on the Siksika (Cree Nation) Reserve. When clearing snow from the ground to build a fire, we uncovered last fall's bright red cranberries. The size of peppercorns and puckery tart, they were delicious with fresh-baked bannock and fire-simmered tea.

Cranberries and their relative blueberries are the only native fruits of the far north—imagine what treasures they were to subarctic peoples. Apparently they're also a treat to sandhill and whooping cranes, after whom they are named.

---

up to two months refrigerated. They are at their peak in November.

Dried cranberries make a colorful and tangy raisin substitute. They are sugar sweetened.

See **Fruit.**

CRANBERRY BEAN
(Phaseolus vulgaris)

A variety of the common bean, the size and shape of a pinto, the cranberry bean is beige with pinkish red blotches. The color turns a uniform beige when cooked.

See **Beans and Legumes.**

CREAM OF TARTAR
Potassium Bitartrate

I remember the time I made grape jelly and tried a shortcut by not straining the juice after it sat overnight. The result was tasty but unexpectedly—and unpleasantly—crunchy, with little slivers of tartrate crystals that had separated out from the juice.

Cream of tartar is a mildly acidic salt that is a byproduct of wine making. Today, I keep it on hand for homemade baking powder, and to hold the foam in beaten egg whites for meringues, soufflés, and cakes. Cream of tartar is also used in laxatives.

CREAM OF WHEAT See Farina.

CREMINI
Italian Brown Mushroom
(Agaricus)

A vareity of the common white mushroom, the cremini differs from it both in color—it ranges from light tan to rich brown—and in flavor. The cremini has a deeper, denser, earthier flavor.

See **Mushroom Family.**

CRENSHAW See Melon.

CRESS
Garden Cress
(Lepidium sativum)

Faster than radishes—and sometimes hotter—cress is ready for the table in a mere two weeks after sowing. This diminutive, peppery-pungent salad ingredient originated, and still grows wild, in western Asia.

Health Benefits The mustard oil in cress makes it stimulating and cleansing to the lung and colon meridians. Cress is a tonic herb and diuretic; it stimulates the appetite, and is an antianemic. It is also high in vitamin C.

Use Cress is not cooked or dried; its peppery taste is volatile and doesn't withstand heat or moisture. It is interchangeable with watercress in raw dishes and as a sandwich and salad ingredient.

Buying Cress doesn't have a large commercial demand but is sometimes available in the sprout section of markets or as one ingredient in a sprout combination.

See **Cabbage Family.**

CROOKNECK SQUASH
(Cucurbita pepo melopepo)

This thin-skinned summer squash has a yellow bumpy skin and, generally, a crooked neck. Compared to a zucchini (yellow or green), a crookneck is less easily packed and the plant is less productive, and so crookneck squash is usually less available than others. Its optimum size is seven inches or less.

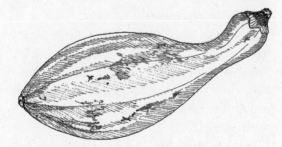

See **Squash; Summer Squash.**

CRUCIFER See **Cabbage Family.**

CUBAN SQUASH See **Calabaza.**

CUCUMBER
Gherkin
(Cucumis sativus)

The cucumber is one of humanity's earliest food crops; cultivated cucumber seeds carbon dated at 7750 B.C. were excavated near the Burma-Thailand border. Introduced eventually to India, China, and Europe, the cucumber remains a popular vegetable worldwide. In fact, the Roman Emperor Tiberius was so fond of cucumbers that he planted them in carts and his slaves wheeled them from one sunny spot to the next to catch maximum sunshine. Lacking slave power, I just plant mine and they prosper— even the gherkins that climbed up a nearby cornstalk and so were partially shaded.

Health Benefits A cucumber contains over 90 percent water (more water than any other food except its relative, the watermelon). This water keeps its internal temperature several degrees cooler than the surrounding atmosphere. No wonder a cucumber is a cooling food that clears heat, quenches thirst, relieves edema, and is an effective diuretic.

Cucumbers are considered an alterative, that is, a food that tends to restore normal health because of its ability to cleanse and purify the blood and gradually alter the excretory process to restore normal body functions. It affects the heart and stomach. Cucumbers contain a digestive enzyme, erepsin, that breaks down protein, cleanses the intestines, and helps expel intestinal parasites, especially tapeworms.

Cucumbers are not advised for someone with a damp condition such as candida, cancer, or diarrhea. For someone with an excessively cold or sluggish digestion, use cucumber in moderation or seeded and cooked or seasoned with warming flavorings such as garlic, onion, and pepper.

Cucumber is used topically for minor burns—simply rub a slice over the burn—and also as a facial ingredient for clearing blemishes and for smoothing and softening the skin. Holding a cucumber slice over an itchy, inflamed eye brings relief.

Regarding the Department of Agriculture's Recommended Daily Allowance of critical nutrients, there's little going for a cucumber except that it contains negligible fat and calories. This, of course, makes it a popular dieting food.

Cucumbers are, however, a superior source of silicon, which is integral for calcium absorption and which is generally lacking in the modern diet. Silicon also helps reduce cholesterol, and it strengthens the nerve and heart tissue.

Cucumbers reduce *vata* and *pitta*.

Use In the United States, cucumbers are mainly eaten raw in salads or pickled. In Asia, they are cooked, as they were in the United States until this century. To make them more digestible, slice in half lengthwise and scoop out and discard the seeds.

If old or if raised without adequate water, cucumbers are bitter. To eliminate bitterness, cut off each end. Dip the end in salt and rub it against the exposed cucumber until foam appears. Discard the ends and rinse the foam from the cucumber.

Buying Select cucumbers that are firm, almost hard to the touch, and plump and heavy for their size. Avoid those that are pliable, have yellow on the skin or soft spots, or are withered at the stem end.

The most common cucumber, medium size with a dark green skin, is sold waxed to preserve its shelf life. A waxed cucumber, which cannot be pickled, has a shiny look and waxy feel; unwaxed, the skin is duller. Small pickling cucumbers, as well as hydroponic or the long English or burpless cucumbers individually wrapped, are not waxed.

Immature cucumbers (English cucumbers excepted) are spiny and slightly warted. As a cucumber matures, its skin smoothes out, it becomes softer, and its seeds grow larger. Gherkins, kirby cucumbers, lemon cucumbers—there are several varieties available, including round and white-skinned ones.

See **Gourd Family.**

CULTURED FOOD See **Fermented Food.**

CUMIN
(Cuminum cyminum)

Cumin is a member of the carrot family with strongly aromatic fruits, commonly called seeds. Popular in India and the Near East since antiquity, today it is produced mainly in India, Iran, Indonesia, China, and North Africa.

Health Benefits Cumin is pungent and bitter tasting, with a cooling nature. It benefits the digestive system, improves liver function, promotes the assimilation of other foods, and relieves abdominal distention, gas, and colic as well as digestive-related migraines and headaches. Cumin is *tridoshic*.

Use I use whole cumin seeds and find that, unlike such larger spices as peppercorns or coriander seeds, whole cumin blends into a long-simmered dish. Ground cumin quickly loses its essence and becomes bitter tasting. When not using the whole seed, use freshly ground cumin.

To heighten the cumin aroma, toast it in an unoiled skillet. A required ingredient in curries and masalas, it's especially popular throughout Asia and in Latin America and North Africa. I, for one, don't know how to cook a pot of beans or make a jar of pickles without adding a generous pinch of cumin. Its flavor, however, can dominate, so use sparingly unless you desire a strong cumin flavor.

Buying Ground cumin has a yellowish hue; it is ground from whole cumin that is light tan in color. Black or wild cumin, called *kala* in India, is a smaller, darker, more intensely flavored seed; it is often confused with the small black spice nigella.

See **Carrot Family; Herbs and Spices.**

CURLY CHICORY See Frisée.

CURLY ENDIVE See Frisée.

CURLY KALE See Kale.

CURRANT
Zante Currant
(Vitis vinifera)

Dry the tiny seedless champagne grape (formerly called zante grape) and you'll have a tiny raisin with a pleasing tart and tangy flavor.

The term currant is actually a derivative of Corinth, the Greek city once known for its small grapes and raisins. Currant cultivation expanded to the nearby isle of Zante, thus providing currants with their alternate name.

I prefer zante currants to raisins in most baked goods, especially cookies, because their tiny size better holds the moisture and their shape is less compromised in mixing.

See **Dried Fruit; Fruit; Grape; Raisin.**
See also **Black Currant.**

CUSTARD APPLE See Cherimoya.

CYMLING See Pattypan.

DAHLIA
(Dahlia)

The flashy dahlia is San Francisco's official flower and popular in backyard gardens across the country. Its tuber is eaten like a potato in central Mexico and, since the mid-1980s, as a natural sweetener and coffee substitute in the United States. Dahlia is a member of the sunflower family.

Health Benefits A sweet juice is extracted from the dahlia tuber and cooked at low temperatures to produce a syrup that is 93 percent inulin, a complex carbohydrate that is caloriefree. Since inulin doesn't stress the pancreas or result in an increase in sugar in the urine, it is of use for diabetics.

Buying Roasted dahlia extract is marketed in beverage products as a natural brown colorant, and as a chocolate and coffee substitute; the latter is marketed as DaCopa.

See **Coffee Substitutes; Sunflower Family.**

DAIKON
Japanese Radish
(Raphanus sativus longipinnatus)

One of my favorite vegetables is the giant daikon. I love its flavor, crisp texture, and great versatility. Daikon is a pearly white root that's shaped like a carrot and can be as long as your arm. It's an easy—and rewarding—vegetable to grow due to its surprisingly hefty yield.

Health Benefits A sweet and pungent tonic, daikon tonifies the lung and liver meridians. Fresh daikon contains diuretics, decongestants, and the digestive enzymes diastase, amylase, and esterase. It is effective against many bacterial and fungal infections and it contains a substance that inhibits the formation of carcinogens in the body. Daikon reduces *vata* and *kapha* and can be eaten in moderation by *pitta*.

Use It is not necessary to peel daikon. Wash and grate it to use raw or cut it into the desired shape and cook it as you would a carrot in soups or sautéed, simmered, baked, or braised dishes. Or cut into a fanciful shape and add it to a grilled kabob. Daikon is also a tasty pickle ingredient and condiment. Because daikon aids digestion, in Japanese cuisine it always appears alongside hard-to-digest or fatty foods.

Use the inner, younger daikon greens like turnip greens, but not in lightly sautéed dishes since their texture is rather course. In my garden, I harvest a few leaves from my row of daikon to enjoy the flavor long before I actually harvest the root.

Buying Look for heavy, hard roots with a fresh, vibrant appearance. A withered, flabby, light for its size, discolored daikon is not worth the purchase price. It will be exceedingly sharp tasting and probably pithy. Refrigerated, the root holds well for up to ten days, but is sweetest when fresh.

Daikon is shipped with its leaves attached but, as the vegetable ages, the greengrocer removes and discards the greens. When available, buy daikon with its tops intact.

DAIKON CONDIMENT

This condiment has a bright, fresh taste that clears the palate. Serve it with any meal that contains cheese, a fatty fish, or meat.

¼ cup freshly grated raw daikon
¼ teaspoon soy sauce
¼ teaspoon mirin (optional)
¼ teaspoon fresh ginger juice (see page 144) or a pinch of ground ginger powder

Combine the ingredients, mound on a small condiment plate, and serve immediately. Serves 2.

Some daikon varieties are green skinned at the very top and in some Chinese varieties the green covers half of the root. Daikon is available year-round. In Asian and natural food markets, both dried and pickled daikon is available.

See **Cabbage Family; Radish.**

DAISY FAMILY See **Sunflower Family.**

DAL
Dhal

Remove the seed coat of any legume, split it, cook it with a full contingent of spices, and you've got dal, an Indian dish as basic as rice and chapati. In fact, dal is a standard accompaniment to both. Since it is refined, dal has the shortest prep time of any dried legume, and it is easy to digest.

Buying The most readily available dal in natural food stores is made from red or white lentils. In Indian markets, there's a wide variety—such as *urad, moong, chana* or *toovar*—made from any pea, bean, or lentil that's split and decoated; dal, in India, also refers to any dried legume.

My favorite Indian cookbook, *The Art of Indian Vegetarian Cooking,* by Yamuna Devi, notes there are two ways to split dal, dry (without soaking) and wet. The more costly mechanical process, dry split, gives the most delicious dal; it is easily identified because both the flat inside and rounded outer side are smooth. Wet-split dal, on the other hand, is made by soaking, decoating, sun drying, and then splitting; the legume shrinks on the flat side, leaving a visible depression.

See **Beans and Legumes.**

DAL ENERGY

Dal is not a viable seed. Take any seed, remove its seed coat, crack it in half, and it won't germinate. In my experience, a dish of dal imparts less vital energy than does a similar serving of whole beans.

Nevertheless, dal is an ideal protein dish for a scorching July day because it cooks so quickly and it sits light on the stomach, making it easy to digest. Some people who find beans hard to digest have no complaints with dal.

DALMATIAN BEAN See Jacob's Cattle Bean.

DANDELION
(Taraxacum officinale)

Despite tons of herbicides designed to eliminate it, dandelion reigns indomitable on suburban lawns and byways. That gives a clue as to the prowess of this vegetable and to the reason that the French and others esteem it.

The dandelion is Eurasian in origin and today grows wild throughout the temperate world. The dandelion's deeply notched leaves explain its Middle Latin name, *dent leo*, tooth of the lion.

Health Benefits Dandelion, both root and leaves, is a remarkable bitter tonic for the spleen-pancreas, stomach, kidneys, and liver. While the greens are cooling, the root is considered cold or very cooling. Dandelion is an effective diuretic (its French nickname *piss-en-lit* means wet the bed), laxative, and antirheumatic. It stimulates liver function, reduces swelling and inflammation, and improves digestion. Dandelion is antiviral and useful in the treatment of AIDS and herpes. It treats jaundice, cirrhosis, edema due to high blood pressure, gout, eczema, and acne. It is used to treat (and prevent) breast and lung tumors and for premenstrual bloating. Herbalist Michael Tierra calls it one of the best remedies for the treatment of hepatitis. Dandelion root contains inulin, which lowers blood sugar in diabetics. Dandelion reduces *pitta* and *kapha*.

A cup of dandelion greens provides nearly a day's requirement of vitamin A in the form of antioxidant carotenoid and a third of the daily vitamin C requirement. It contains more calcium than broccoli and is an excellent source of potassium.

Use Fresh commercial or foraged dandelion greens (early spring) with a vinaigrette make an excellent salad alone or with other garden greens. If leaves are foraged after the plant blossoms, parboil them to reduce their bitter flavor. From late fall to very early spring, use the bittersweet root as you would a carrot, in stir-fries, soups, or simply sautéed with an onion and garlic. Or use either the root or greens—fresh or dried—in combination with other herbs for medicinal tea.

Buying/Foraging Dandelion cultivars are bred to be more tender and less bitter than the wild plant. Their light green leaves are so large and long that they hardly resemble the darker, small, and jagged-toothed wild dandelion. Cultivated dandelion greens are available in specialty markets and natural food stores.

I prefer wild dandelions—greens, crowns, and roots—gathered in the spring before they blossom. The roots and greens are also tasty in the late fall; otherwise, they're mostly bitter. For mild dandelions, pick those protected by shade or partially mulched over by leaves. Gather dandelions before the buds open and use the whole plant.

Last fall, I dug up a dandelion taproot, planted it in a pot of soil, stored it in a dark, cool closet, watered it as needed, and enjoyed tender, blanched leaves throughout the winter. The idea came from Darcy Williamson's *The Rocky Mountain Wild Foods Cookbook;* now that I've tried it, I'm going to follow her instructions more explicitly—I'm going to fill a wooden crate.

See **Sunflower Family.**

DASHEEN See **Taro.**

DATE
(Phoenix dactylifera)

The date evokes images of camel caravans plodding through barren sands toward a beckoning oasis shaded by date palms. These palms provided not only shade and fruit but some apparently thirst-quenching palm wine made by tapping the trees. The sugary sweet fruit, technically a berry, is one of the most ancient food plants of the Middle East. A tree of dry subtropical areas, the date tree thrives in—and today is planted in—areas like North Africa, Iraq, Iran, and the Coachella valley in California near Palm Springs.

Virginia Johnson, of Oasis Date Gardens in Thermal, California, recently rattled off a whole list of different date varieties that they produce, from "green" fresh dates to pocket dates dry enough to carry in your pocket but still moist enough to bite into. Her personal favorite, Halawy, "is what mother used in her fruitcakes."

Health Benefits Dates are sweet and nourishing; they influence the stomach meridian and help harmonize the liver. Unlike refined sweeteners, they build up a person and so are used for weakness, symptoms of aging, and lack of semen and impotence. On the other hand, they are not recommended for people with diabetes, obesity, yeast infections, or respiratory infections. Although dates are *tridoshic, kapha* types should use them in moderation.

As a date dries, its fructose changes to sucrose, so the drier the date, the sweeter it is. The chief nutritional value of dates is their high sugar content, which varies from 60 to 75 percent. Dates are a good source of niacin, iron, and potassium. Present in small amounts are calcium, chlorine, and magnesium, and vitamins A, B_1, and B_2.

Use Dates, either dried or fresh, are eaten as an out-of-hand snack or chopped and used to sweeten baked goods, puddings, granola, and confections. Dates are often stuffed with almonds or served alongside kumquats. Roasted date pits are used as a coffee substitute.

Buying Dates, today as in antiquity, dry naturally on the tree, making this sweet an unusual natural treat, especially when the dates are organic. Domestic dates may be dusted with sulfur to control a mite. Imported dates are fumigated.

By degree of dehydration, dates are classified in one or more of the following four types.

- **Fresh Dates** While not exactly juicy, fresh dates are higher in moisture content and lower in sugar than other dates. The yellow Bahri date is hand harvested before it dries and turns brown. This fresh date is available in some specialty markets in the fall; it is high priced. Purchase fresh dates that are plump, well colored, and have glossy skin (free from sugar crystals). Refrigerate until use.

- **Soft Dates** Allowed to sun dry on the tree, soft dates, usually the Medjool and Khadrawy varieties, are then hydrated with steam to plump them back up. The Medjool date, which many regard as the best-tasting date, is Moroccan in origin, but a virus has totally eliminated it from its native soil. Morocco hopes to replace its Medjool palms but needs seed stock from the United States. Domestic American date farmers, however, are currently enjoying their exclusive position.

- **Semidry Dates** With a low moisture, these dates have a long shelf life and are available year-round. One variety accounts for 85 percent of domestic production—the Deglet Noor, which means "date of light." Other varieties include Khadrawy, Barhi, Halawy, and Zahidi.

- **Dry Dates** This driest and least sticky date variety, the Thoory, is often called the bread date. It has a firm skin, chewy flesh, and is a staple in the diet of nomadic Middle Eastern peoples.

See **Date Sugar; Dried Fruit; Fruit.**

DATE SUGAR

Date sugar is made from 100 percent pitted dehydrated (3 to 5 percent moisture) dates that are coarsely ground; it is made from cosmetically inferior dates. Date sugar is about 65 percent fructose and sucrose. If consumed in excess, it upsets the blood sugar balance just as white sugar does. Used in moderation, though, date sugar is a quality sweetener, certainly more natural and unrefined than most. It contains all the nutrients of dried dates.

Use Date sugar is coarse and it is mainly used in two ways. One is as a sprinkle to top foods like yogurt, breakfast cereals, and baked goods (add after baking to prevent burning). The other is to dissolve date sugar in hot water to make a syrup and then, as natural foods consultant Margaret M. Whitenberg, author of *Good Food: The Complete Guide to Eating Well*, advises, use it in a similar fashion to honey, maple syrup, or rice syrup.

See **Dates; Sweeteners.**

DELICATA SQUASH
Sweet Potato Squash
(Cucurbita pepo)

Compared to other winter squash, the delicata—as its name suggests—has a more delicate flavor suggesting the sweetness of sweet corn. This small squash is shaped like a fat yellow cucumber with orange stripes. Its pale yellow flesh is moist and creamy. It's a type of acorn squash but, unlike acorn, its thin skin is edible.

See **Acorn Squash; Squash; Winter Squash.**

DENDÊ See Palm Oil.

DEVIL'S DUNG See Asafetida.

DEWBERRY
Trailing Blackberry
(Rubus caesius)

A dewberry is similar to a blackberry, but its black fruit is rather squat with a whitish bloom and the plant fruits earlier in the season. Dewberry vines, because of their less sturdy stems, grow closer to the ground than other related berries.

See **Blackberry; Fruit.**

Ø DEXTROSE

A corn-derived sweetener added to granulated cane or beet sugar to create a cheaper sugar. If sugar in the supermarket is not labeled as pure cane or beet sugar, it has been cut with dextrose. Not recommended.

See **Sweeteners.**

DHAL See Dal.

DILL
Dillweed
(Anethum graveolens)

The most popular American pickle takes its name not from what's pickled—the cucumber—but from the herb that punches up the flavor of this otherwise bland vegetable, dill. Dill is an aromatic herb with delicate lacy leaves similar in appearance to its relative fennel. As with another of its relatives, cilantro, both the leaf and seed of dill are used.

Dill's name comes from an old Norse word *dilla*, which means "to lull" because dill is a mild soporific, which is used to soothe colicky babies. In the 1800s in America, dill seeds—called "meetin' seeds"—were given to children to chew in church to help keep them quiet. The plant is native to Eurasia.

Health Benefits Dill is a pungent, warming herb that tonifies the stomach, spleen-pancreas, and liver. Its seeds are more tonic than its leaves. Dill calms the spirit, aids digestion and insomnia due to indigestion, and relieves hiccups and intestinal gas. It controls infection, is a diuretic, promotes lactation, and alleviates menstrual difficulty. Dill's warming properties help it dry overly moist conditions and therefore helps treat viral conditions. Dill is *tridoshic*.

Use Dill is milder than caraway but sweeter and more aromatic than anise. It is popular throughout Europe and much of Asia, but it is most prized in Scandinavian, Russian, and Polish cooking, where it appears in breads, sauces, salads, and with fish. In the United States, dill is most often used in pickles.

The featherlike greens are added toward the end of cooking because heat diminishes their flavor. Ideally, use fresh dill; using dry, add generously since drying diminishes its flavor. Dill seeds are flat and oval and more intensely flavored than the leaf.

Buying In August and September, yard-long stalks of fresh dill are available in supermarkets and roadside vegetable stands. Year-round, it has the same availability as other culinary herbs.

See **Carrot Family; Herbs and Spices.**

DILLISK See Dulse.

DILLWEED See Dill.

DINKEL See Spelt.

DINOSAUR KALE See Kale.

DIOSCOREA See Jinengo.

DIXIE SPECKLED BUTTER BEAN See Lima Bean.

DOU GOK See Yard-Long Bean.

DRIED BLACK FUNGUS See Wood Ear.

DRIED FRUIT

As sweet as—and more satisfying than—a candy bar, dried fruit is a natural winner. Drying food is one of the oldest ways of preserving the harvest for the lean months ahead, and though no longer the necessity it once was, it remains popular. Raisins—not grapes—are essential to an oatmeal cookie, and prunes—not plums—are a morning choice for some people seeking regularity.

Dried fruits are concentrated. Six pounds of fresh apricots, for example, yield one pound dried. A dried fruit has enough moisture removed (from 75 to 95 percent) that it is not subject to decay. To dehydrate a food, its moisture is extracted, either naturally or artificially, by air or heat or both. This darkens the color, changes the texture, destroys the vitamin C, and concentrates the sugar, minerals, and flavor.

Some fruit is still sun-dried, which is certainly the most natural method and, where labor is cheap, the most economical method. Solar drying, recently introduced on a commercial level, intensifies the sun's heat; the fruit retains more flavor and nutrients and is more tender. The United States is the largest producer of raisins and prunes.

Health Benefits In moderation, dried fruits are nutritive, they tonify the spleen-pancreas, help build muscles, and nurture body mass. Dried fruit is a concentrated source of sugar and if eaten in excess causes the blood sugar to fluctuate, compromising the pancreas. Because dried fruit is a concentrated and sticky sugar, brushing your teeth after eating it helps deter caries.

Dried fruits are easier to digest when rehydrated (especially for *vata* types). If eating dried fruits in their dry state, be sure to consume liquid, for they've a tendency to block the gut.

Use Dried fruits are a healthy sweet snack, delicious on their own, combined with nuts, added to a trail mix, or as a baking ingredient. When hydrated, they're used in fruit salads, compotes, or puréed for fruit soups and sauces.

If dried fruits are too sticky to cut with a knife, try using kitchen shears or cleaning the knife blade frequently. To plump fruit, cover with boiling water and allow to soak until softened, or gently simmer until soft, or soak overnight. The time varies depending upon the size and thickness of the fruit.

Buying It's prudent to favor domestic, organic dried fruit. When a fruit is dried, not only are its sugars concentrated but also any chemical contaminants. Most commercial fruits are grown with chemical herbicides, insecticides, and fertilizers. In addition, if the fruit is imported, it has been fumigated, and many tropical commercial fruits are adulterated with sugar.

- **Sulfured Fruits** Light rather than dark in color. If it's a golden raisin or a pale apple, apricot, or banana, it has been sulfured. This is a sobering thought, especially considering that the FDA in 1986 banned the use of sulfites on fresh produce but still permits it in dried fruits, wine, and pick-

---

HONEY-DIPPING A MANGO IS LIKE GILDING THE LILY

Corn syrup or sugar is routinely added to tropical fruits even though the label may say "honey-dipped," "unsweetened," or "fruit-juice sweetened." The fruit is soaked in a sugar-water solution until it is saturated to 80 percent sugar. Such fruits may appear in granola and trail mixes.

Emily Eterson, writing for the *Natural Foods Merchandiser* (February 1995), noted that tropical fruits that are exceptionally sweet, that have a translucent or glazed quality, or that leave a gritty residue when rubbed between your fingers are probably sweetened. Apparently customs officials check for contraband, infestation, and quality but rarely check that labels and products match.

les. Sulfur compounds destroy all the B vitamins. In sensitive individuals, they cause allergic reactions and, in some cases, death. Asthmatics are especially at risk.

- **Potassium Sorbate**   Often added to prunes and figs to keep them moist and chewy. If a dried fruit has a high moisture content, you can assume that it has a preservative; otherwise, it would be moldy.
- **Propylene Glycol**   Frequently added to coconut to retain moisture.

See **Apple; Apricot; Banana; Blueberry; Cherry; Cranberry; Coconut; Currant; Date; Fig; Guava; Jackfruit; Litchi; Mango; Mulberry; Papaya; Peach; Pear; Pineapple; Prune; Raisin; Sour Cherry; Star Fruit.**

DRIED SWEET CORN See Chicos.

DULSE
Dillisk
(Palmaria palmata)

This inexpensive food that tastes similar to jerky is an unlikely tavern snack food, but the seaweed dulse was served in Boston pubs—especially in Irish neighborhoods—through the 1920s. Today, you're not apt to find it in a bar crawl, but do try dulse at your own table. Tear the attractive red-purple fronds into bite-size pieces, mix with a bowl of salted peanuts, set out with some microbrewery beer, and see which goes first.

Dulse grows in smooth, hand-shape fronds; its Latin name means palm. It grows from the temperate to the frigid zones of the Atlantic and Pacific oceans and, oddly enough, it is one of the few seaweeds available in North America that is not eaten in Asia.

Health Benefits Medicinally, dulse is a cooling food with a salty flavor. It's used to strengthen the blood, adrenals, and kidneys and to treat herpes. For temporary relief of irritated gums or a sore tooth, pack a small piece of dulse between the lip and the painful area.

Dulse is a superior source of iron and iodine. Even though it tastes salty, it contains only 122 mg. of sodium per serving. It also contains phosphorus, potassium, magnesium, protein, and vitamin A. Dulse is a good source of vitamins E, C, and B-complex (including B_{12}), and numerous trace elements. It is about 25 percent protein, 45 percent carbohydrate, and 4 percent fat. It reduces *vata*.

Use Dulse was a popular food to eat out of hand in Ireland and Alaska. It's chewy at first, but tears or cuts easily, and has a pleasing slightly tangy, salty flavor. Dulse complements savory dishes, vegetable, grain, and fruit dishes; it is not suited to sweet or delicate dishes or baked beans.

To toast dulse, pick it over to remove any foreign material and toast it in the oven until it is crisp and the color turns slightly greenish (2 minutes at 350 degrees). Use this as a condiment, sprinkle, or addition to savory nut mixes. Toasted dulse imparts a light sea flavor to breads and casseroles.

When quickly rinsed under running water, dulse holds its color and is tender and delicious in a green salad, dressings, or as a garnish. My favorite use of dulse is as a bacon substitute in a BLT sandwich. Added to a soup, it gives a seafoodlike flavor but it should be added at the last minute since it dissolves after five minutes of cooking. In stir-fries, too, add rinsed dulse at the last minute for it to maintain its red color and texture.

Buying Dulse is available packaged in fronds, which are easily torn to the desired size. It's also available as flakes or powder for use as a condiment.

See **Seaweed.**

DURIAN
(Durio zibethinus)

An equatorial tree native to Southeast Asia, the durian bears a large fruit covered with a semihard green, formidable-looking, spiny shell. Its aroma is so fetid—it's been compared to sewer gas—that some airlines and hotels refuse to admit it. People who can get beyond its sulfurous perfume rank the durian supreme of all fruits. The durian currently has limited availability in the United States.

Use Overripe durians split along seams that are faintly visible among the spines. To open a durian, insert a stout knife into such a line. Durians have about five segments, each containing several seeds surrounded by a rich, juicy custardlike aril, which may be spooned out and eaten as is or used in baking or in a milk-based beverage, ice cream, or custard. Frozen and baked preparations diminish the aroma.

A popular Indonesian side dish, *tempoya*, is fermented durian. Half-ripe fruit is used in soups. Durian seeds are toasted and eaten.

Buying Pick a fruit that is intact, comparatively light, and with a large and solid stem. When you shake a mature durian, you should hear the seeds moving and it should exude a strong—but not sour—aroma. If it passes these tests, insert a knife in the center; if a sticky knife comes out, it is ripe.

See **Tropical Fruit.**

DURUM WHEAT See **Wheat.**

DUTCH-PROCESS See **Chocolate.**

E

EDAMAME See Green Soybean.

EDDO See Taro.

EDIBLE BLOSSOMS See Flower Blossoms.

EDIBLE CHRYSANTHEMUM See Garland Chrysanthemum.

EFAs See **Essential Fatty Acids.**

EGGPLANT
Aubergine
(Solanum melongena)

The Swedish botanist Linnaeus gave eggplant the Latin name *Solanum insanum,* because Europeans were then convinced that eating eggplant caused—on the spot—insanity. Its name has since been changed to *melongena,* which refers to its dark color. The eggplant was introduced into Europe in the thirteenth century by the Arabs in Catalonia, and its alternate name, aubergine, comes from the Arabic *al-badingan.* The first egg-

plants were the size and shape of eggs, providing our name for it.

The eggplant is a native of tropical Asia and was first cultivated in India. It is actually a berry and a member of the nightshade family. The most common eggplant in the United States is large, pear shaped, and purple with shiny patent leather–like skin. Several smaller, slender Japanese or Chinese varieties, white, lavender, gold, and green, are becoming increasingly available. They range in size from as large and slender as a cucumber to as small as an olive.

Health Benefits Eggplant is cooling and clears heat. It has a sweet flavor, reduces yang energy, and influences the stomach and large intestine meridians. It renews arteries, treats dysentery, and is used for bleeding problems and to influence blood in the lower part of the body. Eggplant brings energy and blood to the uterus while removing any congealed blood. Because of this, in Asia pregnant women are advised to eat eggplant sparingly if at all because it can cause miscarriage. Bob Flaws and Honora Wolfe, two Western authorities on Chinese medicine, in their book, *Prince Wen Hui's Cook: Chinese Dietary Therapy*, report that these same properties are medicinal in cases of sexually transmitted diseases, ovarian cysts, uterine tumors, and menstrual irregularities (including painful or suppressed menstruation). In moderation, eggplant reduces *kapha*.

Eggplants are mostly water, 90 percent, and therefore low in calories and other minerals, potassium excepted.

Use Because an eggplant is spongelike in structure with many intracellular air pockets, it soaks up oil like a sponge. When cooked until the eggplant collapses, the absorbed oil is exuded back. People wishing to reduce calories and still enjoy eggplant favor baked or simmered dishes.

An eggplant's fleshy, meaty texture makes it a favorite in numerous vegetarian dishes. In fact, eggplant is best when combined with other vegetables—especially strongly flavored vegetables—rather than with meat, fish, or poultry. It may be fried, stir-fried, sautéed, baked, or simmered.

Buying Eggplant is available year-round but is at its peak in summer. Purchase only firm and unblemished eggplants; discoloration or dents indicate a bitter fruit. Avoid spongy-to-the-touch or large eggplants. The smaller varieties generally have a thinner skin, firmer texture, sweeter flavor, and few if any seeds.

Male eggplants have fewer seeds than the female plants, and the seeds are often bitter, according to Sharon Tyler Herbst, author of *The Food Lover's Tiptionary*. The blossom end

---

AN OLD-FASHIONED TECHNIQUE THAT WORKS

To improve the flavor and digestibility of eggplant, salt and press it to draw out its acid and bitter juice. This step is especially useful for large eggplants. Cut the eggplant into half-inch slices and sprinkle generously with salt. Place on absorbent paper, cover with additional paper, place a cookie sheet or a cutting board topped with weights such as full jars or cans, and press for 30 minutes (without the weight, press for 45 minutes). Rinse off the salt, drain or pat dry, and cook as directed.

---

of a female plant is generally indented while that of the male fruit is rounded.

This highly perishable fruit should be purchased no more than two days before use. Store in a cool, not cold or hot, area. Summer and fall eggplants are grown commercially in the United States. Those available in the winter and spring are from Mexico.

See **Nightshade Family**.

ELEPHANT GARLIC
Giant Garlic
(Allium ampeloprasum)

Technically not a garlic but a close relative of the leek, elephant garlic is milder than garlic and doesn't store as well. Its cloves, the size of an apricot, are used as a vegetable rather than a flavoring agent.

See **Onion Family**.

EN CHOY See **Amaranth Greens**.

ENDIVE
(Cichorium endiva)

A heading chicory that looks much like a loose-leaf lettuce. Its leaves are narrower and more serrated than escarole but wider than frisée.

See **Chicory.**

ENGLISH PEA See Pea, Fresh.

ENOKI
Enokitake, Snow Puff
(Flammulina velutipes)

The creamy white enoki mushroom has a long, threadlike stem with a diminutive round cap; it grows in dense clusters. Its length and color are comparable to a bean sprout but its gestalt is fairy rings. It is a popular Japanese mushroom.

Health Benefits Enoki inhibits tumor growth and may prevent, as well as cure, liver disease and gastroenteric ulcers, according to herbalist and mushroom expert Christopher Hobbs, Lic.Ac. He advises against eating them raw with any frequency. Enoki contains flammutoxin, a protein toxic to the heart, which is rendered harmless when cooked.

Use Unlike other mushrooms, the enoki is not earthy but has a delicate fruity flavor. Trim and discard the base. Separate the mushrooms, rinse, and add enoki to any sautéed vegetable, grain, or meat dish. Add them at the end of cooking or cook them separately and arrange them in the finished dish so they visually stand out, for therein lies most of their enchantment. A few enoki mushrooms floating in a consommé or clear broth are exquisite.

Increasingly, enoki mushrooms are found raw in salads and salad bars; if eating enoki raw, do so only occasionally.

Buying Enoki mushrooms, packaged with their root section intact, are available in most supermarkets and natural food stores. Purchase those that are firm and white. Refrigerate, in the package, for up to two weeks.

See **Mushroom Family.**

ENOKITAKE See Enoki.

EPAZOTE
Mexican Tea, Pazote, Wormseed
(Chenopodium ambrosioides)

Epazote is indigenous to the Yucatán peninsula but now grows throughout warm European countries and the United States. Its name is taken from the Aztec word for skunk, *eptal*, and sweat, *tzotl*, which aptly describes its intense, musky-sour aroma. Epazote, a very close relative of lamb's-quarters, is a nondescript weed that grows several feet high and has irregularly toothed green leaves, sometimes splotched with red or purple.

Health Benefits An acrid and astringent herb, epazote increases perspiration and relaxes spasms. It's not used during pregnancy because it stimulates downward motion in the pelvis. Epazote, as its popular name, wormseed, suggests, is a safe and reliable vermifuge for roundworms. For a vermifuge protocol, see Michael Moore's *Medicinal Plants of the Desert and Canyon West*. Moore does not recommend it as an abortifacient or a menstrual stimulant, despite its reputation as such. "There have been many cases of poisoning from taking large amounts of the tea or the distilled oil, and it seldom works. On the other hand, all parts of the plant are effective externally for fungal infections, barber's itch, athlete's foot, and ringworm, as well as being somewhat antibacterial." It reduces *vata*.

HANGOVER SOUP

Copeland Marks, in *False Tongues and Sunday Bread: A Guatemalan and Mayan Cookbook*, gives an epazote and egg soup recipe traditionally used as a hangover cure, *Caldo de huevo para la goma*. Epazote's ability to increase perspiration would indeed help detoxify, and if you've got the shakes, it would help there as well. Hangover or otherwise, this is a delicious and easy-to-make soup.

2 cups water
½ teaspoon chile powder
¼ cup chopped tomato
2 chopped scallions
½ cup chopped fresh epazote leaves
2 eggs

Bring all the ingredients but the eggs to a boil. Simmer for 15 minutes. Drop the eggs into the simmering soup and poach until firm, about 10 minutes. Take care not to break the yolks. Serve hot. Serves 2.

Use Epazote has a mild antiseptic flavor that is ingratiating. Foods, especially beans, but also soups, meats, and vegetables, are seasoned with epazote leaves to enhance digestibility, add flavor, and reduce flatus levels.

Buying/Foraging Look for fresh epazote in regional southwestern markets and in Asian stores. Look for it dried in herb stores, natural food stores, and mail-order suppliers. Or refer to a food foraging book as odds are it's growing in a nearby vacant lot.

See **Goosefoot Family; Herbs and Spices; Lambs-Quarter.**

EQUAL See Aspartame.

ESCAROLE
(Cichorium endiva)

Escarole is a bitter-tasting chicory that looks like a loose-leaf lettuce. Its leaves are broader and less curly than endive and more sturdy. It is more readily available than endive or frisée.

See **Chicory; Endive; Frisée.**

ESSENTIAL FATTY ACIDS (EFAs)

In decreasing order of importance, the nutrients our life depends upon are air, water, carbohydrates, protein, essential fatty acids (EFAs), fats, then vitamins; last are minerals and micronutrients. EFAs, as their name suggests, are an essential nutrient. Although all nutrients are important, consider spending your grocery dollar on quality EFAs before spending it on vitamin or mineral supplements.

There are two critical EFAs. The most

fragile, and most lacking EFAs in our diet, are Omega-3s. Counting up, Omega-6 fatty acids are more stable and more available in most diets. (Omega-9 fatty acids are the most stable and are not lacking in American diets.) To concentrate on Omega-3 and Omega-6: The primary Omega-3 fatty acid is alpha-linoleic acid, and flax seed oil is its richest source. It is also found in hemp seeds, canola seeds, chia seeds, pumpkin seeds, walnuts, and dark leafy vegetables. Two derivatives of Omega-3 fatty acids exist: EPA (eicosapentaenoic acid) and DHA (docosahexanenoic acid), and their food sources include microalgae, fish-liver oil, and cold-water fish such as wild (not farmed) salmon, tuna, herring, mackerel, and sardines.

The primary Omega-6 fatty acid is linoleic acid, and its food sources include sesame seeds, pumpkin seeds, safflower oil, sunflower oil, and many nuts. Two subcategories of Omega-6 fatty acids exist: gamma-linoleic acid (GLA), available in evening primrose oil, borage oil, and black currant oil, and arachidonic acid, available in meat and other animal products.

Health Benefits When there is an EFA deficiency, the whole body declines and eventually dies. These acids are needed for healthy cell function, brain development, nerve coverings, hormones, bile acids, and prostaglandins. EFAs help maintain healthy blood, circulation, and immune and nervous systems. They transport fat-soluble vitamins, promote normal growth and healthy skin, and contribute to the fatty tissue that surrounds, protects, and holds the organs in place.

EFA deficiency is associated with cardiovascular disease, atherosclerosis, inflammatory bowel disease, cystic fibrosis, brain and behavioral dysfunction, strokes, hypertension, celiac disease, kidney failure, pressure in the eye and joints, water retention, allergic response, multiple sclerosis, and cancer. By adding EFAs back to the diet, many of these maladies are ameliorated.

Use Many people take a tablespoon per day of unrefined flax oil or a blend of flax and other oils that provide the ideal essential fatty acid balance. Use this as a nutritional supplement or as a dressing for salads, baked potatoes, or steamed vegetables. Because of their high Omega-3 content, do not heat unrefined flax or flax oil blends.

Barry Sears, in *The Zone*, offers a different approach for vegetarians, especially women, to stabilize EFA metabolism. It is to consider using some meat medicinally.

Coconut oil, olive oil, and sesame oil are the three best Omega-9 vegetable oils for culinary use because they contain no fragile Omega-3s. While coconut oil withstands higher temperatures, use olive oil and sesame oil only for light sautéing and stir-frying over low to medium heat (325 degrees).

Buying Because EFAs have a limited shelf life and are destroyed by light and heat, take the following precautions. Purchase any oil that contains EFAs in small quantities. Purchase only Omega-3 oils that list their date of manufacture and a "best if used by" date stamped on the container. Purchase oils bottled in opaque, black, inert plastic bottles.

See **Fat and Oil.**

ETROG See Citron.

EVAPORATED CANE JUICE See **Rapadura;**
Sugar.

EVENING PRIMROSE OIL
(Oenothera biennis)

Not until dusk in the late spring or early
summer does the primrose unfurl its delicate
petals. Then to compound the wonder, in the
moonlight they glow luminescently. On the
waterways of sage-covered areas, it's always
a thrill to come upon the evening primrose,
a plant native to North America. In the West,
their four-petaled blossoms are a white-
green whereas in the eastern and central
states the blossoms are yellow.

Health Benefits An oil extracted from
primrose seeds contains gamma-linoleic acid
(GLA); it is successful in treating a wide
range of medical problems, including arthritis, premenstrual syndrome, obesity, cardiovascular ailments, hyperactivity, diabetes,
skin disease, and allergies.

Supplementing the diet with evening
primrose oil or other GLA-containing substances may be appropriate for some. Prudent for all would be to avoid those
substances that create biochemical obstacles
to the body's own formation of GLA. That
would include a diet heavy in saturated fats
and cholesterol, processed vegetable oil, and
alcohol. Even if your consumption of alcohol
and saturated fats is minimal, consider that
virtually all baked goods, chips, salad dressings, and restaurant foods contain processed
vegetable oils.

Use The primrose root is a long, fleshy
taproot with firm, white flesh, rather like salsify. It is a tasty vegetable but one that requires that you forage it or grow it yourself.
As with burdock, harvest just the first
year's roots.

See **Essential Fatty Acids; Fat and Oil;**
Gamma-Linoleic Acid.

FARINA
Cream of Wheat

"Middlings," or small hard bits of wheat, are sold as a hot breakfast cereal. In the past, after the germ and bran were removed from wheat, it was ground and then bolted, or sifted through a coarsely woven fabric for the end product, flour. The middle product was farina, granular nubbins, too coarse to go through the cloth. Farina is the Italian word for meal or flour.

See **Wheat**.

FARRO See **Spelt**.

FAT AND OIL

Fat is sexy. Oil—fat in a liquid state—is sexy, too. Here's why. A most critical part of any plant is its seed's fatty acids, which store sunlight energy to start anew. No wonder these delicate oils found in the plant's reproductive parts contain more flavor and aroma than the rest of the plant.

Consider, for example, an eight-foot-tall corn plant including its root system. Only the kernels of this huge plant contain oil, and, at that, each kernel contains only 5 percent fat. One huge plant yields only a few grams of oil. It's precious stuff. From the point of view of human health, oil is even more precious. Every single living cell in our bodies requires essential fatty acids for construction and maintenance.

Befitting their preciousness, oils require careful handling. Light and heat quickly destroy them, and consuming denatured oils accelerates our aging and damages our immune system. We can't live well without oils, and if they are denatured, we can't live well with them. The choice is obvious. Consume quality fats and oils.

Unfortunately, consuming only quality oils requires vigilance. Almost all restaurant foods and baked goods, soups, salad dressings, and prepared foods that you buy contain a denatured oil. In the United States, up to 40 percent of calories consumed are in the form of fat—it's a billion-dollar industry.

There are three different types of fat: saturated, monosaturated, and polyunsaturated.

Any given fat or oil is a blend of one or more of these types. The predominately saturated fats, like butter and coconut oil, are solid at room temperature. Olive oil, a monosaturate, thickens when chilled but is fluid at room temperature. Canola and sunflower oil, primarily polyunsaturated fats, remain liquid when chilled.

Health Benefits We all need fat. Dietary fats produce body fat needed to insulate and keep us warm and to protect and hold our vital organs in place. The fat-soluble vitamins—vitamins A, D, E, and K—need fat to be bioavailable. Fats help us feel grounded; they impart a sense of feeling soothed and comforted; and they help provide energy and warmth.

Ø Refined fats, however, are carcinogenic; they suppress the immune system; they cause gastric distress and irritated lungs and mucus membranes; and they speed aging. Overconsumption of fats—whether unrefined or refined—can cause a person to be mentally, physically, or emotionally heavy, overly materialistic or grasping. Excessive fats and/or poor quality fats challenge the liver and exacerbate cancer, candida, tumors, cysts, edema, obesity, and some forms of high blood pressure.

Use I recommend butter and coconut oil for baking and sautéing because of their stability and great flavor. For light sautéing, I recommend extra virgin olive oil and unrefined sesame oil, which withstand moderate heat because they contain no fragile Omega-3 fatty acids. For salads, marinades that will not be cooked, and to dress steamed vegetables or grains, use your favorite unrefined nut or seed oil.

FOOLPROOF TEST OF GOOD OIL

It doesn't take a Ph.D. in chemistry to discern good oils from bad. It's as simple as taste and smell. Compare a superior extra virgin olive oil with a pure olive oil. If the oil smells and tastes like the food from which it was pressed, that's one indication of quality. If it leaves a fresh, rather than an acrid, burning, or metallic taste in your mouth, it passes a second test. There is also a third indicator, how the oil feels in your mouth.

Within seconds of swallowing a teaspoon of vital oil, your mouth feels fresh and clean. It's as if your body, knowing that good oil is indispensable, invites it right in. Conversely, an oil denatured by oxygen or high heat (due to shoddy production or storage) has a greasy taste, coats the mouth, and isn't readily soluble. The body doesn't want to absorb it. If denatured oil tastes greasy in your mouth, imagine how it gums up arteries and challenges the liver, the organ primarily responsible for fat metabolism.

To safely sauté with sesame, coconut, or olive oil, all you need to do is smell. Pour some oil into a sauté pan. Heat it until it is aromatic, then quickly add and sauté other ingredients. If heated until slight ripples form, the oil is too hot and close to the smoke point. This toxic level of heat is, according to Madeleine Kamman in *The New Making of a Cook*, ''when the oil releases a bluish smoke. If the smoke develops to the point of irritating eyes and throat, acrolein

OIL GLOSSARY

- **Cold Pressed** This marketing term is without regulation or accepted meaning.
- **Expeller Pressed or Pure Pressed** Cooked seeds or grains are mechanically pressed in an expeller (screw) press at such a high speed that high temperatures result. Because of this heat, and the exposure to light and air, the oils begin—from the moment of their pressing—to oxidize and deteriorate. These oils may be termed *unrefined*. However, after pressing, they may be deodorized at temperatures exceeding 500 degrees.
- **High Oleic** Seeds that are genetically manipulated to decrease their essential fatty acids yield an oil with a longer shelf life, one that withstands higher heat. I pass on all genetically modified organisms (GMOs) and strongly encourage you to do the same. Some high oleic oils, however, are derived from hybrid, rather than GMO, seeds. Examine the oil label for the manufacturer's stand on GMO material.
- **Refined** To increase an oil's shelf life, its color, flavor, and aroma are removed through a multistepped, high-tech refining process that uses toxic solvents, caustic soda, bleaches, and phosphoric acid. In addition, supermarket oils typically contain synthetic antioxidants and chemical defoamers. Sometimes these oils bear a health food label. Buyer beware.
- **Solvent extracted or cold processed** Mashed seeds are bathed in a petroleum solvent to separate the oil from the meal. It's the most efficient and least healthful method of oil production because not all of the solvents may be recovered. If the oil label does not indicate how it was extracted, you may assume that solvents were used.

has formed and . . . you are very close to the flash point, which is reached when the mixture of smoke and air spontaneously ignite."

If the oil does smoke, remove the pan from the heat and allow it to cool. Wipe out all traces of the damaged oil. Start over. Heat the oil, and when it's aromatic, add other ingredients.

An even more healthful—but less thermally warming—alternative to sautéing is to water-sauté. To preserve the integrity of sesame or olive oil, Michael A. Schmidt, M.D., in his book *Smart Fats: How Dietary Fats and Oils Affect Mental, Physical and Emotional Intelligence*, recommends the following. Heat a small amount of water in a pan or skillet, add and sauté food, and, at the end of cooking, add oil. "This shortens the time the oil is in contact with the heat, yet preserves the flavor of the food."

Some health literature recommends that vegetable oils high in Omega-6 such as safflower, sesame, and sunflower may be baked at 325 degrees because the interior temperature will not exceed 212 degrees, the temperature at which Omega-6s are denatured.

What, I ask, about the exterior of that muffin? The fatty acids in the crust will be toxic. I bake only with fats that withstand higher temperatures—butter and coconut oil.

Buying With the exception of *quality* extra virgin olive oil in a can, I do not buy or recommend buying bottled oils from the shelf—even if they say unrefined. Other quality oils produced by several different companies are refrigerated or are available by mail order (see page 400) and they have the following guarantees on their label:

- Pressing temperature (buy only if pressed under 115 degrees).
- Pressed in the absence of light and oxygen.
- Packaged with an inert gas to protect it from air.
- Bottled in a black, opaque, inert plastic bottle to protect it from light, or, optionally, in the case of olive or plam oil, in a can.
- Date of manufacture and "best if used by" date listed.

Less common oils not discussed separately include: almond, apricot kernel, avocado, hazelnut, poppy seed, and pumpkin seed. As with all oils, use them only if they meet the listed criteria for quality, and if they taste and smell like the food from which they were pressed.

See **Butter; Canola Oil; Clarified Butter; Coconut Oil; Corn Oil; Cottonseed Oil; Essential Fatty Acids; Flax Oil; Ghee; Grape Seed Oil; Hemp Oil; Margarine; Olive Oil; Palm Kernel Oil; Palm Oil; Peanut Oil; Rice Bran Oil; Safflower Oil; Sesame Oil; Soy Oil; Sunflower Oil; Walnut Oil.**

FAVA BEAN
Broad Bean, Horse Bean
(Vicia faba)

As the words "broad" and "horse" suggest, the fava bean is big—larger even than a lima bean. It also has an Old World hearty quality. The fava is one of the most ancient cultivated vegetables; it has been found with Iron Age relics in various parts of Europe. Prior to Columbus, and the subsequent introduction of the American *vulgaris* bean varieties to the other major continents, fava beans were a mainstay throughout much of the world. Today, with innovative American chefs, the fava is a popular spring and early summer shell bean.

Health Benefits The fava bean is neutral in its thermal nature, has a sweet flavor, and tonifies the spleen-pancreas and kidney meridians. It improves blood circulation and water metabolism. Lui Jilin, in *Chinese Dietary Therapy*, notes this historical Chinese use of fava beans: For loss of appetite and loose stool owing to weakness in the spleen and stomach meridians, take powdered broad bean mixed with boiling water and brown sugar. For edema and difficult urination due to a deficiency of the spleen-pancreas function, drink tea made of broad beans. A small number of people, mostly boys and especially of Mediterranean origin, can develop acute hemolytic anemia, or favism, after eating fava beans. Fava beans reduce *pitta*.

Use Fresh favas are available in the spring. Immature pods, up to three inches long, may be cooked whole. The large coarse green pod is shucked to get at the beans, which have a delicate, slightly earthy flavor. They are usually peeled, especially as the beans become more mature. This may be done before cooking or the beans may be blanched and peeled.

Buying Fresh favas are increasingly available in Mexican, Italian, Middle Eastern, and farmers' markets. Favor small, crisp pods with a bright green color and minimal discoloration. Don't, however, bypass larger and more mature specimens; although the pods aren't edible, the beans themselves are flavorful if slightly less delicate tasting. One pound of pods yields only ½ cup of beans, so purchase accordingly. Although fresh favas may be stored refrigerated (in a paper bag, not plastic) for a few days, plan to use them quickly.

Purchase dried favas, either whole or skinned and split, from a market with a wide selection of dried beans or from a specialty market. Some such markets also sell fava flour.

FEIJOA
Pineapple Guava
(Feijoa sellowiana)

Native to southern Brazil and northern Argentina, the feijoa (fay-JOH-ah) is a subtropical evergreen tree that bears small, bumpy fruits that look like fuzzless kiwis. The fruit is lime green in color and has a tart, tutti-frutti flavor. A feijoa's strong perfume suggests pineapple, strawberry, spruce, quince, and mint. It has a granular but creamy whitish flesh that surrounds a jelly-like central cavity filled with tiny edible

---

BEANS AND THE FATHER OF MATHEMATICS

Pythagoras, a Greek philosopher of the fifth century B.C., discovered the numerical relationship of musical tones and is considered the father of mathematics. He's also remembered for founding a religious brotherhood with prohibitions against eating beans because, he maintained, they caused cloudy thinking.

It is believed that Pythagoras suffered from favism, a congenital adverse reaction to fava beans. It made sense for him and other such sensitive people to avoid this tasty bean, but pity the rest of his buddies.

---

seeds. The U.S. commercial supply is grown in California and New Zealand.

Health Benefits The feijoa is a rich source of water-soluble iodine compounds, ranging from 1.5 to 4 milligrams per kilogram of fresh fruit.

Use When the fruit is slightly soft and ripe, peel or spoon the flesh out of the shell and enjoy it as is or in almost any preparation calling for bananas or apples. The feijoa is tasty in yogurt, fruit salads, compotes, and other deserts. It may be made into jam or jelly. Puréed, it is an excellent flavoring for ice cream, sherbet, flans, or puddings. Note, however, a feijoa's strong fragrance overpowers milder-tasting ingredients.

Buying Select a feijoa with a full fruity aroma. If it is not as tender as a peach, ripen at room temperature until it is soft, then refrigerate and use within a day and two. Immature feijoas are bitter. Domestic feijoas are available in the fall; imported fruits are available in the spring and early summer.

See **Tropical Fruit.**

FENNEL
Finocchio, Florence Fennel, Sweet Fennel
(Foeniculum vulgare var. dulce or azoricum)

There are two distinct varieties of fennel, a Mediterranean parsley relative. Wild fennel (*F. vulgare*) has the small flat seeds, technically the fruits, which are used as a spice; the greens are used as an herb. Sweet or Florence fennel (*F. vulgare* var. *dulce*) is used as a vegetable. This type has a large, bulblike base, hollow stalks, and threadlike leaves. Sweet fennel has a pleasing licorice flavor.

Health Benefits Sweet and spicy with some bitter tones, fennel is a warming herb. Although the whole plant is used medicinally, the seeds are highest in the volatile oil anethole, which treats indigestion, gas, and spasms of the digestive tract and increases peristalsis. It helps expel phlegm from the lungs. Fennel is weakly estrogenic and helps stimulate lactation and menstrual periods and facilitate birth. It also contains the antioxidant flavonoid quercetin and is therefore anticarcinogenic and of special use for cancer patients following radiation or chemotherapy. Fennel is considered *tridoshic*.

Use Fennel seed is used throughout the northern hemisphere as an ingredient in curries, breads, crackers, pickles, vinegar, vegetable and grain dishes, sausages, liqueur, and

---

PERSIANS AND FENNEL TROMPED UPON AT FIRST MARATHON

In 490 B.C. in a fennel field some 26 miles from Athens, the Greeks defeated the Persians. An Athenian runner bearing this welcome news raced backed to town. Since then, the length of a marathon race has remained the same as from the fennel field into town, or 26 miles and 385 yards. The Greek name for fennel is marathon.

---

to season apple pie. In Indian restaurants, a saucer of fennel seeds is served after a meal as a digestive. Wild fennel leaves are also used as an herb in the Mediterranean.

As a vegetable, fennel has been used mainly in the Mediterranean region and only recently in the United States. I use the whole vegetable—cooked or raw—in any recipe calling for celery. Its feathery leaves can serve both as a garnish and as a flavoring agent. Cooking softens its licorice flavor.

Buying Peak season for sweet fennel is fall through spring. Select unblemished bulbs, which look crisp and have fresh blue-green leaves. The bulb should be medium size, well developed, firm, and white. Trimmed stalks indicate an old vegetable.

See **Carrot Family; Herbs and Spices.**

FENUGREEK
(Trigonella foenum-graecum)

Fenugreek is a member of the large legume family, but it is used as a spice. Fenugreek seeds are mustard yellow, rhombic (unequal adjacent sides) in shape, and smaller than a grain of wheat. Fenugreek is potent indeed, not currently a popular spice in Western countries but one of the oldest known and most valued medicinal plants.

Health Benefits Fenugreek is a bitter aromatic. It tonifies the liver and kidneys and the male sexual organs. It increases milk flow, stimulates the uterus (not for use in pregnancy, though it is excellent for postpartum use), enhances digestion, helps treat allergies, and has antiparasitic and antitumor effects. Fenugreek is helpful for wasting diseases, gout, anemia, and debility. In clinical studies, fenugreek reduces cholesterol and is therefore useful for preventing atherosclerosis. It also helps regulate sugar levels of non-insulin-dependent diabetics. Today, it is an ingredient in some oral contraceptives. Fenugreek balances *vata* and *kapha*.

Use Raw fenugreek seeds have a nasty, uncooked-bean taste. Toasting reduces the bitter taste and gives the seeds a pleasant aroma and flavor. If overtoasted, however, they become bitter, so just lightly toast them until aromatic. If you inadvertently overtoast fenugreek, one taste will tell; from then on, you will have a sense of how much is enough.

In Ethiopia and throughout the Middle East and in India, fenugreek is a common spice in pickled dishes and spice blends. Sprouted fenugreek seeds may be substituted for alfalfa sprouts in salads and sandwiches. Indians use fresh fenugreek leaves (*methi*) as a spinachlike vegetable and sometimes add them to chapatis. In the Middle East and India, dried fenugreek leaves are used to flavor vegetables and baked goods.

See **Herbs and Spices.**

FERMENTED FOOD

A baby in utero has a sterile digestive tract. Within two days of birth, cultures of microorganisms from his mother's milk have established themselves in his gut—by adulthood, there will be four hundred species of bacteria in the colon. Consumption of certain fermented foods helps build and maintain the population of intestinal flora. Fermentation increases digestibility, adds flavor, increases nutrition but not calories, and enhances texture.

Health Benefits Fermentation, in a manner of speaking, is the predigestion of foods before consumption. Molds, yeast, and bacteria break down the complex components of the original ingredients and synergistically create a superior food. Lactic acid bacteria are among the principal bacteria active in food fermentation; they contribute to the sour flavor and aroma of fermented foods and inhibit the growth of unfavorable organisms. Lactic acid bacteria in fermented foods help the body produce natural antibiotics, natural anticarcinogenic compounds, and even compounds that retard or inactivate toxins and poisons. Lactobacilli help prevent cholesterol formation and completely eliminate an antinutritional factor in soybeans. Undesirable phytic acids found in grains, beans, and seeds are totally removed when fermented.

YOUR 100 TRILLION INTIMATE FRIENDS

No one has done an exact nose count, but your gastrointestinal tract provides room and board to more enzymes, fungi, and bacteria (100 trillion) than there are people in the world. By the pound, that adds up to three and a half pounds of intestinal flora in the healthy adult intestine. The question is: Are these critters doing their job of assimilating food and maintaining your vitality or are they wreaking havoc?

If you're in robust health, then your numerous colonies of various microorganisms dwell in a balanced, harmonious environment. If, however, you've taken antibiotics, which kill both the good and the bad bacteria, then the odds are that one or more communities of microorganisms are growing out of control. This creates a toxic internal environment.

To rebuild your population of digestive partners, use a quality fermented food daily; you may also wish to use a probiotic supplement. A probiotic supplement repopulates the digestive system with healthful microorganisms essential to proper digestion; it thereby strengthens the immune system and inhibits cancer, bowel disease, and pathogens. A probiotic supplement also aids in the digestion of protein, fats, and carbohydrates and the assimilation of vitamins. When selecting a probiotic supplement, choose one that lists the viable cell count and identifies the organisms. Most probiotic supplements require refrigeration.

Substances that decimate intestinal flora include broad-spectrum antibiotics, some other medications, antiseptic mouthwashes, alcoholic beverages, and chlorinated drinking water.

Buying Unfortunately, the fermented foods most often found in markets and restaurants are dead—rather than living—foods. The microorganisms they contained were killed by heat and/or additives to create a consistent product with increased shelf life.

Quality fermented foods available in most natural food stores and with entries in this book are listed below. Other fermented foods that may augment intestinal flora—providing they're unpasteurized—include micro-brewery beer, traditionally aged cheese from unpasteurized milk, kefir, wine, yogurt, and naturally brewed soft drinks (see page 402). Homemade vegetable pickles such as dill pickles, kim chee (see recipe, page 78), and sauerkraut do the same, providing they're not canned or cooked. There is one brand of raw sauerkraut available in the refrigerated section of many natural food stores that is produced by Rejuvenative Foods (see page 402).

See **Amasake; Apple Cider Vinegar; Brown Rice Vinegar; Kombucha; Miso; Natto; Olive; Soy Sauce; Tempeh; Umeboshi.**

FIDDLEHEAD FERN
Ostrich Fern
(Matteuccia struthiopteris)

Tightly curled fern embryos look like the scrolled end of a violin and taste like asparagus with woodsy tones. This wild food treat enjoyed in northern climes worldwide includes the new green shoots of ferns in general, but particularly the ostrich fern. This variety grows along stream banks and in moist pastures, woods, and shaded mountain slopes. The fiddlehead is thus far not cultivated. It is a foraged food with limited availability.

Butch Wells, Jr., of W. S. Wells & Son in Wilton, Maine, is a fourth-generation fiddlehead processor of canned and freeze-dried local items. A good season for Wells is to process 40 tons of fiddleheads brought to his plant by local foragers in large green trash bags. In *Edible Native Plants of the Rocky Mountains*, H. D. Harrington reports that in Japan and Korea fiddleheads are parboiled, sun dried, and set aside for winter use. In Siberia and Norway, fiddleheads are fermented into a type of beer.

Use Fresh fiddleheads are a remarkable delicacy, likened to asparagus, artichokes, and morels. Eat them raw as a trail food if you're out in the woods.

To cook fiddleheads, first soak them in cold water and then lightly brush or rinse them to remove their brown, flaky casings. Sauté in butter or steam them for 5 minutes, or until tender. Season with salt and a little lemon juice. Because they lose flavor rapidly, use them within a day of picking or purchasing.

Buying/Foraging "When the flocks of geese have flown over and danger of frost is almost past," advises Frances Hamerstrom, author of *Wild Food Cookbook*, "it is time to look for fiddleheads. . . . Often they are one of the dominant ground cover plants in young woods, and they may invade pastures and meadows in abundance." If fiddleheads grow in your area, by all means forage. Collect the tightly coiled plants when they're under four inches in diameter.

Fresh, freeze-dried, and canned fiddleheads are available in specialty markets. Look for small, vital, jade green young shoots, tightly furled. In the market, avoid any that are wilted, rotted, or more than two inches in diameter.

Caution: Food writer Elizabeth Schneider, in *Uncommon Fruits and Vegetables*, warns against the bracken fern (*Pteridium aquilinum*), which may be extremely carcinogenic. It is consumed both domestically and in Japan. Schneider cites Dr. John Mickel, fern curator at the Bronx Botanic Garden in New York, as "adamant that the fern, the fiddlehead commonly marketed, is the only one that is definitely noncarcinogenic."

FIG
(Ficus carica)

Botanically, the fig is fascinating. Bite into the small opening (ostiole) at the bottom of a fig—dried or fresh—and surrounding the hole you'll see the threadlike male stamen. Beyond that opening, hundreds of seeds fill the fig's cavity. Imagine these when immature as hundreds of miniature buds, which blossomed, were pollinated (although some varieties

Fig • *129*

self-pollinate), and then matured into seeds. It reminds me of a secret harem hidden inside the oval fruit.

Wind and insects usually pollinate blossoms. Pollinization occurs inside the Smyrna fig in a unique way. A female, gnat-size fig wasp (*Blastophaga psenes*) hatches inside an inedible caprifig. As the wasp crawls out of the ostiole, it gets covered with pollen. Once inside a Smyrna fig, the wasp futilely attempts to lay her eggs, but her ovipositor is too long. The wasp goes into a death frenzy, and the flowers become pollinated. As the fruit ripens, its enzymes assimilate the dead wasp. Smyrna fig growers caprify their figs by placing a branch of wasp-infected caprifigs near their blossoming Smyrna trees.

The fig originated in southwestern Asia and was one of the first cultivated fruits from Asia to the Mediterranean. A species of fig, the bo, is the tree under which Siddhartha Gautama sat and Buddhism was born. Most domestic figs are grown in the orchard country surrounding Fresno, California, which calls itself the Fig Capital of the World.

Health Benefits Figs are neutral in their thermal properties. They increase energy, reinforce the stomach and spleen-pancreas meridians, and are lubricating to the lung and large intestine meridians (and are therefore useful in the case of a dry cough and as a mild laxative). Figs aid digestion by cleansing and soothing the intestine; they also treat dysentery. In England, Syrup of Figs is a well-known medicinal preparation for constipation; it is included in the British Pharmaceutical Codex. An old Italian kitchen remedy for a lingering cough is lightly roasted dried figs eaten just before bedtime. Figs are *tridoshic,* but dried figs best balance *kapha* and fresh figs best balance *vata.*

Of the common fruits, the fig has the highest sugar content. Dried, a fig is about 50 percent sugar; fresh, about 10 percent. Dried figs have more dietary fiber than prunes, and—ounce for ounce—are higher in calcium than cow's milk. Figs have a notable amount of protein, and abundant magnesium, phosphorus, and potassium.

Use Figs can be enjoyed fresh, dried, or canned. The soft juicy texture has a sweet, nutlike flavor. Roasted, they make a rich addition to hot beverages.

Buying Round or pear-shape fresh figs are available in shades of white, green, purple, and red. Because of their fragility, they're seldom available fresh, except in Cal-

By what miracle
does this cracker
made from Kansas wheat,
this cheese ripened in French caves,
this fig, grown and dried near Ephesus,
turn into Me?
My eyes,
My hands,
My cells, organs, juices, thoughts?

Am I not then Kansas wheat
and French cheese
and Smyrna figs?
Figs, no doubt,
the ancient Prophets ate?

—Judith Morley

ifornia and a few southern states where they are grown and in specialty markets. Select plump, soft figs with the skin intact and with a fresh aroma. Figs that are starting to dry are acceptable. The new crop is available in late August to early September.

Dried figs should be sweet smelling and slightly moist. The two dried fig types most commonly available in the United States are the light-colored Calimyrna and the dark purple Mission fig. The former was a Turkish native, Smyrna, and was named Calimyrna to acknowledge its ancestry and its new California homeland. The Mission fig took its name from the Spanish missionaries, who introduced it to California.

See **Dried Fruit; Fruit.**

FILBERT See **Hazelnut.**

FILÉ See **Sassafras.**

FINOCCHIO See **Fennel.**

FLAGEOLET
(Phaseolus vulgaris)

Called the Rolls-Royce of Beans by Sheryl and Mel London in *The Versatile Grain and the Elegant Bean,* the flageolet is a medium-size, kidney-shape bean, pale green in color. Cultivated primarily in France and Italy, it is an American variety bean that is harvested and dried before it reaches maturity. The flavor is very delicate and creamy, with an herblike essence. Flageolets are pricey.

For a homegrown quasi-flageolet substitute, allow green beans to mature in the pod just beyond their best eating stage. For authentic flageolets, purchase their seeds from a seed company that offers European varieties. Or buy them dried or canned, as a French import. Flageolets are delicious, fresh or dried, cooked until tender, drizzled with olive oil, and served warm.

See **Beans and Legumes.**

FLAT CABBAGE See **Tatsoi.**

FLAX OIL

Flax oil is considered a drying oil because it readily combines with oxygen, then thickens and hardens. Available by its industrial name, linseed oil, it makes an excellent varnish; stir in pigment and you've got a paint that will dry to a hardened gloss. Our interest in flax oil is, however, culinary.

In northern European countries too cold to produce the more stable olive oil, freshly pressed flax oil was the primary culinary oil until World War II. It was sold, freshly pressed, by street vendors, who made weekly rounds through a neighborhood; a fresh and healthful product was assured. For the four decades following the war, fresh flax oil was not commercially available because large commercial oil mills produced cheap oil with a long shelf life.

Then in the 1980s, investigative reporters like Udo Erasmus, author of *Fats and Oils,* disclosed how damaging refined oils are. He, research scientists, and people in the natural foods industry helped encourage the production of quality flax oil, which is once again commercially available.

Health Benefits Unlike flax seed, the oil

doesn't have laxative or expectorant properties. The oil can be used daily, however, as a reliable source of Omega-3 fatty acids. As such, it plays a critical role in healthy brain function and structure. Flax oil helps support proper thyroid, adrenal, and hormone activity. It strengthens the immune system and helps maintain healthy blood, nerves, arteries, skin, and hair. Flax oil helps transport fat-soluble vitamins and cholesterol and also helps to break down cholesterol.

Use Do not heat flax oil since heating denatures its fatty acids. Use flax oil in dressings and uncooked marinades or drizzle over steamed vegetables. Some people take flax oil, by the spoonful or in capsules, as a dietary supplement. If flax oil tastes at all acrid, is intensely bitter, or feels scratchy in the throat, it is old and should be discarded.

See **Fat and Oil.**

FLAX SEED
Linseed
(Linum usitatissimum)

Flax is a bright plant with small blue flowers topping slender but tough stems—a soothing sight to see. And when the seeds are encased in a small silk eye pillow (available in health food stores), they soothe tired eyes. The fibrous flax stems are spun into linen and used in paper making. Linen and linseed oil have culinary and industrial uses. But in terms of health, the tiny, flat, brown seeds are most outstanding, for flax is the richest source there is of Omega-3 fatty acids.

Flax was used by late Stone Age lake dwellers in what is now Switzerland and cultivated in Babylon around 5000 B.C., making

---

> ### EGG SUBSTITUTE FOR BAKING
>
> Flax seeds lend richness to baked goods, according to Lorna Sass, in *Recipes from an Ecological Kitchen*. Ground flax seeds blended with water develop a texture akin to egg whites, and, as a result, they bind the ingredients in a batter to provide a modest amount of leavening.
>
> Grind 3 tablespoons flax seeds in a blender or spice mill. If using a spice mill, transfer to a food processor or continue by hand. Add ½ cup water and blend until the mixture is slightly gummy, about 30 seconds. If using a food processor, add the water and process until slightly thickened, about 60 to 90 seconds. Or whisk the ground seed and water mixture vigorously by hand about 100 times. Use in place of 2 large eggs.

---

it one of mankind's earliest food supplies. In the eighth century, Charlemagne considered flax so essential for health that he passed laws requiring its use.

Health Benefits Flax seeds are a sweet, thermally neutral food that tones the stomach and colon meridians. Flax seeds contain up to 40 percent oil, primarily linoleic and linoleic acids, which are vitally important for strengthening immunity, helping prevent cancer, clearing the heart and arteries, and alleviating rheumatoid arthritis. Flax is a superior source of lignan, a mildly estrogenic compound that helps normalize a woman's menstrual cycle and that has anticancer, antibacterial, antifungal, and antiviral properties.

Flax seeds are highly mucilaginous, and when they come in contact with liquid, they become soft and jellylike. This soothing property makes them highly useful as an intestinal cleanser and bowel regulator for diverticulitus and to soothe coughing, sore throats, and chronic bronchial complaints.

Flax seed contains prussic acid, which in small amounts stimulates the respiration and improves digestion but in excess causes respiratory failure and death.

Flax seeds reduce *vata* and *kapha* and can be used in moderation for *pitta*.

Use Historically, flax seeds were cooked or pressed for oil, processes that inactivate their toxins. Use flax seed as a seasoning in baked goods as the Scandinavians do, or as an egg substitute. Some contemporary health advocates recommend grinding flax for use as a raw condiment or supplement. Please use in moderation.

Buying Compared to other culinary seeds, flax is inexpensive. Purchase it in bulk from a natural food store.

See **Seeds**.

FLORENCE FENNEL See **Fennel**.

FLOUR
Meal

Most people think that flour means ground wheat. Not so. There is a whole realm of nonwheat flours that offer delicious flavors. Each flour excels in its own way and can transform what might otherwise be a mundane dish into a new or even exotic dish. Although most flour is milled from cereal grains, there are also flours made from other grains, legumes, starchy vegetables, and nuts.

Health Benefits Healing diets recommend limited use of flour products as they tend to be more mucus forming and difficult to digest than whole grains, beans, and nuts. Soft flour products, such as noodles, dumplings, and hot breakfast cereals, are easier to digest than baked flour products, especially easier than baked goods that contain a fat or oil and/or sweetener.

Each individual grain, legume, or nut is an integral, balanced food. When a grain is broken down into minute flecks of flour, it loses its vitality and its essential fatty acids become denatured. Make these flecks into a dough and bake it, and energetically each speck gets baked solidly into place. Digestive enzymes have a hard time getting at these cemented flecks. Whole foods, on the other hand, demand longer chewing, which means they're more fully mixed with digestive enzymes and therefore easier to assimilate.

Buying The type of mill that grinds grains has a surprising effect on the flour's performance, flavor, and nutrition. You can easily verify this for yourself by purchasing different flours and testing them in the same recipe.

The best flour comes from stone mills where layers are flaked off the grain. This is a cool milling process, and essential fatty acids are not damaged. Stone-ground flour is labeled as such at the market. Or purchase a home stone flour mill, either hand operated or electric. The mills are available in either synthetic or natural stone.

The majority of commercial mills are hammer mills or blade mills. The hammer mill smashes grains into bits. The blade mill is like a gigantic blender, which chops grains into particles. Unless a commercial flour is labeled stone ground, you can assume that it was milled by the more economical hammer or blade method.

Any whole grain, bean, or nut flour has a limited shelf life. When buying such flour, purchase it from a local retailer who has quick turnover and who refrigerates the flour. Once home, store the flour in a covered container in a cool, dark place or refrigerate it.

If you have the luxury of having your own grain mill or like the people in Creston, British Columbia, have access to a village mill, grind your own flour twelve hours prior to use. Until then, it is "green," as they say, and performs poorly. Soybeans and nuts, because of their high fat content, may not be ground in a stone grain mill, as their fat adheres to and gums up the stones.

See **Amaranth Flour; Arrowroot; Barley Flour; Buckwheat Flour; Cassava Flour; Chestnut Flour; Chickpea Flour; Corn Flour, Grits, Cormeal, and Pinole; Millet Flour; Oat Flour; Pinole; Quinoa Flour; Rice Flour; Rye Flour; Soy Flour; Tef Flour; Wheat Flour.**

FLOWER BLOSSOMS

Like the faces of children, flower blossoms invite the eye and delight the heart. Their fragrance and essential oils, which are related to warmth, add a magical warming touch to a meal. Indeed, a blossom's inner temperature is higher than the temperature outside, though sometimes only a micro-thermometer will show this. Blossoms invite a pause and a deeper breath. They uplift the spirit and somehow make the whole meal taste better.

Health Benefits Blossoms, often the brightest and most striking part of the plant, convey the most energy. Sweet-tasting flowers (like honeysuckle) calm *vata* and *pitta;* pungent blossoms (like nasturtium) reduce *kapha*. Bitter and astringent flowers (like marigold) reduce *pitta* and *kapha*.

To sensitive individuals, blossoms may cause allergic reactions. Moreover, some are poisonous. Do not eat Oriental lilies, lily of the valley, sweet pea, or any of the narcissus family (daffodils, narcissus, paper-whites, and jonquils).

Use Flowers often taste similar to how they smell and are mainly used raw in salads or as a garnish. Because flavors differ from variety to variety, always taste blossoms before use. For example, some roses taste alluringly sweet and others sour, bitter, or metallic. Tasting first also tells you how much—and which parts—to use. The center disk in some flowers, like a daisy or sunflower, is bitter and is not used. Likewise, discard the base or cup of a chrysanthemum, carnation, or dandelion.

Some small- and medium-size blossoms are used whole. Unless stuffed, large blossoms—like the nasturtium or squash—may be sliced or torn. Susan Belsinger, author of *Edible Flowers,* recommends stuffing nasturtiums with guacamole for stellar flavor, color, and texture.

Consume only organic blossoms. Do not

use flowers from the florist, which are grown and treated with chemicals. Edible flowers include:

- **Decorative Flowers** Carnation, chrysanthemum, daisy, daylily, fuchsia, geranium (scented), gladiolus, hibiscus, hollyhock, honeysuckle, johnny-jump-up, lavender, lilac, marigold (taste first, some varieties are very bitter), nasturtium, pansy, pinks, rose, viola, and violet. The flowers of some bulbs, such as daffodils and tulips, may be toxic, and so it is best to avoid flowers from bulbs.
- **Fruit Blossoms** All blossoms of edible fruits. Orange, cherry, and strawberry blossoms are a special delicacy.
- **Herb Blossoms** Bee balm, borage, calendula, chamomile, chive, dandelion, dill, garlic, marjoram, mint, mustard flowers, oregano, rosemary, savory, and thyme.
- **Vegetable Blossoms** All blossoms of the cabbage, bean, and gourd families are edible.

Buying/Foraging With the exception of squash blossoms and some flowering cabbage family members, edible blossoms are usually not available from the greengrocer. Harvest blossoms from an organic garden or orchard and, when possible, collect just prior to use. Some blossoms—but not all—may be held for a day or more. To enhance storage of some varieties (but not others like squash blossoms or nasturtiums), submerge them in tepid water for five minutes, drain, wrap in plastic, and refrigerate.

See **Nasturtium; Squash Blossom.**

FLOWERING CABBAGE
Chinese Flowering Cabbage, Choy Sum
(Brassica parachinensis)

Similar to broccoli rabe, flowering cabbage is a small, nonheading vegetable with white stalks. Like bok choy, the stalks are fleshy, crisp, and sweet but these are deeply grooved; in addition to dark broad leaves, the central stalk holds beautiful yellow flowers. Flowering cabbage is milder than broccoli rabe but otherwise its use and properties are similar.

See **Cabbage Family.**

FOOD YEAST See Nutritional Yeast.

FRACTIONATED PALM KERNEL OIL See Palm Kernel Oil.

FRENCH BEAN See Green Bean.

FRENCH SORREL See Sorrel.

FRISÉE
Curly Chicory, Curly Endive
(Cichorium endiva)

This salad green, which looks like a tangled mop, has a crisp texture and a bittersweet flavor. Frisée is small and loose heading with slender lime-colored outer leaves and lemon yellow inner leaves. The leafstalks are white and the leaf itself is deeply serrated. Frisée is more delicate in flavor than other endives.

See **Chicory; Endive.**

Ø FRUCTOSE

Fructose is a natural monosaccharide that occurs in fruits and honey. In whole fruit, it is an excellent energy source. Pure fructose may be derived from fruit, but this is not financially expedient. Commercial fructose is available in either liquid or crystal form. Liquid fructose is made by splitting the two components of corn syrup. High-fructose corn syrup may contain as much as 55 percent sucrose and (diabetics, please note) it requires insulin for its metabolism. Crystalline fructose is made from intensely refined cane and beet sugar.

Since fructose has a tendency to convert into fat (rather than glycogen, the storage form of glucose in the liver and muscle cells), too much of it in the diet may lead to elevated triglyceride levels in the blood and increase the risk of arteriosclerosis. Commercial fructose contains no nutrients and is about 60 percent sweeter than sugar. As with other highly refined substances (fructose is 90 percent pure), the body reacts to it more like a drug than a real food. Some people experience allergic reactions to fructose; it aggravates blood sugar problems and may increase cholesterol buildup.

Food manufacturers who "naturally" sweeten their products with fructose are, to say the least, misinformed.

See **Corn Syrup; Sweeteners.**

HAVE YOU CONSUMED THIS WEEK'S TWO-POUND QUOTA?

In 1993, the per capita consumption of sweeteners was more than two pounds per week per person according to the USDA. Corn sweeteners led with 79 pounds annual consumption per person. Next was cane or beet sugar at 65 pounds per year. Less than one pound per year of honey and maple syrup were consumed.

Western science is yet to establish a direct correlation between diabetes and sugar consumption. Oriental medicine, however, has long described an association between excessive consumption of sweets and damage to the kidneys and spleen-pancreas. People suffering from hypoglycemia, obesity, tumors, and edema are advised to eat little, if any, refined sweeteners.

FRUIT

Sensory, sweet, saucy, and (when sun ripened and fresh) utterly irresistible—these are but a few ways to describe fruit. Botanically, a fruit is the ripened ovary of a flowering plant consisting of one or more seeds and surrounding tissue. Grains, legumes, nuts, and seeds are fruits with skins that become hard and dry when mature. The succulent fruits, in contrast, consist of a ripened ovary with soft, fleshy skin; this description includes the gourd family of cucumbers, squash, and melons as well as what fills our fruit bowl. Tomatoes, peppers, and eggplants, which we think of as vegetables, are also fruits, technically speaking.

Health Benefits Medicinal uses vary according to the fruit; generally, however, they are refreshing and therefore tend to reduce inner heat. For high-energy, "hot-blooded" people who are physically active and who eat many heating foods such as meat and fried foods, fruit helps bring balance. Conversely, for people with low energy, who tend to feel cold or who suffer from debilitating weakness or wasting diseases, all sugary foods, including fruit, are best used in moderation.

Temperate climate fruits, such as apples, plums, and other stone fruit, and berries, range from 10 to 12 percent sugar. Tropical and subtropical fruits (citrus excepted) range from 20 to 60 percent sugar, are higher in vitamin C, and are more cooling than fruits that require four seasons to grow to maturity (an exception is the warming tropical fruit, papaya). Cooking a fruit modifies its cooling properties.

Since fruits are digested more quickly than other food, they are best assimilated when eaten alone. Digestion is especially problematic when fruits are eaten with grains and protein food, because the fruit is digested first, and the other foods start to ferment. Fruit makes an ideal between-meal snack. For fruit as a dessert, consider first washing the dinner dishes, then sitting down to dessert.

An excellent source of natural sugar (fructose), fruits provide quick energy and their fiber aids digestion. They are low in protein and fat. Potassium and vitamin C excepted, most fruits are a negligible source of minerals and vitamins.

Use Almost all fruits can be enjoyed raw, juiced for a beverage, used in frozen desserts or cooked desserts, preserved, or dried.

Buying Fruit, due to its high sugar and water content, is more perishable than other fresh produce. For maximum flavor and sweetness, most fruits should be picked when fully ripened. Since when fruit reaches its peak of ripeness it starts deteriorating, most commercial fruits are picked before peak maturity. Allow immature fruits to ripen at room temperature, then eat them or refrigerate them and use as soon as possible. If a fruit is picked when too green, it will never become sweet. For the most flavor, serve fruit at room temperature. Some fruits, such as apricots and grapes, do not continue to ripen if picked immature.

When selecting fruit, consider smell, feel, and weight. Ripe fruits smell lightly fruity and fresh; if their aroma is dank or cloyingly sweet, they have started to rot. A gentle press with your thumb will cause ripe fruit to give a bit. Mature fruits are heavy, rather than light, for their size.

On a per-pound basis, smaller fruits contain more nutrients and flavor than larger ones. This is because in most fruits (and vegetables) the nutrient and flavor components are concentrated in the skin or just under it; the smaller the fruit, the more surface there is in relation to total mass.

See **Apple; Apricot; Asian Pear; Blackberry; Black Currant; Blueberry; Boysenberry; Cherry; Citrus Family; Cranberry; Currant; Dewberry; Dried Fruit; Feijoa; Fig; Fruit Conserves; Fruit Juice Concentrate; Gooseberry; Grape; Nectarine; Peach; Pear; Persimmon; Plum; Pomegranate; Prickley Pear; Quince; Raspberry; Rhubarb; Sour Cherry; Star Fruit; Strawberry; Tropical Fruit; Watermelon.**

FRUIT CONSERVES

Life without jam and jelly is hard to imag-

CELIBATE FRUITARIANS

There were two small groups in the 1970s, one in Florida and the other in southern California, that advocated a fruitarian diet as the most natural and healthful. I found it interesting—but not surprising—that their literature idealized celibacy as the spiritually correct choice. Fruit is cooling and, in excess, chills the libido. Many people who have fasted on fruit juice can attest to the subsequent diminishing of sexual appetite.

Food writer Annemarie Colbin observes in *Food and Healing*, ". . . a fully fruitarian diet seems to support contentment, gentleness, lack of competitiveness, as well as a certain detachment and perhaps even celibacy." Colbin writes that while fruit eating supports artistic expression, it doesn't "encourage creativity in more mundane areas, such as business or urban planning."

ine. These fruit products embellish bread and toast, plus numerous desserts and entrées, with nutrition, color, flavor, and pizzazz. The FDA, however, requires a high level of sugar concentration for jam, preserves, and jelly. For people seeking more healthful alternatives, apple butter or fruit conserves made from 100 percent fruit are available.

Fruit conserves that are a blend of fruit and fruit juice concentrates bill themselves as a healthful alternative. Read about fruit juice concentrate and then determine for yourself.

Ø FRUIT JUICE CONCENTRATE

Here's a hype. Take a cheap, commercial fruit juice and remove most of its flavor, acid, and color through deionization. All that remains is sugar water with a trace of minerals and, if the fruit wasn't organic, chemical contaminants. Manufacturers blend this sugar water in a "healthy" product and then label the result "natural, fruit juice sweetened." It sounds good. And for the manufacturers, it's been a highly profitable scam since 1990. Fruit juice concentrate appears on the ingredient list as the fruit (or fruits) it was derived from followed by the word concentrate. The two most common are white grape concentrate and pineapple concentrate. There is also mixed fruit juice concentrate.

Health Considerations Jeffrey Bland, Ph.D., president of Functional Medicine Research Center (HealthComm Intl.) in Gig Harbor, Washington, an author and a national lecturer, observes, " 'Fruit juice sweetened' sounds wonderful, so environmentally and physiologically friendly. But, speaking as a nutritional chemist, when we get down to chemical compositions and investigate how these things are processed, they start to look very similar to refined sugars from other sources. They are not a significant source of nutrition, and may actually sap the body of minerals." Fruit juice–sweetened baked products often taste acidic and are hard to digest.

Buying Fruit juice concentrate appears in beverages, including juice blends, frozen orange juice, natural sodas, and flavored bottled water. It's a common sweetener in cold breakfast cereals, candy, energy bars, frozen desserts, crackers, fruit conserves, and cookies.

Organic fruit juice concentrate products are a grade better than commercial concentrate. Deionized fruit juice products are found in supermarkets as well as natural food stores.

See **Sweeteners.**

FU

Imagine the toast part of milk toast, and you've got the comforting, soft texture of cooked fu. This easily digested Chinese and Japanese product, dehydrated wheat gluten, is available as fresh and fresh-frozen dough, fully cooked and ready to use, or fully cooked and dried and thus requiring hydration before use. In natural food stores, it is typically available cooked and dried, wrapped in cellophane and looking like a cracker or like round melba toasts. High in protein, unseasoned fu has little flavor of its own but takes on the flavor of soups or stews and lends a succulent texture. To prepare dried fu, soak it in water until it softens. Squeeze out the extra water, add fu to a soup, adjust the seasonings, cook for two to three minutes, and serve. Fu reduces *vata* and *pitta*.

See **Gluten; Seitan; Wheat.**

GAI LAAN See Chinese Broccoli.

GALANGAL
Greater Galangal, Thai Ginger
(Alpinia galanga)

Greater galangal is a pungent-tasting tuber used in place of ginger in Thailand and Laos and imported to Europe since the time of Marco Polo. Its small black fruits are used as a cardamom substitute.

Lesser galangal (*Alpinia officinarum*), yet another ginger family member, is used primarily as a vegetable and medicinal ingredient. It is also called kencur.

Both galangal types are available dried, ground, pickled, and occasionally fresh in Asian markets.

See **Ginger Family; Herbs and Spices.**

GAMMA-LINOLEIC ACID (GLA)

An essential fatty acid that is needed for growth and repair of cells and for production of hormonelike substances; it is normally produced by the body. In cases of deficiency, however, supplement with GLA-rich substances like borage, black currant, or evening primrose.

See **Essential Fatty Acids.**

GANDULE See Pigeon Pea.

GARBANZO See Chickpea.

GARDEN CRESS See Cress.

GARDEN HUCKLEBERRY
Sunberry
(Solanum intrusum syn. S. nigrum guineense)

Last summer, in a far garden corner that didn't benefit from regular watering, weeding, or fussing over, one of the community gardeners planted garden huckleberries. I didn't think they'd have a chance, but by summer's end, handsome, three-foot-high bushy plants had filled in the whole corner; they had purple-black fruits about the size of a cherry. We appreciated everything about the plant but the fruits. They were bitter, acid, and harsh on the tip of the tongue.

Two contemporary English references (the *Random House Book of Vegetables* and *The New Oxford Book of Food Plants*) claim that with adequate sugar garden huckleberries are a good pie ingredient and that they are used primarily in North America. I stewed one cup that turned a creepy indigo and tasted disgusting. I tossed the mess. Agronomist Duane Johnson at Colorado State University told me that their new food products development lab failed to find a commercial application for garden huckleberries. He knows of no domestic commercial use. Johnson warned me—now too late—that after one experimental crop they've remained a problem weed in his garden.

See **Nightshade Family.**

GARDEN PEA See **Pea, Fresh.**

GARDEN SORREL See **Sorrel.**

GARLAND CHRYSANTHEMUM
Chop Suey Greens, Chrysanthemum
(Chrysanthemum coronarium)

An annual Mediterranean herb related to the daisy, the spicy-tasting leaves of the garland chrysanthemum are widely used in Asian cuisine as a vegetable. They are either lobed or deeply dissected. Like broccoli and kale, garland chrysanthemum is unusually high in protein. Its slightly perfumed taste lends itself to rich dishes. Garland chrysanthemum is commonly cooked like collards. Some varieties are also grown for their edible flowers. The flower of *C. morifolium*, for example, is a classic Chinese remedy for alleviating migraine headaches. In Ayurvedic medicine, it is used for the treatment of gonorrhea.

See **Sunflower Family.**

GARLIC
(Allium sativum)

> Now bolt down these cloves of garlic.
> Well primed with garlic you will
> have greater mettle for the fight.
> Aristophanes, *The Knights*

The Greeks used garlic for more than fueling the fighting spirit; they also set garlic on stone piles at crossroads to propitiate Hecate, the underworld goddess of magic, charms, and enchantment.

Garlic is a universal seasoning agent and home remedy. And it's been a favorite from the dawning of Egyptian, Indian, and Chinese civilizations. In fact, it's been cultivated for so long that garlic is no longer found as a wild plant and its seeds are no longer fertile. It's propagated by clove: Plant one clove in the fall or spring and it yields one bulb. Ninety percent of our domestic garlic supply comes from California.

Health Benefits Garlic has a pungent and sweet flavor, is warming in thermal nature, is a stimulant, and tonifies the spleen-pancreas, stomach, kidney, and lung meridians. Garlic stimulates metabolism and is used for both chronic and acute diseases. It's antibacterial, anticarcinogenic, and antifungal. It reduces ear troubles, sinusitis, influenza, blood pressure, and cholesterol. Garlic helps stabilize blood sugar levels. Garlic lowers fever by increasing perspiration. It is antiparasitical, and it promotes the growth of healthy intestinal flora. It eliminates toxins from the body ranging from snake venom to poisonous metals, such as lead and cadmium. It increases body heat and thus may act as an aphrodisiac.

Garlic is not recommended when there are menopausal hot flashes or excessive heat typified by a red face and eyes, thirst, and a sense of feeling too hot. Excessive garlic may damage the stomach and liver. Use moderately during pregnancy, as it mildly stimulates the uterus. Garlic reduces *vata* and *kapha*.

Use To quickly remove the papery scales that enclose each garlic clove, place a clove on a hard surface and—using the flat side of a knife blade—crush it. If you use a wooden cutting board and don't want everything else to taste like garlic, then you have two options. Reserve a board for garlic and its kin. Or wet the board before cutting strong-smelling foods; the water acts as a buffer and protects the board from absorbing flavors.

Garlic may be mashed, pounded, pressed, diced, sliced, minced, or left whole. "What you *do* to garlic is what you *get* from garlic," according to Lloyd J. Harris, author of *The Book of Garlic*. A whole clove cooked slowly has a mild and nutty flavor because the heat has destroyed the enzyme responsible for the odoriferous sulfur compound. Heat, then, is one factor.

A second is how many garlic cells are exposed to oxygen. Exposed cells release sulfides that oxidize on contact with the air. Therefore, a thoroughly mashed garlic clove is more potent than one sliced or chopped.

When sautéing with garlic, take care not to brown the garlic, or it will become bitter. Garlic has probably been featured in every known savory dish—some people even add it to fruit chutneys and ice cream.

Dried powdered or granulated garlic? "Not to be used by anyone truly interested in the flavor of garlic, or in the food value of garlic (including the medicinal properties)," reports Harris.

Buying Select garlic bulbs that are plump and firm—smaller ones tend to be more pungent. There are numerous garlic varieties ranging in color from a pure white to lavender or pink bulbs.

See **Elephant Garlic; Onion Family.**

GARLIC AWAY JET LAG

Garlic and ginger are effective folk remedies for jet lag. Eat generous amounts (or take in capsule form as the bottle recommends) several days before the trip, the day of the trip, and one day after a trip. The day of travel drink adequate liquid but avoid coffee, carbonated beverages, and alcohol. Favor easy-to-digest, grounding foods, including potatoes and other root vegetables. That night, a hot bath and oil massage—especially of the feet—help ease jet lag.

GARLIC CHIVE
Chinese Chive, Oriental Garlic, Yellow Chive
(Allium tuberosum)

Unlike common tubular chives, garlic chives have larger (up to 10 inches long), flat, blade-like leaves, and a sweet garlic flavor.

Health Benefits Sweet in flavor, warming and tonifying for the kidney and bladder, stomach and liver meridians, garlic chives whet the appetite and counter blood stasis. When raw, garlic chives are more building; when lightly cooked, better at dispersing stagnation. Garlic chives are a traditional remedy for urinary incontinence, male impotence due to kidney weakness, or low back pain. Not recommended for people with fever, ulcers, or eye disorders. Garlic chives reduce *vata* and *kapha*.

Use In the West, garlic chives are used to add a light garlic flavor to any savory dish. In Asia, garlic chives are not used as a garnish but as an important vegetable, and the buds are considered a delicacy.

Buying Look for garlic chives in farmers' markets or Asian markets in the warm months. In the winter, blanched garlic chives, which look like a clump of pale straw, are available in Chinese markets.

See **Onion Family.**

GHEE

Ghee is a premier Ayurvedic cooking fat made of pure butter fat. It is an anticarcinogen, makes food easier to digest, enhances their medicinal action, gives food a clean-looking appearance, and it imparts an ambrosial flavor to both sweet and savory dishes.

Because ghee is cooked longer than clarified butter, the milk solids are allowed to brown before being strained out; this imparts a nutty flavor to the fat. Organic ghee is available in natural food stores, but it is so easily made at home and so much more delicious homemade. I recommend it to you for sautéing as well as baking.

See **Butter; Clarified Butter.**

NITER KIBEH

I favor the Ethiopian *niter kibeh* over unflavored ghee because the medicinal properties of the spices become more bioavailable. It's also an incredible time saver since your supply of cooking oil is seasoned all at once, rather than with each use. If you want to have plain ghee, use only butter in the following recipe. Otherwise, pick and choose those spices you enjoy. Here's one of my favorite cool weather spice combinations. In hot weather, I eliminate the ginger, nutmeg, and cinnamon. As the remaining spices are satvic (onions and garlic excepted) and support digestion, they're good to use year-round.

> 1 pound cultured unsalted organic butter
> 1 small onion, chopped
> 2 cloves garlic, chopped
> 1 teaspoon minced ginger
> 1 teaspoon cumin seeds
> 1 teaspoon coriander seeds
> ½ teaspoon asafetida
> ½ teaspoon turmeric
> 1 cinnamon stick piece, about 1 inch long
> 1 bay leaf
> ¼ teaspoon whole cardamom
> ⅛ teaspoon ground nutmeg or mace

Place all the ingredients in a saucepan and slowly melt the butter over medium

---

heat. When the butter comes to a boil, reduce the heat and simmer, uncovered and undisturbed, for about 30 minutes. As the temperature reaches the boiling point of water, the butter's water content vaporizes, foaming and making tiny, sharp crackling noises. It will be ready when the crackling noise stops and the sound becomes a rounder, boiling sound. The foaming almost ceases; the butter turns a lovely, clear golden color and the white sediment (milk proteins and salts) that forms on the bottom turns a light tan color. Immediately remove from the heat since the ghee can easily burn. (If it burns, it will begin to foam rapidly again and turn brown instead of golden.) Cool slightly. Pour hot ghee through a stainless steel mesh tea strainer. When cool, cover tightly. *Niter kibeh* (and ghee) stores for 4 months or more at room temperature. Makes 1½ cups.

GHERKIN See **Cucumber.**

GIANT GARLIC See **Elephant Garlic.**

GINGER
Ginger Root, Stem Ginger
(*Zingiber officinale*)

Ginger ale, ginger beer, candied ginger, gingerbread, ginger snaps, and the pale pink, paper-thin slices of pickled ginger mounded next to sushi—there's no other spice that helps define so many dishes, East and West.

Second only to salt as an Asian condiment, as a medicinal, ginger is even more remarkable. Herbalist Deni Bown notes that ginger occurs in about half of all Chinese and Ayurvedic prescriptions and in Ayruveda is known as *vishwabhesaj*, or "universal medicine." Equally valued in the West, it was listed as a taxable commodity by the Romans in A.D. 200.

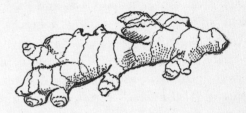

Ginger in medieval England was understood to "quycken the remembraunce," writes Lorna Sass in *To the King's Taste: Richard II's Book of Feasts and Recipes.* The medieval kitchen was not limited as we are to one variety but could choose between green, white, columbine, and string ginger.

Ginger is actually a rhizome, or enlarged underground stem. It grows in the shape of a palm with fingers, called a hand of ginger. It's a small plant with slender stalks. Ginger is native to tropical India, and today grows throughout tropical and subtropical areas and in greenhouses in temperate regions.

Health Benefits Ginger has a peppery, pungent taste. It is warming, stimulates digestion, and boosts circulation, respiration, and nervous system function. By increasing circulation, it helps effect a systemic cleansing through the skin, bowels, and kidneys. Ginger treats colds and fevers and is an effective remedy for motion sickness, nausea from chemotherapy, and sometimes morning sickness. It is anti-inflammatory and destroys many intestinal parasites. It normalizes blood pressure and helps support the liver. It eases congestion in the throat and lungs, relieving symptoms of cold and flu, and helps alleviate menstrual discomfort. To relieve headaches, rub a few drops of ginger juice over the affected area. Ginger reduces *vata* and *kapha;* dry or ground ginger is especially not recommended for *pitta.*

There are no adverse side effects listed in current pharmacopoeias, reports a recent issue of *HerbalGram;* a sixteenth-century Ayurvedic text, however, advises not to use ginger with some skin diseases, difficult urination, and hot symptoms, nor in the summer and autumn.

Use Ginger gives a clean, fresh taste to foods and is warming. Dried ground ginger is very heating and is not interchangeable with fresh. I use ground ginger in middle-of-the-winter breads, cookies, and puddings but otherwise favor fresh. If necessary, substitute ⅛ teaspoon ground ginger for one tablespoon of freshly grated ginger.

An easy way to use ginger is to grate it on a fine grater, then, using your fingertips, press out the juice. A plump, fresh knob of ginger is surprisingly juicy with 1 tablespoon of finely grated pulp yielding 1 teaspoon of juice. As the root dehydrates, its juice yield decreases. The Japanese have a handy grater especially for ginger called an *oroshigane,* available in porcelain or metal, which I recommend. I prefer the small porcelain grater. Even though the metal grater contains a con-

venient curved surface to catch the just-grated ginger, in time the ginger corrodes the metal.

Young, pink-tinged stem ginger is pickled, candied, and used as a fragrant vegetable in Asian stir-fried dishes. Stem ginger is less spicy than mature ginger.

Buying Stem ginger has pink-tinged tips and is available in Asian markets in the spring and fall. It should be used immediately.

Mature ginger is readily available year-round. Look for firm, plump hands or fingers of ginger with clean, smooth skin. The pale yellow flesh is very juicy when fresh, but as it ages it becomes fibrous. Avoid wrinkled, discolored, or moldy ginger. The

---

TO PEEL OR NOT TO PEEL

Some cooks peel ginger and, in the process, waste much of its flesh. Peeling is unnecessary unless you're making candy or pickles, and even then the tough skin is removed only for cosmetic and sensory reasons. Whether you use ginger by the slice and remove it prior to serving or finely grate it to express the juice, peeling is superfluous. If you mince, shred, or cut ginger into matchsticks, the minuscule bits of skin soften with cooking and are undetected in a finished dish, so it's not worth peeling. When a whole knob of ginger needs to be peeled, use the edge of a spoon to scrape the ginger. The skin—and only the skin—almost rolls off.

young, smaller fingers have the most delicate flavor.

Refrigerate ginger, unwrapped, in the vegetable drawer (if tightly covered, it becomes moldy). If storing a large quantity, bury it in a bucket of clean sand in a cool spot, and the ginger will keep for several months. Ginger is also available pickled and candied.

See **Galangal; Ginger Family; Herbs and Spices.**

GINGER FAMILY
(Zingiber)

As a good description of ginger's flavor and action, ginger also means spirit, liveliness, and verve. While the ginger family is named for its most famous member, its other familiar culinary members—cardamom, galangal, and turmeric—are equally distinctive and spirited. The zingiber genus, native to tropical Asia, has reedlike stems and aromatic rhizomes. They make excellent houseplants.

See **Cardamom; Galangal; Ginger; Turmeric.**

GINGER ROOT See **Ginger.**

GLA See **Gamma-Linoleic Acid.**

GLASSWORT
Marsh Samphire, Samphire, Sea Asparagus, Sea Bean, Sea Pickle
(Salicornia europaea)

Glasswort is one of a handful of delicious wild vegetables with occasional market availability. Buy it when you see it. Or better yet, harvest it from clean Pacific or Atlantic coasts, salt marshes, or alkaline Nevada and Oregon soils. The plant grows about sixteen inches high and looks like a leafless, skinny, branching succulent. Its leaves are like scales, which give the branches a bumpy look. In the spring and summer, it's green, but by fall it turns orange red.

Elizabeth Schneider tells the charming story of its name. Because this vegetable grows in cliff crevices, the French called it *Saint-Pierre* for Saint Peter, the rock upon which Christ built his church. Along the way the name became *sampyre* and then samphire (a name shared by an old-fashioned parsley relative that also grows in rocky places). The name glasswort comes from the use of a related plant, *S. stricta*, which was used in glass manufacturing.

Use Glasswort has a juicy, salinelike flavor and a pleasing crunch. Use it raw as a trail nibble, an attractive garnish, or salad ingredient, or pickle it, a favorite historical use. When cooking glasswort, trim the roots, then prepare and serve them like asparagus. Take care, however, to cook the greens just until the color brightens, so that their texture is not compromised.

Buying/Foraging Glasswort is occasionally available in specialty markets during the summer and early fall. The plants should be firm, dry, and bright. When foraging, harvest the plant tips from late spring until early summer. The mature plant has a fibrous center, which you may eat around, but glasswort is superior when younger.

GLOBE ARTICHOKE See Artichoke.

GLOBE ONION See Onion.

GLUCOSE

A monosaccharide sugar common in most plant and animal tissue, glucose is the body's major energy source. Honey is primarily composed of glucose and fructose. Commercial glucose is a colorless, syrupy mixture of chemically derived sugars and water.

See **Honey**; **Sugar**; **Sweeteners**.

GLUTEN

Chew one teaspoon of hard wheat berries for several minutes or until all that remains is the water-insoluble, gumlike endosperm protein—that's gluten. Without gluten, yeast can not perform its leavening function: When wheat flour is made into a dough, this protein becomes elastic and traps gas bubbles released from yeast. Hard wheat is higher in gluten than soft or pastry wheat. Spelt has a water-soluble gluten that quickly softens in your mouth.

Barley, kamut, oats, rye, and triticale also contain gluten but in lesser amounts than wheat. People who are allergic to gluten can use glutenfree grains like amaranth, buckwheat, corn, millet, quinoa, rice, and wild rice.

See **Fu**; **Seitan**; **Wheat**.

GOA BEAN See Winged Bean.

GOBO See Burdock.

GOLDEN HUBBARD See Hubbard Squash.

GOLDEN NUGGET See Gold Nugget Squash.

GOLD NUGGET SQUASH
Golden Nugget
(Cucurbita maxima)

The winter squash that looks like a miniature pumpkin is a Gold Nugget. It ranges from tennis ball to grapefruit size and when fully ripe has a mildly sweet squash flavor. If picked before maturity, Gold Nugget has a shiny rind (rather than dull) and is bland and tasteless. It keeps well.

The Gold Nugget is treacherous to cut because of its size and extremely hard shell. Bake it whole, then cut into desired shapes, season, and serve.

See **Squash**.

SOUP TUREENS

Golden Nuggest squash is the perfect size for an individual soup tureen. Allow one squash per person. Rub the shell with oil and bake at 350 degrees for 30 minutes. Remove from the oven, cut off and reserve the top to serve as a lid. Remove the seeds and fibers. Add hot soup (cream of celery goes especially well) and replace the lids. Bake for another 15 to 20 minutes, or until the squash is just cooked. Watch carefully—overcooked squash loses its shape and eye appeal. Sprinkle the soup with a green garnish, such as chives. Serve hot, with or without the lid.

GOOSEBERRY
(Ribes grossularia)

Tart describes the gooseberry. Very tart. A

black currant relative, the gooseberry grows wild in Europe and the Americas; the plant—a bush—was domesticated a short five hundred years ago. Most gooseberries are small with a translucent skin, smooth or downy, enclosing a number of seeds in a juicy flesh. The color varies from white through shades of green to purple, with the darker colors having a sweeter flavor.

Gooseberries are mostly used in pies, preserves, and sauces for their tart flavor. They are available in specialty markets in late summer. Recently it has been discovered that their oil is rich in gamma-linoleic acid.

See **Fruit**.

GOOSEFOOT FAMILY
(Chenopodiaceae)

The goosefoot, or chenopod, family of plants is found throughout the world. The name is derived from the Greek words for goose (*khen*) and foot (*podium*) because the triangular shape of the leaf looks like the webbed foot of a goose.

See **Amaranth; Beet; Chard; Epazote; Lamb's-Quarter; Orach; Quinoa; Spinach.**

GOURD FAMILY
(Cucurbitaceae)

The gourd family is an important food plant family that grows throughout the warm regions of the world. It includes numerous and diversified foods that grow on trailing or climbing plants with tendrils and lobed leaves. The blossoms are edible. Chayote, squash, and pumpkins evolved in the Americas. Cucumbers, gourds, and melons originated in Africa and Eurasia.

See **Bitter Melon; Chayote; Chinese Winter Melon; Cucumber; Kiwano; Loofah; Melon; Pumpkin; Squash; Watermelon.**

GRAINS
(Gramineae)

Grains, as members of the grass family, are the most complex and highly evolved plant species. Unlike most other plants, which have a separate fruit and seed, the fruit and seed walls of a grain unite in a single unit. By sheer number, the grasses—including bamboo, cane, wild grasses, and even suburban lawns—are the most dominant botanical species; they cover more of the earth's surface than any other plant species. Three seeds that are not members of the grass family are commonly considered along with grains because their use is similar. They are amaranth, buckwheat, and quinoa.

Humankind, the most developed life form of the animal species, coevolved with grains. An examination of the human digestive system and teeth indicates that we evolved eating predominantly a grain-based diet. Almost all peoples have revered a grain as their sacred mother, kept it at the heart of their diet, and made it central to their ritual. Even today grains remain the primary calorie source in most of the temperate world. In terms of alleviating world hunger, grains hold the greatest promise.

Health Benefits Grains are nutritive and sweet and help build body mass. The complex carbohydrate—and to a lesser extent quality pasta or bread made from their flours—content of whole grains helps stabilize blood sugar.

Grain consumption, as Annemarie Colbin notes in her classic book, *Food and Healing*,

SOME GRAINS ARE EASIEST TO
DIGEST—AND SWEETEST—WHEN
PRESSURE COOKED

I endorse pressure cooking the harder grains—whole barley, whole oats, brown rice, sweet brown rice, both types of wild rice, and rye and wheat berries. Pressure cooking softens their otherwise hard-to-digest bran and yields a sweeter-tasting grain. To pressure cook these grains, use the accompanying chart but reduce the water level by two tablespoons and the cooking time by five or ten minutes, or until the steam escaping from the pressure valve smells aromatic. Place grain, water, salt, and any seasoning into the pressure cooker. Lock the lid in place. Place over high heat and bring to high pressure. Lower the heat just enough to maintain medium pressure. Cook for the designated time. Remove from the heat and allow the pressure to come down naturally for ten minutes. Remove the lid, tilting it away from you to allow any excess steam to escape.

Cooking two cups or less of grain in a large pressure cooker (few pressure cookers are small) often produces grain that's dry on the top and scorched on the bottom. An easy remedy is to use an insert. Put the grain, water, salt, and any seasonings inside a heat-resistant glass bowl and cover it tightly. (A foil-covered oven-proof measuring cup works fine.) Place the insert inside the pressure cooker. Add two inches of water to the pressure cooker, lock the lid in place, and cook as above. A ceramic pot with a convenient rope handle that doesn't retain heat is designed as a pressure cooker insert; it is available from the mail-order resources on page 399.

"also has certain nonphysical, psychological, or spiritual effects [that] can foster a holistic worldview. Ancient Central American Indian lore has it that grains facilitate socialization and social intercourse; and in the West, breaking bread with one's neighbor is the ultimate symbol of a spiritually strong social connection. Time and time again I hear from my students that a change of diet [to include more whole grains] has helped dramatically in changing their perception of life—from a fragmented, alienated, self-centered view to one of connection, integration, and oneness."

Grains, along with legumes, are the only foods that contain all the major nutrient groups needed by the body: carbohydrates, protein, fats, vitamins, minerals, and fiber.

Use With the exception of muesli and some grain sprouts, grains are always cooked. Cooking is the first step to making them bioavailable; chewing them is the second. For grains to be well digested, they must be mixed with the digestive enzyme ptyalin, which is found only in the mouth.

The accompanying chart lists water proportions and cooking times for one cup of grain. If the grain amount increases to three cups or more, slightly reduce the water. This chart is only a guideline: The level of heat, the type of pot, and your individual prefer-

COOKING WHOLE GRAINS

1 CUP GRAIN	WATER MEASUREMENT (IN CUPS)	TIME (IN MINUTES)	(YIELD IN CUPS)
Amaranth	1½	20	2
Barley (pearl)	2½	40	3½
Barley (whole)	3	60 (1 hour)	3½
Buckwheat	2	12	3½
Bulgur (medium)	2	20	3
Millet	2¼	20	4
Oats (whole)	2	45	2½
Quinoa	2	15	3
Rice (brown sweet)	1½	40	3¼
Rice (long brown)	2¼	60 (1 hour)	3½
Rice (long white)	2	20	3
Rye	2¼	60 (1 hour)	3¼
Tef	1½	15	3
Wheat	2½	60 (1 hour)	2½
Wild rice (cultivated)	2½	60 (1 hour)	3½
Wild rice (wild)	1¾	45	3½

To cook a grain, combine it and the water in a heavy pot, preferably an enameled one. (Sweet rice excepted, I always add a pinch of sea salt for each cup of grain, and I typically add a one- or two-inch strip of kombu. Adding oil, ghee, or spices is optional.) Bring the grain to a boil, cover the pot, reduce the heat, and simmer, without stirring, until the water is absorbed. Remove from the heat and allow the grains to stand, still covered, for ten minutes before serving. If you are using a thin pot or an electric range, placing a flame distributor (available from hardware and cookware stores) under the pot helps prevent scorching.

ence—some like grain wet; some like it dry—will make a difference.

I disagree with the many recipes that sug-gest cooking brown rice 50 minutes or less. To soften the bran of brown rice enough that it is digestible and to bring out the full flavor of the rice requires one hour of cooking time. Like brown rice, whole barley, rye, wheat, and cultivated wild rice require a full hour of cooking. If you prefer a softer texture for these grains, or if you are cooking an especially impervious grain because of its variety or age, add additional water and increase cooking time as necessary.

Presoaking and light toasting enhance the flavor and digestibility of all grains (and sometimes reduces the cooking time of longer-cooking grains). I recommend lightly toasting the grain in a light pot or wok and soaking it for several hours or overnight. I soak grains in their measured amount of water in a glass measuring cup. When ready to cook, I note the water level of the soaked grain, strain out the soaking water, add fresh water to the same measure, and cook as described. However, I don't soak tef or quinoa because quinoa quickly sprouts, and tef's symbiotic yeast triggers fermentation.

Buying The advantages of purchasing grain from bulk bins are price and quality; it also lets you see your purchase. Good-quality grain is whole and contains few broken, scratched, or deteriorated grains.

See Amaranth; Barley; Buckwheat; Corn; Flour; Job's Tears; Kamut; Millet; Oats; Quinoa; Rice; Rye; Sorghum; Tef; Triticale; Wheat; Wild Rice.

GRAM FLOUR See Chickpea Flour.

GRANDMA'S BEAN See Lima Bean.

Ø GRANULAR FRUIT SUGAR
This is grape juice concentrate mixed with rice syrup, yet another attempt to satisfy the

> ### Song of the Taste
>
> Eating the living germs of grasses
> Eating the ova of large birds
>
>   the fleshy sweetness packed
>   around the sperm of swaying trees
>
> The muscles of the flanks and thighs of
> soft-voiced cows
>   the bounce in the lamb's leap
>   the swish in the ox's tail
>
> Eating roots grown swoll
>   inside the soil
>
> Drawing on the life of living
>   clustered points of light spun
>   out of space
> hidden in the grape.
>
> Eating each other's seed
>   eating
>   ah, each other.
>
> Kissing the lover in the mouth of bread:
>   lip to lip.
>
> —Gary Snyder

sweet tooth while claiming that a product is more healthful than sugar. Such a case may be made for rice syrup but not for grape juice concentrate.

See Fruit Juice Concentrate.

GRAPE
(Vitis vinifera)
Vitis vinifera translates as "the vine that

bears wine." The grape seems to have originated in the southern Caucasus, "more or less where Noah, famous as the first of all drunkards, is supposed to have landed his ark after the Flood: a pleasing coincidence," reports French culinary writer Maguelonne Toussaint-Samat.

Grapes are berries, which grow on a woody vine. A symbiotic yeast naturally grows on grapes. This makes grapes a natural choice for fermentation, as their historical use attests. The fermented fruit of Bacchus is associated not only with frivolity but also with fine cuisine, excess, and Jewish and Christian religious use.

Wine making, the largest fruit industry of the world, is based on the one and only Eurasian grape, *V. vinifera*, which now has more than eight thousand cultivars. In contrast, there are more than 25 different species native to North America, several of which are cultivated or may be foraged today. American varieties, including the popular Concord, have a softer, juicier flesh and less sugar than Eurasian ones.

Grapes do not tolerate extended periods of freezing or tropical heat, but they grow throughout the world in mild, temperate climates. More than two-thirds of all grapes are produced for wine, about 20 percent for table use, 10 percent are dried, and 1 percent are used as fruit juice. The volume of U.S. grape production ranks only under that of apples and oranges, with California produc-

ing the bulk of the U.S. crop. In fact, after almonds, grapes are California's largest food export.

Health Benefits Grapes have a sweet-and-sour flavor and astringent action; they are neutral in thermal properties; and they act upon the kidney, liver, and stomach meridians. Grapes increase vital energy and are used to build blood and body fluids and to cleanse the glands. Grapes are good to treat thirst, menopausal heat symptoms, difficult urination, edema, and dry cough. Grape juice is used to treat liver malfunctions, including jaundice and hepatitis. They relieve inflammations of the throat, mouth, gums, and eyes.

Grapes contain vitamins A, B-complex, and C. They have potassium and other trace minerals, and are high in natural sugars. Grapes are easily digested and are said to be medicinal to the lungs and to be strengthening to the internal organs. Grapes reduce *vata* and *pitta* and in moderation can be used by *kapha*.

Use Grapes are a perfect size for tidy, out-of-hand snacking. They are delicious in fruit salads and, when poached, add flavor and good texture to compotes and soups.

Grape leaves are a tasty vegetable and wrap. Gather the leaves in the spring just when they reach their full size. Use like other green potherbs or as a wrap for savory food morsels.

Buying Grapes cease ripening when harvested, so select a mature bunch. If the stem and the area where the grape attaches to the stem look fresh, the grape will be fresh as well. Look for well-colored, plump grapes with a powdery bloom (which serves as a natural waterproofing) on their skins. Avoid soft or wrinkled grapes or grapes with stems that are brown and brittle. Since grapes are unfortunately one of the most chemically treated fruits, you may wish to favor organic grapes, raisins, and wines. The peak season for domestic grapes is September to November and when stored under controlled atmospheric conditions they are available until May. However, imported grapes from South America are available in the spring and summer.

Table grapes are available with seeds or without. The three most popular seedless varieties are Thompson, flame, and ruby.

Green table grapes (as opposed to grapes grown for beverages or to dry) are sweetest when their color has a yellow cast with a tinge of amber. Red varieties are prime when one color predominates on all or most of the berries. Like red varieties, purple and blue-black varieties are at their prime when one color predominates.

See **Fruit; Grape Seed Oil; Raisin.**

GRAPEFRUIT
(Citrus paradisi)

> There's a lot more juice in a grapefruit than meets the eye.
>
> —Anonymous

The largest of the citrus family was so named because its fruits are borne in clusters, somewhat like grapes. Grapefruit is the most important citrus to have originated outside of Asia; it was hybridized in the West Indies and has been cultivated commercially for one hundred years.

Health Benefits Grapefruit is cooling and cleansing in its action. Its sweet-and-sour flavor acts upon the liver and stomach meridians. It treats poor digestion and jaundice and is a popular diet food. Its most abundant nutritive property is vitamin C. It is especially calming to *vata*.

Use A tasty variation of a plain halved grapefruit is to drizzle it with maple sugar and broil it. Or splash it with orange juice, which neutralizes the acid and makes the grapefruit sweeter, and broil. My favorite way of eating grapefruit—the way my grandmother did—is to peel it like an orange and then using a paring knife, extract each segment from the membranes and savor it on the spot. Grapefruit segments are also good in salads or fruit salads.

Buying Although there are many varieties of grapefruit, consumers are primarily interested in white or red ones, with or without seeds. Rubies, with pink flesh and a pink blush on the yellow skin, are grown in Texas; they are generally larger and sweeter than whites. Florida grows 70 percent of the world's supply of grapefruit, mainly the white variety.

Select a heavy grapefruit with a thin—rather than puffy and thick—peel, which means there is more edible fruit. The skin should be firm and smooth to the touch. Surface marks do not affect the fruit's flavor; avoid bruised fruit, however.

See **Citrus Family; Pummelo.**

Ø GRAPE SEED OIL
Grape seed oil is a drying oil used, according to Jean Anderson and Barbara Des-

kins in *The Nutrition Bible*, to improve the looks of commercial quality seeded raisins and keep them from clumping together. It is also used as a culinary oil. Until there is an organic, unrefined grape seed oil available, please avoid this product. Here's why: Chemical toxins are concentrated in a plant's fatty acids; and a plant's fatty acids are concentrated in its seeds. Considering that commercial grapes are grown with many chemicals, oil from their seeds is tainted.

See Fat and Oil.

GRASS FAMILY See Grains.

GREATER GALANGAL See Galangal.

GREAT NORTHERN BEAN
(Phaseolus vulgaris)

This medium-size white bean is similar to a navy bean, only larger. Great northerns or navies are standard in baked beans and pork-and-bean dishes.

See Beans and Legumes.

GREEN BEAN
Filet Bean, French Bean, Haricot Vert, Runner Bean, Snap Bean, String Bean, Wax Bean
(Phaseolus vulgaris)

Any bean eaten in its pod stage as a vegetable is green; that is, immature as compared to the fully mature seeds, which are known as beans. The pod of green beans is usually green, but varieties with a purple pod are also called green beans. French beans, sometimes called filet beans or—more usually—haricots vert, are straight, very slender beans about seven inches long. Yellow beans are sometimes called green beans, more often wax beans. These beans used to be called string beans because of the fibrous string running the length of the pod seam; it was removed before cooking. Modern cultivars are stringless.

A beautiful crop that either grows in bushes or climbs poles and fences, green beans are a seasonal favorite. They are delicious fresh and lend themselves to canning and pickling. If there are extras, let them fully mature on the vine and shuck them for succulent fresh beans.

Health Benefits Green beans are neutral in their thermal nature. They are sweet and tone the spleen-pancreas and kidneys. Green beans increases yin of the body (its fluids, hormones, and structure); they are diuretic and help treat diabetes. Dry or poorly cooked green beans irritate *vata;* otherwise, they are *tridoshic.* Fresh beans have ample vitamin A, B-complex vitamins, and calcium and potassium.

Use When beans are green and immature, they are easier to digest than dried beans. Heirloom varieties have strings, which must be removed prior to cooking. It's a time-consuming process; on the other hand, many old varieties have more flavor than modern cultivars.

Compared to most other vegetables, once harvested green beans age quickly, so plan to use them quickly. They can be blanched or steamed and served on their own or used in salads, casseroles, soups, and stir-fries—either whole, cut into lengths, or sliced into small rounds. To french beans (cut them into ribbon-thin lengths), trim the beans and, using a vegetable peeler with a frenching end, cut the beans into thin strands. This works best with very fresh beans.

Buying Select green beans that are firm, whole, and crisp, without rust spots. A fresh bean snaps crisply and feels velvety to the touch. Old beans are bulging and leathery. Those with greatest commercial availability include plain green beans, Italian (flat Romano), purple podded, wax beans, which are usually yellow, and yard-long beans.

See **Beans and Legumes.**

GREEN HOKKAIDO See **Kabocha Squash.**

GREEN ONION See **Scallion.**

HUFFING AND PUFFING IN YOUR VEGETABLE CRISPER

Growing plants take in carbon dioxide and give up oxygen, but once picked, fruits and vegetables do the opposite. The technical term is respiration, according to Dr. Robert Shewfelt, one of the world's authorities on postharvest care of fruits and vegetables. While a potato gives off a mere 8 milliliters of carbon dioxide per kilogram per hour, green beans top the vegetable respiration rate by giving off 250 milliliters. The faster the respiration rate, the faster a vegetable expires. To keep vegetables fresher longer, limit their oxygen supply by wrapping them in plastic, recommends Shirley O. Corriher, in *CookWise: The Hows & Whys of Successful Cooking.*

GREEN PEA See **Pea, Fresh.**

GREEN SOYBEAN
Edamame, Sweet Bean
(Glycine max)

Vibrantly green soybeans in their pods make a fun finger food and a tasty snack. It's like shelling peanuts. Several varieties of soybeans are grown for eating cooked from the pod when the beans are full size but still green. They are an inexpensive—and nutritious—snack.

Health Benefits Green and immature soybeans are easy to digest and are exceptionally high in fiber. They reduce *pitta.*

Use Steamed in salted water and served as a snack, green soybeans (called edamame) are available fresh in Asian markets, frozen in specialty stores, and as finger food in sushi bars.

See **Soybean.**

GREEN TEA See **Tea.**

GRISTLE MOSS See **Irish Moss.**

GRITS

Grits may refer to any broken cereal grain, most often buckwheat and corn. When a grain is broken, its germ is exposed to light, so it will oxidize and turn rancid. To store grits, refrigerate tightly covered. Grits made from degerminated corn have an indefinite shelf life.

GROAT

A term referring to any hulled grain, it most often refers to oats and buckwheat.

GROUND CHERRY
Chinese Lantern, Cape Gooseberry, Husk Cherry, Strawberry Tomato
(Physalis pruinosa, P. alkekengi, P. pubescens)

At first glance, this small fanciful fruit looks like a tomatillo, but it is not. Neither is it, as its numerous names suggest, a cherry, gooseberry, lantern, strawberry, or tomato, though it is a nightshade family fruit, closely related to the cape gooseberry and tomatillo. The ground cherry is fully encased in its papery husk (calyx) that is thinner than that of a tomatillo; its fruit is smaller than both the tomatillo and cape gooseberry.

The ground cherry is native to North America, was eaten by most Native Americans, and still grows rampantly as a weed. Ground cherries are also cultivated throughout the world.

Health Benefits The ground cherry supports the digestion of fats and proteins. It helps reduce fever, ease rheumatic discomfort, and increase urine volume. High in pectin, ground cherries also contain iron, niacin, and vitamin A.

Use Green or immature wild ground cherries may be toxic. Use only those that are yellow or yellow-orange and have a fresh-looking husk. Remove the husk just prior to eating, or, if you are using the fruit as a garnish, pull back the husk and leave it intact. Ground cherries have a distinctive sweet, slightly acidic taste; they are used in jams, jellies, pies, tarts, sauces, and salsas.

See **Nightshade Family.**

GROUNDNUT See **Peanut.**

GUAVA
(Psidium guayava)

The guava is a relative of cinnamon and feijoas and its fruit is grainy and pearlike in texture. But what's most memorable is its floral aroma, which fills tropical and subtropical markets when guavas are at their prime. The rounded or ovoid fruits have yellow or chartreuse skin with white, salmon, or crimson-blushed flesh. There are more than a hundred guava species, which range in size from a tangerine to an orange—and like citrus may be loaded with inedible seeds or seedless.

Originally from Peru and Brazil, the guava grows on a small evergreen tree or large bushy shrub. Today, guavas grow throughout the tropical world. Our domestic supply comes from Hawaii, California, and Florida.

Health Benefits The guava is known for its astringent and laxative properties; it tonifies the lymphatic and skeletal systems. It is an excellent source of vitamin C as well as potassium.

Use Remove the skin and the seeds, if any. Guava is delicious raw, in ice cream and sherbet, stewed, and as a sauce or preserve. Guava makes an excellent juice and nectar, by itself or blended with other fruit juice.

Buying Guava is most readily available during the summer. Using your nose is the best way to choose a guava. Select one with a rich aroma, and since the flavor varies considerably from guava to guava, select one with the aroma most enticing to you. A guava with a rank, foul smell is immature and not worth purchasing. To finish ripening a guava, wrap in a paper bag with a banana and leave out at room temperature until the guava is soft to the touch. Do not refrigerate until it is fully ripe and then use it within two days.

See **Tropical Fruit.**

GUMBO See **Okra.**

GUNGA PEA See **Pigeon Pea.**

HABANERO PEPPER See Chile Pepper.

HAMBURG PARSLEY See Parsley Root.

HAMLIN ORANGE See Tangor.

HARICOT VERT See Green Bean.

HATO MUGI See Job's Tears.

HAZELNUT
Avellan, Cobnut, Filbert, Noisette
(Corylus americana)

The hazelnut is Oregon's official state nut, with good reason—99 percent of the entire U.S. commercial crop is Oregon grown. The mild Willamette valley, stretching from Eugene to Portland, provides the perfect eco-niche for the hazelnut. Long before it arrived in the Willamette, however, it was a favorite European nut. The Celts regarded the hazel as the tree of knowledge, and—as water witches know—a forked hazel branch is the best divining rod for finding underground water. The hazelnut originated in Turkey and is so closely related to the filbert that their names are used interchangeably.

Health Benefits The Greek physician Dioscorides in his book titled *De Materia Medica* written in the first century A.D. observed, ''It cures chronic coughing if pounded filbert is eaten with honey. Cooked filbert, mixed with black pepper, cures the cold.'' Of the various nuts, hazelnuts are second only to almonds as a good calcium source. They reduce *vata*.

Use The sweet, somewhat toasty flavor of hazelnut has been likened to browned butter. Indeed, the French word for browned butter, *noisette*, also means hazelnut. Ground hazelnuts are an old favorite for pastry cooks, who add them to tortes, cookies, and candies. Hazelnuts are particularly delicious with chocolate. They're also good in salads, stuffing, breading, and as a garnish.

For full flavor, roast hazelnuts before using them. To remove the skins, rub the

---

TRUE OR FALSE: HAZELNUTS NEED BEES?

While fruit- and nut-bearing trees rely upon the birds and bees and other flying things for pollination, hazelnuts don't. In the dead of winter, the trees sprout bright yellow male catkins, and with the help of wind and gravity the pollen reaches the inconspicuous red female flowers. This union remains quietly dormant until warm weather. Then, as temperatures rise, the fertilized ovum quickens and the hazelnuts take form.

---

warm nuts with a rough cloth or between your hands, and the skins will flake off.

Buying While all nuts have a fragile shelf life, hazelnuts especially do. Purchase a year's supply in the late fall—ideally, in the shell—wrap the nuts tightly, and freeze until use.

See **Nut and Seed Butters; Nuts**.

HEADED MUSTARD CABBAGE See Wrapped Heart Mustard Cabbage.

HEAD LETTUCE See Iceberg Lettuce.

HEMP OIL
(Cannabis sativa)
The Latin name for marijuana means "useful hemp," and useful it is. Long before Flower Children smoked it for its psychotropic effects, hemp provided humans with edible greens, seeds, oil, and medicine as well as fiber for clothing, tents, sails, ropes, and paper. Our word for a painter's canvas comes from the word *cannabis*: Mona Lisa smiles from a coarse hemp cloth. In the 1930s, more than twenty-five hundred products were manufactured from hemp.

Health Benefits Dr. Andrew Weil, a hemp oil advocate, notes that at 81 percent it is richer in essential fatty acids than flax

---

MARIJUANA GREENS AS A SPRING TONIC

According to Don Wirtshafter, founder of the Ohio Hempery, a company that promotes hemp oil, it is only a small subspecies of the cannabis plant (*Cannabis sativa* subsp. *indica*) that produces the psychotropic alkaloid, and since the alkaloid is a recessive gene, it is quickly lost if the plant cross-pollinates with other hemp plants. Other hemp plants abound in rich soil throughout much of the world. In the United States, nonpsychotropic hemp is a common ditch weed. Wirtshafter observes that in the States nobody bothers to pick it because it won't make you high.

Elsewhere in the world—Asia, Europe, and, historically, in the Americas—the tender shoots are foraged as a spring green, cooked and eaten like spinach. The seeds are gathered in the fall for culinary purposes. In India, pounded hemp greens are mixed with honey and milk to make *bhang*, a cleansing spring tonic.

---

oil. He notes that "unlike flax oil, hemp oil also provides 1.7 percent gamma-linoleic acid (GLA). . . . My experience is that it stimulates growth of hair and nails, improves the health of the skin, and can reduce inflammation." Applied topically, hemp oil ameliorates eczema, psoriasis, and minor skin irritations. In Ayurvedic medicine, it reduces *vata* and is used externally for rheumatism.

Use Dr. Weil is equally enthusiastic about hemp oil's use: He uses it "on salads, baked potatoes, and other foods and would not consider putting it in capsules. Like flax oil, hemp oil should be stored in the refrigerator, used quickly, and never heated."

Buying Due to Drug Enforcement Agency regulations, hemp oil produced in the United States must be made from sterilized or irradiated seeds. Therefore, to obtain vital hemp oil, purchase only imported oil that specifies it is made from untreated seeds.

HEN-OF-THE-WOODS
Maitake, Sheep's Head
(Grifola frondosa)

The Japanese word maitake means dancing mushroom because, so tradition tells us, when people found maitake they would dance for joy. What was so joyous about this fungi? For one thing, it was worth its weight in silver.

Hen-of-the-woods clumps grow at the base of tree stumps in the woods. The stalks of their fan-shape caps fuse together at the base to form a mass sometimes as large as a football. Hen-of-the-woods grows wild throughout the northern hemisphere. Since 1990, it has been successfully cultivated.

Health Benefits The polysaccharide in Hen-of-the-woods, Beta 1, 6-Glucan, is a unique and potent immunostimulant, apparently helping to neutralize tumors and to ameliorate cancer, AIDS, chronic fatigue, and problems of obesity. It lowers blood pressure and benefits diabetes sufferers by lowering blood glucose. Historically, this mushroom was valued for promoting longevity and maintaining health. As medicine, a standard dosage is three to seven grams daily as a tea, supplement, or cooked vegetable.

Use Hen-of-the-woods is excellent when thinly sliced and sautéed in butter with herbs. It may also be baked, grilled, or added to a casserole or soup. When using it dried, rehydrate in water for at least 30 minutes, or until softened. Substitute about one ounce of the dried mushroom for each eight to ten ounces of fresh mushrooms.

Buying Fresh from the hothouse, hen-of-the-woods is available year-round in fine food shops.

Hen-of-the-woods mushrooms are available by mail order and in natural food stores for use as a vegetable. Also listed as maitake, the mushrooms are available as a medicinal supplement with or without other ingredients.

See **Mushroom Family.**

HERBS AND SPICES

Herbs and spices are often said in the same breath and may be stored in the same cupboard, but technically they differ. Herbs are the leaves of herbaceous plants. Spices may be the bark, root, bud, fruit, or berry of a plant. Herbs remain primarily regional in use, depending on local availability. Spices played a significant role in religion and global economics. Spices instigated Marco Polo's travels and turned the small city-state of Venice into a great power. They launched Columbus's voyages, and the wealth from their trade formed the Dutch Empire.

Use The use of herbs and spices to flavor foods and as kitchen remedies is as old as cooking itself. Cuisine worldwide is defined more by spices and herbs than by food staples. For example, rice, beans, and vegetables are universal Asian ingredients but it's the seasoning that identifies a dish as Punjabi, Korean, or Szechuan.

As a cook, one of my greatest pleasures is using spices and herbs in my daily cooking. To season by taste, here's a trick from Joanne Saltzman, culinary instructor and author of *Amazing Grains*. Crush an herb or spice you suspect might go well in the dish you are preparing. Now smell the herb at the same time you taste the dish. If you like the way they meld, then it's a combination worth trying.

Fresh herbs lend a more delicate and refreshing flavor to foods than dried herbs. When substituting dried herbs for fresh herbs, use 1 teaspoon dried herb for 1 tablespoon fresh.

Buying For maximum herb flavor, grow your own and snip them just prior to use. If you don't have a garden, consider a kitchen window herb garden: It requires minimum space and care. Best of all, when fresh herbs are at hand, using them is easy. Snipping at-hand chives is certainly more pleasurable and efficient than this alternative: Write

"chives" on a shopping list, purchase them, refrigerate them, remember to use them before they're past prime, find them in the refrigerator, unwrap them, and, finally, dispose of their package.

For maximum spice flavor, buy spices whole and grind them prior to use. "A whole spice," according to herb and spice wholesaler Ann Wilder from Vanns Spices, Ltd., in Baltimore, "is pretty much immortal. Once ground, its oils deteriorate. Cardamom, for example, looses fifty percent of its aroma and flavor in one week."

By FDA ruling, all imported herbs and spices must be sterilized. According to Wilder, however, this FDA ruling is not enforced. Ethylene bromide and ethylene oxide, potentially hazardous treatments banned in Europe, are the principal domestic fumigants; irradiation is also used. Fumigation reduces the oil and denatures the alkaloids in certain plants. Quality purveyors flash-freeze or use a superhot steam process to sterilize imported herbs and spices.

According to Wilder, price is not an indicator of quality and—with imported product —verifying organic is impossible. A quality spice purveyor lists the country of origin and offers fresh product that looks vibrant and has a fresh, clean, fragrant, and strong scent. Stale herbs easily crumble between your fingers, have little or an "off" aroma, and taste bitter and flat.

See Angelica; Anise; Annatto; Asafetida; Basil; Bay Leaf; Borage; Caraway; Cardamom; Chamomile; Chervil; Chile Pepper; Chive; Cilantro; Cinnamon; Citrus Peel; Cloves; Cumin; Dill; Epazote; Fennel; Fenugreek; Galangal; Garlic; Ginger; Horseradish; Juniper Berry; Lavender; Lemon Balm; Lemon Grass; Licorice Root; Lovage; Mace; Marjoram; Maté; Mint; Mustard Seed; Nigella; Nutmeg; Oregano; Parsley; Pepper; Perilla; Rosemary; Saffron; Sage; Sassafras; Savory; Star Anise; Tarragon; Thyme; Turmeric; Vanilla; Wasabi.

HICKORY NUT See Pecan.

HIGH-FRUCTOSE CORN SYRUP See Fructose.

HIJIKI See Hiziki.

HING See Asafetida.

HIZIKI
Hijiki
(Hizikia fusiforme)

The most mineral-rich of all seaweeds are the narrow ribbons of black hijiki. It grows near the low-water mark along the Japanese coast and is harvested in the winter and spring. Hiziki is sun dried, boiled, and dried again. Hijiki strands are several inches long, slightly bulbous in the middle, and pointed on both ends.

Health Benefits Hiziki has a salty flavor and cooling action and is a superior kidney food. It acts as a diuretic, helps stabilize blood sugar, helps detoxify the body, and supports the thyroid and bones. In Japan, hiziki is valued more so than other seaweed as a food that increases one's beauty and strengthens and adds luster to the hair.

An extremely rich source of calcium and iron, one cup cooked hiziki contains calcium and iron—more calcium, in fact, than the same amount of milk. It is high in other trace elements, and a good source of protein, vitamin A, and the B vitamins. Hiziki, like all seaweed, is low in calories. It especially reduces *vata*.

GINGER CARROTS AND HIZIKI

I've yet to serve this to students and have leftovers. It seems that when a food is very good for you, it also tastes very good. Bright orange and glistening black, this dish has a deep, mineral-sweet flavor.

- ¼ cup hiziki, loosely packed
- 1 teaspoon unrefined oil
- 1 clove garlic, pressed or minced
- 1 teaspoon minced ginger
- 1 small onion, sliced
- 1 small carrot, cut into matchsticks
- 1 tablespoon tamari soy sauce
- 1 tablespoon mirin or sweet wine (optional)

Rinse the hiziki and soak it in ½ cup water for 10 minutes. Drain, reserving the soaking water, and chop the hiziki. Warm the oil in a skillet, add and sauté the garlic, ginger, hiziki, onion, and carrot for 5 minutes. Add the tamari and soaking water, cover, and simmer for 15 minutes. If any liquid remains, uncover and cook until the liquid evaporates. Add the mirin, if using, adjust the seasoning, and serve. Makes 2 servings.

Use Available dried, hiziki is black when dried or cooked. It is a deep brown when fresh or hydrated. Soaked hiziki expands to more than four times its original volume, so start with a small quantity. Sautéed or simmered with other vegetables, this seaweed has a unique flavor. If you're new to hiziki, try the accompanying recipe.

See **Seaweed**.

HOKKAIDO PUMPKIN See **Kabocha Squash**.

HOMINY See **Posole**.

HONEY

We had some colonies of bees and I had been keeping track of progress and it was time to take off the apple-blossom honey before the white clover burst. I think the apple-blossom honey flow is the finest kind and look forward all winter to the supremacy of a comb on a pan of hot biscuits.

—John Gould,
Christian Science Monitor

A worker bee foraging for flower nectar, a disaccharide, visits up to a hundred blossoms before returning to the hive. There the enzymatic action in the stomachs of the bees processes the nectar to a highly concentrated and refined sugar. One bee's lifetime foraging yields only a twelfth of a teaspoon of honey. What precious stuff. No wonder domesticated beekeeping dates back to the Bronze Age.

Some people exalt honey, others disparage it as comparable to white sugar, and vegans won't touch it because it's an animal product. Whatever your stance, savor it for its marvelous flavor and use it in moderation, as with all sweeteners.

Bees are subject to a variety of illnesses and some are treated with antibiotics, traces of which may show up in honey. The FDA periodically monitors honey for drug residues, adulteration (some fraudulent producers cut their product with high-fructose corn syrup or invert sugar), and botulism. A form of botulism (*Clostridium botulinum*) is associated with honey consumption and causes some infant botulism deaths. Do not give honey to children under the age of two. Most commercial honey is produced in California, the Midwest, and Florida.

Health Benefits Energetically, honey acts upon the stomach, spleen-pancreas, and lungs. It tonifies, soothes, and nourishes and has laxative properties. It is also useful in cases of fluid retention. Ayurvedic medicine has long observed that the beneficial properties of honey are destroyed when it is heated and that, furthermore, it becomes mucus forming. Raw honey reduces *vata* and *kapha*.

Honey contains up to 60 percent more sugar than white sugar. (There is no industry standard for honey because the composition of each kind varies according to its nectar source.) Seventy-five percent of honey is glucose and fructose. It is thus quickly absorbed and produces hypoglycemic symptoms. Honey is not, however, as empty of nutrients as is sugar since it contains minuscule amounts of enzymes and minerals.

Use Honey can be stirred into herbal tea, spooned on hot cereal, or smeared on toast. Honey is used as an ingredient in spreads,

---

HONEY FOR SUGAR

To use honey as a sugar replacement in baked goods, substitute ⅔ cup honey for 1 cup white sugar, reduce the liquid by ¼ cup, add ¼ teaspoon baking soda per cup of honey, reduce the oven temperature by 25 degrees, and increase baking time as necessary.

---

sauces, marinades, and dressings. Since honey absorbs and retains moisture, homemade baked goods made with honey as a sugar substitute stay fresher longer. Honey also reduces crumbliness in cookies and scones.

Buying Honey is available mainly in liquid form but is also available in the comb or creamed. I favor a local source of unpasteurized wild flower honey. Some healthcare experts believe that consuming local honey may decrease the allergic response for people with pollen allergies. The best-quality honey, either dark or light, has not been heated to temperatures over 105 degrees; it is cloudy because of minimum filtration and clarification. The darker the honey, the more mineral rich it is, also the stronger in taste.

Most commercial honey is a blend from several different nectar sources. The single most common honey available is from clover; it has a pleasing, mild flavor and varies in color depending upon the clover variety from very light to amber. Other popular types include alfalfa, basswood, buckwheat, eucalyptus, orange blossom, tupelo, and wildflower.

Storage Store honey at room temperature away from direct sunlight. Do not refrigerate honey; refrigeration speeds crystallization, which thickens the honey and turns it cloudy and grainy. To reliquefy, remove the lid, place the honey container in a saucepan with water, and heat slowly until all the crystals are dissolved.

See **Sweeteners.**

HONEYBALL See Melon.

HONEYDEW See Melon.

HONEY LEAF See Stevia.

HONEY TANGERINE See Tangor.

HOP YEUNG QWA See Chayote.

HORN CHESTNUT See Horned Water Chestnut.

HORNED CUCUMBER See Kiwano.

HORNED MELON See Kiwano.

HORNED WATER CHESTNUT
Horn Chestnut, Water Caltrop
(Trapa bicornis)

This handsome Asian vegetable, aptly named in Latin "two fruit horns," looks like a play mustache. Each horned point contains a seed, but it's the crisp, starchy central part (16 percent starch) that is cooked and used like a water chestnut and, historically, as a grain substitute. The horned water chestnut is an aquatic plant that grows in marshes and lakes. Its leaves form a nosegay on the water surface and bear small white flowers; as the plant matures, the chestnuts form under the water surface. A fresh horned water chestnut is plump with firm, creamy colored, unblemished flesh.

This aquatic oddity is new to our markets, but it has been used in both Europe and Asia since the Stone Age. In India, it is called *Singhara* or *paniphal* and when sun dried and ground its flour is used in batters, flatbreads, and pudding. The European variety (*T. natans*) has four horns rather than two and was called the Jesuit's nut. In Europe, it is still foraged.

To use, shell with a nutcracker. Steam, stir-fry, braise, add to soup, or cook in a honey syrup as a sweetmeat.

HORN-OF-PLENTY See Trumpet Mushroom.

HORSE BEAN See Fava Bean.

HORSERADISH
(Armoracia rusticana)

Horseradish is one of the five bitter herbs of the Jewish Passover Seder, but it is far more pungent than bitter. The predominant—and immediate and overpowering—sensory experience in fresh horseradish comes from fiery pungent mustard oil. The oil is so volatile that when exposed to air it oxidizes and within 30 minutes starts to become bitter. This gnarled, forked taproot is a cabbage family member, thought to be Russian in origin. It remains popular in Europe and western Asia. Although once common

in American gardens, it has been displaced by chiles.

Health Benefits Horseradish is pungent and stimulating to the lung and colon meridians. It inhibits bacterial infection, increases perspiration and circulation, and acts as a diuretic. Horseradish is an excellent source of iron and potassium. Some use it in weight-reduction programs. It reduces *kapha*.

Use An intact horseradish root is not remarkable in appearance or action. Grate it, however, and your eyes will water and your nose will burn. Horseradish's oil dissipates within 30 minutes after exposure to air, and it is destroyed by heat, so use it raw and freshly grated. To temporarily preserve its intensity, mix it with a sour ingredient like lemon juice, vinegar, or sour cream.

Horseradish root is generally served as a condiment for meat. The leaves when young make an excellent salad green.

Buying Horseradish is available from the fall through the spring; look for plump, firm, crisp roots; it stores well for months when buried in damp sand.

See **Cabbage Family; Herbs and Spices.**

HOT PEPPER See Chile Pepper.

HUBBARD SQUASH
Golden Hubbard, Warted Hubbard
(Cucurbita maxima)

The thing I remember most about Hubbard squash from my childhood is my father chopping into it with a hatchet. Hubbard was an autumn standby in our home, but whatever else was baked alongside it was eaten first. This large (often weighing over 25 pounds) winter squash has dark green or reddish orange pebbly skin. Today, smaller sizes are available, perhaps reflecting the smaller-size family. The Hubbard looks something like an oversize crookneck squash, or it can be more rounded in shape. A Hubbard's flesh is more mustard colored than orange. I find the texture dry, and compared to many other winter squash, the flavor lacking.

HUCKLEBERRY See Blueberry.

HUITLACOCHE
Corn Smut, Cuitlacoche
(Ustilago maydis)

This somewhat scarce corn product is a parasitic fungus that attacks corn and other cereal grains. It is found worldwide on corn, wheat, rye, and other grains during the rainy season.

Health Benefits Huitlacoche is cold in thermal properties; it is a tonic for the liver, stomach, and intestines. It has a long tradition in both Asian and Western medicine for enhancing uterine contractions during labor and for postpartum use to control bleeding. It also is used to regulate and tonify the uterus and ovaries.

Use Huitlacoche is a true delicacy that tastes something like mushrooms and corn. Prepare it as you would mushrooms, sautéed with other vegetables, or as a side dish.

Buying Commercially, huitlacoche is available in Mexico dried, canned, and fresh in the markets. Locally, ask corn growers—especially during a wet season—to watch for it and save you some.

HUNGARIAN PAPRIKA See Paprika.

HUSK CHERRY See Ground Cherry.

HUSK TOMATO See Tomatillo.

ICEBERG LETTUCE
Imperial Lettuce, Head Lettuce

What other green could remain crisp and flavorless when compressed between a burger and bun? Iceberg is indeed unto itself. After potatoes, this head lettuce is the second most consumed vegetable in the United States. Through the mid-1900s, iceberg was synonymous for shoppers with lettuce. Iceberg is 90 percent water and stores longer than other lettuce varieties. In Asian cuisine, it is valued for its cooling properties.

See **Lettuce.**

IMBE
(Garcinia livingstonei)

A small, Day-Glo orange tropical fruit from East Africa, now also grown in Florida, the imbe is a thin-skinned, juicy fruit with sweet, mildly acidic flesh. More seed than fruit, the imbe is eaten fresh and used in beverages. Available September through March.

See **Tropical Fruit.**

IMPERIAL LETTUCE See Iceberg Lettuce.

INDIAN FIG See Prickly Pear.

INDIAN LONG PEPPER See Long Pepper.

INDIAN SAFFRON See Turmeric.

IRISH MOSS
Carrageen, Rock Moss, Sea Moss, Gristle Moss
(Chondrus crispus)

Found near the low-tide mark throughout the Atlantic and Pacific coasts, Irish moss is a beautiful, densely tufted, reddish purple to greenish white seaweed. One bushy head grows from a two- to four-inch holdfast, which clings on rocks, shells, or wood pilings. Classified as a red algae, Irish moss has a long culinary history throughout Europe and the United States.

Irish moss is easily foraged. Collect storm-cast greens from a clean beach or rake it by hand at low tide from small boats. It is produced in Massachusetts, the Canadian Maritimes, Hawaii, Ireland, and Brittany.

Health Benefits Long noted for its medicinal properties, Irish moss is used in cough preparations; for digestive disorders (including ulcers), kidney ailments, heart disease, and glandular irregularities; and as a bowel regulator. Irish moss is exceptionally high in vitamin A and iodine. It is highest in vitamin A when harvested in summer. Irish moss also contains iron, sodium, copper, and numerous trace minerals, as well as protein and vitamin B_1. It reduces *vata*.

Use The high sulfur content of Irish moss gives it a sea odor much stronger than that of other seaweeds. Rinsing it several times and soaking it reduces this strong odor. Before adding it to a delicately flavored or sweet dish, soak it for twenty minutes or more. For a savory dish, a ten-minute soak is adequate.

Irish moss provides an excellent gel, softer than agar gel. Its extract, often called carrageenan, has numerous culinary uses. An essential ingredient in blancmange, it is used in beer, ice cream, salad dressings, candy, and puddings or is added to soups and stews as a vegetable. It is an ingredient in a traditional bread of northern France, *pain aux algues*.

Buying Irish moss is occasionally available dried in natural food stores. It is more commonly found as an ingredient in prepared foods.

See **Seaweed**.

ISRAELI COUSCOUS
Grande Couscous, Pearl Pasta

It's not really couscous, but it is from Israel. This almost pea-size cereal product is extruded from refined hard wheat flour and then toasted in an open-flame oven to heighten its flavor and color. (Couscous is rolled from semolina and is not toasted.)

During a recession in Israel in the 1950s, rice was scarce but not hard wheat flour and an inventive cook created this *faux* grain. Israeli couscous is most often sautéed with flavorful ingredients to create an al dente minipasta. It may also be cooked like couscous or an instant risotto. Israeli couscous, a comfort food in Israel, has recently captured the attention of American chefs.

See **Wheat**.

Ø ISOMOL

Isomol is a highly refined, nonnutritive sweetener made from beet sugar—one I do not recommend.

See **Sweeteners**.

ITALIAN BROWN MUSHROOM See **Cremini**.

ITALIAN CHICORY See **Radicchio**.

ITALIAN KALE See **Kale**.

ITA WAKAME See **Wakame**.

JABORANDI PEPPER See **Long Pepper**.

JABOTICABA
(Myrciaria cauliflora)

Not limited to twigs—this subtropical fruit sprouts directly from the tree trunk and large branches of a Brazilian tree. The jaboticaba is like a purple grape in taste, size, shape, and juiciness. Its sugary flesh, however, is milky, and its skin, though edible, is tougher than a grape's and high in tannin. Its small seeds are edible. Available spring through fall, the fruits are eaten fresh and used in preserves, sauces, desserts, and wine. Refrigerated, the jaboticaba stores for up to two weeks; at room temperature, it quickly ferments.

See **Tropical Fruit**.

JACKFRUIT
(Artocarpus heterophyllus)

The jackfruit tree, native to India and Malaysia, currently grows in Florida and most tropical countries. A relative of breadfruit and figs, it is a vegetable staple in many Asian countries; when ripe, it is eaten as a fruit and has a banana- and pineapplelike flavor. The jackfruit is among the largest fruits of any tropical plants and can measure up to three feet in length, nearly two feet in diameter, and weigh up to 65 pounds. Its green skin is covered with short, sharp spikes. It is a composite fruit consisting of large bulbs of yellow flesh enclosing a smooth oval seed, surrounding a central pithy core.

Health Benefits Jackfruit pulp and seeds are considered a cooling, nutritious, tonifying food that helps counteract the influence of alcohol. The ripe fruit has laxative properties. Dried seeds contain B-complex vitamins, calcium, iron, and sulfur.

Use When immature, the jackfruit is boiled and used as a vegetable, added to chutneys, or dried and ground into a starchy meal. Its cooked seeds taste something like chestnuts and are added to soups or ground into flour. When mature, jackfruit is eaten raw as a fruit, juiced, added to salads, or served with yogurt. Cooked, it may be puréed for a sauce or preserved in syrups. Jackfruit is also dried. The fruit's skin, core, and the uncooked seeds are inedible.

Buying There are two main jackfruit varieties: soft flesh with sweet, juicy pulp; and a crisp variety that is less juicy and sweet. Purchase a fruit that is without bruises or soft spots. Because of its size, jackfruit is often sold precut.

Storing As jackfruit continues to ripen after it is picked, store a whole, immature jackfruit at room temperature for three to ten days. When ripe, its spikes stand clear of one another, its color changes from lime green to yellow or brown, and it has a heavy aroma similar to rotting onions. Its cut flesh, however, has a sweet tropical perfume. Refrigerate when ripe.

See **Tropical Fruit.**

JACOB'S CATTLE BEAN
Dalmatian Bean, Trout Bean
(Phaseolus vulgaris)

Jacob's cattle bean has a creamy white background with one large purple splotch and numerous purple speckles. An heirloom New England bean variety, it has excellent flavor and a slim kidney shape. Jacob's cattle bean is similar in appearance and use to the anasazi bean.

See **Beans and Legumes.**

JAGGERY

Jaggery is a thick brown sugar from India, made from palm or cane juice, usually sold in round cakes.

See **Rapadura; Sugar.**

JALAPEÑO See **Chile Pepper.**

JAPANESE HORSERADISH See **Wasabi.**

JAPANESE MEDLAR See **Loquat.**

JAPANESE PLUM See **Loquat.**

JAPANESE PUMPKIN See **Kabocha Squash.**

JASMINE
(Jasminum officinale)

Jasmine blossoms, with their heady, tropical scent, are an important herb in both Chinese and Ayurvedic medicine. Jasmine is used to relieve depression, calm the nerves, and dissolve damp problems such as edema and candida. Its roots and oil, as well as its blossoms, are useful in treating cancer and headaches. Jasmine is also considered an aphrodisiac. It reduces *pitta* and *kapha*.

There are several jasmine varieties with one, Arabian jasmine (*J. sambac*), used primarily to flavor green tea. These sweet blossoms are so aromatic that simply storing them alongside delicate green tea is all that's needed to permeate the tea leaves with the scent of jasmine. Other blends of jasmine tea are predominantly green tea mixed with a few jasmine blossoms.

JASMINE RICE
(Oryza sativa)

Imported from Thailand and now also grown in the United States, jasmine rice has a floral aroma and a tender, silky texture. It is a long-grain, crystal-clear white rice that is soft and slightly clingy when cooked.

See **Rice.**

JELLY MELON See **Kiwano.**

JERUSALEM ARTICHOKE
Sunchoke
(Helianthus tuberosus)

The Spanish named the ubiquitous Native American sunflower *girasol*, because from dawn to dusk its blossoms turn from east to west following the sun. Presumably, this word sounded like Jerusalem. That, together with the tuber's sweet, almost artichokelike flavor when cooked, is probably how it earned the unlikely name of Jerusalem artichoke.

Its edible tuber looks like a small potato but with multiple knobs, like ginger. The flesh is sweet, crisp, and white or yellow. The skin is light tan and sometimes has a purplish tinge. The plant, which has narrower leaves and smaller heads than the common sunflower, is widely distributed throughout the United States. This tuber, cultivated by numerous Native American tribes prior to colonization, is frost-hardy and, unlike potatoes, may be harvested year-round.

Health Benefits Jerusalem artichokes are a superior source of inulin, a natural fructose that is medicinal for diabetics. This sweet tuber relieves asthmatic conditions, treats constipation, and nourishes the lungs. Dr. K. M. Nadkarni, Ayurvedic author of the *Indian Materia Medica*, considers Jerusalem artichokes an aphrodisiac and an enhancer of semen production. It balances *pitta* and *kapha*, and may be used in moderation for *vata*. Jerusalem artichoke also contains vitamins A and B-complex, potassium, iron, calcium, and magnesium. Unlike most root vegetables, it contains no starch.

Use Jerusalem artichokes may be sautéed, baked, pickled, or served raw in salads. They do not can or freeze well, and if overcooked (more than twelve minutes) they toughen and become rubbery. As with a potato, peeling them is optional. Although most people can easily digest Jerusalem artichokes, some people experience digestive disomfort.

Buying The Jerusalem artichoke is at its peak in flavor and availability in fall and winter. Select firm tubers; avoid limp, wilted, or sprouting ones. Modern cultivars, such as the Fuseau, are less knobby than heirloom varieities.

See **Sunflower Family.**

JEUNG QWA See Chayote.

JICAMA
Yam Bean, Sa Kot
(Pachyrhizus erosus)

A Central American root vegetable, jicama (HEE-kuh-muh) is the underground tuber of a legume; it looks like a beige, oversize turnip. Jicama skin is easily peeled to reveal crisp, slightly sweet flesh that's similar to water chestnuts—only crunchier.

Health Benefits An excellent food for dieters, jicama is low in sodium and is a good source of potassium. Jicama balances *pitta* and *kapha* and can be used in moderation for *vata* conditions.

Use Jicama may be eaten as you would water chestnuts, Jerusalem artichokes, or potatoes and, although its flavor diminishes with cooking, it doesn't lose its crunch. Peel the tan outer skin and the fibrous inner layer. Because of its bland flavor, jicama goes with almost any other vegetable. Raw, jicama retains its hint of sweet and lends itself well to both fruit and vegetable salads or as a crudité. A popular Latin American preparation is to season raw slices with lime juice, salt, and chile pepper to taste.

Buying Select firm, heavy roots that are fresh looking and relatively unblemished. Smaller roots up to three pounds in weight are juicier than the larger ones. Store jicama at room temperature for a few days or refrigerate for up to two weeks. Do not freeze.

See Legume Family.

JINENGO
Dioscorea, Long Potato, Mountain Yam, Wild Yam, Yamaimo
(Dioscoreaceae opposita, D. villosa)

Native Americans and Asians all value the jinengo as food and as medicine. It's a slightly hairy, buff-colored tuber, skinny as a cucumber, that grows to lengths of three feet. There are many varieties.

Health Benefits Sweet tasting and warming, jinengo contains hormone precursors that affect the female menstrual cycle and help to reduce pain. In fact, jinengo extract was the original source for diosgenin in birth control pills; currently, it is synthesized. Jinengo contains allantoin, which is medicinal for stomach ulcers and asthma. It yields the anti-inflammatories steroids and cortison, which treat rheumatism. It strengthens the lungs, spleen-pancreas, and kidneys; increases stamina; rejuvenates; supports the liver and gallbladder; and is used for treatment of various digestive disorders. Jinengo contains even more starch-digesting enzymes than daikon does. In Ayurvedic medicine, jinengo is used for sexual and hormonal problems.

Use Grated raw jinengo is gooey and slimy. Season this goo with a splash of soy sauce and you have a potent digestive aid with a sweet taste. Jinengo may be cooked like potato chips or potato patties, or used as a binder to hold other ingredients together. When cooked, it loses its mucilaginous quality.

Buying Purchase jinengo dried for use in medicinal teas. It is also used as a strengthening ingredient in some prepared Japanese foods such as soba noodles. You'll find jinengo root stored in sawdust in Asian markets. Break off as large a section as you wish to purchase. Refrigerate it. Although the cut ends become discolored, the jinengo will keep for a week or more.

See **Yam.**

JOB'S TEARS
Hato Mugi, Yi Yi Reu
(Coix lacryma-jobi)

This heirloom grain has been cultivated in Africa and Asia for centuries. It looks like a large ebony teardrop, and it is strung for rosary beads and other prayer beads. Its black, impervious hull, which makes it a sturdy bead, is inedible. Once hulled, this grain looks like a giant pearl gray barley, and has a sweet flavor.

Health Benefits Job's tears strengthen the stomach and spleen-pancreas. The grain cools and reduces inflammation and pain and is useful for arthritis and urinary problems. In macrobiotic literature, the grain Job's tears is acclaimed for its anticancer properties; it is considered too strong to consume during pregnancy and menstruation. In Ayurvedic medicine, it is used as a blood purifier.

Buying You can purchase Job's tears from herb stores, Chinese pharmacies, and full-service whole foods suppliers and as a prepared cereal or beverage from Asian markets.

Use Soak Job's tears prior to use. This grain requires longer cooking than barley and is less sticky than either rice or barley. Combine it with rice or another grain or add it to long-cooking soups.

See **Grains.**

JUNIPER BERRY
(Juniperus communis)

Gin, the alcohol, is flavored with juniper berries, and the names Jenny, Genviève, and Geneva, Switzerland, all refer to the juniper tree. The small, dusky or dark purple berry-like cones of the common evergreen juniper tree have a sharp pine flavor and are a popular medicinal and culinary agent.

Health Benefits Juniper berries are bitter tasting and antiseptic. They improve digestion and are used for urinary tract cystitis and urethritis, arthritic-type complaints, poor digestion, and neuralgia. They are not to be used for kidney inflammation. Juniper berries reduce *pitta* and *kapha*.

Use Juniper berries are used to season strong-flavored dishes such as meat marinades—especially for game meats—pâté, pork, sauerkraut, and pickles. To use, remove any seeds, crush the berry, and add as a seasoning ingredient. Ten berries season one pound of meat.

Buying/Foraging Juniper trees are among our most common landscape greenery. When foraging, do not harvest berries from red or savin cedars, as their oils are too toxic for internal use. Juniper berries are also available in the spice section of well-stocked health food stores.

See **Herbs and Spices.**

KABOCHA SQUASH
Baby Red Hubbard, Green Hokkaido, Hokkaido Pumpkin, Japanese Pumpkin, Red Kuri
(Cucurbita maxima)

To my palate, kabocha squash is a strong contender for the ultimate sweet. It's satisfyingly rich, almost nutty, and never cloying like chocolate or sugar. Kabocha's sweetness makes me feel both nurtured and content. It's a good keeper—I keep a stash under the spare bed in my basement. Kabocha skin is either slate green or a loud orange-red. Its flesh is mustard yellow and its texture is similar to buttercup squash but it's drier, flaky (if overbaked), and never stringy. Delicious baked, sautéed, in a soup, with grain, beans, or vegetables, or in a pie.

See Winter Squash.

KAFFIR LIME
Makrut Papeda, Wild Lime
(Citrus hystrix)

The species name for Kaffir lime, *hystrix* (Greek for porcupine) refers to the plant's many thorns. The wrinkled, rough, yellow fruit has an aggressive lemon aroma and little culinary use. The leaves and rind, on the other hand, are popular seasoning ingredients in Southeast Asia, where the tree originated. When gently rubbed, the richly perfumed leaves release a luscious citrus scent.

Use Kaffir lime leaves are often added to Thai soups, stir-fries, and curries, along with garlic, galangal, ginger, chiles, and fresh Thai basil. Although lime or lemon peel is the nearest approximation, Kaffir lime's strong perfume cannot easily be duplicated. The rind, powdered or grated, is available in Asian markets. German herbalist Gernot Katzer notes that the fruit's juice, which is intensely sour and has the same fragrance as the leaves, is sometimes added to fish or poultry dishes in Malaysia and Thailand.

Storage Because dried Kaffir lime leaves lose their flavor readily, they are best kept frozen.

See Chile Pepper; Citrus Family; Galangal; Garlic; Ginger.

KALE
Dinosaur, Italian, or Tuscan Kale, Ornamental Kale, Salad Savoy, Scotch or Curly Kale, Siberian or Russian Kale
(Brassica oleracea acephala)

Kale is the grandmother of the whole cabbage family. One would expect such an old-timer to be hardy, and indeed kale is. It has a strident flavor, a sturdy appearance, and the pluck to withstand frost and even snow. In fact, kale is sweetest after a good frost or, in mild climates, after it has wintered over. Like a collard green in size and shape, a kale leaf is crisp and tightly curled—like curly parsley.

Health Benefits Kale is warming and when fresh has a sweet and slightly bitter-pungent flavor. When old, its bitter tone increases. Kale eases lung congestion, benefits the stomach, and is a specific healer for the liver and the immune system. Its juice is medicinal for treating stomach and duodenal ulcers. Overall, it's a strengthening vegetable. Kale reduces *pitta* and *kapha*.

Kale contains the nutraceuticals lutein and zeaxanthin, which protect the eyes from macular degeneration, and indole-3-carbinol, which may protect against colon cancer. It is an exceptional source of chlorophyll, calcium, iron, and vitamins A and C.

Use Substitute kale for cabbage whenever you want a bright green color and additional chlorophyll. Use the very young leaves in salads. Garden-fresh kale may be lightly steamed; if older, it requires longer cooking.

Buying Kale is available year-round but is best in the cold months. Select crisp—not limp—kale with a bright, fresh color and no signs of yellow or decay. Among the kinds of kale being marketed are:

- **Dinosaur, Italian, or Tuscan Kale** is an old variety with narrow, almost black-green savoylike leaves and a sweet, mild flavor.
- **Ornamental Kale** grows like a flat bouquet of ruffly-edged violet and cream leaves; it is more dramatic than many flowers. Not as flavorful as the more modest varieties, it is most typically used as a garnish or as a border along a flower bed.
- **Scotch or Curly Kale** is dark green or even blue-green with very curly leaves.
- **Siberian or Russian Kale** has broader, deeply serrated leaves that may or may not be curled. It is available in green or red varieties. This is the largest growing variety.

See **Cabbage; Cabbage Family.**

KALONJI See Nigella.

KAMUT
(Triticum durum)

Large, plump, and blond, this heirloom durum wheat has a buttery flavor due to its high percentage of lipids. Cooked whole, it is the most tasty wheat berry; when ground, it makes rich-tasting breads, pasta, and baked goods. And it makes a delicious Sicilian-style bread. For homemade pasta, I always favor kamut flour. Many people who are allergic to common wheat are able to tolerate kamut.

See **Grains; Wheat.**

KING TUT'S WHEAT

A Montana airman stationed in Portugal in 1949 was given 36 kernels of a giant wheat that had been gathered from a stone box in an excavated tomb near Dahshur, Egypt. The airman mailed the seed to his wheat-farming father, who grew them and showed them off at the county fair as "King Tut's wheat."

The grain was not as high a producer as modern hybrid wheat, and so it soon went to cattle feed and was forgotten. Forgotten, that is, until 1977, when Bob Quinn, an organic wheat farmer, remembered seeing King Tut's wheat at the fair in his youth. Quinn ferreted out a single pint of the giant wheat, and named the grain kamut, which means "wheat" in Egyptian. It is available today as a grain, a whole grain flour, and in products such as breakfast cereal, bread, and pasta.

The story of this grain being preserved since the time of the pyramids makes a good tale, but unfortunately a tale is all it is. All seeds have a limited life span due to their fragile fatty acids. Kamut is an heirloom Egyptian wheat. Fortunately, it was saved from the destructive wake of the "green revolution" that created high-yield hybrid seed and that is responsible for the loss of thousands of irreplaceable genetic strains.

KANTEN
(Gelidium amansii)

Kanten is a blend of agar varieties used as a gelling agent in Japan. It is available flaked—in small packets—or in an eight-inch bar that looks and feels like cellophane. Kanten is prepared using a centuries-old traditional method that includes outdoor freeze-drying in the winter. One bar of kanten (or three tablespoons of agar flakes) will gel two cups of liquid. Agar, available in bulk in most natural food stores, is a less pricey gelling agent than kanten.

See **Agar; Seaweed.**

KARELA See **Bitter Melon.**

KASHA See **Buckwheat.**

KASHI

Contrary to what some people believe, Kashi is not a grain. It is a trademarked blend of whole grains.

KAU FU See **Seitan.**

KAVA
(Piper methysticum)

Early Christian missionaries in the South Pacific vilified kava, presumably for its cultural and symbolic value . . . or was it for the pleasure it brings? Who knows. Despite the missionaries' best efforts, kava drinking couldn't be squelched. Indeed, the peoples of the far-flung Oceania communities—from Australia to Hawaii—remain linked in their kava-drinking customs. Today, North Americans value it as a relaxant. Kava is extracted from the pounded roots of a black pepper relative of the same name.

Health Benefits One difficulty in addressing the medicinal properties of kava is that there are at least nine distinct chemotypes (each with different chemical properties). In general, however, kava is recognized by European health authorities as a relatively safe remedy for anxiety. Kava is a muscle relaxant, and counters insomnia, fatigue, asthma, and rheumatism. It acts as a diuretic and has some local anesthetic properties. While kava is apparently not addictive, daily use for several months or more may cause skin lesions.

Use To make a kava beverage, place 2 tablespoons powdered kava in a coffee filter or four layers of cheesecloth, pour 1 cup of cold water through the kava, and drink immediately. The flavor of kava is peppery with sour and bitter overtones.

Buying Kava is available in capsules, tinctures, chopped root, and in a powdered form, with or without added flavors. Ask for it in natural food stores. Store in a dry, dark area.

KELP
Brown Algae
(Laminaria)

Giant pumpkins weigh more than 800 pounds and a Douglas fir can reach 400 feet—puny compared to giant kelp, which sprawls up to 1,500 feet in length. No wonder kelp is also called "oar weed."

The kelp family, which includes kombu, sea palm, wakame, and arame, is the largest, most studied, and most widely consumed of the seaweeds. Kelp is also a generic term for seaweed.

Health Benefits Medicinally, kelp is used for blood pressure regulation, for weight loss, as a digestive aid and colon cleanser, and to alleviate kidney, reproductive, circulation, and nerve problems. Kelp reduces *vata*.

One serving provides the recommended daily allowance of iodine and has only 15 calories. Kelp is high in calcium, iron, and all the major minerals. It is a plentiful source of trace elements such as copper, zinc, and chromium. It contains sugar, starch, and various vitamins, including A, B_6, B_{12}, C, D, and K.

Use Kelp is most commonly sold as powder or in tablet form. Some people use powdered kelp as a salt replacement in savory dishes. Kelp has numerous commercial uses

---

"YOU CAN'T HATE WITH KAVA IN YOU"

Claims are made for using kava as a spiritual aid, and indeed it was originally used only for religious rites by traditional peoples throughout Oceania. Today, rituals and community functions begin with a bowl of kava. An old account from Fiji attests, "It gives a pleasant, warm and cheerful, but lazy feeling, sociable, though not hilarious or loquacious; the reason is not obscured."

A researcher in Tonga wrote, "The head is affected pleasantly; you feel friendly, not beer sentimental; you cannot hate with kava in you. Kava quiets the mind; the world gains no new color or rose tint; it fits in its place and in one easily understandable whole."

as a stabilizer, an emulsifier, a suspending agent, and a thickener. When hydrated, its volume increases by almost 40 percent. Kelp does not complement milk, melon, or delicately flavored desserts. It does, however, complement just about everything else, including seafood, vegetables, grains, beans, squash, potatoes, and meat.

Raw, it has a slightly acrid, salty taste. It becomes sweeter with cooking. Check dry fronds for foreign material and toast until brittle (about 2 minutes at 350 degrees) to make a tasty snack food. Pan-fry kelp in oil until crisp and crumble to sprinkle on salads or as a condiment for grains. Or hydrate and cook until tender, about 15 minutes.

See Seaweed.

KEY LIME See Lime.

KIDNEY BEAN
Mexican Bean, Spanish Tolosana
(Phaseolus vulgaris)

The red, medium-size kidney bean derives its name from its kidneylike shape. A smaller red variety is used in chile con carne and other Latin American dishes. Kidney beans have a full-bodied robust flavor and a creamy texture. The white Italian kidney bean is called cannellini.

See Beans and Legumes.

KING BOLETE See Bolete.

KIWANO
Horned Cucumber, Horned Melon, Jelly Melon
(Cucumis metuliferus)

Kiwano, the African melon that resembles a multispiked spacecraft, is weird-looking. It has a brilliant orange-yellow skin and a seedy flesh that might remind you of lime Jell-O. It's the size of a fist, with a bland, unremarkable flavor vaguely reminiscent of bananas and cucumbers.

Health Benefits The kiwano is a cooling fruit that helps relieve thirst. It is over 90 percent water and is high in vitamin C.

Use The most spectacular use of a kiwano is to halve it, scoop out its flesh, and use its shells to hold individual servings of fruit soup or salad. Or peel the skin and add the flesh to salad, soup, sorbet, or yogurt. When sweetened, its juice makes a tasty summer beverage. A kiwano is best eaten raw.

Buying Select a bright yellow or orange kiwano with firm spikes and firm undamaged skin. Do not purchase one with dull-colored skin. Today, kiwanos are grown in New Zealand and California and are available year-round in specialty sections of supermarkets. When handled with care, kiwanos will store at room temperature or in the refrigerator for several weeks. They are most delicious, however, when used within a week.

See Gourd Family; Tropical Fruit.

KIWI
Chinese Gooseberry
(Actinidia deliciosa, syn. A. chinensis)

A kiwi looks like a furry brown egg, with a sweet but acid-tasting, brilliant green flesh. Tiny edible black seeds surround a creamy yellow center. A native of China, kiwifruit is now grown in New Zealand, Australia, and California. Since domestic kiwifruit is harvested in October and available through May and imported kiwis arrive during the summer months, kiwis are available year-round.

Health Benefits Kiwis are cold in nature and therefore clear heat. They help promote the production of fluids and so help induce urination and relieve a dry mouth or throat, or even thirst for those with feverish diseases. They support the stomach and bladder meridians. To aid in the passage of kidney stones, the Chinese recommend eating kiwis or drinking kiwi juice. They are too cooling for a person with cold or stagnant energy in the spleen-pancreas and stomach meridians. Kiwi reduces *vata*.

According to a nutritional analysis made by the Rutgers University Food Science Department, kiwis are the most nutrient-dense of our common fruits. They have nearly twice the vitamin C of oranges, are a significant magnesium source, and are higher than bananas and oranges in potassium. At 45 calories per fruit, kiwis are a low-calorie food.

Use Kiwis are eaten out of hand—peeled or unpeeled. They can also be served juiced, in ice cream, and in fruit salads. They are often used in mixed-fruit tarts. They make a bold garnish and, cooked, are tasty in compotes and preserves.

Buying Look for firm, plump, unwrinkled fruit. Some kiwis appear to have "water-stains" on their skin; this is normal. Allow to ripen by leaving at room temperature for a few days or until the fruit feels like a ripe pear and gives to gentle pressure. A kiwi will also ripen gradually if it is refrigerated for several weeks.

See **Tropical Fruit.**

KNOB CELERY See Celeriac.

KOHLRABI
(Brassica oleracea gongylodes)

Don't be put off by the kohlrabi's octopuslike appearance. A key staple in eastern Europe until it was deposed by the potato, this delicious bulbous vegetable has a radishlike bite, a crisp turnipy texture, and a sweet cucumber taste. Either pale green or bold purple, kohlrabi grow as a bulbous swelling (or corm) on the plant's stem—one kohlrabi per stem. *Kohl*, which is German for cabbage, aptly indicates which family this vegetable belongs to.

Health Benefits Kohlrabi improves energy circulation and eases stagnancy; it reduces damp conditions and

---

> **KIWI AND JELL-O DON'T SET TOGETHER**
>
> Have you ever added kiwi to gelatin or kanten and then wondered why it wouldn't gel? Raw kiwi contains actinic, an enzyme similar to papain in papayas, and bromic acid, which breaks down proteins and prevents gelatin and agar from setting. It also changes the composition of many dairy dishes. Several minutes of cooking destroy these enzymes.

so is effective for edema, candida, and viral conditions. It helps stabilize blood sugar imbalances and is used for hypoglycemia and diabetes. Kohlrabi reduces swelling of the scrotum and balances *kapha*. It is an excellent source of vitamin C and potassium. Kohlrabi is high in fiber and low in calories.

Use Some people first cook kohlrabi and then remove its skin. Using a sharp knife, I peel the vegetable first—but I remove only the tough, fibrous skin at the vegetable's base. Raw and sliced thin, kohlrabi is a delicious crudité served with a vegetable dip. Or grate it or cut it into matchsticks for salads. It can be steamed, stir-fried, baked, braised, added to soups and stews, or—as the Hungarians do it—stuffed. Kohlrabi, unlike cabbage, does not become sulfurous with long cooking. The leaves, when young, are similar in flavor to kale or collards.

Buying Although kohlrabi can grow up to 40 pounds, they're sweetest when smaller, about the size of a tennis ball. Large kohlrabi tend to be pithy or woody. Look for firm, crisp bulbs with no sign of cracking and with fresh, green leaves.

See **Cabbage Family.**

KOHREN See **Lotus Tea.**

KOJI

The "yeast" of Japan, koji is the fermenting catalyst for amasake, miso, sake, soy sauce, tamari, and several pickles. Ready-made koji is available in Asian markets, some natural food stores, and by mail from G.E.M. Cultures (see page 402). It is often packaged with simple instructions for making miso and amasake. Refrigerated koji has a life span of a year or more.

KOMBU
(Laminaria augustata, L. dentigera, L. japonica)

To the uninitiated, kombu doesn't *look* like comfort food, but it is. Like a secret bouillon replacement, it enhances the flavor and nutrients of any savory dish that's stewed, simmered, boiled, or baked. I put it in most everything but desserts. Before ladling the soup to someone prejudiced against seaweed, simply remove the spent kombu as you would a bay leaf.

Health Benefits Kombu, like other seaweeds, is cooling and moistening. It reduces or softens masses (such as tumors and cysts) in the body, but it is therefore not to be eaten excessively during pregnancy. Kombu reduces *vata* and *pitta*.

Kombu is very high in sugar, potassium, iodine, calcium, and vitamins A and C. It also contains appreciable amounts of B-complex vitamins, glutamic acid, starch, and trace minerals.

Use Kombu is the easiest seaweed to use, and it is versatile. Put it in any soup stock and every pot of beans. Add it to stews, or use it as a wrap for food morsels. It also stands on its own baked, deep-fried, or boiled. Kombu, when rehydrated and cooked with liquid, becomes mucilaginous, and after several hours of cooking it will break into small pieces. When crisped (without hydration) for a few minutes in the oven, it becomes a delicious chip. If the kombu blisters, it was overtoasted and will taste bitter.

Buying Commercial supplies of domestic kombu foraged near Mendocino, California, and in Maine are available in natural food stores and by mail order. Kombu from Asia is available in Asian markets and natural food stores. Store covered, in a cool, dark cupboard, and it will be good for several years. The most commonly used kombu comes in strips several inches wide and of varying lengths. Other forms of kombu include:

- **Natto Kombu** Kombu that's been sliced into very fine strands, natto kombu is used in soups and vegetable dishes.
- **Ne Kombu** The kombu holdfast (or root) is a strengthening food particularly beneficial in treating cancer and dysfunction of the intestines, kidneys, and reproductive organs. Ne kombu is recommended for breaking down fatty acids in the body and reducing cholesterol and high blood pressure. It requires long soaking and cooking.
- **Sweet Kombu** A premier kombu, harvested only from the Pacific during a one-week period, sweet kombu has sporadic availability. It has a deliciously sweet mineral taste.
- **Tororo Kombu** Fine, almost powdery kombu filaments seasoned with rice vinegar, tororo kombu may be used as a condiment or added to soups just before serving. It is tasty and mucilaginous.

See **Kelp; Seaweed.**

NATURAL MSG ENHANCES FLAVOR *AND* HEALTH

In Japan in the 1940s, glutamic acid was extracted from kombu to make monosodium glutamate (MSG). Just as kombu enhances flavor and tenderizes food, so does MSG. However, MSG is now composed of synthetic glutamic acid and health-conscious people know to avoid it. Laboratory-produced MSG is toxic. The naturally occurring glutamic acid in kombu, on the other hand, improves overall health.

KOMBUCHA
Manchurian Mushroom, Tea Kvass, Tea Mushroom
(Fungus japonicus)

A fermented beverage with a winelike taste, kombucha is an old-time folk remedy. Really old-time: It's been used in China for more than two thousand years. The mushroom, a brown culture that looks like a jellied pancake, replicates itself with each new batch. Kombucha is easy to make: Brew a jug of black tea, stir in some sugar, add the culture, and let it ferment for a week.

Health Benefits This ancient elixir is extolled in popular literature as a cure for everything from cancer to arthritis. Kombucha sounds as good as it tastes. Many secondhand reports state that kombucha is a potent liver detoxifier and has antibiotic properties. Still, Christopher Hobbs, Lic.Ac., in his comprehensive research, has found no published chemical analysis of kombucha tea that identifies such properties.

In some cases, kombucha supports digestion and may help prevent the common cold. It is used for edema, arteriosclerosis, gout, constipation, mental fatigue, kidney stones, and general convalescence. Contrary to popular accounts, kombucha is not recommended for candida and yeast-type overgrowths.

Buying Notices for free kombucha cultures are often posted on bulletin boards of health food stores. A mail-order source is G.E.M. Cultures (see page 402). Some prepared beverages (reconstituted and dry) contain kombucha. There are reports of contaminated kombucha starters; to prevent contamination, do not use a culture with pink, green, or black mold. Considering its ancient history, however, as well as the countless hands that have brewed it and passed it on, one can safely assume that a culture cared for with rudimentary hygiene will produce a beneficial elixir. One guideline for fermented foods: If it smells or tastes repugnant, don't consume it!

Curiously, or not so curiously, Hobbs reports that smoking in the same room where kombucha is fermenting causes the culture to dissolve or to mold and putrefy.

KUDZU
Kuzu
(Pueraria thunbergiana)

In Georgia, the legend says
That you must close your windows
At night to keep it out of the house.
The glass is tinged with green, even so,
As the tendrils crawl over the fields.
—James Dickey, ''Kudzu''

Pronounced KUD-zoo between clenched teeth, kudzu was introduced to the southern United States to control soil erosion. It does more than control erosion. According to the locals, turn your back on this green menace

---

MACROBIOTIC CURE-ALL

The morning after a birthday party, Halloween, or any good indulgence, my children invariably requested an *ume-shoyu-kudzu*. I'd make servings for all—earned or otherwise—and we'd each savor our portion down to the last sticky drop. This effective kitchen remedy revitalizes energy and relieves colds, flu, headaches, diarrhea, hangovers, and digestive problems. Make it thin and sip from a mug, or thick and spoon it up. Your choice.

Ume-shoyu-kudzu

1½ tablespoons kudzu powder
1½ cup water or twig tea
1 teaspoon umeboshi paste or ½ umeboshi plum
1 teaspoon soy sauce, or to taste
½ teaspoon freshly squeezed ginger juice or ¼ teaspoon powdered ginger

Put the kudzu in 1 cup cold water or tea and stir to dissolve. Add the umeboshi, soy sauce, and ginger. Bring to a boil, stirring constantly, and simmer for 1 minute, or until the liquid turns from milky to opaque. Thin, if necessary, with the remaining liquid to the desired texture. Drink hot.

and it overgrows your car, barn, and even telephone lines. Officially classified as a noxious weed in 1970, kudzu has been valued on the other side of the globe for two thousand years as an important food and medicine. Aficionados—myself included—often pay $20 a pound at natural food stores for the powdered, chalklike root of the vine.

Health Benefits In Chinese medicine, kudzu root and flowers are used to relieve acute pain, stiff neck and shoulders, intestinal and digestive disorders, headaches, fever, colds, and hangovers. Recent research confirms its traditional use for suppressing the desire for alcohol. A cooling, tonic herb, kudzu induces perspiration. It prevents the eruption of rashes and clears the skin. It reduces *pitta*.

Use I use kudzu as a thickener, rather than cornstarch or arrowroot, because of its superior essence. To measure kudzu, crush the lumps with the back of a spoon, then substitute for cornstarch in any recipe requiring a thickener. Kudzu enhances the flavor of sauces, desserts, and soups. As it cools, a kudzu sauce thickens; a sauce thickened with arrowroot, on the other hand, thins as it cools.

Buying Currently, this starch is available only as an expensive Japanese import. Surely some day some industrious individual will harvest and market domestic kudzu. This kudzu available in natural food stores is a pure product, while in Asian markets it may have been blended with potato starch.

Kudzu is sold in capsules and tablets as an even more expensive dietary supplement that I find quite unnecessary. It's such an easy-to-use, and delicious, culinary agent.

FOR ALCOHOLICS, OLD NEWS IS GOOD NEWS

In 1993, Harvard biochemists discovered that a dose of kudzu made alcoholic hamsters cut their imbibing by 50 percent. Apparently the compound *daidzin*, found in the root, leaves, and flowers of kudzu, reduced the rodents' craving and significantly lowered their blood levels of alcohol, even taking into account their lower consumption. Similar studies found that kudzu works on mice in Japan, and human alcoholics in China. In fact, after a month of herbal treatment, 80 percent of the Chinese alcoholics in one study reported that they no longer craved alcohol and had no adverse side effects from the withdrawal. This information was published in the *Proceedings* of the National Academy of Sciences, November 1993.

But then, this is not really news. *The Divine Husbandman's Classic of the Materia Medica* from the later Han period (207 B.C.–A.D. 220) prescribed kudzu to treat drunkenness and hangovers.

KUKICHA See **Twig Tea.**

KUMQUAT
Limequat, Meiwa, Nagami
(Fortunella)

Kumquats, which look like date-size oranges, are eaten whole, skin and all. The skin is spicy-sweet (with some bitterness) while the juicy flesh is tart—quite a puckersome tidbit. If you enjoy bold flavors, chances are you'll adore kumquats.

The kumquat is not a true citrus, but its pollen pollinates citrus blossoms and vice versa, creating crosses, such as limequats, lemonquats, and more.

Kumquats originated in China, and their name, in Cantonese, translates as "gold orange." More cold-resistant than citrus, our domestic crop comes from Florida and California; kumquats are also imported from Brazil.

Health Benefits Kumquats are warming and energize the lungs, stomach, and liver. They help alleviate phlegm, relieve coughing, and move energy (*chi*). A traditional Chinese remedy for a cough that has settled in the lungs due to inner cold, is to infuse sliced kumquat and fresh ginger in boiling water. When the cold is from a fever, drink an equal mixture of kumquat and turnip juice. Kumquats reduce *vata* and, in moderation, *kapha*.

Use Serve kumquats whole on a fruit-and-cheese platter or to accompany salted nuts. Or slice, quarter, halve, or stuff them as a bold garnish and a welcome flash of color. The seeds are easily removed with a knifepoint.

Cooking releases the full aroma of kumquats, inviting their use in sauces, compotes, ice cream, and preserves. I candy kumquats in a honey syrup and keep a jar in the refrigerator to accompany game or to serve as a sweetmeat. To serve kumquats with greens, grains, or salads, simmer them whole for 15 minutes to tenderize them.

Buying Available in the winter months, the best kumquats are firm, not soft and moist. Their thin skin makes this petite fruit more perishable than citrus. Left at room temperature, they will mold, so refrigerate (do not wrap in plastic) and use within two weeks.

See **Citrus Family; Tropical Fruit.**

Kuzu See **Kudzu.**

LADY'S FINGER See Okra.

LAMB'S LETTUCE See Mâche.

LAMB'S-QUARTERS
Chinese Spinach, Pigweed, Redroot, White Goosefoot, Wild Spinach
(Chenopodium album)

Four thousand years ago in North America, the cultivated seeds and greens of lamb's-quarters were staple foods, until corn became the dominant crop around A.D. 1200. Of necessity, the greens regained popularity during the 1930s Depression when lamb's-quarters were foraged and eaten in both rural and urban areas and also canned for winter use. A "mess of greens" often meant a meal of lamb's-quarters fried in lard and served with a splash of vinegar. Lamb's-quarters are found—and eaten—in temperate regions worldwide; from April through September, you're apt to find these tender greens in my salad or soup bowl, by choice rather than necessity.

Health Benefits Lamb's-quarters, like other wild foods, are more energizing than cultivated foods—as you can tell from eating them, as well as by comparing nutrient profiles. Lamb's-quarters contain more vitamin A by weight than carrots and three times the calcium of broccoli. Lamb's-quarters have a slightly slippery texture and so are useful in treating constipation, especially in the elderly. The leaves of lamb's-quarters help cleanse the blood and have a positive action on the liver and lungs. They are *tridoshic*. The seed is effective in treating dysentery, diarrhea, and eczema. It also acts as a vermifuge.

Use Very young lamb's-quarters are mild tasting with a hint of lemon and can be used in salads. Once the plant sets seed, however, the leaves are bitter. Young leaves are used as a potherb or as a spinach substitute in any recipe. As with spinach, cooking greatly diminishes their volume.

Buying/Foraging This mild-tasting green is increasingly available in farmers' markets. But better than buying it, find a patch of lamb's-quarters in early spring while the shoots are just inches high. The leaves are trilobed, like a goose foot, and when young are about the size of a pansy leaf, with a

---

BEFORE CORN IT WAS "PASS THE LAMB'S-QUARTERS, PLEASE"

Lamb's-quarters seed remained a food source for some of the Tohono O'Odham into the twentieth century as I once read in Ruth Underhill's *Papago Woman*.

We always kept gruel in our house. It was in a big clay pot that my mother had made. She ground up seeds into flour. Not wheat flour—we had no wheat. But all the wild seeds, the good pigweed (goosefoot) and the wild grasses. . . . Oh, good that gruel was! I have never tasted anything like it. Wheat flour makes me sick. I think it has no strength. But when I am weak, when I am tired, my grandchildren make me a gruel out of wild seeds. That is *food*.

Out of curiosity, I've collected and cooked lamb's-quarters seed. The harvesting is easy—bend a stalk of mature, dried lamb's-quarters into a bag and, with one sweep of your hand, strip off its seed—but the winnowing and cleaning out leaf debris is time-consuming. The flavor of the seed is wild and potent. I recommend it.

---

silvery cast that looks almost fuzzy. Pinch off the tender green tops for your table. Repeat this harvest weekly, and you'll have abundant greens throughout the growing season. At maturity, the stems reach five feet. Following the first good frost, the seeds may be collected.

See **Goosefoot Family**.

LAUREL See Bay Leaf.

LAVENDER
(*Lavandula angustifolia*)

The name lavender comes from the Latin *lavare*, "to wash." If you love the feminine, floral lavender scent in toiletries, try a pinch of these blossoms in a soup. A color was named for the minuscule blossoms of this mint family member; the aroma takes me back to my grandmother's sachets. Lavender is an occasional culinary herb with potent aromatic and flavoring properties.

Health Benefits Taken internally as a tea or culinary herb, lavender is used for indigestion, depression, anxiety, exhaustion, irritability, headaches (including migraines), and bronchial complaints. Lavender relaxes spasms, benefits digestion, and stimulates peripheral circulation. It also lowers fevers. Externally, lavender is used for burns, sunburn, muscular pains, cold sores, and insect bites. Lavender's essential oils contain a substance called perillyl alcohol that, in laboratory studies, has antileukemia and antitumor effects for the liver, pancreas, and breast. Lavender is *tridoshic*.

Use The spice blend characteristic of southern France, *Herbes de Provence*, contains lavender. Its distinctive floral essence can easily overpower, though, so use it sparingly.

Crystallize lavender flowers and use them as an elegant decoration or add fresh flowers to jams, ice cream, and vinegar. Or use the flowers, fresh or dried, in an infusion or with an herb tea blend.

See **Herbs and Spices.**

LAVER
(Porphyra umbilicalis)

A variety of red algae, laver is hand harvested in the northern Atlantic and Pacific from rocky beds at low tide during July and August. The plants are picked over and spread on nets to dry in the sun or in a drying shed. Laver blades may be from an inch to three feet long and are only one to two cells thick. When cultivated, laver is termed nori.

When I lived in London in the early 1970s, I bought freshly foraged laver from the outdoor market in the small coastal town of Barnstaple. Already marinated with vinegar, it was black, with an unappetizing, sludgelike texture, but its taste was delicious with a fresh sea essence and nutty, sweet-and-sour mineral flavor. Traditionally, the British use laver in oat bread, as a seasoning agent, and as a condiment. In Hawaii, cooked laver is used as a relish. The California Kashaya Pomo tribe called it *mei bil* (sea leaf) and favor it above other varieties.

Health Benefits Laver is cooling and salty. It helps soften tumors and lumps; it helps eliminate all toxins—from radioactive elements to phlegm. Like other seaweeds, laver promotes water passage. As with all wild foods, laver is more energizing than cultivated nori. It contains all the minerals and trace elements required for optimum health. Laver is an abundant source of vitamins, particularly A and all the B vitamins. It's high in chlorophyll, beta carotene, and enzymes. Laver contains more total dietary fiber and soluble fiber than oat bran. It's higher in protein than land vegetables, and it contains no fat. It reduces *vata*.

Use Before using laver, pick it over for occasional small shells or pebbles, which may be lodged in the fronds. Roasting tenderizes laver and enhances its nutty flavor. Spread the laver on a cookie sheet and bake at 350 degrees for 5 to 8 minutes or toast in a skillet until crisp but not burned. A second way to tenderize laver is to marinate it in vinegar or lemon juice for up to 24 hours. Add marinated laver to salads, sandwiches, or salad dressings. Because laver has not been processed, as is nori, you cannot use it for making sushi.

Buying Wild, hand-harvested laver is available from natural food stores or by mail order directly from people who harvest seaweed (see pages 403–04).

See **Nori; Seaweed.**

LEAF LETTUCE See Loose-Leaf Lettuce.

LEEK
(Allium porrum)

The leek, the sweet cousin of the onion, is one of my favorite root vegetables—for more reasons than the flavorful white bulb, which is the only part that most recipes call for. I use not only the leek's green leaf but also its many tiny rootlets, which look like a string mop. These mineral-dense filaments add valuable flavor and nutrients.

Health Benefits As with onions and garlic, the sulfur compounds in leeks account for some of its healing action. But unlike those cousins, leeks are an excellent source of the lesser known carotenoids lutein and zeaxanthin. Because leeks are milder than onions and garlic, they are less stimulating and therefore better suited to young children and people with a fiery, hot temper. Leeks reduce *vata* and *kapha*.

As a stalk-like vegetable, leeks energetically support movement. Next time you're feeling physically, emotionally, or mentally stuck, favor leeks and other such vegetables. They subtly tonify and support energy movement.

Use Leek roots contain flavor and minerals that are far more bioavailable than mineral supplements. Cut them—as a cluster—from the root base. Soak this cluster to loosen any embedded sand, then carefully rinse. Mince the rootlets and use in any soup, sautéed, or simmered vegetable dish; they are too fibrous to add to salads or lightly cooked dishes.

Trim off the dehydrated tips of the leaves or any large, tough leaves. Slice the remaining vegetable in half lengthwise. Wash, taking care to remove any dirt lodged in the leaves. (If a leek is unusually gritty, cut it lengthwise into quarters, for more thorough cleaning.) I use rootlets, bulb, and leaf in soups, sautéed dishes, pilafs, and casseroles. Cockaleekie is a Scottish soup that contains, as its name suggests, chicken and leeks. In the country of Georgia, they pickle leeks; in Portugal, they grill young leeks.

Buying Look for brightly colored, firm (not wilted or flabby), fresh-looking leeks—preferably with untrimmed tops and bottoms. While large leeks, up to ten inches or more, are more readily available than small leeks, the smaller ones are more tender and flavorful.

See **Onion Family; Ramp.**

LEEN NGAU See **Lotus.**

LEGUME FAMILY
(Leguminosae)

The French call any vegetable a *légume*. A nutritionist names any bean, pea, peanut, or lentil a legume. Botanists consider a leguminous fruit one that splits into two halves.

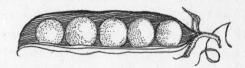

See **Beans and Legumes; Jicama; Lentil; Pea, Dried/Fresh; Peanut.**

LEMON
(Citrus limon)

As a world-class seasoning ingredient, the lemon is second only to salt and pepper. Be it a Brazilian prawn soup (*sopa de camarão*) or a Ukrainian yeasted roll (*mandryky*) with a cherry glacé, count on a squeeze of tart lemon to tune your dish's flavor just so.

Lemons have less sugar and more acid, primarily citric acid, than does other citrus. The juice and rind of this small citrus are both valued for their refreshing, sour flavor.

The lemon originated in India and may actually be a citron and lime hybrid. The lemon is more sensitive to frost than other citrus. Most of the U.S. lemon supply comes from places with even temperatures like California's coastal areas and southern Arizona. Newer varieties now flourish in Florida's humid climate and are able to withstand Florida's occasional cold snap.

Health Benefits As a medicinal agent, the lemon is remarkable. It has a cooling effect and so is good for fevers. It constricts body tissues, dries damp conditions, resolves stagnation, and dispels sputum. Lemon aids digestion by stimulating the flow of saliva, thus easing the work of the liver. It acts as a laxative and as a diuretic, and it has important antiseptic and antimicrobial properties. It treats colds, flu, coughs, and parasite infestation. Lemon benefits bile formation and therefore supports liver function; it improves the absorption of minerals, cleanses the blood, and is useful in treating high blood pressure. It relieves sore throats and hiccups, assists with weight loss, and alleviates flatulence. Externally, lemon juice helps heal sores; relieves itching from insect bites and sunburn; and even softens corns. Lemon reduces *vata*.

Like limes, lemons are high in citric acid, making them a good vinegar substitute. They are also used as a remedy for acidosis as their alkaline content is five times greater than their acidic content. A lemon has less than 1 percent sugar—even a lime has more. It is an outstanding source of vitamin C, and is high in potassium and vitamin B_1 as well.

Buying Unlike other citrus fruits, which are tree ripened, most lemons are picked green in the cold months and then left to ripen and cure in storehouses. Storage mellows the acid, thickens and toughens the skin, and gives the lemon a bright silky

---

A MORNING ELIXIR

Gently invite your energy up from its down time with this morning elixir. It aids in restoring balance and rehydrates the body, helping you to feel alert without that coffee jolt.

If your body feels stiff and your mind cloudy as you turn off the alarm, then your liver is complaining. It didn't complete its middle-of-the-night task of blood cleansing. In this case, modify your elixir by substituting ¼ teaspoon turmeric for the honey. Better yet, care for your liver by avoiding chemicals, alcohol, refined oils, and too much meat or fried food. Also avoid overeating and eating after dusk.

Morning Elixir

  1 cup boiling water
  2 tablespoons freshly squeezed lemon
    juice
  honey to taste

Simply stir ingredients together, and sip away.

yellow finish. Storage also makes it possible to have a year-round lemon supply for ample lemonade and lemon sorbets during hot spells. Lemons with a pale or greenish yellow color are fresh and more acidic than darker lemons.

Organic lemons are available seasonally in some markets. Commercial lemon skins are dyed and waxed. Avoid lemons with a darker yellow or dull color or with hardened or shriveled skin, which indicates old age. Soft spots, mold, or broken skin indicate decay.

The main domestic lemon varieties have a long nipple at the blossom end and a thick neck at the stem end—but other varieties are round. Some varieties are seedless, and some are juicier than others.

See **Citrus Family; Citrus Peel.**

LEMON BALM
Melissa
(Melissa officinalis)

As a medicinal herb, lemon balm is cooling with a sour and spicy flavor. It supports the lungs and liver and thus aids digestion and treats depression, flatulence, insomnia, and nervousness. It is often helpful in treating attention deficit disorder (ADD). As a culinary herb, one that is coming back into fashion, lemon balm gives a lemony flavor to vegetable, fish, and poultry dishes. It makes an effective garnish for lemon-flavored dishes by heightening the lemon aroma. It may be substituted for some of the basil in pesto. Lemon balm is a relative of mint.

See **Herbs and Spices.**

LEMON GRASS
Sereh, Serei
(Cymbopogon citratus)

Ten years ago, I was walking on an empty beach near Tepiac, Mexico, and developed a hankering for a cup of herbal tea—though I doubted its availability. I eventually came to a makeshift café and was surprised to hear, *''Sí, tengo té de herba.''* The cook took one step off the covered kitchen platform, cut a stalk from a spiky plant, and, that fast, delighted me with a pungent, flowery cup of lemon grass tea.

This reedlike grass, which tastes just as it sounds, is becoming increasingly available as a fresh herb for use in Bali, Thai, Vietnamese, and Cambodian cuisine. Its pleasing bouquet scents many cosmetics, perfumes, and even Ivory soap.

Health Benefits This tropical grass is rich in citral, the active ingredient found in lemon peel. Lemon grass cools, aids digestion (especially in children), and increases perspiration. It relieves spasms, muscle cramps, rheumatism, and headaches and is also effective against infections. Lemon grass is *tridoshic.*

Use The pleasant flavor of lemon grass is never dominating. Although it can be substituted for lemon balm, it is not a lemon substitute.

The entire stalk is usable. Peel away the fibrous outer layer and use it like a bay leaf, to season but not to eat. The tender center section is also fibrous, but less so, and can be minced and added to sauces, soups, and stews. The lemony flavor increases with cooking, so use it sparingly. The stalk may also be chopped into sections and infused for tea.

Buying In Asian markets, specialty markets, or the specialty produce section of large supermarkets, look for fresh-looking, scallion-shape stalks about ten inches long. If not available fresh, look for it in the freezer section. Once dried, lemon grass quickly loses its flavor and aroma, so I favor it fresh.

Store any portion that you will use within a week in plastic in the refrigerator, then tightly wrap and freeze the remainder. Slice off a piece as needed and return the unused portion to the refrigerator or freezer.

See **Herbs and Spices.**

LENTIL
(Lens culinaris)

Early astronomers named their double convex optic glass after lentils (latin, *lens*) because of this legume's disk shape. Judging from the French name for lentil soup, *potage esau*, it dates back to the book of Genesis and the hungry Esau who sold his birthright to Jacob for a thick bowl of lentil soup. For eight thousand years, lentils have remained an important dietary staple in Europe, the Middle East, and India. The U.S. domestic supply of lentils comes primarily from eastern Washington and northern Idaho.

Health Benefits Unlike beans, lentils have no sulfur and so produce very little wind. Lentils have a mild diuretic action, are neutral in thermal properties, and benefit the heart and circulatory systems. They increase kidney vitality. Lentils rank just under soy as the top legume protein source. Lentils help

to reduce blood cholesterol, to control insulin and blood sugar, and to lower blood pressure; they contain neutraceuticals that inhibit cancer. In addition, they help regulate colon function and may help in the prevention of hemorrhoids. Lentils are high in calcium, magnesium, sodium, potassium, phosphorus, chlorine, and vitamin A. They reduce *kapha*.

Use Lentils are handy to keep on hand as they cook much more quickly than beans. They are mild tasting and lack that characteristic "beany" flavor. Most Americans think of lentils in terms of soup, but they're also great as a salad, in a vegetarian pâté, or cooked with or without vegetables as a side dish. For inspiration in seasoning lentil dishes, peruse any Indian or Middle Eastern cookbook.

Buying Like many Americans, I grew up knowing only one lentil variety—a brown and rather bland-tasting legume. Today's selection is larger, especially if you shop in a specialty, natural foods, or Indian market. India has more than 50 multicolored lentil varieties to choose from, either whole or split and husked. A tasty tiny green French lentil, Le Puy, which has a velvety texture and a spicy flavor, is now available, along with an increasing number of heirloom varieties.

See **Beans and Legumes; Dal.**

LETTUCE
(Lactuca sativa)

Wild lettuce, the precursor to cultivated lettuce, is found throughout the world as a common weed. It's not a weed for your salad bowl, however, since wild lettuce, even when young, is intensely bitter. Cultivated since ancient Egyptian times and popular throughout Europe, lettuce came to America with the early settlers. Today, lettuce accounts for almost 25 percent of the fresh vegetable consumption in the United States. It is a member of the sunflower family.

Health Benefits Lettuce leaves secrete a milky latex when the plant bolts or goes to seed. In another example of like curing like, lettuce helps increase mother's milk. Its cooling powers, prized for centuries, are used to tame fevers, liver inflammations, and—in the language of the old texts—lust.

Long valued for its soporific properties, lettuce contains the sedative lactucarium, which relaxes the nerves. It is also a superior source of magnesium, which contributes to its soothing properties. Lettuce is cooling in its thermal nature. Its flavor is bitter and sweet. It acts as a diuretic, and is drying, and so treats edema, candida, and damp conditions. Lettuce contains the highest amount of silicon of the common vegetables, and so it specifically supports pancreatic function.

Lettuce, and salads in general, are balancing for *pitta* and *kapha*. *Vata* people do better with a cooked or warm salad; by combining their lettuce with warming herbs such as arugula, watercress, and nasturtium; or with a more warming salad dressing that might include fennel, garlic, or ginger.

Use Indispensable in salads, garnishes, and on sandwiches, lettuce is primarily used raw; it is valued for its refreshing, crisp nature. Sturdier varieties may be wilted or lightly cooked.

Buying The best selection of lettuce greens is in the spring and fall. Look for

WHY DID APHRODITE SLEEP UPON A BED OF LETTUCE?

According to the ancient Greeks, Aphrodite, the Goddess of Love, was so distraught over the death of handsome Adonis that, for sedation, she slept upon a bed of lettuce.

Too much sedation, however, is never a good thing. Eating a large quantity of bolted lettuce (that which has gone to seed) has been known to cause comas. Not to worry: You won't find bolted lettuce in the store, and, if it is in your garden, it will taste too bitter to eat.

bright, vibrant lettuce with no signs of rust or dehydration. Many "exotic" salad greens, actually heirloom varieties, are coming back into favor. Experiment with these "new" lettuces, which range in color from red and yellow to blue-green. Textures range from buttery soft to crisp and flavors from mildly bitter to distinctly bitter, with some nutty and sweet tastes as well.

See **Butterhead Lettuce; Celtuce; Iceberg Lettuce; Loose-Leaf Lettuce; Mâche; Mesclun; Romaine; Sunflower Family.**

LICORICE ROOT
(Glycyrrhiza glabra)

Black jelly beans and licorice candy ropes and whips contain a black extract of licorice root. For more than two thousand years throughout the temperate world, both wild and cultivated licorice were a valued medicinal, and sometimes culinary, herb. Until, that is, it was synthesized and used as an effective ulcer-healing medication that caused side effects in some people. Since then, the Western medical community disregards its long record as a safe herb and warns about using the root, as Robert A. Barnett reports in *Tonics: More than 100 Recipes that Improve the Body and the Mind.*

Health Benefits Licorice is a soothing, moist, sweet root that has a positive action on all organs and so is used as an energy tonic in Chinese medicine. It is a mild sedative, is anti-inflammatory, controls coughing, and has hormonal effects for women. It detoxifies and protects the liver and inhibits breast, colon, and prostate cancer. Licorice treats chronic hepatitis and immune deficiency disease; it is used for arthritis, allergic complaints, asthma, and Addison's disease. Licorice is not given to pregnant women or to people with high blood pressure or kidney disease, because, in excess, it may cause water retention and raise blood pressure.

Licorice contains glyceritinic, a neutraceutical that's 50 to 100 times sweeter than sucrose. It's one of the most common ingredients in Chinese herbal formulas, for it moderates the strong effects of other ingredients and makes them more effective. Licorice reduces *vata* and *pitta.*

Use A common flavoring ingredient in tobacco, beer, soft drinks, and medicines, licorice has an anise- or fennel-like aroma with a strong, dominating sweetness. This taste overwhelms both sweet and spicy dishes, except when minute quantities are blended with other spices—a pinch of powdered licorice added to fruit juices or punch adds an interesting note of flavor.

LIC(K) SMOKING

Years ago, when I stopped smoking cigarettes but still craved them, chewing on a piece of licorice root was an effective aid. It's the same size as a cigarette, with a funky, sweet taste, and it kept my fingers and mouth similarly (sort of) occupied. Licorice's adaptogenic properties also helped ameliorate the nicotine craving.

Today when hiking, I take licorice root chips. A couple of chips held in the mouth, and occasionally chewed, last all the way up to the next ridge and are a great thirst quencher. I share these chips with fellow hikers, who always appreciate them.

Buying Licorice root that resembles a brown pencil is available in three- to five-inch lengths or cut into chips. It's also available powdered and in extracts.

LIMA BEAN
(Phaseolus limensis, var. P. lunatus)

The lima, a favorite South American bean, takes its name from the capital of Peru. Limas come in two sizes. The large one, fordhook bean, grandma's bean, madagascar, or rangoon, is the largest of the common beans. The small lima (*P. lunatus*) is also called baby lima, butter bean, Dixie speckled butter bean, or sieva. The U.S. domestic supply of limas is grown in California, Florida, and Delaware.

Health Benefits The dried lima bean is cooling in nature and has a sweet, starchy flavor, almost like chestnuts; it is beneficial to the liver and lungs. It neutralizes acidic conditions and so is an excellent legume for people who have eaten a poor diet high in refined and fatty foods. The lima is less fatty than most other beans but starchier. Like common white beans (the navy bean and great northern), lima beans are especially medicinal to the liver. They reduce *pitta* and *kapha*.

Use Fresh limas are pale green and sweet. Fresh, they are popular in succotash. Dried, they're used in soups and casseroles or mashed like potatoes.

See **Beans and Legumes.**

LIME

The bright green, seedless Persian lime (*Citrus aurautifolia*) most commonly found in U.S. supermarkets is a subtropical fruit; it is also called the Tahiti lime. The smaller, mottled yellow-green, heavily seeded Key or Mexican lime (*Citrus aurantifolia*) is a tropical fruit; it is sometimes called a West Indian lime. All limes are harvested before they ripen. If left to mature on the tree, they lose their acidity, become sweet, and turn yellowish.

Health Benefits Limes are just less acidic than lemons and exhibit a more pronounced action on the liver. In other respects, limes are comparable in medicinal action.

Use Limes may be substituted for lemons in most dishes. They are a signature ingredient in tropical marinades, beverages, and, in the case of Key limes, pie. An authentic Key lime pie consists only of Key lime juice, egg yolks, and condensed milk in a graham cracker crust.

Buying Key limes are less available in temperate climes, but buy them when you can; they have a very perfumed flavor, which is accentuated by cooking. Key limes are the size of a golf ball, thinner skinned than Persians, and therefore more fragile.

Unlike most commercial lemons, which are dyed a uniform color, limes are not colored. Limes are the thinnest skinned and most fragile of the citrus fruits; refrigeration causes the skin to brown. Select limes that are heavy for their size with a glossy skin. Limes with a dull, dry skin are old and therefore less acidic than fresh limes.

See **Citrus Family; Kaffir Lime.**

LIMEQUAT See **Kumquat.**

LING ZHI See **Reishi.**

LINSEED See **Flax Seed.**

LITCHI
Lychee
(Litchi chinesnis)

> The lychee is to a table grape as a haiku is to pop music.
> —Norman Van Aken

One September, a mere two dollars in New York's Chinatown bought me a small bag of a valued—food writer Elizabeth Schneider says "revered"—Chinese fruit. I'm now a believer. The litchi is the size of a small round plum. Peel its strawberry-red, warty, leathery rind and its smooth and milky fruit is as juicy as a muscat grape. The litchi has an uplifting sweetness and an aroma that suggests lavender, jasmine, and rose.

Litchis grow in clusters upon evergreen trees prized for their stately beauty and native to tropical and semitropical southeastern Asia. Only after a tree is ten years old will it produce fruit, and even then production is erratic. Litchis are now grown in semitropical areas worldwide, including Florida and California, and this hopefully will guarantee greater availability in coming years.

Health Benefits In Chinese medicine, litchis are recommended for the spleen-pancreas, stomach, and liver meridians. They help promote body fluids and ease thirst, reinforce spleen *chi*, and replenish blood. They are quite cooling. The fruit contains vitamins B and C as well as folic acid, citric acid, malic acid, and arginine.

Use Litchis are easy to eat out of hand. The flesh easily separates from the peel and from its large, mahogany-colored seed. Both peel and pit are inedible. Litchis are at their best eaten fresh and need no accompaniment; they are also excellent combined with other fruits and may be gently stewed. Their sweet acidic flavor makes them a popular last course to a Chinese meal.

Buying Litchis are primarily available in midsummer. The red peel turns brown soon after harvest, but don't pass over brown-skinned fruits as long as they are plump and heavy. Avoid shriveled or cracked fruits. Best if not chilled, litchis can be refrigerated for up to two weeks, although this will incur some loss of flavor and texture. Some reports suggest freezing unpeeled litchis. Litchis are available canned in syrup in Asian markets.

Dried litchi fruits are like raisins in texture; they have a pleasingly nutty flavor.

See **Dried Fruit; Tropical Fruit.**

LOGANBERRY
(Rubus ursinis loganbaccus)

The loganberry was discovered growing wild in California in 1881; it may be a natural raspberry and blackberry hybrid or its own species. It is a large, lackluster red berry with an intensely acid taste due to its high content of citric acid. Too acid to eat raw, loganberries are used in preserves and, with plenty of sugar, as a raspberry substitute.

See **Blackberry; Boysenberry; Raspberry.**

LOLLO BIONDO See Loose-Leaf Lettuce.

LOLLO ROSSO See Loose-Leaf Lettuce.

LONG BEAN See Yard-Long Bean.

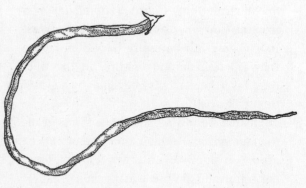

LONG PEPPER
Indian Long Pepper, Jaborandi Pepper, Pipali
(Piper longum)

Long pepper is an invaluable Ayurvedic

and Chinese medicinal plant worth getting to know. A relative to black pepper, long pepper is actually a cluster of tiny berries that merge to a single rodlike fruit about 1½ inches long and a mahogany brown. It is typically available ground and is hotter, but less aromatic, than black pepper.

Health Benefits Hot and warm with sweet overtones, long pepper has a higher content of piperine (the primary micronutrient in black pepper) than black pepper. It aids digestion and has decongestant, antibiotic, and analgesic effects. Long pepper improves absorption in the intestines and helps protect the liver from free-radical damage. The Chinese use it externally for toothache. It reduces *kapha* and *vata*.

Use Since long pepper is more pungent than black pepper, add it carefully—unless you like fiery food. Crush the rods before use. Or use the clusters whole as a pickling spice. *Trikatu*, the most important stimulant and digestive tonic in Ayurvedic medicine, is made of equal parts black pepper, long pepper, and ground ginger. Combine ½ teaspoon of this blend with 1 cup of hot water and a teaspoon of honey. It's a great morning wake-up drink that doesn't have the side effects of caffeine.

Buying Long pepper is typically available ground and combined with Asian and North African spice blends. Adriana's Caravan (see page 402) offers the whole rods.

LOOFA See **Loofah.**

LOOFAH
Loofa, lufa
(Luffa cylindrica)

While most people imagine a loofah floating in their bath rather than in their soup, it's more delicious in a soup. When immature, this Asian gourd is sweet with a pale green flesh and a slightly spongy texture. When grown to maturity and dried, its fibers make a pleasingly abrasive bath sponge to stimulate circulation and scrub the skin.

Health Benefits Loofah acts on the lungs, liver, and stomach. It's an astringent, painkilling plant that controls bleeding and promotes circulation. It's used specifically for backache, hemorrhoids, and rheumatism. Loofah reduces *pitta* and *kapha*.

Use If the loofah is ridged, peel only the ridges; if the vegetable is tough, peel the whole thing. Cut it into chunks or slice it, and cook as you would a zucchini in soups, stir-fries, and braised or baked dishes.

Buying There are two types of loofahs. One is slightly curved and ridged and the other is straight, smooth, and slightly thickened at the blossom end, resembling a baseball bat. Select a loofah that is about two to three inches thick, fresh-looking, and pliant rather than brittle. They are available in Asian markets and specialty food stores.

A loofah's flavor is best when it is fresh, so plan on using it within five days. Wrap in perforated plastic; if the loofah becomes too moist, it will soften and may become moldy.

See **Gourd Family.**

LOOSE-LEAF LETTUCE
Leaf Lettuce
(Lactuca sativa)

Rather than a compact head, loose-leaf lettuce has leaves that are easily separated. This structure makes it ideal for a garden patch since you can pluck the outer leaves as needed, while the plant continues producing throughout the growing season. The satisfaction of a daily garden-fresh salad is easily yours.

The loose-leaf lettuces are more tender and fragile in texture than romaine or iceberg lettuce, or chicory.

Buying The more fragile structure of loose-leaf lettuce means it doesn't ship or store as well as other kinds. Plan to use loose-leaf lettuce quickly. An ever increasing variety of leafy lettuces is becoming available, including Lollo Biondo, a bright, almost lime green lettuce with a distinctive frilly edge; Lollo Rosso, which is darker green than the Biondo, with red-edged leaves; and oak leaf lettuce, which is reminiscent of an oak leaf in shape and comes in green and red varieties.

See Lettuce.

LOQUAT
Japanese Medlar, Japanese Plum
(Eriobotrya japonica)

Like an apricot in size and color but like a pear in shape, the loquat bruises so easily that you'll probably not find it fresh outside of California or Florida, where it grows. It is also available in its native Asia as well as in Mediterranean countries. A loquat tastes something like a dead ripe (and therefore rather sweet) sour cherry and has a crisp but tender, juicy texture.

An apple relative, a loquat contains one or more large seeds.

Health Benefits Loquats are cooling in action and support the lung and stomach functions. They help relieve coughs and ease thirst and a dry throat. A famous Chinese patent medicine, Honey Loquat, available in Asian markets and health care sections of most natural food stores, is a syrup of loquat, honey, and fritillaria.

Use Loquats are delicious eaten fresh out of hand or added to fruit salads or made into sauces, jams, or jellies. They are also baked or poached. The seeds and—depending upon its toughness—skin are discarded. In Bermuda, a loquat liqueur is made.

Buying This highly perishable fruit is available early in the spring. Hold at room temperature until completely ripe, then refrigerate. Use within a few days.

LOTUS
Leen Ngau; Renkon
(Nelumbo nucifera)

Lotus roots, looking like connected sausage links, grow submerged in the mud of tropical ponds and paddies. From this mire, they send up leaves and exquisite pink blossoms that float on top of the water. The blossom, a Buddhist symbol of enlightenment, appears throughout Indian and Asian art. It is a promise that even though we come from muddy, sticky places we, too, can blossom and become fully realized, loving persons. The lotus blossoms—as well as its leaves, roots (actually rhizomes), stems, seeds, and the embrionic sprout within the seed—are delicious and valued medicinal foods. The roots and seeds are more readily available.

See **Lotus Root; Lotus Seed; Lotus Tea.**

LOTUS ROOT

An individual lotus root (technically, a rhizome) is shaped like a fat cucumber and colored like old ivory with some brown streaks. When it is sliced into rounds, the root's hollow air chambers make a beautiful lacy design.

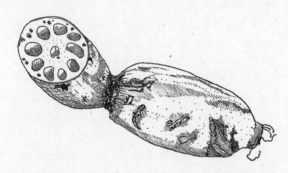

Health Benefits In Ayurvedic medicine, lotus root is primarily used for cooling function. In Oriental medicine, it is used to support the spleen-pancreas and stomach; to astringe the intestines; and to nurture the heart. It promotes the production of fluids; is useful for hemorrhages, nosebleeds, excessive menstruation, and diarrhea; and enriches the blood. It is prescribed for lung-related ailments, to increase energy, to neutralize toxins, and to treat anorexia. It reduces *pitta* and *vata*.

Use The lotus rhizome is fun to use because of its beautiful shape; its crunchy texture (similar to a jicama), which holds up to cooking; and its mildly sweet flavor. Slice it thin and braise, steam, or stir-fry it, or float it on top of soups. For a dramatic-looking dish, stuff the chambers of a whole root with a brightly colored filling, cook it, and then slice it. Some cooks peel lotus; I never do since the skin is tender and mild tasting.

Buying Lotus is in season in the fall, winter, and early spring. Select firm, cream-colored roots free of bruises or discoloration. Uncut, the root stores well if refrigerated, in plastic, for up to a week. Once cut, it should be used within three days.

Dried lotus root is available in Asian markets. It is packaged in thin rounds. Reconstitute by soaking in water for two hours prior to use. It may be substituted for fresh lotus in long-simmered dishes.

LOTUS SEED

The cream-colored lotus seed, similar in size and shape to a cooked chickpea, is a tasty food with a pleasant nutty flavor. It can be bought dried from Asian markets. When soaked and split open, notice its unusually large embrionic sprout that looks like a miniature lotus plant.

Health Benefits Lotus seeds increase kidney energy and overall vitality. They aid digestion, nourish the heart, counter insomnia, and soothe the nervous system. They're used for vaginal discharge, cloudy urine, or seminal emission. They contain 20 percent protein and so are highly nourishing. Lotus seeds reduce *pitta* and *vata*.

Use Lotus seeds require soaking and cooking, like beans. In fact, when I want to give an energy boost to a pot of beans, I'll often add three or four lotus seeds per cup of dry beans, soaking and cooking them together. Be-

---

**THOUSAND-YEAR-OLD SEED
GERMINATED BY U.C.L.A. PLANT
PHYSIOLOGIST**

The viability of most seeds is—depending
upon storage conditions—a decade or so,
and the percentage of seeds that germinate decreases with each passing year.
The scientific world was astounded when
an ancient lotus seed not only sprouted
but grew to maturity. A lotus seed radio-
carbon dated to 1288 B.C. (give or take
220 years) from a dry lake bed in China
was germinated in 1994 by Jane Shen-
Miller. According to her, the seed's natural preservative, together with the oxy-
genfree environment in the lake bed,
helped maintain its viability. This enzyme
helps repair age-damaged proteins—no
wonder lotus seeds are considered an
important vitality-building food in Asia.

---

fore cooking, remove any seeds that float to
the top; they have a bitter taste. Use lotus
seeds in vegetable, bean, soup, or grain, dishes.

LOTUS TEA
Kohren

Lotus tea, made from fresh or powdered
dried lotus, is an excellent medicinal beverage.
Regular use of lotus tea builds overall strength
and specifically strengthens the heart, lungs,
kidneys, and digestive system. When ginger is
added to this tea, it treats enteritis, nausea, digestive disorders, and difficulty in swallowing.
To quench thirst during a fever, sweeten
with honey.

To make lotus tea, mix 2 teaspoons of
dried lotus powder (or 2 tablespoons of
freshly grated lotus root) into 1 cup of water.
Add a pinch of salt and heat over low heat
just to the boiling point. Drink hot. The powder is available in Asian markets, natural
food stores, and from full-service whole
foods suppliers.

LOVAGE
Love Parsley
(Levisticum officinale)

A parsley relative that tastes like strong
celery, lovage is a favorite in herb gardens
and one of the first to green up in the spring.
It is a tall perennial with hollow stems and
leaves that resemble celery leaves. As a medicinal and culinary agent, lovage is popular
in southern and central Europe.

Health Benefits Lovage is a bittersweet
sedative that aids digestion, increases perspiration, and acts as a diuretic and expectorant.
It strengthens the immune system, and is
useful for indigestion, and for relieving flatulence, kidney stones, and painful menstruation. Do not use during pregnancy, as it
promotes the onset of menstruation. Lovage
reduces *kapha* and *pitta*.

Use In Slavic regions, lovage root is peeled
and used as a vegetable. Roots at least three
years old are used for extractions and tinctures. Young stalks are eaten as a vegetable
and used as a straw for beverages. Its seeds
are used as a spice; its leaves as an herb.
Lovage leaves pep up soups, stews, and pickles; they hold up well to heat and so may be
simmered for a long time.

See **Carrot Family; Herbs and Spices.**

LOVE PARSLEY See Lovage.

LUCERNE See Alfalfa.

LUFA See Loofah.

LUPINE
(Lupinus albus, L. luteus, L. varius, L. mutabilis)

An old European legume, the lupin is bit-ter tasting but high in protein—as high as 44 percent. A sweet lupine, developed in the United States, is available in natural food stores in the form of a nutritious pasta. Once cooked, lupine pasta is more fragile than wheat pasta.

See **Legume Family.**

LYTCHEE See Litchi.

$\mathscr{M}$

MACADAMIA NUT
(Macadamia integrifolia)

The name of this most buttery, sweet nut once evoked for me visions of a faraway, lush, tropical Macademian realm. Then I learned that the nut was named for a Scotsman, John Macadam.

The texture of a macadamia nut is similar to a Brazil nut but more meltingly tender. This creamy-colored nut originated in northeastern Australia and is the only native Australian plant that has been domesticated, according to Jared Diamond's fascinating history *Guns, Germs, and Steel*. In the past few decades, Hawaii and California have become the main producers of the U.S. domestic supply. Availability of the macadamia is increasing.

Health Benefits Oil is the only vegetarian food higher in fat and calories than the macadamia, which contains a whopping 70 percent fat content. One pound of nuts is over 3,500 calories. Macadamia nuts reduce *vata*.

Use For possibly the most sumptuous nut flavor there is, substitute macadamias for any nutmeat in entrées, desserts, or confections.

Buying Because the macadamia is nigh impossible to crack by hand, it is sold shelled. See **Nuts**.

MACE
(Myristica fragrans)

This spice, quite out of fashion for several decades, is staging a modest comeback. Mace is the yellow-orange aril, or lacy husk, of the nutmeg seed. Like nutmeg, mace has a peppery, cinnamonlike flavor, but is sharper and distinctly unique.

Health Benefits Mace is warming and supports digestive functioning; I tend to favor it during the colder months. It reduces *vata* and *kapha*.

Use This pleasing and somewhat old-fashioned flavoring agent is mostly used in desserts but is also delicious in soups, in sauces, and with poultry. I also like to add it to flavored butter.

Buying Mace is sometimes sold in blades but is most often sold ground; it is difficult

GRANDMA THEURER'S MACE CAKE

Years after Grandma died, my Aunt Anna Theurer happened to visit an old grammar school friend, Shirley. Shirley's daughter came in and requested a mace cake. Aunt Anna, who had never heard of a mace cake, asked about it. Shirley pulled out her mother's old recipe, and—to their mutual surprise—found that the recipe was called "Mrs. Theurer's Mace Cake." It has since become—apparently once again—one of our family's favorites. I bet even Grandma would prefer the rich, round flavors of my whole food substitutions for the angular taste of white sugar and refined salt and the flat flavor of white flour.

    1 cup unsalted butter
    1½ cups rapadura
    5 eggs, separated
    2 tablespoons milk
    2 cups whole wheat pastry flour
    ¼ teaspoon sea salt
    ½ teaspoon ground mace
    2 teaspoons lemon juice
    1 teaspoon grated lemon zest
    2 tablespoons finely chopped black
        walnuts or pecans

Preheat the oven to 325 degrees. Cream together the butter and rapadura. Add the egg yolks and milk and beat well. Sift dry ingredients together and stir into the wet ingredients. Add the lemon juice and zest and beat well. Beat the egg whites to peaks and fold them in. Put in a greased tube pan or 4 × 10-inch or 5 × 8-inch loaf pan. Sprinkle the top with the nuts. Bake for 1 hour. Leave right side up to cool.

to grind the blades at home. Unlike many ground spices, mace holds its flavor well.

See **Herbs and Spices; Nutmeg.**

MÂCHE
Corn Salad, Lamb's Lettuce
(Valerianella locusta)

What was available at the turn of the century as corn salad is back again as mâche. This attractive blue-green salad green, a valerian family member, has been cultivated since neolithic times. It has a mild, nutty flavor and a downy texture. Compared to lettuce, it is slightly chewy and firm. The largest of its diminutive leaves are five inches long and about one and a half inches wide. This hardy vegetable thrives in cold, wet regions and even grows through frost and snow. Mâche is one of my favorite garden plants, for once established, it produces long after and long before other salad greens.

Health Benefits Like other dark leafy greens, mâche is an excellent source of beta carotene and an excellent liver food. Its ability to survive harsh winters is a good indicator that it is more nutrient-dense than lettuce and other fragile salad greens. Mâche reduces *pitta* and *kapha;* in moderation, it also reduces *vata.*

Use Mâche is often found in salad mixes. It lends itself to arranged salads and is delicious by itself with a simple dressing. Historically it was used as a potherb—a use that I also recommend.

Buying Mâche is available as separate leaves or as a whole plant, roots intact, which is the size of a small nosegay. Select fresh heads with unblemished leaves, and use it immediately.

Ma Chi Xian See Purslane.

Madagascar Bean See Lima Bean.

Maitake See Hen-of-the-Woods.

Maize See Corn.

Makrut See Kaffir Lime.

Malanga See Yautia.

Ø MALITOL

A refined, non-nutritive sweetener made from corn, malitol is a more costly version of sorbitol; it is currently being touted as a "healthful" sweetener. If malitol is eaten excessively, it may cause gas or other digestive disturbances. Not recommended.

See **Sorbitol; Sweeteners.**

Malt See Barley Malt Sugar; Barley Malt Syrup.

MALT VINEGAR

Made of sprouted and fermented barley, malt vinegar at 5 to 6 percent acetic acid is too strongly flavored for salad dressings. The English liberally splash it on fish and chips to help cut the oil. When malt vinegar is distilled to a clear white, instead of amber brown, it is excellent for pickling.

See **Vinegar.**

MAMEY SAPOTE
(Pouteria sapota)

A tropical fruit native to the West Indies, the mamey sapote is just now gaining a market position. It is a fruit to watch for. It's shaped like a large pointed peach with gritty skin and striking flesh that ranges from pink to salmon in color. The mamey's memorable tropical flavor is a blend of honeyed pumpkin and almond essence. Ripen at room temperature until it is soft to the touch and use as you would a mango. Available in the summer, mamey sapote is grown extensively in the Caribbean, Mexico, and South America. The single pit is toxic.

See **Tropical Fruit.**

Manchurian Mushroom See Kombucha.

MANDARIN
(Citrus reticulata)

Mandarin is a citrus group encompassing fruit from the tiny tangerine to the large ugli. Its Latin name, *reticulata*, means "netted" and refers to the fibrous strands located under the thin, loose-fitting peel, which easily detaches from the fruit. Clementines, mineolas, and satsumas are the most readily available mandarin types. In the citrus trade, "tangerine" refers to the smaller mandarins with a deep red-orange peel and many seeds, and a low acid content.

Health Benefits Cooling and refreshing, mandarins are sweet and sour; they act upon the lungs, stomach, and spleen-pancreas. They are used to build energy, to clear heat, and to quench thirst. Mandarins are useful in the treatment of chest congestion, vomiting, diabetes, and hiccupping.

Mandarin peel from a ripe fruit aids digestion and transforms phlegm while peel from an immature fruit treats liver congestion. Mandarins are used for mastitis and breast cancer and pain in the liver, chest, or breasts. They reduce *vata*.

See **Citrus Family.**

MANGO
(Mangifera indica)

Sensuously sticky and lush, the mango is one of the most popular tropical fruits, after the banana and coconut. It is a cashew relative and grows on an evergreen tree. The mango has a smooth, leathery skin colored green, yellow, or red. Mangos are generally round to oval and vary in weight from six ounces to one and a half pounds. The juicy orange-colored flesh clings to a large, flat stone. The U.S. domestic crop, which grows in Florida, California, and Hawaii, is in season during the summer. Out-of-season mangos are imported.

Health Benefits A mango's thermal property is cooling, thus it is useful in clearing heat from the body and in quenching thirst. Ripened mangos are *tridoshic*. This delectable fruit is a superior source of vitamins A and C and provides a good source of potassium. It is moderately high in calories.

Use In mango-producing areas, the fruits are often available from sidewalk vendors, peeled and skewered upon a stick, and are better than a lollipop. The stick enables you to tease away the sweet flesh that clings to the pit. Otherwise, removing the flesh from the pit is a slippery affair. The best way is to slice the fruit lengthwise all around the stone. Cut slices and pull them away from the stone, then peel and discard the skin.

Contrary to what some people suggest, a mango (like other fruits) is most flavorful at room temperature. If the mango has an off taste at room temperature, chilling will indeed mask the foul flavor. But why not just toss it?

With or without a squeeze of lime, use raw mango, sliced or cut into chunks, for vegetable, fruit, and meat salads, fruit kabobs, parfaits, and puddings; or purée mango for ice cream and smoothies. This all-around fruit is equally delicious cooked in tarts, cakes, and cobblers, or even made into jelly. Immature mangos are a classic chutney, relish, and pickle ingredient.

Buying Select mangos that are firm, plump, and fresh-looking and that have a pleasant, spicy aroma at the stem end. If there is no scent, the fruit will be flavorless. Ripen at room temperature in a brown bag until the fruit yields slightly to pressure, like a ripe avocado. As the mango ripens, the

---

WHAT MANGOS AND POISON IVY HAVE IN COMMON

Four botanical relatives—mangos, poison ivy, poison oak, and poison sumac—all contain urushiol. For people with allergies, this toxic resin can cause contact dermatitis or blistering skin. The peel and juice of a mango seem to be more of a problem than the flesh—especially immature fruits. Eating mangos to excess may cause itching or skin eruptions.

---

skin color intensifies (green-skinned mangos excepted). Once ripe, a mango may be refrigerated for several days. As imported mangos are heat treated to kill fruit flies or pests, I favor domestic mangos.

See **Tropical Fruit.**

MANGOSTEEN
(Garcinia mangostana)

Many people say that this Malaysian berry, with its exquisite milky, sweet juice, is maybe the most delicious tropical fruit there is. Like a tangerine in size and structure, a mangosteen is covered by a tough, thick, brownish purple rind; it contains from five to six orangelike segments. Carefully cut through and discard the rind. Because mangosteen propagation is difficult and because its flavor is best when fresh, availability is sketchy in the United States. Keep cool and dry.

See **Tropical Fruit.**

MANIOC See **Cassava.**

Ø MANNITOL

The powdery dust on sticks of chewing gum is mannitol; it is a synthesized form of corn sugar. When used in excess, mannitol has been implicated in kidney and gastrointestinal disturbances. Not recommended.

See **Sweeteners.**

MAPLE SUGAR

Granulated like white sugar but buff color, maple sugar is made by evaporating the water from maple syrup. This premier sweetener is nearly 100 percent sucrose with a pleasing flavor. Maple sugar is available in natural food stores in packages, as well as in cake, cookie, and icing mixes. It is often found molded into the shape of a small maple leaf for sale as a novelty food or tourist item.

Use Substitute maple sugar for white sugar, cup for cup, in any recipe. It yields a less intensely sweet but more flavorful dish.

See **Maple Syrup.**

MAPLE SYRUP

Using technologies learned long ago from Native Americans in the Northeast, 80 percent of today's maple syrup is still produced by small family operations. As agribusiness encroaches, however, reverse osmosis is now used to process some syrup. By either method, it takes 40 gallons of sap to make one gallon of syrup; the sap is collected over three months.

In early February, a small tap hole is drilled into a sugar maple tree trunk, and the seeping sap is collected; at 3 percent sucrose, it is barely sweet. But boiled down to reduce its water content, it turns into a liquid treasure.

Health Benefits Compared to white sugar with its 99 percent sucrose content, maple syrup at 65 percent sucrose is obviously a more healthful choice. Like white sugar, however, it may still cause insulin and adrenaline reactions. Maple syrup is damp producing, and so is best used in moderation if at all by people with candida, malignancies, tumors, cysts, or a compromised immune system. It reduces *vata* and *pitta*.

Use Real maple syrup is utterly delicious on so much more than just pancakes and waffles. I use it in place of sugar for some candies and in many baked goods where it adds a wonderful maple flavor, moisture, and density. It is less intensely sweet than honey or white sugar. To substitute maple syrup in a recipe calling for sugar, replace 1 cup of sugar with ½ to ⅓ cup of maple syrup and reduce the recipe's liquid measurement by ¼ cup for a more flavorful, moister, denser crumb. Easier yet, and to get the same "sugar crumb," use maple sugar.

Buying To the connoisseur, the flavor of maple syrup varies depending upon when the sap is drawn. Sap harvested in February yields a light-colored and most delicately flavored syrup—a syrup considered premium. As the weather warms, the mineral and bacteria content of the maple sap increases, and when it is cooked down, it more readily caramelizes into a darker, more robustly flavored syrup. The USDA has recently standardized these grades of syrup: U.S. Grade A, categorized as light, medium, or dark; U.S. Grade B, darker in color and more

commonly available to the consumer in half-gallon sizes or larger.

Because the quality of pure maple syrup varies dramatically, favor certified organic maple syrups. Some syrup producers place a formaldehyde pellet in the tree's tap hole to prolong sap flow. This contaminates the sap. The Canadian government, the state of Vermont, and organic certification codes prohibit use of these pellets.

Maple syrup may also be contaminated with high levels of lead. This may be from the lead seams in the metal cans it is marketed in or from the evaporating pans used by most producers. Since the FDA limits the lead content of imported maple syrup, Canadian brands can be considered safe as can certified organic brands.

Maple syrup is the one sweetener that is usually refrigerated. Refrigeration is necessary, however, only in a very hot climate.

See **Sweeteners.**

SNOW CANDY

Grandma stood by the brass kettle and with the big wooden spoon she poured hot [maple] syrup on each plate of snow. It cooled into soft candy, and as fast as it cooled they ate it. . . . There was plenty of syrup in the kettle, and plenty of snow outdoors. As soon as they ate one plateful, they filled their plates with snow again, and Grandma poured more syrup on it.

—Laura Ingells Wilder, *The Little House in the Big Woods*

Ø MARGARINE

Not recommended. Even if margarine is sold in a health food store, even if it's made from "good" ingredients—leave it on the shelf. It's a synthetic food containing from 25 to 51 percent toxic transfats. A transfat forms when a hydrogen molecule bonds to a liquid vegetable oil, changing it into a solid fat. Transfats challenge the digestive system and liver; raise cholesterol (by increasing low-density lipoproteins and decreasing the high-density lipoproteins); raise the risk of heart disease and cancer; and contribute to obesity.

See Butter; Fat and Oil.

MARINE ALGAE See Seaweed.

MARJORAM
Sweet Marjoram
(Origanum majorana)

Related to oregano, marjoram is a native of the Mediterranean region; it is the milder of the two herbs. When dried, its flavor is further reduced, and so this herb is often passed over in favor of its more robust relative. Favored fresh in French, Greek, and Italian cuisine, marjoram is at its best when added just at the end of cooking.

Health Benefits Medicinally, marjoram is valued for its ability to relieve menstrual cramps, calm stressed nerves and muscles, to relieve insomnia, and for bronchial complaints. As a flavoring agent or in tea, it aids digestion. It reduces *vata* and *kapha*.

Use Both the leaves and blossoms of marjoram are used to infuse oils and vinegar and to season pasta, tomato, bean, and meat dishes.

See Herbs and Spices; Oregano.

MARSH SAMPHIRE See Glasswort.

MASA

Masa means dough in Spanish; in the Americas, it refers to a wet dough made from posole (hominy or slaked corn). Masa is a base for tortillas, tacos, enchiladas, tamales, or corn chips (see page 207). Commercially available masa is made from white corn; blue corn masa products, however, have increasing availability; and yellow masa is usually used for chips and tortillas. Masa is available frozen—and sometimes fresh—from Latino markets. Fresh masa is available in two grades: fine (*masa para tortillas*) and coarse (*masa para tamales*).

See Corn; Masa Harina; Posole.

MASA HARINA

Harina means flour in Spanish. Masa harina is ground dried masa. It is readily available in supermarkets as well as in specialty food stores.

See Arepas; Masa; Posole.

MATÉ
Yerba Maté
(Ilex para)

Maté comes from a Quechua word meaning a gourd vessel used for brewing and drinking a type of holly tea—but it has come to mean the tea itself. This holly originated in Paraguay, and the tea remains a popular beverage there as well as in Uruguay, Argentina, Chile, and Brazil.

Health Benefits Maté is a mildly caffeinated beverage. It reduces feelings of fatigue and hunger. Maté acts as a diuretic, relaxes spasms, clears toxins, and is mildly

A TASTE TEST FOR CORN CHIP CONNOISSEURS

Taste a Cheerio, Wheat Chex, or Fritos corn chip. It's hard to find the flavor of, respectively, oats, wheat, or corn. When extruded under high heat and pressure, a grain's subtle flavors are lost, and its heat-vulnerable nutrients are denatured. This high-tech process forms the *O* of a Cheerio, the weave of a Chex, and the curl of a Frito but about all you can taste is the seasoning agents—not the grain.

In the case of corn chips, however, there are tasty and healthful options to extruded products. Traditional corn chips are made of masa harina and not extruded. Their giveaway triangular shape with sharp angles marks them as wedges cut from tortillas. Their real masa flavor is the best giveaway. The rounded corners on some triangle-shape corn chips reveal extrusion.

LA BOMBILLA

Slurping maté, the definitive South American tea, from a dried gourd through a *bombilla* is satisfying to the soul. The *bombilla* is a metal straw that ends in a spoon-shape sieve. The sound made while sucking the dregs to savor one last sip is deliciously barbarous. The irregular-shape gourd—which is both brew pot and drinking cup—is soft in the hand and adds ambiance. Maté and sometimes maté gourds and *bombillas* are available in natural food stores and specialty food markets.

MATSUTAKE
Pine Mushroom
(*Armillaria ponderosa, A. edodes*)

One of the most appealing edible mushrooms, the matsutake has a sweetly scented pine aroma and a superb flavor. The stems are thick and meaty and the slightly pointed, unopened caps are enclosed in a veil, making them look distinctively phallic. As the caps flare open, the market price declines.

Health Benefits Matsutake mushrooms thin blood and thus lower cholesterol and help prevent strokes and heart attacks. By stimulating the immune system, they help prevent cancer and other degenerative conditions. Matsutake contain germanium, which increases oxygen efficiency and counters the effects of environmental pollutants.

Use In Asia, matsutake mushrooms are traditionally broken into pieces rather than sliced. To best reveal their spicy aroma, they are simmered in broth. While they can flavor

analgesic. It is said to help relieve headaches, arthritic pain, mild depression, and neuralgia. Maté reduces *kapha*.

Use Maté has a pleasing, light flavor and is drunk in South America at all hours. People who are caffeine-sensitive might favor it in the morning.

Buying Maté is available packaged, in bulk herb departments, in natural food stores, and as an ingredient in herbal tea blends.

See **Herbs and Spices.**

many savory dishes, they are usually show-cased alone or in a simple preparation. To reconstitute dried matsutake mushrooms, soak in water or an unsalted, seasoned broth for 20 minutes, or until softened.

Buying/Foraging Matsutake mushrooms are foraged near stands of red pine in China, Japan, and the Pacific Northwest. They are recently under limited cultivation; this factor, plus their short foraging season, makes them extremely expensive. Dried matsutake have limited availability; drying diminishes their flavor.

See **Mushroom Family.**

Maui Onion See Onion.

Meal See Flour.

Meat Analog See Textured Vegetable Protein (TVP).

Meat Extender See Textured Vegetable Protein (TVP).

Medicine Plant See Aloe Vera.

Meiwa See Kumquat.

MEKABU WAKAME
(Undaria pinnatifida)

The reproductive part of the seaweed wakame is called mekabu wakame. It is the leafy blade that bears the plant's spore and it grows in a spiral fashion on a thick stipe. Mekabu wakame is highly mucilaginous; for many people, it is an acquired taste. Mekabu is considered an excellent female tonic. It requires longer cooking than wakame. It is available in Asian markets and from full-service whole foods mail-order sources.

See **Wakame.**

Melissa See Lemon Balm.

MELON
(Cucumis melo)

Melons do their share to usher in—and give relief from—the dog days of summer. They have come a long way from their original state. Wild melons the size of oranges and bland tasting still grow in Africa. In Roman times, melons were eaten as part of green vegetable salad. During the Renaissance, the monks at the Pope's summer residence Cantalupo coaxed this watery food into the sugary, flavorful fruit we know today.

As the seed structure indicates, melons are members of the gourd family, relatives of cucumbers and squash. There are two types of melons—the muskmelon and the watermelon. The latter has its seeds imbedded in its juicy flesh like a cucumber; in muskmelons, the seeds are contained in a hollow central cavity, like a squash or a pumpkin. These muskmelons so readily interbreed among themselves that there are many varieties, with many more likely to be developed—and endless confusion about nomenclature as a result. Muskmelons' flesh color ranges from a honeydew's lime green to a Crenshaw's pink-salmon hue.

Health Benefits Of late, melons, especially the orange-fleshed varieties, have received much press for their excellent beta carotene content, which puts them high on the list of anticarcinogenic foods. Melons are also an excellent potassium source, and since they have a negligible amount of fat, are perfect for those concerned with high blood pressure. In addition, they have an anticoagulant ingredient, adenosine, which offers support for those with heart disease and may help bring on menstruation.

Melons are a cooling food useful for hot conditions such as fevers accompanied by chills or dry coughs. They also have diuretic properties and may relieve mental depression. Melons are best avoided when there is abdominal swelling or watery stools. Melons in general reduce *vata* and *pitta*, though watermelon increases *vata*.

Use Melons, with a water content of about 94 percent, are digested very rapidly. It is therefore best to eat melon alone. If melon is combined with another food, digestion is slowed, and fermentation—rather than assimilation—results. Melons do not withstand cooking but are delicious in fruit salads, fruit soups, ices, or sorbet. They may be juiced, or served standing on their own, with or without a squeeze of lime.

Buying A melon's sugar content does not increase after picking, so avoid immature fruits. A ripe melon is heavy for its size with a firm rind, a slight softening, and a sweet aroma at the blossom end (casaba excepted). Avoid an overly ripe melon or one with dark, soft, or sunken spots. The flavor of a fresh local melon far exceeds that of an out-of-season melon, which, of necessity, was picked immaturely.

- **Cantaloupe** Most available of the melons. Cantaloupe is usually sold when mature but not dead ripe. Purchase a cantaloupe with no stem or stem fragment. Hold it at room temperature until it has a pleasant cantaloupe aroma and yields slightly to light thumb pressure on the blossom end, and when the rind's netting is pronounced with a dull yellowish cast. Avoid purchasing an overripe melon, which is soft with a pronounced yellow rind.
- **Casaba** Round like a pumpkin but pointed slightly at the blossom end. The rind has shallow, irregular furrows running from blossom end to stem end. Some have a pale green rind and pale yellow flesh; others have a light orange to dark green rind with gold flesh. When ripe, it has a slight softening at the blossom end. A ripe casaba has no aroma until cut.
- **Crenshaw** Easy to identify because of its large, ovoid size and pointed stem end. The rind of the Crenshaw melon is smooth, golden, and slightly corrugated. The thick flesh is a bright salmon color. A Crenshaw is ripe when it has a sweet aroma and the rind is a deep golden yellow, yielding slightly to moderate pressure at the blossom end. When ripe, the flesh has a spicy-sweet taste.
- **Honeyball** Similar to the honeydew but smaller.
- **Honeydew** Large with a smooth, very pale green skin and sweet light-green flesh. A slight "bloom," faint netting, and a slightly sticky feeling on the skin indicate a ripe honeydew. If it is hard with a white or green-

white rind, the honeydew was picked prematurely and will not become sweet.

- **Persian** Similar to a cantaloupe but more nearly round, with a finer netting. The flesh is thick, finely textured, and orange.

See **Gourd Family; Fruit; Watermelon.**

MESCLUN
Misticanza

Mesclun is a mix of tender young lettuces, herbs, and (sometimes) edible blossoms used for salad greens. It's as delightful to the eye as it is to the palate. Butterhead lettuce, loose-leaf lettuce, chicory, red romaine, cress, and frisée are the commonly used greens. Mesclun, a French term (*nisticanza* is the Italian), is increasingly available, both loose and in cellophane packs; it is best used the day of purchase. Packets of mesclun seed mixes are available for home gardeners.

MESQUITE
(Prosopis veluntina)

Aromatic mesquite meal is an ingredient I keep on hand for more than its malty sweet flavor and many energy properties. Its taste evokes for me the fresh, clean smell of the desert in blossom.

Most people associate mesquite with a novelty charcoal for grilling or a honey with a desert bouquet. But it is much more. Mesquite has been perhaps the single most important plant food of Southwest native peoples. A leguminous, drought-resistant small tree or shrub, mesquite produces wood that's highly valued for furniture, crafts, and charcoal making. As a result, the fragile desert ecosystem throughout the Southwest and northern Mexico is being threatened as mesquite is stripped from it. Hopefully this destruction will cease and the desert will be restabilized.

Health Benefits Regarded as a high-energy food, mesquite meal is a key ingredient in pinole, the dietary staple of the world-famous Tarahumara runners who ate pinole to sustain them in their legendary hundred-mile mountain marathons.

Mesquite pods, as well as their leaves, twigs, and bark, make a strong disinfectant wash for broken-skin injuries. Decoct in boiling water. Or drink this tea for its astringent, antimicrobial action. Mesquite inhibits diarrhea and intestinal inflammations including ulcers, colitis, and hemorrhoids. For pinkeye or conjunctivitis, infuse five washed and crushed pods and half a teaspoon salt in two cups of boiling water.

Mesquite is high in lysine and rich in calcium, magnesium, potassium, iron, and zinc. It reduces *vata*.

Use The meal ground from mesquite pods is so sweet that I sometimes use it as a sweetener replacement in corn bread, muffins, puddings, sauces, and even pie crust. It doesn't work well in pancakes or waffles, though. Mesquite meal does not contain gluten, so it is best when combined with wheat in baked goods. If you have whole pods, you may make, as do some Native Americans, a thin syrup of the pods by simmering them, covered in water, for a day, then straining out the pods and reducing the liquid.

Buying/Foraging According to Michael

Moore, author and herbalist who specializes in plants of the Southwest, if you are in any part of the Colorado, Mojave, Sonora, or Chihuahua desert, then mesquite, the most common shrub in all of the Southwest, is nearby. Mesquite meal is available in some specialty shops by mail order and from PRO-NATURA (see page 401). Mature mesquite pods are foraged in the fall directly from the tree or from the ground below.

MEXICAN BEAN See **Kidney Bean.**

MEXICAN BREADFRUIT See **Monstera.**

MEXICAN LIME See **Lime.**

MEXICAN PARSLEY See **Cilantro.**

MEXICAN TEA See **Epazote.**

MICHIHLI CABBAGE See **Chinese Cabbage.**

MICROALGAE

Photosynthesis, the conversion of sunlight into food, is possible because of chlorophyll. With this miraculous substance, the plant kingdom manufactures its food from basic elements and sunlight. All life is dependent on the chemical reactions made possible by chlorophyll, which is often referred to as the "blood of plants." Given that as the molecular structure between hemoglobin (red blood cells) and chlorophyll is similar, it is not surprising that chlorophyll enriches our blood.

The most intense concentrations of chlorophyll are found in freshwater algae. These algae exist on the edge between the plant and animal kingdoms and offer more than just chlorophyll. They are higher in protein, beta carotene, and nucleic acids than any other food. Their nucleic acids benefit the renewal of human cells and help to reverse aging. Three exceptionally nutritious algae widely available in natural food stores are chlorella, spirulina, and wild blue-green algae. These cooling foods have cleansing, detoxifying, and healing effects upon our bodies.

MILK SUBSTITUTES

As awareness of lactose intolerance increases, milk substitutes multiply. Soymilk was the first to gain popularity in the 1980s; now there's a wide assortment, including soymilk, rice milk, amasake, rice-soymilk, oat milk, and almond milk. These beverages come plain and flavored with different degrees of enrichment. Found in the refrigerated section, in liquid form in shelf-stable packaging, and powdered, each product varies in quality. While these milk substitutes are useful foods, those that are highly processed are certainly not deeply nourishing or strengthening. The powdered products, energetically speaking, are superior to the liquid beverages in shelf-stable packaging (see page 317).

MILLET
(Panicum miliaceum)

Most corn is fed to cattle; most barley is brewed for beer; and most millet is used as birdseed. The eastern Colorado town of Otis's (population 700) claim to fame is as Bird Seed Capital of America.

Elsewhere in the world, millet is a generic term for at least five different small and unrelated cereal grains. In the United States, the word millet refers to proso, and it is this strain that we find in natural food stores, in some progressive supermarkets, and in parakeet feed.

Proso was among the earliest cultivated cereals. The first written reference to this millet is dated at about 2800 B.C. and lists the five sacred crops of China as rice, soybeans, barley, wheat, and millet. Millet seems to have been brought overland by the Mongols into the Middle East and the Mediterranean basin. Frequently noted in the New Testament, millet flourished throughout the Roman Empire and into the Middle Ages, during which time it was a dominant food crop before being supplanted by modern wheat.

Health Benefits Millet is a cooling grain good for the stomach and spleen-pancreas and for healing gastrointestinal irregularities. Cooking it with winter squash increases its medicinal value to the stomach and spleen-pancreas. Millet is the preferred grain in the treatment of blood sugar imbalances and one of the best grains for those suffering from thrush. A European remedy for relieving rheumatic and some arthritic pains is to apply a poultice of hot (but not so hot as to burn the skin) millet porridge to the affected area. Millet reduces *kapha*.

Of all the true cereal grains, millet has the richest amino-acid protein profile and the highest iron content. It is very rich in phosphorus and the B vitamins. It is glutenfree and due to its high alkaline ash content, the easiest grain to digest. This unusual makeup allows millet to be cooked without salt and yet be alkaline rather than acidic.

Use If millet is cooked with little liquid (1 cup millet to 2¼ cups liquid), it makes a

---

STEAMED MILLET

Millet is quick, easy to prepare, and versatile. It can be served with any gravy, sauce, topping, or condiment as a grain entrée or as a side dish or with honey and milk for breakfast. Form leftover millet into small cakes with moistened hands, season with soy sauce, and pan-fry in oil or butter.

  1 cup millet
  2¼ cups boiling water or stock
  ¼ teaspoon sea salt
  1 tablespoon oil or butter (optional)

Put the millet in a heavy-bottomed saucepan over medium heat. Toast, stirring constantly, for about 5 minutes, or until the millet is lightly aromatic and begins to pop. Reduce the heat, if necessary, to prevent scorching. When the millet is toasted, remove from the heat. Pour into a strainer and rinse under running water for 15 seconds, or until the water runs clear. Shake out excess water. Meanwhile, bring water or stock to a boil. Add salt and oil, if using. Return to a boil, cover, and simmer for about 20 minutes, or until all water is absorbed. Turn off the heat and let stand, covered, for 5 minutes. Fluff the millet with a fork and serve immediately.

light, dry, fluffy pilaf. Increase the liquid to 3 cups and it has a smooth texture like mashed potatoes or polenta. Millet can be eaten alone as a cereal or side dish or cooked in combination with other grains in breads, soups, stews, stuffing, and even desserts.

Buying As millet has a more fragile shelf life than the other grains, purchase it in small quantities from a natural food store that has a high turnover and store it in a cool pantry or refrigerate. Millet has a mild, nutty flavor. If it has an acrid, harsh aftertaste, it is rancid and should be discarded.

See **Grains.**

MILLET FLOUR

Millet flour lends a dry, delicate, cakelike crumb and a pale yellow color to baked goods. Fresh millet flour has a distinctive sweet flavor. When old, it is bitter and should be discarded. Millet flour is sold in natural food stores, but since it turns rancid and bitter quite rapidly, it is best to grind it as needed in a spice grinder or grain mill.

Because millet has no gluten, the flour is best combined with wheat flour for cookies, cakes, and bread. For sauces and some cookies and flatbreads, it may be used alone.

See **Flour.**

MINEOLA See **Tangelo.**

MINERAL WATER See **Water.**

MINT
(Mentha)

Even if you were blindfolded in a garden, your nose would draw you right to mint.

Mint is a fragrant presence not only in the garden but in the kitchen and medicine cabinet as well.

There are more than five hundred known mint varieties, the two most common culinary mints being peppermint and spearmint. Although used interchangeably, peppermint is the more cooling and stimulating of the two. Spearmint is slightly warming.

Health Benefits The pungent menthol flavor of mint helps disperse pathogens such as viruses or bacteria, invigorates by promoting circulation of energy, blood, and lymph. These properties make mint a useful ingredient in many herbal remedies, especially where there is excessive heat, such as in mastitis, painful menstruation, and hives. In cases of painful menstruation due to cold blockages, mint is not recommended.

Peppermint relieves spasms, increases perspiration, and tones the digestive system, especially the colon. It is not, according to herbalists, to be used for infants at any time. Spearmint, on the other hand, is a common remedy for feverish childhood illnesses as well as for hiccups, indigestion, and flatulence. Both peppermint and spearmint are *tridoshic*, though they are considered especially calming to *pitta*.

Use Mint's menthol is too intense an aroma and taste to go with subtly flavored savory dishes. But it's a great addition to tea, sugary foods, chocolate, and candy. Mint jelly or sauce is a traditional accompaniment to lamb. Because of its cooling properties, in hot weather I strew it in teas, boldly flavored chilled soups, and in rice, tabbouleh, and couscous salads.

See **Herbs and Spices.**

MIRIN

Quality mirin is an ambrosial cooking wine. Like sake, it is naturally brewed and fermented from sweet brown rice, koji, and water. The 13 to 14 percent alcohol in mirin evaporates quickly when heated—but not before it has imparted a mild sweetness. Mirin rounds out and gives a signature Japanese flavor to many dishes.

Inexpensive, commercial-quality mirin, available in Asian markets, is chemically brewed to quicken production time and is sweetened with sugar or corn syrup. The sweet rice wine found in natural food stores, however, is usually a natural and high-quality product. Use mirin for a glaze on pie crusts, pastries, and barbecued dishes. It is excellent in vinaigrette, in fish or vegetable dishes, or in sauces and dips.

See **Koji.**

MIRLITON See Chayote.

MISO

Miso is a fermented paste with a texture like peanut butter. It's made of soybeans, a koji inoculant, salt, and a grain—most commonly rice or barley. Just as grapes may be fermented into a wide range of differently flavored wines, soybeans may be fermented into a vast range of differently flavored misos, from meaty and savory to delicate and sweet.

Prior to the 1970s, miso was an unknown word—and taste experience—to most Americans. Today, this traditional Japanese food has become an important staple in haute cuisine as well as in healthy diets.

Health Benefits Miso, an anticarcinogen, is also effective in reducing the effects of radiation, smoking, air pollution, and other environmental toxins. The darker the color, the more potent its medicinal properties. While all naturally fermented foods are invaluable digestive aids, miso is one of the most remarkable—probably because soybeans, already a nutritive food, are further enhanced through fermentation.

Miso is a concentrated protein source, which contains a rich amino-acid profile of the eight essential amino acids. Miso's protein content ranges from 12 to 20 percent, depending upon the kind. It is also low in fat but high in salt, thus used best in moderation. Miso reduces *vata.*

Use Miso may be used in place of Worcestershire sauce, salt, and soy sauce as a seasoning agent. Miso's most typical use is in soup, where it serves as a rich and flavorful bouillon, but it is also used in sauces, dressings, and even some desserts.

Before adding miso to a soup, thin it with soup stock. Add this thinned purée to the soup, and then allow it to simmer very lightly for one minute. Longer cooking or boiling destroys miso's beneficial microorganisms.

Buying Thanks to enterprising health-conscious Americans who learned how to make traditional miso from miso masters in Japan, quality domestic miso is now available. The more expensive, traditionally made miso—which is aged for up to eighteen months—is superior to high-tech miso with chemically induced, and therefore shortened, fermentation periods.

I favor domestic, unpasteurized, and natu-

MISO, THE RADIOPROTECTIVE FOOD PAR EXCELLENCE

A remarkable and widely reported account comes from the Japanese medical doctor Shinichiro Akizuki, director of Nagasaki's St. Francis Hospital, which was located only a mile from the center of the atomic bomb blast in 1945. This report comes from *Fighting Radiation with Foods, Herbs, and Vitamins* by Steven R. Schechter, N.D.

The staff at Saint Francis treated hundreds of people for radiation sickness in the aftermath of the explosion. He [Dr. Akizuki] and his hospital staff remained at St. Francis; however, none of his staff members became ill—a remarkable occurrence since they were so close to the epicenter of the explosion and were exposed to enormous doses of radioactivity. Akizuki hypothesized that it was the daily consumption of miso soup taken by him and his staff that protected them from the effects of radiation.

rally fermented (rather than chemically processed) miso, which is available in the refrigerated sections of natural food stores. Many Americans prefer the lighter-flavored misos, which are yellow or creamy beige in color, to the red, dark amber, and brown misos, which are stronger in taste.

Kept in an airtight—preferably glass—container, refrigerated miso will last for a year or more. As a convenience item, packets of additivefree, freeze-dried instant miso soup are available in natural food stores; they are great for travel.

See **Fermented Foods.**

MISTICANZA See **Mesclun.**

MIXED FRUIT JUICE CONCENTRATE See **Fruit Juice Concentrate.**

MIZUNA
Siu Cai
(*Brassica rapa, Japonica* group)

Mizuna, yet another leafy green of the cabbage family, is unlike most of its relatives in that it can be eaten raw as well as cooked. It has deeply serrated, almost lacy leaves. Mizuna is less sulfurous than bok choy, but energetically is otherwise quite similar. It reduces *kapha*.

Mizuna is an excellent potherb or salad or sandwich green. It makes an exceptionally beautiful garnish. Mitzuna is interchangeable with spinach in any recipe. The stalks, more fibrous than the leaves, need to be coarsely chopped before serving.

MOCHA

The highly fragrant—almost winy—and distinctively flavored—almost gamey—mocha coffee bean takes its name from the town of Mocha in Yemen, although the beans are actually grown in Ethiopia. Today, mocha is also a term commonly used to describe coffee-and-chocolate-flavored beverages and dishes.

See **Coffee.**

MOCHI

When Japanese children look at the full moon, they don't see the man in the moon; rather, they see a rabbit pounding mochi. Look and you'll see the rabbit's ears at the top right as she faces left with a long pestle in hand, pounding cooked sweet rice until it becomes glutinous. Mochi is such a favorite Japanese food that New Year's Day feasting includes mochi as a harbinger of good in the coming year.

Health Benefits Mochi is beneficial for pregnant and lactating women and for children. It becomes so elastic with the pounding that, as macrobiotic teacher Aveline Kushi used to say, "it supports our being flexible." Mochi strengthens the kidneys, builds blood, and helps regulate blood sugar. Mochi also reduces *vata.*

Use Mochi is my favorite "instant" natural food on the market. Flavored or otherwise, it may be baked, broiled, or fried until it puffs. I like it best sliced into thin (¼ inch) pieces and baked in a waffle iron. It puffs up into an airy, crunchy but moist, satisfying waffle. Serve hot with a sweet or savory dipping sauce. To make mochi from scratch, pound cooked sweet rice with a pestle or beat it in a heavy-duty mixer until it becomes glutinous. Enjoy it fresh or form it into a flat cake, dust with arrowroot flour, and refrigerate until use.

MOCHI POUNDING PARTY

In my community, a pregnant woman is cause to pound mochi. It's especially good for pregnant women. I cook up a pot of sweet rice, call in women friends, and pull out a wooden baseball bat. Then we take turns pounding the hot rice to a sticky, gooey consistency. For some reason, hand-pounded mochi tastes better than machine-made mochi. Next, with moistened fingers, we tear off bite-size pieces, roll them in a savory condiment or in chopped nuts, and then feast. At such a feast, we include a Blessing Way, borrowed from Navajo tradition, in which we offer wishes and a small talisman for good birthing and a healthy babe.

Buying Richly flavored whole grain mochi is available in the refrigerated or frozen section of natural food stores. The white rice mochi available in Asian food markets puffs beautifully but lacks flavor.

See **Sweet Rice.**

MOLASSES

This thick, strong-flavored syrup (56 to 76 percent sucrose) is used most often as an old-fashioned sweetener in traditional recipes. Several different kinds and grades are available. So-called table syrup may be placed on the table and poured directly over a stack of pancakes. Other molasses grades are used as an ingredient.

Health Benefits Most sweeteners have

negligible mineral content, but molasses—especially dark molasses—is an exception. Blackstrap molasses is rich in calcium, iron, and potassium. Medium molasses and light molasses are considerably less rich in minerals.

In the Oriental Five Element system, molasses tonifies *chi*, strengthens the spleen-pancreas, eases coughing, and lubricates the lungs. Molasses reduces *vata*. For a mellowing *vata* tonic, stir a teaspoon of molasses and a few drops of vanilla into a cup of yogurt and savor slowly.

Use Use molasses for its heat-resistant flavor—rather than its sweetness—in gingerbread, baked beans, spice cookies, and other strongly flavored dishes. Dark molasses is used commercially in baked beans, licorice, soy sauce, and chewing tobacco. Molasses with lighter flavor and color is used in toppings, syrups, and baked goods. Health enthusiasts in the 1950s and 1960s liberally used molasses in baking, as well as in health beverages, because of its high mineral content.

Buying Organic, unsulfured molasses is made without the use of synthetic chemicals. The more concentrated and darker a syrup is, the higher the percentage of minerals, the stronger the flavor, and the lower the percentage of sugar.

- **Barbados Molasses** Made from the first press of sugarcane. Lighter in color and more delicate in flavor than blackstrap molasses. One tablespoon of Barbados molasses is about 70 percent sugar and has 2 percent of the RDA of iron.
- **Unsulfured or Blackstrap Molasses** Made from the last pressing of the sugarcane. The darkest, most nutritious, and most intensely flavored. One tablespoon of blackstrap molasses contains about 46 percent sugar and 20 percent of the RDA of iron.

Ø Commercial-quality molasses is a byproduct of cane sugar manufacturing and is processed with sulfur dioxide. I do not recommend it. As a concentrated byproduct, the chemical contaminants (including pesticides, industrial toxins, and sulfur) are also concentrated.

See **Sorghum Molasses; Sweeteners.**

MONSTERA
Ceriman, Mexican Breadfruit
(Monstera deliciosa)

The monstera plant, a biological curiosity, belongs to the only plant family that has natural holes in its large, elegantly lacy leaves. Far more curious than the leaves, its conelike fruit resembles a huge primeval green banana covered by hexagonal scales. These scales, or platelets, conveniently fall off as the fruit ripens to indicate which part to eat. With a knife, scrape the creamy flesh away from the core. Wait for more scales to fall off before harvesting the next portion, since underripe monstera contains irritating acidic crystals and a nasty flavor.

A Mexican native, monstera is eaten fresh or in fruit desserts. Today, it is grown in Florida and California.

See **Tropical Fruits.**

MONUKKA RAISIN

An especially large grape, the monukka is an old variety used specifically for drying. It makes a large raisin with a pleasing, mellow sweetness. Compared to the more intensely sweet common raisin (made from Thompson grapes), monukkas are pricier and more subtly flavored.

See **Raisin**.

MOREL
(Morchella esculenta)

The morel is a small, conical mushroom crisscrossed with irregular pale brown ridges that produce a spongelike appearance. When fresh, the stalk is whitish; it darkens when old. The flavor of the morels is hard to pinpoint. Food writer Elizabeth Schneider comes close: "It may suggest warm autumn leaves, hazelnuts, or even nutmeg. As with truffles and caviar, tasting is believing."

Health Benefits Considered a tonic to the digestive system, morels reduce phlegm, regulate the flow of energy, and inhibit the formation and growth of tumors. The Ayurvedic *Indian Materia Medica* by A. K. Nadkarni considers morels an "aphrodisiac and narcotic."

Use Roasting concentrates their flavor and they are especially elegant when cooked in parchment paper with pine nuts and butter. They're also tasty sauteed, marinated, broiled, or used in stuffings. Compared to shiitake or other dried fungi, dried morels quickly rehydrate because of their hollow center and airy structure.

Buying Terry Farms Technology Division in Auburn, Alabama, is the only farm in the world currently producing morels. According to vice president Rod Sorensen, their weekly morel harvest of three thousand pounds is air freighted to high-end restaurants, resorts, and signature stores in destination cities around the globe. A small percentage of the crop is available in natural food stores and other specialty markets. Select fresh morels that have a sweet, earthy smell and are firm but not slimy. Fresh morels may be purchased directly from Terry Farms (see page 403).

See **Mushroom Family**.

MOUNTAIN SPINACH See Orach.

MOUNTAIN YAM See Jinengo.

MULBERRY
(Morus)

A native of western Asia, the mulberry is a stately tree best known because the leaves

---

THE THRILL OF THE FIND

I still remember one June morning when I headed out the back door of my Colorado mountain home and down South Crestone creek. There, in a grassy meadow, I found several dozen morels. It's always a thrill to find freely given treasures. I gathered them up, and within the hour some were drying while others were gently sautéing in butter with a splash of tamari. After one taste, my then young children turned up their noses . . . and I had no recourse but eat them all myself!

of the white mulberry (*M. alba*) are the sole food source of the silkworm. The inexplicably refreshing, delicately perfumed purple berries of the black mulberry (*M. nigra*), which look somewhat like a blackberry, stain everything—fingers, lips, clothing—with their vivid purplish red juice. Berries of the white mulberry are white or pinkish purple when ripe but lack the sweetness of the black mulberry.

Health Benefits Mulberries are one of the few fruits that strengthen and replenish constitutional kidney energy in Chinese medicine. In addition, mulberries quench thirst, have detoxifying properties, and are said to nourish the blood, calm the spirit, and relieve constipation in the elderly. For medicinal purposes, white mulberries are harvested just before they are fully ripe. Fresh mulberries reduce *pitta* and *vata* and, in moderation, *kapha*.

Use For culinary purposes, use fully ripened mulberries. Eaten out of hand, black mulberries are irresistible. Sweet but never cloying, these berries are excellent in jam or wine; they can be substituted for other berries in any dessert or salad recipe. The dried fruits may be substituted for raisins.

Buying/Foraging In recent years, mulberries have become somewhat available in natural food stores and specialty food markets. Fresh mulberries are too fragile to have commercial availability, so count yourself lucky if there's a mulberry tree in your neighborhood.

MUNG BEAN
(Phaseolus aureus)

This small, khaki green, cylindrically shaped legume is Indian in origin. An important staple throughout Asia, mung beans are sprouted, cooked as a legume, or made into a pasta that looks like cellophane. Of sproutable seeds, mung beans rank with alfalfa seeds at the top—easy to sprout, tasty, and multipurpose. A black mung variety is popular in the West Indies.

Health Benefits Compared to common beans, mung beans are readily digestible. Their thermal property is more cooling than common beans. In Southeast Asia and India, mung beans are often served during hot seasons for their ability to disperse body heat. According to Donna Gates, author of *The Body Ecology Diet*, mung beans are the one sprout that ferments, and so they're not advised in an anticandida diet. Mung especially reduces *vata* and *pitta*, and, in moderation, is considered *tridoshic*.

Use Mung beans may be used like any other legume. In Southeast Asia, they are a popular soup ingredient. Mung beans are also excellent puréed and seasoned with curry like a dal. In the United States, mung beans are most often sprouted. If you purchase mung beans for cooking and then use them for sprouting, carefully cull through and remove any broken or split mung beans beforehand. Young mung pods may be cooked and served like green beans.

Buying Mung beans are available packaged and in bulk bins of natural food stores. Mung sprouts are available in supermarkets, Asian stores, and natural food stores. Whole mung beans suitable for sprouting, with a high germination rate and no broken seeds, are available in natural food stores with other designated seeds for sprouting. Young mung pods are available in Asian markets.

See Beans and Legumes; Sprouts.

MUNG BEAN PASTA
Cellophane Noodles

Popular throughout Asia, mung bean pasta is a translucent noodle made only of mung bean starch; it needs no cooking. Simply cover the mung bean noodles with boiling water and let stand until softened. Then marinade and combine the noodles with other flavorful ingredients as a side dish or soup, or use them to fill Vietnamese spring rolls. Mung bean pasta is even more cooling and refreshing than mung beans themselves.

MURCOTT HONEY ORANGE See Tangor.

MUSCAT RAISIN

Made from the large, seed-bearing muscat grape, this raisin is extra sweet with a distinctive fruity flavor; the seeds are mechanically removed. Muscat raisins, about twice the size of other raisins, have limited availability; they are more easily found in the fall and winter months. Muscats are prized for baking, especially in fruitcakes.

See Raisin.

MUSHROOM FAMILY
(Agaricus campestris, A. bisporus, et al.)

What we recognize as a mushroom is actually the fruit of the fungus. This may not sound appetizing but it sure tastes good. These savory fruits are indeed among the most costly, delectable, and medicinal of foods.

In popular usage, the common mushroom (A. campestris) is termed "cultivated," while the other varieties—which today are also cultivated—are termed "wild." Do not, however, consume truly wild, foraged mushrooms unless you are positive of their identity. Several varieties are lethal.

Health Benefits Other vegetables contain chlorophyll and convert sunlight into food; mushrooms do not. These primitive fungi scavenge upon other organic matter. That's why in nature they are found growing on decaying wood or even out in the pasture under cow patties. Rather than cringing at this image, use it to understand why mushrooms so effectively detoxify: In nature, mushrooms draw upon that which is decaying; in the human body, mushrooms are said to absorb and then safely eliminate toxins.

These toxins include undesirable fat in the blood, pathogens, and excess mucus in the respiratory system. The common button mushroom is milder in action than other varieties. In Asia, some mushrooms, such as the reishi, are regarded as increasing longevity. Because of how and where they grow, mushrooms are disparaged in traditional Ayurvedic medicine. They reduce *pitta* and *kapha*.

Mushrooms are a rich source of glutamic acid (the natural version of the flavor enhancer monosodium glutamate) and so enhance the flavor of any savory food that they are cooked with. They are high in protein and a good source of vitamin B_2 and zinc.

Use The contemporary practice of eating

raw mushrooms lacks historical precedence—and with good reason. Carcinogenic compounds found in raw common mushrooms are destroyed in cooking. Just before use, clean fresh mushrooms with a damp paper towel.

Drying intensifies the flavor of the mushrooms and is a convenient way to keep favorite varieties on hand. While all foraged mushrooms may be dried, not all commercial varieties are available dried. Dried mushrooms may be rehydrated and used in most applications (grilling excepted) like fresh mushrooms. Use about 1 ounce of dried mushrooms for each 8 to 10 ounces of fresh mushrooms called for in a recipe. To reconstitute dried mushrooms, soak in water or wine diluted with water until softened, 20 minutes or longer, depending upon variety. For maximum flavor, I soak them overnight.

Mushrooms soak up the essence of whatever they are cooked in; the more finely they are sliced, the more flavor they absorb. Mushrooms are excellent simply prepared and they add a rich flavor to sauces, soups, stuffing, and stir-fried dishes. The larger varieties are meatlike sliced and grilled. Roasting concentrates their flavors.

Buying/Foraging As with other lifeforms, the quality of a mushroom is greatly determined by the quality of its nourishment. Foraged mushrooms have a flavor superior to commercial varieties grown in a sterile medium of organic waste (straw, corncobs, sawdust, bark, gypsum, and potassium) in windowless, controlled–atmosphere sheds. Many mushrooms are available dried.

Except for morels and chanterelles, select

THE WILD SIDE

Puffballs, tooth fungi, fairy-rings, shaggy manes . . . there are hundreds of wild mushrooms—oddly named or not—free for the taking. (There are also deadly poisonous varieties, so do *not* forage without a reputable field guide.) There's the thrill of the find, the joy of returning home laden with bounty, and finally the hedonistic pleasure of feasting upon mushrooms incomparable to cultivated ones.

Many cities have mycological clubs that organize foraging expeditions and provide information about the local harvest season.

---

smooth, plump, and uniformly colored mushrooms that are firm and not slimy and that have a sweet earthy smell. For medicinal purposes, favor button mushrooms with tightly closed caps that hide the gills. (Exposed gills indicate a mature mushroom and dispersed spore.) For taste alone, mushrooms with exposed gills are more intensely flavored but have a shorter shelf life.

You can grow your own mushrooms indoors with the purchase of a small kit containing mushroom spores (see pages 402–03).

See **Bolete; Chanterelle; Cremini; Enoki; Hen-of-the-Woods; Kombucha; Matsutake; Morel; Oyster Mushroom; Portobello; Reishi; Shiitake; Trumpet Mushroom; Wood Ear.**

MUSKMELON See Melon.

MUSTARD FAMILY See Cabbage Family.

MUSTARD GREENS
(Brassica juncea)

The mustard is a pungent, bright green plant with leaves so curly that they ruffle. While numerous mustard plants grow wild throughout the world, the one readily available at greengrocers throughout the United States is relatively mild when fresh. Seed companies and some Asian markets have mustard varieties that make a jalapeño chile seem mild. Its fire quotient depends upon its mustard oil content.

Health Benefits Like other dark leafy greens from the cabbage family, mustards are a superior anticancer vegetable. As their bite indicates, they help move stuck energy and so are beneficial for people with colds, arthritis, or depression. Mustard greens reduce *kapha*.

Use For most people, the mustard's pungent flavor is too strong when raw or steamed, but it quickly mellows with parboiling or sautéing. Mustard greens are especially good when sautéed with garlic and also may be added to soups and stews.

Buying Mustard greens are available all year long. Select young, fresh-looking greens. They fade more quickly than collards or broccoli, so plan to use them within several days.

See Cabbage Family.

MUSTARD SEED
(Brassica)

Mustard seeds are cabbage family members, be they black (*B. nigra*), brown (*B. juncea*), or white (*B. hirta*) in color. The most common use of mustard seed is in the prepared condiment, indispensable for slathering on a hot dog, which has remained popular since Egyptian times and is still comprised of the same ingredients: ground mustard seed, vinegar, oil, and salt to taste. Both ground and whole, mustard seed as a culinary ingredient is popular in pickles and dressings in Western and Asian cuisine.

Health Benefits Mustard seed acts as a diuretic, a blood purifier, and a stimulant for body energy, circulation, and heat. Ground mustard seed is also used as a topical plaster to increase blood flow to the skin and draw out deep-set inflammation and congestion— as in the case of rheumatism, sprains, colds that have settled in the chest, and arthritis. Mustard seed reduces *vata* and *kapha*.

See **Herbs and Spices**.

𝒩

NAGAMI See **Kumquat.**

NAPA CABBAGE See **Chinese Cabbage.**

NASTURTIUM
(Tropaeolum majus)

A favorite edible blossom because of its brilliant orange, red, or yellow color and its peppery, cresslike bite, the nasturtium is native to South America. As beautiful in the garden as in the salad bowl, nasturtiums are enjoying increasing commercial availability. These pungent blossoms are fragile and best used the same day they are purchased or plucked. More warming than lettuce, nasturtium blossoms enhance salad digestion for people with cold or deficient digestive energy.

See **Flower Blossoms.**

NATTO

Powerful-tasting natto, steamed and fermented soybeans, is an unusual food. Fondly called the limburger of soy, this traditional Japanese condiment looks like innocuous brown soybeans until you dip a spoon in and out; hundreds of hair-fine strands will stretch from the bowl to your spoon—up to ten inches in length. These strands contain countless enzymes, bacteria, and fungi. For some people, natto is an acquired taste. Others love it from the first encounter, including my children who often asked for "string beans."

Use When serving natto as its own dish, mix it with mustard, soy sauce, and chopped scallions to taste. Allow one tablespoon per serving as a condiment for rice or other grains. Natto is also tasty stirred into soups and noodles.

Health Benefits Natto is a potent digestive aid because it is fermented and because its own culture of enzymes assists in the digestion of other foods. Natto is considered medicinal for the regenerative organs and it helps regulate blood sugar. This condiment contains no salt; it is an excellent source of protein.

Buying Natto is available frozen in well-stocked natural food stores and Asian markets and the starter is available from G.E.M. Cultures (see page 402). I often make it from scratch—it's as easy to make as yogurt—by simply inoculating cooked soybeans with a starter and incubating it.

Keep natto frozen until ready for use. Once defrosted, cover tightly and refrigerate for up to five days.

See **Fermented Foods; Soybean.**

NATURAL SUGAR See **Rapadura.**

NAVEL ORANGE See **Orange.**

NAVY BEAN
(Phaseolus vulgaris)

> The Army gets the gravy but
> The Navy gets the beans, beans,
> beans, beans . . .

These century-old lyrics explain how this small white bean was named. The navy bean is smaller than the great northern bean but has a similar hearty flavor and is interchangeable in recipes. When immature, it can be eaten pod and all, like a green vegetable.

See **Beans and Legumes.**

NECTARINE
(Prunus persica)

The drink of the gods—at least the Greek gods—was "nekter," and indeed the nectarine tastes divine. It is a kind of smooth-skinned peach only it's more of everything—sweeter, richer, more distinctively flavored, stronger smelling, and more brightly colored. The flesh of a nectarine is also firmer than that of a peach, and it is often smaller in size. The leaves, trees, and seeds of peaches and nectarines are indistinguishable; the fruit may be either freestone or clingstone—that is, loose from the stone or attached to it.

In Mesa County, the peach heaven of Colorado, nectarines are outlawed because their rootstock has disease potential that could harm peach trees. Nectarines are mostly produced in California. They are in season from late summer through September; out-of-season nectarines are imported from South America.

Use Nectarines are enjoyed raw, cooked, or dried. They can be used interchangeably with peaches and apricots in fruits salads and other desserts. Because of the fuzzless skin, a nectarine doesn't need peeling. The flesh of a nectarine will discolor after being cut, so slice just prior to serving or toss with lemon juice.

Buying A ripe nectarine is too fragile to be shipped, so nectarines are harvested when immature. Once picked, a nectarine does not increase in sweetness. This surely explains why buying nectarines directly from the farmer's roadside stand is the only guarantee for getting good ones. If only everyone had such a stand in the neighborhood! Unfortunately, nectarines do not grow in moist climates. All things considered, it's understandable that nectarines are costlier and generally less available than peaches.

Look for a plump nectarine with a rich (rather than a bright) color, and a slight softening along the "seam" of the fruit. Russeting or staining of the skin does not affect the fruit's quality.

See **Fruit; Peach.**

NELIS See Pear.

NETTLE
Stinging Nettle
(Urtica dioica)

As I write this, the aspens are turning gold and it has snowed once here at my cabin at 8,500 feet in Colorado—and still I feasted on steamed fresh nettles for lunch. They are growing in a protected corner. With luck, the weather will hold for a few more days, so that I can enjoy another mess of this delicious wild green. Used throughout the world to build vitality, nettles are delicious and—if you're in a moist area—free for the grabbing. But do grab carefully!

Health Benefits Stiff, bristly hairs protrude from the leaves and stems of nettles; if they penetrate the skin, they inject a stinging fluid, which causes temporary burning and irritation. This injection, which like an ant's bite, contains formic acid, increases circulation, and provides external treatment for arthritic pain, gout, sciatica, neuralgia, hemorrhoids, and scalp and hair problems.

Internally, nettles are a kidney tonic with diuretic properties. They afford allergy relief, enrich the blood, and thicken the hair. Nettles are good for hypoglycemia, as they help reduce blood sugar levels, and they also ameliorate high blood pressure. Used for anemia and excessive menstruation, nettles also build overall energy and *chi*. Nettles reduce *pitta* and *kapha* and can be used, in moderation, by *vata*.

Use Prepare nettles as you would spinach. Nettles are delicious sautéed alone or with

---

SHOW NO FEAR AND THEY WON'T STING

Ideally, you'll have gloves along to protect yourself from stinging nettles' pricks when harvesting. Many a time I've glovelessly happened upon a stand of nettles and gladly endured burning fingertips for the treasure at hand. Next time, however, I'll try talking to them as did Tom Brown's Apache grandfather, as reported in *Tom Brown's Guide to Wild Edible and Medicinal Plants*.

"To my amazement, Grandfather carefully began to gather some of the smaller plants, grabbing them at the base and plucking them from the ground with his fingers. In astonishment, I asked him how he could touch those damn plants without getting stung and why the hell would he want to pick the little monsters. He simply said, 'If you talk to them and show no fear, they won't sting.' He also informed me that they were not little monsters but would soon be his supper."

other vegetables such as onions and carrots. Add to soup or casseroles or parboil. Nettles may also be made into a tea to drink hot or cold. Do not, as some old texts indicate, use nettles raw in salads. Heat and drying destroy nettles' sting.

Buying/Foraging Dried nettles and nettle extracts are available in natural food stores. Bottled nettle-flavored teas and beverages are appearing in specialty food markets. If you want to enjoy nettles as a vegetable, however, head for a sunlight-dappled stream bank or a wooded rural area. Collect young shoots before they flower or harvest the tender stem tops. Older leaves contain gritty deposits of calcium oxalate and are bitter in taste.

NEW ZEALAND SPINACH
(Tetragonia expansa)

This native New Zealand green is not related to spinach, although it does have a similar—but more intense—taste. New Zealand spinach leaves are tougher, coarser, and smaller than spinach leaves. When the hot summer sun wilts garden spinach, lettuce, and other delicate greens, this vegetable thrives and so it has endeared itself to home gardeners. It's an excellent source of beta carotene and a good source of vitamin C and potassium. Cook as you would spinach, or use raw in a salad. In recent years, New Zealand spinach lacks commercial availability.

See **Spinach.**

NEW ZEALAND YAM See Oca.

NIGARI

If you extract salt and water from sea water, the residue that remains is primarily magnesium chloride with additional trace minerals. This residue, nigari, is the traditional coagulant used in making tofu, and it makes the most delicately sweet product. Today, commercial tofu is also made with calcium sulfate and Epsom salts or calcium chloride.

At home, tofu may be made with nigari, vinegar, and lemon juice. Nigari is available in natural food stores and in Asian markets for people who want to make tofu from scratch.

NIGELLA
Kalonji
(Nigella sativa)

A popular spice in India and the Middle East, nigella seed is as small as a sesame seed and ebony black. In ancient Rome, it was used as a pepper-type condiment long before the introduction of pepper. It is often mistakenly called black cumin.

Health Benefits Nigella is pungent tasting; it aids digestion, reduces inflammation, eases bronchial complaints, stimulates lactation, and eases painful menstruation and postpartum contractions. It has laxative properties.

Use The seeds are used, ground or whole, to season beans, vegetable dishes, baked goods, curries, chutneys, and meat dishes. They impart exotic flavor and, when whole, a pleasant crunch. Nigella is an ingredient in the Indian spice mixture panch phoron. I like to use nigella to punch up the flavor of beans and in spice mixes like garam masala.

See Herbs and Spices.

NIGHTSHADE FAMILY
(Solanaceae)

Nightshade plants are so named because they grow in the shade of the night rather than, like other plants, in the light of the sun. (Corn, a remarkable evolutionary exception, grows during both day and night.) Most nightshades originated in the fertile altiplano region of South America and were introduced to the rest of the world in the fifteenth century. They include three primary crops—potato, tomato, and tobacco.

The nightshades contain a toxic alkaloid, solanine, which seems to adversely affect human calcium balance and may be implicated in health complaints ranging from headaches to arthritis. Both macrobiotic and Ayurvedic medicine recommend using the nightshade vegetables in moderation, especially tomatoes and potatoes, if at all.

In his book *The Nightshades and Health*, Norman F. Childers, Ph.D., professor of horticulture at Rutgers University, reveals a correlation between rheumatoid arthritis and nightshade consumption. According to his studies, when some people eliminate these foods from their diet, their arthritic symptoms are alleviated or even disappear.

See **Chile Pepper; Eggplant; Garden Huckleberry; Ground Cherry; Pepino; Peppers; Potato; Sweet Pepper; Tamarillo; Tomatillo; Tomato.**

NIXTAMAL See Posole.

NOISETTE See Hazelnut.

NOPAL
Beavertail Cactus, Cactus Pad, Cactus Paddle
(Opuntia ficus-indica and other O. species)

The prickly pear cactus stem, shaped like a beaver tail, is a popular Mexican vegetable called nopal or nopalito. Its soft, pulpy texture and pleasant flavor make this vegetable worth experimenting with, especially given its splendid medicinal properties.

Health Benefits A skinned nopal pad may be substituted for aloe vera as a drawing poultice for contusions, bruises, and burns. It is also an anti-inflammatory and a diuretic. Its most remarkable use, however, is as a hypoglycemic tonic. Recent clinical studies confirm the oral tradition that nopales are effective for adult-onset diabetes and hypoglycemia. They reduce *pitta*.

Use Most cultivated nopales are without spines and may be easily peeled with a vegetable peeler or a sharp knife. Wild nopales still have their spines. Grasp such a nopal with tongs, pare off the outer edges, cut off the prickers with a sharp knife, then peel and discard the skin. Nopal enhances egg, tomato, and cheese dishes. Add narrow strips of nopales to soups and stews twenty minutes prior to serving and cook until tender. Like okra, nopales serve as a thickener, besides imparting a pleasing flavor.

Buying/Foraging Look for nopales that

GRILLED NOPALITOS

In west-central Mexico, according to chef and author Rick Bayless, grilled nopalitos are a favorite delicacy. Score nopales several times on each side, brush with vegetable oil, sprinkle with salt and lime juice, and grill over a medium-low charcoal fire for 15 minutes, turning occasionally. Or oven roast nopales for 25 minutes at 350 degrees. Cool, cut into strips, and serve as is or dice and add to casseroles, pilafs, and vegetable dishes.

are stiff, firm, fresh-looking (never droopy), and around eight inches long and four inches wide. Larger ones are available but tend to be fibrous. Nopales are available in some supermarkets and in Latino markets. Unlike most green vegetables, nopales may be refrigerated in plastic for several weeks. I do not recommend canned nopalitos; they have little flavor and a compromised texture. If you live west of the Appalachians and south of British Columbia, you can forage this widespread desert food.

See **Prickly Pear.**

NORI
(Porphyra tenera)

Nori, dried seaweed, is ebony colored, paper-thin, and crisp. A sheet of nori makes an excellent toddlers' first finger food. Fascinated by its crinkly texture, they gum it until it softens, besmearing fingers and face—a visible and healthy food experience. Nori also has more elegant applications. It's indispensable for sushi and can be made into dramatic garnishes.

Nori is actually several varieties of cultivated laver. Nori spores are scattered over shallow inlets where nets have been sunk on bamboo poles—a contraption something like an underwater volleyball net. Months later, mature nori is hand harvested, washed, chopped, and spread over bamboo mats to dry into sheets. Nori is also available in flakes.

Health Benefits Like all seaweed, nori is medicinal for the kidneys, strengthens the nervous system, and contributes to a sense of groundedness because it is so mineral rich. Nori is a natural complement to fried foods, since it emulsifies fat and aids digestion.

Nori contains more vitamin A than carrots. It is very rich in protein, higher than soybeans, milk, meat, fish, or poultry. It is also high in B vitamins and vitamins C and D, and it is a good source of calcium, iron, potassium, iodine, and many trace elements. Nori reduces *vata*.

Use Sheets of nori are used to wrap sushi and rice balls; they can be cut or torn and used as a garnish or in soups. Nori may be used as is or lightly toasted by slowly waving it over an open flame or the burner of an electric stove. It has a tasty, delicate, nutlike flavor. Nori flakes can be sprinkled over salads, popcorn, grains, and vegetable dishes.

Buying The price of nori varies greatly and directly reflects quality. Superior-quality nori is almost black; lesser-quality is green. Chemical fertilizers are used on inexpensive qualities. Wild North American laver is sometimes marketed as wild nori.

See **Laver; Seaweed.**

NUÑA
Popping Bean
(Phaseolus vulgaris)

Just like popcorn, nuñas, or popping beans, pop. They don't explode like popcorn but, when heated for a few minutes in a hot skillet or air popper, will burst from their seed coats with a bang. The popped beans are soft and taste a bit like roasted peanuts. They're a great snack food and certainly take a lot less time to cook than a pot of beans. I enjoyed eating nuñas so much when I was in Peru that I later tried (unsuccessfully) to grow them in my garden. Nuñas are brightly colored and have a hard shell but otherwise look similar to other common beans. Nuñas' availability outside of the Andes is currently limited, although agronomists at Washington State University in Pullman, Washington, are working to develop a domestic crop.

See **Beans and Legumes.**

NUT AND SEED BUTTERS

Many seeds and nuts are ground into paste as a culinary ingredient. The all-American favorite, peanut butter, is also the most economical. Other butters include almond, cashew, macadamia, hazelnut, sunflower, and sesame. Sesame is unique in its duality: Hulled sesame seeds yield sesame butter; unhulled sesame seeds yield tahini. Soy nut butter is not recommended.

Health Benefits Freshly ground, natural nut and seed butters have the same nutritional value as the foods from which they were ground. But that's not the whole story. They're also harder to digest. Therefore, people with digestive or liver complaints or in a weakened condition are advised to use nut butters rarely, if at all. Because seed butters are less fatty, they are easier to digest. Most nut and seed butters are calming to *vata*.

Use Nut and seed butters make for nutritious additions to sauces, dips, spreads, salad dressings, cookies, icings, and candies. Roasting nuts not only increases flavor but it reduces their fattiness and the effects of rancidity. Homemade butters are easily made with your favorite seed or nut or a combination. Grind lightly roasted nuts in a blender, a meat grinder (use the finest attachment), a steel (not stone) grain mill, or a nut butter machine. A pinch of salt will increase shelf life and flavor. If the paste seems dry, stir in a little oil.

Buying Because nut butters quickly become rancid, buy them in small quantities or make your own. Most commercial peanut butter contains sugar and other additives and lacks the flavor of natural peanut butter, which is made only from peanuts and maybe a pinch of sea salt. Some natural food stores have grinders for customers to grind peanut butter fresh. Note that the oil of natural butters separates to the top, but it can be stirred back in.

NUTMEG
(Myristica fragrans)

A popular and pleasant spice, nutmeg evokes images of a warm hearth with just-baked spice cookies on a cooling rack. The nutmeg is not a nut but the brown seed of an Indonesian evergreen tree. This one tree produces two separate spices: nutmeg and mace, which is more strongly flavored than nutmeg.

Health Benefits Warming nutmeg is considered an aid to digestion. It can help

---

BRING YOUR OWN NUTMEG

It was once used as an embalming ingredient in ancient Egypt, as a perfume in Arabia, and as a medicine in the West. It was also a culinary "security blanket" in the seventeenth century. The fashionable French carried their own nutmeg and grater when going out to dine. Better to be prepared than to take the chance of a dinner short on nutmeg.

---

relieve coughs, reduce pain, and even relieve flatulence acting as a carminative. The essential oil of nutmeg is added to hot bedtime drinks or toddies as a sedative. The oil may also be rubbed into an arthritic joint to ease pain. Nutmeg reduces *vata* and *kapha.*

Use Irish I'm not, but like the Irish I love the way one sprinkle of nutmeg enlivens a whole bowl of hot oatmeal. Heat diminishes nutmeg's flavor and so, if possible, add this spice at the end of cooking. Its pungent and slightly astringent flavor complements other warming spices such as allspice, cardamon, cinnamon, cloves, ginger, and black or white pepper. Sprinkle nutmeg over casseroles, boiled potatoes, spinach, cauliflower, fruit, pasta, or any whole grain dish.

Buying Once ground, nutmeg's volatile essential oils dissipate, and therefore does its flavor and aroma. If you purchase ground nutmeg, buy it in small quantities and replace it often. Better yet, invest in a nutmeg grater or mill and enjoy its full fresh flavor on demand.

See **Herbs and Spices.**

NutraSweet See **Aspartame.**

NUTRITIONAL YEAST
Brewer's Yeast, Food Yeast, Primary-Grown Yeast

A popular "health" ingredient, nutritional yeast does have an impressive vitamin B profile as well as an extremely rich protein content. It's grown on mineral-rich molasses or wood pulp and pasteurized; then many varieties are blended with a wide range of artificial flavors. Nutritional yeast can challenge a weak or yeast-infected digestive system. Although it's not a "natural" food, many people and animals seem to benefit from it.

NUTS

It's easy for me to sense why nuts are such a powerful food when I'm in my father's garden, standing under the wide canopy of his hundred-foot-tall English walnut tree. A smattering of nuts in almost any dish kicks up its flavor, interest, and overall satisfaction. Be it a curried pilaf with cashews or a quinoa-hazelnut pudding, nuts impart energy. And they do it with style—a rich flavor and a creamy, meaty texture. Hmm, sprinkle in some more.

A nut, popularly speaking, is any oily kernel within a hard-shelled fruit. Technically speaking, not everything we call a nut is a nut: almonds and pistachios are fruits; peanuts are a legume; and pine nuts and Brazil nuts are seeds.

Health Benefits Nuts energize. Traditional folk medicines associate this burst with sexual energy—a kind of energy not associated with rational behavior; nutty, in a word.

In addition, nuts are the most concentrated vegetable source of oils and, if eaten in excess, challenge the liver. An overtaxed liver may lead to another kind of nutty behavior—spring fits and a restless spring fever.

That's the excessive side of nuts. In moderate quantities, however, for high-strung and nervous people, nuts are a calming food. The trick is how to determine the dose—and that will depend upon your ability to digest oil. Nuts are best used sparingly—if at all— for people with a compromised liver or digestive system, an overweight problem, or a sluggish condition (such as candida or yeast or viral problems, edema, tumors, or cysts). Such people would do best to favor the less fatty nuts.

Valued as a restorative and warming food in both Ayurvedic and Chinese medicine, nuts help build body mass and strength. In the Ayurvedic system, nuts reduce *vata.*

Nuts are superior sources of vitamin E and essential fatty acids, which are critical for human health. Moreover, nuts are high in protein, with some nearly as protein-rich as meat. Most nuts are good sources of calcium, phosphorus, magnesium, and potassium.

Use Before chopping those nuts, carefully pick them over. A hollow-centered almond, Brazil nut, or other nut is rancid. Toss it. Rancid nuts are too toxic to feed to the dog.

Not too often found in soups but in everything else from salads to tortes to beverages, nuts enhance many traditional and contemporary recipes. Nuts and some seeds are often interchangeable in recipes.

For full flavor—and to heighten digestibility—toast nuts and seeds just prior to use. I prefer to toast them in a hot, dry (unoiled) wok while stirring constantly. This takes only a few minutes, and I can control the degree of toasting, taking care not to denature their oils by letting them scorch or smoke. To oven roast, spread the nuts in a shallow pan and roast at 275 degrees for 15 to 20 minutes.

Soaking nuts overnight initiates the sprouting process, making them even easier to digest. Once they've been soaked, drain the nuts and use as is or toast or roast them.

Buying Because of their high oil content, nuts are prone to rancidity. The most healthful—and tasty—purchase is nuts in their protective shell. In addition to offering protection from light, shells shield the kernel against fu-

WHEN YOU WANT NUTS—BUT NOT FAT—CHOOSE CHESTNUTS	
NUT	GRAMS FAT PER 100 GRAMS EDIBLE PORTION
Macadamia	72
Pecan	71
Brazil Nut	67
English Walnut	65
Hazelnut	62
Black Walnut	59
Almond	54
Pistachio	54
Peanut	48
Pine Nut	47
Cashew	46
Coconut	35
Acorn	5
Chestnut	2

migants and other chemical treatments. Nuts in the shell keep for about a year if stored in a cool, dry place.

When purchasing shelled nuts, buy them whole and refrigerate or freeze them in airtight containers. Nuts exposed to light and sliced, broken, roasted, or blanched are rancid. Nuts completely contained in their protective skin like almonds and hazelnuts are better protected than are other nuts.

See **Acorn; Almond; Black Walnut; Brazil Nut; Cashew Nut; Chestnut; Coconut; Hazelnut; Macadamia Nut; Nut and Seed Butters; Peanut; Pecan; Pine Nut; Walnut.**

OAK LEAF LETTUCE See Loose-Leaf Lettuce.

OAT BRAN

The fibrous outer layers of oats—the bran—is what makes cooked oatmeal sticky, and it's this sticky stuff that reduces serum cholesterol levels. Studies vary in their conclusions as to whether oat bran or oatmeal is the more effective cleanser. I prefer the whole food over the refined because it is filling, warming, and energizing.

See Oats.

OAT FLOUR

Oat flour yields a sweet, cakelike crumb that retains its freshness far longer than wheat flour products because oats contain a natural antioxidant. Substitute up to 20 percent oat flour for corn, wheat, or rice flour in quick breads, cakes, and muffins. To my taste, a waffle containing oat flour is unsurpassable. For a dairyfree but milklike base, use oat flour in soups, sauces, and roux. (Rolled oats, rather than oat flour, best enhance yeast breads.)

When purchasing oat flour, favor stone-ground flour. Or to mill 1 cup fresh oat flour, grind ⅔ cup oat groats in a flour mill. For coarser flour, you may use a spice or coffee grinder or a blender. Or substitute 1½ cups oatmeal for the ⅔ cup oat groats for the same yield of flour; note, however, that flour made from an already flaked or cut grain will be less flavorful and nutritious than that made from whole grain.

OAT MILK

As a nondairy substitute for people who are allergic to soy or rice, oat milk is available. Its texture is most comparable to rice milk. As with any dairy substitute, its healthfulness reflects the ingredients it contains and the degree of processing it's undergone.

See Milk Substitutes.

OATS
(Avena sativa)

There is great healing power in the sight of oats, the faintly blue color of their stems, the knack of each seed head to hold a single, radiant drop of moisture after rain.

—Tom Ireland, *Birds of Sorrow*

Cultivated oats are native to northern Central Asia but found a permanent home in the British Isles as well as other cold, damp climates. That the Celts' staple grain, or daily bread, was oats is reflected by the number of oat dishes that have been handed down, including bannock, brose, and farl. The U.S. domestic supply of oats is grown primarily in the northern Midwest.

Health Benefits Because of their high fat content, oats impart stamina and warmth, making them excellent cold-weather fare. Oats are the one adaptogen grain, meaning that they improve resistance to stress and thus support the system being in a healthy state of balance. Oats help stabilize blood sugar, regulate the thyroid, soothe the nervous and digestive systems, reduce the craving for cigarettes, and reduce cholesterol. Medicinally, they're an amazing food. Cooked oats reduce *vata* and *pitta;* dry oats, as in granola or energy bars, calm *kapha.*

Oats contain the highest percentage of sodium and fat (unsaturated) of any grain. High in protein, they have an amino acid content similar to that of wheat. Only the outer husk is removed during milling, so oat products retain more of their original nutrients than refined wheat products.

Use Whole oats may be used in pilafs, stuffings, and casseroles, as well as in porridge. Steel-cut oats are less gummy than whole or rolled oats and are a tasty addition to a grain salad in place of bulgur, rice, couscous, or pasta.

Besides the obvious hot cereal dish, rolled oats are the basis of muesli and granola, and are the secret ingredient in Mrs. Field's chocolate chip cookies.

Buying Unlike other grains, oats must be steamed before their two inedible outer hulls can be removed. As with other grains, the more processed oats are, the more their fla-

---

OATS AND INVINCIBILITY

The Romans conquered the English but found the wild Scotsmen invincible. One old account I read attributed the Highlanders' prowess and guerrillalike mobility to their staple food. Each Highlander carried a pouch of oatmeal and dinner was as quick as mixing sea water with it to form a cake that baked in minutes on a hot stone over an open fire.

Eighteen centuries later, Samuel Johnson in his famous English dictionary defined oats as "A grain which in England is generally given to horses, but in Scotland supports the people," to which a Scotsman replied, "England is noted for the excellence of her horses; Scotland for the excellence of her men."

vor and nutrients are compromised. Oats are available in three basic forms.

- **Whole Oats** About the size of long-grain rice, whole oat groats take as long to cook as brown rice. They're rarely cooked whole.
- **Steel-Cut Oats** Cut an oat groat into two or three pieces and you've got a steel-cut oat. Steel-cut oats require less cooking time than whole oats and have a pleasing texture. Also called Scottish or Irish oats.
- **Rolled Oats** Made by pressing whole oats between two rollers. Rolled oats vary from old-fashioned or thick flakes, each of which is one flattened oat groat to tiny particles for "instant" cooking.

See **Grains; Oat Bran; Oat Flour.**

OCA
New Zealand Yam, Papa Roja
(Oxalis tuberosa)

In Bolivian Indian markets, I marveled at the ocas, boldly colored small tubers. Small and cylindrical with multiple bulges and deep grooves, they look like a stubby carrot. Among root crops, they're second only to potatoes in the altiplano.

Today ocas are also grown in Mexico, where they're called *papa roja*, or red potato, and in New Zealand, where they're called New Zealand yam.

Use Some ocas have a slightly acidic taste; others are so sweet that they're sometimes sold as fruits. Boiled, baked, fried, candied,

or used as a salad ingredient, ocas are more versatile than potatoes.

See **Chuño.**

OIL See **Fat and Oil.**

OIL PALM See **Palm Kernel Oil; Palm Oil.**

OKARA

When cooked soybeans are pressed to extract soymilk, the remaining fibrous mass, or dregs, are called okara. Okara has a mild, almost neutral flavor, and it is used in second-generation soy products such as soy sausage or soy burgers. It is available frozen in some Japanese food stores. If you make soymilk or tofu from scratch, you can use the resulting okara in muffins or scramble it with eggs.

OKRA
Gumbo, Lady's Finger
(Hibiscus esculentus)

The size and shape of okra suggest their alternative name, lady's finger, a description that doesn't consider their lime green color. In Louisiana, it's called gumbo. Like cotton, okra originated in Ethiopia and its seeds are pressed for oil.

Health Benefits Okra is high in carotene and contains B-complex vitamins and vitamin C. Its slippery gel effectively lubricates the intestines and thus helps to ease constipation. Okra is *tridoshic*, balancing to all Ayurvedic types.

Use Sliced into rounds, okra looks like fanciful little wheels. Nevertheless, some people are put off by the sticky, mucilaginous texture of okra. Garden fresh okra can be lightly steamed, seasoned, and eaten like green beans; or it can be pickled, broiled, fried, or baked. Okra goes well with tomatoes and highly seasoned vegetable dishes; it serves as an excellent thickener in soups and stews. Do not cook it in aluminum or cast iron. Just before preparing, trim the woody stem ends.

Buying Okra, a hot-weather food, is available from midsummer into Indian summer. Select small, crisp okra, preferably under three inches long. Okra longer than seven inches is tough and fibrous. This mildly sweet vegetable does not store well. Refrigerate it and use it within a few days.

OLIVE
(Olea europaea)

And the dove came in to him in the evening; and, lo, in her mouth was an olive leaf plucked off: so Noah knew that the waters were abated from off the earth.

—Genesis 8:11

The fruit of the slow-growing, picturesque olive tree, with its leathery leaves and fragrant blossoms, has been valued since antiquity. What has it been valued for? In a word—fat—and fat spells flavor.

As a fruit, olives are never enjoyed in their raw state. Green olives are inedible due to a bitter glucoside, which is removed by soaking olives in a lye solution prior to curing. (When olives are pressed for oil, this glucoside remains in the mash.) Strong-tasting black olives are cured in dry salt or salt brine, and the lactic acid fermentation reduces the bitter flavor.

Health Benefits Olives contain up to 20 percent fatty acids. The only other whole foods containing more fats are nuts and seeds. Avocados and soybeans are close contenders at 17 percent fat; a few other foods (mostly grains and beans) contain 1 or 2 percent of fat; but the vast majority of all other vegetables and fruits contain less than 1 percent fat.

As with any fatty food, olives tend to slow down body functions and processes. They are considered obstructive and therefore medicinal for a person with high-strung, nervous energy or for someone with diarrhea. A slow-moving person with blocked or stuck energy patterns or one who has a tendency for cysts and tumors might use olives less frequently. Olives reduce *vata;* in moderation, black olives can be used by *pitta.*

Olives have acquired a bad reputation from some sodium- and calorie-conscious people because of their high salt and fat content. Phooey! To write off a food because of two nutritive characteristics—out of hundreds—is, at best, naive; at worst, food fundamentalism.

Use There are few foods that olives, a signature ingredient in Mediterranean fare, do not enhance. American cuisine has come a long way from the 1950s when olives were

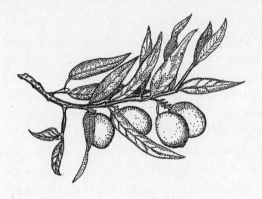

little more than a pimiento-stuffed cocktail snack. Today, many kinds of olives enhance spreads; breads; and meat, grain, and vegetable dishes.

Buying The flavor of an olive depends upon the variety, climate, soil, time of harvest (green olives are picked unripe), and curing method and whether it was processed whole, cracked, or pitted. Experiment with Spanish, Greek, French, Italian, Moroccan, and California olives to discover your favorites.

Green olives are soaked in a lye solution and then cured in a salt solution. They may or may not be pitted and stuffed. Ripe, or black, olives are cured directly in salt or in a salt brine. Once cured—be they green or black—they may be packed in olive oil. To enhance the flavor of brined or salted olives, rinse them, pat dry, pack into a sterile jar, and cover with a quality extra virgin olive oil.

Until the past decade, the only quality olives were imported from the Mediterranean region. California now also produces excellent olives as well as the cheap, canned black olive that is not made from ripened olives.

> ### ALMOST AS IMPORTANT AS YOUR HOME, OX, AND CAMEL
>
> After the ox *Aleph*, the house *Beta*, and the camel *Gamma*, the olive or *Zai* was the symbol denoting the fourth letter of the most ancient alphabets. Flocks and herds, housing, transport, and agriculture were the four poles of a thriving civilization. And out of all cultivated plants, the olive tree was chosen as a symbol rather than any of the cereals, which may well seem surprising. However, dealing in olive oil was the backbone of the import-export trade in the ancient world.
> —Maguelonne Toussaint-Samat, *History of Food*

Immature olives are dipped in ferrous gluconate, soaked in lye, and then canned in a brine solution. Because they are not allowed to ferment and because it is heat (rather than salt and fermentation) that preserves them, they are bland tasting.

See **Fat and Oil; Fermented Foods; Olive Oil.**

OLIVE OIL

For 25 centuries, olive oil has remained the "fat" of Mediterranean peoples. It has an assertive, bright, fruity aroma and a rich, nutty, woodsy taste, with a hint of pepper. Olive oil enhances the flavor of many foods.

Health Benefits Olive oil's most remarkable property is that, after coconut and palm oil, it's the most stable vegetable oil, which is due in part to its high vitamin E content.

Nearly three-quarters of its fat content is monosaturated fat, which lowers the so-called bad cholesterol (LDL or low-density lipoproteins) and leaves the good cholesterol (HDL or high-density lipoproteins) undisturbed.

Throughout the alternative health care community, extra virgin olive oil is highly regarded for its ability to support liver and gallbladder functions. Olive oil reduces *vata* and can be used, in moderation, by *pitta* and *kapha*.

Use Extra virgin olive oil is my choice to drizzle on steamed vegetables or delicate fish. Blend it with herbs for fine vinaigrettes and marinades or use it for low-temperature stir-frying and sautéing. This is contrary to the popular advice to cook with the less expensive refined, and therefore denatured, olive oil. By not heating extra virgin olive oil above 325 degrees, you can enjoy its greater health and flavor benefits.

Buying Since extra virgin oil costs from $5 to $100 per quart, it pays to be an informed consumer. Superior olive oil depends upon the variety of olive, how and where it was cultivated, where it was picked, and—most importantly—how it was processed.

The first cold pressing of olives yields the best-tasting and most healthful oil. Only oil containing less than 1 percent acids can be labeled extra virgin olive oil. If its acid content is a little higher, 1 to 3 percent, it is termed virgin olive oil.

Pomace, the acidic mash of olive pulp and seeds from which the quality olive oil was pressed still contains oil, but mere pressure is not enough to extract it. Pomace is heated to temperatures exceeding 450 degrees and the oil is chemically extracted. This process removes all trace nutrients, flavor, and aroma and denatures the fatty acids. An unregulated amount of extra virgin oil is added to this bland, tasteless oil to give it some flavor, and it is then labeled pure or natural olive oil. So-called light olive oil contains even less virgin oil. For optimum health—and flavor—avoid refined oils and/or denatured oils. Extra virgin olive oil, preferably organic, is the best choice.

Extra virgin olive oil is quite stable and may be stored for up to a year in a cool cupboard in a tightly closed container that keeps out all light. Refrigeration is not necessary; in fact, it causes the oil to solidify, and the frequent warming and chilling brought on by pulling it out and in of the fridge instigate rancidity. Olive oil's remarkable storage properties lend itself to bulk purchase and thus significant savings. Don't add new oil to a used oil container.

See Fat and Oil; Olive.

OMEGA-3, OMEGA-6, AND OMEGA-9 FATTY ACIDS See Essential Fatty Acids.

ONION
(Allium cepa)

Called the "rose of the roots," the onion is actually not a root vegetable—it's a bulb, but its sulfurous perfume is as distinctive as the rose's. Its sulfur compound (propenethial-s-oxide), concentrated in the base or root-end, makes an onion hot and irritates the eyes.

Onions grown in regions where the soil and water are low in sulfur produce a sweeter onion. The Vidalia onion, for example, is as sweet as a fruit—with a sugar content of 12.5 percent versus about 7 percent sugar in a generic onion.

Health Benefits The onion is valued for its medicinal properties, which include improving kidney function and lowering cholesterol. The onion is an exceptionally strong antioxidant and contains numerous anticancer agents. It is anti-inflammatory, antibiotic, and antiviral. Onions also help remove parasites and heavy metals from the system.

The onion and its relatives are prohibited in yogic diets because they increase appetite and body heat. Raw onions reduce *kapha*, and when cooked they balance *pitta* and *kapha*. Well-cooked, sweeter onions calm *vata*.

Onions contain about 90 percent water and are low in calories. They have vitamins A, B-complex, and C.

Use Most people add onions to any conceivable cooked savory dish and some people love them raw in salads and on sandwiches. But one question to consider is the type of onion. Are the new sweet varieties interchangeable with the standard yellow? Not according to Madeline Kamman, author of *The New Making of a Cook,* who states that the sweeter onions "will taint anything with their sugars." I agree. Just because a food is sweet doesn't make it better. Kamman says "only the mean 'crying' yellow onion should be used to flavor cooked dishes of European origin; the red onion should go mostly in salads or compotes. . . . Cook several types of onions separately in a bit of oil or butter and establish which corresponds best to your own personal taste."

Buying Select firm onions that have a papery, dry skin with little or no neck and no soot. Avoid onions that are light for their weight or are beginning to sprout.

- **Cipolline** Small, 1 to 1½ inches in diameter, with flattened ends and a mild, sweet flavor. They are delicious grilled or used on kabobs.
- **Globe Onion** Also called yellow or white onion depending upon skin color. Globes, the best-keeping onions, are available year-round. They are a good all-purpose onion. Small and medium-size globes are pungent; larger globes tend to be sweeter. The more expensive white onion is more mild than the yellow onion.
- **Pearl** Also called pickling onion, this radish-size miniature onion affords great eye appeal in fancy dishes. You can expedite peeling by parboiling first.
- **Spanish and Bermuda Onions** Purple-red in color and sweeter and milder tasting than the globe. These onions are flavored in pickles and condiments and are excellent grilled. With long cooking, they turn gray in color as they alkalinize. To maintain or even intensify their red color, keep them in an acid base (use lemon juice or vine-

---

NOT CRYING OVER ONIONS

Techniques for preventing tears while peeling onions are as numerous as cures for hiccups. Some people cry just looking at a raw onion; others can chop onions for hours and stay dry. Freshly harvested onions and those past their prime are the most sulfurous and therefore the most irritating. To reduce tearing, try any—or all—of the following:

- Cut with a sharp knife.
- Peel under running water.
- Chill the onion and then peel it.
- Trim the root end last.
- Burn a candle, and the flame will consume the sulfur.
- Wear contact lenses or goggles.
- Hold the nonstriking end of a wooden matchstick between your teeth.

---

gar). These onions are higher in moisture and do not store as well as globes.

- **Sweet Onion** Types of sweet-tasting, extra-yellow onions, such as the Vidalia, Walla Walla, Maui, Sweet Imperial, and the Texas Sweet, also known as the 1015 because it is planted on October 15, are becoming more available. They are juicy—and therefore don't store well—and have a low sulfur content that makes them ideal for salads and sandwiches.

ONION FAMILY

Unequivocally the most outstanding characteristic of the onion, or Liliaceae, family is a strong taste and sulfurous odor. The onion and its relatives have been used by humanity for more than six thousand years; it probably originated in Asia Minor. Onions grow throughout the world and are the most universally used vegetable and flavoring agent. Although many cuisines and individuals find the onion family indispensable, there are some who disdain the whole clan or specific members. Onions and garlic are the most potent of this group.

See **Chive; Elephant Garlic; Garlic Chive; Leek; Onion; Ramp; Rocambole; Scallion; Shallot.**

ORACH
Mountain Spinach
(Atriplex hortensis)

Orach, one of the earliest cultivated Eurasian vegetables, was a standard vegetable in North America from Colonial times until this last century when spinach displaced it. Today, orach is resurfacing among home gardeners as an enjoyable and tasty heirloom crop that is hardier than spinach.

Health Benefits Orach is valued historically in Europe for its ability to soothe sore throats, ease indigestion, treat gout, and cure jaundice. It stimulates the metabolism and is used internally to dispel sluggishness. Orach reduces *kapha*.

Use Less acid than spinach, tender young orach shoots are used like spinach, sorrel, or its relative, lamb's-quarter. Add raw orach to salads or sandwiches. Steam it as a side dish or combine it with other ingredients in soups, vegetable, grain, and pasta dishes. Do not use older shoots, as they contain excessive saponin, a mild irritant.

Buying There are three main types of orach divided according to color. Purple, white (actually pale green), and green. White orach is the sweetest and most tender. Look for orach in a farmers' market or purchase the seed from an heirloom seed supplier (see page 402).

ORANGE
(Citrus sinensis)

An orange is a berry—originally a bitter berry. But after three thousand years of cultivation, sweet varieties now predominate. This fruit of a subtropical evergreen tree, Malaysian in origin, has blossoms with a hauntingly sweet perfume.

Health Benefits For frail people, those who have low energy, who tend to be cold, or who have arthritic-type problems, and/or who live in cold climates, I recommend oranges and their juice as an occasional treat rather than as a dietary staple. On the other hand, oranges are a helpful treatment for those with hot, inflammatory diseases. Oranges have medicinal properties for those with liver weakness; they help cleanse the blood and liver. They balance *vata* and, if sweet and eaten in moderation, are good for *pitta*.

The aromatic peel of an orange aids digestion. Oranges are famed for their high vitamin C content. They also contain potassium and some calcium and are a good source of pectin. The interior white orange membrane is a superior source of bioflavonoids that enhance the absorption of iron from plant foods, defend against cancer, and have antioxidant properties.

Use Nearly 80 percent of sweet oranges are grown for juice; the remainder are eaten fresh. Prepared orange juice imported from South America is becoming increasingly available in the United States.

Oranges are easiest to digest when eaten alone or with other tropical or subtropical fruits. They challenge the digestive system when eaten with carbohydrates, sweets, or dried fruits.

For optimum health, choose eating an orange over drinking orange juice. The mineral-rich pulp helps buffer the citric acid, and it also slows down absorption of the fruit's sugar into the bloodstream. A fully ripened orange contains as much as 10 percent fruit sugar.

Buying Oranges are tree ripened—in fact, state regulations require that oranges be mature before being harvested—and therefore skin color, be it green or orange, is not a reliable index for quality. A greenish cast or green spots indicate that the orange was not colored or gassed for a uniform color. Some fully ripened oranges even turn greenish late in the marketing season. Do avoid oranges with dark brown spots, soft spots, or a puffy-looking peel. Select those heavy for their size. Store loose in a dry and cool, but not cold, place. Do not wrap in plastic.

Navel and Valencia oranges are the two most popular orange varieties grown in the United States.

• **Blood Oranges** An exceptionally sweet and juicy orange with dramatic red-orange flesh. The flesh color may be spotted or totally colored with a flamboyant red. The skin color may be uniformly orange or a combination of orange and red. This pipless orange is mostly imported from southern Spain, Italy, or Israel, although more are coming from domestic orchards than in the past.

- **Navel Orange** Seedless, named for the belly-button-like spot at the blossom end. Native to Brazil and favored for eating rather than juicing, the navel's bumpy skin indicates a thick, easy-to-peel rind. Peak season is from November to May.
- **Valencia Orange** Favored for juicing, with numerous pips (seeds), a sweet and juicy pulp, and thin and smooth skin. Valencias are at their peak from late March through June.

See **Bitter Orange; Citrus Family; Tangor.**

ORANGE ZEST See **Citrus Peel.**

OREGANO
(Origanum vulgare)

A hardy perennial herb, oregano, whose name derives from the Greek "joy of the mountains," gives a punchy, almost peppery uplifting flavor to countless Greek and Italian dishes, especially tomato-based ones. Unlike more delicately flavored herbs, which lose much of their flavor when dried, oregano holds its flavor well.

See **Herbs and Spices; Marjoram.**

ORNAMENTAL KALE See **Kale.**

OSTRICH FERN See **Fiddlehead Fern.**

OYSTER MUSHROOM
Pleurotte
(Pleurotus ostreatus)

This velvety, fawn or gray mushroom is shaped like an oyster, has a silken texture, and almost no stalk. In the wild, the oyster mushroom grows in shelflike clusters on poplars, aspens, and elms throughout the world. It is also cultivated. In various world cuisines, the oyster mushroom is valued for its excellent aroma, its thick, sweet flesh, and its medicinal properties.

Health Benefits The protein profile of the oyster mushroom is remarkably high,

---

ORANGE OVER JUICE

Can you start the day with*out* OJ? Orange juice is one of the ten most common allergens and thinking that it's a must is one allergy indicator.

Allergic or otherwise, you might consider choosing the fruit rather than its juice. As with most foods, a whole food gives better nutrition than a part of it does. Orange juice, along with other fruit juices, is a concentrated sugar and—like sugar—causes the blood sugar to jump and then fall in the well-known rollercoaster effect. Too much juice contributes to hypoglycemia or blood sugar imbalance. According to Oriental medicine, hypoglycemia is the first step—and an avoidable one—toward diabetes.

Unlike juice, a whole orange provides fiber and a powerful antioxidant called glutathione.

nearly comparable to protein from milk or meat. It is an excellent blood builder due to its significant percentage of iron. In Oriental medicine, this fungus is used in the treatment of numbness and tendinitis.

Clinical studies show the oyster mushroom's effectiveness in inhibiting tumors, lowering cholesterol, and protecting the liver from alcohol consumption. This tasty food also binds with and removes heavy metals from the digestive system.

Use The flavor and texture of the oyster mushroom is vastly improved when cooked. When sautéed, alone or with other ingredients, it's at its perfection.

Buying/Foraging Watch for cultivated fresh oyster mushrooms in your market or cultivate them from home kits. If you're *positive* of their identification, forage them in the fall.

As with other mushrooms, refrigerate until use, stored in their original container or in a paper or cloth bag covered with a damp paper towel. Do not store mushrooms in plastic. Dried oyster mushrooms are not

---

STRING A STRING OF OYSTER GEMS

If you're fortunate enough to find a large clump of oyster mushrooms (be positive of their identification), odds are you'll have more than you and your friends can eat fresh. Trim the mushrooms, cut into ¼-inch slices, and, using a needle and thread, string the rest. Regular sewing thread will hold about a cup of mushroom slices. For longer strands, use heavier thread or unflavored dental floss. Hang the string indoors and out of the sun to dry. Once dry, store in a covered jar in a cupboard. To reconstitute, soak the mushrooms in water, or water and wine, for about 20 minutes or until hydrated.

---

commercially available, but you can dry your own.

See **Mushroom Family.**

OYSTER PLANT See **Salsify.**

PACKHAM PEAR See Pear.

PAK CHOY See Bok Choy.

PALM KERNEL OIL
Fractionated Palm Kernel Oil, Oil Palm
(Elaeis guineensis)

The African oil palm tree, which looks like a coconut tree, is unique in that its fruit contains two types of oil—palm oil and palm kernel oil. Palm oil is pressed from the fibrous fruit and palm kernel oil from the seed. The oil from the fruit is a vivid red color and constitutes 90 percent of the plant's oil. The oil from the seed, on the other hand, is colorless and yields the remaining 10 percent of the plant's oil.

The oil palm produces more oil per acre than any other vegetable crop. In volume of worldwide production, palm oil is second only to soy oil. Although this palm originated in West Africa, it is now grown throughout the tropics with Malaysia and Indonesia producing the most for export.

Health Benefits Palm kernel oil is a highly saturated (82 percent) tropical plant oil. When unrefined, this high saturation gives it stability, making it a superior culinary oil for cooking at high temperatures. Today, palm kernel oil is still denigrated because of its high saturation; and rightly so when it is *refined* palm kernel oil. The saturation in both palm and palm kernel oil enable it to be used for manufacturing purposes without hydrogenation.

Use Unrefined palm kernel oil is excellent for baking, deep-frying, and sautéing at high temperatures.

Buying Unrefined palm kernel oil is available in Indian, Latino, and Asian markets.

As a cheap chocolate substitute, palm kernel oil is chemically fractionated to be

100 percent saturated. This prevents candy coatings from melting at room temperature or in your fingers.

Ø Avoid *refined* palm kernel products, including margarine, vegetable shortenings, nondairy coffee creamers, dressings, dips, whipped toppings, carob products, confections, baked goods, and prepared waffles.

See **Fat and Oil.**

PALM OIL
Dendê, Oil Palm
(Elaeis guineensis)

Palm oil, like palm kernel oil, comes from the African oil palm tree. Both are liquid when warm, solid at room temperature, and healthful when unrefined—and their similarities end there.

Health Benefits While palm kernel oil is predominantly saturated, the oil from the palm fruit is 44 percent saturated and 40 percent monounsaturated oleic acid. The most remarkable nutritional property of palm oil is, however, that it's the richest source of beta carotene, which, incidentally, is what gives it its vivid red-orange color. Palm oil has fifteen times more beta carotene than carrots. It is also an excellent source of vitamin E (both tocopherol and tocotrienol). Its vitamin E content helps retard oxidation, making it a naturally stable oil.

Palm oil reduces the tendency for blood to clot, which may lessen the risk of heart diseases. It does not raise blood cholesterol; rather, it increases the level of "good" HDL cholesterol and lowers the "bad" LDL cholesterol.

Use The Bahians of northeastern Brazil call palm oil *dendê*. Its color, unmistakable aroma,

and flavor are as integral to their cuisine as olive oil is for the Italians. I anticipate American cooks finding innovative uses for this quality oil as its availability increases.

Buying Unrefined palm oil is available in Indian, Asian, and Latino markets. Look for its cans rather than bottles, as the cans are light protective.

Ø Avoid the pale-colored refined palm oil found in commercial products and do not use it in cooking.

See **Fat and Oil.**

PANELA See Rapadura.

PAPA ROJA See Oca.

PAPAYA
(Carica papaya)

A native of Central America, the papaya tree, which is similar to a palm tree, bears pendulous fruits weighing from one to twenty pounds. Columbus called it a melon tree, and this fruit is indeed melonlike in shape and taste. Papayas have a dense, silky texture and a mild, refreshing taste. Its lush pink-to-orange flesh contains many black seeds in a central womblike cavity; the seeds look like oversize caviar and have culinary and medicinal properties.

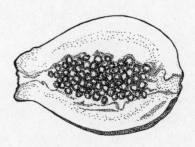

Domestic papayas are grown in Hawaii and, to a lesser extent, southern Florida. Papayas also come from Puerto Rico and Mexico.

Health Benefits Medicinally, papayas are remarkably different from other fruits in two significant ways. First, along with cherries, they are warming in thermal nature, rather than cooling or neutral like most other fruits. Second, the enzyme papain, which aids digestion, is found in high levels in unripe papayas and their seeds. Papain is used in commercial meat tenderizers to break down proteins.

Ripe papayas moisten and lubricate the lungs and so are generally helpful to relieve coughs and asthma. This fruit is also considered beneficial for easing stomach ulcers, rheumatism, and liver and spleen-pancreas dysfunction, and as an anticarcinogen. Papaya seeds are an effective vermicide. Papayas reduce *vata*. Papayas are an excellent source of vitamins A, C, and E, and are rich in calcium, iron, potassium, and phosphorus. They are low in calories and, when ripe, contain about 8 percent sugar.

Use Green, immature papayas are used throughout the tropics as a squashlike vegetable. A ripe papaya with a squeeze of lemon or lime juice to heighten its flavor is delicious in fruit salads, kabobs, and frozen desserts. Do not use raw papaya in a gelatin or agar dish, since papain prevents gelling. Cooking, however, deactivates the enzyme.

The peppery papaya seeds make a tasty salad dressing ingredient. Purée the seeds in a blender and add oil, vinegar, and your choice of seasoning.

Buying Although some varieties remain green when ripe, the skin of most papayas turns yellow or orange. A ripe papaya, like an avocado, is slightly soft to the touch. If green, it will ripen at room temperature. Once it has ripened, refrigerate it. Peak season is from January to April, but papayas are found year-round.

See **Tropical Fruit.**

PAPAYA NEUTRALIZES MOSQUITO BITES

A home remedy to reduce mosquito bite irritation is to rub the bite with a piece of green papaya, its seeds, or a meat tenderizer made of papain. The papain digests or breaks down the irritating proteins injected by the insect. If you have allergic reactions to insect venom, do *not* use this kitchen remedy.

PAPEDA See **Kaffir Lime.**

PAPRIKA
Hungarian Paprika, Pimiento

Back when the American pepper came to Europe in the 1600s, the Hungarians figured a way to sun dry and grind the pimiento, a sweet red variety; ever since then, paprika has helped define Hungarian national cuisine and has become a universal seasoning agent. Spanish paprika lacks the subtlety of Hungarian paprika.

Use To heighten paprika's flavor, lightly toast it in a dry skillet for a few minutes until it is aromatic.

At my local farmers' market, thick-fleshed pimientos are available in the late summer.

They have a much sweeter flavor than other sweet peppers, and I substitute them freely for sweet pepper in soup, pilaf, or salad. Slivers of pimiento are used to stuff green olives.

Buying Too often in the United States, paprika is a bland red pepper powder. For rich-tasting paprika that gives an appealing flavor and a warm accent to foods, purchase imported Hungarian paprika, which is so labeled.

Fresh pimientos are deep red, fist sized, and as broad as they are tall.

See **Chile Pepper; Herbs and Spices.**

PARSLEY
(Petroselinum crispum)

The world's most popular herb, parsley, originated in Sardinia, and Sardinian coins, until recent times, were minted with a parsley imprint. The name parsley comes from the Greek, meaning "rock celery" (parsley is a celery relative); banqueting Greeks wore parsley crowns to stimulate the appetite and promote good humor.

A biennial plant, once established in your garden, parsley will come back year after year.

Health Benefits When Peter Rabbit had overeaten Mr. McGregor's vegetables and was "feeling rather sick, he went to look for some parsley." Parsley, as certainly Beatrix Potter knew, is a digestive aid.

Parsley is a warming food and a blood purifier that helps stimulate the bowels, and treat kidney and gallstones, deafness, and ear infections. Parsley is an anticarcinogen. A sprig of it also freshens the breath.

Dried parsley tea is a diuretic and ameliorates kidney function (do not use for inflamed kidneys though) and strengthens the teeth. It stimulates the uterus but is not used by pregnant women, although after delivery, it helps contract the uterus and encourages milk flow. Parsley reduces *pitta* and *kapha*.

Two sprigs of parsley contain 10 IUs of vitamin A. Parsley has three times as much vitamin C as oranges, and twice as much iron as spinach; it is also a good source of copper and manganese.

Use Do more with parsley than garnish. You can serve it as a vibrant ingredient in steamed and blanched vegetable dishes, as a base for salad dressings, as a sauce ingredient, or generously strewn in soups and casseroles. Unlike the tops, cooked parsley stems do not color a dish, so chopped fine, they are good for a white sauce.

Buying There are two main types of parsley: the strongly flavored flat-leaf parsley (also known as Italian parsley), which stands up well to heat; and the mildly flavored curly parsley, which is a better keeper. Flat-leaf parsley is a deep blue-green; curly, a lighter green. Select parsley with no sign of wilting. Dried parsley offers little flavor and less color.

See **Carrot Family.**

PARSLEY ROOT
Hamburg Parsley
(Petroselinum crispum var. tuberosum)

It's a red-letter day when I find parsley roots at the supermarket. This Old World vegetable, still popular in Germany and enjoying increased availability in the United States, is a parsley variety grown for its root. Parsley root looks like a dwarf parsnip and is usually sold bunched with its rather coarse, broad-leaf parsley greens attached. It tastes similar to celeriac or like a combination of celery heart and parsley.

Health Benefits Parsley root is medicinal for the stomach; it treats anemia and rheumatism, promotes lactation, and helps contract the uterus. It is a good source of vitamin C and rather high in sodium. It reduces *pitta* and *kapha*.

Use I like parsley root in almost any soup that I'd put celery into; it's also delicious cooked with hiziki and onions. Germans often steam the root until tender and serve it with butter or a cream sauce. Russians and Poles use it in borscht.

Buying Parsley root is a fall and winter crop. Select parsley roots that are firm and preferably have the greens attached. Remove the greens and use in soup stock or in place of parsley.

See **Carrot Family; Parsley.**

PARSNIP
(Pastinaca sativa)

When I was a high schooler, the Russian who filled my daydreams was the poet and author of *Dr. Zhivago*, Boris Pasternak. When I discovered that parsnip is *pasternak* in Russian, that further endeared both the author and vegetable to me. The parsnip is a carrot relative that looks like an oversize albino carrot, but its flavor is much sweeter and nuttier. Wild parsnip is still abundant in Europe and the Caucasus, where it originated. In Europe, the parsnip was an important staple until it was replaced by the blander and more versatile potato.

Health Benefits Parsnips are high in sili-

con and insoluble fiber and offer some vitamin A and vitamin C, calcium, and potassium. Ounce for ounce, boiled parsnips have about 31 percent as much calcium as milk. Sweet, moist, and heavy, parsnips are medicinal for the stomach and spleen-pancreas; they clear heat from the liver and improve bowel action. Parsnips reduce *vata* and *pitta*.

Use Because of their strong, dominating flavor, use parsnips with discretion in soups and stews. They may be boiled, simmered, steamed, baked, used in puddings, or in making wine. Peeling parsnips is, I believe, unnecessary. Steam, rice, or mash them as you would potatoes, and serve with a pat of butter and freshly grated black pepper.

Buying The parsnips available in supermarkets are too often old and flabby and rarely worth purchasing. No wonder so few people use them today. A parsnip that is allowed to remain in the ground at least two weeks past the first frost is unbelievably sweet and satisfying, so they're best in the late fall and winter. Look for straight, smooth-skinned roots that are a tan or creamy-white color, firm and fresh-looking, without gray, dark, or soft spots. Large roots tend to be woody.

See **Carrot Family.**

PASSION FRUIT
(Passiflora edulis)

If the name of the heavenly scented, intensely sweet passion fruit evokes erotic images, you're off track—at least, off the official track. Named for the passion of Christ, the blossoms' twelve white petals are for the Apostles, its bright red stamens look like the five wounds, and the disk floret holds three nails and crown of thorns.

A native of Brazil, passion fruit is now widely planted in the tropics and is hardy enough to grow in some Mediterranean countries. It comes from a perennial climbing plant.

Use Passion fruit has a spicy flavor; sweet, golden flesh; and many black edible seeds, which, like tomato seeds, have little flavor and cannot be separated from the pulpy flesh unless it is strained.

Passion fruit may be eaten like a cantaloupe from its sliced-open shell; made into juice; or puréed and used as a sauce to decorate and flavor desserts, sorbets, and ice cream. Bottled passion fruit juice is a popular beverage base.

Buying This dull purple fruit, originally from Brazil, has the shape and the size of an egg. Look for passion fruit that is heavy for its size, with a firm, smooth shell. Keep at room temperature until it becomes wrinkled, appears old, and sounds liquidy when shaken next to your ear. It is then ready to eat—or it may be refrigerated for up to a week.

See **Tropical Fruit.**

PASTA

We're living in an age of pasta. It's quick to prepare, nutritious, and readily digestible. While wheat—both whole wheat and refined—is the most common pasta ingredient in the West, in Asia pasta is also made from buckwheat, mung beans, potatoes, rice flour, and jinengo.

Health Benefits Pasta is as nutritious as the ingredients from which it is made—almost. Almost, that is, because it is made from flour and therefore lacks the vitality that whole, intact, unground grains impart. You can experience this subtle energetic difference by eating only pasta and other refined grain products for a week, then eat whole grains.

Compared to bread, cookies, and other baked flour products, pasta is easier to digest because it is cooked in water. To further enhance its digestion, serve it in a soup or with broth. Whole wheat pasta contains nearly four times as much fiber as white pasta. Wheat and rice pasta usually calm *vata* and *pitta*. Corn, quinoa, and buckwheat pasta reduce *kapha*.

Use One pound of pasta serves four as a main course. Pasta may be an entrée or a side dish; it is tasty in soups, casseroles, salads, and desserts, or alone with a sauce. There are hundreds of types and shapes to choose from. The rule of thumb for matching a pasta with a sauce is that chunkier sauces go best with chunkier pastas, while thin strands better receive a smooth sauce.

Buying As with another wheat product, bread, the quality of pasta ranges from superb to dismal. Good-quality whole grain pasta is available and worth seeking out.

The best American and European pasta is made from durum wheat, a hard wheat grown specifically for pasta making. Noodles made from whole durum flour are more filling and have more fiber and a nutty flavor. Because they are a whole grain product, they should be used within a few months of purchase, or the oil in the germ will become rancid. Semolina pasta is made from refined durum wheat. Like white flour, which also lacks germ and bran, it has a long shelf life.

- **Durum/Semolina Pasta** The hard starch in durum wheat enables pasta to hold together in boiling water and yield a toothsome, soft but firm cooked noodle. All other grains tend to disintegrate in a boiling bath. If a pasta label says "farina" (Italian for flour) or "wheat," it was made of common wheat flour, which turns cooking water cloudy when its starches are released to yield a soggy, inferior pasta.

- **Wheatfree Pasta** For pasta-loving people who are wheat-sensitive, pasta made of buckwheat, corn, quinoa, rice, and wild rice is available. Depending upon the brand and variety, these are acceptable wheat pasta substitutes and, in the case of 100 percent buckwheat pasta, a superb pasta in its own right; extra care needs to be given, however, not to overcook a nonwheat pasta to keep it from turning to mush.

- **Sesame Pasta** A durum wheat pasta flavored with sesame meal, which is a byproduct of sesame oil production and therefore makes an inferior product.

- **Spinach or Vegetable Pasta** Pasta flavored with spinach—or tomato or artichoke—is wheat based but flavored and/or colored with an added ingredient.

- **Asian Noodles** Glutenfree noodles made of mung beans, rice, yams, potatoes, or cornstarch are clear and springy when cooked. The better known Chinese and Japanese bean thread pastas are called *fen si* and *sai-fun,* respectively.

- **Oriental Wheat Pasta** Ramen, udon, mian, or mein are made of soft white wheat flour rather than durum; their flavor and texture differ greatly from American and Italian pasta.

PATTYPAN
Cymling, Scallop Squash
(Cucurbita pepo melopepo)

Among vegetables with fanciful shapes as well as names, the pattypan ranks high. The fruit of this summer squash looks like a squat pincushion with scalloped edges. The pattypan has a pale green skin when immature, which turns white or cream when the squash ripens. Some varieties are speckled green. Small pattypans, under four inches in diameter, are superior in flavor and texture to larger ones.

See **Squash; Summer Squash.**

PAZOTE See Epazote.

PEA, DRIED
(Pisum sativum)

Peas are an ancient legume that have been used in Europe and Asia since prehistoric times. Pea varieties grown for drying are starchier than those used fresh; the starch enables them to dry better and, after rehy-

---

A SURFEIT OF PEAS

A favorite childhood memory of mine is pea harvesttime in rural northern Utah. As farmhands pitchforked green peas, vines and all, onto trucks for transport to the canneries, my father would bounce our car down dirt lanes to the harvest site and ask for a fork full. Two scoops and the backseat of our old Dodge coupe was brimming with a mountain of green pea vines and filled with their heady aroma. Back home, my family would loll under a shady tree, pulling pods from the vines, shucking and eating peas, setting some by for Mom to freeze.

---

dration, to cook up to a more creamy consistency.

Dried peas are generally yellow or green and may be whole or split. When split, their outer seed coat is removed and they are called dal in Indian cuisine. The main producers of dried peas in the United States are Wisconsin and Washington.

Health Benefits Split peas, as with any broken seed, are not able to sprout, grow, or regenerate, so they impart less vitality than a whole pea does. But then, they do cook in half the time. Dried peas are lower in protein than are other legumes.

Dried peas reduce *pitta* and *kapha*. They are medicinal for the spleen-pancreas and stomach.

Use Dried peas have a distinctive sweet flavor and quickly cook into a soft, grainy texture that is ideal for soup and purées. In the United States, green peas are favored while in Europe the nuttier-flavored yellow split peas are preferred. When whole, dried peas may be served as a side dish. Whole or split, dried peas do not require presoaking.

Buying Select vibrantly colored whole yellow or green peas with few broken pieces. When purchasing split peas, favor those that are cleanly split in half with few chips.

See **Beans and Legumes.**

PEA, FRESH
English Pea, Garden Pea, Green Pea
(Pisum sativum)

> I eat my peas with honey,
> I've done it all my life.
> It makes the peas taste funny
> But it keeps them on my knife.
> —Anonymous

When brought straight from the garden to the table, peas are a vegetable unsurpassed in delicacy of flavor. Once the peas are picked, the sugar content starts converting to starch and their flavor fades. This conversion is delayed in edible-podded peas, which are protected by the pod.

Health Benefits Peas, with or without their pods, reduce *pitta* and *kapha* and are medicinal for the liver and stomach, spleen and pancreas. Green peas are high in vita-

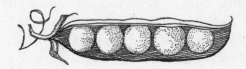

mins A and B-complex and are a good source of calcium and potassium.

Use Shuck green peas just prior to cooking and save the pods for soup stock. The flavor of fresh peas is distinctive, elusive, rich, aromatic. Even the blossoms are edible and are a beautiful garnish for salads. Some golden yellow peas are available as fresh peas.

Buying In the market, look for small, crisp, shiny pods that squeak when rubbed together. Refrigerate and use immediately.

See **Pea, Dried; Snow Pea; Sugar Snap Pea.**

PEACH
(Prunus persica)

The peach is an unusually fine fruit—juicy, fleshy, sweet, and yet tart. The peach tree, which originated in China, was the Tree of Life to the ancient Chinese, and the emperor's royal scepter was made of peachwood. In China, the peach still symbolizes virginity and fertility. Its cultivation moved along caravan routes to Persia and eventually to Europe and the Americas. The peach is a member of the plum family.

Unlike many fruits, peaches are produced in most of the states, 36 to be exact. Georgia claims the title of the Peach State because it was one of the first states in the commercial peach industry in the 1800s, but California produces 99 percent of all cling peaches.

Health Benefits Peaches—as well as nectarines—have a sweet-and-sour flavor and are cooling in thermal nature. They help to build body fluids in the case of dry coughs and to lubricate the intestines in the case of constipation. Peaches and nectarines reduce *vata*. In moderation, they can be eaten by *pitta*.

The peach kernel, which contains amygdalin, a naturally occurring cyanide/sugar compound, in minute quantities, is used in Oriental medicine to strengthen the blood. However, cases of poisoning after eating peach pits in quantity have been reported. Peach leaves and bark are used as a medicinal tea for chronic bronchitis, coughs, and gastritis. Peach leaf tea is used for morning sickness, to purge intestinal worms, and to cleanse the kidneys.

Both peaches and nectarines are subacid fruits and low in calories. They contain fewer calories than apples or pears, and they aid in elimination. They are high in vitamin A (especially the darker-colored peaches) and vitamin C and, unlike most fruits, contain calcium.

Use In the United States, the peach is among the most popular fruits for eating out of hand; it's also popular canned, dried, or made into preserves, sauces, butter, chutney, confections, and liqueurs. For easiest peeling, blanch peaches in boiling water for a few seconds, then plunge into cold water until cool enough to handle; the skin will slip right off. To keep sliced peaches from discoloring, mix them with a little lemon juice or ascorbic acid.

Buying Since peaches are seasonal, buying locally grown fruit is the best way to get good peaches, so watch fruit stands and farmers' markets. Peaches harvested for shipping are unripe when picked and their flavor never fully develops. Hard, out-of-season peaches and those with greenish skins do not

BOOKCLIFF ESPALIER

Renaissance gardeners, like Chinese gardeners, used to plant peach trees against a wall with southern exposure, painted white to cast back the warmth and light of the sun, and trained the trees to grow flat. This espalier technique protects the trees from frost, hastens their ripening, and, according to gardeners, produces a superior-tasting fruit.

The peach capital of Colorado, my neighboring community of Palisade, abuts the towering Bookcliffs, a sheer 3,000-foot escarpment, which, though too steep for vegetation, absorbs heat from the sun and beams it out to warm the orchards. I can attest to the sweetness of Palisade peaches.

ripen or become sweet. A red blush indicates variety and not ripeness. A peachy aroma indicates ripeness, as does softness; choose a peach that gives slightly to palm pressure.

There are two main types of peaches, determined by whether the flesh clings to the pit (clingstone) or breaks free of it (freestone). Freestones are preferred for eating fresh; most clingstones are commercially processed and not available fresh in retail markets. There are also yellow- and white-fleshed varieties, with the lighter-colored peaches ripening earlier. Different types of peaches vary greatly in ripening, from early summer to fall.

See **Fruit.**

PEANUT
Groundnut
(Arachis hypogaea)

The peanut was cultivated by the Aztecs and the Maya, then introduced to Africa, Europe, Asia, and North America. Like other legumes, peanuts are an inexpensive protein source, and an important food for many people throughout the world. China and India together grow more than 50 percent of the world's supply. Peanuts are a nutritious, all-American favorite snack food.

In the early 1900s, botanist George Washington Carver mechanized peanut cultivation and developed more than three hundred ways to use peanuts in food. Since his pioneering work, peanuts have become an important crop in the United States.

Technically a legume, the peanut is unusual in two ways. After the flower is pollinated, the flower-bearing stalk elongates, forcing the young pod down into the soil, where it matures. This explains the English name for peanuts, groundnuts. Its second curious feature is that while other legumes store starch, peanuts store fat and so are more like a nut than a bean.

Health Benefits Here's an unusual kitchen remedy to strengthen the kidneys. Simmer raw peanuts in the shell for one hour, add salt to taste, simmer for ten minutes more, and drain; shell and eat while still moist and warm.

Peanuts are one of the ten most common food allergens, and people with delicate liver conditions, cancer, gout, or candida would do best to avoid them. Peanuts are a grounding food and excellent for people with a fast metabolism. They are also useful for increasing the milk supply of nursing mothers. They have a laxative effect and may cause gas in *vata* types. Peanuts reduce *pitta* and are unfavorably regarded in Ayurvedic medicine for all body types.

Like other legumes, the peanut is a good source of protein, but unlike other legumes, it is high in fat, of which a small percentage is saturated. Peanuts are the second highest

---

Ø PEANUT CROPS ROTATED WITH COTTON

Peanuts are a leading U.S. crop but unfortunately one of the most chemically adulterated crops. Most southern peanut fields are crop rotated with cotton. Plagued by the boll weevil, cotton, a nonfood crop, is treated with chemicals too toxic to be permitted on food crops. A field of cotton may receive up to sixteen applications of various pesticides annually. These chemical residues affect next year's peanut crop. Some people who are allergic to commercial peanuts find that they are able to enjoy organic peanuts.

Furthermore, the USDA allows a low percentage of the carcinogenic mold aflatoxin in peanut products. Peanuts grown in the humid Southeast invariably develop some mold while drying in the field. Peanuts grown in arid areas, like eastern New Mexico, are free of aflatoxins because mold cannot form in desertlike conditions.

---

source of pantothenic acid. They are high in the B vitamins (thiamine, riboflavin, and niacin), vitamin E, and iron.

Use Unlike nuts and seeds, which may be eaten raw, peanuts—a legume—require cooking to be digestible. To roast peanuts, spread in a thin layer and bake at 350 degrees for about 15 to 20 minutes for shelled peanuts, about 25 minutes for unshelled peanuts. Stir as necessary to assure even roasting. Or toast shelled nuts in a dry skillet over high heat, stirring constantly, until the peanuts start to brown. Reduce the heat to low and continue stirring until the peanuts are uniformly colored a shade darker.

Buying Because peanuts are heavily treated with powerful chemicals, it's critical to purchase only organic peanuts. Since peanuts exposed to heat and air easily oxidize and become rancid, choose unshelled peanuts with clean, unbroken shells that don't rattle when shaken. Peanuts in the shell will hold for six months when stored in a cool, dry place. About 1½ pounds of unshelled peanuts yield about one pound of shelled nuts. If purchasing shelled peanuts, purchase those with no additives and refrigerate until use.

The most popular domestic varieties are the small Spanish, the Valencia, which is primarily used for peanut butter, and the larger, more oval Virginia, which is mostly used whole in roasted nut blends.

PEANUT BUTTER

A "P.B. & J." sandwich is almost synonymous with childhood—and some of us have a delayed childhood. I hope your P.B. & J.

is made with the real thing. One taste comparison of natural peanut butter with a commercial variety provides ample argument. Most commercial peanut butter contains 10 percent poor-quality sweeteners, hydrogenated oil, and salt. It tastes bland and sugary compared to the rich peanut flavor of natural peanut butter.

Natural peanut butter contains only ground nuts and sometimes sea salt. Its oil may separate to the top, but is easily stirred back in. Some natural brands of peanut butter now add lecithin, which prevents separation.

Health Benefits Though nutritious, peanut butter is hard to digest, especially for someone with a delicate digestive system, or a congested gallbladder or liver. It is grounding and good for persons wishing to gain weight.

Use According to the National Peanut Council, adults actually eat more peanut butter than children do. In fact, it is one of the most commonly purchased food items in supermarkets. Peanut butter, one of the least expensive protein sources, is most often used on sandwiches, although it also finds its way into candy and onto celery sticks.

To make your own peanut butter, process 1 cup roasted peanuts in a food processor or blender until the nuts are finely ground. Add 1½ teaspoon unrefined oil and ¼ teaspoon sea salt and continue processing until the peanut butter reaches the desired degree of smoothness. For chunky peanut butter, stir in ¼ cup chopped roasted peanuts.

Buying Due to its fat content, peanut butter becomes rancid when exposed to light and heat or with long storage. Refrigeration retards rancidity but firms the butter, making spreading a challenge that's only measured in proportion to the bread's fragility.

See **Nut and Seed Butters; Peanut.**

PEANUT OIL

In theory, the peanut is an excellent oil food because it is about half oil. However, I cannot fully recommend this product. Commercial peanut quality is poor, and I've yet to see organic peanut oil. It also lacks the shelf life of olive and sesame oil.

If you deep-fry peanut oil, at 20 percent saturation, it will withstand higher temperatures than other liquid vegetable oils. It is low in linoleic acid and vitamin E and high in monounsaturated fats, with a low trace mineral content.

See **Fat and Oil; Peanut.**

PEAR
(Pyrus communis)

There once was a duke who, according to a sixteenth-century Italian manuscript, was into pears—and more than just Bartlett or Anjou. During a one-year period, 209 different pear varieties were served to the Grand Duke Cosmo III.

Once called "butter fruit," the pear is a fall fruit and is similar to its apple relative in its seed core, but with a texture that is both more melting and grittier. The pear is native to the Middle East and the subalpine zones of Kashmir. Some pears are the distinctive pear shape, while others are elongated, and still others are round. The Romans introduced this fruit to Europe. Today, 95 percent of American-produced commercial pears are grown in Washington, Oregon, and California.

Health Benefits Pears clear heat and energize the stomach and lungs. The pear is used in the treatment of diabetes, hot cough, gallbladder obstruction, and constipation. Pears reduce *pitta* and *kapha*, though a dry pear best reduces *kapha*.

Pears are a good source of fiber, particularly pectin, as well as potassium and boron. They are low in sodium and have small amounts of phosphorus and vitamin A. The pectin reduces serum cholesterol and cleanses the body of environmental and radioactive toxins.

Use Sweet, melting, and juicy describe pears preferred for eating out of hand. Varieties that are more firm and crisp, almost like apples, are canned or pickled. Pears may also be juiced, puréed, used in salads, brandied, frozen, dried, made into preserves, or distilled into liqueur or wine. To prevent cut pears from browning, sprinkle with lemon juice.

The two main categories of pears are Bartletts and winter pears. Bartletts change color when ripe; color change in the winter pears is negligible.

Bartletts are available from mid-July through December; winter pears are available from early fall to early spring.

Buying Unlike most tree fruits, pears are best ripened off the tree. Select firm—not hard—pears with a noticeable pear aroma. Ripen at room temperature in a closed paper bag until the flesh at the stem end yields to gentle thumb pressure. Because pears soften from the inside out, a pear that is really soft on the outside is overripe.

- **Anjou** Egg shaped, with almost no neck; green to yellow-green; and spicy-sweet and juicy. A red Anjou remains maroon red when ripe. The Anjou is good fresh and better baked or poached than in a pie. Available from October through May.

- **Bartlett** Red or yellow; juicy and with a definite aromatic flavor. Bartletts are bell shaped, medium to large, and often have a red blush when fully ripe. There are two types of red-skinned Bartletts—those that turn bright red when ripe and those that remain dark red. An all-around pear, the Bartlett is good for eating fresh, cooking, and canning.

- **Bosc** Long with a long, narrow neck; dark yellow with brown-russet skin; firm but buttery, highly aromatic, nutty, and flavorful. The Bosc is unsurpassed in pies, muffins, and quick breads and baked or poached. Available from August through April.

- **Comice** This superlative winter pear is often featured in gift boxes of fine fruit. The Comice is mild flavored and buttery textured with a round shape and a short neck. When ripe, it is incredibly juicy. It is a medium yellow with pink or brown tinges. A red Comice pear is also available. The Comice is delicious with cheese, in fruit salads, and baked. As an out-of-hand variation, cut it open and eat with a spoon. It is available from September to April.

- **Conference** Very similar in texture, color, and flavor to the Bosc pear, the

Conference pear has a juicy, sweet flesh that is creamy white and granular.

- **Nelis** A Russett pear with a squat shape, dull green skin, and a firm crisp flesh that has a spicy, rich flavor. Good out of hand and in quick breads. Available from September through April.
- **Packham** An Australian variety that is a Bartlett cross, the Packham is a large pear with a small neck and green skin that becomes pale yellow as the fruit matures. Its flesh is white, juicy, and sweet.
- **Rocha** A medium-size Portuguese pear that is round with a short, brownish neck. When ripe, the Rocha is buttery soft.
- **Seckel** Green to russet, small, often bite sized; ultrasweet and dense flesh. Pickled whole, Seckels are an eye-catcher. Best eaten fresh or in salads. Available August through February.

Never store a pear sealed in plastic. Without freely circulating oxygen, the core will turn brown and brown spots will develop under the skin.

See **Pear**.

PEARL ONION See **Onion**.

PECAN
Hickory Nut
(Carya illinoensis)

Our most important native American nut crop, the pecan, was an important staple for Native Americans, known to the Algonquian, Cree, Ojibwa, and Abenaki peoples. Pecans are a relative of walnuts and a member of the hickory genus. Of the eleven hickory species native to North America, only the pecan has commercial availability. All nuts of the hickory family are, however, edible, and are an important food for wildlife, from bears to blue jays.

The state tree of Texas, the pecan is indigenous to the Mississippi River basin; pecans are an essential ingredient in southern cookery. A mature tree produces about five hundred pounds of nuts a year.

Health Benefits Second only to macadamia nuts in fat, pecans are an exceptionally warming food. High in iron, calcium, phos-

---

A GIFT OF THE WILDS

At a graduation party of my cooking school, Jayme Gregley brought some native pecans. On the counter, an assortment of cakes, cookies, and puddings overshadowed her bowl of pecans, which were smaller and darker than commercial pecans. Until, that is, we tasted—as Jayme calls them—the wilds. Their sweet, meaty, robust flavor bursts in the mouth, turning the taste memory of thin-shelled, commercial pecans into cardboard.

On her visit home to Tulsa, Oklahoma, Jayme gathered these from a stand of scrubby, wild pecans, cracked them with a hammer, and lightly toasted and salted them. When she was a girl, she told us, the money she earned from foraging "the wilds" paid for her first pony.

phorus, and potassium, pecans contain vita-mins A, C, E, and B-complex. Pecans decrease *vata*.

Buying These oblong nuts have a smooth light brown, sometimes mottled brown, shell. If the shells are red, they've been dyed. Because of the high fat content, shelled pecans have a shorter shelf life than other nuts. Consume them, ideally, shortly after they are shelled; if this is not possible, refrigerate shelled nuts in tightly sealed plastic containers for a month or two. Freezing holds them in top condition for six months or longer.

See **Nuts**.

PECAN RICE
(Oryza sativa)

This partially scarified rice (see page 290) is pale gold and long-grain. Grown in Louisi-ana, it has an aroma and flavor reminiscent of pecans.

See **Rice**.

PEPINO
Melon Pear
(Solanum muricatum)

My first morning in a friend's home in Lima, Peru, I sat at the breakfast table facing a large bowl filled with fruits I'd never seen before. Which to choose? And then, how to eat it? A pepino drew me—it's neatly con-tained in the palm of the hand, and its bright yellow, glossy skin with its jagged eggplant purple streaks gives it allure. I found its aro-matic, gold flesh similar to honeydew melon—watery, subtly flavored, and not overly sweet.

This native Andean fruit that grows on a bushy evergreen shrub is now produced in New Zealand and California. It's a trendy fruit in Japan.

Health Benefits Pepinos, a subacid fruit, are as good a source of vitamin C as many citrus fruits. They are a fair source of vitamin A and are low in calories.

Use A pepino's many seeds, contained in a central cavity, are inedible but are easily removed. Its tough skin is slightly bitter and is easily peeled from the fruit. South Ameri-cans and the Japanese eat pepinos almost ex-clusively as a fresh dessert. Its versatility in New Zealand, however, is compared to a to-mato; it goes into soups, juices, sauces, or alongside fish and meat. It will be interesting to see how its use in North America develops.

Buying Pepinos are available in winter and spring. Select a fruit that has a light, sweet aroma, yields to the touch but is not soft, and has a golden, pink undercolor. Use immediately.

See **Nightshade Family; Tropical Fruit**.

PEPITO See **Pumpkin Seed**.

PEPPER
Peppercorn
(Piper nigrum)

Elias Derby, the first United States mil-lionaire, made his fortune importing black peppercorns—a fortune that endowed Yale University. Long before Yale, pepper was the most important spice in world trade; indeed, it was the single most important factor that brought Columbus to America. Black and white peppers, native to India's Ganges River valley, are the small fruits of a climbing vine. Like grape vines, they are cultivated on props. They are harvested in May, June, and July on the west coast of India. Today, India remains the primary producer, but pepper is also cultivated in Indonesia, Malaysia, and Brazil. Most of the U.S. domestic supply comes from Brazil.

Health Benefits Historically in Eurasia, pepper was valued to aid digestion, to cause sneezing, and to relieve gas. It stimulates the flow of energy and blood to the body and, because it opens the pores for sweating, it is good at the onset of a common cold.

Clinical evidence shows that a major pepper compound, piperine, has antifertility effects, depresses the central nervous system, acts as an anti-inflammatory, protects the liver against solvents like tetrachloride, and acts as a parasite inhibitor. Pepper is a good source of chromium and, in action, reduces *kapha.*

Use Preferably grind pepper to taste; once ground, its flavor rapidly deteriorates. Preground pepper, furthermore, is toasted, and once toasted, it acts as an irritant. Store ground pepper in a dark-colored glass container and use within three months.

At its best, pepper is hot and pungent with sweet or gingery flavor notes. Pepper has more taste than aroma. Once ground, its pungent flavor becomes bitter with long cooking—so add it at the end of cooking. Or place whole peppercorns in a cheesecloth bag, add to a long-simmering dish, and remove prior to serving. Today, we use pepper to enhance the flavor of savory dishes; in Roman times, it was also used in sweet dishes. It adds zing to herbal teas.

Pepper connoisseurs select their pepper by region. Tellicherry, Lampong, and Sarawak produce the finest-quality pepper; Malabar and Brazilian pepper are overly hot and sharp.

- **Black Peppercorns** Picked when mature but still green in color, not red, and sun dried. The flavor is hot with a hint of sweetness and spice.
- **Green Peppercorns** Picked when mature but still green, cleaned, and packed in brine or dried.
- **White Pepper** All white pepper is picked when fully mature and then it's soaked in brine to remove its red outer skin. Because much of pepper's pungency is in its skin, all forms of white pepper are milder than black pepper. Aroma, however, is a different matter, with the fragrance of white pepper excelling over that of black pepper.

  Whole, brined white pepper is available packed in brine or vacuum packed. It is most commonly available when, following the brining step, it is sun dried. Sun drying intensifies white pepper's pungency.
- **Red Peppercorns** Tiny rose hips from the tropical Bayles rose are added to peppercorn mixes for eye appeal, but they're effective for both eye and tastebud. These rose hips taste sweet and mildly pungent.

PEPPERMINT See Mint.

PEPPERS
(Capsicum)

Columbus unsuccessfully voyaged to find pepper, and rather than acknowledge his failure, he named the most pungent New World food "pepper." Capsicum peppers are not related to black pepper.

Even though pepper varieties are legion, they neatly fall into two categories. Chile peppers and sweet peppers are both members of the capsicum family, which is Latin for box, aptly describing their hollow, boxlike form. The difference between the chiles and the sweet peppers is that chiles contain fiery capcaisin and are used primarily as a spice; sweet peppers lack capcaisin—and therefore heat—and are used primarily as a vegetable.

The penchant of peppers to cross-pollinate and develop new varieties is matched by our penchant for new and exotic foods. We are apt to see more new pepper varieties as time goes by.

See **Chile Pepper; Nightshade Family; Sweet Pepper.**

PERILLA
Beefsteak Leaf, Shiso
(Perilla frutescens crispa)

Used by the Koreans, Vietnamese, and Japanese, this light green or reddish purple leaf looks like a large basil leaf. It tastes like a tart, minty cinnamon and it has crinkly, sometimes serrated, leaves.

Health Benefits The volatile oil in perilla leaves is two thousand times sweeter than sugar and eight times sweeter than saccharin. The seed oil is high in linoleic acid. Perilla seeds, especially seeds of purple perilla, have been used medicinally in China since A.D. 500 as a warming herb for colds, nausea, abdominal pain, constipation, food poisoning, and allergic reactions. The leaves are exceptionally high in iron and calcium and build blood hemoglobin.

Use Red perilla both colors and flavors pickled ginger and umeboshi, the Japanese pickled plum. Green perilla, which is more strongly flavored, is favored as a fresh herb to season fish, meat, tofu, or vegetable dishes. Perilla sprouts, tiny and spicy, often accompany sushi dishes.

Buying Fresh perilla leaves are available in Asian markets; they should be used within two days of purchase. They're also available salted and dried as a condiment. Perilla is easy to grow and makes an attractive border plant.

See **Herbs and Spices.**

PERSIAN LIME See Lime.

PERSIAN MELON See Melon.

PERSIMMON
(Diospyros kaki, D. virginiana)

I liken eating an unripe persimmon to having the business end of a vacuum cleaner in my mouth—and the sensation lingers even after spitting out the fruit. Ah, but eating a ripened persimmon is as pleasurable as eating an unripened one is horrible.

—Lee Reich, *The New York Times*

The persimmon, a glossy, bright red-orange fruit that looks like a plastic tomato, is native both to North America (*D. Virginiana*) and Asia (*D. kaki*). When it is mature, its flavor is a blend of apricots, plums, pumpkin, and honey. Immature, its astringency causes one big pucker. The word persimmon comes from Algonquian *pessemin;* dried and ground, it was mixed with wild nuts and jerked game as pemmican.

Persimmon is one of the few trees of the ebony family that grow in a temperate region, and its hard and durable wood is highly valued for golf club heads and weavers' shuttles. Native persimmons are not commercially available but may be found growing wild. Food historian Raymond Sokolov reports that the "powerfully fragrant" wild persimmon is superior in taste to the Japanese, and about the size of a small lemon.

Health Benefits A ripe persimmon is cooling and moistening and so helps counter dry weather or dry conditions in the body, such as a dry, hacking, or unproductive cough. It also relieves bleeding, including bleeding hemorrhoids and constipation. An astringent, or underripe persimmon, cooked, treats diarrhea. Chinese medicine advises against combining persimmon and crab at the same meal, which can produce extreme diarrhea.

Ayurvedic cuisine notes that the persimmon helps promote clarity but in excess can create pain and stiffness. It reduces *pitta* and *kapha.*

Persimmons are a good source of vitamin A and potassium, containing 60 percent more potassium than orange juice.

Use Eat a persimmon as you would eat a ripe mango—out of hand. Cut the persimmon in half and spoon out the meltingly soft flesh, add it to a fruit salad, or purée it for beverages and fresh fruit sauces. Cooked, it is tasty in compotes, puddings, and quick breads. Or, like the Algonquian Indians, dry your persimmons; they are a delicious and versatile dried fruit and, unlike most other dried fruits, hold their brilliant gold color without the assistance of a sulfur treatment.

For no-fuss persimmon "sherbet," halve a persimmon, wrap it tightly in plastic, and freeze it for at least four hours, then eat it out of the shell with a spoon. Freezing is not recommended for other applications, because it reduces the pulp to mush.

Buying The Asian persimmon originated in China. It is widely cultivated by the Japanese, who consider it their national fruit. Japanese cultivars, now grown in California and some southern states, include the large Tanenashi and the Hachiya, which is pointed like an acorn at its base. Both of these become very soft when ripe. The smaller, tomato-shape Fuyu is nonastringent and remains firm when ripe.

Select plump fruits that have a smooth skin, intact green cap, and are soft (Fuyu excepted). Persimmons are mainly available in the late fall and early winter.

See Fruit.

PICKLING ONION See Onion.

PIE CHERRY See **Sour Cherry.**

PIGEON PEA
Gunga Pea, Gandule
(Cajanus cajan)

The yellowish brown pigeon pea, which originated in Egypt, is ¼ inch long, plump, with a mildly pungent flavor. This is a popular bean throughout the Caribbean and among Latino peoples in semitropical and tropical areas. A relative of the cowpea, the pigeon pea has a tough outer skin and requires longer cooking time than other, more common bean varieties.

See **Beans and Legumes.**

PIGNOLI See Pine Nut.

PIGWEED See Amaranth Greens; Lamb's-Quarters.

PIMIENTO See Paprika.

PINEAPPLE
(Ananas comosus)

The pineapple, which originated in Brazil, is not a fruit in the ordinary sense of the word. It is a multiple organ that forms when the fruits or berries, the indented "eyes" of a hundred or more separate flowers, coalesce together. Its high sugar content and lush flavor make it one of the most popular tropical fruits. Early Spanish explorers named this fruit *piña* because it is shaped like a pinecone.

The pineapple is a symbol of hospitality and often appears in household art motifs. Start noticing these pineapples and you'll soon see them on everything from brass door knockers to light fixtures.

Health Benefits The pineapple is cooling; it aids digestion of starches and protein; and it destroys intestinal parasites. Pineapple juice relives chronic bronchitis and has a soothing effect on a sore throat, possibly because it contains the anti-inflammatory enzyme bromelain. This bromelain, a protein-digesting enzyme, literally digests foreign microbes or diseased cells in the bronchial tissues. Pineapple reduces *vata* and *pitta*.

Unlike most fruit, pineapple contains negligible vitamins A and C. It is remarkable for its high percentage of the important trace mineral manganese, which is an essential component of digestive enzymes for proteins and carbohydrates.

Use If a pineapple is acidic and not pleasingly sweet, do not eat it. Ripe pineapple is at peak for a day, and then rapidly deteriorates. You can improve its overall flavor by storing the pineapple upside down for a day or two before cutting it. As its sugar is more concentrated at its base, inversion enables the sugars in the stem end to develop. Once cut, or if purchased cut, use within a day or two.

Bromelain in fresh pineapple lowers a food's capacity to retain water. It is therefore an effective meat tenderizer but it turns milk sour, and prevents gelatin or agar from gelling. Fresh pineapple has no effect on yogurt or ice cream but, if allowed to sit in a fruit salad, the salad will become soggy. Since bromelain is neutralized by cooking, canned or cooked pineapple may be used freely in salads and gelatins.

Thickly peel a pineapple to eliminate its eyes and slice it. Add to salads or eat by the slice. Use as a garnish or purée and as a topping. Broiling heightens pineapple's flavor.

Buying A sweet, fragrant aroma is the

single most important key to selecting a ripe pineapple. (If there's little or no aroma, don't buy it.) A ripe pineapple smells sweet, especially at its base, and feels firm when squeezed. Also look for glossy, golden orange skin; a small, compact, and fresh-looking (rather than dried) leafy crown; a fruit that is heavy for its size; and eyes that are flat and almost hollow. An overmature pineapple is soft and mushy.

Unlike some other fruits and vegetables that, once picked, become sweeter by converting their starches to sugar, pineapple has no stored starch, and so its sweetness doesn't increase after it is picked, though its acidity decreases when it is stored at room temperature. Pineapple is available throughout the year, with peak supplies in the springtime.

See **Tropical Fruit.**

PINEAPPLE GUAVA See Feijoa.

PINE NUT
Piñon, Pignoli
(Piñus pinea)

In rural northern New Mexican cafés, my favorite purchase is pine nuts by the shot glass. The thin shell is easily removed by cracking it between your teeth. Pine nuts are rich, both in taste and in price. As the name suggests, they come from pine trees, specifically those that have seeds large enough to be edible. Such varieties grow in various parts of the world. The U.S. domestic supply comes mainly from the Mediterranean stone pine and a Chinese pine. The piñon of the Southwest is foraged and available locally at roadside stands and in regional markets.

Health Benefits Pine nuts lubricate the lungs and intestines. They help alleviate coughs and constipation. Like all fatty nuts, they aggravate all conditions when eaten in excess. Piñon reduces *vata.*

The Mediterranean stone pine nut is much higher in protein than any other nut or seed, and lower in vitamins and fat than the domestic piñon. The piñon is richer in vitamin A and the B vitamins and minerals, and it contains 14 percent protein.

Use Whole pine nuts are eaten as a snack,

WASH UP WITH MAYONNAISE

Since childhood, piñon foraging has been one of my favorite fall expeditions. Watch the pine jays—when they cluster in the piñon and start pecking at cones, don't delay. Wearing old clothes, shake piñon branches with a rake or long stick until the cones fall to the ground. Collect the cones in something disposable like burlap bags or boxes (plastic doesn't work because the gum tars it stuck). At home, place the tightly closed cones on a foil-lined cookie sheet and bake at 350 degrees for 10 minutes, or until the cones open and the house is filled with a heady pine fragrance. Allow to cool. Shake or pick out the pine seeds from each cone, crack them individually, and savor.

To clean your clothing and hands of the pine pitch that gums up *everything* it touches, wash with salad oil or mayonnaise, and then soap and water. Once the cones bake, the sap hardens to a varnishlike sheen and is no longer sticky.

either raw or roasted and salted. They are a main ingredient in pesto and are tasty in cakes, crackers, candies, casseroles, and, when ground, in soups. Because of their high price and limited availability, pine nuts are used sparingly. I follow the old Roman custom of seasoning pine nuts in asafetida.

Buying When purchasing pine seeds in the shell, look for dark-colored shells—the light-colored shells contain undeveloped seeds. When purchasing shelled nuts, look for creamy white, plump kernels; refrigerate until use to retard rancidity.

See **Nuts.**

PINK BEAN
Pinquito
(Phaseolus vulgaris)

In 1980, I first found these little pink beans in an open-air market in a Mexican mountain village in Michiocan. The vendor extolled his *pinquitos* above all the others. I bought some and cooked them over a camp stove in my hotel. Ever since that first bowl, *pinquitos* have remained one of my favorites.

These small heirloom beans are a regional favorite in central Mexico and have increasing availability in U.S. markets. Sweet, meaty, and flavorful, they're the size of a navy bean but boast character.

See **Beans and Legumes.**

PINOLE

Pemmican (a mixture of ground jerky, nuts, and fruits) was a staple and trail food of hunter-gatherer Native Americans; pinole was a similar staple and trail food for the early maize-growing cultures. Pinole's pri-

mary ingredient is a fine corn flour that can be made only from soft or flour corn, not from dent or flint corn. It is cooked with water into a cereal or beverage or eaten in dry pinches as a trail food. I recommend it all three ways.

Additional pinole ingredients vary from region to region, from season to season, and from cook to cook. I've made pinole using ground berries, seeds (chia, sunflower, or pumpkin), pine nuts or other nuts, and mesquite meal.

The pinole available today in small packets in specialty food departments usually contains sugar and other flavoring agents in addition to the corn. As a beverage, stir 2 tablespoons of pinole into 1 cup of water or milk and simmer for 5 minutes. To make a breakfast cereal, increase the pinole to ¼ cup to 1 cup liquid and cook, stirring as necessary, for 5 minutes.

PIÑON See **Pine Nut.**

PINQUITO See **Pink Bean.**

PINTO
(Phaseolus vulgaris)

What bean is associated with tacos? The pinto. Indeed, the pinto is nearly synonymous with southwestern-style cooking. This kidney bean family member is identified by its buff to pink color that, contrary to what its name suggests, is not splotched like a pinto pony. Next to the soybean, the pinto is the most common bean grown in the United States. It is my least favorite bean.

A high-yield pinto bean was hybridized in

the 1930s and soon, with encouragement from agricultural colleges and county farm agents, bean growers favored the more-bushel-per-acre pinto over regional heirloom varieties. There's nothing wrong with a pinto, but if you're interested in greater flavor range and vitality, consider a nonhybrid, such as pinquito, anasazi, or Jacob's cattle bean.

See **Beans and Legumes.**

PIPALI See **Long Pepper.**

PISTACHIO
(Pistacia vera)

The fruit of a small evergreen tree and a cashew relative, the pistachio originated in Asia Minor before recorded time. It is prized for its pleasant, mild flavor and fetching green color.

Health Benefits Pistachio tonifies the liver and kidneys and eases constipation. Compared to other nuts, the pistachio is a superior source of protein, calcium, and vitamin A and the best source of iron and potassium. Like most nuts, it reduces *vata*.

Use A favorite way of eating pistachios is out of hand or as a cocktail nut. They are also an ingredient in pistachio ice cream, Turkish delight, nougat, and halvah. Pistachios may be substituted for other nuts in recipes. One cup of unshelled pistachios yields about ½ cup of nutmeats.

Buying Iran, Turkey, and Afghanistan are the largest producers of pistachios, and Americans consume nearly 90 percent of the world's supply. Commercial crops were planted in California in 1968, and today California is the world's second largest pistachio producer. California pistachios are generally larger than those from the Middle East. Imported pistachios are fumigated with methyl bromide or phostoxin.

Almost all pistachios are sold roasted and salted. Because the shell of pistachios splits open as the nut matures, they do not have as lengthy a shelf life as other whole nuts do. Don't bother to crack unsplit nuts, as the kernel is immature.

The preferred Afghan pistachio shell has a natural pink tint; other varieties are tan. Some pistachio growers and importers dye the nut red, which exposes the kernels to the chemical dyes. Favor plain Jane pistachios over Day-Glo reds.

See **Nuts.**

PLANTAIN
(Musa paradisiaca)

The astringent, oversize banana called the plantain figures prominently in Latin American and Asian cookery, where it is used as a starchy vegetable. Unlike the ubiquitous sweet banana, the plantain is never eaten raw.

Health Benefits Plantains with yellow skins are high in vitamin A. They contain a fair amount of vitamin C, are an excellent source of potassium, and are high in calories. Plantains are cooling, reduce *pitta*, and soothe the intestines. When astringent in flavor, they also calm *kapha;* when sweet, they reduce *vata*.

Use As with a banana, peel just prior to use, unless, of course, you wish to bake or grill it in its skin. To peel a plantain, cut off both ends, slit the peel along one side, and remove. The fresh color is creamy yellow or bright pink. The starchy, bland green plantain may be used as a potato—fried, baked, simmered, sautéed, or mashed.

A yellow-ripe plantain may be prepared like the green plantain or with apples or sweet potatoes as a sweet dish. A black-ripe plantain may be cooked as you would a ripe banana; unlike the banana, a plantain will hold its shape and texture.

Buying Do not be intimidated by a black or brown peel: As the plantain ripens, it darkens. A ripe plantain is not hard; it has give like a banana and a sweet flavor. Avoid any that are cracked or overly soft. They are available in Asian and Latino markets and, increasingly, in supermarkets, natural food stores, and greengrocers.

Store plantains at room temperature and do not refrigerate unless absolutely soft (refrigeration stops their ripening). Plantains are available year-round.

See **Banana; Tropical Fruit.**

PLEUROTTE See **Oyster Mushroom.**

PLUM
(Prunus domestica)

> Green plum—
> it draws her eyebrows together.
> —Buson

The juicy, sweet-tart plum is a cousin to the peach and the cherry and grows on every continent except Antarctica. The plum has been used by man since prehistoric times. California supplies 90 percent of the U.S. commercial crop.

Health Benefits Plums are an excellent food for people suffering from liver problems and for diabetics. Plums aid digestion, relieve dehydration and thirst, and help stabilize energy flow. According to Chinese tests, they relieve the feeling of "steaming bones" and build body fluids.

Purple plums are more cooling and better for nervous disorders than are yellow plums, which are slightly warming. An acid fruit, plums are not recommended for people with stomach ulcers or inflammations. Plums, sweet or sour, reduce *vata*. Sweet plums reduce *pitta*.

Due to their high content of oxalic acid, eat plums in moderation; otherwise, they may deplete calcium from the body. Plums provide sugar but no starch, some potassium, vitamins A and C, and a fair amount of silicon.

Use Plums' sweet-tart bite make them especially delicious in pies and tarts; sweet they are also eaten fresh, stewed, and made into preserves, wines, and liqueurs. Sloe, a wild plum (*P. spinosa*), is used to make sloe gin. A prune is a dried plum. Cooking plums in an acid base like lemon juice intensifies their color; cooking them with an alkaline base like baking powder reduces their color.

Buying/Foraging The test for a good plum is temperature. Pass your hand over a bin of fresh plums, and they emit a perceptible coolness. If not, they're old and will taste insipid. I rarely find freshly picked plums in the supermarket but have better chances with roadside vendors.

Of the thousands of plum varieties in existence, about twenty are grown commercially, most classified as European or Japanese. Purple or blue European plums are small and firm. Red, yellow, or green Japanese varieties are generally larger and juicer.

Purchase plums that are slightly soft to the touch, especially at the tip, and have a powdery bloom on the skin. They should be plump but not shriveled, split, overly soft, leaky, or bruised. If not fully ripened, leave plums out at room temperature for a few days (they won't become sweeter but will soften), then refrigerate for three to five days.

CHILDREN KNOW BEST

"Don't eat those sour plums," parents admonish, "they'll give you a bellyache." And children go right on eating them.

Immature plums (and apples) stimulate the production of digestive enzymes that support the function of the stomach, liver, and gallbladder. Immature plums are pickled in salt and sold throughout Mexico and Asia. They're sold fresh in Greece and other Balkan countries. In the country of Georgia, sour plums are made into a highly flavored sauce, *tkemali*.

Unripe plums and apples are rich in citric, malic, and succinic acids, and contain phenolic compounds and hydrolyzable tannins, which help increase hydrochloric acid levels.

Wild plums proliferate throughout temperate regions and may be found in abandoned lots, wooded land, or open spaces. If you ever come across a thicket of plums—wild trees are scrubby, not stately—with ripe fruit, sample fruits from more than one tree. The flavor varies dramatically from one to another, and though most will be tart, odds are you'll find a tree or two with remarkably sweet fruit.

See **Fruit**; **Prune**; **Umeboshi**.

POBLANO See **Chile Pepper**.

POI See **Taro**.

POLENTA See **Corn**.

POMEGRANATE
(Punica granatum)

> Eat the pomegranate, for it purges the system of hatred and envy.
> —Muhammad

When I lived in New Mexico, a pomegranate tree grew by the backyard fishpond, and the hummingbirds could not get their fill of the brilliant, salmon red blossoms. It seems hard to get a fill of the fruit's edible seeds, which have little pulp but lots of juicy, ruby red juice.

The word pomegranate means "many-grained apple." From China to the Mediterranean, the many-seeded pomegranate symbolizes fecundity. A Turkish bride throws the fruit to the ground, and the number of seeds that pop out predicts how many children she

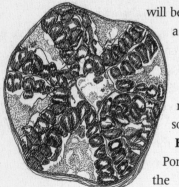

will bear. This unique fruit, a Persian native, is now widely cultivated in the tropics, subtropics, the Mediterranean region, and southern California.

Health Benefits Pomegranates promote the production of red blood cells; expel tapeworms; strengthen the bladder (especially for the elderly) and the gums; and soothe ulcers in the mouth and throat. The peel is used as a home remedy for treating chronic dysentery. A kitchen remedy for burning eyes is to place a drop of pomegranate juice in each eye before sleeping. Pomegranates reduce *pitta* and *kapha*.

Pomegranates are a superior source of potassium, are high in citric acid, and have moderate amounts of vitamin C and the B vitamins.

Use Pulling pomegranate seeds from the fruit is a sticky task but a sweet one—and best if not hurried. The juice is easier to extract: Bruise the fruit by rolling it on a hard surface, then puncture its end, insert a straw, and drink. The juice makes a permanent stain, so protect your clothing with a bib apron.

The fruit is primarily eaten raw and is a common ingredient in Spanish, Italian, Middle Eastern, and Latin American cuisines. It may be used in jelled desserts, sauces, conserves, and syrups. As a garnish, a few of its ruby red seeds sprinkled in a fruit cup or even risotto add dramatic flare.

Grenadine is a popular pomegranate nonalcoholic sweet liqueur. It adds a sweet tang to sauces, marinades, and dressings, and its red color looks great in sorbets and ice

---

GRENADINE

Today's commercial grenadine contains pomegranate extract, and flavoring, as well as red dye and preservatives. The real thing is easy to make. Briefly process 2 cups of pomegranate seeds (first remove the bitter-tasting white membrane from around the seeds) with 2 cups sugar. The mixture need not be a smooth consistency. Place in a glass jar or bowl and allow to sit for 24 hours. Bring to a boil in a nonaluminum pan. Simmer for 2 minutes, stirring constantly. Strain out the seeds and press the pulp to extract all the juice. Pour into a sterile jar and refrigerate for up to 6 months.

---

cream. Pomegranate molasses, made by boiling down and concentrating the juice, is used in Persian cuisine.

Buying Look for fresh-looking, plump, heavy fruit with a hard red skin. Pomegranates are at peak supply in the fall. Store in a cool, dark place for up to a month, or refrigerate for up to two months. Grenadine is sugar sweetened; pomegranate syrup available in Middle Eastern markets is unsweetened.

See **Fruit.**

POMELO See **Pummelo.**

POPCORN
(Zea mays praecox)

[E]ach Grain burst and threw out a white substance of twice its bigness.
—Benjamin Franklin

Many things American—from pop music to Levi's—are popular elsewhere in the world, but popcorn isn't one of them. Munching popcorn at the movies and at home remains primarily an American pastime. Popcorn is not only native to the Americas, but it is the original grandmother of all corn. In her book *The Story of Corn*, Betty Fussell described the remarkable 1948 discovery that established corn's origins. In Bat Cave, Catron County, New Mexico, Harvard anthropologists dug through layers of more than two thousand years of accumulated trash, garbage, and excrement. "The deeper they dug," writes Fussell, "the smaller and more primitive the cobs, until they reached bottom and found tiny cobs of popcorn in which each kernel was enclosed in its own husk, the 'pod popcorn' . . . identified as the genetic ancestor" of modern corn.

The husk of the first corn was just like the husk or hull that encloses each grain of wheat, rice, and all other grains. Early farmers' development of corn varieties in which the husk covered several kernels was an amazing advancement. It also makes corn dependent upon farmers to remove the husk and plant the seed. All other grains can reseed themselves.

Popcorn, a corn variety unto itself, is typified by a hard hull and endosperm that seals in moisture content. About 14 percent of the kernel is water. When popcorn is heated, the trapped moisture becomes steam, which builds up until the kernel explodes.

Health Benefits Popcorn is light and dry, and its thermal property is hot. The Doctrine of Signature suggests that while its good for moving stuck energy, it may be best avoided by someone with an explosive temperament.

One cup of popped corn has 54 calories and two grams of protein. Its nutritional value can be greatly enhanced by sprinkling it with kelp and herbs. Popcorn reduces excess in a person and therefore aids *kapha*.

CARAMEL CORN

For those times when you're hungry for a quick and satisfying snack, here's a fantastic one. It brings out the kid in me.

- 1 cup honey, sorghum molasses, rice syrup, *or* maple syrup
- 4 quarts popped corn, unsalted
- 1 cup toasted almonds or peanuts (optional)

Place the sweetener in a medium saucepan over medium-high heat. Bring to a boil. When boiling, lower heat to medium and boil, without stirring, for about 5 minutes, or until the syrup reaches 270 degrees on a candy thermometer. (The syrup's appearance as it cooks also indicates readiness—initially, it is frothy, then as the froth recedes, the syrup becomes thicker, denser. When it's a shade darker, it's ready.)

Pour the hot syrup over the popped corn and nuts, if using. Stir to coat, taking care to not touch the burning hot syrup. To make popcorn balls, butter your hands and quickly form the warm candied corn into desired size. Makes 4 quarts.

Use Place popcorn in a heated, covered pan over high heat for 3 minutes or until kernels pop. Shake the pan as necessary to prevent burning. Or pop in a hot air popper according to the manufacturer's directions. One cup of popcorn yields one quart of popped corn.

If popcorn is dehydrated, place popcorn in a sealed jar, add ¼ teaspoon water per cup of corn, set aside for several days, then pop.

Buying Most popcorn is yellow, but red, blue, and white kernels are also available. Today, popcorn is hybridized to expand up to 40 times the kernel's original size and to have a high percentage of kernels that pop. Some manufacturers guarantee having under 1 percent of unpopped kernels.

See **Corn.**

POPPING BEAN See **Nuña.**

POPPY SEED
(Papaver rhoeas)

The minuscule slate blue seed (nine hundred thousand per pound) of the poppy is a favorite seasoning agent. It has a mildly spicy aroma, a distinctive nutty-sweet, pungent flavor, and a crunchy texture. The milky sap from the unripe seed pods of a different variety, the opium poppy, yields opium and its derivatives, morphine and codeine. Poppies originated in the Middle East, although today most culinary poppy seed comes from Holland.

Health Benefits Poppy seeds are soporific, which means that they sedate and calm the nervous system. They also relieve coughs

---

> ### AS SOOTHING AS MOTHER'S MILK
>
> A slice of poppy seed cake today can cause tomorrow's urine analysis to test positive for opium or an opium derivative. No wonder poppy seed cake soothes. The seeds are so soothing, in fact, that they used to be given to infants and young children to quiet them. Thus the Latin name for poppy comes from the word *pap*, or teat, which also explains our word for infant cereal, pabulum.

and are considered medicinal for the colon. Poppy seeds help reduce *vata* and *kapha*.

Use The seeds have a long culinary tradition, especially in Middle Eastern, Central European, Slavic, and Balkan cooking. Use them as a topping for breads, in cakes, or as a filling in pastries.

Buying Store poppy seeds tightly covered in a cool, dark cupboard for up to a year. If they develop an acrid, sharp, bitter, or unpleasant flavor, they've become rancid. Toss them. In addition to slate blue poppy seeds, there are yellow and brown varieties with some limited availability.

See **Seeds.**

PORCINO See **Bolete.**

PORTOBELLO
(Agaricus bisporus)

A common mushroom variety that is large, dark, and meaty in flavor and texture, the portobello tastes more like a wild meadow mushroom than a white supermarket button mushroom—though all three types are the same species. Because of its substantial size, the portobello holds, refrigerated, for up to ten days. Grilled or sautéed, it is a great substitute for roast beef in a sandwich or entrée.

See **Mushroom Family.**

PORTULACA See **Purslane.**

POSLE
Arepas, Hominy, Nixtamal, Pozole, Samp, Slaked Corn

In New Mexico, posole refers to soup cooked for traditional feast days, and it also refers to the slaked corn that goes into the soup. This corn is possibly the most amazing Native American food.

Throughout the Americas, most corn was processed into posole, enhancing the flavor, shortening preparation time, and increasing its mineral and vitamin content. To make posole, whole dried corn is boiled with wood ash or slaked lime until the hull is softened and washed off. It is this hull, the same one that gets stuck in your teeth when eating popcorn, that makes cooking whole dry corn nigh impossible.

Health Benefits Posole is from 20 to 300 percent higher in calcium than dried corn, depending upon what it was slaked with. In one study, one-half cup of blue corn contains 1 mg. calcium; when slaked in juniper wood ash it contains 334 mg. calcium. Slaking dramatically increases both calcium and niacin. The niacin in posole is also more bioavailable than from dried corn. Posole and posole

products support the heart and also the kidneys due to their mineral concentration. They reduce *kapha.*

Use Soak dried posole overnight or for several hours, drain it, and cook it for an hour, or until the kernels "butterfly" or splay open. Use this as the base for a grain pilaf or salad or turn it into a soup using your favorite soup ingredients, with or without meat or beans. It makes a very satisfying soup, to which I usually add onion, winter squash, celery, and a strip of kombu; for a one-dish meal, I add beans.

Buying Posole, made from white corn, is available dried and often frozen in supermarkets, natural food markets, and Latin American markets. It is also available canned as hominy, but this unfortunately tastes more like the can than like the hominy.

See **Arepas; Corn; Masa; Masa Harina.**

POTATO
(Solanum tuberosum)

Americans eat about a potato a day, according to USDA figures. One in every three restaurant meals includes potatoes. I find that boring. When I dined upon potatoes in their place of origin, the Peruvian Andes, they were not boring. These tiny *papas* were like Jerusalem artichokes in shape and size. The colors were stupendous—black skinned with bright yellow flesh, or with rose-colored skin and flesh, or in all shades of purple and blue. Even more memorable were their earthy, sweet, bright flavors, which varied from variety to variety. Only in texture were they comparable to our common potatoes.

One of the world's most important foods

today, potatoes were introduced into Europe some four hundred years ago. Fortunately, heirloom varieties are available in seed catalogs, and are finding their way into our markets.

Health Benefits Unless a diet is high in meat and sodium, both macrobiotic and Ayurvedic cuisine recommend using the potato infrequently, especially in the case of rheumatoid arthritis.

Potatoes reduce inflammations (except in some arthritic conditions), treat acidosis, and neutralize body acids. Their juice has antibiotic properties, helps lower blood pressure, and treats stomach or duodenal ulcers. For people with compromised digestion, potatoes are easiest to digest when consumed with nonstarchy vegetables instead of with meat, beans, or grains. Potatoes are considered beneficial in function for the spleen-pancreas and reduce *pitta* and *kapha*.

Potatoes, a complex carbohydrate food, are 2 percent protein. Just beneath the potato skin are significant quantities of manganese, chromium, selenium, and molybdenum. They are a good source of vitamin C, B vitamins (especially vitamin B_1), and potassium. From 10 to 50 percent of a potato's potassium may be lost during boiling; steaming, baking, and frying do not significantly reduce the potassium.

Use I find almost every potato preparation, from mashed potatoes to potato salad to hash browns, works well with the skin intact. And the skin provides important nutrients and fiber.

Do not eat the potato sprouts ("eyes") or any green-colored flesh or greenish skin;

they contain the poisonous alkaloid solanine. This alkaloid, a nerve poison, can cause drowsiness, itching, diarrhea, and vomiting. A potato that causes a sharp, burning sensation on the tongue has excessive alkaloid levels.

Buying Select firm potatoes that are clean, firm, smooth, and free from soft spots or darkened areas. There are several types of potatoes, each of which is better suited to certain types of cooking than to others.

- **Fingerlings** Shaped like long, chubby fingers, these yellow, pinkish, purple, or white potatoes are superlative. An heirloom Peruvian crop now grown in the United States, fingerlings have a silky fine texture and a creamy, pleasing flavor.
- **New Potato** Not a specific variety

LIFE WITHOUT LUMPS

Mashing potatoes in a food processor or electric mixer does not work well. The result is as gummy as packaged instant mashed potatoes. A potato masher works better. Best of all is a ricer, which produces long, silky, light potato strands. Either way, using your energy—rather than machine energy—takes but a minute, is easier to clean up than a food processor mess, and each mash makes a satisfying "thwocking" sound. Have a go at it.

but, rather, any freshly harvested potato with thin, flaking skins and a sweet flavor. New potatoes require less cooking than mature potatoes; they hold their shape better after cooking, and are best boiled or steamed within one week of purchase.

- **Purple Potato** They are similar in flavor and shape to the russet with an indigo skin and a lighter purple flesh. When fried, purple potatoes turn a dingy gray color, so boiling, steaming, or baking is recommended.
- **Red Potato** Characterized by a thin, reddish skin, ranging from pink to dark red in color. Moister than a russet or long white potato with a waxy, white, crisp flesh. The red potato is best boiled, but it can also be roasted or fried.
- **Russet Potato** Also called Idaho potato or baking potato. An elongated cylinder with yellowish brown skin. Its dry, floury, or mealy texture suits it to baking, frying, and potato pancakes or dumplings.
- **White Potato** Round or long with a smooth, tan-colored skin and a firm texture. The white potato is an all-purpose potato for baking, steaming, mashing, and frying.
- **Yellow Finn** Also called Finnish Yellow Wax. A waxy, yellow-fleshed potato, excellent for salads and soups.

See **Chuño; Nightshade Family.**

POZOLE See **Posole.**

PRICKLY PEAR
Cactus Pear, Indian Fig, Tuna
(Opuntia ficus-indica)

> Here we go round the prickly pear
> Prickly pear, prickly pear
> Here we go round the prickly pear
> At 5 o'clock in the morning.
>> T. S. Eliot, *The Hollow Men*

The sweet and juicy fruits of the opuntia cactus are popular in local cuisines worldwide. As its name suggests, the fruit is shaped like a pear and covered with glasslike prickles. Remove these little spines along with their coarse skin—which is colored green, orange, red, or mauve. The tangy pulp, which contains many hard edible seeds, is most often a ruby red.

Health Benefits Prickly pears are astringent and tonifying to the colon and lungs. They are high in ascorbic acid, magnesium, and bioflavonoids. For *pitta*, they are powerfully cooling and reducing.

Use Although the spines are mechanically removed before the fruits are marketed, inevitably a few hard-to-see ones remain. Skewer a fruit on a fork and lightly singe the skin (like singing pinfeathers from poultry) to permit handling. Or skewer the fruit, and holding it firmly on a cutting board, peel the skin and the spines.

To serve prickly pear, slice and serve raw in a salad or fruit cup; as a garnish; or as the base for an unusual salad dressing. Or purée the pulp and sieve it to make a dramatically colored jam, syrup, ice, or beverage from the juice.

Buying Prickly pears are available in Latino markets, the specialty produce section of some supermarkets, and specialty food markets, except during the summer. Select those which are tender and fresh-looking. Refrigerate for up to a week.

See Fruit; Nopal.

PRIMARY-GROWN YEAST See **Nutritional Yeast.**

PRUNE
(Prunus domestica)

All prunes are plums, but not every plum can become a prune. The deciding factor is moisture content. Try drying a juicy plum, one that still contains the pit, and fermentation will spoil it before it can dry; a drier plum, like a damson or the French d'Agen, will dry without fermenting. Traditionally, ripe plums were sun dried for several days and finished in bakers' ovens. Today, they are dehydrated to 21 percent moisture in special ovens immediately after harvest.

Valued from ancient times, the premier prune was produced mainly in southwestern France until this century. California now supplies 70 percent of the world's supply. Almost all of the crop is the California French prune (originally from the Aegen area).

Health Benefits Prunes are an excellent tonic for a sluggish liver. They are a high-fiber food; ounce for ounce, they contain more food fiber than dry beans. The fiber in prunes, together with its oxalic acid, stimulates the colon. To relieve constipation, prunes are most effective simmered in water until plump rather than eaten dried. Prunes are an excellent source of vitamin A and are a B-complex vitamin source. They are also an excellent source of iron (nonheme or vegetable quality), providing more than a third as much iron as an equal serving of liver. Prune fiber lowers blood cholesterol. Prunes reduce *pitta* and *kapha.*

Use Besides stewed, prunes can be used in stuffing, cakes, salads, confections, and soups. Prune butter, or puréed prunes, makes a good fat replacement in baked goods. Substitute ½ cup prune butter for every cup of fat in cakes, cookies, and brownies. For superior flavor, make a low-fat rather than fat-free baked good. To make your own prune butter, combine 1⅓ cup pitted prunes (8 ounces) with ⅓ cup water and process or blend to form a soft paste.

Buying Choose prunes that are slightly soft and somewhat flexible, with a black skin that is blemishfree. Purchase tightly sealed packages. Prunes are available whole, with or without the pit, dried in paste form; or as a juice. Size varies from 20 prunes per pound to 80 per pound, and is a factor only of size, not variety.

Commercial prunes are preserved with the innocuous potassium sorbate (the potassium salt of sorbic acid) to protect against mold and yeast spoilage. Organic prunes contain no additives.

See **Dried Fruit; Plum.**

PSYLLIUM
(Plantago psyllium)

Plantain—no relation to the bananalike plantain—is a small, low-to-the-ground leafy weed found in most lawns throughout the United States. It's one of the most important greens to forage because of its versatility both in the salad bowl and in herbal blends, poultices, and infusions. The seed of one plantain variety, psyllium, and sometimes just its husk, is possibly the most popular herb for people suffering from bowel irregularities.

Health Benefits Psyllium seed and its husk are highly demulcent and swell when mixed with liquid. This gives a mucilaginous coating to the intestines as well as providing bulk to the stool. Psyllium, therefore, facilitates bowel movement. For constipation, stir 1 teaspoon into a cup of water or place in a jar, cover, and shake. Drink immediately. For diarrhea, stir into buttermilk. By moistening membranes, psyllium soothes irritation and absorbs digestive toxins. Psyllium reduces *pitta*.

See **Seeds.**

PUMMELO
Pomelo, Shaddock
(Citrus maxima)

Grandmother of—and double, or even treble, the size of—the grapefruit, the pummelo is teardrop in shape with a very thick, coarse peel. Like a grapefruit, its skin and segmented flesh varies from yellow to pink and may be seedless or full of seeds. The pummelo is generally less juicy, acidic, and bitter than a grapefruit.

See **Citrus Family; Grapefruit.**

PUMPKIN
(Cucurbita pepo)

Go to sleep now, my pumpkin,
I will cover your toes.
If you sleep now, my pumpkin,
You'll turn into a rose.

—Lullaby

The pumpkin, an indigenous American fruit, was a staple of Native Americans, who dried it and made it into flour. Today, its use is primarily limited to baking pies, making jack-o'-lanterns, and competing to see who can grow the biggest one, by now well over six hundred pounds.

Health Benefits Pumpkins help regulate blood sugar metabolism; support the spleen-pancreas; and relieve bronchial asthma. In moderation, they help to reduce *vata*. The major nutrients supplied by pumpkins are vitamin A and potassium.

Buying For eating, choose small pie pumpkins for flavor and tenderness. Their shape may be round or oblong. Look for those that are heavy for their weight with a firm rind without soft spots. Although orange is the traditional color, new varieties are buff or white.

See **Squash; Winter Squash.**

PUMPKIN SEED
Pepito
(Cucurbita pepo)

The pumpkin seed, the largest and costliest of seeds, is not from the jack-o'-lantern pumpkin variety. They are from a South and Central American squash that is grown specifically for its seeds. The smaller seeds from domestic pumpkins may be eaten like pepitos but are not available commercially.

Pumpkin seed oil is dark brown, pleasantly flavored, and popular in Austrian cuisine. It has recently become available in the United States.

Health Benefits Pumpkin seeds are higher in protein (29 percent) than many other seeds and nuts, and they are a valuable source of the important Omega-3 fatty acids. An excellent source of iron, zinc, phosphorus, and vitamin A, they also contain calcium and some of the B vitamins. Raw pumpkin seeds are recommended by some to expel pinworms or other intestinal parasites. Considered medicinal for the liver, colon, and spleen-pancreas, pumpkin seeds are *tridoshic,* or balancing to all body types, when used in moderation. They are most calming to *vata.*

Use Pepitos have a slight crunch, an interesting green color, and a mildly nutty flavor. Pumpkin seeds are available roasted and salted or raw. Light roasting improves their flavor and digestibility.

To use your own pumpkin or winter squash seeds, remove the pulpy fibers; season to taste with a little salt, soy sauce, or curry; spread in a buttered pan and roast in a preheated 350 degrees oven for 15 minutes, or until brown and crisp.

See **Pumpkin; Seeds.**

PURSLANE
Ma Chi Xian, Portulaca, Pussley, Verdolaga
(Portulaca oleracea)

A near relative of the garden flower portulaca, or moss rose, purslane is valued in Asia and Europe both as a potherb and as a medicinal herb. Purslane grows wild throughout the United States. When I taught cookery in New Mexico, my older Latino and Native American students fondly recalled *verde lagos,* as they called purslane, as a staple green from their childhood—a small, slow-growing annual herb with numerous branches and succulent leaves that looks something like a

---

MY CHICKENS AND CHOLESTEROL-REDUCING EGGS

Egg yolks from chickens that were fed purslane contained ten times the amount of Omega-3 fatty acids, which reduce cholesterol, as yolks from supermarket eggs, according to a study at the National Institute on Alcohol Abuse and Alcoholism in Bethesda, Maryland. Of all leafy green vegetables, purslane is the richest known source of the important Omega-3 fatty acid.

After reading this information in Kay Young's *Wild Seasons: Gathering and Cooking Wild Plants of the Great Plains,* I went outside to observe my small clutch of banties scratching up a weedy part of my garden where purslane flourishes. Without even having heard of the Bethesda chickens, they did me proud and pecked away at the purslane.

---

jade plant. It makes an attractive ground cover in a flower garden.

Health Benefits Purslane is used externally to remove toxins from eczema, insect bites, and boils. Internally, it's used for dysentery, hemorrhoids, and postpartum bleeding. Do not, however, use it during pregnancy or for people with digestive problems. In moderation, purslane is *tridoshic.*

Use A German friend, Karen Di Giacomo, once showed me how to pickle purslane seeds in vinegar as "poor woman's capers." They were smaller than capers, but quite tasty. More often, though, I add purslane leaves and stems—raw or blanched—to salads or simmer or stir-fry them in any vegetable dish.

Buying/Foraging Dried purslane is available in Chinese pharmacies. Fresh purslane is sometimes found in food specialty shops or farmers' markets. Odds are, however, that it's outside your back door. Although you may harvest purslane throughout the summer, its flavor is superior before it flowers.

PUSSLEY See **Purslane.**

QUINCE
(Cydonia oblonga)

I once inherited an old, unruly bank of quince; I trimmed the trees back, and every fall thereafter they produced a few precious, primitive-looking, furry green fruits. The quince, resembling a misshapen apple or pear, is called "the ugly duckling of the apple family." The dazzling, salmon pink blossoms, however, are one of the most beautiful spring blooms.

An Asian native, the quince was once a staple in many homes in the northern hemisphere. Thanks to its generous amount of pectin, it is unparalleled in preserving jellies and as a confection. When home preserving and candy making became unfashionable, so did quince. Happily, the current interest in so-called exotic produce is bringing it back to market.

Health Benefits The astringent taste of quince produces a drying, choking sensation, like an unripe banana or crabapple. Quince treats diarrhea, but an excess may exacerbate constipation, dryness of the mouth, difficulty of speech, and palsy symptoms. Astringent foods in moderation reduce *pitta* and *kapha*.

This high-pectin fruit provides a fair amount of vitamin A and potassium and is a good source of fiber. Pectin helps lower cholesterol.

Use The quince is unusual among fruits in that it is always eaten cooked. Raw, it is exceedingly astringent, hard, and bland. Stewing, baking, or braising brings out its unique, perfumed flavor, which complements meat, savory, or sweet dishes. If a quince is on hand and I'm baking apples or making an apple pie, I always include quince slices; their lush flavor, texture, and aroma enhance the apples.

Since the fruit maintains its shape even with long cooking, it encourages experimentation. Remove the quince peel, which tends toward bitterness. For jams or jellies, use the fruit alone or in combination with low-pectin fruits, such as berries or grapes. A candylike fruit leather made of quince purée and sugar is a great specialty in Sicily, Hungary, and France, and in Germany, where it is called *Quittenwurst*. With cooking, the quince's flesh turns from yellow-white to a delicate pink or red, a reminder in the fall of their exquisite spring blossoms.

Buying The availability of quince is best in the fall. Select firm fruits that are smooth skinned. Handle carefully because, despite their hardness, they do bruise easily. The quince has a powerful aroma, which when the fruit is left at room temperature will perfume a room for several weeks. Quinces store well and may be refrigerated for a month or more.

See **Fruit**.

QUINOA
(Chenopodium quinoa)

Native to the high valleys of the Andes, the grainlike quinoa (pronounced KEEN-whah) was revered by the Incas as their mother grain. The Spanish squelched its cultivation, but, fortunately, it endured in remote locations. The plant flourishes under extreme ecological conditions, including high altitude, thin cold air, hot sun, radiation, drought, frost, and poor soil. Although most quinoa varieties grow best at 10,000 feet and above, some varieties grow as low as sea level.

I've sown, weeded, harvested, and threshed quinoa. It's a beautiful plant. Its boldly colored leaves, stalks, and seeds are as flamboyant and varied as the traditional clothing of the former Incas, the Quechua and Aymara. At the very least, I recommend the plant to you as an ornamental.

Quinoa, a member of a goosefoot family, is not a true cereal grain but is used as one. About the size of millet, the periphery of each disk-shape grain is bound with a narrow germ or embryo. When cooked, the wispy germ separates from the seed, and its delicate— almost crunchy—curlicue makes a great contrast to the soft grain.

Health Benefits Quinoa is a high-energy grain that, because it is easy to digest, is an ideal endurance and fitness food. It is drying and warming, strengthening to the kidneys and heart, as well as the whole body. It decreases *kapha*. *Vata-* and *pitta*-type people may use it in moderation.

The United Nations World Health Organization reports that quinoa is at least equal to milk in protein quality. Quinoa has the highest protein of any grain (16 percent) and, unlike other grains, is a complete protein with an essential amino acid profile similar to milk. It contains more calcium than milk and is high in lysine, an amino acid that is scarce in the vegetable kingdom. Quinoa is a rich and balanced source of many other vital nutrients, including iron, phosphorus, B-vitamins, and vitamin E.

Use Quinoa is so easy to prepare and quick cooking that it readily becomes a favorite grain staple of people regardless of their culinary preferences. Wash quinoa well before cooking to remove the bitter saponin that coats it. Because the seeds are so small, it's imperative to use a strainer. Place the quinoa in a bowl, add water to cover, and, using the palms of your hands, lightly scrub for about 10 seconds. Strain out the washing water and repeat this process. Pour all of the quinoa into the strainer and run fresh water over for 5 to 10 seconds, or until the water runs clear.

Imported quinoa takes two cups of stock or water per cup of grain. Our smaller domestic quinoa requires 1½ cups stock or water per cup of grain. Both yield about three cups of cooked grain and take about 15 minutes to cook.

As versatile as rice, quinoa can be substituted freely for rice, millet, or couscous in any recipe. It's also good plain as a side dish or as an ingredient in soups, pilafs, and casseroles. For an unusual pudding, substitute quinoa for the rice in your favorite rice pudding recipe.

Buying Imported quinoa was first marketed in the United States in 1984 and is now available in many supermarkets as well as in natural food stores. Although quinoa will not set seed east of the Rocky Mountains, commercial crops are grown in several western states and Canada. Occasionally, black quinoa is available; its rich, nutty flavor is superior to the lighter colors.

See **Grains**.

QUINOA FLOUR

Quinoa flour, used primarily by people with wheat allergies, adds interest to quick breads, cookies, and cakes.

Because quinoa is a soft grain, you can

MOTHER GRAIN STAGES A COMEBACK

When I visited Bolivia and Peru in 1987 to research my book *Quinoa: The Supergrain*, I admired the quinoa sold in the open-air Aymara and Quechua Indian markets (quinoa was not then available in restaurants or in stores). These gentle people, proud of their other merchandise, were reluctant to speak of their quinoa. The Spanish had denigrated quinoa as chicken feed and as food fit only for the poor. For over four hundred years, these people believed that if they fed quinoa to their children, it would make them stupid. As soon as these indigenous people could afford it, they chose foods of the upper and middle classes, pasta and white bread. And Bolivia, at that time, had the highest rate of infant mortality.

Fortunately, North American interest in quinoa is helping reinstate the status of the mother grain in its homeland. Today, quinoa is available in restaurants and stores throughout the Americas.

---

pulverize it to a flourlike consistency in a coffee mill or blender. A grain mill, however, gives superior results. If the quinoa has a bitter taste, then wash it and dry it before grinding. Quinoa flour, which has had its bitter-tasting saponin removed, is available in natural food stores and some supermarkets.

RADICCHIO
Italian Chicory, Red Chicory
(Cichorium intybus)

Magenta-colored radicchio (rah-DEEK-ee-o) is a heading type of chicory with firm crisp leaves and an arresting flavor bordering on sweet and bitter. The most dramatic variety, radicchio di Verona, looks like a little red cabbage with thick white veins. Radicchio di Treviso has long, narrow leaves and is better than Verona for cooking.

Health Benefits Radicchio is a cooling food. Its bitter properties and red color make it a heart food that's cleansing to the blood and supports circulation. Radicchio also encourages bile production and aids digestion. It reduces *pitta* and *kapha*. This salad green is a good source of vitamins A and C and is also high in calcium.

Use Radicchio is most commonly thought of as a winter salad green, but its sturdy leaves afford much wider use. Freely substitute radicchio in any chicory or endive recipe. Braise, add to soups, or grill. Individual leaves can be used as cups or wrappers for holding a salad or to wrap food morsels.

Buying As this vegetable, available throughout the year, gains in popularity and availability, its price is dropping into the reasonable range. Select fresh-looking radicchio with a firm white core. Its bitterness increases with each passing day, so use quickly.

See **Sunflower Family.**

RADISH
(Raphanus sativus)

Grown in Egypt since at least 2780 B.C. and originally black, the radish helped fuel the slave labor on the pyramids. Several centuries later, Asia developed a range of red, green, and white radishes. And what a range—from our petite cherry radish that matures in a mere three weeks to a 40-pound daikon, which takes up to three months to mature. Larger radishes inspire culinary artists wielding a sharp knife to carve garnishes as fanciful as radish ''butterflies,'' with wings so delicate that they ''flutter'' as they are set upon the table. Radishes belong to the cabbage family.

Health Benefits A cooling food that's pungent and sweet in flavor, radishes stimulate the appetite and are an excellent digestive aid. They have antibacterial and antifungal action.

In the West, radishes are commonly used in a salad or as an hors d'oeuvres to stimulate the appetite; in Asia, they're served at the end of the meal, especially a fatty meal. European folk medicine recommends eating radishes—several a day—on an empty stomach to help melt gallstones and kidney stones. Radishes reduce *vata* and *kapha*.

Radishes contain vitamin C, potassium, and other trace minerals.

Use The pungent, peppery taste of radishes make them a popular salad ingredient and snack. Cooking transforms their tangy bite into a delicate sweet kiss. Radish greens add flavor and nutrition to soups, and when tender may be used as a stir-fry ingredient.

Buying Select firm, crisp radishes with bright, fresh-looking greens. Avoid limp or oversize radishes, which tend to be pithy and overly hot. Also avoid those that are split and have leaked their flavor.

- **Easter Egg Radish** A rainbow-colored collection of small globe radishes.
- **Icicle Radish** White and several inches long, comparable to a red radish in bite and texture.
- **French Breakfast Radish** Red with a white tip, this small cylindrical radish has a mild flavor.
- **Red Radish** Cherrylike in size and shape, the most common radish variety; an elongated red radish is more pungent than a round one.

See **Black Radish; Cabbage Family; Daikon.**

RADISH SOLITAIRE

Here is a gorgeous—but simple—soup. The radish color softens to a rich pink, set off by one green leaf nestled in among a few shimmery strands of translucent noodles.

4 small red radishes with greens
5 cups vegetable stock
2 small fresh shiitake mushrooms, thinly sliced
½ ounce fine bean thread noodles
Sea salt and freshly ground pepper to taste

Trim away all but the innermost leaf from each radish. Place the stock, mushrooms, and noodles in a soup pot, bring to a boil, and simmer for 2 minutes, or until the noodles are almost tender. Add the radishes and simmer for 2 minutes, or just until the radish turns from red to pink. Adjust seasoning. Divide the soup among individual soup bowls. Serve immediately before the radish color fades. Serves 4.

RAISIN

Take four pounds of grapes and remove most of their water, and you'll have one pound of raisins. The other components of the grape, most notably the sugar, remain intact. The high sugar content of raisins has made them a popular food since time immemorial. Until the European medieval period, when cane sugar was imported, raisins were second only to honey as a sweetener.

You may be eating more raisins than you imagine since more than one hundred processed foods use raisin paste or juice. Because of their natural sugars, flavor enhancers (tartaric acid), and preservatives (propionic acids), raisins are a valuable ingredient in yogurt, ice cream, and baked goods.

Virtually all of our domestic raisins are produced in California's San Joaquin valley, within a hundred-mile radius of Fresno. Harvested in August, grapes are spread on paper trays and sun dried for two to three weeks in the vineyard, then the stems are removed and they're sorted and package.

Health Benefits In 1985, the *Journal of the American Dental Association* reported that raisins, because of their large amount of fermentable, sticky sugars, support the growth of cavity-causing bacteria.

Valued as a high-energy food, raisins are rich in potassium, phosphorus, magnesium, iron (ounce for ounce, they have as much iron as cooked hamburger), and calcium. They are a good source of vitamins A and B-complex. Oxygen-sensitive vitamin C, abundant in grapes, disappears in the drying process.

Raisins reduce *kapha* and *pitta,* and when soaked or stewed, are least aggravating to *vata.*

RAISIN RELATIVITY

What's neat about raisins is that they're still cured the old way, in the sunshine rather than in commercial ovens. As we know, the sun imparts its own energy and sun-cured foods (including fruits, couscous, and bulgur, as well as grains that once cured in sheaves) taste better. What's not so neat is that grapes are grown with more chemical fertilizers, pesticides, and growth hormones than any other fruits. Thus raisins, which are concentrated grapes, contain the highest level of pesticide residue of any fruit.

Organic raisins are free of toxic residues. Rather than being fumigated with methyl bromide, organic raisins are frozen to −5 degrees to achieve insect kill.

Use A popular ingredient in baked goods, stuffings, and chutneys, raisins are also enjoyed out of hand, in trail mixes, and with salted nuts. For chocoholics, there are even chocolate-covered raisins.

Before using raisins in baked goods, plump them by soaking them in water, rum, wine, or brandy for 15 minutes or simmer them for several minutes. A plumped raisin doesn't become overly dry when baked.

Buying Thompson seedless grapes make up 95 percent of U.S. domestic raisins. Golden raisins (called sultanas in England) are Thompsons treated with sulfur dioxide to prevent their darkening.

A new raisin crop is available each September. Look for plump raisins that show no signs of being overly dried or sugary. Store raisins in a dark, cool cupboard to prolong their shelf life and prevent flavor and texture deterioration. If refrigerated for more than six months, they become sugary. Store raisins away from brick or concrete walls, as raisins can absorb moisture from these surfaces.

See **Currant; Dried Fruit; Grape; Monukka Raisin; Muscat Raisin.**

RAMBUTAN
(Nephelium lappaceum)

A tropical fruit from Malaysia, rambutan's name aptly means "hair of the head." The plum-size rambutan is red orange and covered with soft green spines. A relative of the litchi, the rambutan's inner white flesh surrounds a single seed. It has an appealing, sweet, slightly acidic taste and is usually eaten raw by itself or in a fruit salad. Rambutans may also be stewed. The seeds are roasted and eaten as a snack. Rambutans are available from midsummer through early winter in Asian markets and specialty food stores. Select fruits that show no sign of moisture and have a fresh smell. Refrigerate and use within three days.

See **Tropical Fruit.**

Ramen See **Pasta.**

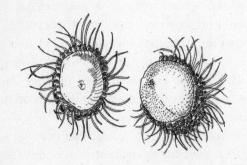

RAMP
Wild Leek
(Allium tricoccum)

In springtime, the wild leek, or ramp, is foraged in the Northeast woodlands; it is occasionally available in a farmers' market. A ramp has a strong onion-garlic taste and may be used as an alternative to a scallion, but in smaller quantities in view of its stronger flavor. The size of a large scallion, the ramp has broader leaves like a leek, although, unlike leek leaves, these leaves splay open.

See **Onion Family.**

Rangoon Bean See **Lima Bean.**

RAPADURA
Unrefined, Evaporated Cane Juice

Unrefined, evaporated cane juice is a natural sweetener that has all of the sugarcane's minerals, vitamins, and micronutrients intact. Marketed today under its Brazilian name, *rapadura*, it is called *panela* in Spanish-speaking South and Central America and *jaggery* in India. Historically, evaporated rapadura was associated with low-income populations.

Rapadura is made by a simple technology. Juice is pressed from sugarcane and cooked to reduce its water content. Today's organic rapadura is then granulated at low temperatures. When traditionally made, this hot concentrated cane juice is poured into cones or blocks that harden when cool and require grating before use. *Rapa* in Portuguese means to grate; *dura* means hard. In Latin America, rapadura may also be made from palm sugar.

Health Benefits Rapadura is 82 percent

sucrose; it is high in chromium, the nutrient that diabetics are deficient in. Like sugar, unrefined cane juice can ease spasms, relieve pain, give a sense of ease and nurture, and, in the short term, boost energy. Because its vitamins, minerals, and micronutrients are intact, though, rapadura does not pass as quickly into the bloodstream as sugar does. If used in excess, however, it contributes to the same health problems as sugar. Rapadura reduces *vata* and *pitta*.

Use Use granulated rapadura, measure for measure, as you would use white sugar. The end product will not be as sugary sweet; it will be lightly colored and will have a more rich and satisfying flavor. If using rapadura in its molded form, grate it prior to use or melt it in a saucepan, strain, and serve as a syrup.

Buying Today, I'm aware of only one domestic brand of unrefined, evaporated cane juice. This granular organic rapadura is available at natural food stores or by mail order from Rapunzel Pure Organics (see page 404). Panela and rapadura in chunks or cones are available in Latino markets. Jaggery is available in blocks in Indian markets.

Avoid the numerous highly refined sugar products that mimic rapadura (see Sugar). Unfortunately, in today's natural food store most of the baked goods, breakfast cereals, candy, frozen desserts, and flavored yogurts contain refined sugar. Even more unfortunately, they are labeled in a less than forthright manner. The following terms are just another way of saying sugar: cane crystals, dehydrated cane juice, granulated cane juice, milled cane, muscovado sugar, natural milled cane sugar, raw cane juice, Sucanat, and unrefined cane sugar.

See **Sugar; Sweeteners.**

RAPE SEED See **Canola Seed.**

RAPINI See **Broccoli Rabe.**

RASPBERRY
(Rubus idaeus)

As fate would have it, the most delicious fruit of the temperate climate is also the worst traveler. The sweet and tart raspberry is so fragile that it turns to pulp if simply held in the hand too long. This makes local raspberries an expensive and rare summer fruit.

Health Benefits Raspberries and their leaves strengthen both the kidneys and the vision. Ripe raspberries cleanse the blood, benefit the liver, and are a good treatment for diarrhea, mucus conditions, and dysentery. Tea made of raspberry leaf is very strengthening to the female system and is a popular herb throughout pregnancy. It eases childbirth by increasing muscle tone in the uterine walls throughout a woman's cycles, and it reduces menstrual cramps. Raspberries are *tridoshic* in moderation; their astringency makes them especially calming for *pitta* and *kapha*.

Raspberries contain ample pectin to thicken homemade jam. They provide vitamins A, C, and some B-complex and minerals.

Use A sprinkling of fresh raspberries is an

elegant garnish for desserts and fruit dishes. Raspberry vinegar, chocolate-covered raspberries, raspberry corn muffins . . . these bright berries enliven all types of dishes. Among jam connoisseurs, raspberry remains unsurpassed. If you've extra raspberries, freeze them in a single layer on a jelly-roll pan. Once frozen, store in a plastic freezer bag in the freezer.

Buying Select raspberries that are fresh, brightly colored, plump, and well mounded in the package. If the green cap is intact, a raspberry is immature and will never become sweet. If the color is dull, or if the package is stained, or if the fruits are leaking, the berries are overmature. Refrigerate and use within 24 hours. Most local raspberries ripen in July; some varieties, however, bear also in September.

Due to controlled-climate air freight, raspberries from as far away as Chile and New Zealand are available year-round. In flavor, these imports are a poor substitute for local berries.

The most common raspberry is red, but there are yellow, golden, and black varieties. The black one is known as a black cap. The yellow-colored one is called a white raspberry, and is rarely available because it is particularly soft.

See **Fruit.**

RATTLESNAKE BEAN
(Phaseolus vulgaris)

A new hybrid bean, similar to the pinto but gray with black streaks and a squarish, blunt shape, the rattlesnake bean may be substituted freely for any of the common beans.

See **Beans and Legumes.**

RAW SUGAR See **Sugar.**

RED BEAN

Red beans are comparable to kidney beans in color and use but are smaller in size.

See **Beans and Legumes; Kidney Bean.**

RED CHICORY See **Radicchio.**

RED-EYE BEAN See **Soldier Bean.**

RED KURI See **Kabocha Squash.**

RED PEPPER See **Chile Pepper.**

RED RICE
(Oryza glaberrima, O. sativa)

Red rice is any rice variety with a red bran layer covering a white endosperm. While most are Asian (*O. sativa*), some are African (*O. glaberrima*). Asian red rice varieties with increasing availability are from southern

---

HOW MANY FRUITS DOES ONE RASPBERRY CONTAIN?

Raspberries and blackberries are not true berries. Each tiny bump on a raspberry or blackberry is actually a minuscule fruit, or drupelet. A drupelet is a fruit with a soft outside and a single, hard stone within. Thus a peach is a drupelet, while a raspberry is a cluster of 80 drupelets.

India, Sri Lanka, Bhutan, and Nepal. They are typically scarified, or coarsely milled, so that only part of their colorful bran layer is removed. Lundberg Family Farms' Wehani, a large, plump red rice, is whole rather than scarified.

See **Rice**.

REDROOT See Lamb's-Quarters.

REISHI
Ling Zhi
(Ganoderma lucidum)

Called the "herb of spiritual potency," the reishi outshines many other mushrooms for its well-documented medicinal properties. Although it grows throughout the world, the reishi is best known and valued in China and Japan, where it has been used in folk medicine more than four thousand years.

Health Benefits Reishi indeed sounds like a cure-all. An immunostimulant, it is helpful for people with AIDS, leaky gut syndrome, Epstein-Barr, chronic bronchitis, and other infectious viruses. It is used as an aid to sleep; as a diuretic; as a laxative; and to lower cholesterol. Reishi mushrooms are antioxidants and liver protectants.

Use Reishi mushrooms are not produced for the commercial market and are not available fresh. Dried, they may be reconstituted and prepared as other fungi. They are primarily found as an ingredient in herbal preparations.

Buying In the past two decades, cultivation has increased the availability of this heretofore wild, priceless, hard-to-come-by fungus. A boletus type of mushroom, the re-

ishi is found wild in various colors. The red reishi, the most potent medicinally, is the one that is now cultivated. It is available dried, in tinctures, in tablets, and in liquid form in natural food stores and from Chinese herb dealers.

RENKON See Lotus.

RHUBARB
(Rheum rhaponticum)

Tightly furled, scarlet, primitive-looking rhubarb sprouting up out of the garden heralds spring—and with it, the springtime ritual of strawberry-rhubarb pie. Rhubarb is not ready to eat until its large reddish celerylike stalks are a foot in length and its forest green leaves are the size of elephant ears. Rhubarb root is a prized medicinal herb, but it's the tart, astringent stalk that we sweeten and use as a spring dessert. This old-fashioned food remains a local vegetable that is available only when it's in season. Rhubarb, along with its relative, buckwheat, is northern Asian in origin.

Health Benefits Rhubarb leaves are poisonous. Eating them has caused deaths, probably because of the leaves' high oxalic acid content. Even the fleshy stalks are high in oxalic acid, and so it is a food that should always be eaten in moderation and is *not* recommended for people who form calcium oxalate kidney stones, or for those with inadequate calcium absorption.

Rhubarb is sour, astringent, and cooling. It's an excellent food to cool an inflamed liver and for detoxifying after eating too much meat. Rhubarb has a long-term heating effect on the digestive system. It also relieves constipation and reduces *vata* when used a little at a time.

High in vitamins C and A, and in potassium, rhubarb also contains tannin, the astringent substance responsible for making your mouth pucker up.

Use Trim off the dried stalk ends of the rhubarb, coarsely chop, sweeten to taste, and stew or boil until tender, 10 to 15 minutes. To be edible, this tart vegetable, which is used like a fruit, demands ample added sweetener. Cook it in a nonreactive (stainless steel or glass) pan. Rhubarb is eaten as a compote and is used in pies, dessert sauces, and jams.

Buying Rhubarb stalks are available only in early spring in supermarkets and natural food stores. Select crisp, plump, deeply colored stalks, preferably the smaller stalks, which are more tender. Refrigerate, tightly wrapped in plastic, and plan to use within a few days.

See **Fruit.**

"IN THE PINK" SPRING TEA

Rhubarb tea has a fruity, tangy flavor and a nice pink color. It's an easily made spring cure for liver-related problems. For this remedy to be most effective, do not sweeten. Do not use over five consecutive days, and discontinue if it causes diarrhea.

½ stalk rhubarb, chopped
2 cups water
1 teaspoon mint or chamomile leaves
    (optional)
Honey to taste (optional)

Simmer the rhubarb in a glass or stainless steel (not aluminum) pot for 5 minutes. Remove from the heat. If using mint or chamomile, add and allow to steep for 5 minutes. Add honey, if desired. Sip 20 minutes before breakfast.

RICE
(Oryza sativa)

> Grain upon grain
> Fresh and delightful as frost
> A dazzling jewel
> To what can I compare this treasure?
> —Yang Ji (Ming Dynasty)

Rice is the staple food for more than half the world's population. What an incomprehensible number of people are probably sitting down right now to a bowl of rice. The word *meal* is synonymous with rice in both the Chinese and Japanese languages, just as in English the word *meal* originally referred to our staple food—ground grain. As grain no longer enjoys this prominence in the United States, it is sometimes difficult to appreciate the importance of rice to cultures where it is *the* staple.

Americans eat about 25 pounds of rice per person per year, compared to more than 100 pounds per person per year in the Far East. The United States grows about 1 percent of the world's rice and exports about 60 percent of this crop. Less than 2 percent of the U.S. production is brown or whole grain rice.

Health Benefits Rice generates energy and promotes good digestion. It quenches thirst, relieves mental depression, and stops diarrhea that's been caused by spleen-pancreas deficiency. White rice digests more quickly than brown; however, because it is refined it is not a strengthening food. Basmati rice is *tridoshic.* Brown rice reduces *vata* and may slightly aggravate *kapha* and *pitta.*

Brown rice is the highest of all grains in B vitamins, but somewhat lower than others in protein. It contains iron, vitamin E, amino acids, and linoleic acid. Short-grain brown rice contains less protein but more minerals; it is heartier and more strengthening than the long-grain.

Sweet, or glutinous, rice is more warming, higher in protein, and more easily digested than regular rice. It strengthens the kidneys, spleen-pancreas, and stomach.

Use Rice is unlike such cereal grains as barley, rye, and wheat. It is easy to eat whole, day after day, without tiring of it—whereas most other grains are ground into meal or flour to enhance their palatability. Rice fits in with haute cuisine or with its humble partner, beans. Serve rice with a protein complement, or plain or fried, or in soup, croquettes, casseroles, salad, sushi, and bread and dessert.

Short-grain rice holds moisture better and so cooks up stickier than long-grain rice, which is fluffy and light; medium-grain rice is closer to long-grain in appearance and performance. Brown rice requires more water, longer cooking, and more chewing; it provides a more substantial dish than white rice does.

Buying I recommend purchasing rice, brown or white, from a natural food store that usually has a fast turnover—you will find the broadest and freshest selection in the bulk bins. I do not recommend parboiled (converted) or instant rice.

Our most commonly available rice species (*O. sativa*) include short-, medium-, and long-grain rice varieties. Numerous specialty rice blends are available in a potpourri of rice colors and flavors.

No matter the variety, be it long or short, black or red, regular or sweet, rice for consumption has its inedible outer hull removed. A farmer wants this hull intact for germination, but it is too tough to eat and so it is removed. Once hulled, rice is available to consumers in one of the three ways:

Whole (Brown, Black, or Red) Rice Whole grain rice has its bran layers intact and therefore all its nutrients are present and accounted for. Furthermore, the bran protects the germ's fragile fatty acids. Brown rice is the best example of whole grain rice. Most black and red rice varieties are also available whole because if their bran is removed, they look like ordinary white rice.

Scarified (Partially Milled) Rice

The bran of whole grain rice makes it slow to cook and, for many people, hard to digest. Therefore, historically, most Asians ate partially milled or scarified (scratched) rice that had some bran scoured off to shorten its cooking time and ease digestion.

Depending upon the degree, scarifying compromises some of a grain's vitamins, minerals, and phytonutrients. In addition, removing some of the bran exposes the essential fatty acids to light, and light instigates rancidity. In the past, this was not a problem since the rice was coarsely milled at the local millers, a week's supply at a time. Today, however, it is problematic. Red rice and pecan rice are scarified and available in natural food stores. Ask that your retailers provide the grain's milling date in order to make an informed choice.

White (Refined) Rice With "improved" milling technology, the germ is removed with all of the bran layers. Extended shelf life is one advantage of such rice. However, it is a highly refined food, and therefore it's prudent to enjoy it in moderation.

See **Arborio Rice; Basmati Rice; Black Rice; Black Sticky Rice; Carnaroli Rice; Carolina Rice, Jasmine Rice; Pecan Rice; Red Rice, Sushi Rice; Valencia Rice; Vialone Nano Rice.**

MY FAVORITE KITCHEN REMEDY

Rice porridge, congee, jook, kitchari . . . all of these are names for a rice soup that has been popular throughout Asia for five thousand years. Gruel is a more apt translation, but please don't let that put you off! Western equivalents are the old English and Native American kitchen remedies barley water and atole. Whenever I serve congee in a cooking class, students are amazed at how deeply satisfying it is. There is a substantial difference making the same ingredients into a soup rather than just steaming them.

The Buddha, as recorded in the *Vinayapitaka* [*Book of Discipline*], praised congee as giving "life and beauty, ease and strength. It dispels hunger, thirst and wind. It cleanses the bladder. It digests food." Long cooking makes it easy to assimilate and absorb the ingredients' medicinal properties.

The recipe is simple: Simmer 2 tablespoons rice in 2 cups water over the lowest possible heat (or in a Crock-Pot) for 4 to 6 hours. (You may substitute sweet rice, wild rice, millet, barley, steel-cut oats, spelt, or quinoa.) Add one or more seasonings to taste, such as ghee, nuts, tofu, beans, vegetables, meat, spices, or herbs. White rice will dissolve when used in congee; brown rice and other grains will soften but keep their form. It is an ideal first food for infants, convalescents, people under stress, or those with a weakened digestive or immune system. Congee can be a lifesaving remedy for someone with an inflamed, ulcerated digestive tract or with extreme diarrhea.

In *The Book of Jook*, Bob Flaws has translated specific congee recipes from Chinese medical texts for a wide range of ailments. For example, a teaspoon each of honey and butter are added to the rice and water and cooked together. This builds energy and blood and is used to counter emaciation, a dry cough, vomiting blood, dried skin, and dry, difficult constipation.

Ø RICE BRAN OIL

I do not recommend any highly refined oil, including rice bran oil. It is praised by some for containing a fatty acid–free lipid, which apparently blocks the production of LDL cholesterol. Once refined, however, this lipid contributes to the formation of free radicals. Unrefined rice bran oil is not available and would be prohibitively expensive to make.

RICE FLOUR

Unlike the bran of wheat, the bran of brown rice is an insignificant colorant; therefore, white and brown rice flour may be used interchangeably in any recipe. Because rice flour is glutenfree, it cannot be used to make bread dough.

Brown rice flour imparts a lively, seedlike flavor to baked goods. Since brown rice flour, like other whole grain flours, starts to oxidize as soon as it's milled, it should be used fresh. (Whole grain flour is rancid if it tastes or smells strong and acerbic.) White rice flour doesn't become rancid; it has a slightly smoother texture, and less flavor.

There is a significant performance difference between rice types. Unfortunately, packages do not always specify which is which;

LEMON-DROP COOKIES

These sunshine-colored cookies have a refreshing lemon flavor. The rice flour gives it an airy, delectable crumb.

3 cups medium- or short-grain brown rice flour
½ teaspoon baking soda
½ teaspoon sea salt
8 tablespoons (1 stick) unsalted melted butter
½ cup honey or maple syrup
1 teaspoon pure vanilla extract
Juice and grated zest of 1 organic lemon
15 blanched almonds, halved

Heat oven to 375 degrees. Sift the flour, salt, and baking soda together. Combine the butter, honey or maple syrup, vanilla, lemon zest, and juice. Mix the wet and dry ingredients. With your fingers, form into small rounds. Place on a greased cookie sheet and press each down with moistened fork tines (or damp fingers) to 2½ inches in diameter and ⅓ inch thick. Press nut meat into the center of each cookie. Bake for 10 to 12 minutes, or until the bottoms are lightly browned. Makes 30 cookies.

you may assume it is multipurpose medium- or short-grain rice flour unless the package specifies that it is not for use in baked goods.

- **Long-Grain Rice Flour** Suited to breadings, sauces, and use as a thickener; it is not good for baking since it yields a wet, soggy product with a large crumb.
- **Medium- and Short-Grain Rice Flour** Multipurpose. Can be used as a thickener and in cookies, crackers, and quick bread. It gives a sandy crumb that is similar to corn flour in its dryness. It is excellent for dusting bread dough when shaping it into loaves because it dries the dough's surface without adhering to it, so that any excess may be brushed off.
- **Sweet Rice Flour** Yields a moist, dense texture that's unsurpassable in brownies and Japanese-style dumplings.

Buying Mail-order suppliers and full-scale natural food stores carry the largest selection of rice flours. All-purpose white rice flour is available in most supermarkets.

See **Flour.**

RICE MILK

Although rice milk is tasty, it is less nutritious and strengthening than soy or almond milk. It is made by converting rice into a sweetener and then into a beverage. Rice milk is also available flavored and frozen as an ice cream substitute.

See **Milk Substitutes; Soymilk.**

RICE NOODLES
Brown Rice Pasta, Mei Fun, Rice Sticks, Rice Vermicelli

A popular Asian pasta, dried rice noodles are made of fine white rice flour. Slender rice noodles are soaked in hot water for two minutes and then heated in a soup. Wider rice noodles may also require boiling for one or two minutes. If deep-frying rice noodles, do not presoak.

Brown rice pasta, which is cooked like, and substituted for, semolina pasta is available for people on glutenfree diets. The texture is gummy.

See **Pasta; Rice.**

RICE STICKS See Rice Noodles.

RICE SYRUP

Rice syrup is a mildly sweet syrup with an almost butterscotch flavor. I've made it from scratch the traditional way by substituting 5 percent of sprouted barley as an enzymatic starter to a pot of cooked rice and then incubating it. The U.S. domestic supply of rice syrup is produced in Manteca, California.

Health Benefits Rice syrup is considered a healthful sweetener because it is predominantly maltose, a slow-digesting carbohydrate that enters the bloodstream steadily over a two-hour period. This protects against problematic rapid fluctuations in blood sugar levels caused by the ingestion of simple sugars (fructose, glucose, and sucrose) that are found in sweet fruits, fruit juice, sugar, corn syrup, honey, molasses, and maple syrup. It reduces *vata* and *pitta*.

Use For most palates, rice syrup is not an

adequate honey or sugar substitute in baked goods, since its sweetness is easily overpowered by other flavors. It is excellent, however, in caramel corn (see page 269). Straight from the jar, rice syrup makes a delicious topping for sandwiches, waffles, toast, and crackers.

Buying Available organic or nonorganic, plain or fruit flavored, rice syrup is carried in many stores. All rice syrups have about 50 percent complex carbohydrates, but their glucose-to-maltose proportion differs. Ones with higher glucose are sweeter than ones higher in maltose.

Rice syrup has a long shelf life and requires no refrigeration. Unlike honey, it does not crystallize. If syrup hardens in cold weather, set the jar in warm water until the syrup softens.

RICE VERMICELLI See Rice Noodles.

RICE VINEGAR See Brown Rice Vinegar; Vinegar.

ROCAMBOLE
Sand Leek, Spanish Garlic
(Allium scorodoprasum)

The flower stalk of this garlic relative develops an attractive spiral twist that's topped with a cluster of purple bulblets, or bulbils. The rocambole bulb—and its bulbils—is milder tasting than garlic. It is an attractive plant used in floral arrangements and available primarily in farmers' markets.

ROCHA PEAR See Pear.

ROCKWEED See Bladder Wrack.

ROCKET See Arugula.

ROCK MOSS See Irish Moss.

ROMAINE
Cos Lettuce
(Lactuca sativa)

The second most popular lettuce after iceberg is romaine. This tall lettuce has crisp, dark green outer leaves and is sturdier than other lettuces.

Health Benefits Romaine is a cooling vegetable, with a slightly bitter taste. It is used in the treatment of alcoholism. It calms *pitta* and *kapha*.

Buying Romaine is best during colder seasons. Red-leafed romaine is becoming increasingly available. An overly large or mature romaine is unpleasantly tough.

See Lettuce.

ROQUETTE See Arugula.

ROSEMARY
(Rosmarinus officinalis)

There's rosemary, that's for remembrance
　　—William Shakespeare, *Hamlet*

Rosemary is native to the Mediterranean region. In ancient times, it symbolized both love and death and was a frankincense substitute for the poor. A perennial in mild climates, rosemary is often used as a landscape plant as well as a culinary herb.

Health Benefits An excellent stimulant, rosemary is a warming herb that improves poor circulation; lowers cholesterol; eases muscle and rheumatism pains; and treats lung congestion, sore throat, and canker sores. Rosemary stimulates the nervous system, supports mental functions and memory, helps relieve a sluggish gallbladder, and is often used in penetrating liniments. It is not recommended during pregnancy. Rosemary reduces *vata* and *kapha*.

Rosemary tea and twig tea are the two beverages I know of that buffer or alkalinize an overly acidic stomach. Rosemary tea is also a good aspirin alternative for treating headaches, gas, and fevers. To make the tea, steep 3 tablespoons dried rosemary or 4 sprigs fresh rosemary in 1 cup just-boiled water for 10 minutes. Strain, sweeten if desired, and drink.

Use With its pinelike, camphor flavor, rosemary is more potent than most herbs and a little rosemary seasons chicken, lamb, and pork, and it often is added to breads, black olives, and biscuits. Its flavor is not reduced with cooking. It is available fresh and dried.

See **Herbs and Spices.**

ROYAL MANDARIN See **Temple Orange.**

RUCOLA See **Arugula.**

RUNNER BEAN See **Green Bean.**

RUSSIAN KALE See **Kale.**

RUTABAGA
Swede, Swedish Turnip
(Brassica napus napobrassica)

Rutabaga, a turniplike vegetable, is probably a cross between a wild cabbage and a turnip. The skin is purple toward the top and golden yellow at the point. Its golden flesh is firmer and sweeter than a turnip, but unlike a turnip, it is not pungent.

Health Benefits Like other root vegetables, rutabagas are a warming food that strengthens the digestion, especially the stomach and spleen-pancreas; they also help detoxify the liver. They reduce, and are thus beneficial for, *vata* and *pitta.* Their nutritional properties are comparable to turnips, but, unlike turnips, they do contain vitamin A.

Use Rutabagas make a pleasant purée; they may be substituted for, or used alongside, carrots in any soup, or stir-fried, braised, or steamed dish. Rutabagas are always cooked before eating—trim as necessary.

Buying Select rutabagas that are firm and fresh looking, with smooth, unblemished skin. Avoid those that are withered or light for their size. There are also white-fleshed rutabagas.

See **Cabbage Family.**

RYE
(Secale cereale)

Unlike other grains, rye appeared quite abruptly in the Iron Age as a grain field weed in Asia Minor. Rye soon flourished in northern soils and soils that had been depleted by annual crops of wheat. Rye reigned in western Europe through the Middle Ages, and still flourishes in eastern Europe and across the Russian plains.

Like a slender wheat in shape, rye has blue gray overtones, and a robust, tangy flavor. The United States produces only 2 percent of the world's rye.

Health Benefits Rye's strong, almost bitter flavor seems to match its strong, weedlike hardiness. Rye is said to build muscles and promote energy and endurance, and is medicinal for the liver. A broth or congee (see page 290) made of rye often relieves a migraine headache. Rye reduces *kapha.*

Nutritionally, rye is similar to wheat, but it contains less gluten. Of the common grains, rye has the highest percentage of the amino acid lysine. It contains eleven B vitamins, vitamin E, protein, iron, and various minerals and trace elements.

Use The main use of rye in the United States is in rye whiskey and, to a lesser extent, in bread. Rye berries are rarely cooked whole by themselves, but it is a dish that I occasionally enjoy. The secret is to toast the grains first and then to cook them as you would brown rice. Flaked rye is used like rolled oats for a breakfast cereal and in granola; it is unfortunately not a fast-moving product, so is apt to be stale.

See **Grains.**

RYE FLOUR

Rye flour from supermarkets, labeled dark, medium, or light, is degermed. The dark flour contains the most bran. Whole grain rye flour is a shade darker than whole wheat flour; it is available mainly in natural food stores.

Rye flour is mildly sweet, and I often combine it with another flour to make quick bread, corn bread, muffins, and waffles. The most popular rye bread, sourdough rye, gains its characteristic sour flavor from the starter, not the rye. Pumpernickel bread is colored by something besides rye, usually caramel, to give it its characteristic dark brown color. Bread containing rye stays moist longer than an all-wheat loaf and slices thinner. Traditional gingerbread desserts were made of rye flour. About the only other place you'll find rye commercially is in Swedish hardtack crackers.

SAFFLOWER OIL

Safflower oil is acclaimed by many people for its 78 percent polyunsaturated fatty acid content; they are misinformed. The ratio—not the percentage—of polyunsaturated fatty acids is the critical factor. Safflower contains predominantly Omega-6 fatty acids and is therefore low on the list of desired oils. Tradition substantiates this view since safflower has a poor reputation in Ayurvedic medicine. Another telling indicator is that it lacks the historical value of the quality oils: olive, sesame, coconut, and palm.

The new oleic-rich safflower oil has 80 percent monounsaturated fatty acids, which gives it greater heat stability. It therefore appears to be an improvement over regular safflower oil. If using oleic-rich safflower oil, however, be sure to purchase one with a label guaranteeing that it is not made from genetically modified plants.

The safflower, a thistlelike sunflower relative, prefers a semiarid climate; California and Arizona are the principal U.S. safflower growers.

See **Fat and Oil.**

SAFFRON
(Crocus sativus)

Saffron was once used to dye the robes of Buddhist monks because its brilliant golden yellow color signifies illumination. Also valued as a spice, a cosmetic, and a medicine since the tenth century B.C., saffron is the stigmas of a special crocus, a cousin of our common garden flower.

Saffron's current wholesale price is $70 per ounce. It has always been almost literally worth its weight in gold both because it must be hand harvested and because one flower yields but three tiny stigmas. To collect one pound of saffron requires plucking stigmas from 75 thousand crocus. Imagine that.

Health Benefits Saffron is used medicinally as a blood cleanser, liver detoxifier, and nerve and heart tonic. Long considered an aphrodisiac, saffron is reputed to increase sperm count. I think of saffron as silky and add a few threads to a cup of tea when I'm ready for a soothing, luxuriating respite.

Use saffron in *small* amounts, no more than several threads once per day, since larger amounts can be toxic or even lethal. Saffron is *tridoshic*.

Use The smallest pinch of saffron gives dishes a brilliant golden yellow color, a deep aroma, and a unique flavor. To draw out its maximum flavor and color, crumble saffron threads in a small amount of tepid water, soak, then add at the end of cooking (heat destroys some of its properties).

The Pennsylvania Dutch of Lancaster County are called the "Yellow Dutch" because of their generous use of saffron in chicken and egg noodle dishes. Saffron is an indispensable ingredient in French bouillabaisse, Spanish paella, and Swedish Christmas bread.

Buying Saffron threads are a brick red color, about one inch long, and wiry. Purchase whole threads. Bypass ground saffron, which is often adulterated with turmeric.

See **Herbs and Spices.**

SAFFRON ON A SHOESTRING

Clarke Hess, in the tradition of her Mennonite "Yellow Dutch" grandmother, reports that saffron crocuses are easy to grow, require little garden space, and are a welcome blossom in October when the rest of the garden is in decline. While a first year's harvest might yield a scant tablespoon of saffron, the bulbs quickly multiply.

Be sure to distinguish *C. sativus*, which has three stigmas, from a similar-looking autumn crocus (*Colchicum autumnale*), which is highly poisonous.

SAGE
(Salvia officinalis)

A perennial herb with a spicy, sharp, and herby aroma, sage is a universal flavoring agent long valued for its medicinal properties. The small bushy plant with downy green or gray-green leaves has small pink, purple, or white blossoms. It is not to be confused with the larger, similar-smelling sagebrush (*Artemisia tridentata*), which covers much of the high deserts of the western United States and is too overpowering to add to food. If you have a garden or room for potted herbs, consider keeping sage. It grows as easily as thyme and, once established, requires little attention.

Health Benefits Sage's action focuses on the mouth, the throat, and the female reproductive system. Sage is a decongestant whose antimicrobial properties make it an effective gargle; an astringent for abraided or inflamed skin; and a treatment against colds, flu, and fevers. It also increases estrogen and helps treat menopausal sweats. Sage is also a muscle relaxant for nervous disorders, including tics. If pregnant or epileptic, do not use sage.

Sage stimulates and helps regulate bile flow and so is often combined with fatty meats. Michael Moore observes that the classical use of sage to decrease lactation "works fine if the tea is drunk cool and the breasts are washed with the tea as well. Several goat keepers I know of use the tea whenever a particular female needs her milk slowed or stopped." Sage reduces *vata* and *kapha*.

Use The bold, almost camphorous aroma of sage becomes even more potent when dried, so use dried sage in small amounts. Young, freshly minced leaves are mild enough to be used in salad. Dried sage goes well with other assertive flavors, such as rosemary, thyme, and bay. It is a traditional flavoring in stuffing and sausages.

See Herbs and Spices.

SAINT JOHN'S BREAD See Carob.

SA KOT See Jicama.

SALAD SAVOY See Kale.

SALSIFY
Oyster Plant
(Tragopogon porrifolius)

With some imagination, salsify is said to have an oysterlike flavor, which accounts for its alias. My hunch is that the oyster association comes from the milky fluid that oozes from a cut in the fresh greens. To me, salsify tastes like a tame burdock. This long, buff-skinned taproot looks like an undernourished and hairy parsnip, with white, mildly sweet flesh that's similar to burdock but not as flavorful. Salsify is a member of the sunflower family and is closely related to scorzonera.

Health Benefits Salsify contains inulin, a natural insulin, which explains why old European kitchen remedies regard salsify as strengthening to the digestion. It also nourishes the kidneys and intestines.

Use Tender young salsify leaves are a good salad ingredient. The purple buds are reminiscent of asparagus in flavor and may be cooked as a potherb. The root can be boiled, sautéed, baked, or simmered in soups and stews. Salsify's flavor is best after a frost, so look for it in the late fall or winter.

Before cooking, give salsify a good scrub and then cut it into the desired shape. Salsify becomes mushy if cooked too long or peeled.

Buying/Foraging Salsify is occasionally available commercially and is readily available wild. Look for it along country lanes and as a sturdy weed in gardens. If you are foraging salsify, dig only the taproots of first-year plants, which have not yet sent up their flower stalk.

In the market, select roots that are firm and crisp rather than soft. The root will be up to eight inches long and will have many tiny rootlets. Large roots tend to be pithy.

See **Sunflower Family**.

SALT See **Sea Salt**.

SALT PLUM See **Umeboshi**.

SAMP See **Posole**.

SAMPHIRE See **Glasswort**.

SANDLEEK See **Rocambole**.

SAND PEAR See **Asian Pear**.

SAPODILLA
(*Manilkara zapota*)

The sapodilla, a native Central American fruit, looks like a furry brown kiwi. The sapodilla tree yields a valued hard wood and chicle as well as this tasty fruit. The fragrant and melting blond flesh of the sapodilla has the subtle flavor of pure maple syrup. Commercial crops are now growing in Florida and other subtropical regions.

Use Cut open the sapodilla, remove its barbed black seeds, and then peel and slice or spoon out the soft flesh. Season with lime juice and serve alone or with other fruits in any fresh fruit dish, sauce, or frozen dessert. When dead ripe, the pulpy flesh may be used in puddings or baked goods.

Buying If possible, select a sapodilla that is soft as a peach. The fruit, sharp and astringent when immature, is palatable only when fully ripe. To test for ripening, scratch off some of the fuzz; if the skin shows green, hold at room temperature for another day or two or until the skin is brown. Once ripened, it will hold in the refrigerator for two to three days.

See **Chicle; Tropical Fruit.**

SAPOTE See **White Sapote.**

SASSAFRAS
Filé
(*Sassafras albidum*)

An old and respected North American remedy, the root bark of the sassafras tree once flavored root beer. Before that, its dried and ground leaves were used by the Choctaw Indians to make filé powder, a seasoning

---

HOW I LEARNED RESPECT FOR A WHITE SUGAR RECIPE

As a child, soda pop was a rare and exotic treat; homemade root beer was our summer thirst quencher. Into the canning kettle mother simmered sassafras root beer extract (available in supermarkets, and from wine and home brewing suppliers), sugar, and 4 gallons of water. When cooled to tepid, she added yeast, then we funneled it into bottles, and capped it with a capping gadget. It was a sticky but fun family task.

Several weeks later we'd sample a bottle to judge its progress. If not fully aged, root beer tastes "green" or yeasty. When the yeast is spent and sugar fermented—with carbonation as the by-product—the brew is ready to drink.

When my children were young, mother—with the old bottle capper in hand—came to visit and headed up a brewing project. The result was as refreshing as I had remembered. Fermented and aged root beer is more mellow, smooth, and satisfying than commercial root beer that is merely mixed and injected with carbon dioxide. Look for naturally brewed soft drinks in the refrigerated section of your natural food store.

I upgraded our next batch with a natural sweetener; then, not sure of its sucrose content, I added extra yeast to compensate. Two weeks later from the cellar we started hearing explosions. A second before each glass-shattering blast there had existed an over-carbonated bottle of naturally sweetened root beer.

agent that remains an essential ingredient in the Creole stew, filé gumbo.

Health Benefits Safrole, a component of sassafras oil that was declared carcinogenic by the FDA, is no longer available as a food additive. Safrole is, however, an ingredient in natural unguents used to relieve rheumatic pain and as a natural insect repellent.

Sassafras bark tea is an excellent blood purifier, which stimulates the liver to clear toxins from the system. Its ability to cleanse the blood explains its usefulness as a treatment for various skin disorders. The bark is also used as a seasoning agent in cordials and medicines. Do not consume more than two cups of sassafras tea per day, as larger quantities may be overstimulating. Sassafras, and filé powder to a lesser extent, reduces *vata* and *kapha*.

Use The principal use of filé powder is as a thickening agent in gumbo, in sauces, and in gravy. If the filé is boiled, it becomes stringy, so it is stirred into a soup or sauce immediately after cooking. Or the gumbo may be ladled into individual bowls, and each person stirs the filé powder into his or her own portion while it's still piping hot.

As available, tender young sassafras leaves and winter buds may be added to green salads.

See Herbs and Spices.

SATSUMA
(Citrus reticulata)

A large Japanese seedless mandarin, the satsuma is less round than an orange, peels very easily, and has a slight green tint to its thin skin. Satsumas are similar to, but less aromatic and flavorful than, clementines.

See **Citrus Family; Mandarin.**

SAVORY

There are two kinds of savory, summer savory (*Satureja hortensis*) and winter savory (*S. montana*). Both have a peppery taste. Native to the Mediterranean region, winter savory is a hardy perennial low shrub; the leaves have a strong, sharp flavor. Summer savory, an annual plant, is milder tasting; it is the more popular of the two. Savory is a member of the mint family.

Health Benefits Savory aids digestion, especially of fatty foods, beans, or acidic foods like tomatoes. It reduces *vata* and *kapha*.

Use Almost thymelike in flavor, savory goes with bean, pea, and potato dishes. A few chopped fresh leaves are good in a salad, but more would be overpowering. Dried or fresh, savory is a common ingredient in tomato-based dishes, sausages, dressings, and herb blends such as *Herbes de Provence*.

See **Herbs and Spices.**

SCALLION
Green Onion, Spring Onion
(Allium cepa)

The mildest of the famed onion family, the scallion is the immature stem and bulb of an onion. The scallion is valued for its bulb and leaves. I go a step further and use the stringy rootlets.

Health Benefits Like its onion relatives, the scallion has antifungal and antimicrobial effects, but to a lesser degree. Scallions are useful in alleviating chest and heart pain; they promote urination and sweating; and they serve as a digestive aid. In addition, a scallion bulb is an old kitchen remedy for earache. Slice off the rootlets and base, leaving enough of the stalk attached to use as a handle, and place the bulb in the affected ear. Cooked scallions reduce *vata*. A moderate use of scallions, cooked or raw, reduces *kapha*.

The green part of a scallion is high in vitamin A. The bulb contains vitamins A, B-complex, and C; it also has some calcium, magnesium, and potassium.

Use Both the scallion bulb and leaves are used either as a garnish or as an ingredient for salads, soups, and stir-fries. They add lightness, both of flavor and appearance, and make a heavy or fatty dish more digestible. I often use the rootlets, washed well and chopped fine, in soup; they are a concentrated source of minerals and add flavor.

Buying Scallions are available year-round, but they are more perishable than mature onions. Look for firm scallions with their long rootlets intact, and unblemished leaves that show no signs of withering or slime.

See **Onion Family.**

SCALLOP SQUASH See **Pattypan.**

SCHAV See **Sorrel.**

SCORZONERA
Black Salsify
(*Scorzonera hispanica*)

A native plant of Spain, scorzonera is similar to salsify in size, use, and flavor, but with a chocolate brown skin and broader leaves.

While it is easy to cultivate in a vegetable garden, scorzonera is low in demand and current market supplies are only imported from Belgium during the colder months. Select roots that are firm and smooth.

See **Salsify; Sunflower Family.**

SCOTCH KALE See **Kale.**

SEA ASPARAGUS See **Glasswort.**

SEA BEAN See **Glasswort.**

SEA LETTUCE
(*Ulva lactuca, U. fasciata*)

Emerald green patches of gossamer thin—literally two cells thick—blades of sea lettuce cover rocks on the intertidal zone. This seaweed, which feels like wax paper, has a flavor similar to nori. As its name suggests, it may be added raw to salads or sandwiches. Dried, shredded, crumbled, or rehydrated for 5 minutes and chopped, sea lettuce adds its distinctive flavor to any savory dish. It is available by mail order (see pages 403–04).

See **Seaweed.**

SEA MOSS See **Irish Moss.**

SEA PALM
(*Postelsia palmaeformis*)

Last spring, one of my students, all fired up about the virtues of sea palm, served it in a stir-fry to her husband and two adolescent children. "Black pasta," she said, when asked its identity—and they've been eating it ever since. The texture, appearance, and flavor of sea palm fits right into family fare.

Sea palm, which looks like a miniature palm tree, is a brown seaweed found on the north Pacific coast of North America.

Health Benefits Cooling in thermal nature, sea palm helps reduce blood cholesterol, soften hard masses, and support normal thyroid function. Like other brown sea vegetables, it contains algin, which fixes and removes radioactive particles and heavy metals from the body.

Use Mildly sweet, with a pleasing al dente texture, sea palm comes in long, flat, ribbed strands. I buy it by the pound and keep two jars close at hand. I keep long strands in one jar to use in sautéed and simmered dishes. I crunch the others with a pestle (sea palm can also be pulverized in a blender) and then strew the dark, confettilike flecks into soups; grain, braised, and stewed dishes; condiments; and/or any pot of beans that's wanting enhanced flavor, mineral enrichment, and eye appeal.

Buying Only domestic sea palm is available. Purchase it from natural food stores or by mail order (see pages 403–04).

See **Seaweed.**

SEA PICKLE See **Glasswort.**

SEA SALT

Rye bread and salt—two valued staples—are traditional housewarming gifts in eastern Europe. Throughout history and until this past decade, humanity highly valued salt (sodium chloride). More essential than currency, it was wages for Roman soldiers, *salarium*, from *sal*, Latin for salt, thus our term for salary.

Sea salt is concentrated ocean, with its water evaporated and its impurities removed. This is also true for salt mined from the earth, the deposits being remnants of ancient salt lakes and oceans. While primarily sodium chloride, sun-dried sea salt contains all trace elements—including iodine—balanced in the same ratio as sea water. Because iodine, a mineral needed for proper thyroid function, is less stable than the other minerals, it dissipates from refined, washed, or kiln-dried salt. To make iodine stick to processed salt requires chemical manipulation.

Health Benefits Our blood, lymph, and extracellular fluids are like a miniature sea with a composition of sodium and trace minerals similar to ocean water. Should the normal saline count in our bodily fluids fall below 1 percent, disorders of the nervous system, glands, and organs would develop.

Because we lose these minerals daily through normal body processes, they must be replaced. Using quality sea salt, which contains up to 10 percent trace minerals, is an easy way to do so. Furthermore, the minerals from natural sea salt are far more easily assimilated than mineral supplements are.

Sodium, the primary constituent of salt, is one of the three vital electrolyte minerals; it helps convey energy and the spark of life itself. It is this electrical charge that enables nerve impulses and muscle contraction; it is vital for every living cell's function.

From an energetic point of view, salt is the most grounding culinary substance and gives foods an earthy substantial quality. Too much salt, however, is too grounding and may make one grasping or greedy.

Salt is considered medicinal to the kidneys, although overuse of salt can damage them. Excess salt can also interfere with calcium and nutrient absorption, cause excessive thirst and edema, and contribute to high blood pressure. Energetically speaking, a person who overuses salt may then be somewhat fearful and paranoid and demonstrate a lack of joy and happiness. Salt favorably reduces *vata*.

Use Throughout the world, salt is the primary flavor additive. It heightens, deepens, and unites savory flavors. Salt not only aids in the digestion of grains, beans, bread, and potatoes, it also transforms them from flat tasting to flavorful. It acts as a natural preservative, masks the taste of stale or poor-quality foods, and it whets the appetite. Salt has an estimated ten thousand uses.

Less than ½ teaspoon would satisfy our current daily salt requirements, but Americans typically consume 3½ teaspoons of salt per day. Seventy percent of this excess comes from processed foods.

Buying Purchasing sea salt at a natural food store is not a guarantee of purchasing quality.

Quality salt is evaporated from pristine, rather than polluted, waters. Leslie salt and Morton salt, for example, both extract salt from the San Francisco Bay. In a recent phone interview with the Hain Pure Food Company, I asked the source of their sea salt and was told that it is "near San Francisco." The company spokesperson refused to be more specific, indicating that ocean water is ocean water, period.

After determining its source, look at how the salt was processed to determine quality. Most salt is refined to 99 percent sodium chloride and then, by FDA standards, may contain up to 2 percent additives. Commercial salt is kiln dried at temperatures exceeding 1,200 degrees. This intense heat causes the sodium molecules to split into a cosmetically uniform size with diminished bioavailibility.

Fortunately, there are several small companies that manufacture quality natural sea salt. Superior natural sea salt brand names include

---

TASTE TESTING SALT

I always have my students taste salt. Many hundreds of students later, the results remain consistent. A few grains of commercial salt taste acrid, metallic, and harsh; by contrast, a few grains of hand-processed, Celtic sea salt taste mellow, flavorful, and sweetly salty.

Here's the quick story of Celtic sea salt. For more than nine hundred years, the Breton *paludiers* (salt makers) have harvested natural sea salt from the marshes in Guérande on the Atlantic. Proclaimed a National Treasure by the French government in 1991, the salt is solar evaporated and hand-harvested using traditional wooden scoops. Three grades of Celtic salt are available. The premier grade and the choice of many chefs is Fleur de Sel. The tiny crystals form only when the wind blows from the east and when the salt is carefully harvested, a gentle fragrance of violets is said to fill the air. The price of Celtic Fleur de Sel is over $30 per pound, while coarse Celtic sea salt is under $10 a pound.

Celtic, Lima, Malden, Muramoto, and Si. Quality natural sea salt is available from a natural food store or by mail order (see page 399). Two quick guidelines for determining quality are taste and, to some extent, price. The mellower the taste, the better the quality, and quality salts involve some degree of hand processing—hence price is a factor.

Storage Since salt draws moisture from the air, store sea salt covered tightly to retard solidifying or caking. Do not store salt in silver saltshakers or saltcellars because the salt's chlorine reacts with the silver, causing a green discoloration.

SEA VEGETABLES See Seaweed.

SEAWEED
Marine Algae, Sea Vegetables

A Piece of Sea Weed serves for a Barometer;
it gets wet and dry as the weather gets so.
                                    —William Blake

Must be our sensual nature that sends us into the blustery dawn of the full moon's ebb tide to gather our spring salad. . . . Gingerly step over the icy granite rocks. Past the slimy ones, tidal pools lined with frizzy Irish moss, the leafy florescence of sea lettuce, the swaying dulse palms, delicate purple laver, down to the fleecy crashing ocean roll: our cup overflows. Bending now. Wrist flick of the stick looses the streaming fronds from their holdfasts. Into the baskets.

                            —Anne Franklin Harris

Even if you swear you'll never eat seaweed, you already have. It's a ubiquitous ingredient in ice cream, baked goods, jelly, salad dressing, chocolate milk, beer, wine, and toothpaste. These are earth's first vegetables and have often figured in the human diet, and with good reason. Vegetables from the sea are not only the most singularly nutritious food—they're also delicious. Although they're more popular in Asia—especially Japan—they have been valued by many cultures throughout the world. That the Irish, the Inuit, and other coastal peoples use them makes sense. I was amazed, however, to find new-to-me seaweed varieties in open-air Indian markets in landlocked Bolivia. Foods of exceptional value have remained trade items from time immemorial.

The nutritional content of all plants reflects their immediate environment. A carrot grown in deficient soil, for example, is nutritionally deficient compared to one grown in good soil. Seaweeds are continuously bathed in the mineral-rich sea brine. These greens are a direct transformation of sea water, and their mineral content is from 7 to 38 percent of their dry weight!

Ranging from microscopic plankton to giant kelp with fronds more than 1,500 feet long, seaweed is one of the world's most underutilized foods. It's also the world's most abundant food.

Algae is classified according to color as green, brown, red, or blue-green. The color

WILDCRAFTING IN WET SUITS

Dressed in a wet suit, I foraged salad greens at dawn. In a low, −8.5-foot tide, while gulls squawked and the full moon dissolved into the Pacific fog, I sloshed through tidal pools, sidestepped starfish, and took care to remain on this side of the crashing surf. I cut and bagged sturdy kombu, elegant sea palm, and satiny, purple nori. I nibbled as I worked—these greens are irresistibly delicious.

For me, a highlight of last summer was harvesting seaweed on the Mendocino coast with the wildcrafters who have supplied North Americans with tasty sea greens for the past twenty years. Before that time, I settled for Japanese varieties, some of which are cultivated. (For a listing of our five cottage craft industries, see pages 394–95.) Commercial seaweed is harvested off the coast of southern California in large boats, which mow through the waters indiscriminately chopping whatever lies in their path.

Using a grape harvester's knife with a curved blade, eighteen-year-old Shanti Lewallen, who has harvested seaweed with his family since childhood, showed me which plants were at their prime for harvest and how much to trim without stressing the plant's reproductive cycle. The morning crew included Shanti's twelve-year-old brother, Loren, his parents, and two other helpers. We placed our harvest into onion bags (the loose weave holds the weed but not the sea),

hauled them to the beach, carted them to the parking lot, filled the back of a small pickup, and then headed to the sunny inland drying racks and lines. There, the small varieties—like sea palm, dulse, and nori—were spread onto mesh trays and the longer strands of kelp, alaria, and sea whip were clothespinned onto lines, making a beautiful sea green display. We worked quickly to have it all sun drying by noon, then we pulled out picnic hampers and took refuge in the shade of the surrounding redwood forest. I napped while the sun dried the harvest. By late afternoon, we bagged this invaluable food and made plans for the next day's foraging (the tide is low enough only for three to four days per lunar cycle). Could they count me in? Yes, unequivocally.

is determined by the spectrum of light available to the plant for photosynthesis. Thus the most light receptive, the reds (*rhodophyta*), are found as deep as 2,000 feet because they are able to absorb sunlight's shortest frequencies (blue and ultraviolet). The reds also flourish at the shoreline just below tidemark.

Health Benefits The documented medicinal properties of seaweed are voluminous. Benefits include reducing blood cholesterol, removing metallic and radioactive elements from the body, and preventing goiter. Seaweed also has antibiotic properties known to be effective against penicillin-resistant bacteria. Seaweed counteracts obesity; it also strengthens bones, teeth, nerve transmission, and digestion. Seaweed softens hardened masses or tumors, and so it is used to treat lumps, swollen lymph glands, fibroid tumors, and edema. Furthermore, seaweed is a beauty aid, helping maintain glowing, healthy skin and lustrous hair; it is also credited with anti-aging properties. The thermal property of seaweed is cooling; its flavor is salty. In Ayurvedic medicine, seaweed reduces *vata*.

Ounce for ounce, seaweed is higher in vitamins and minerals than any other class of food. It supplies all the minerals needed for human health in proportions very similar to those found in human blood. The most significant elements are calcium, iodine, phosphorus, sodium, and iron. Seaweed is an extremely rich protein source containing up to 38 percent protein. Seaweed is a better than average source of vitamins A, B, C, and E.

It's not surprising that the iodine and iodine compounds in seaweed reduce enlarged thyroid glands (hypothyroidism) caused from insufficient iodine. Eating seaweed also alleviates hyperthyroidism by inhibiting the metabolic rate of the disease.

Use The sea garden contains hundreds of nutritious sea vegetables. These highly versatile foods are easily incorporated into numerous styles of cuisine and complement many dishes from soup to dessert. Those that invite beginners' use are agar, dulse, kombu, nori, and sea palm.

Buying/Foraging My first choice is seaweed that I've wildcrafted at its prime from clean coastal areas. My second choice is the same quality available in natural food stores, and by mail order (see pages 403–04). Third

is seaweed from reputable natural food distributors who import top grades. The commercial quality seaweed in Asian markets may be indiscriminately harvested; however, as a novelty, some of these markets offer fresh seaweed. Fresh seaweed will keep, refrigerated, for two to three days. Dried seaweed keeps for several years when stored, tightly covered, in a cool, dry place.

As our seas become more polluted, some people worry that seaweed is contaminated. According to laboratory analysis, pollutants are not concentrated in seaweed.

My favorite seaweed wildcrafting book so captures the essence of each vegetable that reading it I can almost smell sea brine. It is by John and Eleanor Lewallen, *Sea Vegetable*

FINING BEER AND DETOXING PLUTONIUM

For centuries, beer meisters tossed Irish moss into their vats of beer. The seaweed, which was discarded before kegging the beer, bonded with impurities to discharge toxins. In a like manner, a helping of seaweed will chelate with toxins and discharge them with normal body waste. Amazing stuff. Seaweed not only detoxifies radioactive elements and heavy metals, it also counter the effects of X rays. Such established journals as *Radiation Research*, *Health Physics*, *Nature*, and the *International Journal of Radiation Biology* are among the many that have published papers on this topic.

Gourmet Cookbook and Wildcrafter's Guide (see page 407).

See **Agar; Alaria; Arame; Bladder Wrack; Dulse; Hiziki; Irish Moss; Kanten; Kelp; Kombu; Laver; Mekabu Wakame; Nori; Sea Lettuce; Sea Palm; Sea Whip; Wakame.**

SEA WHIP
Bullwhip Kelp
(Nereocystis leutkeana)

When I was a child, at the seaside we played jump rope with a twenty-foot-long, greenish brown stipe of sea whip that ended in a large bulb with attached fronds. We never thought to nibble on our rope. It has, I have since discovered, a crispy, celerylike texture and taste. It is the sea whip fronds, however, that I'm wild about.

Sea whip fronds are the reproductive organs of this large seaweed. Each frond, a foot or so in length and several inches wide, contains dark oblong patches of spore that, upon maturation, dissolve into the ocean. When fresh, on the ragged frond ends you can see where the spore has been released. When dried, if you look carefully, you can see these patches.

Health Benefits Sea whip is remarkable in that it is delicious to nibble on dried and therefore a superior source of fluorine. While all seaweed contains this important nutrient, which boosts the immune system and strengthens bones and teeth, even minimal cooking destroys it. Sea whip is especially strengthening to the reproductive system. In other medicinal respects, it is similar to seaweed.

Use Undoubtedly one of the easiest sea-weeds to use, sea whip is as thin as a layer of phyllo dough and, when crumbled into a soup or grain or vegetable dish, is quickly absorbed. To benefit from its fluorine content, however, stir it into soups or moist grain or vegetable dishes just prior to serving. As a snack, sea whip is like potato chips in terms of crunch and flavor, but unlike the chips, concentrated essence of sea whip leaves you satisfied after a few nibbles.

Buying Sea whip is available by mail order (see pages 403–04).

See **Seaweed.**

SECKEL See **Pear.**

SEEDS

A seed, like a fertilized egg, is the self-contained embryonic plant, which holds the potential for propagation of the species. This power is reflected in a seed's superior nutritional and energetic properties. It is no coincidence that seeds are a hiker's favorite trail food.

While technically all grains, beans, and many fruits and nuts are seeds, the seeds considered in this entry are oil-rich seeds used in oil production or similar to nuts in culinary use.

Health Benefits Because of their oil content, seeds are high in calories and are a warming and energizing food. That oil content may also make them a digestive challenge for people with a compromised liver. Seeds are an excellent protein and mineral source and are higher in iron than nuts. They contain vitamins A, B-complex, E, and D and are outstanding sources of calcium.

Seeds are high in unsaturated fats; if eaten raw, they are a superior source of fatty acids. Seeds usually reduce *vata*.

Use The seeds most often substituted for nuts and eaten as a snack food are sesame, sunflower, and pumpkin seeds. Other culinary seeds include alfalfa, chia, flax, hemp, poppy, and psyllium.

Buying Select vital-looking, debris-free seeds. With larger seeds like sunflower and pumpkin, you can cull out discolored, broken, or rubbery seeds. Taste is the best way to determine the quality of small seeds like poppy and sesame. The seeds should taste fresh and full bodied, with no off flavor.

See **Alfalfa; Black Sesame Seed; Canola Seed; Chia Seed; Flax Seed; Poppy Seed; Psyllium; Pumpkin Seed; Sesame; Sunflower.**

SEITAN
Kau Fu, Wheat Gluten

Seitan (say-TAN), or wheat gluten, is a chic meat substitute that is versatile, hearty, and wholesome. A traditional Asian food, "wheat meat" is eaten by vegetarians and some religious groups such as the Seventh-Day Adventists.

Health Benefits Seitan tonifies spleen-pancreas and kidney function. High in protein, it helps build body mass, strengthen muscles, and it engenders overall strength and vitality. When freshly made with quality ingredients, seitan is an energizing food. It calms *vata* and *pitta*.

Use Seitan is easily made at home by water extracting the gluten (protein) from wheat flour. First make flour and water into a dough and then, under running water, knead out the wheat starch and bran until only gluten remains. The gluten is seasoned, cooked, and ready for use in a variety of dishes as a meat replacement. The complete method, plus many recipes for using it, is described in *Cooking with Seitan* by Leonard and Barbara Jacobs.

Buying Seitan and seitan products are available in natural food stores, refrigerated or in jars. I do not recommend canned gluten products. It is available as kau fu in Asian markets.

See **Fu; Gluten; Wheat.**

SEMOLINA See **Pasta; Wheat; Wheat Flour.**

SEREH See **Lemon Grass.**

SEREI See **Lemon Grass.**

SERRANO See **Chile Pepper.**

SESAME
(Sesamum indicum)

All it takes are a few hulled sesame seeds topping a bread crust to lend a lively flavor and visual appeal to your loaf. No wonder this minute seed has remained an important food since prehistoric times. It is the oldest known plant grown for its seeds and oil and has been especially valued in Mediterranean, African, and Eastern cultures.

Health Benefits Sesame seeds are a remarkable source of calcium, but this calcium, which is bonded with oxalic acid, is not bioavailable. Soaking the seeds overnight and then toasting them reduces their oxalic acid

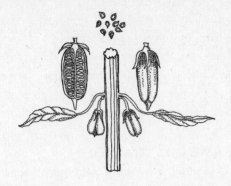

content. While hulling the seeds actually eliminates the oxalic acid, it also eliminates most of the calcium. Moreover, hulled sesame seeds lose their fiber and calcium oxalate, and much of their potassium, iron, and vitamins A and B_6, folacin, and thiamine. If the hulls are removed with caustic alkali rather than mechanically, the nutrient loss is even greater.

There is some concern that consuming whole sesame will adversely affect calcium reserves. Current scientific thought—and years of gastronomic experience—indicate that whole sesame enjoyed in moderation will not interfere with calcium absorption in healthy individuals.

In Oriental medicine, sesame seeds are used to build a deficient liver and/or kidneys when there are symptoms of premature graying, dizziness, and general weakness. They have similar but milder action than black sesame seeds. Sesame seeds reduce *vata*.

Sesame seeds contain over 35 percent protein, more than any nut; they are about 50 percent oil, and are high in vitamin E, which makes sesame oil and butter highly stable and resistant to oxidation. Sesame contains as much iron as liver, and it's rich in phosphorus, niacin, and thiamine. It has a unique surplus of two amino acids, methionine and tryptophan, which are usually lacking in popular vegetable protein foods.

Buying If purchasing hulled sesame seeds, purchase only those that have had their hulls mechanically removed. If the hulled seeds are not organic, you can assume that caustic lye was used to dehull them, thus denaturing nutrients and flavor. According to Paul Pitchford, overuse of hulled sesame seeds and hulled sesame products like tahini may contribute to liver and gallbladder stagnation. The whole seed is the healthful choice.

Use Whole sesame seeds are used in baking and in condiments, confections, salads, and vegetable dishes. Washing the seeds removes any bitter taste, and toasting them enhances their flavor. To wash, place the seeds in a bowl and fill with water; pour the seeds into a strainer, being careful to not pour out any of the sand or grit (if there is any) that may have settled in the bottom of the bowl.

See **Black Sesame Seed; Seeds.**

SESAME BUTTER

Sesame butter is made of whole roasted sesame seeds and may be used interchangeably with peanut butter. It differs from the better known tahini, which is made of hulled raw sesame seeds, and is therefore refined and denatured. Of the two, tahini is lighter in flavor and color and has more culinary applications. Sesame butter is used as a spread and may also replace tahini as a more wholesome ingredient.

QUICK AND CREAMY SALAD DRESSING

4 tablespoons sesame butter
¼ cup water
¼ cup minced fresh oregano leaves
2 tablespoons lime juice
1 garlic clove, pressed
½ teaspoon sea salt

Combine all the ingredients. As different brands of sesame butter vary in consistency, you may need to add additional water to reach desired consistency. Use as a vegetable dip or to dress vegetable, grain, or chicken salads or steamed vegetables. Dressing, covered tightly, holds refrigerated for 5 days.

Sesame butter is high in vitamin E and therefore has a longer shelf life than other nut butters. Once opened, sesame butter should be refrigerated, where it will hold for about 6 months. If it tastes or smells harsh, it is rancid and should be discarded.

See **Nut and Seed Butters; Tahini.**

SESAME OIL

In Africa, the Middle East, and the Orient, the use of nutrient-dense sesame oil dates back to antiquity, and it remains one of the most valued oils for its inimitable flavor, excellent stability, and resistance to oxidation. Even though sesame contains 41 percent of the unstable—but valuable—polyunsaturated fats, it also contains a natural antioxidant that enhances its stability. Along with extra virgin olive oil, sesame oil remains the most healthful culinary oil available.

Use Quality sesame oil can be used in sauces and dressings, or for sautéing or baking at temperatures below 325 degrees.

See **Fat and Oil; Sesame.**

SESAME OIL, TOASTED

A distinctive Asian condiment, toasted sesame oil, made from toasted seeds, has a rich dark color and a heady aroma. It burns when heated directly and so is used as a seasoning agent rather than a cooking oil. Use a few drops to garnish a cooked stir-fry or soup or as an ingredient in a cold sauce or dressing.

SESAME PASTA

A pasta made from semolina and flavored with sesame meal—here's a pasta I don't recommend even though it's commonplace in natural food stores. Sesame meal is a byproduct of the sesame oil industry, and the consumer has no way of knowing how processed, denatured, or stale it might be.

SEVILLE ORANGE See **Bitter Orange.**

SHADDOCK See **Pummelo.**

SHAKER DRIED CORN See **Chicos.**

SHALLOT
(Allium cepa)

The aromatic shallot is sweeter, milder, and more subtly flavored than other members of the onion family. It is an important ingredient in French and New Orleans cuisine.

Health Benefits Shallots reduce *kapha* and, when cooked, *vata*.

Use Considered indispensable for such classic sauces as béarnaise, the shallot cooks down to a creamy, thick consistency. Shallots can also be roasted whole or added, finely chopped, in a salad dressing.

A shallot bulb, when peeled, divides into two halves. When a recipe calls for one shallot, it refers to both halves.

Buying Yellow, red, and gray shallots are available year-round. Currently, most are imported and therefore pricey, but domestic crops have increasing availability. Look for plump and firm bulbs. See **Onion Family.**

SHEEP'S HEAD See Hen-of-the-Woods.

SHIITAKE
Black Forest Mushroom, Chinese Mushroom
(Lentinus edodes)

The second most widely produced edible mushroom, the shiitake has a rich woodsy flavor and a meaty texture when cooked. The shape of a shiitake is similar to a common white mushroom—only its brown cap is peaked at the center like an umbrella and its gills are tan.

Health Benefits Shiitakes strengthen, detoxify, and restore. They contain two potent substances with proven pharmacological effects as immune regulators and antiviral and antitumor agents; they also positively affect the cardiovascular system. Shiitakes treat diseases involving depressed immune function including cancer, AIDS, environmental allergies, candida infections, and frequent flu and colds. In addition, they soothe bronchial inflammation, regulate urine incontinence, and reduce chronic high cholesterol.

Shiitakes are rich in vitamins D, B_2, and B_{12}, and are a good source of minerals when grown in a mineral-rich medium. They contain about 2.5 percent protein.

Use Cooking, especially roasting, sautéing, or grilling, enhances the flavor of shiitakes. The longer the cooking, the more water they lose and the denser and chewier they become. Use in soups, stir-fries, pasta sauces, entrées, and side dishes.

To reconstitute dried shiitake, soak in warm water for at least 2 to 3 hours or, preferably, overnight. Use the soaking water for stock. But discard the woody portion of the stem.

Buying When purchasing fresh shiitakes, look for firm, fleshy mushrooms with a dry, blemishfree surface. Select thick mushrooms with their peaked caps intact over flat, or broken, mushrooms. The more aroma the mushrooms have, the more flavor.

Dried shiitake are readily available in Asian, natural food, and specialty food markets. Top-quality shiitake, called *donko*, or "flower petal," in Japanese, are very costly because they are grown outdoors on hardwood. Most commercial shiitake grow in a few weeks in warm conditions on artificial substrate.

See **Mushroom Family.**

SHISO See Perilla.

SHOYU See Soy Sauce.

SIBERIAN KALE See Kale.

SIEVA BEAN See Lima Bean.

SLAKED CORN See Posole.

SNAP BEAN See Green Bean.

SNOW PEA
(Pisum sativum macrocarpon)

Pea seeds found in archaeological digs in Anatolia (Turkey) date from 5700 B.C., making this legume as ancient as wheat and barley. By comparison, the tender-crisp, jade snow pea is new—the first mention of it was in 1597. Rather than having a stiff pod the snow pea (like the sugar snap pea) has a pod that's as succulent as the peas it contains.

Health Benefits Snow peas are high in vitamins A and B-complex and are a good source of calcium and potassium as well as iron and phosphorus. Snow peas nourish the liver, stomach, and spleen-pancreas. They reduce *pitta* and *kapha.*

Use Snow peas need only to have their tips removed. They're used in soups, salads, stir-fries, and more. They are a classic ingredient in Asian cuisine.

Split open and spread with a delectable tofu or cheese filling, snow peas make a showy hors d'oeuvre.

Buying Purchase snow peas that are squeaky fresh. When withered at the tips or when the peas are large and round (rather than small and in a flat pod), the vegetable is past its prime. Snow peas are available year-round in some markets but are least costly in the spring.

SNOW PUFF See Enoki.

SOBA

A flavorful tan- or dark-colored Japanese noodle made of buckwheat or a blend of buckwheat and wheat.

See **Buckwheat Flour; Pasta.**

SOLDIER BEAN
Red-Eye Bean
(Phaseolus vulgaris)

This dull white bean with a red eye shaped like a soldier's silhouette is called the soldier bean. It is an heirloom bean from New England.

See **Beans and Legumes.**

Ø SORBITOL

Sorbitol masquerades as a healthful sweetener, but I suggest tasting—*really* tasting—a sorbitol-sweetened candy. Its lingering aftertaste is harsh, unpleasant, and metallic. People using sorbitol have reported health problems, especially of the digestive tract. Highly processed from corn syrup, sorbitol is an artificial sweetener to avoid.

See **Sweeteners.**

SORGHUM
(Sorghum vulgare)

Sorghum, a nutritious milletlike grain, has been a staple grain in Africa and Asia since time immemorial. The large plant looks like a thin-bladed corn plant, and the seed looks like large, dark-colored millet. Unfortunately, the only domestic varieties grown today are used for cattle feed or sorghum molasses—neither of which is savory to the human palate.

I once was given five pounds of table sorghum, a variety grown for human consumption. It was delicious with a robust and nutty flavor and excellent texture. It was hard not to exhaust this small stash very quickly. May table sorghum one day soon be readily available to you. In the meantime, it is easily grown in a home garden.

Health Benefits Sorghum's sweet and slightly astringent flavor make it medicinal for the spleen-pancreas and stomach. It helps to alleviate diarrhea and to restore a flagging appetite. To heighten its medicinal properties, toast it prior to cooking. In addition to protein, fat, and sugars, sorghum contains calcium, phosphorus, iron, vitamins B_1, B_2, and niacin. Sorghum is nutritionally similar to corn. As a sweetener, sorghum calms *pitta* and *vata*.

Use Sorghum may be cooked whole or ground into flour for flatbreads. To prepare whole, add 1 cup sorghum and a pinch of salt to 2 cups of water and simmer, tightly covered, for 40 minutes.

SORGHUM MOLASSES

Sorghum molasses was a chief sweetener in American homes in the eighteenth and early nineteenth centuries. Sorghum molasses is made from the sorghum stalks. It has a smoky, sweet taste and a thick texture, not unlike table molasses made from sugarcane.

Health Benefits Sorghum molasses is comparable nutritionally to blackstrap molasses and has similar effects on body metabolism. Sorghum is high in iron and is a fair source of calcium. It is 65 to 70 percent sucrose.

Use Sorghum molasses may be used as a table sweetener over pancakes, French toast, or waffles or as a substitute for molasses in baking and cooking.

Buying Sorghum molasses is easiest to find in southeastern states and in some well-stocked natural food stores and specialty shops. As its availability is sporadic, buy it when you find it.

See Molasses; Sweeteners.

SORREL
French Sorrel, Garden Sorrel, Schav, Sour Dock
(Rumex acetosa)

In the 1885 edition of the classic *Vegetable Garden*, Madame Vilmorin-Andrieux observed that "garden sorrels may be ranked among the plants which have been least modified by cultivation, as most of them are little, if anything, better than wild plants of the same species growing under favorable conditions." The same is true today. There is nothing tame about this sour-tasting perennial potherb, an old favorite in European cuisine.

The name sorrel comes from a Germanic word for sour. The bright triangular leaves of sorrel grow up from a clump; they are like spinach in size.

Health Benefits Used as a spring tonic throughout Europe, sorrel stimulates the liver and aids digestion, especially of rich food. It is high in oxalic acid and a rich source of iron and potassium and vitamins A and C. Sorrel reduces *vata*.

Use A few slivered young sorrel leaves perk up any salad or sandwich. Sorrel is very easy to purée, and the purée makes an ideal base for a sauce or soup. Strip the stems, shred the leaves, and simmer in very little water. Within minutes, sorrel melts into a purée. It reduces even more than spinach in volume.

Creme of sorrel soup is a famous Old World dish; salmon with sorrel sauce is popular in France; and a sorrel and egg yolk soup, *schav*, is a favorite Jewish dish. Due to its high acid content, sorrel discolors if cut with a carbon steel knife, cooked in aluminum or iron pots, or served in a silver dish.

Buying Sorrel is available in specialty food markets in spring. Look for bunches of light green arrow-shape leaves that are firm and not limp. The smaller leaves are less acidic. Plan to use it within a few days.

SOUR CHERRY
Pie Cherry, Tart Cherry
(Prunus cerasus)

A wild cherry found in both European and American Stone Age sites developed into today's cherry, both sour and sweet. The sour cherry is the smaller and more astringent of the two. Their color is a bright cherry red compared to the darker sweet cherry. "Acid cherry" would be a more apt name than sour. By any name, it takes just one to reap a serious pucker.

Health Benefits Opposite of the sweet cherries, which are warming, sour cherries are cooling and astringent and support liver function. Sour cherries are remarkably high in vitamin A and folic acid. They are low in calories. In moderation, sour cherries reduce *vata*.

Use The primary use for sour cherries is cherry pie. In any recipe calling for cooked cherries, the texture of sour cherries outperforms sweet cherries. Serve sour cherries as a cold soup, with game, and in any dessert or preserve that calls for cherries. Unlike sugary sweet cherries, which often don't require additional sugar in a recipe, sour cherries demand it.

Buying/Foraging Hardy sour cherry trees are prolific bearers—one small tree produces more bushels of tart fruit than any one family could use—so pie cherries often fall to the

---

CHERRY PIE BAKING CONTEST

In high school in 1960, I won a cherry pie baking contest that took me to a national competition in Chicago. Each state was represented and the Sheraton Blackburn Hotel ballroom was fitted out with 50 ranges and worktables, and several supply tables loaded with lard, sugar, and sour cherries. The winner would travel to the White House kitchen to bake a pie for President Eisenhower. Leading up to the Chicago trip, how I practiced my technique, confident that, if given the opportunity, Ike would love my pie. I didn't win—but I sure ate a lot of sour cherries.

ground for lack of anyone to harvest them. What a waste. Is there an un- or under-harvested sour cherry tree in your neighborhood? There's no harm in asking to pick a few bags full.

Sour cherries are so juicy and perishable that they bruise at a touch and are thus difficult to market. They can always be found canned or frozen in a thick sugar syrup, but with increased interest in unusual fruits, fresh sour cherries are once again becoming available, if only in regional markets. Look for them at farm stands and farmers' markets in July following the sweet cherry harvest. Use immediately.

See **Fruit.**

SOUR DOCK See **Sorrel.**

SOUR ORANGE See **Bitter Orange.**

SOYBEAN
(Glycine max)

In five-thousand-year-old Chinese texts, the soybean was described as one of the most important crops. Not much has changed since then, except that today it is valued worldwide. This versatile Asian pea is the least expensive source of protein in virtually every country. In fact, an acre of soybeans produces more than twenty times more usable protein than if that land were used to raise beef cattle or grow their fodder. The United States produces about 75 percent of the world's soy crop. It is used primarily as animal food.

Health Benefits Isoflavones, a type of plant estrogen usually occurring in soybeans, are credited with slowing osteoporosis, relieving some side effects of menopause, and alleviating many forms of cancer, including breast and prostate cancer, as well as kidney disease and complications from diabetes. Although other plants contain isoflavones, none contain as rich a supply as soybeans do. In addition, soybeans dramatically lower the undesirable low-density lipoprotein blood cholesterol while raising the desirable high-density lipoprotein level.

The soybean is a good source of easily absorbed iron and is therefore especially beneficial to young children and people with iron-deficiency anemia. In addition to iron, soybeans also contain carotin, vitamins B_1 and B_2, and niacin. The spleen-pancreas and stomach meridians are supported by soybean products, which help reduce damp conditions, support detoxification, improve circulation, and promote clear vision. Soybeans reduce *pitta*.

Use In the West, soybeans are cooked whole and eaten in any number of dishes, from minestrone to bean tacos. In Asia, however, the soybean is not cooked and served whole. Why? If merely boiled, soybeans inhibit the digestive enzyme trypsin; they are a bear to digest. Asian cuisines have devised numerous healthful methods to tame this bean into an easily digested food.

I do not recommend hard-to-digest Western soy products, which have not had the trypsin inhibitor removed. These products include soy flour, soy grits, soy flakes, soy nuts, and soy nut butter. Neither do I recommend superrefined soy products, such as lecithin, soy isolates, soy protein, TSP (textured soy protein), and TVP (textured vegetable protein). TSP and TVP are made from defatted soybeans using thermoplastic extrusion.

See Beans and Legumes; Black Soybean; Green Soybean; Miso; Natto; Okara; Soy Sauce; Tempeh; Tofu; Yuba.

SOY SPLICED WITH HERBICIDES IS PROBABLY ON YOUR PLATE

Today, our food chain is permeated with Roundup Ready Soybeans, biogenetically engineered by Monsanto. We're talking more than tofu. Soy appears in foods ranging from infant formula to meat extenders. Furthermore, soy products like oil, flour, and lecithin are ubiquitous in prepared, packaged, and restaurant foods.

There's only one way to tell whether the soy ingredient in your soup is natural or genetically engineered: Purchase only certified organic foods or products with a manufacturer's statement that it uses *no* GMOs (genetically manipulated organisms). Otherwise, you're most probably ingesting Roundup Ready Soybeans spliced with an herbicide that enables the plant to survive otherwise toxic doses of chemicals. I wish this were a joke. It is not.

SOYBEAN CURD See Tofu.

SOYBEAN PASTE See Miso.

SOY CHEESE

I've given up trying to find a palatable soy cheese. When I'm in the mood for Parmesan, real Parmesan satisfies. If, however, you're reducing or eliminating dairy foods and if you find some dishes unacceptable without cheese, then soy cheese *is* an alternative. A second choice is to up the quality of the other ingredients, then the cheese is not missed.

Soy cheese is available in types ranging from soy cheddar to soy mozzarella. Experiment with different brands since quality varies dramatically. Soy cheese contains no cholesterol but does contain oil and may or may not contain casein, a cow's milk derivative.

Ø SOY DELI FOODS

Be it a soy-based burger, cold cut, bacon, hot dog, or sausage, the familiar fatty and meaty mixture of these soy foods appeals to many people who are reducing their consumption of meat. Made of highly refined soy isolate and textured vegetable protein, they are not whole foods, and they usually lack savor.

Ø SOY FLAKES AND SOY FLOUR

I do not recommend using soy flakes or flour. The trypsin inhibitor is not removed from these products (see Soybean), making them hard to digest. It's unfortunate that many so-called health recipes call for soy flour, mistakenly thinking that if it ups the protein, it's good for you. Many commercial products use soy flour because it's dirt cheap.

Ø SOY ISOLATE

Whenever soy isolate is an ingredient in a food, isolate that food from your diet.

Here's how it's made. When oil is pressed from soybeans, the dregs or meal is bathed in chemical and alcohol solutions to eliminate all the carbohydrates. This soy isolate is used in imitation cheese and ice cream and other highly processed soy products.

SOYMILK

Concurrent with the increasing incidence of milk allergies is the growing popularity and availability of soymilk. In terms of flavor, milk from the bean is a fair approximation of milk from the cow, but of course it is not an exact duplication.

Health Benefits Bill Shurtleff, author of *The Book of Tofu* and fondly called the Johnny Appleseed of Soy, observes this about fresh soymilk: "Many Japanese doctors view it as an effective natural medicine and prescribe it as a regular part of the diet for diabetes, heart disease, high blood pressure, hardening of the arteries, and anemia. They also use it to strengthen the digestive system and fortify the bloodstream.

Nutritionally, soymilk contains the same amount of protein as cow's milk and is superior in the following ways. It has approximately one-third the fat, fewer calories, no cholesterol, many essential B vitamins, and fifteen times as much iron. Because it is lower on the food chain, it contains one-tenth the amount of chemical residues. Cow's milk, however, is higher in calcium.

Soymilk reduces *pitta*, and, when warm, it reduces *kapha* and can be used in moderation by *vata*.

Use Freely substitute soymilk for cow's milk in any recipe, for breakfast cereal, or by the glassful as a beverage. It adds flavor, body, and nutrients to casseroles, soups, puddings, pancakes, and quick breads.

You can clabber soymilk (that is, allow it to become sour and separate) to make a healthful buttermilk substitute. To 1 cup of soymilk add 1 tablespoon lemon juice and let stand for 5 to 10 minutes, or until it thickens.

Buying Soymilk is available fresh, packaged in aseptic containers, and powdered. Its

---

A NIFTY HOME APPLIANCE

Nutritionally, soymilk has an impeccable profile, be it fresh or aseptically packaged. Nutrition, however, does not tell the whole story. Any highly processed food with a lengthy shelf life—even soymilk—imparts neither energy nor strength. To make shelf-stable soymilk, soybeans undergo up to fourteen mechanical steps, some at high temperatures.

If you frequently use soymilk, consider purchasing a soymilk machine. Add soaked soybeans and water to this large blender-size unit, and 20 minutes later you'll have a tasty and healthful beverage that costs less than 25 cents a quart to make. Make a quart a week for a year and you'll recoup the price of the unit (see page 404).

You may also make fresh soymilk from scratch by boiling ground beans and straining them; it is, however, a sticky, time-consuming process and the resulting milk has a rather beany flavor.

quality and flavor varies considerably from brand to brand, so read labels and experiment until you find the brand that suits you best.

Fresh soymilk is available in the refrigerated section of natural food stores and is superior to packaged soymilk since it is minimally processed. Fresh soymilk has a shorter shelf life than cow's milk or highly processed soymilk. When purchased in a plastic container, it can be transferred at home to a glass container, covered, and refrigerated to increase storage time. Should fresh soymilk clabber, use it like buttermilk or yogurt in cooking and baking.

Shelf-stable aseptic cartons of soymilk have a shelf life of a year; once opened, the milk holds for a week if refrigerated.

See **Okara.**

Ø SOY NUTS AND SOY NUT BUTTER

I do not recommend these hard-to-digest bean products. Real nuts or nut butter taste so much better.

Ø SOY OIL

Soy oil is the most prevalent oil used in commercial food production. This oil, a by-product of the soy industry, is highly refined. Unrefined soy oil is no better. It has an unpleasantly intense aroma and flavor; it is considered toxic in traditional Chinese medicine, and it is difficult to digest.

SOY SAUCE
Shoyu, Tamari

Soy sauce, indispensable to Asian cookery, has a salty, sweet, slightly tart flavor and a rich, fermented fragrance. Even a few drops of quality soy sauce bring out the natural sweetness and subtle hidden flavors of almost any food but dessert. If soy sauce to you means a cheap, harsh-tasting liquid condiment, then you've never experienced the real thing.

Both soy sauce and tamari are made of soybeans, salt, and water. Soy sauce, however, also contains a wheat koji and so has a milder flavor. Tamari originally referred to the liquid that rises to the surface of aging hatcho miso; today, it refers to wheatfree soy sauce. If traditionally made, both sauces are aged for a year or more. Commercial rotgut soy sauce is chemically brewed in a 24-hour process.

Action Soy sauce and tamari are nutritious natural flavor enhancers and an excellent source of amino acids and glutamic acid. Because they are fermented, they enhance digestion. Plain salt contains two grams of sodium per teaspoon, while the same amount of natural soy sauce contains 286 milligrams of sodium, about a seventh as much.

In low-sodium circles, soy sauce has a bad name because of its high salt content. This reputation would be warranted if it was consumed by the glassful—which of course is not the case. Soy sauce's wide range of flavors allows richer seasoning with less salt than if straight salt were added to a dish. Soy sauce and tamari have more than twenty identified flavor components. Soy sauce and tamari reduce *vata*.

Use Much of the sweet aroma and flavor of soy sauce is lost during long cooking, so it is best to use it to season during the last few minutes of cooking. Do *not* boil soy sauce. Strongly flavored tamari, on the other hand, holds up to long simmering, which actually rounds out its flavor.

Use tamari or soy sauce in place of table salt in soups, stir-fried vegetables, dressings, and marinades. They're also good to season grilled and fried foods, be they Asian or Western in flavor.

Buying Excellent soy condiments are made in the United States, but the most flavorful are aged in cedar kegs and imported from Japan. If these imports are not available at your natural food store, they are available by mail order (see page 402).

To preserve the flavor of quality soy sauce or tamari, purchase it in small quantities and store it, tightly covered, in glass in the refrigerator.

To meet the low-sodium demand, reduced-sodium soy sauce with 8 percent sodium is available (soy sauce usually contains from 16 to 18 percent). *Caution:* Some low-sodium brands may contain a preservative.

SOY YOGURT

Soy yogurt is as versatile as yogurt with a fair-to-middling approximation of the flavor. "Soygurt," a lactose- and cholesterol-free product, is available commercially. It is easy to make at home. Any unpasteurized dairy yogurt may be used as a starter; nondairy cultures are available in health food stores or by mail order.

Prepare, store, and use soy yogurt as you would dairy yogurt. Soygurt has a comparable nutritional profile to soymilk but has enhanced digestibility because it is fermented. Soy yogurt reduces *vata*.

SPAGHETTI SQUASH
(Cucurbita maxima)

The spaghetti squash is pale in flesh and flavor, like a summer squash, but it has the storage capabilities of winter squash. Its memorable property is that when it is cooked, the flesh may be coaxed into spaghettilike strands, which some people adore. Others (like me) find the vegetable all texture and no taste.

See **Squash; Winter Squash.**

SPANISH GARLIC See **Rocambole.**

SPANISH ONION See **Onion.**

SPANISH TOLOSANA See **Kidney Bean.**

SPEARMINT See Mint.

SPELT
Dinkel, Farro
(Triticum spelta)

Spelt, an ancient red wheat that thrived in the Middle Eastern Mediterranean more than nine thousand years ago, is mentioned by name in both Exodus and Ezekiel in the Bible. Despite pressures to use hybrid wheat, people remained loyal to spelt in the European Alps because of its excellent flavor. Spelt became available in America in the 1980s.

Today, spelt products include bread, breakfast cereal, and pasta. I can recommend the bread and cereal, but since spelt is a

bread wheat, spelt pasta is dense and stodgy. Spelt is a boon to people who are allergic to common wheat but can tolerate spelt.

See **Grains; Wheat.**

SPICES See **Herbs and Spices.**

SPINACH
(Spinacia oleracea)

Spinach is a popular green vegetable throughout temperate regions. Its thick, juicy leaves, cooked or raw, have a velvety quality. Spinach originated in the Middle East, where wild varieties still grow.

Health Benefits Spinach supports the functions of the large intestine, stomach, and liver. It moistens, quenches thirst, and supports vision; it is especially useful for easing constipation for frail or elderly people. It is not recommended for someone with a tendency toward loose stools or urinary incontinence.

Because spinach contains a large amount of oxalic acid, people prone to kidney stones or gallstones are advised to eat spinach sparingly. An Ayurvedic remedy for a chronic cough is to eat spinach soup seasoned with ginger two times a day on an empty stomach. Spinach reduces *kapha*.

Spinach, a fast-growing member of the goosefoot family, contains carotin, vitamin C, calcium, and phosphorus. It is higher in protein than most vegetables, but despite Popeye's admonition—is not higher in iron than other dark leafy greens. Why, then, did Popeye mislead us? Before his time, a typist misplaced a decimal point, making spinach look almost as good as iron filings.

SAINT HILDEGARD'S CURE-ALL

Saint Hildegard of Bingen, a twelfth-century mystic, cured every imaginable ailment with spelt. "When someone is so weakened by illness that he cannot eat," she wrote, "then simply take whole spelt kernels and boil them vigorously in water, add butter and egg. . . . Give this to the patient and it will heal him from within like a good healing salve."

Modern science has supported Saint Hildegard's theories by showing that spelt's water solubility is remarkably different from that of common wheat. Hold a few spelt kernels in your mouth and—unlike other types of wheat—they immediately soften. Spelt is also, therefore, readily assimilated into the body.

Use Surely the bad reputation spinach had was due to canned or overcooked spinach, which is indeed without savor. Lightly cooked spinach (cooked only until it begins to go limp), on the other hand, is a delicacy, which absorbs any seasoning agent and doesn't impart its flavor to other food. Spinach can be eaten raw as a salad green. Avoid cutting spinach with a carbon blade knife, cooking it in aluminum, or serving it in silver, for it discolors these metals. Spinach grows in sandy soil, so it needs several washings prior to cooking.

Buying Spinach is available throughout the year; in the winter its taste is stronger than in the summer. Look for crisp bright green leaves with short stems. Avoid spinach that is yellow, wilted, slimy, or with stem ends that show drying.

Savoy spinach (with crinkled leaves) is the most commonly available. There are also flat-leafed varieties.

See **Goosefoot Family.**

SPIRULINA
(*Spirulina platensis*)

Spirulina, a microalgae, is a remarkable chlorophyll source with an intense chlorophyll flavor. Unlike macroalgae (like kelp), spirulina is microscopic and derives its name from the spiral shape of its filament. One of the most primitive forms of plant life, spirulina was used by the Aztecs and some Africans as an important food staple.

Health Benefits Spirulina lowers cholesterol, suppresses fatty accumulation in the liver, prevents tumor formation, enhances the immune system, protects kidneys from mercury poisoning, is useful in treating obesity, and aids digestion by increasing the levels of beneficial bacteria in the intestines. Spirulina is very cooling and therefore not advised for people who tend to be cold and have accompanying "damp" conditions in the lower body, such as water retention, candida-type infections, or cysts.

Spirulina is an excellent source of nucleic acids (RNA/DNA), gamma linoleic acid (GLA), vitamin A, other B vitamins, vitamin E, iron, selenium, and other trace minerals. It consists of 60 to 70 percent protein (of which 85 to 95 percent is digestible). One acre of spirulina ponds produces more than twenty times the protein produced by an acre of soybeans, the next best protein crop.

Use The easiest way to consume spirulina is in a capsule or tablet; to be fully digested, the tablets must be chewed. It's less expensive to purchase the powder and to stir it into a glass of water or juice. Spirulina is also found as an ingredient in such products as pasta and energy bars.

See **Chlorella; Essential Fatty Acids; Gamma-Linoleic Acid; Microalgae; Wild Blue-Green Algae.**

SPRING ONION See **Scallion.**

SPROUTS

The ultimate in springtime food, the tender sproutlets of grains, beans, and seeds burst with energy and nutrients. Used for thousands of years in Asia, sprouts have been commonplace in the West since the 1970s.

Broccoli sprouts have recently made news.

A recent study found that one ounce of broccoli sprouts contains more isothiocyanates, a potent anticarcinogenic neutraceutical, than two pounds of broccoli. This study from Johns Hopkins University was released in September 1997, and within three months broccoli sprouts were selling fast in U.S. markets. Despite their bitter tang, broccoli sprouts are a tasty addition to a salad or sandwich.

Health Benefits A sprouted seed is easier to assimilate than the seed itself. People who have a hard time digesting beans, for example, can easily digest bean sprouts or even beans that have started to sprout.

Sprouts are valued for their cooling properties and their ability to detoxify the body, especially the liver. They are, however, to be used in moderation and should preferably be cooked for someone with a cold or a deficient or weakened condition. Mung bean sprouts are best avoided by someone with candida or other yeast-type infections. Sprouts of all kinds reduce *pitta* and *kapha*.

In the process of sprouting, seeds attain higher levels of protein, sugar, enzymes, hormones, vitamin C, and some B vitamins. Sprouts are low in fat and calories.

Use To make sprouts at home, use organic seeds from a natural food store or by mail order (see page 404) that are whole and preservative-free (seeds from a feed store are often chemically treated). Place in a wide-mouthed jar, add water to cover, cover the jar's mouth with a piece of cheesecloth, nylon, or fine mesh, and secure with a rubber band or screw-on jar ring. Soak overnight. The next morning, strain out the water, rinse the seeds, and strain again. Repeat, if necessary, until the water runs clear. Turn the jar upside down to drain on the counter as light increases the seeds' chlorophyll. Rinse and drain the seeds twice a day.

Sprouts may be made of legumes, vegetables, herbs, oil seeds, or of wheat or rye. Any legume will sprout, but unlike other sprouts, legume sprouts (exception alfalfa) need to be cooked prior to eating. The carbohydrates in grain convert to sugar; they may become alcoholic and develop an unpleasant sweetness if allowed to grow longer than the length of the grain.

Buying Choose fresh and vibrant-looking sprouts with no signs of brown discoloration, slimy texture, or musty aroma.

Some of the more common and easy-to-sprout seeds include:

- **Alfalfa Sprouts** Queen of sprouts, ubiquitous at every salad bar. Two tablespoons of seed yield one quart. This tiny sprout is high in minerals, protein, and vitamins A, B-complex, C, D, E, and K. Not to be consumed by lupus patients. At harvest, their length should be one to two inches. Growing time is from four to six days, depending upon room temperature.
- **Broccoli and Cabbage Sprouts** Ready to eat when the sprout is an inch long. Sprouting may take up to five days.
- **Chickpea Sprouts** Require up to sixteen hours soaking time. Three-fourths of a cup yields one quart of sprouts. Best when the sprout is just

under one inch, they are ready in about four days.

- **Clover Sprouts** Popular for sprouting, especially red clover. Sprouting instructions are the same as for alfalfa.
- **Fenugreek Sprouts** An aggressive flavor not everyone appreciates. One tablespoon yields about a quart. Ready when they're an inch long, fenugreek sprouts are ready in about four days.
- **Lentil Sprouts** Require only four hours of soaking. Most nutritious if sprouted to half an inch but tastier if allowed to grow longer. Three-fourths of a cup yields one quart of sprouts.
- **Mung Bean Sprouts** Popular and a mainstay of Chinese cookery. One-half cup yields one quart. They are ready in about five days.
- **Radish Sprouts** Sprouted like cabbage sprouts but may take a day longer.
- **Soybean Sprouts** Require more rinsing than other sprouts; the rinsing water should be discarded. Best when under one inch in length, they are ready in three to five days. Soybean sprouts need to be eaten cooked, not raw.
- **Wheat Sprouts** Flavor is sweetest if the sprout does not exceed the length of the grain, but the finished length may be from one-quarter of an inch to one inch, depending upon how you will use the sprouts. They are ready in about four days.

Ø *Caution:* Children, the elderly, and people with weakened immune systems should not eat raw sprouts. When sprouts are grown in contaminated environments, they may contain food-borne diseases that put vulnerable consumers at risk. Tainted alfalfa sprouts caused a 1998 outbreak of food poisoning in California. Currently, the International Sprout Growers Association is seeking methods to kill dangerous bacteria before they germinate during sprout production. In the meantime, favor cooked sprouts or sprout your own.

SQUASH
(Cucurbita)

The Narraganset and Iroquis said *askutasquash* and *isquotersquash;* the Pilgrims heard squash. Indigenous to the Americas, squash is a member of the gourd family. Squash neatly falls into two categories, summer and winter, but there's less agreement about their names and, because squash rampantly cross-fertilize, hybrids are endlessly created.

- **Cucurbita Pepo** Includes all of the summer squash as well as acorn, delicata, pumpkin, spaghetti, sweet dumpling, and turban squashes. Except for pumpkin, the winter pepos are usually small, deeply ridged, and yellow fleshed when ripe; they require little or no curing time. The five-sided stem gradually enlarges as it nears the fruit. The flavor of pepos fades with long storage, and they become fibrous.
- **Cucurbita Maxima** Next to ripen.

Maximas have leathery skins, round stems that do not expand at the fruit, and deep yellow-orange dry flesh. Maximas include banana, buttercup, gold nugget, hubbard, kabocha, red kuri squash, and spaghetti squash. The flesh is flaky when cooked but becomes smooth when puréed or mashed.

- **Curcurbita Moschata** Best keeper and the last to mature. Butternut is the best known of the moschatas. The rind is easy to cut and the five-sided, narrow, woody stem expands right at the fruit. The moist, deep orange and richly flavored flesh requires six weeks curing after harvest to fully sweeten. If a butternut is too old or was not properly cured and stored, its interior color will fade to white and will become pithy.

See **Acorn Squash; Banana Squash; Buttercup Squash; Butternut Squash; Delicata Squash; Gold Nugget Squash; Gourd Family; Kabocha Squash; Pumpkin; Spaghetti Squash; Summer Squash; Turban Squash; Winter Squash.**

SQUASH BLOSSOM

The large, vivid golden blossom of any squash and pumpkin is edible and long a favorite in Native American and European cuisine.

Use A squash blossom can be sliced and tossed in salads, sautéed, stuffed, and baked, and batter coated and deep-fried. If the blossom is more than a few hours old, its central section becomes slimy, so pinch it out. Like-

---

HOW TO TELL THE BOYS FROM THE GIRLS

Does harvesting squash blossoms mean that you'll have less fruit? Nope, you can have your blossoms and your crooknecks, too. All flowers of the gourd family are edible, whether male or female. When gathering squash blossoms from your garden, pick only male flowers, leaving a few on each plant for a bee or bug to do its pollinating work.

How to tell male from female? It's easy. The male blossoms are narrow stemmed, while the female blossoms attach to the stem with a large bulge, which is, in fact, the nascent squash.

---

wise, if you are going to stuff the blossom and the stamen is overly large, remove it.

Buying Look for squash blossoms from late spring through early summer in farmers' markets or ethnic markets. Select fresh blossoms with closed buds; expect them to be as soft and limp as silk lingerie. The cost per pound is high, but a few ounces are probably all you need.

See **Flower Blossoms.**

SQUASH SEED

Roasted winter squash seeds are a superior source of fiber and zinc. They are so

---

A HIGH-FIBER SNACK

1 cup winter squash or pumpkin seeds
½ teaspoon curry powder
Sea salt to taste
1 tablespoon melted butter (optional)

Preheat the oven to 350 degrees. Separate the squash seeds from the stringy pulp. Toss the seeds with the curry, salt, and butter, if using. Spread in an even layer in a small baking pan. Bake for 10 minutes, or until the seeds become crisp and lightly browned.

---

chewy that some people find them bothersome to eat; others find the succulent kernel well worth the exercise. Depending upon the squash variety, you may either eat the seed and hull together, or crack a seed between your teeth and use your tongue to extract the nutmeat from the hull. Use seeds from winter squash or pumpkins, or purchase them toasted and seasoned from Latino food markets.

See **Pumpkin Seed.**

STAR ANISE
Chinese Anise
(Illicium verum)

Star anise, the beautiful, star-shape dried fruit of a small Chinese evergreen, is a favorite spice in Vietnamese and Chinese cuisine. Star anise contains anethole, the same essential oil as anise does—just stronger. Star anise is used to flavor anisette and other licorice-flavored liqueurs and is an ingredient in five-spice powder.

Medicinally, star anise is a stimulant and a diuretic; it aids digestion, relieves pain, and has antifungal properties. Star anise tea is soothing for a cough.

STAR FRUIT
Carambola
(Averrhoa carambola)

The banana yellow star fruit is a Disney-like creation that slices into perfectly shaped stars to delight the eye and spirit. A native of Indonesia, where the fruit still grows wild, the star fruit is now grown in Florida.

This oval, deeply ribbed fruit, from three to five inches long, has a thin, edible waxy skin and its citrusy, juicy flesh is almost translucent.

Health Benefits Star fruit is cooling and astringent and thus clears excess heat. It allays biliousness and diarrhea. Star fruit is a good source of vitamin C and potassium. It is low in calories.

Use Sweet star fruit can be eaten out of hand, used in salads and desserts, or as a garnish. Tart star fruit may be used as a lemon or lime substitute or in jams and chutneys.

Buying Look for star fruits that are evenly colored and without brown spots. Narrow-ribbed fruits are tart; fleshy ribbed fruits are sweet. Leave at room temperature until their full fruity aroma is apparent, and then refrigerate for up to one week. Star fruits are available from late summer and through early winter. Dried star fruit is available in some natural food stores.

See **Tropical Fruit.**

STEM GINGER See Ginger.

STEM LETTUCE See Celtuce.

STEVIA
Honey Leaf
(Stevia rebaudiana)

Imagine a healthful herb that is 30 times sweeter than sugar, nonnutritive, and essentially noncaloric. Stevia, which the Guarani Indians of Paraguay call *caa-hee* (honey leaf), is such a plant. Its leaves and flower buds contain two glucosides that are two hundred and three hundred times respectively sweeter than sucrose, and which cannot be metabolized in the human digestive system. In 1995, the FDA reversed its ban on stevia, provided it is labeled for use as a dietary supplement.

Health Benefits Stevia has a long history of use in South America and current widespread use in Japan where clinical data indicates that it suppresses dental bacteria. It apparently regulates blood sugar and therefore may be of use for people with hypoglycemia and blood sugar imbalances. It assists with weight loss, regulates blood pressure, and reduces mental and physical fatigue. There is currently no evidence of adverse reactions to stevia.

Stevia is the one sweetener people suffering from candida and yeast-type conditions can tolerate. As sweetened foods exacerbate an overly hot and moist internal environment, which fosters yeast overgrowth, people on anticandida diets must forego all sweets. Stevia is the sweet exception. Ayurvedic cookbook author and nutritionist Amadea Morningstar, however, recommends that stevia be used in moderation for candidatype health problems until we've had a longer time to observe its properties. Stevia reduces *pitta* and *vata*.

Use Do not expect stevia-sweetened products to have the same flavor or texture as sugar-sweetened foods, but do expect it to imbue light-colored foods with a green tint. Stevia is not affected by heat. To extract the sweetness from the leaves, soak 1 teaspoon of stevia in 1 cup of water overnight and strain. Use to sweeten beverages and desserts. Refined stevia—as a clear liquid or white powder—won't color your food green, but it is not as healthful as the whole leaf products. Two drops of stevia liquid extract sweeten 1 cup of liquid. One speck of refined stevia sweetens 1 cup of liquid.

Buying Stevia is available in natural food stores as a cut herb, in leaf form, as a liquid extract, as a pure powdered extract, and blended with rice syrup powder as a granulated sugar substitute. Store stevia tightly covered in a cool, dry place.

STRAWBERRY
(Fragaria x ananassa)

> Doubtless God could have made a better berry, but doubtless God never did.
>
> —William Butler

I hope that everyone knows of at least one wooded path that promises wild strawberries. It takes time, down on the knees, to ferret out these tiny jewels. The payoff, in volume, is negligible—but that's no deterrent.

The strawberry is an ancient plant that grows wild throughout Europe and North America. It is an unusual fruit in that its seeds are embedded on its surface. At their best, strawberries have a musky aroma and are sweet but acidic, almost pineapplelike in flavor. They are plump, juicy, and soft as a baby's cheek. California provides 80 percent of the nation's fresh and frozen strawberries. Strawberries are one of the foods permitted irradiation.

Health Benefits Research has determined that strawberries have a tranquilizing effect; that's why surgical gloves for dentists and masks for children's anesthesia are often perfumed with a strawberry scent.

Strawberries are an excellent spring tonic, beneficial to the spleen-pancreas, and used to break down excess toxins in the liver. They increase the appetite and are moistening and lubricating. Strawberries have clinically proven antiviral properties. Some people suffer from hives when they eat strawberries that were not vine ripened.

A kitchen remedy to remove tartar and strengthen teeth is to rub a halved strawberry on the teeth and gums and leave on for 45 minutes. Rinse with warm water.

Strawberries in moderation reduce *vata* and *kapha* and, to a lesser degree, *pitta*. Strawberries provide vitamin A, as much vitamin C as oranges, and some B-complex vitamins, as well as silicon, some potassium, and fiber.

Buying Buy local strawberries, fully red and slightly soft, with hulls intact. Since strawberries do not ripen off the vine, local vine-ripened strawberries will be the most aromatic and flavorful. Out-of-season or out-of-region strawberries may *look* like strawberries, but that's about all. Peak season is from late spring through early summer. Do not remove the green caps until after washing the fruit and just before serving.

See **Fruit**.

STRAWBERRY TOMATO See **Ground Cherry**.

STRING BEAN See **Green Bean**.

Ø SUCANAT

Sucanat, the trademarked acronym for sugarcane natural, is the evaporated and granulated juice of sugarcane and blackstrap molasses. It sucrose level is 90 percent. Although once an unrefined product, it no longer is.

See **Sugar**.

Ø SUCROSE

A simple sugar molecule, sucrose is found in many plants. It is extracted primarily from sugarcane and sugar beets. White sugar contains 99 percent sucrose and rapadura contains 82 percent sucrose. In addition to widespread use as a sweetener, sucrose is used as a preservative in the manufacture of plastics.

See **Sugar; Sweeteners**.

Ø SUGAR

Sugar, by name or under any of its guises, is highly refined by chemical processes from sugarcane, beet sugar, or corn. It contains over 90 percent sucrose. Fortunately, rapa-dura (unrefined, evaporated cane juice) is a healthful, natural alternative. If you do purchase sugar, favor cane sugar—preferably organic—over the more highly processed beet or corn sugar found in generic sugar packages at the supermarket.

Health Benefits Sugar can ease spasms, relieve pain, give a sense of ease and nurture, and, in the short term, boost energy. Sugar acts upon the spleen-pancreas, stomach, kidney, and liver meridians. It passes quickly into the bloodstream, shocking and weakening the digestive system, to result in a blood sugar imbalance that causes a craving for more sugar. Sugar consumption creates an acid condition that consumes the body's minerals and causes calcium loss. Refined sugar use is implicated in all of our contemporary degenerative health problems.

Use Sugar is a primary ingredient in desserts and confections; it is a ubiquitous ingredient in prepared, packaged, and restaurant foods.

Buying Numerous highly refined sugar products attempt to convey a healthful image. These names include, but are not limited to: brown sugar, cane crystals, evaporated cane juice, Demerara sugar, dried cane juice, granulated cane juice, milled cane, molasses, muscovado sugar, natural milled cane sugar, plantation white, raw cane juice, Sucanat, turbinado sugar, unrefined cane sugar, and yellow-D sugar.

See Rapadura; Sweeteners.

SUGAR SNAP PEA
(Pisum sativum macrocarpon)

The sugar snap pea, a cross between a snow pea and a green pea, offers the best of both. Its tender but crisp pod is edible, as are the sugary, plump little peas.

Health Benefits Sugar snap peas are medicinal for the liver and stomach and spleen-pancreas. They are high in vitamins A and B-complex and are a good source of calcium and potassium as well as iron and phosphorus. They reduce *pitta* and *kapha*.

Use Sugar snap peas need only to have the tips removed. They can be cut and added to salads, stir-fries, soups, and more, but possibly the best way to eat them is straight from the garden out of hand.

Buying Sugar snap peas are deep green with peas that are well formed but smaller than green peas. The sugar snap pea is available primarily in the fall and spring.

See **Snow Pea.**

SUMMER SAVORY See **Savory.**

SUMMER SQUASH
(Cucurbita pepo melopepo)

A welcome summer vegetable is the tender, brightly colored summer squash, which comes in a variety of fanciful shapes. Soft-skinned summer squash is mild but flavorful when small and garden fresh. The flavor rapidly diminishes as the size and age increase.

Health Benefits Squash are cooling; they are an excellent summertime food and also balancing for a person with too much heat. Squash contains a fair amount of vitamins A and C, potassium, and calcium. Summer squash is *tridoshic*.

Use Garden-fresh baby summer squash can be served as crudités or finely sliced in salads. Squash longer than three inches is most flavorful when cooked. Size, however, is not always an indication of maturity. An overly mature summer squash has a tough skin, hard seeds, and dry flesh, which makes it best suited to stuffing and baking. When I have an abundance of garden zucchini and yellow squash, I pickle them whole like dill pickles. Summer squash is a popular ingredient in stir-fries, casseroles, and soups, or neat, steamed or sautéed.

Buying The prolific summer squash plants produce continuously throughout the growing season. In the garden, I harvest summer squash just when the blossom withers, for then its flavor is developed, but its flesh is still tender.

Even though zucchini and other summer squash are available from warmer climates during the winter months, they lack flavor. When squash is fresh and seasonal, choose those with brightly colored skin free from discoloration.

See **Bitter Melon; Crookneck Squash; Pattypan; Squash; Zucchini.**

SUNBERRY See **Garden Huckleberry.**

SUNCHOKE See **Jerusalem Artichoke.**

SUNFLOWER FAMILY
(Composita Asteraceae)

One of the largest botanical families, the compositae family (also called the sunflower or daisy family) actually provides us with relatively few food plants. The chief distinguishing characteristic of the plants is that each blossom is composed of two kinds of flowers. The center is composed of individual flowers, each of which becomes a seed. Surrounding this flower are the ray petals. Some of this family also have a milky juice called latex. Many roots of this family contain inulin, a complex carbohydrate that helps diabetics lower blood sugar.

See **Artichoke; Burdock; Cardoon, Celtuce; Chamomile; Chicory; Dahlia; Dandelion; Endive; Garland Chrysanthemum; Jerusalem Artichoke, Lettuce; Salsify; Scorzonera; Sunflower Seed; Tarragon.**

SUNFLOWER OIL

Sunflower oil has the heady aroma of the sunny blossom itself. The sweet, nutty oil, pressed from sunflower seeds, is, when unrefined and fresh, a good source of Omega-3 fatty acids and therefore may not be heated. Use to dress salads or to dress cooked grains or vegetables.

See **Fat and Oil; Sunflower Seed.**

SUNFLOWER SEED
(Helianthus annus)

More than any other flower, the sunflower suggests the glory of the summer sun itself. Wild, it lines roadways and gilds whole fields with its stunning, sun-colored mandalas. Cultivated in home gardens, it towers to impressive heights of fifteen feet in or more and boasts a flower up to two feet in diameter. A showy plant indeed.

This daisy relative, which originated in western North America, is more than just show. Both sunflower seeds and sunflower tubers (Jerusalem artichoke) were important Native American foods. Sunflowers were introduced in Europe in the 1500s and have become a staple in Russia. Until the popularization of health foods in the United States in the 1960s, its domestic use was primarily for bird feed; hence its once common name "polly seed." Sunflower seeds are also nicknamed "sunnies."

The shells may be white, brown, black, or black with white stripes. The U.S. commercial supply comes primarily from the Red River valley of Minnesota.

Health Benefits Sunflower seeds are an energy tonic and nurturing food used to treat constipation. Sunflower seeds contain more protein than beef and 20 percent fat, most of which is unsaturated. A good source of calcium, phosphorus, and iron, as well as vitamins A, D, E, and several of the B-complex, they also contain a trace of fluorine, which may explain the Russians' claim that they are good for the teeth. Sunflower seeds are *tridoshic* used in moderation; in larger quantities, they primarily reduce *vata*.

Use Shelled sunflower seeds can be substituted for nuts in many recipes. The seeds may be ground into a butter similar in use to peanut butter. They are a popular snack food and ingredient in trail mixes and energy bars. To heighten their flavor, toast the seeds lightly in a skillet before eating and season them with soy sauce, if you like.

Buying Sunflower seeds are available shelled or unshelled, roasted and salted, or raw. Whole seeds have a good shelf life but once hulled they need to be refrigerated. Look for unbroken, even-colored seeds. Avoid discolored or rubbery seeds.

See Jerusalem Artichoke; Seeds; Sunflower Family.

SUSHI RICE
(Oryza sativa)

A short-grain, glutinous rice that, contrary to many foods, is prized for its neutral flavor. Since sushi rice doesn't overpower the palate, it doesn't detract from the alluring flavors of raw fish. Rather than each cooked grain being fluffy and distinct, cooked sushi rice sticks together; thus, when formed into an artful sushi morsel, it holds its shape.

See Rice.

SWEDE See Rutabaga.

SWEDISH TURNIP See Rutabaga.

SWEET BEANS See Green Soybean.

SWEET BROWN RICE See Rice.

SWEET CORN
Corn on the Cob
(Zea mays saccharata)

On or off the cob, we think that sweet

corn is as American as apple pie—but it's actually a newcomer to the scene. Popular for only the past hundred years, the first recorded sweet corn was collected from the Iroquois in 1779. The distinguishing characteristic of sweet corn is a defective gene that prevents its sugars from being completely transformed into starch. In other words, sweet corn stays sweet, while other varieties become starchy at maturity.

Buying Fresh sweet corn has vibrant (rather than dry and matted) silk, dark green, compact husks; and firm, full ears. Keep the husks intact until just before cooking. For the sweetest and most delicious dish, fresh and slightly immature (rather than overmature) corn is best. Even though available year-around, sweet corn is primarily a seasonal food because of the superior taste of local, fresh corn. New hybrid varieties have a higher and more durable sugar content that lasts up to ten days after picking; their actual corn flavor is, however, modest.

See **Chicos; Corn.**

SWEETENERS

Mother's milk is sweet. Maybe this is where it all starts, for most everyone loves sweets. This doesn't have to be a problem as long as attention is paid to quality and quantity.

Health Benefits The sweetness found in grains, dairy, meat, legumes, and some vegetables like squash, carrots, and yams strengthens the spleen-pancreas and helps build energy. These foods satisfy the sweet tooth.

"Empty sweets," to use a Chinese medical term, are those primarily composed of simple sugars (sweet fruits, juices, honey, sugar, and other sweeteners). These foods give a short-term energy boost by increasing the amount of sugar in the blood. When concentrated or used in excess, sweets damage the spleen-pancreas. Excessive use leads to chronic fatigue, bodily weakness, edema, and various digestive problems.

Sweeteners composed of maltose, a complex carbohydrate, are relatively more healthful. Barley malt and rice syrup, for example, take longer to assimilate than the more simple sugar molecules do. Unrefined sweeteners reduce *pitta* and *vata*.

Other sweeteners contain glucose, fructose, and sucrose and are more problematic because they are quickly absorbed into the bloodstream, stress the whole metabolism, and suppress the immune system. Such sweeteners cause the pancreas to secrete more insulin to monitor the amount of sugar going into the blood, and extra adrenaline from the adrenal glands is also mobilized to monitor the blood sugar level. Simple sugars provide a few hours of increased energy, which are followed by energy depletion and an emotional low aptly known as the "sugar blues." Thus sweeteners that contain sucrose are best used occasionally and with discretion. These include carob, date sugar, honey, maple syrup, rapadura, and sorghum molasses.

Ø The following list of "Not Recommended" sweeteners is by no means inclusive, since the industry is endlessly coming up with a "better" sweet. (The list does include the sweeteners you're most apt to find in the natural food store, which may currently be promoted as "healthful.") Strive to avoid fructose, fruit juice concentrate, granular fruit sugar, isomol, malitol, mannitol, sorbitol, and xylitol. Because of its widespread use, there's also a brief entry on Aspartame.

See **Aspartame; Barley Malt Sugar; Barley Malt Syrup; Carob; Date Sugar; Fructose; Fruit Juice Concentrate; Granular Fruit Sugar; Honey; Isomol; Malitol; Mannitol; Maple Sugar; Maple Syrup; Molasses; Rapadura; Rice Syrup; Sorbitol; Sorghum Molasses; Stevia; Sugar; Xylitol.**

SWEET FENNEL See Fennel.

SWEET IMPERIAL ONION See Onion.

SWEET LAUREL See Bay Leaf.

SWEET MARJORAM See Marjoram.

SWEET PEPPER
(Capsicum)

During Indian summer, sweet peppers rival all other produce at market displays in terms of their flashy hues. Plump and glossy, the peppers range from delicately sweet and peppery to very sweet in taste. They come in a variety of shapes as well as colors. The pepper is so adept at cross-pollination that we can anticipate many more new colors, shapes, and flavors in the future. Florida, California, and Texas supply most of the peppers except during the winter months, when they are imported from South America.

Health Benefits Peppers are cooling and improve the appetite; their frequent use, however, is not recommended for people with weak digestion or for those in frail health. Peppers reduce *pitta* and *kapha*.

Use Sweet peppers can be served raw in salads and as finger food; they can be roasted, sautéed, or stuffed, or they can be added to soups and stews. This Native American food now figures prominently in ethnic cuisine throughout the world.

Buying The color of pepper depends on the variety. Many peppers are green through most of their development but turn red as they reach full maturity. Others are black, purple, brown, or yellow at maturity. The riper the pepper, the greater its flavor and nutrition. Select firm, glossy peppers with stems intact. Avoid those with soft spots or shriveled, pale skin, signs that they are past their prime. In general, those with thinner skins are more peppery; those with thicker skins, sweeter.

- **Banana Pepper** Long and tapered, usually bright yellow but also green or orange-red, with a thin wall. It is preferred by many over the bell pepper. The banana pepper, also called Hungarian pepper, may be fried or served raw.

- **Bell Pepper** Boxy in shape and green, red, yellow, or purple in color, with a thick wall. Crisp with a refreshing taste, the bell pepper is equally good cooked or raw. Red bell pepper, a fully mature green bell, is the sweetest of the bells; it tastes excellent raw or cooked. The yellow bell pepper is pleasantly sweet but less flavorful than the banana pepper. The purple bell pepper is eggplant colored on the outside and green inside. Cooking may render its purple flesh an unappetizing gray, so it is most often served raw.

- **European Sweet Pepper** Similar to the bell pepper in shape but larger with tapered ends; green, red, yellow, purple, or even brown. Very thick fleshed.
- **Pimiento** Small to medium, squat, and dark red, with thick flesh.

See **Chile Pepper; Nightshade Family.**

SWEET POTATO
Boniato, Yam
(Ipomoea batatas)

The sweet potato is sweet. It is native to South America, a member of the morning glory family, and related to that horrible garden nuisance, bindweed. The sweet potato is actually not related to the potato nor to the yam, though very sweet, and dark sweet potatoes are called yams. True yams are native to Africa and are very popular in tropical and subtropical countries.

Health Benefits Higher in sugar than potatoes, sweet potatoes are also an excellent source of carotenoid antioxidants; they also contain calcium. They are high in vitamins A and C, with a fair amount of thiamine. In Oriental medicine, sweet potatoes are valued for nourishing the spleen-pancreas, stomach, and large intestine meridians; for quenching thirst; and for lubricating dry conditions. Sweet potatoes are also valued for building the kidneys; overconsumption, however, may cause abdominal swelling and indigestion. Sweet potatoes reduce *pitta* and *vata*.

Use Cooking converts most of the sweet potato's starches and softens it into a sweet and soft, or dry vegetable, depending upon the variety. While candied yams are a classic holiday dish, sweet potatoes can be eaten throughout the year; they can be substituted for squash or carrots in soups, salads, pilafs, and baked goods. Sweet potato pie is a southern classic.

Buying Select smooth-skinned sweet potatoes with tapered ends and no bruises or harvesting scars. Size is of no concern in terms of sweetness or storage capability. Sweet potatoes bruise easily, so handle with care. Store in a cool, dry area. Sweet potatoes are at their peak in late fall. The sweet potato is denser than a potato, so allow a somewhat smaller serving size per person.

The Jersey or dry sweet potato has a buff skin with a firm yellow flesh. When cooked, it has a fluffy dry texture, similar to a potato, and a delicate (rather than overpowering) sweetness. This potato is more favored in northern states.

The deep orange or purple-skinned sweet potato—also called jewel or garnet yam—has soft, moist flesh colored a flamboyant orange. This sugar-sweet vegetable is suitable as a dessert or as a winter squash substitute.

SWEET POTATO SQUASH See **Delicata Squash.**

SWEET RICE See **Rice.**

SWEET RICE WINE See **Mirin.**

SWISS CHARD See **Chard.**

TAHINI

Tahini is a creamy smooth paste ground from hulled sesame seeds (as opposed to sesame butter, which is ground from whole, or unhulled, sesame seeds). This high-protein spread is a culinary staple in Middle Eastern and some Asian cultures.

Use Tahini is an oily ingredient used in dressings, sauces, and desserts. In some recipes, tahini serves as an oil, egg, and/or milk replacement. In whole foods recipes, sesame butter replaces tahini. Tahini is an essential ingredient in halvah, hummus, and baba ghanoush.

Buying The best tahini is made from mechanically hulled seeds and is sweet and nutty tasting. Commercial tahini, made from seeds hulled and processed in caustic chemical baths, tastes bitter and slightly soapy.

See **Sesame; Sesame Butter.**

TAHITI LIME See Lime.

TAI GOO CHOY See Tatsoi.

TAI SAI See Bok Choy.

TAMARI See Soy Sauce.

TAMARILLO
Tree Tomato
(Cyphomandra betacae)

The tamarillo is an attractive fruit. The size and shape of an egg, it has a patent leather–like red or yellow skin. Its dense, copper-colored flesh is pleasantly bitter and contains a number of soft, small magenta-colored seeds. Not surprisingly, this tomato relative has an aroma like a tomato.

Health Benefits The tamarillo is a good source of vitamins A and C and is low in calories. As a member of the nightshade family, it contains the toxic alkaloid solanine.

Use The aromatic tamarillo requires peeling. Its meaty texture is best when cooked in relishes, chutneys, and sweet and savory sauces. Tamarillo may also be sliced and served with other fruits in a salad or cooked in a compote.

Buying Tamarillos are primarily available

as a New Zealand import from early summer through the fall. Choose a firm, heavy tamarillo as you would select a tomato and allow it to soften at room temperature. Then refrigerate for up to a week. The more yellow the fruit, the sweeter it is.

See **Nightshade Family.**

TAMARIND
(Tamarindus indica)

Tamarind pulp is used in Sri Lanka, India, Mexico, and other tropical regions the way lemon is used as an acid seasoning agent in the West. This sticky brown fruit from the tamarind tree tastes like apricots and dates. The pulp, contained in a luguminous pod with a tan, papery skin, surrounds inedible seeds.

Health Benefits Tamarind is astringent; it aids digestion, lowers fever, and has antiseptic and laxative effects. It reduces nausea in pregnancy, and treats jaundice, fever, and dysentery. Tamarind reduces *vata.*

Use The secret seasoning in Worcestershire sauce, tamarind is also used as a curry ingredient and by itself to season meat, vegetable, and bean dishes as well as tropical beverages. Tamarind fruit is also made into confections and eaten fresh.

To use, remove the hard outer shell and strings from the tamarind pods. Boil in water to cover for 2 minutes. Allow to cool. With your fingers, press the seeds from the pulp. Discard the seeds and pods. Using a fork, purée the pulp with the water to create an extract. Use as directed in recipes. The extract can be stored in a closed jar in the refrigerator for up to a week.

Buying Tamarind is available in the specialty section of supermarkets. In Indian, Asian, and Mexican markets, the pulp is available in an easy-to-use paste form. The paste may be stored for a year or more. Tamarind is also available powdered.

See **Herbs and Spices; Legume Family; Tropical Fruit.**

TANGELO
(Citrus paradisi x C. reticulata)

Cross a mandarin and a grapefruit and you get a tangelo, an easy-to-peel fruit, which tastes like an orange and mandarin. The mineola tangelo contains few seeds, is sweet, and has a nipple at the stem end. The Orlando variety is smaller, rounder, and without an enlarged neck; it has more of a grapefruit's tang.

See **Citrus Family; Grapefruit; Mandarin.**

TANGERINE
(Citrus reticulata)

Named for the Moroccan port Tangier, where it was first marketed, this small mandarin citrus fruit is deep red orange in color. The most popular variety is the Dancy.

See **Citrus Family; Mandarin.**

TANGOR
(Citrus reticulata x C. sinensis)

A cross between the tangerine and the sweet orange, the tangor is sweet and tangy—and thus its name, tangor. Like a tangerine, this fruit is loosely skinned. The most readily available tangors are the Hamlin, honey tangerine (also called the Murcott honey orange), pineapple orange, and the Temple orange.

See **Citrus Family.**

TANNIA See Yautia.

TAPIOCA

Tapioca, a traditional Brazilian food, is extracted from a cassava variety rich in starch but with a bitter and toxic hydrocyanide content. The purified starch, or *tipioca* in the language of the Tupi peoples of the Amazon region, makes an excellent thickener and pudding. Tapioca was widely used in puddings in the United States until displaced by easier-to-use gelatin and agar products.

Health Benefits Tapioca is soothing, nutritious, and easy to digest. It's medicinal for convalescents and anyone with a compromised digestive system. Tapioca reduces *pitta* and *kapha*.

Use When set, the starch in tapioca, amylopectin, is crystal clear and glossy, which makes it an ideal glaze. However, tapioca thins if reheated. With exposure to air, tapioca loses its thickening action over time. Unlike instant tapioca or tapioca flour, pearl tapioca must be soaked for 45 to 75 minutes before being cooked.

Buying When processed from cassava, tapioca forms small pearls, which are graded into varying sizes and available as pearl tapioca. Or tapioca may be precooked and ground, flaked, or granulated into instant tapioca. Pure tapioca powder is available in Asian markets. Quick tapioca is available in supermarkets and some natural food stores.

See **Cassava**.

TARO
Albi, Dasheen, Eddo
(Colocasia esculenta)

Taro is a potatolike tuber with widespread use throughout Asia and the tropics. It has a shaggy, barklike brown skin circled with distinct rings. Its crisp white, cream, or almost lilac flesh has a mild flavor, tasting something like chestnuts. Hawaiians ferment the taro to produce their "staff of life," poi.

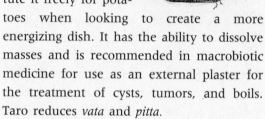

Health Benefits In Chinese medicine, taro is used to strengthen the stomach and spleen-pancreas and for loss of appetite and fatigue owing to weak digestion. I substitute it freely for potatoes when looking to create a more energizing dish. It has the ability to dissolve masses and is recommended in macrobiotic medicine for use as an external plaster for the treatment of cysts, tumors, and boils. Taro reduces *vata* and *pitta*.

High in potassium and a fair source of calcium and iron, the taro contains vitamins B_1, B_2, and C. Taro is always cooked to deactivate its calcium oxalate crystals, which otherwise irritate the mouth and throat.

Use As a food, taro may be substituted for potatoes, but expect a drier, sweeter, nuttier flavor. My favorite use for taro is in soups, where it holds its shape nicely and absorbs other flavors. Taro may be baked, steamed, or broiled. It is crisp and delicious when thinly sliced and pan- or deep-fried. Wear gloves when peeling taro, to avoid skin irritation.

Buying This plant produces two types of tubers. One is a large turnip-shape and turnip-size "corm," from which the leaf stalks grow. There are also smaller, subsidiary cormels, the size of an egg, which grow attached to the main corm by rootlets. Select corms that are moist and plump and show no sign of withering. Store as you would potatoes—in a cool, well-ventilated place—and use before they start to soften.

Taro is available in Asian markets and some large supermarkets.

TARRAGON
(Artemisia dracunculus)

Believed an antidote for bites of venomous animals, tarragon's name probably comes from the Greek *drakon* for "little dragon." The aromatic, long, delicate, polished gray green tarragon leaves are a favorite in French cuisine. Its flavor and aroma are reminiscent of anise but more briskly tart. The only common culinary herb from the important artemisia genus, which gives us sagebrush, mugwort, and wormwood, tarragon originated in Russia.

Health Benefits Tarragon is a bitter, warming herb that supports the digestive system and helps expel parasites in children. It has diuretic properties and helps lower fevers, but is not recommended during pregnancy. Tarragon reduces *vata* and *kapha*.

Use A classic ingredient in tartar and béarnaise sauces, fresh tarragon enhances salads and dressings and vegetable, poultry, and fish dishes. It is especially compatible with beans, mushrooms, squash, and eggs and is a favorite herb for flavoring vinegar. Use sparingly, as its flavor easily overpowers other ingredients.

Buying Tarragon is available both fresh and dried. Even more so than other herbs, dried tarragon has less flavor than fresh and

---

FORMERLY FERTILE

Tarragon flowers are always barren. There is, coincidentally, an ever increasing number of foods that are incapable of reproducing themselves at all or of reproducing themselves true to form due to hybridization or infertility. If we are what we eat, possibly our rapidly increasing consumption of sterile foods—from eggs and beef to bananas and seedless grapes—may be implicated in the increasing rate of human infertility.

In the case of tarragon, several hundred years ago the plant produced fertile seed, but because cultivars propagated by division or root cuttings were favored, the fertile plants were irretrievably lost.

---

is hardly worth the bother of drying it or of purchasing it dried. French tarragon, also called true tarragon, has less of a bite than Russian tarragon.

See **Herbs and Spices.**

TART CHERRY See **Sour Cherry.**

TATSOI
Flat Cabbage,
Tai Goo Choy
(Brassica
rosularis)

In my garden, these small, flat nosegays of deep forest green are a favorite crop. As with its nearest cousin, bok

choy, tatsoi is good in almost any cooked preparation, and its young leaves are also delicious raw. Compared to arugula, tatsoi is sweeter and lacks the bite. Tatsoi leaves are a common mesclun ingredient. Primarily available in farmers' markets and Asian markets.

See **Bok Choy; Cabbage Family.**

TEA
(Camellia sinensis)

According to legend, tea—which has eye-shape leaves—sprang from the eyelids of the Bodhidarma. This semimythical Indian who introduced Chen Buddhism to China in the first century A.D. vowed to meditate for nine years straight. Despite his most firm resolve, he dozed. In anger, Bodhidarma cut off his own eyelids and threw them to the ground. From that spot emerged the tea plant, whose leaves help us remain alert.

Second only to water, the world's most widely consumed beverage comes from a small, native Chinese evergreen tree with stiff, shiny, pointed leaves. Its leaves—and, to a much lesser extent, its blossoms and twigs—are used as a refreshing and mildly stimulating infusion.

Just-harvested tea leaves make an insipid, thin, raw-tasting brew, and so must be processed. Tea is grown and processed on large tea plantations throughout China, Japan, Taiwan, Indonesia, India, and Sri Lanka. Tea from the tea bush is not to be confused with herbal drinks or tisanes, also called teas.

Health Benefits The therapeutic benefits of tea are impressive. Recent research shows that both black and green tea inhibit tumor cells, help prevent heart disease, strengthen the immune system, have antioxidant activ-ity, reduce cavities, and retard atherosclerosis. This broad array of health benefits is derived from tea's rich supply of polyphenols. Green tea is a better source of polyphenols and is generally considered the more medicinal of the two kinds of tea.

Green tea is considered cooling, black tea more warming. Strong tea, in excess, is mucus forming. When milk is added to tea, either green or black, the milk totally inhibits the tea's antioxidant activity. Tea aids digestion, relieves thirst, and is a diuretic.

Like coffee and chocolate, tea affects the central nervous system with three stimulants: caffeine, theophylline, and theobromine. Caffeine predominates in coffee, theophylline in tea, and theobromine in chocolate. Tea also contains from 5 to 20 percent tannin. Tannin, which gives tea its body, is a growth depressant—and therefore tea is not recommended for children. Also, excessive tea consumption can deplete iron, yet another reason children should not drink tea. Neither is it advised for people with a tendency toward forming calcium oxalate kidney stones.

Tea contains the B vitamin folacin, vitamin C, fluoride, and magnesium. It reduces *kapha.*

Use Tea etiquette ranges from the highly stylized and formal Japanese tea ceremony to a rushed, microwaved, generic orange pekoe in a Styrofoam cup at the local convenience store. Granted, tea bags make brewing a tidy event. If the bag dangles from a plastic strip, however, consider removing that strip, since, as you may well imagine, infused plastic does *not* enhance the flavor of tea.

Buying For tea connoisseurs, several factors determine quality besides its being organic. These include the leaves' age and the season they were harvested in, as well as the elevation and geographical region they were grown in. The size of the leaf also makes a difference in quality and whether it's whole, broken, or bruised. Brick tea, with leaves that are compressed into a solid mass, is considered inferior to loose tea.

There are hundreds of tea varieties. They are either fermented or nonfermented (green). The most popular fermented tea is black; partially fermented tea is red (oolong or yellow).

- **Black Tea** Leaves are fermented through enzymatic oxidation. Leaves darken and release their bitterness, producing a tea that is more robust in body, aroma, flavor, and color. These teas are primarily produced in India and China; they comprise over 95 percent of world production.
- **Green Tea** Leaves are steam heated to deactivate their enzymes and dried immediately after harvest. They have a thin, mild, fruity but sometimes astringent flavor and a pale yellow color. Japan and China produce green tea.
- **Red Tea** (Also called yellow or oolong.) Lighter in color and less fermented than a black tea, red tea is lighter in flavor, body, and character than black tea. Red tea is grown in Formosa and China.
- **White Tea** The most subtle tea in flavor and color, the leaves only are dried. They are neither steam heated

---

WHY A PROPER CUP OF TEA REQUIRES JUST BOILED WATER AND FAVORS LOWER ELEVATIONS

If made from reheated or overboiled water, which has lost some oxygen, tea tastes flat. To treat yourself to an excellent cup of tea, use just-boiled water. At high elevations, the water boils at a lower temperature and so getting a full extraction is difficult. Here are aids to making an excellent cup of tea.

Good tea requires quality tea, good water, an enamel or glass pot for boiling the water, a ceramic teapot, and a relaxed atmosphere in which to sip. Use loose tea so the hot water can better circulate, coaxing out the tea's maximum flavor. (Stainless steel infusing spoons, tea balls, or strainers inhibit adequate water circulation through the leaves.)

Warm the teapot with hot water and then drain it. Bring water to a boil. Add a teaspoon of tea for every cup desired, plus one for the pot, to the warmed pot. Just as the water comes to a full boil, immediately pour it over the tea, cover, and allow to steep for 3 to 5 minutes. Serve, straining if necessary, as is, or with lemon or milk. Sit back, relax, sip, and savor.

nor fermented. This Chinese product is expensive and has limited availability.

- **Flavored Tea** Tea may be flavored with floral, spice, fruit, or chemical extracts or agents. Flavored teas are prepared in a range of ways, from adding flower blossoms, such as jasmine, to flavoring with the citrus oil bergamot, as for the classic Earl Grey tea. Making your own house blend is as easy as putting a cinnamon stick, cardamom pod, or other flavoring agent in a tea container, closing it, and letting the flavors meld for several weeks or more.

- **Decaffeinated Tea** Tea decaffeinated with ethyl acetate is not recommended. Buy only water-processed decaf tea.

- **Instant Tea** Like instant coffee, instant tea is made by spray drying a tea infusion.

See **Twig Tea.**

TEA KVASS See Kombucha.

TEA MUSHROOM See Kombucha.

TEF
Teff, T'ef
(Eragrostis tef)

In the rugged Simian Mountains, at the source of the Blue Nile, grows a tiny cereal grain, tef. This prized Ethiopian staple was virtually unknown outside of Ethiopia until this century. Tef is so small that 150 grains weigh the same as a single kernel of wheat. For a grain, it has a uniquely sweet and ro-

bust flavor. Because tef has zero economic value in the world market, the Ethiopian government discourages its cultivation. In addition, the cultural disruption brought on by the warfare and famine of the last several decades has caused the irretrievable loss of many valuable tef varieties.

Thanks to the recent interest in underutilized grains—and the demand by Ethiopian immigrants—tef is now grown in the United States (Caldwell, Idaho, to be precise) and is available in natural food stores.

Health Benefits Ayurvedic writer Amadea Morningstar observes that tef is definitely *sattvic* (helps the mind become clear and stay focused). Because of the grain's sweet flavor and its high mineral concentration, I find it supportive to the kidneys, stomach, and spleen-pancreas function. Tef reduces *vata* and *pitta* and in moderation can be used by *kapha*. As an ancient grain like quinoa and amaranth, it is often well tolerated by people with O blood type.

Tef is a remarkably rich source of calcium and is an excellent source of iron, zinc, and copper. It is, for a grain, high in protein.

Use For people who like small grains like amaranth—and I admit I am one—the texture of tef is enjoyable. Others, who object to the tiny size of the whole grain, will enjoy tef flour. In fact, traditionally, tef is used as a flour rather than as a whole grain.

To cook whole tef, lightly toast 1 cup in a dry skillet for about 3 minutes, or until it starts to pop and emits a pleasant aroma. Add 1½ cups boiling seasoned stock or water, cover, and simmer for 15 minutes. Serve with a condiment or as a side dish.

Buying Tef is available in bulk or packaged from most natural food stores and some specialty foods stores, or by mail order (see page 401). It comes in various colors, including ivory, red, and a deep chocolate brown. The most flavorful available is the brown. Store tef, tightly wrapped, in a cool, dark cupboard for up to a year.

See **Grains**.

TEF FLOUR

The Ethiopians use tef flour to make their staple, injera, which is a large—up to two feet in diameter—flatbread. The dough is fermented for three days, and the injera is soft and limp like a crepe but with a moist spongy texture and a decidedly sour flavor. When ordering injera in an Ethiopian restaurant, request a tef injera if you want the real thing; otherwise, the injera will be made of a less expensive millet or wheat flour. Tef injera calms *vata*.

Use To my palate, sweet and nutty flavored tef flour is a superior flour for cookies, cakes, and quick breads. My favorites include spicy banana-nut muffins, waffles, and a gingery cake. I substitute tef flour for part or all of the wheat flour in these recipes.

Please don't add tef flour to a yeast bread, however. Like grapes, tef has its own symbiotic yeast, and the synergy between the two is wild. The dough runs amuck and creates a fetid stench that takes hours to air out of the house.

Buying Tef flour is available from many natural food stores. The grains are too small to be ground in a blender or a small grinder. Making your own requires a flour mill.

See **Flour**.

TEMPEH

Tempeh is a traditional Indonesian food made by splitting, cooking, and fermenting soybeans. More versatile than tofu, tempeh's hearty texture holds bold flavors and lends itself to vegetarian burgers, kabobs, mock chicken salad, and the like. William Shurtleff and Akiko Aoyagi, in *The Book of Tempeh*, tell this food's history and also give complete instructions for making it from scratch.

Health Benefits With an easily assimilable protein content of 19.5 percent (50 percent more than hamburger), tempeh is an energy-building food, especially good for people with low energy. Homemade tempeh is one of the world's richest sources of B_{12}. This vitamin is not available in commercial tempeh. Tempeh contains the important Omega-3 fatty acids. Tempeh is bound together with a mycelium of branching, threadlike enzymes. This mycelium makes the soy easily digestible, provides many valuable B vitamins, and produces a natural antibiotic, which supports immune system function. Tempeh reduces *pitta*.

Use Tempeh is not eaten raw. Steamed, baked, grilled, broiled, or fried, tempeh appeals to all palates, especially fried or grilled, when it becomes reminiscent of southern fried chicken or seafood fillets. Assertive seasonings like garlic, ginger, curry, and coriander complement it; souring agents such as wine, lemon juice, or vinegar enhance it. Seasoned tempeh cutlets that can go directly onto the grill are also available.

Buying Available in thin, eight-ounce cakes in the refrigerator or freezer section of natural food stores. Fresh tempeh is preferable to frozen tempeh. Fresh tempeh smells mushroomlike and its cottony mold is either white, gray, or black. Compost tempeh that has an unpleasant ammonia aroma or with any other color of mold.

Grains or other foods, such as rice, wild rice, arame seaweed, coconut, or peanuts, may be fermented with soy to make a variety of tempeh blends.

See **Fermented Foods; Soybean.**

TEMPLE ORANGE
Royal Mandarin
(Citrus reticulata* x *C. sinensis)

A medium-large cross between an orange and a tangerine with a pebbly skin that easily peels off, the Temple orange is juicy and has a snappy, sweet flavor.

See **Citrus Family; Tangor.**

TEXAS SWEET ONION See **Onion.**

TEXMATI RICE See **Basmati Rice.**

Ø TEXTURED SOY PROTEIN
Meat Analog, Meat Extender, TSP

Textured soy protein (TSP) is a shoddy product that's often confused with textured vegetable protein (TVP) because they are similar in appearance and use. According to soy expert and author Dana Jacobi, TSP has a slight edge over TVP because it's less apt to cause gastric distress. However, few stores or labels distinguish between the two products, which are both produced from commercial (rather than organic) soybeans by the giant food processor Archer-Daniels-Midland.

See **Soybean; Soy Isolate.**

Ø TEXTURED VEGETABLE PROTEIN
Meat Analog, Meat Extender, TVP

Here's an ingredient to avoid for two good reasons. One, textured vegetable protein (TVP) is a highly refined byproduct of soy oil production. Two, it often causes gastric distress because it contains the hard-to-digest oligosaccharides found in soybeans.

TVP is made from soy isolate, soy protein that's chemically extracted from defatted soy meal. It is extruded under high pressure and spun into bits or chunks of marketable foodstuffs. TVP chunks are firm and chewy like meat, but unlike meat they are bland tasting. When flavored and colored, however, TVP imitates a wide variety of animal proteins.

In natural food stores TVP is available in bulk bins and packaged in granules, flakes, or chunks that look like dry dog kibble. As an ingredient, it is found in countless products from vegetarian burgers to an extender in chile con carne. TVP is used as a cheap filler in fish, nut, and vegetable dishes as well as in sauces, lasagna, frozen desserts, and breakfast cereal.

For healthful and excellent-tasting, low-technology meat analogs consider fu, seitan, tempeh, tofu, or yuba. Or cook up a pot of beans.

See **Soybean; Soy Isolate; Textured Soy Protein.**

THAI BLACK STICKY RICE See **Black Sticky Rice; Rice.**

THAI GINGER See Galangal.

THYME
(Thymus vulgaris)

> Wind-bit thyme that smells like the perfume of the dawn in paradise.
> —Rudyard Kipling

Balmy, aromatic thyme, a native of southern Europe, is a very small undershrub, with slender woody stems and gray-green leaves. There are over one hundred species of this herb, whose name comes from the Greek for "to burn as incense." Thyme was valued by the ancient Greeks and Romans as an aphrodisiac and for instilling bravery and courage. Or, in the words of Euell Gibbons in *Stalking the Healthful Herbs,* "According to ancient tradition, if a girl wears a corsage of wild thyme flowers, it means that she is looking for a sweetheart; and according to another tradition, if a bashful boy drinks enough wild thyme tea, it will give him courage to take her up on it."

Health Benefits The primary fragrant oil of thyme, thymol, is a powerful antiseptic used in Listerine mouthwash, cough drops, and vapor rubs. It is medicinal for the lungs, liver, and stomach and relieves lung congestion, whooping cough, candida, and indigestion. It destroys some intestinal hookworms and roundworms. In aromatherapy, thyme is used to relieve mental instability, melancholy, and nightmares and to prevent memory loss and inefficiency. Thyme reduces *vata* and *kapha.*

"Taken before sleeping, it is a remedy against nightmare," according to Michael Tierra in *Planetary Herbology.* "It has both stimulant and relaxant properties so that it tends to regulate the system as needed."

Use Thyme is one of the most popular herbs for flavoring soups, stews, stuffing, and sauces, either alone or in a *bouquet garni.* It performs especially well in slowly cooked dishes, and it doesn't overpower other flavors. Among the many different varieties of thyme are lemon thyme and caraway-scented thyme.

Thyme leaves are tiny and their stems are woody—so instructions for using the fresh

---

THYME-HONEY COUGH SYRUP

This is so very easy to make and so much more soothing than a ready-made cough syrup. I hope you'll try it. One teaspoon taken every hour will relieve a cough.

    2 cups boiling water
    3 tablespoons dried thyme
    1 cup honey

Bring the water to a boil in a small saucepan. Remove from the heat. Add thyme, cover, and steep until cool. Strain. Stir in 1 cup honey. Store in a covered glass jar, refrigerated, for several months.

herb range from tying thyme up in cheese-cloth to stripping the leaves through the tines of a fork. Here's my method: Cook thyme sprigs in the dish and then discard the sprig as you would a bay leaf.

See Herbs and Spices.

TOFU
Bean Curd, Soybean Curd

Tofu, the best known soy food in America, has moved from an obscure curiosity to a common staple in American cuisine over the past few decades—and with good reason. It has a mild, unimposing, delicate flavor and a chameleonlike ability to take on the flavor of whatever food it is cooked with. Tofu has the consistency of a firm custard. It is made from soymilk curdled with nigari or calcium sulfate. Tofu originated in China, but the product generally available in the United States is Japanese-style tofu.

Health Benefits Tofu supports the colon and lung systems, is a cooling food, and, when lightly cooked, is especially good for people who feel too hot or who have high blood pressure. Tofu is said to neutralize toxins. Used as a poultice, it is excellent to reduce fever or to reduce congestion from a concussion or a bump on the head.

When combined with grains, tofu yields easily digested high-quality protein. Tofu is cholesterolfree and low in saturated fats. It is an excellent source of calcium; depending upon the coagulant used, it can equal milk in calcium content. It is a good source of other minerals such as iron, phosphorus, potassium, and sodium. It also contains essential B vitamins, choline, and fat-soluble vitamin E.

Tofu reduces *vata*, *pitta*, and, when well spiced, *kapha*. Depending upon their constitutional type, *vata*s may or may not tolerate tofu well.

Use Drain tofu, and if using it in dressing or in a sauce, blanch it in boiling water for one minute. Or cut tofu to desired size and pan-fry, bake, broil, steam, or simmer with ingredients and flavors of choice. For a meatier texture, freeze tofu for at least two weeks. Thaw, squeeze out the water, break into small pieces, and sauté with robustly flavored seasoning agents.

Buying Tofu is available extra firm, firm, or soft, according to the percentage of water contained. Soft tofu is more delicate and is better suited to soups and desserts. Harder tofu holds its shape better in stir-fried and grilled dishes.

TEMPERATURE OF SEX

If you were to describe good sex in terms of temperature, would it be "hot" or "cold"?

Cooling foods, like tofu, tend to temporarily reduce the blood flow to the regenerative organs. This explains why tofu was used by some Buddhist monks to abate their sexual desires.

If it's a cold day and you're feeling cold and in the mood for tofu, then prepare it with warming foods such as onions, ginger, and garlic; it will warm you. Traditionally, tofu was served as a savory dish, rather than (as many do in the West) sweetened (which makes it cooling) as a dessert ingredient or even as an ice cream substitute.

Water-packed tofu from the refrigerated section of a supermarket or natural food store has a superior flavor if it's made with the traditional coagulant, nigari. (The coagulant calcium sulfate increases tofu's calcium content significantly.)

I do not recommend tofu in shelf-stable (not refrigerated) packages. This highly processed product lacks palatability. Nor do I recommend purchasing water-packed tofu in blocks from open buckets, which are subject to contamination. And, of course, do not purchase tofu if it is past the expiration date on the package.

Store water-packed tofu refrigerated in its package until use. Once opened, store unused tofu in a covered plastic tub or glass jar, with water to cover. If you change the water every few days, the tofu will last up to a week. If the tofu develops a sour flavor, discard it.

See **Okara; Soybean; Yaki Tofu.**

TOMATILLO
Husk Tomato
(*Physalis ixocarpa*)

The tomatillo comes wrapped in a fanciful parchmentlike husk, and the enclosed fruit, which ranges in size from a cherry tomato to a small egg, is yellow when ripe. Most often it is used green.

In texture and flavor, the tomatillo is like a green plum—sweet and sour but with a delightful aroma of fresh-mown hay. Its lemony balm and gelatinous texture lend body and flavor to a variety of sauces.

Use This member of the nightshade family is featured in southwestern and Mexican cuisine. Cooking enhances its flavor and softens its skin. Tomatillos are primarily used in salsa and sauces, but they may also be added, raw, to salads.

Buying Look for tomatillos throughout the year. If they're not in your supermarket, you'll find them in Latino food stores. Select those that are firm and evenly colored, with intact dry husks. They hold refrigerated for several weeks. Husk just prior to use.

See **Nightshade Family.**

TOMATO
(*Lycopersicon esculentum*)

Botanically speaking, tomatoes are a fruit, but technically they're a berry, since they are pulpy and contain one or more soft seeds. According to an 1893 United States Supreme Court ruling, however, the tomato is legally classified as a vegetable because it is used as a vegetable. Now, there's some logic.

After potatoes and iceberg lettuce, tomatoes are the most commonly consumed vegetable in the United States. But tomatoes rank above all produce in terms of popular fervor, which upholds them as a dietary necessity. Considering that 80 years ago most Americans regarded this South American food as an oddity, or even as poisonous, this is a remarkable about-face. Controversy regarding its healthfulness, or lack thereof, remains.

Tomatoes are produced in all states; our primary sources are Texas, California, Florida, and Ohio. From January through April, many tomatoes are imported from Mexico and Cuba.

Health Benefits Tomatoes have both a sweet and sour flavor, are cooling, and act on the stomach and liver meridians. They clear heat, promote body fluids, nourish yin, and cool and detoxify the blood.

Even though the tomato is acidic, after digestion it alkalizes the blood and is useful in some cases of gout and rheumatism. However, because they upset calcium balance due to their solanine content, tomatoes are best avoided by people with arthritis or osteoporosis.

Tomatoes are on the macrobiotic "use almost never" list because they are too yin, too acidic, and therefore—with long term use—weakening to the gastrointestinal tract. According to Dr. Bernard Jensen, author of the popular *Foods That Heal,* the acids of green tomatoes are especially detrimental to the kidneys.

In the Ayurvedic tradition, tomatoes are problematic for two reasons. They are *rajasic,* stimulating outward motion, creativity, aggression, and passion—a food recommended to warriors before battle. Secondly, their sour *vipak,* or postdigestive effect, makes them stay sour after metabolism, which—with extended or excessive use—irritates the gut, to which any person with an ulcer or an already sensitive stomach will attest. When cooked with warming spices like cumin or mustard, they are a more balanced food. The peel and seeds are most aggravating to *vata.*

The highest concentration of vitamin C is in the jellylike substance that surrounds each seed. Vine-ripened tomatoes are an excellent source of vitamin C and a good source of vitamins A and B-complex and of potassium and phosphorus. A hothouse-grown tomato has half the vitamin C as a field-grown one. Tomatoes are rich in sugar (fructose, glucose, and sucrose), have a moderate fiber content, and are devoid of starch. They contain lycopene, flavonoids, and other phytochemicals with anticarcinogenic properties.

Use The easiest way to slice a tomato is with a serrated knife. To retain its juice, slice lengthwise from stem to blossom end rather than crosswise. Because tomato seeds are hard to digest, it is best to remove them; because the skin is tough, it can also be removed. To seed a tomato, cut it open, set a strainer over a bowl, and squeeze the tomato firmly enough to push out the seeds. Discard the seeds and reserve the juice.

Never cook tomatoes in aluminum or cast iron; their acid binds with these metals, and this will impart a metallic flavor to the tomatoes.

Buying Because ripe tomatoes are fragile and don't withstand shipping, the commercial crop is picked and shipped when green and then "hard-ripened" with ethylene gas, which turns the skin red by eliminating the chlorophyll. Such a tomato has negligible flavor and aroma. If tomato seeds, or any part of its fleshy interior, are green, then it was picked green, despite its cosmetic red facade.

The best assurance of a delicious tomato is to purchase it from a local grower during tomato harvest season, which is, in temperate regions, roughly from mid-July up to the first frost. Hydroponic and hothouse tomatoes lack the flavor and nutrition of vine-ripened field tomatoes, but at least they may

$25,000 TEST-TUBE TOMATO

Calgene, Inc., of Davis, California, has spent twelve years and at least $25 million developing a genetically engineered Flavr Savr tomato. Scientists reversed the gene responsible for softening tomatoes and then injected it back into the tomatoes. Now all the tomatoes descended from this test-tube baby have a genetically scrambled code that makes them tough enough to withstand cross-country shipping. The advantage of the Flavr Savr to producers is obvious; its advantage to consumers less clear.

be grown (and in some areas, purchased) locally twelve months of the year.

Purchase tomatoes that are firm but yield slightly to pressure and have an even, bright red color and a rich tomato aroma. Avoid those with bruises, cracks, and dark spots. To ripen immature tomatoes, put them in a closed paper bag or in your fruit bowl for about three days, or until fully ripened. Use fresh. Do not refrigerate tomatoes; refrigeration drains their flavor and gives a mealy texture.

See **Nightshade Family.**

TOMATOES, DRIED

Drying does not enhance the flavor of most vegetables, but it does concentrate and enhance the flavors of fruits, including tomatoes. Dried tomatoes have a sweet, roasted flavor. They are a popular ingredient in Mediterranean cuisine. They are available packed in oil or dry-packed. The former need only to be drained; the latter need to be rehydrated in a 2-minute-long boiling water bath.

Domestic and organic dried tomatoes are available in quality food stores, but they may also be sun dried or oven dried at home.

TRAILING BLACKBERRY See Dewberry.

TREE EAR MUSHROOM See Wood Ear.

TREE TOMATO See Tamarillo.

TRITICALE
(Triticum x Secale)

A laboratory hybrid of wheat and rye, here's a dud that has all but slipped into oblivion. Touted as "science's gift to the world" because of its high protein content, triticale was developed in the late 1800s in Sweden. One reason that consumers have never fully embraced triticale, despite periodic press on its behalf, is that it's tricky to turn it into a good loaf of bread.

See **Grains; Wheat.**

TROPICAL FRUIT

It is curious that fruits from temperate regions may be eaten whole (melons, watermelons, and pomegranates excepted) but not tropical and subtropical fruits. Bananas, oranges, pineapples, and most other tropical fruits have a thick, inedible peel.

Tropical and subtropical fruits are more thermally cooling, and they're often more lush and sugary, than temperate region fruits. Apples, plums, berries, and many temperate region fruits are delicious cooked as well as raw. Tropical fruits, however, are more frequently eaten raw, and many collapse when cooked. Lastly, compared to temperate region fruits, tropical fruits have negligible mineral content.

We all enjoy lush tropical fruit, and we don't have to go without them. It's useful to remember that fruits are not tissue builders, especially tropical fruits. People who are trying to build (this includes the very young) or conserve their energy might, however, favor temperate region fruits over tropical and subtropical fruits. Even though some subtropical fruits, like kiwis, are now grown in more temperate regions, they are more cooling than native fruits.

See **Atemoya; Banana; Breadfruit; Cherimoya; Citrus Family; Durian; Feijoa; Ground Cherry; Guava; Imbe; Jaboticaba; Jackfruit; Kiwano; Kiwi; Longan; Litchi; Mamey Sapote; Mango; Mangosteen; Monstera; Papaya; Passion Fruit; Pepino; Pineapple; Plantain; Rambutan; Sapodilla; Star Fruit; Tamarillo; Tamarind; White Sapote.**

TROUT BEAN See Jacob's Cattle Bean.

TRUFFLE
(Tuber magnatum, T. melanosporum)

The most famous fungus of the West, the magically aromatic truffle is so flavorful and hard to obtain that it sells for $350 per pound. The white truffles from Piedmont (*T. magnatum*) and the black truffles from Perigord (*T. melanosporum*) are the best known. Truffles had defied cultivation until the 1970s; now, 90 percent of the crop is cultivated in oak or hazelnut orchards in France, New Zealand, and North Carolina.

Franklin Garland, of Garland Gourmet Mushrooms and Truffles Company, Hillsborough, North Carolina, favors growing his black perigord truffles on hazelnut trees. An

---

EUROPEANS USE PIGS, NORTH AMERICANS USE RAKES

Because truffles grow underground, some European truffle hunters use a female pig to sniff them out, a practice in use since Greek and Roman times. But why a pig? A truffle emits an aroma that is also found in a male pig's saliva; this musky aroma, which makes a sow amorous, propels her through the woods to a truffle site. (The same chemical hormone is also secreted, as it happens, in the underarm sweat of human males.)

Pat Rawlinson, Director of the North American Truffling Society, forages both white and black truffles with a rake. She looks for signs of animal digs under a Douglas fir, hemlock, oak, alder, or pines that have nothing growing under them, as if the area were burnt out. Rawlinson and her colleagues, who are collecting samples for studies at Oregon State University, rake from three to five inches of the tree's litter from the trunk to the tree's drip line and, in the process, unearth truffles. Rawlinson urges any forager to positively identify truffles before eating them, as they could be mistaken for a poisonous mushroom.

inoculated hazelnut seedling produces truffles in four to five years (an inoculated oak sapling produces in ten years). According to Garland, domestic black truffles are better tasting than European truffles because they're fresher.

Health Benefits The almost meaty flavor of truffles is due to their high glutamic acid content, which not only enhances the flavor of other foods but also acts as a tenderizer. The truffle has long been considered an aphrodisiac for humans as well as for sows.

Use Truffles are excellent in risottos, grain dishes, or salads but they are famous with pasta. Their essence is also available in flavored oils, a splash of which magnificently rounds out a pasta dish or salad.

Buying Truffles vary from marble sized to as large as an orange. They are a firm, dense, knobby mass, which may be black or white in color. The black are black skinned with jet black or gray marbled interior. In specialty stores, they're available fresh, bottled, or dried. Or plant a truffle-inoculated hazelnut tree available from Garland Gourmet Mushrooms and Truffles (see page 402). Wait five years and then harvest your own.

See **Mushroom Family.**

TRUMPET MUSHROOM
Black Chanterelle, Horn-of-Plenty
(Craterellus cornucopioides, C. fallax, C. cinereus)

The newest mushroom with commercial availability, the trumpet mushroom has a trumpetlike shape and a buttery woodsy flavor.

See **Mushroom Family.**

TSAMPA See **Barley.**

TSP See **Textured Soy Protein.**

TUNA See **Prickly Pear.**

TURBAN SQUASH
Warren Turban
(Cucurbita pepo)

The turban, with its bright orange red rind, looks like a variation of the buttercup squash. The turbanlike swirl on its blossom end is variegated orange, red, and white. It's more beautiful to look at than to eat. As other *C. pepo* winter squash, like the pumpkin and spaghetti, its flesh lacks savor.

See **Squash; Winter Squash.**

TURMERIC
Indian Saffron, Yellow Ginger
(Curcuma longa)

The rhizome, or root of turmeric, is bright orange but otherwise has the skin and shape of its relative, ginger. Turmeric is boiled, peeled, dried, and ground into a powder. This powder is an essential ingredient in Indian cuisine. It is also used as a yellow dye for clothing (especially the robes of Buddhist monks), and as a dye for margarine and some dairy products. Turmeric originated in India.

Health Benefits Turmeric is the highest known source of beta carotene. It tones the spleen-pancreas, liver, and stomach. It strengthens the immune system, enhances digestion, and helps dissolve uterine tumors, cysts, and gallstones. Turmeric is antibacterial and may be used to regulate blood sugar for diabetics.

The bright yellow pigment in turmeric appears to inhibit the development of colon cancer. Turmeric may also be used topically to reduce canker sores and cold sores. Apply the powder directly to the afflicted area or mixed with water to form a paste.

Combined with coriander and cumin, turmeric aids in the digestion of complex carbohydrates. It also aids in the assimilation of protein and so is good to combine with milk for very young children. Turmeric is *tridoshic* in moderation; in excess, its astringency can agitate *vata*.

Use In addition to its mustard yellow color, turmeric lends to food a warm, musky aroma and flavor that's slightly astringent. The yellow color may stain clothing, and it will temporarily color counters, wooden spoons, and other kitchen surfaces that it comes in contact with. To improve its flavor and medicinal properties, sauté it briefly in ghee or oil before cooking it with other ingredients. As an essential ingredient in curry, turmeric may be used to add color and flavor to any vegetable or grain dish. I sometimes add a little to breads to make them more digestible.

Buying Light quickly reduces the color, flavor, and aroma of turmeric, so purchase in small quantities and store tightly covered in a dark glass jar. Turmeric has, however, excellent heat stability.

See **Ginger Family; Herbs and Spices.**

TURNIP
(Brassica rapa rapifera)

The turnip has a rustic character, and—among those people who have not tasted it at its prime—a low reputation. This inexpensive white root grows in impoverished soils and keeps well—features that have endeared it to the poor and given cause for the uninformed to scorn it.

I, on the other hand, am an unabashed fan of the turnip. I love its sweet, tender but crisp flesh, its mild bite, and sweet flavor. I adore a cooked turnip's funky, earthy mustard oil aroma. I also find the dark leafy greens delicious.

The turnip originated in northern Asia and has been used throughout Asia and Europe since prehistoric times. It is a member of the famed brassica (cabbage) family. The turnip is similar in many respects to its near relative, the rutabaga, which has pale yellow flesh and yellow-and-purple skin and is generally larger in size. The turnip is white fleshed, shaped like a radish, and has a white skin with a purple collar.

Health Benefits Raw grated turnip serves as a digestive aid, much the same as radish and daikon. Turnips clear heat, dissolve phlegm, moisten, and cool and strengthen the blood; they are good for general detoxification. Turnip juice reduces mucus and catarrh.

While the whole cabbage family is valued for its anticarcinogenic glucosinolates, turnips and rutabagas are exceptionally high in these important nutrients. Likewise, they contain mustard oil, and, when overcooked, release a sulfurous aroma—but not as intensely as cabbage and Brussels sprouts do. Turnips contain vitamins B and C, potassium, phosphorus, calcium, and other trace nutrients. They have more naturally occurring sodium than most vegetables. Turnips reduce *kapha*.

Use Use fresh young turnips in salads as you would a radish. Cooking further sweetens turnips and mellows their bite. When cooked with other foods, turnips have the remarkable ability to absorb other flavors, which allows them to become particularly succulent and rich. Their starchy properties are somewhat reminiscent of potatoes. Peel turnips only if they are overly large and less than fresh. Turnips can be used in soups and casseroles, steamed on their own, roasted, baked, and puréed.

Buying A turnip past its prime is bitter and pithy and has nothing to recommend it. A fresh, small turnip, no longer than three inches in diameter, grown in the spring or fall, is sweet with a mild bite like radish when raw. Turnips grown in the hot months, or without adequate water, are decidedly more pungent.

Select turnips that have root end and stem base intact. If these parts are trimmed away and yellowed at the incision, the turnip will lack flavor. Look for smooth, firm roots, preferably small or medium small. Reject flaccid, discolored, or withered turnips.

See **Cabbage Family.**

TURNIP GREENS
(Brassica rapa rapifera)

Turnip tops are just as delicious as their bottoms. There are even some varieties of turnips grown just for their dark, leafy greens, which look like exceedingly large radish leaves.

Health Benefits Turnip greens are similar to collard greens in medicinal properties.

Use Turnip greens have a milder flavor than mustard greens and kale and only a hint of bitterness. They are too coarse for salads, but light cooking (light being the operative word) turns them into a succulent green.

Buying Turnip greens are sporadically available in the supermarket, usually near the collards and kale. At a farmers' market, you can sometimes find turnips with their tops. Purchase those that are a vibrant deep green and show no sign of yellowing. Refrigerate in a plastic bag for up to five days.

See **Turnip.**

TUSCAN KALE See **Kale.**

TVP See **Textured Vegetable Protein.**

TWIG TEA
Bancha tea, Kukicha
(Camellia sinensis)

Twig tea is to the macrobiotic diet what milk is to the standard American diet. Kukicha is Japanese for twig tea; it is made only from the twigs and stems of the tea plant. Bancha tea contains some tea leaves as well as twigs, and therefore has a slightly higher caffeine content.

By commercial standards, kukicha is the poorest grade tea because it is very low in stimulants. While the finest green tea is made from the first new leaves in the spring, kukicha contains no leaves, and it's harvested in the fall when the caffeine content is minimal. Then it is roasted in cast-iron cauldrons to lessen its bitterness and to decrease its tannin.

Health Benefits Twig tea is a digestive aid; it helps neutralize an overly acidic digestive system because it is high in minerals and low in caffeine. It reduces *kapha*.

Use Unlike other grades of tea, which are infused, twig tea is simmered for up to 20 minutes. This gives it body and a deep flavor and makes it a more warming drink. For a more cooling beverage, it is steeped.

See **Tea.**

UGLI FRUIT
Unique Fruit
(Citrus paradisi x C. reticulata)

The ugli fruit is a grapefruit and mandarin cross, so named because its skin is, well, ugly: puffy, misshapen, pale orange, and baggy fitting. The fruit tastes like a sweet orange and mandarin. Look for this native Jamaican fruit in the winter and early spring months.

See **Citrus Family.**

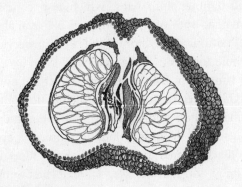

UMEBOSHI
Salt Plum
(Prunus mume)

A Japanese seasoning agent that ranks right under soy sauce and miso in use and versatility is the pickled plum umeboshi. Sour, immature plums are partially sun dried and then fermented in salt with the herb perilla for a full year. Perilla is high in iron, acts as a natural preservative, and imparts the characteristic pink color to the plums.

Health Benefits A highly alkaline condiment, umeboshi is high in citric acid and antibiotic in action. It eliminates lactic acid (which contributes to fatigue, colds, flu, viruses, diseases, and chronic illnesses) from the body. It increases hydrochloric acid levels and therefore enhances digestion and helps to strengthen blood quality. It relieves indigestion due to overeating, alcohol overindulgence, or morning sickness. Umeboshi calms *vata* beautifully.

Use Umeboshi may replace salt and vinegar in salad dressings, spreads, seasonings, and sauces, or it may be cooked with grains and vegetables. I favor it in spring and summer cooking, as its sour flavor lightens hot-weather dishes. In colder seasons, I add it to tea as a quick energy boost or digestive aid. (See *ume shoyo kudzu* recipe on page 181.)

Buying Whole umeboshi plums contain the pit and perilla; remove the pit and crack it, and then savor its sweet-and-sour pickled kernel; chop and use the perilla along with the plum. Umeboshi is also available in a less expensive and more convenient paste form (without the pit and perilla).

I purchase umeboshi from a natural food market to be assured that it is additivefree and traditionally fermented for one year (a chemically induced fermentation period lasts only a few weeks).

In paste form or whole, umeboshi keeps for several years at room temperature. Hold in a glass jar with a tight-fitting lid to prevent dehydration. If old, salt crystals may form; these may be rinsed off prior to use.

See Plum; Umeboshi Vinegar; Ume Plum Extract and/or Balls.

UMEBOSHI VINEGAR
Ume Su

Umeboshi vinegar is a pink brine with a deep, cherry aroma and fruity sour flavor; it is a byproduct of umeboshi making. Technically, it is not a vinegar because it contains salt; nevertheless, it may be substituted for vinegar and salt in any recipe. Umeboshi vinegar imparts a light, refreshing citric flavor, which enhances salad dressings and steamed vegetables. Its medicinal properties are comparable to, but less potent than, umeboshi.

See Umeboshi.

PICKLED PLUM WORKSHOP

The beloved Japanese healer, the late Sensi Naboru Muramoto, gave a plum pickling workshop in my Boulder home in 1979. As the plum variety used for ume does not grow in the Americas, we used the nearest equivalent—immature apricots. The fruits were partially sun dried on bamboo mats for several days, then mixed with perilla and Sensi's own hand-harvested sea salt. This mixture was packed into a 20-gallon ceramic crock, topped with a wooden lid, weighted down with heavy stones, and stashed in the basement to ferment for a year. These "apriboshi" and their brine—umeboshi vinegar—were wonderful.

UME PLUM EXTRACT AND/OR BALLS

A black, almost tarlike extract of sour green plums, ume plum extract is a highly concentrated source of citric acid. This concentrate is also available in convenient pills called ume plum balls, which also contain jinengo. Both of these products are available in natural food stores and by full-service whole foods suppliers (see page 399).

Ume plum balls and ume extract are both highly effective natural medicines for both children and adults. They treat indigestion, morning sickness, fatigue, liver- and stomach-related problems, asthma (due to kidney yin deficiency), labored breathing, and shock.

See Umeboshi.

UME SU See Umeboshi Vinegar.

UNIQUE FRUIT See Ugli Fruit.

UNREFINED, EVAPORATED CANE JUICE See Rapadura.

UNSULFURED MOLASSES See Molasses.

URAD
Black Gram
(Phaseolus mungo or *Vigna mungo)*

The urad bean, sometimes incorrectly identified in natural food stores as a black aduki bean, is a cousin of aduki as well as of the mung bean. It is small, plump, and slightly kidney shaped with a white hilum, or eye. While usually black, the urad bean may also be grayish, dark green, or brownish. Urad is an extremely popular bean in India.

Health Benefits Urad beans are high in protein, sodium, beta carotene, and folic acid. They support kidney function, help reduce blood cholesterol, control insulin and blood sugar, lower blood pressure, and regulate colon function.

Use Prepare urad beans whole as a side dish or puréed in soups. Urad is especially complimented by ginger, chiles, turmeric, and fresh coriander or mint. In India, split and husked urad beans are soaked and fermented with rice, then ground for feather-light steamed dumplings (*idlee*), pancakes (*dosai*), and fried savory breads (*bada*).

Buying Urad beans are available whole, split, split and skinless, and as a flour in Indian and Middle Eastern grocery stores. In natural food stores, I've found them only whole.

See **Beans and Legumes; Dal.**

VALENCIA ORANGE See Orange.

VALENCIA RICE
(Oryza sativa)

A medium-grain Spanish rice that is featured in paella, a stovetop dish seasoned with saffron that includes fish, chicken, meat, and vegetables. It is available in specialty stores. Valencia rice is similar to Italian Arborio rice.

See **Rice**.

VANILLA
(Vanilla planifolia)

Of all flower species, the beautiful, delicate orchid is, botanically speaking, the most highly evolved. Of the many orchid varieties, there's only one with an edible fruit: the vanilla orchid. In its natural environment, a very small hummingbird and a tiny bee once pollinated this orchid. Both bird and bee are now extinct. Today, all vanilla is hand-pollinated, and pollination must occur within a few hours of the flower's opening. The orchid fruit then takes seven months to mature into a long, skinny green pod.

The green vanilla pod has little flavor until it is cured, and then a smidgen of it imbues foods with a rich, floral aroma and flavor. A superior-flavored vanilla takes up to six months to cure and ferment; it is cold—rather than heat—extracted. Hand pollination and the lengthy maturation and fermentation period explains why, after saffron, vanilla is the most expensive seasoning agent.

Today, vanilla is produced throughout moist tropical areas within 20 degrees of the equator. Vanilla orchids grown north or south of this zone will flower but will not produce pods. Native to southern Mexico, vanilla was used by the Aztecs long before it became popular elsewhere in the world.

Health Benefits There are 36 aromatic compounds in vanilla, and vanillin, the most active component, is mildly toxic in both its natural and synthetic forms. The FDA, however, considers it safe because such small amounts are used. Workers who daily handle large quantities, however, may be afflicted with vanillism, which causes headaches and allergic skin reactions.

Vanilla is a digestive aid and *tridoshic* in action.

In aromatherapy, vanilla's consoling aroma is used to support self-confidence, to dissolve pent-up anger and frustration, and to access sensuality.

Use Vanilla is heat sensitive and so, whenever possible, it should be added at the end of cooking. Its most common use is in baked goods, desserts, and fruit dishes, but it also may effectively flavor savory dishes. Vanilla combines well with chocolate, a combination that the Aztecs first used.

Buying Choose dark brown vanilla pods or beans that are supple, plump, and tender, with a strong but round vanilla aroma. Quality beans are covered with a fine white powder, which is crystalline vanillin. Vanilla beans in an airtight glass jar stored in a cool, dark place will keep for about six months.

Pure vanilla extract contains at least 35 percent alcohol. Best-quality vanilla is nothing but vanilla extract and alcohol, and its flavors mature and develop as it ages. An excellent organic vanilla is now available. Lesser-quality extracts may contain sugar or corn syrup, glycerin, and/or propylene glycol. Vanilla extract in an airtight glass jar will store indefinitely in a cool, dark place.

Many people come home from Mexico with a quart of Mexican vanilla that cost only a few dollars. If it has a coarse aroma and acrid, bitter aftertaste, don't use it. By U.S. law,

---

HOMEMADE VANILLA

Commercial vanilla, even from a natural food store, is often harsh tasting and adulterated with shoddy ingredients. It's effortless and inexpensive to make your own quality vanilla extract. Here's how:

Vanilla Brandy Extract

   2 whole vanilla beans, split and
      chopped into 1-inch pieces
   1 cup good-quality brandy (or vodka
      or rum)

Place the ingredients in an 8-ounce dark bottle, cover, and allow to steep for 1 month before using. As the extract is used, refill with brandy a second time. The third time you make the extract, remove the spent beans and use fresh beans.

To make vanilla sugar, place the spent beans in 2 cups of rapadura, cover tightly, and set aside for a week or more.

---

vanilla extract must be derived from *V. planifolia*. If the vanilla label does not say vanilla extract, it's probably a sulfite waste byproduct from the paper industry, a chemically extracted compound known as coumarin. This substance, a potential toxin, was outlawed as a food ingredient by the USDA.

VEGETABLE OIL See **Fat and Oil.**

VEGETABLE PEAR See **Chayote.**

VEGETABLES

The vegetable realm includes any edible part of a plant—leaf, stem, tuber, root, bulb, berry, and seed. The vegetable realm therefore includes grains, legumes, nuts, seeds, fruits, and sea vegetables; technically it excludes mushrooms, which are a fungus. In common usage, however, vegetables refer to fleshy, edible plants, which are more mineral rich and less sugary than fruits.

See Avocado; Cabbage Family; Carrot Family; Goosefoot Family; Gourd Family; Legume Family; Mushroom Family; Nightshade Family; Onion Family; Seaweed; Sunflower Family.

VERDOLAGA See Purslane.

VERMICELLI See Pasta.

VIALONE NANO RICE
(Oryza sativa)

A short, round (*nano* means dwarf in Italian) white rice that is favored in risotto. Vialone nano is available in specialty shops.

See Rice.

VIDALIA See Onion.

VINEGAR

For about ten thousand years throughout the world, vinegar has been an important seasoning agent, preservative, medicine, beauty aid, and antibiotic. The word vinegar comes from the French *vin* meaning "wine" and *aigre* meaning "sour." Indeed, vinegar may be made from any sugar-containing liquid that can be fermented to less than 18 percent ethyl alcohol, including honey, maple syrup, and other sugars; fruit and coconut; vegetables such as beets and potatoes; grain and malted grain; and whey.

Traditionally, whatever local sugar-containing food source was in abundance was turned into the predominant vinegar of a region: malt in England, grapes in France and Italy; rice throughout Asia; and apples in North America.

Health Benefits Vinegar has a sour and sweet flavor, it energizes the stomach and liver meridians, assists with digestion, and moves blood stagnation. Vinegar is warming and detoxifying; it quickly resolves liver congestion and can significantly reduce mental depression. In Ayurvedic medicine, vinegar is considered *rajasic,* and is best used sparingly. It calms *vata.*

Vinegar is a common ingredient in many kitchen remedies. Applied topically, vinegar relieves sunburn and may ease arthritis and insect bites or stings.

Traditional, unpasteurized, unfiltered vinegar contains as many as 50 different nutrients, amino acids, and trace elements, which contribute to vinegar's distinctive taste and also its medicinal properties. The amino acids counter the effect of lactic acid buildup in the blood and help prevent the formation of toxic fat peroxides, which contribute to aging, fatigue, and irritability and to cholesterol formation on blood vessel walls.

Use Much of vinegar's volatile pungency is lost when it is heated, so if you wish to retain its acid flavor, stir in vinegar after removing the dish from the heat. When cooking with vinegar, do not use aluminum, copper, or cast-iron cookware; vinegar's 4 to 6 percent acetic acid is corrosive.

Vinegar is used in commercial bread and cheeses as well as in dressings, marinades, seasoning agents (from salsa to mustard), soups, pickles, olives, bean dishes, and various ethnic cuisines.

Buying For eons, delicious and healthful vinegar has been made using slow fermentation over a several-month period. In this century, "significant technological advances" have enabled vinegar production to go from scratch to market in a quick 24-hour process. As one producer told me, "Who, today, can afford to keep a product in storage for one year before selling it?"

Labeling laws do not require that manufacturing processes be listed. Key words that indicate traditional process include "unpasteurized," "unfiltered," "traditionally brewed," "traditionally fermented," or "aged in wood."

To the best of my knowledge, there are only a few traditionally made vinegars with commercial availability. Shopper beware: Most vinegar is a high-tech product even if it's made from organic ingredients.

Storing Vinegar is a solvent. Therefore, vinegar stored in plastic or metal becomes enriched with polycarbons or metallic ions. I

Ø **I'LL PASS ON PICKLES SPIKED WITH PETROLEUM**

Please do *not* use distilled vinegar. By FDA regulations since the 1950s, it may be synthetic ethanol made by direct chemical oxidation of wood or fossil fuels. Distilled and other highly processed vinegars are mineral deficient and, when consumed, pull calcium and other minerals from the bones and tissues. Also, look closely at labels of salad dressings, pickles, and packaged food products that contain vinegar. If the ingredient simply states "vinegar," you may assume it is the least expensive quality. Consider, too, the foods, such as cheese and bread, in which vinegar is used in processing but is not listed on the label.

---

purchase traditionally made vinegars aged in wood and bottled in glass (rather than plastic or cans). When cooking with vinegar, I use nonreactive cookware, such as an enameled pot, as opposed to a metal one.

See **Apple Cider Vinegar; Balsamic Vinegar; Brown Rice Vinegar; Malt Vinegar; Umeboshi Vinegar; Wine Vinegar.**

WAKAME
(Undaria pinnatifida)

Wakame is a versatile and salty variety of the sea vegetable kombu. Most of the North American supply of wakame comes from northern Japan; however, our domestic equivalent, alaria, is harvested in Maine and northern California. Olive green in color, wakame grows in fronds in deep and shallow water.

Health Benefits Like other seaweeds, wakame contains alginic acid, a polysaccharide compound that has the ability to chelate or bind heavy metals like lead and radioactive elements, as well as excessive sodium. It reduces *vata*.

After hiziki, wakame is the seaweed highest in calcium; it is also rich in iodine, protein, iron, and niacin. It also contains numerous trace minerals and vitamins A and C.

Use Wakame acts as a tenderizer and so increases the digestibility of beans and any other fibrous foods it is cooked with. A pop-ular soup ingredient, wakame may also be used as a green vegetable in salads and other dishes. When toasted in a 350-degree oven for 7 minutes or until crisp, then crumbled, it makes a tasty condiment. Or pulverize toasted wakame in a blender and use it as a seasoning agent or salt replacement.

Wakame flakes may be crumbled into a broth and simmered for one or two minutes before serving. Wakame fronds should be soaked in cold water to hydrate and the fibrous stipe cut out and reserved for soup stock. Once hydrated, wakame should be cooked for 10 minutes, or until softened.

Buying Except for seasonal fresh wakame from an Asian market, most wakame is available dried. Ita wakame is an exceptionally fine quality. Wakame may or may not be precooked; the latter is usually available as wakame flakes. When purchasing wakame in fronds, note that the younger, more tender plants have a thin, rather than wide, stipe. When dried, it is impossible to determine the stipe size, so purchasing reputable brands is

BLOOD ORANGE, WAKAME, AND CUCUMBER SALAD

Crisp cucumber, juicy-sweet orange, and succulent wakame make this an unusually beautiful and refreshing salad. As wakame aids the digestion of fat, it's an excellent side dish for a fatty meal. The unique perfume and bold garnet color of blood oranges is unbeatable, but if they're not available, substitute navel oranges or mineola tangerines.

> 3 fronds of wakame (about ½ ounce)
> 1 cucumber
> 2 medium blood oranges
> 2 teaspoons finely grated ginger
> Sea salt, to taste

Hydrate the wakame in water to cover for about 3 minutes, or until softened. Cut out the center stipe and reserve for soup stock. Chop the wakame into 1-inch pieces and place in a salad bowl.

Peel the cucumber if it is not organic. Slice the cucumber in half lengthwise and scoop out and discard the seeds. Chop the cucumber and add to the wakame.

Peel 1 orange, chop it into small chunks, remove the seeds, and add it to the wakame mixture.

Juice the remaining orange and strain out the seeds. Using your fingertips, squeeze the ginger to express ½ teaspoon ginger juice. Combine the orange and ginger juices and salt to taste. Pour over the salad and toss to combine. Allow to marinate for 5 minutes. This salad is best when eaten within an hour of making it. Serves 4.

the best way to obtain quality wakame. Fresh wakame requires refrigeration and prompt use.

See **Alaria; Mekabu Wakame; Seaweed.**

WALLA WALLA SWEETS See **Onion.**

WALNUT
(Juglans regia)

The most popular and widely used nut throughout the world is the Persian walnut, which, in America, is called the English walnut because of who shipped it here during the Colonial period. Unlike the American native, black walnut, the English walnut is easy to shell and does not stain. Walnut kernels are plump, meaty, and crisp, with a sweet flavor that has bitter aftertones because of the tannic acid in the nut's skin. Most of the U.S. domestic supply—and a significant percentage of the world's supply—of English walnuts comes from California.

Health Benefits The walnut is a warming food and is used as a kitchen remedy to strengthen the kidneys and lungs and to lubricate the large intestines. Sweet in flavor, walnuts are able to reduce inflammation and alleviate pain, which may be due to their Omega-3 oil content. The walnut balances *vata*. The English walnut is fatty (over 60 percent) and contains fair amounts of protein, zinc, calcium, and potassium.

Use To minimize the tannin in the skin and to concentrate the flavors, toast walnuts just prior to use. I toast them in a dry wok, stirring constantly.

Buying For the freshest nut with the most flavor, purchase walnuts in the shell and crack just prior to use. For convenience, purchase shelled, whole walnut halves, but only if they are refrigerated and if their flesh is white rather than yellowed, which would indicate rancidity. Broken, chopped, and/or unrefrigerated walnuts are rancid and bitter tasting. Walnuts may harbor liver flukes, so be sure to toast them or, preferably, use them in cooked dishes.

BRAIN FOOD

According to the Doctrine of Signature, since the walnut looks like the human brain, it is used for brain injuries and mental illness in traditional, plant-based medical systems. The thin, outer green husk, which is removed before the walnuts are marketed, is likened to the scalp. The walnut's hard shell is like a skull. The thin envelope inside, with its paper-like partitions between the two halves of the nut, is like the membrane. The convoluted nut itself represents the human brain's two hemispheres.

Eating a handful of walnuts would not cure a concussion. However, walnuts freshly cooked in a rice congee (see page 290) and eaten daily for a week or more will energetically support the brain's healing.

Commercial walnuts sold in the shell are washed, bleached, and polished to a uniform tan color. Organic walnuts have darker brown shells, and their color varies depending upon how shaded or sunny the branch they grew on was.

Shelled commercial walnuts frequently are treated with ethylene gas, fumigated with methyl bromide, blanched in hot dye or glycerin and sodium carbonate, rinsed in citric acid, and dried to increase shelf life. The result is a uniform nut with reduced flavor and tannic acid. In addition to stocking organic walnuts, most natural food stores also sell a less processed and therefore "lower" baking grade commercial walnut, which has more flavor than the bleached nuts.

See **Black Walnut; Nuts.**

WALNUT, BLACK See **Black Walnut.**

WALNUT OIL

A richly scented and flavored delicacy with a fragile shelf life, walnut oil is best to buy in small quantities with its manufactured date on the label. Keep refrigerated. Use walnut oil in salad dressings or over steamed foods. Do not heat it. Use only unrefined walnut oil.

See **Fat and Oil.**

WARREN TURBAN See **Turban Squash.**

WARTED HUBBARD See **Hubbard Squash.**

WASABI
Japanese Horseradish
(Wasabia japonica)

Eat just a speck of wasabi and immediately it feels as if smoke is pouring from your ears. Some stuff. Wasabi is the gnarled and warty root of a plant of the cabbage family, which is unique to the Japanese islands and highly valued in Japanese cuisine. Its pale green flesh packs a furious wallop. Although it is called Japanese horseradish, wasabi is more fragrant than horseradish and has a cleansing taste.

Health Benefits Wasabi contains protein-digesting enzymes, which make it a digestive aid. It is also used as a kitchen remedy to antidote fish poisoning. It is a heating food. Wasabi is balancing to *kapha*.

Use The digestive enzymes in wasabi quickly dissipate; therefore, grate fresh wasabi, or reconstitute powdered wasabi, just prior to use. Prior to grating, remove the "eyes" and pare away the tough skin. To use the powder, mix with an equal portion of tepid water to form a paste and allow to stand, covered, for about 10 minutes to develop flavor.

Serve wasabi in half-teaspoon amounts as an accompaniment to fatty foods or raw fish dishes. Because it stimulates the palate, it is a useful ingredient in hors d'oeuvres, barbecue sauces, dressings, dips, and condiments.

Buying Fresh wasabi is found in Asian markets in water-filled pans. Select a plump, fresh-looking root, preferably not sprouting.

Powdered wasabi is available in both Asian markets and natural food stores in convenient tiny tins or envelopes. Note that if when reconstituted, the "wasabi" is bright green (rather than a greenish gray), it is powdered horseradish or daikon with green coloring.

See **Cabbage Family; Herbs and Spices.**

WATER

Pure water is critical for maintaining or regaining health. Human embryos are 95 percent water, newborns are about 75 percent water, and most elderly people are about 50 percent water. Whatever your age, let's hope the water you're consuming is good quality.

Unfortunately, getting good water is not as easy as purchasing water in a plastic bottle. The plastic bottle actually "enriches" demineralized water with toxic polycarbons. In addition, a cancer-causing chemical, methylene chloride, has been found in water stored in polycarbonate resin bottles. Store water in glass or inert plastic.

Over 40 percent of American faucets deliver water that's been recycled through a sewer or industrial conduit. Moreover, the water supplies of an increasing number of communities are contaminated by the water-borne giardia parasite. Other water contaminants include radon, which makes water radioactive; old pipes and soldered joints, which contaminate water with lead; such agricultural toxins as nitrates and pesticides; chemical additives such as chlorine and sodium fluoride; and numerous industrial pollutants, including trichloroethylene.

Health Benefits Some people advocate distilled and reverse osmosis (RO) water for cooking and drinking because it is pure H_2O. Others disdain it for the same reason. Food cooked in demineralized water loses a much higher percentage of minerals to the water, due to osmosis. It is the minerals in water that provide taste and character. Demineralized water is not recommended for someone with an energetic or mineral deficiency. To remineralize RO and distilled water, add a scant ⅛ teaspoon unrefined sea salt per gallon of purified water.

Buying Feel fortunate if you have a natural source of deep underground water that tests free of contaminants. Such sources include artesian, spring, and well water. Look under the water entry in the yellow pages of the telephone book to find companies that deliver water and request the laboratory analysis. If more than one brand is available and their data sheets are comparable, then rely on your taste to determine which is best. In general, avoid water with either low or excessive mineral content. Insist that it be delivered to you in glass containers.

Other options are to purchase purified water in a glass jug or to install a home purification unit. The three types of purified water are RO water, distilled water, and filtered water. To reenergize purified water, leave it in a loosely covered glass container exposed to natural light, preferably direct sunlight, for several hours.

- **Reverse Osmosis (RO)** Pure water (H_2O) created through reverse osmosis and distillation. Both processes remove toxins, gases, and minerals. RO water is hard to justify from an environmental vantage point, as it wastes two to five gallons of water for every gallon produced.
- **Distillation** Not all distillation units remove hydrocarbons. Favor a home unit with a charcoal filter that also removes hydrocarbons.

Ø WATER IN PLASTIC CONTAINERS IS NOT A SIMPLE SOLUTION

The ubiquitous bottled water in purses, backpacks, and at the office water stand is probably tainted with toxins. Demineralized water more quickly leaches polycarbons and methylene chloride than mineral-rich water does. Therefore, when using water stored in plastic, do not use distilled or RO water. According to 1996 FDA Labeling Regulations for Bottled Water, water with its minerals intact include:

Artesian Water From a well that taps a confined aquifer or water-bearing underground layer of rock or sand.

Mineral Water From an underground source that is naturally rich in flavor-enhancing minerals; no minerals can be added. Mineral water is often named for its place of origin.

Sparkling Water Naturally contains carbon dioxide, which makes it bubbly. Carbon dioxide may be added to equal but not exceed the amount of carbonization the water contains as its emergence from the source. (Soda water, seltzer, and tonic water are not considered sparkling water.)

Spring Water From an underground source that flows naturally to the earth's surface.

Well Water From a manmade hole in the ground that taps an aquifer.

- **Activated Charcoal-Filtered Water** Water filtered through activated charcoal. The water retains its water-soluble minerals and therefore has more flavor and is more "natural" than demineralized water (RO water and distilled water). Filters do not remove water-soluble toxins such as nitrates, nitrites, and sodium fluoride. If your tap water contains no such toxins, then filtered water is a convenient choice. Under-the-counter or countertop water filters are effective when the filters are replaced as necessary. Once installed, under-the-counter units are the most convenient, as they have their own faucet. Freestanding units, such as the popular Brita filter, require pouring water into the filter. They are as inexpensive as $20 per unit.

WATER CALTROP See **Horned Water Chestnut.**

WATER CHESTNUT
(Eleocharis tuberosa)

The most memorable property of the water chestnut is its crunch. Although jicama and the Asian pear come close in texture, they do not match its refreshing delicacy or its juicy sweet flavor. The water chestnut, which looks like a grubby chestnut in size and shape, actually grows in the mud. It has a black outer peel and a slightly peaked, tufted top. It has been a food staple in Asia since neolithic times.

Health Benefits The water chestnut is a cold and sweet bulb that disperses excess heat from the body. It treats diabetes and jaundice and inhibits infectious diseases, such as staphylococcus and E. coli. It is also said to aid vision. It calms *pitta* and in moderation reduces *kapha.*

The water chestnut is a low-calorie food, containing ample protein, calcium, phosphorus, iron, and vitamins B and C.

Use The water chestnut, like a tree chestnut, may be boiled, roasted, or made into flour. Cooking enhances its flavor, does not detract from its texture, and eliminates the possibility of contamination by water-borne pathogens. Peel the outer skin and any dark spots.

Buying Currently, water chestnuts are not grown commercially in the United States despite several attempts to do so. They are readily available canned but as such have little flavor and a compromised crunch. Look for fresh water chestnuts exported from China and Taiwan in Asian markets and some supermarkets. Select those that are rock hard and free of withered, wrinkled, or soft spots.

See **Horned Water Chestnut.**

WATER COCONUT See **Coconut.**

WATERCRESS
(Nasturtium officinale)

One of my favorite pastimes as a child was gathering watercress from a pure mountain stream or lake. Because of giardia and other water-borne contaminants, however, it is no longer safe to eat wild watercress. What a loss.

Eurasian in origin, watercress was probably introduced in America in the 1600s and now thrives in all 50 states. A cabbage family member, watercress—be it cultivated or wild—comes in only one variety.

Health Benefits Watercress is a pungent, stimulating herb that clears toxins, aids digestion, and is useful for gallbladder complaints or rheumatism. Raw watercress is not recommended for the young, the elderly, or anyone with compromised health, a propensity for yeast infections, or with a history of internal parasites. Watercress balances *kapha*.

Use Watercress has a mustardlike bite and aroma but surprises the palate with a cooling, refreshing effect, rather than a fiery one. Cooking eliminates its bite and leaves a sweet vegetable. When cooked, its volume is reduced by three-fourths, so plan accordingly.

Buying Purchase vibrantly green watercress with no yellowed leaves. Wash watercress with extra care.

See **Cabbage Family**.

WATERMELON
(Citrullus vulgaris)

How perfect that our most watery fruit originated in Africa's hot and arid Kalahari region. There is indeed some logic in favoring your region's native foods; and, when you're not in the Kalahari but it feels like it, then cool down and rehydrate with watermelon. Technically a vegetable, watermelon is more closely related to a cucumber than a cantaloupe. It's a classic picnic food, enjoyed out-of-doors, especially by children and participants in seed-spitting contests. Some new varieties have yellow instead of red flesh and some are seedless. Watermelons range from a few pounds in weight to as large as 40 pounds.

Health Benefits Surprisingly, watermelon has only half the sugar (5 percent) of an apple. It tastes much sweeter, though, because sugar is its main taste-producing element—the rest is primarily water. This makes it a popular diet food and an unexcelled cooling food; it's even more cooling than cantaloupe. Watermelon relieves thirst, mental depression, edema, and it induces urination. It is not recommended for someone with weak digestion and it can inhibit semen production. Watermelon balances *pitta*.

Watermelon is a good source of vitamins C and A and potassium. It is low in sodium and calories and has no fat.

Use Watermelon flesh is enjoyed in fruit salads, in fruit punch, and just by itself. Its seeds may be seasoned, toasted, and eaten as a snack food like squash or pumpkin seeds; and its rind (both the green skin and the white layer) makes a delicious pickle. To make watermelon juice, remove the seeds and process the flesh in a blender or processor to create a uniform pulp, which may be diluted with water or another juice and seasoned to taste.

Watermelon doesn't stand up to cooking or mincing, so use large chunks in combination with other fruit salad ingredients.

Buying As the melon ripens, the white

spot where it rests on the ground turns to yellow, and this will indicate its maturity. A dry, brown stem, rounded ends, and a smooth rind that is neither shiny nor dull are other signs of ripeness. Heft several melons and choose one that is heavy for its size and symmetrical in shape. Also hold the melon in one hand and thump it with the other. If it sounds hollow with a slight ring, it is ripe.

If purchasing a cut watermelon, avoid one with immature white seeds, pale flesh, or white streaks. If overmature, its flesh is mealy and either dry or watery.

See **Gourd Family.**

Wax Bean See **Green Bean.**

Wax Gourd See **Chinese Winter Melon.**

Wehami Rice See **Red Rice.**

West Indian Lime See **Lime.**

West Indian Pumpkin See **Calabaza.**

WHEAT
(Triticum aestivum)

The common ancestor of all wheat is einkorn, first cultivated nearly nine thousand years ago in what is now Iraq. In world trade, wheat is the world's most important carbohydrate crop and the most widely distributed cereal grain; it is grown in nearly every country and in every state in America. In many cultures, wheat is now the staple grain, having replaced amaranth, barley, buckwheat, corn, millet, oats, quinoa, rye, and wild rice.

Health Benefits Wheat nurtures the heart, calms and focuses the mind, and treats a wide range of stress and mental health symptoms. It also supports the spleen-pancreas, liver, and kidney meridians. Like rye, wheat is good for the musculature. Wheat balances *vata* and *pitta*.

Since the late 1920s, wheat has been genetically altered for smut resistance. It is theorized that this manipulation may be a contributing factor in the plethora of wheat allergies. Two readily available heirloom wheat varieties— which some wheat-sensitive people can enjoy with no allergic response—are kamut and spelt.

Whole wheat contains twelve B vitamins, vitamin E, protein, essential fatty acids, and important trace minerals such as zinc, iron, copper, manganese, magnesium, and phosphorus.

Use Wheat berry is the term applied to the whole wheat grain as it is found in natural food stores with just its outer hull removed. Because cooked wheat berries are so chewy, they are rarely eaten whole.

Thousands of wheat varieties exist, but three types are commonly used for human consumption—hard, soft, and durum.

- **Hard Wheat** Has a higher protein (gluten) content. It is used for bread. It is usually rust colored with plump kernels; there are, however, some white (actually buff-colored) varieties.

- **Soft Wheat** Contains more carbohydrate and less gluten than hard wheat. It is not suited to bread making. Also called white wheat, because of its light, golden color, or cracker wheat, it is mainly used for crackers, cakes, and pastries.

- **Durum Wheat** Used primarily for pasta because its hard starch granules hold together even in boiling water. Semolina is refined, or white, durum flour. Most pasta and couscous are from semolina; in the natural food trade, however, excellent whole grain durum products are also available.

CORN DOLLY MADE OF WHEAT

An Old World folk tradition is to weave grain shafts into a talisman, referred to as a corn dolly. She hangs in the kitchen through deep winter as promise of harvest to come. After frost has left the ground, the corn dolly is undone to sow her precious grains.

In Europe, the generic term for all grain is corn, which is derived from the word kernel and means small particle. Thus, for example, biblical references to corn are not about Native American maize but about the cereal crops of the region—barley and spelt. This explains why Christopher Columbus named America's native grain Indian corn.

Hard wheat is also defined by the season it is sown in. Hard spring wheat is sown in the spring and harvested in the fall. It is a fast-growing crop grown where winters are severe. Spring wheat is the grain of choice for bread making, since it generally has the highest protein content. Hard winter wheat is sown in the fall; it germinates; lies dormant through the winter; starts growing again in the spring; and is ready for harvest in June. It is grown where winters are mild. Because it has a longer growing season, it establishes a more extensive root system and is therefore higher in minerals.

See **Bulgur; Couscous; Cracked Wheat; Flour; Fu; Gluten; Grains; Israeli Couscous; Kamut; Pasta; Spelt; Wheat Bran; Wheat Flour; Wheat Germ.**

WHEAT BRAN

Six fibrous protective layers of the wheat berry are resistant to digestion and thus are an effective bowel regulator because they add bulk and fiber to the diet. For those eating refined wheat products, it makes sense to supplement with wheat bran. However, a more commonsense response is to eat the whole grain, which has more vitality and flavor.

Bran accounts for 15 percent of the wheat kernel. In addition to its indigestible cellulose, it is also a rich reserve of nutrients, including niacin, pyridoxine, pantothenic acid, riboflavin, thiamin, and protein.

WHEAT FLOUR

Wheat berries are ground into flour in various forms. The major ones are:

- **Bleached All-Purpose Flour** Made of refined hard and soft wheat and processed with up to 30 chemicals. By law, all refined flour must be enriched with four synthetic nutrients. Self-rising all-purpose flour also contains leavening and salt.
- **Bolted Wheat Flour** Flour sifted through a bolt of coarsely woven cloth to remove hulls and a large portion of the bran and germ, a refining technique developed by the Romans. Bolted flour retains 20 percent of its bran and all of the germ but has limited availability today. It yields a bread with a higher volume than a 100 percent whole wheat flour does.
- **Bread Flour** A high-gluten blend of 98 percent refined hard wheat flour, which contains malted barley to improve yeast activity. It may or may not contain potassium bromate to increase the gluten's elasticity.
- **Durum Flour** Made of 100 percent durum wheat. Used primarily for whole wheat pasta.
- **Cake Flour** A fine-textured, soft wheat flour, low in gluten. Makes light and airy cakes and pastries. A cup of self-rising cake flour contains 1½ teaspoons baking powder, ½ teaspoon salt, and cornstarch as an anti-caking agent.
- **Gluten Flour** A high-protein hard wheat flour with a reduced starch content and a gluten content of at least 55 percent. Bakers often add a small amount of gluten flour to bread dough to produce a lighter loaf. I don't recommend gluten flour because it is highly processed and it toughens bread.
- **Semolina** Ground from refined durum wheat. Used primarily for pasta.
- **Unbleached All-Purpose Flour** Made from wheat refined of its bran and germ. By law, it must be chemically enriched, but at least it is a less processed food than bleached flour. For people who find 100 percent whole wheat products too heavy, including some unbleached white flour yields a lighter product.
- **Whole Wheat Flour** Made from whole hard wheat berries. This flour contains all of the 40-plus nutrients of wheat and has a rich, full taste. Once milled, however, the fatty acids in the wheat germ start to oxidize and become rancid. Therefore, purchase whole wheat flour in small quantities from a store with a brisk turnover or, better yet, purchase it from a natural food store that refrigerates its whole grain flours. At home, wrap tightly and refrigerate or freeze until use.
- **Whole Wheat Pastry Flour** Made from whole soft wheat berries. Preferred for pastries, crackers, cakes, cookies, pie crusts, and other delicate baked goods. Because it is low in gluten, it is unsuitable for bread. This flour requires the same care as whole wheat flour.

See **Flour.**

WHEAT GERM

Wheat germ is the heart or the embryo of the wheat. It comprises only 2 to 3 percent of the whole wheat berry but is nutritionally the richest part. Rich in insoluble fiber, B vitamins, vitamin E, and calories, wheat germ also contains octacosanol, which promotes oxygen utilization and therefore reduces fatigue and enhances overall stamina and endurance. Octacosanol extracted from wheat germ is available as a supplement.

Wheat germ is highly susceptible to rancidity. Some people maintain that wheat germ must be used immediately after milling to obtain its vitamin E. Toasted wheat germ has a delicious nutty flavor, although some nutrients are destroyed by toasting.

WHEAT GLUTEN See Fu; Seitan.

WHEAT GRASS JUICE

Available fresh in some natural food stores, the juice from young, seven-inch-long wheat grass is high in chlorophyll, potassium, calcium, and magnesium. Imagine a flavor so aggressively sweet that it borders on astringency. Few people claim to enjoy this flavor and so wheat grass juice is generally mixed with another juice. Wheat grass is also available powdered and in tablet form. It is a potent detoxifer, especially for the liver and gallbladder.

See Barley Grass Juice.

WHITE GOOSEFOOT See Lamb's-Quarters.

WHITE MUSHROOM
(*Agaricus brunnescens*)

The most widely available mushroom va-

riety, the white mushroom ranges in color from creamy white to light brown and in size from small to jumbo. Its mild, woodsy flavor increases with cooking and is more developed in mature mushrooms.

See Mushroom Family.

WHITE SAPOTE
Zapote, Zapote Blanco
(*Casimiroa edulis*)

The semitropical white sapote looks like a large pointed peach. A coreless fruit, it has an ambrosial vanilla-and-peach aroma, a sugary taste, and a soft and juicy texture. Commercial crops are being developed in California and Florida, and of the many new and exotic fruits, this seems destined to gain in popularity as the "peach of the tropics."

Enjoy it out of hand, or use it in preserves, frozen desserts, or fruit sauces. It is delicious alone or in combination with other fruits. Look for sapote during the fall months. Choose firm fruits that are free of bruises and green or yellowish green in color. Allow sapote to ripen and soften at room temperature until it is softer than a ripe avocado, then refrigerate. Peel off the skin and discard the seeds.

See Tropical Fruit.

WILD BLUE-GREEN ALGAE
(*Aphanizomenon flos-aquae*)

A microalgae that grows wild in Klamath Lake, Oregon, wild blue-green algae is a potent superfood and, as such, is best used with care. It is available as a supplement and in protein beverages.

Health Benefits Cooling, drying, a neurostimulant, antidepressant, and relaxant, wild blue-green algae is of special benefit to people who have robust energy. It is not advised for people who are cold or weak, have trouble gaining weight, and/or who have chronic diarrhea. It reduces *kapha*.

See **Chlorella; Microalgae; Spirulina.**

WILD LEEK See **Ramp.**

WILD LIME See **Kaffir Lime.**

WILD RICE
(Zizania aquatica)

> All that is around us is animate. As such it has spirit. I'm very careful when I harvest [wild rice] because I must reckon with that spirit. I must reckon with an aspiration to harvest. Because you are respectful when you harvest, this ensures that you are able to continue harvesting. It is not because you're smart or clever; it's because you're respectful. The value of eating and harvesting the same way that our ancestors have done cannot be quantified. Both spiritually and culturally, it reaffirms those things which are ours and those things which make us strong as a community. We're not a wealthy people in terms of monetary income. We are wealthy in terms of our culture.
>
> —Winona La Duke

Winona La Duke of the Ahnishinabe Ojibwa, who lives on the White Earth reservation in Minnesota, harvests 150 pounds of rice a year. "We eat it plain and I put it in everything—omelets, muffins, and casseroles," she says. "Rice has always been a staple on the reservation. And I'm not talking Uncle Ben's."

A staple food for the Ojibwa, Chippewa, and Algonquian tribes, who called it *manomin*, wild rice has a wondrous flavor that is a complex blend of nutty sweet with a hint of spice. Even a small amount of this black cereal grain imparts its distinctive character to other ingredients.

Health Benefits Wild rice is a warming and drying food that strengthens the kidneys. Energetically, "wild" wild rice is preferred over the tamed commercial crop. Wild rice balances *vata*.

Wild rice is richer in protein, minerals, and B vitamins, and higher in carbohydrates than wheat, barley, oats, or rye.

Use Most wild rice used commercially serves as a flavoring agent in rice pilafs, soups, or mixes; most home cooks use it the same way. I invite you to use it neat, on its own, as a wild rice entrée or side dish. The bounteous flour of wild rice is something to savor again and again.

The cooking time and water measurement for foraged and commercial wild rice is different because the foraged wild rice has its bran layer partially removed (scarified). Cook 1 cup of foraged wild rice in 1¾ cups of water for 45 minutes. One cup of commercial wild rice requires an hour (sometimes an hour and ten minutes) cooking in 2½ cups water. Because the cooking times vary, wild rice recipes usually suggest cooking with extra water and draining off the excess liquid—but this drains off flavor and nutrients. Instead, prepare the grain without

WHEN A LABEL DOESN'T SAY ALL

Grey Owl organic wild rice brand from Canada, popular in natural food stores, is "Indian Harvested." But that's just part of the story. It is hybrid seed mechanically introduced to lakes far north of the traditional rice lakes, and it is harvested in airboats by Native Americans.

Look for the original thing, which will state on its label "hand-havested" or "lake harvested." Purchasing this natural, organic rice supports the traditional folkways of Native Americans who have hand-harvested this rice for several thousand years in the Great Lake regions. You may also purchase hand-harvested wild rice directly from Leech Lake reservation (see page 401).

extra water. It is cooked when it is tender but not mushy and when some of the grains have "butterflied" or burst open. Ideally, at this point, the liquid will be totally absorbed. If liquid remains, drain it, measure it (reserving it for stock), and next time add that much less liquid.

Buying Two distinct types of wild rice are available today: foraged wild rice from the rivers and lakes of the Great Lakes region, which comprises less than 20 percent of the market share; and hybrid wild rice, which is farmed mainly in California paddies but also in northern Idaho, Saskatchewan, Manitoba, and Ontario.

The heirloom wild rice is unique in that it is the only foraged cereal grain with commercial availability. All other cereal crops throughout the world have been cultivated and selectively bred for thousands of years and therefore have a limited gene pool. Wild grasses, including foraged wild rice, are more robust, nutritious, and flavorful. The heirloom rice is scarified (to remove part of its bran and so is mottled brown, gray, and black).

Tame wild rice is one of four hybrid varieties selected for responsiveness to petrochemical fertilizers, herbicides, insecticides, and fungicides, as well as for ease of mechanical harvesting and factory production. The Canadian hybrid rice is typically an inch long and is ebony black in color.

See **Grains.**

WILD SPINACH See Lamb's-Quarters.

WINE VINEGAR

Wine vinegar is an excellent condiment when traditionally made from organic ingredients and aged traditionally, without the use of preservatives.

See **Vinegar.**

WINGED BEAN
Goa Bean
(Psophocarpus tetragonolobus)

Tropical in origin, the winged bean is billed as a "new soybean" because it's an excellent and inexpensive food source. The bean is like a plump, long green bean with four ridges, or wings, running lengthwise down the pod. Thus, when cut in cross sections, the bean pieces are square.

Use Unlike other beans, the whole winged bean plant is edible—pods, leaves, seeds, shoots, and tubers. Its green pods are the most available; cook as you would green beans. The flavor is mild and pleasant, the texture almost meaty. Winged beans may be substituted for soybeans in tofu, tempeh, and soymilk.

Buying As cold-resistant varieties are developed, expect to see greater availability of this bean. Currently, their availability is erratic in the United States.

See **Beans and Legumes**.

WINTER MELON See **Chinese Winter Melon**.

WINTER SAVORY See **Savory**.

WINTER SQUASH
(Cucurbita maxima, C. moschata, C. pepo)

The word squash aptly describes this vegetable's cooked texture, but it doesn't hint at its sweetness. A good winter squash packs a wallop of flavor. Winter squashes have dark yellow to orange flesh and a thick rind. The sweetest squashes are generally those with the most deeply colored flesh.

Health Benefits Squash is considered a warming food that is medicinal to the spleen-pancreas and stomach; it improves energy circulation. Compared to summer squash, winter squash is a better source of natural sugars, carbohydrates, and beta carotene. Winter squash is exceptionally high in complex carbohydrates and is medicinal for diabetics and for those with digestive problems. It provides vitamins A and C, potassium, iron, riboflavin, and magnesium and is very low in sodium. It is an excellent source of pre–vitamin A and often carotenoids, and there-

fore has anticarcinogenic properties; in fact, winter squash, sweet potatoes, and carrots are the vegetables highest in carotenoids.

Most winter squash reduces *vata* and *pitta*, while spaghetti squash reduces *kapha*.

Use Cutting a winter squash requires a sharp knife or, if it's a large hubbard, a hatchet (if you don't have a hatchet, drop it onto the floor to crack it open). You may also purchase a small squash, bake it whole, then cut it with a butter knife. If a round squash doesn't rest firmly on the cutting board, trim a wedge to give stability as you cut the rest. Butternut squash are easily cut in half and then stood on end for additional cutting.

Once cut, taste the squash. If it is bland raw, it will be bland cooked—toss it. Squash can be baked, stuffed, simmered in a little water, steamed, or fried—but boiling in water to cover leaves it flavorless. Puréed, it makes a sweet soup or pie, a sensational spread for waffles or toast, or raw it may be grated and added to cookies, puddings, and cakes.

Buying Select squash that is heavy for its size with a hard rind with mottled markings. The rind should be free of soft spots, cracks, and bore holes. An intact stem indicates better storage properties.

See **Acorn Squash; Banana Squash; Buttercup Squash; Butternut Squash; Calabaza; Delicata Squash; Gold Nugget Squash; Hubbard Squash; Kabocha Squash; Pumpkin; Spaghetti Squash; Turban Squash**.

WITLOOF See **Belgian Endive**.

WOH SUN See **Lettuce**.

WOOD EAR
Cloud Ear, Dried Black Fungus, Tree Ear Mushroom
(Auricularia auricula)

When foraged or fresh, wood ear is jellylike and rubbery; when dried, it's like a piece of black shoe leather. This relatively tasteless mushroom has a very short stalk. Wood ear grows throughout Asia, Europe, and the Americas.

Health Benefits Wood ears are used in Europe for throat and eye ailments and for heart pain. They are an effective immune tonic. They lower cholesterol; clear the body of free radicals; and support brain function. Wood ears energize the lung, stomach, and liver meridians. They help relieve constipation. There is some evidence that they inhibit egg implantation in animals. Do not use when pregnant or when wishing to conceive.

Use Soak wood ear until supple, for at least 20 minutes, or as long as overnight. It will almost quadruple in size when hydrated. Pick it over to remove any bits of bark or debris. Chop and simmer in a soup, stew, or any Asian vegetable or meat dish.

Buying Wood ear mushrooms are occasionally available fresh in Asian markets. Dried, they can be found in supermarkets, natural food stores, and in Asian markets. They're also available by mail (see page 390).

See Mushroom Family.

WORMSEED See Epazote.

WRAPPED HEART MUSTARD CABBAGE
Headed Mustard Cabbage
(Brassica juncea rugosa)

Wrapped heart mustard cabbage looks like a loose-leafed savoy cabbage but it has a mustard-sharp taste. A near relative of mizuna, mustard cabbage needs ample moisture when growing or it becomes too hot to eat. The condiment mustard comes from the seeds of this branch of the cabbage family.

Younger leaves are less fiery than older leaves and can be used in salad. Mature plants are best pickled, stir-fried, or cooked until soft in a soup. The blossoms are edible. Wrapped heart mustard cabbage holds better if it is washed just prior to use.

Ø XYLITOL

A byproduct of the plywood industry, xylitol is extracted from birch cellulose by an energy-intensive chemical process. This non-caloric sweetener may also be made from other hardwood chips, almond shells, pecan shells, cornstalks, or corncobs. Pound for pound, xylitol costs about ten times as much as white sugar but its sweetening power is far greater.

Xylitol is used in sugarfree gum, candy, and jam. In animal studies, it is linked to cancer, urinary kidney stones, and bladder inflammation. Not recommended.

YAKI TOFU
Baked Soybean Cake

A tofu cake baked until it is lightly blackened, yaki tofu is denser, firmer, and more flavorful than regular tofu. Substitute it for tofu in savory dishes but not in desserts or creamy sauces.

See **Tofu.**

YAM
(Dioscorea rotundata, D. cayenensis, D. composita)

One of the most widely consumed foods in the world, the yam was first cultivated more than ten thousand years ago in Africa. It is the tuber of a climbing plant that today grows throughout tropical and subtropical regions and, in the United States, in the deep South. Yams are round or oblong with a thick, often coarse, skin and their starchy flesh may be white, ivory, cream, pink, or purple. The vegetables called yams in supermarkets are, in fact, sweet potatoes. There are more than six thousand species of yams.

Health Benefits Yams have excellent medicinal uses, including treating arthritis, asthma, and spasms. Their plant estrogens ease many low estrogen symptoms, help regulate menses, and work as an agent to prevent miscarriages. Their simple peptide substances bind with heavy metals like cadmium, copper, mercury, and lead and thus assist in metal detoxification of body tissues. Yams that contain diosgenin are used for treating fatigue, inflammation, spasms, stress, and colitis.

Use Yams have more starch than potatoes, but they are like a mealy potato, with a coarse, dry, and rather bland flavor and texture. Also like a potato, yams must be cooked to convert their indigestible starches into sugar. They absorb flavors of other ingredients they are cooked with, and they are tasty boiled, roasted, mashed, and fried. Unlike a potato, however, the skin is not edible. In countries where yams are a staple, they are most frequently seasoned with spices, served with a sauce, or combined with other foods.

Buying Select yams that are firm and intact with no signs of mold or soft, shrunken spots. Smaller yams have more flavor than larger yams. They are most often available in Latino and Asian markets. As with potatoes, do not refrigerate, but store in a cool, dry, dark place.

See Jinengo.

YAMAIMO See Jinengo.

YAM BEAN See Jicama.

YARD-LONG BEAN
Asparagus Bean, Chinese Long Bean, Cow Bean, Dou Gok, Long Bean
(Vigna unguiculata)

If your children don't eat enough green vegetables, bring home some yard-long beans. Blanch and cool the beans, call in the kids, and let them braid, spiral, and tie the long beans. Their art goes on the dinner table along with a vegetable dip—vitamin A handled for the day. The loan bean is a black-eyed variety and a vegetable staple throughout Asia and in other semitropical regions.

Use Long beans are a poor substitute for green beans when boiled or steamed (although a zippy dressing helps). Best sautéed or in a stir-fry, a long bean's texture holds well in stews and braised dishes as well. Remove the stem end, cut into desired lengths, cook, and serve hot or cold. The beans require no stringing. Long beans are more fragile than green beans, and so are best used within a few days.

Buying Long beans are most commonly available in Asian markets. Favor dark green over pale green ones, which are less flavorful. The length—which varies from one and a half to three feet—is not important, but choosing pods with undeveloped seeds is critical. Look for pencil-thin, firm long beans that show no sign of rust.

See Black-Eyed Pea.

YAUTIA
Cocoyam, Malanga, Tannia
(Xanthosoma)

A root crop that food experts believe holds great promise as a nutritious food of the future is the funny-looking, potatolike yautia. When cooked, this tropical tuber has an earthy, almost nutty favor and lush, creamy texture. It originated in the Americas in both dry and swampy soils. Like taro, the yautia is thin skinned and shaggy, but it tends to be larger and is frequently club shaped. Its yellowish or pinkish flesh is visible through its splotchy skin.

Health Benefits As a kitchen remedy, the yautia may be used to regulate energy, support digestion, and disperse congestion. It has a moderate amount of thiamin and riboflavin, and a modest amount of vitamin C and iron. It is high in calories.

Use Do *not* eat yautia raw; cook this tuber as you would taro or potato. A common Ca-

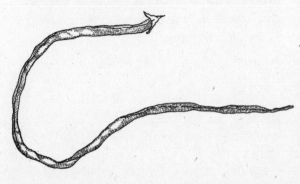

ribbean use of yautia is to peel it, boil it like a potato, and serve it with savory dishes. It is also baked, fried, and ground into flour. In a stew, yautia flavors, thickens, and adds creaminess. If overcooked, however, it tends to disintegrate.

Buying Many supermarkets as well as Latino markets now carry yautia. Select fresh-smelling, firm specimens. Store at room temperature and try to use within a few days of purchase.

YEAST

I recommend purchasing bulk dry bakers' yeast from the refrigerated section of your natural food store, rather than the rapid-action, preservative-containing yeast sold in individual packets or fresh cakes in the supermarket. Besides, the natural food store yeast is more economical. Store it in a closed glass jar in the refrigerator for six months or more.

YEAST, NUTRITIONAL See **Nutritional Yeast.**

YELLOW-EYE BEAN
(Phaseolus vulgaris)

A white bean with a yellowish eye that wraps halfway around the bean, this heirloom New England bean was a staple of the Native Americans in the Northeast.

See **Beans and Legumes.**

YELLOW GINGER See **Turmeric.**

YELLOW WAX BEAN See **Green Bean.**

YERBA MATÉ See **Maté.**

YI YI REU See **Job's Tears.**

YUBA

Yuba is an intriguing soy product that looks like sheets of yellow taffy. It is the skin that forms on the top of hot soymilk when soymilk is being made. This skin is layered, pressed into slabs or cakes, and dried. To use, soak yuba and add it to stews and braised vegetable dishes for its excellent flavor and pleasing texture. It is high in protein and easy to digest. Yuba is available in Asian markets and occasionally in natural food stores.

See **Soybean.**

YUCA See **Cassava.**

YUZU
(Citrus aurantium)

A variety of bitter orange with a unique, limelike fragrance, yuzu yields an extract that is available from purveyors of fine Oriental goods. It is used as a flavoring agent.

See **Bitter Orange.**

Z

ZANTE CURRANT See **Currant.**

ZAPALLO See **Calabaza.**

ZAPOTE See **White Sapote.**

ZAPOTE BLANCO See **White Sapote.**

ZEST See **Citrus Peel.**

ZUCCHINI
(Cucurbita pepo)

The British call it marrow, the French say *courgette,* and in the United States we use the Italian name, zucchini. This best known summer squash is generally dark green when small, but it may develop white stripes as it becomes larger. Yellow varieties are also available.

Use A vegetable of great versatility, the zucchini can be stuffed and baked, fried, broiled, and used in soups. I find that cooking is the best way to coax flavor from a zucchini. I'm lavish with zucchini in zucchini season; otherwise, I've no use for them, for unless they are fresh, they taste insipid.

Buying Zucchini is best when it is under six inches long, local, and fresh. If allowed to grow, it can reach the size of a baseball bat . . . and has comparable flavor. Select those that are firm and shiny.

See **Squash Blossom; Summer Squash.**

Glossary of Terms

ACRID Unpleasantly pungent or caustic.

ADAPTOGENIC Improving resistance to stress and thus supporting homeostasis.

AIDS A severe immunological disorder resulting in increased susceptibility to opportunistic infections and certain rare cancers. AIDS stands for Acquired Immune Deficiency Syndrome.

ALKALOID A plant-based, nitrogen-containing compound that has a potent effect on body function.

ALLERGEN Any substance that produces an allergic reaction.

ALTERATIVE Improves vitality, primarily by enhancing the breakdown and elimination of waste products.

ANALGESIC A natural or synthetic substance that removes or relieves pain.

ANTIBACTERIAL Destroys or inhibits the growth of bacteria.

ANTIBIOTIC Destroys or inhibits growth of microorganisms.

ANTICOAGULANT Prevents or slows clotting of the blood.

ANTIFUNGAL Destroys or inhibits the growth of fungi.

ANTI-INFLAMMATORY Reduces inflammation.

ANTIOXIDANT Inhibits oxidation and thus slows or prevents cell deterioration.

ANTISPASMODIC Reduces muscle spasms and tension.

ANTIVIRAL Inhibits a virus.

ASTRINGENT Firms and contracts tissues (by precipitating proteins from cell surfaces); forms a protective coating; and reduces bleeding and discharges.

AYURVEDA The ancient Indian science of life and self-healing.

BETA CAROTENE The orange-yellow plant pigment that the body converts to vitamin A.

BILE A thick, bitter fluid stored in the gallbladder and secreted by the liver; it aids fat digestion.

BIOENGINEERED Genetic material of an animal or plant that is manipulated, altered, or added to. The industry term is Genetically Manipulated Organism (GMO).

BIOFLAVONOID A plant glycoside that improves circulation and has diuretic, antispasmodic, and anti-inflammatory effects.

BITTER One of the five tastes in Chinese medicine. It is a yin, cooling taste, which clears, improves appetite, detoxifies, and stimulates secretion of digestive juices. It supports heart and small intestine functions.

BLOOD SUGAR The concentration of glucose in the blood.

CARMINATIVE A food, usually an herb or spice, that reduces intestinal gas, pain, and distention; promotes peristalsis.

CATARRH An inflammation of the mucous membrane, most often affecting the nose and throat.

CATHARTIC Strong laxative that initiates rapid elimination.

CHI A Chinese term for the vital energy, or life force, of an organism. Pronounced chee and sometimes spelt qi. It is called *prana* in India and *ki* in Japan.

CHINESE MEDICINE Traditional Oriental medicine based upon thermal property, five flavors, four directions, and the twelve meridians.

CLEANSING The property of improving excretion of waste products from the body.

COOLING The property of clearing toxins and reducing internal heat.

CYSTITIS Inflammation of the urinary bladder.

DAIDZEIN Along with genistein, a plant estrogen and isoflavone uniquely abundant in soy foods; it is an anticarcinogen (especially of breast cancer). In addition, daidzein relieves menopausal symptoms and reduces cholesterol levels.

DECONGESTANT A substance that relieves congestion, especially from nasal passages.

DEMULCENT The property of soothing and protecting damaged or inflamed internal membranes.

DEPRESSANT The property of lowering the rate of vital physiological activities.

DETOXICANT A substance that removes toxins and poisons from the body.

DIAPHORETIC A substance that induces perspiration and increases elimination through the skin.

DIGESTANT A substance that aids the softening and assimilation of foods, such as a ferment, enzyme, or acid; also the bitter taste.

DIURETIC The property of increasing urination by acting upon the kidney and bladder.

DNA A nucleic acid found in all living cells that is important in protein synthesis and the transmission of genetic information. Nutritional sources of DNA and RNA, such as those found in microalgae, are known to benefit cellular renewal.

DOSHA An essential biological energy or structure in Ayurveda. The balance of our three primary doshas, *vata, pitta,* and *kapha,* determine our health.

EDEMA Abnormal accumulation of serum fluid in an organ or body cavity.

EMETIC A substance that initiates vomiting.

EMOLLIENT The property of softening the skin.

ENTERITIS Inflammation of the small intestine.

ESTROGENIC A plant substance similar in effect to the hormone estrogen.

EXPECTORANT A substance that promotes the discharge of phlegm and mucus from the respiratory tract.

FDA Food and Drug Administration, a regulatory branch of the United States Government.

FIVE TASTES The five tastes in Chinese medicine: sour, bitter, sweet (also bland), pungent, and salty.

FUNGICIDE A substance that destroys fungi.

GENETICALLY MANIPULATED ORGANISM (GMO) An organism that contains altered, manipulated, or added genetic material. Also known as bioengineered.

GENISTEIN See daidzein.

GLUTATHIONE An enzyme, a deficiency of which is associated with hemolytic anemia.

GRIT A broken cereal grain, especially buckwheat and corn. Unless degerminated, it oxidizes faster than a whole grain.

GROAT Refers to any hulled grain, most often oats and buckwheat.

HEIRLOOM SEEDS Cultivated seeds that are handed down from generation to generation and valued for characteristics such as flavor, hardiness, natural pest resilience, or ability to thrive in a specific area. Unlike hybrid and bioengineered foods, use of heirloom foods helps preserve genetic diversity.

HERBOLOGY The study of herbs and their use as medicinal and culinary agents.

HORMONE A substance produced in the endocrine glands and transported by the blood to another site to affect a physiological activity such as growth.

HYBRID SEED A cross between different varieties designed to achieve desired cosmetic, nutritional, or harvesting properties. Not capable of reproducing like heirloom seed. With hybrids, the natural integrity and viability of the original seed is lost.

HYDROGENATION A process of treating liquid oil with hydrogen gas to change its molecular structure. This process saturates the fatty acids to render a solid or semisolid product like margarine and shortening. Most processed cheeses and commercial peanut butters also contain hydrogenated oil. Avoid all hydrogenated products.

HYPERTENSION High blood pressure.

HYPOGLYCEMIA A lack of sugar in the blood that causes muscle weakness, sweating, and mental confusion.

IMMUNE SYSTEM The body's system that recognizes and defends against foreign materials such as allergens and infectious organisms.

INDOLE-3-CARBINOL An indole (an anticarcinogen found in cabbage family members) that helps protect against hormone-related cancers such as breast cancer.

INULIN A polysaccharide found in the roots of various sunflower family members that is medicinal for diabetics.

ISOFLAVONE A class of flavonoids that may help prevent hormone-related cancers such as breast cancer.

ISOTHIOCYANATES Sulfur compounds that are among the most effective cancer-prevention agents; they are partially responsible for the pungency of some cabbage family vegetables.

KAPHA Ayurvedic term for a water-like biological energy and constitution that is cold, wet, slow moving, heavy, solid, stable, and enduring. Foods that reduce *kapha* are drying, warm, and eliminative with pungent, bitter, and astringent flavors.

LACTATION Milk secretion from the mammary glands.

LAXATIVE A substance that promotes bowel movements.

LIPIDS Fatty compounds present in most tissues and especially in the blood.

LUTEIN Lutein and zeaxanthin are two antioxidants and yellow carotenoids found in the eye; they filter out harmful blue light and protect against macular degeneration, the leading cause of blindness in people over 65 years of age.

MERIDIAN One of the twelve vital organs and pathways of Chinese medicine. The heart meridian, for example, includes not only the physical heart but blood and circulation throughout the body and the heart's interrelationship with all other systems.

MUCILAGE Soft, slippery substance that protects mucus membranes.

NERVE TONIC A substance that supports the normal functioning of the nervous system.

NUTRACEUTICAL A phytochemical with pharmaceutically recognized healing properties.

NUTRITIVE A food that nourishes the body.

PERISTALSIS Involuntary, wavelike muscle contractions of the digestive tract that move its contents.

PHLEGM Thick mucus, secreted by the respiratory tract lining.

PHYTIC ACID A heat- and acid-stable astringent acid found in cereals, nuts, and seeds (especially in sesame seeds and soybeans) that protects against some cancers and may help control blood sugar, cholesterol, and triglycerides.

PHYTOCHEMICAL A biologically active substance in plants (*phyto*) responsible for giving them characteristics such as color, flavor, and natural disease resistance. Our common foods contain millions of phytochemicals.

PHYTONUTRIENT A nutrient found in plants (*phyto*), which include vitamins, minerals, essential fatty acids, phytochemicals, and nutraceuticals.

PHYTOSEROL Plant sterols that can lower cholesterol and that show anticancer activity.

PITTA Ayurvedic term for fire-like biological energy and constitution, typified as hot, light, clear, sharp, and oily. Foods that reduce excess *pitta* are drying and cooling, with bitter, astringent, and sweet flavors.

PROPHYLACTIC An agent that protects or defends against disease.

PUNGENT (Spicy) One of the fives tastes in Chinese medicine; it is yang (warming, dispersing, and drying). Also called spicy, it moves energy from the interior to the surface; it supports the lung and colon.

PURGATIVE A strong laxative.

RAJASIC Ayurvedic term for fiery foods that excite the appetite and stimulate outward motion, creativity, passion, and aggression; they are best avoided, unless you are seeking these experiences.

REJUVENATE Restore vitality.

RELAXANT A substance that relaxes overactive, tense muscles and tissues.

RESTORATIVE A substance that revives strength.

RNA A nucleic acid found in all living cells that is important in protein synthesis and in the transmission of genetic information. Nutritional sources of DNA and RNA, such as those found in microalgae, are known to benefit cellular renewal.

RUTIN A bioflavonoid obtained from buckwheat and used in the treatment of capillary fragility.

SALTY One of the five tastes in Chinese medicine; it is yin (cooling and moistening); it supports the kidney and bladder system.

SAPONIN A plant substance similar to soap.

SATTVIC Ayurvedic term for foods that are pure and fresh and clear the mind. They are to be favored.

SEDATIVE A substance that reduces tension by lowering the functional activity of an organ or body part.

SOPORIFIC A substance that induces drowsiness or sleep.

SOUR One of the five tastes in Chinese medicine; it is yin (cooling and refreshing) and promotes digestion, enzyme secretion, and liver and gallbladder function.

STIMULANT Increases physiological activity, circulation, and heat; dispels internal chill.

SUSTAINABLE Dietary habits and food production that promote human and environmental well-being. It means favoring organic, seasonal, regional, and whole foods.

SWEET One of the five tastes in Chinese medicine; it is yang (warming, soothing, tonic, building, and nourishing) and it supports the stomach and spleen-pancreas functions. Also called bland.

SYSTEMIC Affecting the entire system or body.

TAMASIC Ayurvedic term for spoiled foods, which increase inner darkness and confusion and depress body functions. They include leftover, processed, refined, frozen, microwaved, chemically treated foods, fast foods, fried foods, frozen foods, and alcohol. Can also denote a very grounding, completing food, like onions or mushrooms.

THERMAL PROPERTY The ability of a food to help regulate body temperature, either up or down. All foods are cooling or neutral or warming by nature. For example, watermelon is cooling, garlic is warming.

TONE The property of strengthening and restoring an organ or muscle to normal fitness.

TONIC A substance that stimulates and increases body tone in the absence of illness.

TONIFY To invigorate, refresh, build, and strengthen.

TOPICAL A skin remedy applied directly to the afflicted area.

TOXIC Harmful or poisonous.

TRIDOSHIC A food that ameliorates all three body types, *vata, pitta,* and *kapha.*

USDA United States Department of Agriculture.

VATA Ayurvedic term for air-like corresponding to biological energy- and constitutional-type movement. It is dry, cold, light, mobile, rough, and clear. Foods that reduce excess *vata* are demulcent, nutritive tonics with a sweet taste and warm energy; they also calm the nervous system.

VERMIFUGE A substance that expels intestinal worms.

VITAMIN P A mixture of bioflavonoids found in vegetables and fruits that reduces the permeability and fragility of capillaries.

VITAMIN U A term given to a factor found in fresh cabbage juice that encourages the healing of peptic ulcers.

WARMING A substance that increases the body's temperature by dispelling cold or hypoactivity and increasing vitality, circulation, and digestion.

YANG Complementary to yin in Chinese philosophy. Yang is the male element associated with the sun, day, dry, hot, exterior, and ascending.

YIN Complementary to yang in Chinese philosophy. Yin is the female element and associated with moon, night, damp, cold, interior, and descending.

ZEAXANTHIN Zeaxanthin is associated with decreased lung cancer risk. In addition, it helps prevent macular degeneration (see lutein).

Appendix I: Storage

All foods deteriorate to some extent during storage, with a diminishing of flavor, color, aroma, and weight. While a raspberry goes in hours, it takes years to lose a chickpea. To minimize deterioration, store foods in a closed, nonreactive container away from light, heat, and moisture and at the temperature appropriate to them.

BEANS

Dried beans have the longest shelf life of our common whole foods. Whole beans are much harder than grains and do not become infested unless they are more than several years old. Split beans are more prone to infestation. For convenience—as well as the delight of seeing their beautiful colors and shapes—store beans in closed glass jars in a cool cupboard.

DRIED FRUIT

To extend the shelf life of dried fruit, refrigerate it in a glass jar or tightly wrapped in plastic.

FATS AND OIL

Olive oil needs no refrigeration; store it in a dark cupboard. All other unrefined oils must be refrigerated, preferably in opaque glass or inert plastic containers. Unlike other oils, flax oil remains liquid when stored in the freezer—thus freezing flax oil extends its shelf life (it is the most fragile oil) and even frozen it is easy to pour.

FRUIT

When fruits are not fully ripened, place them in a closed, roomy paper bag at room temperature and out of direct sunlight. Turn the fruits daily to assure even ripening. Placing an apple or banana in the bag facilitates ripening.

Remove any fruit that shows signs of leaks, bruises, mold, or spoilage, as one bad fruit quickly taints surrounding fruit. Wash fruit just prior to using. Once a fruit is cut or peeled, refrigerate it in a tightly covered container, and use quickly.

- **Apples, Grapes, Loquats, Mangos, Nectarines, Passion Fruit, Peaches, Pears, Pineapples, Plums, Pomegranates, Prickly Pears, Quince, Rhubarb, Star Fruit** Refrigerate in a perforated plastic bag in the crisper drawer. Apples, pears, and quince are excellent keepers and may also be held in a cold (32 to 40 degrees), dry place.
- **Berries, Cherries, Figs** Layer between paper towels, refrigerate, and use as quickly as possible.
- **Kiwis** Refrigerate ripened kiwis, tightly covered in plastic and away from other fruits as the ethylene gas emitted by other fruits will over-soften kiwis.
- **Bananas, Citrus Fruit, Melons, Pineapples** These fruits are compromised by refrigeration; store them in a dark, cool (50 to 65 degree) pantry. Use orange-fleshed melons within a few days. Whole, green-fleshed melons may be stored for a month. Once cut, wrap melons tightly in plastic or their aroma will taint other food, refrigerate, and use within 3 days.
- **Watermelons** Store watermelon in a dark, dry, cool (50 to 65 degree) place for a week. Once cut, cover, refrigerate, and use within 5 days.

GRAINS

Store whole grain in closed glass jars in a cool, dry place. (If you live in a hot, humid area, refrigerate them.) Except for millet, most grains can be stored for a year or more. A prevention to retard insects from hatching is to tuck a bay leaf in the jar.

For optimum flavor, buy small quantities of whole grain products that contain the germ, and keep them refrigerated. These include: rolled oats, steel-cut oats, rye flakes, and whole wheat couscous. If they have little aroma or flavor, or if they have a bitter taste, they're stale. Toss them out.

Grain products that have had their germ removed, like couscous and bulgur, are best stored tightly wrapped in a cool cupboard. Whole wheat pasta has a shorter shelf life than pasta made from refined flour.

To retard oxidization, refrigerate all whole grain flours, tightly covered, and use within a few weeks. Or freeze and use within six months. Flour with a bitter taste is rancid; discard it.

HERBS AND SPICES

To extend their life, immerse stem ends of fresh herbs in water, loosely cover with a plastic bag, and refrigerate. Every other day trim the stem ends.

A rack of spices over the stove may look attractive, but heat and light diminish their essences. Keep spices in dark-colored closed glass containers in a cool, dark place.

Fresh, quality dried herbs are resilient and have a vibrant look. I routinely compost leaf herbs that are more than a year old or that are stale, brittle, and flat-looking. Whole spices have a long shelf life; once ground, their essence diminishes.

MUSHROOMS

Mushrooms respire more actively after harvest than other vegetables and lose nearly half of their sugar and starch within a few days. Refrigerate and use as quickly as possible. Refrigeration in airtight wrapping will slow down respiration, but it will also cause moisture condensation, which speeds spoilage.

Refrigerate mushrooms in the container they were purchased in, in a paper bag or towels, or in a small cotton bag. Should they become dehydrated, place damp paper towels over paper- or cloth-wrapped mushrooms to keep them moist but to permit air circulation.

Store dried mushrooms in an airtight container in a cool cupboard.

NUTS

If you have refrigerator or freezer space, consider purchasing a year's supply of the unshelled new crop in the late fall. Shelled nuts keep in the freezer for up to a year. If rubbery, hollow, moldy, or acrid tasting or smelling, they are rancid and should not be eaten.

Avoid dry-roasted nuts, which often contain sugar, salt, starch, monosodium glutamate, vegetable gums, spices, and preservatives. Also avoid packaged shelled nuts: They are often coated with a preservative, contain excessive salt, and the packaging is typically chemically treated.

Nut and seed butters easily become rancid, so purchase in small quantities and keep refrigerated. A stale, foul aroma and a sharp, burning taste indicate rancidity.

SEAWEED

Seaweed stores well for a year or more. Keep it tightly wrapped in a dark, cool, dry cupboard.

SEEDS

Hulled seeds like sunflower and pumpkin seeds require refrigeration. Whole seeds like sesame, poppy, flax, and others should be stored in a closed container in a dark, cool cupboard.

VEGETABLES

Most vegetables should be stored in the vegetable drawer of the refrigerator. Tomatoes, avocados, potatoes, and sweet potatoes, however, are damaged by the 30 to 40 degree temperatures that other vegetables thrive in. Store these as follows:

Avocados

A ripe avocado holds best at 40 to 50 degrees. If storage at this temperature is not possible, refrigerate a ripe avocado for up to 3 days. Once cut, sprinkle with lemon juice to prevent discoloration, tightly wrap in plastic, and store, refrigerated, for a day or two.

Garlic

Stored in a cool, dry, well-ventilated area,

garlic will keep for several months. Do not refrigerate, as garlic's flavor will taint other foods. If stored in a damp, warm environment, garlic will sprout or become moldy.

Onions

Onions are dormant after harvest and so can be stored without sprouting for, in the case of sharp, yellow onions, 2 to 3 months. Sweet, moist, and/or red onions have a shorter shelf life and may be stored from 2 to 4 weeks. Hang onions in an aerated basket or bag in a cool (ideally, 30 to 40 degrees), dry, well-ventilated place. Do not store onions near potatoes, as onions absorb moisture, which causes potatoes to sprout and rot. Do not refrigerate onions. Once cut, onions oxidize and quickly lose their flavor.

Potatoes

Store new potatoes refrigerated for up to a week. Store mature potatoes and sweet potatoes in a cool (ideally, between 41 and 48 degrees), dry, ventilated, dark area and they will keep up to 2 months. Store in an aerated basket, paper bag, or recycled clean pantyhose. The higher the temperature, the shorter their storage life. Do not store near strongly flavored foods, apples, or onions, as they absorb moisture and flavor.

Roots

Refrigerate roots in a paper or plastic bag. They'll store for several weeks but are at their best within a few days of harvest. Packed in sand, roots hold in a root cellar for several months. Bright greens attached to a turnip or other root vegetable are a welcome sign of freshness. Home from the store, separate greens from roots at the leaf base, but do not cut into the root itself. Leaves left attached to a root draw moisture and flavor from it.

Tomatoes

Store tomatoes in a cool area (ideally, 50 degrees) for up to a week. Do not store in direct sun. If overripe, then refrigerate tomatoes for up to 3 days; however, refrigeration kills their flavor and makes their texture mealy.

Winter Squash

Squash harvested after the first frost keeps until March when stored in a dry, cool, dark, well-ventilated place. Store each squash individually on a shelf; if in a box, wrap each in paper, as direct contact with another squash diminishes shelf life. Butternut is the best keeper, with kabocha, buttercup, and hubbard lasting almost as long. If you do not have a cool storage area, hold the squash at room temperature, rather than refrigerate, and use within a few weeks. Once cut, the unused portion should be refrigerated, wrapped in plastic, for up to five days.

Appendix II: Nutritional Sources

The following is a list of the primary macro- and micronutrients required for optimum health and superior plant sources in which they can be found.

MACRONUTRIENTS

AIR Consumed more than any other element. Regular exercise, which helps fully oxygenate the system, is vital for all people and especially those with sedentary jobs. For all of us who breathe in less than pristine environments, air purifiers are recommended for home, office, and automobile. House plants are remarkable detoxifiers (see sidebar page 9).

Water The second most important element by volume, it accounts for most of our body weight. To support optimum health, drink and cook with pure water (see pages 363–5).

Carbohydrates The next most important nutrient by volume, they are found almost exclusively in plant foods (dairy products are the primary exception). Carbohydrates can be either simple or complex. Carbohydrates with a simple molecular structure are quickly assimilated and cause a rapid fluctuation in blood sugar; they are primarily found in fruits and sweeteners. Because complex carbohydrates take longer to digest, they help stabilize blood sugar; thus they help prevent hypoglycemia and diabetes. Complex carbohydrates are found abundantly in vegetables, whole grains, and beans and legumes.

Fiber, a form of carbohydrate, is abundantly found in all whole vegetable foods. When a vegetable or fruit is juiced, its fiber is removed. Peeling produce and refining grains significantly reduces their fiber content. By favoring a varied whole foods diet, one obtains ample complex carbohydrates, including fiber.

Protein Excellent protein sources include beans and legumes, seeds, grains, and leafy green vegetables. A popular and tenaciously persisting misconception is that animal foods are a superior source of protein because of their amino acid configuration. On the contrary, the amino acid profile in whole grains, beans, and potatoes adequately provides human protein needs. Quinoa and amaranth are unique in the plant realm as their amino acid profile makes their protein equal or superior to milk.

Fat The most concentrated source of energy; it is vital for human health. Oil is fat in a liquid form. Because most Americans consume excessive and/or refined oils, they have fat-related health problems and many struggle to reduce their fat intake. An easier and more healthful option is to switch over to unrefined fats and oils, which satisfy both our nutritional needs as well as hunger, and therefore it is easy to enjoy them in moderation.

MICRONUTRIENTS

Vitamins

Vitamin A microalgae, alaria, barley/wheat grass juice, and deep green or orange vegetables.

Vitamin B_1 (Thiamine) Whole grains (especially brown, red, and black rice), nori, wakame, and beans and legumes.

Vitamin B_2 (Riboflavin) Whole grains, beans and legumes, spinach, nutritional yeast, and hiziki.

Vitamin B_3 (Niacin, Niacinamide, Nicotinic Acid) Whole grains, especially brown, red, and black rice (but not corn), posole, masa, nori, wakame, alaria, peanuts, and nutritional yeast.

Vitamin B_5 (Pantothenic Acid) Whole grains, fresh vegetables, beans and legumes, mushrooms, nuts, and nutritional yeast.

Vitamin B_6 (Pyridoxine) Whole grains, leafy green vegetables, dulse, nori, laver, nutritional yeast, carrots, peas, sunflower seeds, and walnuts.

Vitamin B_{12} (Cyanocobalamin) Nutritional yeast, unpasteurized fermented vegetables, and microalgae.

Biotin Soybeans, nutritional yeast, and whole grains.

Choline Soybeans, whole grains, and beans and legumes.

Folic Acid Microalgae, sprouts, leafy green vegetables, whole grains, nutritional yeast, dates, beans and legumes, mushrooms, oranges, beets, fenugreek, and root vegetables.

Inositol Fruits, vegetables, whole grains, molasses, nutritional yeast, and beans and legumes (especially soybeans).

Para-Aminobenzoic Acid (*PABA*) Whole grains, spinach, molasses, and mushrooms.

Vitamin C (Ascorbic acid) Citrus fruits, bell peppers, chiles, amaranth, berries, cabbage, parsley, potatoes, sprouts, and tomatoes.

Vitamin D The "sunshine" vitamin we obtain from exposure to sunlight. Sunflower sprouts contain vitamin D, and chlorophyll-rich foods perform like vitamin D in the body.

Vitamin E Nuts, seeds, whole grains (especially wheat, oats, quinoa, and brown, red, and black rice); the dark green leaves of cabbage, broccoli, and cauliflower; dandelion greens, sprouts (especially sprouted wheat), asparagus, cucumbers, and spinach.

Vitamin K Alfalfa sprouts, asparagus, blackstrap molasses, dark leafy green vegetables, green tea, kelp, soybeans, oats, rye, and wheat.

Vitamin P (Bioflavonoids) The white pith of citrus fruits, peppers, buckwheat, and black currants.
Vitamin U Cabbage.
Coenzyme Q10 Peanuts and spinach.

Minerals

Boron Seaweed, alfalfa, and unrefined sea salt. To a lesser extent: grains, nuts, leafy green vegetables, grapes, pears, apples, and carrots.
Calcium Seaweed (especially wakame and hiziki, followed by kelp, kombu, and alaria), amaranth, quinoa, oats, beans and legumes, microalgae, leafy green vegetables, almonds, nutritional yeast, sesame seeds, sunflower seeds, figs, dandelion greens, and unrefined sea salt.

Calcium is abundantly provided in a varied whole foods diet. However, our calcium reserves can be depleted by overconsumption of dairy and meat; consumption of refined flours, grains, salt, and sweeteners; and a sedentary lifestyle.
Chromium Seaweed (especially kelp and alaria), rapadura, whole grains (especially wheat), mushrooms, beets, nutritional yeast, beans and legumes, and unrefined sea salt.
Copper Seaweed, whole grains, beans and legumes, raisins, apricots, beets, garlic, nuts, mushrooms, leafy green vegetables, and unrefined sea salt.
Fluorine Seaweed, rye, rice, parsley, avocados, cabbage, and unrefined sea salt.
Germanium Seaweed, garlic, shiitake mushrooms, onions, ginseng, aloe vera, and unrefined sea salt.

Iodine Seaweed and unrefined sea salt. Also, when grown in iodine-rich soil, the following: garlic, asparagus, lima beans, sesame seeds, soybeans, and turnip greens. Similarly, if microalgae is grown in iodine-rich water, it provides iodine.
Iron Seaweed, molasses, whole grains, beans and legumes, nuts, beets, nutritional yeast, sesame seeds, prunes, raisins, dates, and unrefined sea salt.
Magnesium Seaweed (especially kelp and alaria), whole grains (especially amaranth), microalgae, beans and legumes, seeds, chlorophyll-rich foods such as leafy greens, and unrefined sea salt.
Manganese Seaweed, whole grains, nuts and seeds, blueberries, green tea, alfalfa leaf, avocados, and unrefined sea salt.
Molybdenum Seaweed, whole grains, beans and legumes, dark green leafy vegetables, and unrefined sea salt.
Phosphorus Seaweed, whole grains, beans and legumes, dried fruit, garlic, nuts, seeds, and unrefined sea salt.
Potassium Seaweed (especially kelp and dulse), carrot juice, whole grains, beans and legumes, fruit, vegetables, and unrefined sea salt.
Selenium Seaweed, whole grains, beans and legumes, organic garlic, mushrooms, and unrefined sea salt.
Silicon Seaweed, whole grains, lettuce (especially bib lettuce), parsnips, dandelion greens, strawberries, celery, cucumbers, apricots, carrots, and unrefined sea salt.
Sodium Seaweed (especially kelp and alaria), celery, unrefined sea salt, and virtually all foods.
Sulfur Seaweed, cabbage family, beans and

legumes, onions, garlic, nettles, soybeans, and unrefined sea salt.

Vanadium Seaweed, whole grains, vegetable oils, dill, radishes, green beans, and unrefined sea salt.

Zinc Seaweed, whole grains, legumes and beans, nuts, seeds (especially alfalfa and pumpkin), mushrooms, nettles, soybeans, and unrefined sea salt.

Nutraceuticals

Biologically active substances in plants that have pharmaceutically recognized healing properties. Beta carotine is one example of a nutraceutical. There are potentially millions of nutrients with pharmaceutical properties. To obtain adequate nutrients, eat a varied diet of whole foods that, ideally, are sustainably grown, seasonal, and freshly prepared.

Appendix III: Ayurvedic Food Guidelines

To follow Ayurvedic food guidelines, you must first discern which of the three elements (*vata, pitta,* or *kapha*) you predominantly are. By recalling what foods make you feel good and matching them to the elemental types below you may correctly ascertain your predominant type. Or, you may consult one of the many popular Ayurvedic books that provide self-identification guides. A third choice is to visit a qualified Ayurvedic practitioner who will assess your elemental type plus provide a diagnosis, medicinal herbs, and a recommended treatment plan. Note: some people are a combination of types, and one's type(s) may vary over time or even with the season.

These guidelines are just that—guidelines. They are not law. Please bypass them when you choose but then pay attention to how you feel emotionally, mentally, and physically. Better yet, when hungry for a food from the "not recommended" category balance it with other ingredients or dishes that better suit your type.

Rather than limiting your diet and enjoyment of food, these guidelines will help you discern those foods that you most readily digest and that help you feel balanced and at your best.

VATA (air type)

Vata people flourish with a warming, grounding diet composed of strengthening, substantial foods that are moistening and lubricating. For example, a bowl of warm oatmeal with ghee and cinnamon balances *vata,* whereas a granola candy bar or a bowl of granola with cold milk does the opposite. It is important for *vata* types to eat freshly prepared warm foods that, ideally, contain digestion-enhancing herbs and spices such as ginger or cumin. Thus, soups are much more calming to this air type than are salads.

Note that even a food that is "good" for *vata* is upsetting if it is cold, stale, undercooked, eaten with too many other dishes, overeaten, or eaten when stressed.

Flavors that benefit *vata* are sweet, salty, and sour. For example, sour umeboshi plums considerably help *vata* digestion.

Beans and Legumes challenge *vata*, tend to cause gas, and are drying. *Vata* responses to beans and legumes vary widely. Tofu, mung, urud dal, and in small quantities, aduki beans, are generally easy to assimilate. Some vatas do well with lentils, others with split peas, and others with neither of these. To aid bean digestion, soak beans well and cook them until they are well done, moist, and tender. Additionally, cook beans with seaweed, warming herbs and spices, and ghee or sesame oil. Beans are easier to digest when served in modest quantities, or in soup, or when combined with vegetables.

Beverages are important for *vata*. Water may not be substantial enough for *vata* people, although adequate water is necessary to keep *vata* hydrated. To support *vata*, drink warm herbal teas, chai (warming spices with milk), or room-temperature milk, buttermilk, or kefir. In hot weather, enjoy sour fruit juice or water with lemon or lime juice. Small quantities of beer or wine are sometimes helpful.

Fats and Oils moisten, warm, lubricate, and help ground *vata* providing they are unrefined and used moderately. Ghee and sesame oil are the most balancing, followed by almond oil, extra virgin olive oil, butter, and coconut oil.

Fruits moisten and harmonize *vata;* however, they are generally too light to have a grounding effect. Favor regional and seasonal fruits; enjoy them separately rather than combined with other ingredients. Dried fruits, however, challenge *vata* unless they are reconstituted. Watermelon, raw apples, and cranberries are unbalancing.

Grains that are most balancing to *vata* are wheat, oats, and rice. While barley, buckwheat, corn, millet, quinoa, and rye are mildly unbalancing, they can be ameliorated with ghee or sesame oil and digestion-enhancing spices, herbs, or condiments. Additionally, favor one grain dishes (rather than multiple grain combinations). Avoid granola, cold breakfast cereals, crackers, crusty bread, yeast bread, and dried grains.

Herbs and Spices benefit *vata*, as they aid digestion and help dispel gas. They are especially beneficial added to sweet or heavy foods and include: asafetida, basil, bay leaf, cardamom, cinnamon, cloves, coriander, cumin, epazote, fennel, fenugreek, fresh ginger, mace, marjoram, mustard seeds in moderation, nutmeg, oregano, savory, thyme, and turmeric. Very hot spices, such as dried ginger, chiles, or mustard, may aggravate *vata*, especially in hot, windy, or dry climates.

Nuts and Seeds are moistening, heavy, and warming and so nourish *vata* as long as they're taken in small, easy-to-digest quantities. Enjoy them raw or lightly roasted. Avoid nuts and seeds that are dry-roasted, fried, stale, or overly salted.

Sweeteners nurture *vata* when they are natural and used in moderation. Rapadura is especially beneficial. Strive to completely avoid white sugar.

Vegetables cooked support vata. While well-cooked onions and garlic are superior *vata* tonics, raw onions are best avoided as are most other raw vegetables. To make salads more digestible, favor them in hot weather and with an oil-rich dressing and digestion-enhancing herbs or a small amount of garlic. Celery, eggplant, mushrooms, tomatoes, and white potatoes unbalance *vata;* to ameliorate their effects, cook, season, and combine them with cheese.

Vata responses to the cabbage family vary widely. The more tender and watery the cabbage relative, the easier for *vata* to digest. Thus, Chinese cabbage is usually preferred over cabbage. For some *vata* types the cabbage family vegetables with a high mustard oil content such as broccoli, cabbage, and mustard greens will be more challenging than broccoli rabe, cauliflower, or Chinese cabbage.

PITTA (fire type)

Fiery pittas thrive with a diet that is cool, slightly dry, and a little heavy. Typically their digestion is good and they seemingly better tolerate poor eating habits than other types (but indiscretions typically manifest as infectious disease or other toxic blood related problems). *Pitta* does best with bland, mild tasting foods and with flavors that are sweet, bitter, and/or astringent.

Beans and Legumes are easily assimilated by pittas, with the exception of lentils and peanuts. Add herbs and spices to aid digestion, favoring ground coriander seeds and fresh cilantro leaves. Go easy on any added fat or oil cooked with beans and legumes.

Beverages are especially needed by pittas. Favor spring water, black or green tea, astringent herbal teas (such as alfalfa or rasp-

berry leaf), or astringent fruit juices (such as pomegranate), milk, vegetable juices, green drinks (such as wheat grass juice or spirulina). Avoid coffee, spicy tea, alcohol, beer, and wine.

Fats and Oils are warming and therefore best used discreetly by pittas. Ghee and butter are less warming and therefore more harmonious. Favor the more cooling vegetable oils: coconut, corn, and sunflower. Minimize the more warming oils: sesame, peanut, almond, olive, and safflower.

Fruits tend to cool, calm, and harmonize *pitta* as well as relieve thirst. The fruits to favor are sweet flavored ones. Fruits to minimize are those with a sour flavor: grapefruits, lemons, limes, sour cherries, sour plums, peaches, papayas, and apricots.

Grains are well tolerated by *pitta*, as they strengthen but do not overheat. This includes quality bread and pasta. It's best not to use brown rice, buckwheat, corn, or rye as a primary staple or when in an acute condition.

Herbs and Spices are best avoided by *pitta* except those that are not too heating (cardamom, cilantro, cinnamon, coriander, cumin, fennel, mint, parsley, turmeric, and in small quantities, black pepper). Saffron and rose petals calm the *pitta* mind as well as body. Generally, *pitta* does best with a low salt diet except during the summer heat.

Nuts and Seeds are warming and oily and therefore best used in moderation. Favor coconut and sunflower seeds, and less frequently sesame seeds, pine nuts, and pumpkin seeds. Avoid Brazil and macadamia nuts, and use other nuts rarely.

Sweeteners are cooling and more soothing to *pitta* than any other constitution. Rapadura, maple sugar, and fruit-based sweeteners (such as fruit juice, apple butter, or date sugar) are especially recommended.

Vegetables cooked or raw support *pitta*. (But raw vegetables are not recommended in cold weather or when convalescing.) Avoid deep fried vegetables, chiles, raw onions, garlic, tomatoes, and avocados. Also minimize acidic vegetables such as eggplant, potatoes, chard, and spinach.

KAPHA (water type)

Kapha is the water type but with a strong earth influence. It is slow moving, heavy, wet, cold, and enduring and so does best with foods that are light, dry, and warming. The best tastes for *kapha* are pungent, bitter, and astringent. It is important for this type to eat less food and less frequently.

Beans and Legumes support *kapha* as they are drying and increase air. Adukis are particularly diuretic. Chickpeas, however, imbalance *kapha*, as does soy in excess.

Beverages in moderation is the guideline for *kapha*. Avoid all iced and chilled beverages. Green and black tea, and occasionally coffee, are acceptable. Pungent, astringent herbal teas such as ginger, chicory, or dandelion are balancing. Soymilk is preferable to dairy.

Fats and Oils are heavy and damp producing and therefore best used in minuscule amounts. Sunflower, sesame, and olive oil and ghee are tolerated best. If you find yourself yearning for fat, try dressing your favorite steamed foods with a little of these culinary oils or with flax oil.

Fruits increase water, a feature not needed by *kapha* people; however, as fruit is light it often ameliorates *kapha*'s heaviness. Small amounts of dried fruits (dates excepted) balance *kapha*. All fruit is best tolerated alone, rather than in combination with other foods. Sweet fruits such as ripe bananas and watery fruits exacerbate *kapha*, as do fatty fruits such as avocados and coconut. Favor apples, under-ripe bananas, berries, cranberries, cherries, peaches, pears, pomegranates, and persimmons.

Grains that are drying with diuretic properties, such as amaranth, barley, buckwheat, corn, millet, dry oats, and tef, support *kapha*. Puffed or popped grains are drying. Basmati rice is favored over other types of rice. Oats and all wheat products are heavy and increase *kapha*'s tendency to retain fluid.

Herbs and Spices warm and dry *kapha*, increase metabolism, and help prevent fat and water from accumulating. Use sea salt in moderation. *Kapha*'s slow, steady digestion can benefit from digestion-enhancing herbs and spices such as asafetida, basil, black pepper, black mustard seeds, chiles, coriander, cumin, galangal, fresh and dried ginger, fennel, and fenugreek. Kaphas who are not fond of these pungent spices may find themselves better tolerating allspice, cardamom, cinnamon, and nutmeg, which will also support their metabolism.

Nuts and Seeds are heavy, mucus forming, and fatty in nature and therefore best used moderately by *kapha*. Seeds (especially chia, flax, pumpkin, and sunflower) are preferable to nuts. Occasional use of coconut and almonds is acceptable.

Sweeteners such as carob are drying to *kapha*, and curiously enough, so is raw honey, which has warming, drying, and expectorant properties. As much as possible, however, avoid other sweeteners or only use them occasionally.

Vegetables are mostly dry and light and therefore aid *kapha*, especially when they are cooked (except in hot weather) and prepared with little—if any—oil. Indulge in arugula, artichokes, asparagus, baby greens, bitter melon, dark leafy cabbage family greens, endive, mâche, fresh peas, and peppers. When craving starchy foods, kaphas do well with the following root vegetables: beets, carrots, Jerusalem artichokes, potatoes, and rutabagas.

The few vegetables to use in moderation include sweet and juicy vegetables such as cucumbers, seaweed, squash, sweet corn, sweet potatoes, tomatoes, and zucchini.

Appendix IV:
Mail-Order Resources

FULL-SERVICE WHOLE FOODS SUPPLIERS

Gold Mine Natural Food Company
3419 Hancock Street
San Diego, CA 92110
Telephone: 800-475-FOOD
Fax: 619-296-9756

Premier-quality organic and heirloom grains, oats rolled fresh to order, kuzu, mochi, mushrooms, Celtic sea salt, books, and cookware.

GoodEats
P.O. Box 756
Richboro, PA 18954
Telephone: 800-490-0044
Fax: 215-443-7087
Internet: www.goodeats.com

More than 2,000 items with an emphasis on organic foods—a shop-at-home natural food store.

Mountain Ark Trading Company
799 Old Leicester Highway
Ashville, NC 28806
Telephone: 800-438-4730
Fax: 828-252-9479
Internet: www.zibo.com

A full selection of grains, beans, seaweed, salt, pickles, miso, and macrobiotic specialty items including heirloom grain varieties.

Natural Lifestyles Supplies
16 Lookout Drive
Asheville, NC 28804
Telephone: 800-752-2775
Fax: 828-252-3386
Internet: www.natural-lifestyle.com

Specializes in highest-quality organic food staples, miso, tea, and macrobiotic supplies. Provides in-depth articles about product quality on line.

ASIAN AND MIDDLE EASTERN INGREDIENTS

Anzen Oriental Foods and Imports
736 N.E. Martin Luther King Jr. Boulevard
Portland, OR 97232
Telephone: 503-233-5111

Oriental Pantry
423 Great Road
Acton, MA 10720
Telephone: 800-828-0368 or 978-264-4576
Internet: www.orientalpantry.com

Sultan's Delight
P.O. Box 090302
Brooklyn, NY 11209
Telephone: 800-852-5046
Fax: 718-745-2563
Internet: www.sultansdelight.com

BEANS

Phipps Country Store and Farm
P.O. Box 349
Pescadero, CA 94060
Telephone: 800-279-0889
Fax: 650-879-1622

More than 50 varieties of heirloom beans. Also spices, specialty grains, herb vinegars, jams, and jellies.

CULINARY OILS, UNREFINED

Flora Inc.
P.O. Box 73
Lynden, WA 98264-9502
Telephone: 800-446-2110
Internet: www.florainc.com

Twelve unrefined oils. Some are organic; others (pumpkin, toasted sesame seed, and walnut) are tested to meet stringent criteria but are not certified organic.

Loriva Supreme Foods
1981 Pond Road
Ronkonkoma, NY 11779
Telephone: 800-945-6748
Fax: 516-738-9469
Internet: www.loriva.com

Specializes in roasted nut oils (peanut, hazelnut, macadamia, sesame, and sunflower). Loriva features a total of twenty unrefined oils and three infused oils (fresh basil, fresh garlic, and five-pepper hot).

Omega Nutrition
6515 Aldrich Road
Bellingham, WA 98226
Telephone: 800-661-3529
Internet: www.omegaflo.com

Carries eight culinary oils made exclusively from independently certified, organic seed material and five oils containing some organic ingredients. Oils are mechanically pressed in small batches below 92 degrees, no nutrients are removed, and no preservatives or additives are added.

GRAIN AND GRAIN PRODUCTS

Bob's Red Mill
5209 S.E. International Way
Milwaukie, OR 97222
Telephone: 503-654-3215
Fax: 503-653-1339
Internet: www.bobsredmill.com

Mills to order, using only 100-year-old stone mills, and features organic grains. All the grains are available whole or ground into flour, meal, farina, or cracked. Also available: beans, granola, books, mixes, baking equipment. Visit the mill and attend a cooking class if you're in the Portland area.

Indian Harvest
P.O. Box 428
Bemidji, MN 56619
Telephone: 800-346-7032 or 218-751-8500
Fax: 218-751-8519
Internet: www.indianharvest.com
Heirloom beans, wild rice, black barley, black Chinese sticky rice, and other specialty grains.

Leech Lake Wild Rice
6530 U.S. 2NW
Cass Lake, MN 56633
Telephone: 218-335-8317
Fax: 218-335-8309
Hand-harvested from canoes on the Leech Lake reservation, this grain is indeed wild and has an extraordinary flavor range. It is superior in flavor and nutrients to commercial wild rice, and it is competitively priced.

Lundberg Family Farms
P.O. Box 369
Richvale, CA 95974
Telephone: 530-882-4551
Fax: 530-882-4500
Internet: www.lundberg.com
A wide assortment of rice products featuring organic rice, brown rice, rice pasta, and specialty varieties. All products are made from rice grown on the Lundberg Farms.

Friends of PRONATURA
240 East Limberlost
Tucson, AZ 85705
Telephone: 520-887-1188
Mesquite meal available with a membership. Recipe booklet included.

Quinoa Corporation
Box 1039
Torrence, CA 90505
Telephone: 310-530-8666
Fax: 310-530-8764
Imported quinoa, quinoa flour, and quinoa pasta.

Teff Company
P.O. Box A
Caldwell, ID 83606
Telephone and Fax: 208-455-0375
E-mail: teffco.com
Domestically grown organic tef and tef flour, available in brown, red, and ivory varieties. Recipes available.

Western Trails, Inc.
P.O. Box 460
Bozeman, MT 59771
Telephone: 406-587-5489
Whole barley varieties, including bronze, black, and gold. Also sells beans.

White Mountain Farm, Inc.
8890 Lane 4 North
Mosca, CO 81146
Telephone: 800-364-3019
Fax: 719-378-2436
Quinoa from the high-elevation farmers who pioneered quinoa cultivation in North America. Black quinoa has limited availability.

FERMENTED VEGETABLES

Rejuvenative Foods
P.O. Box 8464
Santa Cruz, CA 95061
Telephone: 800-805-7957
Fax: 888-781-9879

Produces raw cultured vegetables that are sold in the refrigerated section of natural food stores. Also provides recipes for making your own.

HEIRLOOM SEEDS, OPEN-POLLINATED SEEDS, AND ORGANIC SEEDS

Johnny's Selected Seeds
310 Foss Hill Road
Albion, ME 04910
Telephone: 207-437-9294
Fax: 800-437-4290 (U.S. only)
Internet: www.johnnyseeds.com

Native Seeds/SEARCH
526 North 4th Avenue
Tucson, AZ 85705
Telephone: 520-622-5561
Fax: 520-622-5591

HERBS AND SPICES

Adriana's Caravan
409 Vanderbilt Street
Brooklyn, NY 11218
Telephone: 800-316-0820
Fax: 718-436-8565 #96
Internet: www.adrianascaravan.com

More than 1,500 items, including every dried herb and spice needed for any ethnic cuisine. Some are available fresh, like galangal, lime leaves, and lemongrass. Also available: ethnic condiments, seasonings, and infused oils.

Penzeys, Ltd.
W19362 Apollo Dr.
Muskego, WI 53150
Telephone: 414-679-7207
Fax: 414-679-7878
Internet: www.penzeys.com

A comprehensive selection of culinary herbs and spices for all ethnic cuisines.

INOCULANTS (Starters for fermented food products)

G.E.M. Cultures
30301 Sherwood Road
Fort Bragg, CA 95437
Telephone: 707-964-2922

Koji, kombucha, natto, and tempeh inoculants are available for making amasake, miso, tamari, sake, kombucha, natto, and tempeh. Also sourdough starters of wheat, kamut, spelt, and rice.

MUSHROOMS

Garland Gourmet Mushrooms and Truffles
3020 Ode Turner Road
Hillsborough, NC 27278
Telephone: 919-732-3041
Fax: 919-732-6037
E-mail: truffleman@mindspring.com

Specializes in black perigord truffles and inoculated tree stock.

Gourmet Mushrooms and Mushroom Products
P.O. Box 515
Graton, CA 95444
Telephone: 800-789-9121 or 707-829-7301
Fax: 707-823-9091
Internet: www.gmushrooms.com

Fresh and dried wildcrafted and commercial mushrooms. Also mushroom oils and extracts.

Mushroom People
P.O. Box 220
Summertown, TN 38483-0220
Telephone: 800-692-6329
Fax: 800-386-4496
Books, videos, and supplies for shiitake and reishi cultivation.

Terry Farms Technology Division
272 Technology Parkway
Auburn, AL 36830
Telephone: 334-826-3200
A 1½-pound minimum order of fresh morels, with shipping charges, costs from $35 to $40.

Western Biologicals
Dept. CC, P.O. Box 283
Alder Grove, BC, Canada 4W 2T8
Telephone: 604-856-3339
E-mail: western@prismnet.bc.ca
Growing supplies and books for shiitake, oyster, morel, maitake, reishi, and other mushrooms. Dried whole reishi and reishi extracts. Also, stevia bedding plants.

PRODUCE
Diamond Organics
P.O. Box 2159
Freedom, CA 95019
Telephone: 888-674-2642
Fax: 888-674-2642
Internet: www.diamondorganics.com
Featuring strictly fresh and organic fruits and vegetables plus a selection of other organic food staples—more than 300 items.

Melissa's World Variety Produce, Inc.
P.O. Box 21127
Los Angeles, CA 90021
Telephone: 800-588-0151
Fax: 323-588-9774
Internet: www.melissas.com
Exotic fruits, specialty vegetables, grains, legumes, mushrooms, chiles, spices, and herbs. Some organic produce. Latin and Asian food staples.

SEAWEED
Maine Coast Sea Vegetables
R.R. 1, Box 78
Franklin, ME 04634
Telephone: 207-565-2907
Fax: 207-565-2144
Internet: www.seaveg.com
Hand-foraged domestic seaweed and some imported seaweed. Candy, pickles, and seasonings made of seaweed.

Maine Seaweed Co.
P.O. Box 57
Steuben, ME 04680
Telephone: 207-546-2875
Fax: 207-546-2003

Mendocino Sea Vegetable Company
P.O. Box 1265
Mendocino, CA 95460
Telephone: 707-937-2050
Internet: www.seaweed.net
Nori, wakame, kombu, sea palm, dulse, fucus, grapestone, and bladder wrack. Also John and Eleanor Lewallen's *Sea Vegetable Gourmet Cookbook and Wildcrafter's Guide.*

Ocean Harvest Sea Vegetables
P.O. Box 1719
Mendocino, CA 95460
Telephone: 707-973-5514

Rising Tide Sea Vegetables
P.O. Box 1814
Mendocino, CA 95460
Telephone: 707-964-5663

Seaweed candies, a trail mix with seaweed, and seaweed sesame salt. Alaria, kombu, nori (laver), sea palm, and other foraged Pacific seaweeds.

SOYMILK MACHINES

Miracle Exclusives
P.O. Box 8
Port Washington, NY 11050-4618
Telephone: 800-645-6360
Fax: 516-621-1997
E-mail: miracle-exc@juno.com

Producers of small kitchen appliances, including an easy to use soymilk machine.

SPROUTING SUPPLIES

The Sprout House
17267 Sundance Drive
Ramona, CA 92065
Telephone: 800-SPROUTS (777-6887)
Fax: 760-788-7979
Internet: www.sprouthouse.com

SOUTHWESTERN INGREDIENTS

Coyote Café General Store
132 W. Water Street
Santa Fe, NM 87501
Telephone: 800-866-HOWL

SWEETENERS, QUALITY

Rapunzel Pure Organics
7 Main Street
Chatham, NY 12037
Telephone: 800-207-2814
Fax: 518-758-6493
Internet: www.rapunzel.com

Producers of granulated rapadura (unrefined, evaporated organic cane juice).

Selected Bibliography

Allgeier, R. J., et al. "Vinegar: History and Development. Part One and Part Two." *Food Products Development* (June/July/August 1974), U.S. Industrial Chemicals Co., Cincinnati.

Anderson, Jean, and Barbara Deskins. *The Nutrition Bible: A Comprehensive, No-Nonsense Guide to Foods, Nutrients, Additives, Preservatives, Pollutants and Everything Else We Eat and Drink* New York: William Morrow, 1997.

Arasaki, Seibin, and Teruko Arasaki. *Vegetables from the Sea: To Help You Look and Feel Better.* Tokyo: Japan Publications, 1983.

Barnett, Robert A. *Tonics: More Than 100 Recipes That Improve the Body and the Mind.* New York: HarperCollins, 1997.

Belleme, John, and Jan Belleme. *Culinary Treasures of Japan: The Art of Making and Using Traditional Japanese Foods.* Garden City Park, NY: Avery, 1992.

————. *Cooking with Japanese Foods: A Guide to the Traditional Natural Foods of Japan.* Garden City Park, NY: Avery.

Bown, Deni. *Encyclopedia of Herbs and Their Uses.* New York: Dorling Kindersley, 1995.

Boyles, Peg. "Dandelion Season." *The Gardener's Companion Newsletter*, P.O. Box 420296, Palm Coast, FL 32142-0296. March 1997.

Brennan, Georgeanne, Issac Cronin, and Charlotte Glenn. *The New American Vegetable Cookbook: The Definitive Guide to America's Exotic and Traditional Vegetables.* Berkeley: Aris Books, 1985.

Brown, Tom, Jr. *Tom Brown's Guide to Wild Edible and Medicinal Plants.* New York: Berkley, 1985.

Carper, Jean. *The Food Pharmacy.* New York: Bantam, 1988.

Castelvetro, Giacomo. *The Fruit, Herbs, & Vegetables of Italy.* New York: Viking Penguin, 1990.

Chalmers, Irena. *The Great Food Almanac: A Feast of Facts from A to Z.* San Francisco: HarperCollins World, 1994.

Colbin, Annemarie. *Food and Healing*. New York: Ballantine, 1986.

Corriher, Shirley O. *CookWise: The Hows & Whys of Successful Cooking*. New York: William Morrow, 1998.

Creasy, Rosalind. *Cooking from the Garden*. San Francisco: Sierra Club Books, 1988.

Cusumano, Camille. *The New Foods: A Shopper's Guide with Recipes*. New York: Henry Holt, 1989.

Devi, Yamuna. *Lord Krishna's Cuisine: The Art of Indian Vegetarian Cooking*. New York: E. P. Dutton, 1987.

DeWitt, Dave, and Nancy Gerlach. *The Whole Chile Pepper Book*. Boston: Little, Brown and Company, 1990.

Diamond, Jared. *Guns, Germs, and Steel*. New York: W. W. Norton, 1998.

Elias, Thomas S. *The Complete Trees of North America: Field Guide and Natural History*. New York: Crown, 1987.

Elias, Thomas S., and Peter A. Dykeman. *Edible Wild Plants: A North American Field Guide*. New York: Borgo, 1991.

Erasmus, Udo. *Fats That Heal, Fats That Kill: The Complete Guide to Fats, Oils, Cholesterol and Human Health* Vancouver: Alive Books, 1993.

Esterson, Emily. "Dried Fruit Labels May Not Tell the Whole Story." *Natural Foods Merchandiser*, February 1995, page 26.

Fitzgibbon, Theodora. *The Food of the Western World: An Encyclopedia of Food from North America and Europe*. New York: Times Books, 1976.

Flaws, Bob. *The Book of Jook: Chinese Medicinal Porridges, A Healthy Alternative to the Typical Western Breakfast*. Boulder: Blue Poppy Press, 1995.

Flaws, Bob, and Honora Wolfe. *Prince Wen Hui's Cook: Chinese Dietary Therapy*. Brookline, MA: Paradigm Publications, 1995.

Frawley, David, and Vasant Lad. *The Yoga of Herbs (An Ayurvedic Guide to Herbal Medicine)*. Twin Lakes, WI: Lotus, 1990.

Fussell, Betty. *The Story of Corn*. New York: Alfred A. Knopf, 1992.

Gagné, Steve. *Energetics of Food: Encounters with Your Most Intimate Relationship*. Santa Fe: Spiral Sciences, 1990.

Gates, Donna. *The Body Ecology Diet: Recovering Your Health and Rebuilding Your Immunity*. Atlanta: BED Publishing, 1996.

Gould, John. "The Home Forum." *Christian Science Monitor*, February 13, 1988, page 17.

Gutman, Robert L., and Beung-Ho Ruy. "Rediscovering Tea." *HerbalGram* (No. 37), pages 33–48.

Hamerstrom, Frances. *Wild Food Cookbook*. Amherst, MA: Amherst Press, 1994.

Harrington, H. D. *Edible Native Plants of the Rocky Mountains*. Albuquerque: University of New Mexico Press, 1974.

Harris, Lloyd J. *The Book of Garlic*. Berkeley: Aris Books, 1980.

Hausman, Patricia, and Judith Benn Hurley. *The Healing Foods: The Ultimate Authority on the Curative Power of Nutrition*. Emmaus, PA: Rodale Press, 1989.

Herbst, Sharon Tyler. *The Food Lover's Tiptionary*. New York: Hearst Books, 1994.

Hess, Clarke. "Saffron on a Shoestring." *The Kitchen Garden*, No. 12, (January 1998), pages 32–35.

Hobbs, Christopher. *Foundations of Health: The Liver & Digestive Herbal*. Santa Cruz, CA. Botanica Press, 1992.

———. *Medicinal Mushrooms: An Exploration of Tradition, Healing, & Culture*. Santa Cruz, CA: Botanica Press, 1995.

Jacobi, Dana. *Natural Kitchen: Soy!* Rocklin, CA: Prima, 1996.

Jacobs, Leonard, and Barbara Jacobs. *Cooking with Seitan*. New York: Japan Publications, USA, 1989.

Jensen, Bernard. *Foods That Heal: A Guide to Understanding and Using the Healing Powers of Natural Foods*. Garden City Park, NY: Avery, 1988.

Jilin, Liu. *Chinese Dietary Therapy*. New York: Churchill Livingstone, English edition, 1995.

Kamman, Madeleine. *The New Making of a Cook*. New York: William Morrow, 1997.

Lad, Usha, and Vasant Lad. *Ayurvedic Cooking for Self-Healing*. Albuquerque: Ayurvedic Press, 1997.

Lewallen, John and Eleanor. *Sea Vegetable Gourmet Cookbook and Wildcrafter's Guide*. Mendocino, CA: Mendocino Sea Vegetable Company, 1996.

London, Sheryl, and Mel London. *The Versatile Grain and the Elegant Bean: A Celebration of the World's Most Healthful Foods*. New York: Simon & Schuster, 1992.

Madlener, Judith Cooper. *The Sea Vegetable Book: Foraging and Cooking Seaweed*. New York: Clarkson N. Potter, 1977.

Mars, Brigitte. "Calm Down with Chamomile." *Delicious!* magazine, November 1995, pages 52–53.

McGee, Harold. *On Food and Cooking: The Science and Lore of the Kitchen*. New York: Charles Scribner's Sons, 1984.

———. *The Curious Cook: More Kitchen Science and Lore*. San Francisco: North Point Press, 1990.

Messina, Mark, Virginia Messina, and Kenneth Setchell. *The Simple Soybean and Your Health: How Soy Foods Can Lower Your Cholesterol and Reduce Your Risk of Disease and Cancer*. Garden City Park, NY: Avery, 1994.

Moore, Michael. *Medicinal Plants of the Desert and Canyon West*. Santa Fe: The Museum of New Mexico Press, 1989.

———. *Medicinal Plants of the Mountain West*. Santa Fe: The Museum of New Mexico Press, 1979.

Morningstar, Amadea. *Ayurvedic Cooking for Westerners: Familiar Western Food Prepared with Ayurvedic Principles*. Twin Lakes, WI: Lotus, 1995.

Nadkarni, M. *Indian Materia Medica*. Bombay: South Asia, 1989.

National Research Council Staff. *Lost Crops of the Incas: Little Known Plants of the Andes with Promise for Worldwide Cultivation*. Washington: National Academy Press, 1989.

Ortiz, Elisabeth Lambert. *The Encyclopedia of Herbs, Spices & Flavorings: A Cook's Compendium*. New York: Dorling Kindersley, 1992.

Phillips, Robert, and Martyn Rix. *The Random House Book of Vegetables*. New York: Random House, 1994.

Pitchford, Paul. *Healing with Whole Foods: Oriental Traditions and Modern Nutrition*. Berkeley: North Atlantic Books, 1996.

Pollan, Michael. "The Call of the Wild Apple." *The New York Times*, November 5, 1998, pages D1, D8.

Reich, Lee. "Upstart American Persimmons Add to Fall Colors." *The New York Times*, September 28, 1997.

Rhoads, Sharon Ann. *Cooking with Sea Vegetables*. Brookline, MA: Autumn Press, Inc., 1978.

Rinzler, Carol Ann. *The Complete Book of Food: A Nutritional, Medical, and Culinary Guide*. New York: World Almanac, 1987.

Root, Waverly. *Food*. New York: Simon & Schuster, 1980.

Ross, Rosa Lo San. *Beyond Bok Choy: A Cook's Guide to Asian Vegetables*. New York: Artisan, 1996.

Saltzman, Joanne. *Amazing Grains: Creating Vegetarian Main Dishes with Whole Grains*. Tiburon, CA: H. J. Kramer, 1990.

Sass, Lorna J. *To the King's Taste: Richard II's Book of Feasts and Recipes Adapted for Modern Cooking*. New York: Metropolitan Museum of Art, 1975.

Schechter, Steven R., and Tom Monte. *Fighting Radiation with Foods, Herbs, and Vitamins*. Brookline, MA: East West Health Books, 1988.

Schneider, Elizabeth. *Uncommon Fruits and Vegetables: A Commonsense Guide*. New York: William Morrow, 1998.

Sears, Barry. *The Zone: A Dietary Road Map*. New York: HarperCollins, 1996.

Shannon, Sara. *Diet for the Atomic Age: How to Protect Yourself from Low-Level Radiation*. New York: Instant Improvement, Inc., 1993.

Shurtleff, William, and Akiko Aoyagi. *The Book of Kudzu: A Culinary & Healing Guide*. Garden City Park, NY: Avery, 1997.

Singh, Yadhu, and Mark Blumenthal. "Kava: Distribution, Mythology, Botany, Culture, Chemistry and Pharmacology of the South Pacific's Most Revered Herb." *Herbalgram* (No. 39), pages 33–56.

Sokolov, Raymond. "America's First Food Writer." *Natural History*, October 1992.

Susser, Allen. *The Great Citrus Book*. Berkeley: Ten Speed Press, 1997.

Tierra, Michael. *Planetary Herbology*. Twin Lakes, WI: Lotus, 1990.

Tiwari, Maya. *Ayurveda—A Life of Balance: The Complete Guide to Ayurvedic Nutrition and Body Types*. Rochester, VT: Healing Arts Press, 1994.

Toussaint-Samat, Maguelonne. *History of Food.* Translated by Anthea Bell. Cambridge, MA: Blackwell Publishers, 1992.

Travers, Rachel. "The Wild and Whorly Fiddlehead." *Christian Science Monitor,* May 2, 1996, page 14.

Tropp, Barbara. *The Modern Art of Chinese Cooking.* New York: William Morrow, 1982.

U.S. Department of Health, Education, and Welfare et al. *Food Composition Table for Use in East Asia.* Washington: UNIPUB, 1972.

Van Aken, Norman. *The Great Exotic Fruit Book.* Berkeley: Ten Speed Press, 1995.

Vaughan, John G., and Catherine Geissler. *The New Oxford Book of Food Plants: A Guide to the Fruit, Vegetables, Herbs and Spices of the World.* New York: Oxford University Press, 1997.

Vilmorin-Andrieux, M. *The Vegetable Garden.* English Edition. Berkeley: Ten Speed Press, 1981.

Webb, Ginger. "Anti-Diabetic Properties of Bitter Melon." *HerbalGram* (No. 39), page 18.

Weil, Andrew. *Spontaneous Healing: How to Discover and Enhance Your Body's Natural Ability to Maintain and Heal Itself.* New York: Fawcett, 1996.

———. "Therapeutic Hemp Oil." *Natural Health,* March/April 1993, pages 10–12.

Williamson, Darcy. *The Rocky Mountain Wild Foods Cookbook.* Caldwell, ID: Caxton, 1995.

Wittenberg, Margaret. *Good Food: The Complete Guide to Eating Well.* Freedom, CA: Crossing Press, 1995.

Wolverton, B. C. *How to Grow Fresh Air: 50 Houseplants to Purify Your Home or Office.* New York: Penguin, 1997.

Wood, Rebecca. *Quinoa: The Supergrain.* New York: Japan Publications, USA, 1989.

———. *The Splendid Grain.* New York: William Morrow, 1997.

Young, Kay. *Wild Seasons: Gathering and Cooking Wild Plants of the Great Plains.* Lincoln: University of Nebraska Press, 1993.

Underhill, Ruth. *Papago Woman.* Reprint ed. Prospect Heights, IL: Waveland Press, 1985.

Index

Recipes